Out for the Count

The 1997 General Elections and Prospects for

Democracy in Kenya

Out for the Count
The 1997 General Elections and Prospects for
Democracy in Kenya

Editors
Marcel Rutten, Alamin Mazrui
& François Grignon

Fountain Publishers

Fountain Publishers Ltd
P. O. Box 488
Kampala
(256) (41) 259-163 (tel), 251-160 (fax),
fountain@starcom.co.ug (e-mail)

Distribution in Europe, North America and Australia by African Books
Collective (ABC), The Jam Factory, 27 Park End St., Oxford OX1 1HU,
United Kingdom +44(0) 1865-72686 (tel), 1865-793298 (fax)

ISBN 9970 02 249 0

04 03 02 01 4 3 2 1

Cataloguing-in-Publication Data

Out for the Count: The 1997 General Elections and Prospects for Democracy
in Kenya / Marcel Rutten, Alamin Mazrui and François Grignon (eds)
Kampala: Fountain Publishers 2001

p. cm.

1. General elections – Kenya   2. Democracy – Kenya

I. Title
324.06'096;'7632
ISBN 9970 02 249 0

Cover design: Marcel Rutten and Fountain Publishers
Cover photos: Catherine Duhamel and Marcel Rutten
Artwork: Charles Hornsby, Marcel Rutten, Fountain Publishers

Dedication

To George Onchara, a 22-year old Kenyan victim of political violence, killed by a large group of raiders in his parents' compound in the Shonda village of Kwale during August 1997. Not tabled in the government's list of the dead, he died without recognition by his own government. His memory is a permanent shame to all political leaders of the country.

Contents

PART 3: REGIONAL ANALYSIS OF THE RESULTS

PART 4: POST-ELECTORAL PROSPECTS

List of Tables

List of Figures

Acronyms and abbreviations

4Cs	Citizens' Coalition for Constitutional Change
AACC	All Africa Churches Conference
ACK	Anglican Church of Kenya (formerly CPK)
ACWIN	African Women and Child Information Network
AEAA	Abaluhya East Africa Association
AFC	Abaluhya Football Club
AG	Attorney-General
AIC	African Inland Church
AP	Administration Police
APP	African People's Party
BBC	British Broadcasting Corporation
BEERAM	Bureau of Education in Electoral Research and Observation
CGD	Centre for Governance and Democracy
CJPC	Catholic Justice and Peace Commission
CLARION	Centre for Law and Research International
CNN	Cable News Network
CPDSG	Central Province Development Support Group
CPK	Church of the Province of Kenya
CPP	Coast Peoples Party
DAP	Democratic Assistance Party
DC	District Commissioner
DCIO	District Criminal Investigations Officer
DCP	Democratic Congress Party of Kenya
DDC	District Development Committee
DDDG	Donors for Development and Democracy Group
DDG	Democratic Development Group
DO	District Officer
DP(K)	Democratic Party (of Kenya)
DSC	District Security Committee
DSG	Donor Steering Group
DSIO	District Security Intelligence Officer
EATEC	East African Tanning Extract Company
EATN	East African Television Network
ECK	Electoral Commission of Kenya
EFK	Evangelical Fellowship of Kenya
EIP	Economic Independence Party
EOC	Election Observation Centre
ERIS	Electoral Reform International Services

EU	European Union
FIDA	International Federation of Women Lawyers
FORD	Forum for the Restoration of Democracy
FORD-A	Forum for the Restoration of Democracy-Asili
FORD-K	Forum for the Restoration of Democracy-Kenya
FORD-P	Forum for the Restoration of Democracy for the People
GAP	Green African Party
GDP	Gross Domestic Product
GEMA	Gikuyu, Embu, Meru Association
GSU	General Service Unit
HIVOS	Humanist Institute for Cooperation with Developing Countries
ICDC	Industrial and Commercial Development Corporation
ICEDA	Institute of Civic Education and Development in Africa
ICJ	International Commission of Jurists
IDs	Identity Cards
IED	Institute for Education in Democracy
IMF	International Monetary Fund
IPG	Inter-Parliamentary Group
IPK	Islamic Party of Kenya
IPPG	Inter-Parties Parliamentary Group
IPU	Inter-Parliamentary Union
IRI	International Republican Institute
IRIS	Interlink Rural Information Services
KABISA	Kamotho, Biwott, Saitoti
KADU	Kenya African Democratic Union
KAMATUSA	Kalenjin, Maasai, Turkana, Samburu
KANU	Kenya African National Union
KAU	Kenya African Union
KBC	Kenya Broadcasting Corporation
KBS	Kenya Broadcasting Service
KCC	Kenya Co-operative Creameries
KEC	Kenya Episcopal Conference
KEM	Kikuyu, Embu, Meru
KENDA	Kenya National Democratic Alliance
KHRC	Kenya Human Rights Commission
KNA	Kenya News Agency
KNC	Kenya National Congress
KPA	Kenya Ports Authority
KPF	Kenya Pastoralist Forum
KPU	Kenya People's Union

KSC	Kenya Social Congress
KTDA	Kenya Tea Development Authority
KTN	Kenya Television Network
KUJ	Kenya Union of Journalists
LEGCO	Legislative Council
LPD	Labour Party Democracy
LPK	Liberal Party of Kenya
LSK	Law Society of Kenya
MCK	Methodist Church of Kenya
MP	Member of Parliament
MUF	Maasai United Front
NADU	National Democratic Union
NAU	New Akamba Union
NCA	National Convention Assembly
NCCK	National Council of Churches of Kenya
NCEC	National Convention Executive Council
NCPC	National Convention Planning Committee
NCWK	National Council of Women of Kenya
NDI	National Democratic Institute
NDIMA	Network for the Defence of Independent Media in Africa
NDP	National Development Party of Kenya
NECEP	National Ecumenical Civic Education Programme
NEMU	National Election Monitoring Unit
NFD	Northern Frontier District
NGO	Non-Governmental Organisation
NHIF	National Hospital Insurance Fund
NSSF	National Social Security Fund
OCPD	Officer in Command of the Police Department
OCS	Officer Commanding Station
ODA	Overseas Development Administration (UK)
OLF	Oromo Liberation Front
PC	Provincial Commissioner
PCDC	Professional Committee for Democratic Change
PCEA	Presbyterian Church of East Africa
PICK	Party of Independent Candidates of Kenya
PO	Presiding Officer
PPK	People's Party of Kenya
PSC	Project Steering Committee
PSIO	Provincial Security Intelligence Officer
PVT	Parallel Voter Tabulation
RCK	Redeemed Churches of Kenya

RECAP	Research and Civic Awareness Programme
RO	Returning Officer
RRP	Republican Reform Party
SAP	Structural Adjustment Programme
SCC	Small Christian Community
SDA	Seventh Day Adventists
SDP	Social Democratic Party
SMB	Strategic Management Board
SNF	Somali National Front
SNV	Netherlands Development Organisation
SPK	Shirikisho Party of Kenya
SPM	Somali Patriotic Movement
SPSS	Statistical Package for the Social Sciences
STV	Stellavision
Supkem	Supreme Council of Kenya Muslims
TOT	Training of Trainers
TSS	Twahir Sheikh Said
UMA	United Muslims of Africa
UMMA	Umma Patriotic Party of Kenya
UNDP	United Nations Development Programme
UNICEF	United Nations Children's Fund
UPF	United Patriotic Front
UPPK	United People's Party of Kenya
USAID	United States Agency for International Development
VoK	Voice of Kenya
VP	Vice-President
YK'92	Youth for KANU 1992

Contributors

Francis Ang'ila Aywa is a programme officer at the Institute for Education in Democracy (IED), Nairobi, Kenya. He holds a Bachelor of Laws (LLB) degree from the University of Nairobi and is currently studying for his Master of Laws (LLM) degree at the same Institution. He has extensive experience in the civil society sector in Kenya and has written public education materials on elections, human rights and the rule of law. He also occasionally authors newspaper articles on current issues on governance in Kenya. At IED, he is in charge of the Electoral Process Monitoring Programme, which manages election observation, voter education, research and publications on democracy generally.

Norbert Braakhuis is a political scientist with a degree in international relations, and a speciality in African affairs obtained at the African Study Centre of the University of Bordeaux. He joined the Dutch Foreign Service in 1981. Having worked on West Africa-related issues, he was from 1995 to 99 posted at the Royal Netherlands Embassy in Nairobi as counsellor and head of the political section. He played an active role in the Donors Democratic Development Group through the Netherlands European Union chairmanship in Nairobi from July 1998 to the end of December 1999. He is currently head of the Middle East Division of the North Africa and Middle East Department at the Ministry of Foreign Affairs in The Hague.

Marren Akatsa-Bukachi is a senior programme officer with the Kenyan Institute for Education in Democracy (IED). She holds a BA degree in sociology from Delhi University. She was employed as Deputy Principal Rehabilitation Officer in the Kenyan Ministry of Social Services before joining the Young Women's Christian Association of Kenya (YWCA) as the National Programme Secretary. In 1995 she joined IED as Programme Officer in the Civic Education Programme and has been instrumental in the design and implementation of civic education projects. She participates in a number of local NGO networks promoting democracy and human rights. She has experience in both domestic and international election observation.

François Grignon is a political scientist and research fellow at the French Institute for Research in Africa (IFRA-Nairobi) and has been working on Kenyan politics and the democratisation process for the past seven years. He holds a PhD from the *Université Montesquieu* in Bordeaux (France). His thesis was on the rural politics of Machakos district. In his recent work, he has concentrated on the return to pluralism in Kenya. He co-edited a volume on Kenya's contemporary society, *Le Kenya Contemporain*, a special issue of the Journal *Politique Africaine* on Kenya, and co-edited with Hervé Maupeu, *L'Annuaire des Pays d'Afrique de l'Est* (2000).

Charles Hornsby is a regional IT manager for a large business in East Africa. He co-authored with David Throup *Multi-Party Politics in Kenya* (1998), and has written several articles on Kenyan electoral politics. His doctoral thesis at Oxford University was on the role of the Member of Parliament in the single party-system in Kenya. For many years he has combined a career in IT with a deep involvement in Kenyan politics.

Joe Kadhi is a journalism graduate of the University of Nairobi and Pacific Western University, California from where he holds a BSc and an MSc degree. He is the former Managing Editor of Kenya's *Daily Nation*. Currently, he lectures at the School of Journalism at the University of Nairobi and is a visiting professor at St Lawrence University. He writes a weekly political column for Kenya's oldest newspaper *The East African Standard* and publishes regularly in the monthly *Expression Today*.

Peter Mwangi Kagwanja is a lecturer in the Department of History and researcher at the Centre for Refugee Studies, Moi University, Kenya. He is also Fulbright fellow and doctoral candidate at the University of Illinois at Urbana Champaign, USA. He has written and published articles on human rights, refugees and labour issues. Currently, he is doing research on human rights, displacement and asylum in Africa with special reference to Kenya.

Karuti Kanyinga is a political scientist and a senior research fellow at the Institute for Development Studies (IDS), University of Nairobi, Kenya. He obtained his BA and MA degrees from the University of Nairobi in 1987 and 1990, respectively. In 1998, he obtained a PhD in social sciences from the International Development Studies (IDS), Roskilde University, Denmark. His dissertation was on the contemporary nature of politics and the land question in Kenya. Kanyinga has published extensively on Kenya's political economy, civil society and development, and electoral politics.

Musambayi Katumanga is an associate researcher and research fellow with the Institute of Policy Analysis and Research (IPAR) and the Series on Alternative Research in East Africa (SAREAT) in Nairobi, respectively. He is currently attached to the *Centre de Recherches et D'etudes sur les Pays D'Afrique Orientale* (CREPAO) at *Université de Pau et des Pays Del'adour* (UPPA) in France where he is undertaking a PhD in political science. He has previously tutored international relations, African politics and political theory at the University of Nairobi and the Catholic University of Eastern Africa, respectively before joining IPAR in 1996. He has written and published on conflicts in eastern Africa and the Great Lakes region of Africa, Kenya's foreign policy and civil society.

Wambui Kimathi holds a graduate certificate from the American University (1997), a graduate Diploma in Journalism (1991) and a BA degree from the University of Nairobi (1986). Currently, she is a programme co-ordinator with the Kenya Human Rights Commission. Until September 1999, she worked with the Institute for Education in Democracy (IED) in charge of the Electoral Process Programme. She co-ordinated the production of publications such as *A Report on the Electoral Environment in Kenya* (1996) and *National Elections Data Book, Kenya 1963-1997* (1997). She has recently written a report for the International Commission of Jurists, Kenya Chapter on 'The Political Economy of the Ethnic Clashes in Kenya' (to be published).

Hervé Maupeu holds a PhD in political science and currently is a lecturer in political science and a research fellow at the Centre for Research on Eastern African Countries, University of Pau (France). For the past fifteen years he has been working on the relations between ethnic identities, religion and politics in Kenya and Tanzania. He is currently co-heading a research programme entitled: 'Nairobi, the Identities of a City' and is the co-editor with François Grignon, of *L'Annuaire des Pays d'Afrique de l'Est* (2000).

Alamin Mazrui is Associate Professor of African American and African Studies at Ohio State University and has a doctorate in linguistics from Stanford University. He has taught at universities in Kenya, Nigeria and the USA and has served as a consultant to non-governmental organisations in Africa on such subjects as language, urbanisation, and language and the law. He has a special interest in human rights and civil liberties and has written policy reports on those subjects. He is also the author of five books, including a play and an anthology of poetry in Swahili. His latest book, *The Power of Babel: Language and Governance in the African Experience* (1998), is co-authored with Ali A. Mazrui.

Kimani Njogu studied linguistics at Nairobi and Yale Universities and is currently a senior lecturer in the Kiswahili and African Languages Department at Kenyatta University. He has written extensively on language, literature and popular culture. He is a council member of the International African Institute of the University of London as well as the chairman of the Kiswahili National Committee. His latest book is *Ufundishaji wa Fasihi: Nadharia na Mbinu*

(The Teaching of Literature: Theory and Method). He is currently working on a study of language and democratisation in Kenya.

Adams Oloo is a political scientist and lecturer at the Department of Government, University of Nairobi, Kenya. He is currently on study leave, undertaking a PhD programme at the University of Delaware, USA. He has authored and co-authored articles on legislative politics and governance in Kenya. His current research projects are on party politics and transition to democracy as well as the impact of ethnicity on electoral politics in Kenya.

Kenneth Ombongi is a historian and currently PhD candidate in medical history at the University of Cambridge, UK. He was trained in Nairobi and New Dehli. He was lecturer at the University of Nairobi, the United States International University (Nairobi) and Catholic University of Eastern Africa (Nairobi) and a researcher with the Wellcome Trust Medical Research Laboratory in Nairobi. His research interests cut across the fields of politics, medical and intellectual history. His PhD research work is on malaria control in Kenya. In this field he has published articles in medical journals.

Marc-Antoine Pérouse de Montclos is a political scientist and researcher with the Research Institute for Development (IRD). He holds a PhD from the *Institut d'Etudes Politiques* (IEP), Paris on urban violence and security in Nigeria and South Africa *(Violence et sécurité urbaines en Afrique du Sud et au Nigeria, un essai de privatisation: Durban, Johannesburg, Kano, Lagos et Port Harcourt).* His main interest is on armed conflicts and forced displacement. From 1996 to 1998 he conducted research on refugees in eastern Africa. He has written articles on Somali refugees in Kenya.

Ralph-Michael Peters holds an MA in political science of the *Freie Universität* Berlin. He is currently a research fellow with the *Institut für Afrika-Kunde*, Hamburg, Germany. He has studied Kenya's civil society and published on this issue (*Zivile und politische Gesellschaft in Kenya; Focus Afrika 5, IAK Diskussionsbeiträge; Hamburg: Institut für Afrika-Kunde*, 1996 and *Die Präsidentschafts- und Parlamentswahlen in Kenya 1997- Hintergründe, Verlauf, Resultate und politische Folgen; Focus Afrika 10, IAK Diskussionsbeiträge; Hamburg: Institut für Afrika-Kunde, 1998).* His current PhD research concentrates on democratisation processes and civil society in Kenya. Other interests are decentralisation and the media in the East African region.

Marcel Rutten is a geographer and senior researcher at the African Studies Centre, Leiden, Netherlands. He holds a PhD in policy sciences and was staff co-ordinator of the Election Observation Centre, the co-ordinating centre of the Western missions during the Kenya 1997 general elections. He has since the mid-1980s done longitudinal research on land tenure, water development and food security especially in semi-arid districts of Kenya. His main publications include *Selling Wealth to Buy Poverty: the Process of the Individualization of Landownership Among the Maasai Pastoralists of Kajiado District, Kenya, 1890-1990* (1992) and *The Diversity of Development* (1997, co-edited). His most recent publication is 'The Kenyan General Elections of 1997: Implementing a New Model for International Election Observation in Africa', in Abbink & Hesseling (2000) *Election Observation and Democratization in Africa*, London: Macmillan.

Preface and acknowledgements

This book, on the 1997 Kenya general elections, is the outcome of a three-day conference held at the African Studies Centre, Leiden, the Netherlands, from 28 to 30 September 1998. The organisation of the conference was a collaborative effort of the African Studies Centre (ASC) and the Nairobi office of the French Institute for Research in Africa (IFRA).

The idea for the book and conference was born within the Election Observation Centre (EOC) that acted as a co-ordinating secretariat of the Donors for Development and Democracy Group (DDDG) – 22 Western diplomatic missions and the European Commission – which observed the Kenyan elections. DDDG members at the time were Australia, Austria, Belgium, Canada, the Czech Republic, Denmark, Finland, France, Germany, Greece, Hungary, Italy, Japan, The Netherlands, Norway, Poland, Portugal, Spain, Sweden, Switzerland, United Kingdom, United States of America and the European Commission.

The staff members of the EOC consisted of four co-ordinators: Dr Judith Geist (USAID), Prof. Palle Svensson (Denmark-Aarhus University), Dr David Throup (British Foreign Office) and Dr Marcel Rutten (Netherlands-ASC). In addition, full-time assistance was provided by Ms Catherine Duhamel (Canada) and Ms Sabitha Raju (UK), while Dr François Grignon (France-IFRA), Dr Charles Hornsby (UK), Mr Peter Njenga (Kenya-SNV) and Mr Ralph-Michael Peters (Germany) contributed to the EOC's operations for short periods. Overall logistics and financial management was in the hands of Ms Laurie Rees (UK).

The main purpose of the EOC was to provide information to the DDDG missions concerning election rules, constituencies to be visited, what to observe, and to co-ordinate the travel plans of the DDDG missions. The main rationale for collaboration was to avoid the duplication of efforts. Another reason for the implementation of this new model of observation was the dissatisfaction with the traditional, short-term election observation by hastily prepared teams of international observers. Moreover, an election is more than just polling day: it includes many phases such as the issuance of ID cards, registration of voters and nomination of candidates.

In Leiden, over twenty specialists on Kenyan politics, local and international observers, international diplomats, NGO-representatives and Kenyan scientists reviewed the elections in detail, debating both technical as well as regional aspects of the elections and the observation methods. Their views were heard by an audience that included representatives of Dutch and foreign NGOs, foreign ministries and Kenyans in the Netherlands, among them Dr Yusuf

Nzibo, the Kenyan ambassador. Prof. Kivutha Kibwana, chairman of the National Convention Executive Council (NCEC) in Kenya, a platform for several groups in the Kenyan society campaigning for a review of the constitution, also attended, courtesy of HIVOS.

In this open-minded and stimulating environment, participants enthusiastically evaluated Kenyan politics and the election observation, happy to skip tea breaks, to take a short lunch and continue till late. Draft chapters presented by the authors were discussed and commented upon, the object being to provide a better understanding of the outcome of the Kenyan elections and to explain the new model for election observation. In addition, a scientific committee consisting of the editors and Charles Hornsby made detailed comments to each and every paper.

The editors would, first and foremost, like to thank all book contributors, discussants as well as participants during the conference. These include Paul Haddow and David Throup who were not able to contribute to this volume. We would also like to acknowledge the logistical support of the administrative staff of the African Studies Centre during the conference. We were equally grateful to HIVOS for enabling the participation of Prof. Kivutha Kibwana. Finally, the editors wish to thank the Royal Netherlands Embassy in Nairobi for their generous financial assistance to the holding of the conference, the participation of many Kenyan scholars and the resulting publication.

The views expressed in this book, however, are those of the authors and do not necessarily reflect the official position of the Dutch Ministry of Foreign Affairs or the Royal Netherlands Embassy in Nairobi. We hope the book has captured the thrilling atmosphere all participants experienced during the conference.

The Editors
January 2000

1

Observing and Analysing the 1997 General Elections: An Introduction

François Grignon, Marcel Rutten, Alamin Mazrui

Kenya held its first multi-party presidential and parliamentary elections since 1966 on 29 December 1992. It followed the footsteps of Zambia which, among the English-speaking African countries, had heralded the transition from single to multi-party politics in October 1991 (Andreassen *et al* 1992). The road to the institutionalisation of a pluralist political system after more than twenty years of a de-facto (1969-82) and then a de-jure (1982-91) single-party system had been a rocky one. The ruling party Kenya African National Union (KANU) witnessed in the 1990-91 years an intense political mobilisation contesting, often violently, the rule of President Daniel Toroitich arap Moi and illustrating the desire of Kenyans to bring about genuine changes in the country. The call by political clerics to restore pluralism or face a Romanian tragedy after the New Year's eve, and the mysterious assassination in February 1990 of Robert Ouko, then minister for Foreign Affairs, led Kenyans to challenge the impunity of their political leaders. *Saba Saba* (seven seven), i.e., 7 July 1990, was the starting point of one week of urban riots that became the symbol of this challenge and ultimately led to the return to multi-partyism. The government in reply established a KANU Review Committee chaired by Vice-President George Saitoti, which toured the country in August and September 1990 and received the grievances from the entire country. When this committee finally delivered its report, it recommended minor reforms like the reintegration of the expelled members of the party or the softening of its internal disciplinary measures. Demonstrating his perennial contempt for the genuine wishes of a population which had expressed loudly its aspirations for change, President Moi had once again despised the appeal. Hence, renewed political turmoil was to be expected. After six months of strategising and tergiversation, the climax of this mobilisation was reached through mass rallies at the Kamukunji independence grounds in October and November 1991. In addition, concerted pressure from the international community – that suspended multilateral aid after several revelations of high level corruption and the implication of State House officials in the killing of Robert Ouko – finally led to the return to multi-partyism in the following month.

The story of the tumultuous 1990-92 years has been dealt with by many scholars in great detail and will not be recalled any further (see e.g., Muigai 1993; Chege 1994; Waruhiu 1994; Grignon 1994, 1998a, 1998b and 1998d; Haugerud 1995; Lafargue 1996; Wanjohi 1997; and for the most comprehensive and detailed account, Throup and Hornsby 1998). Suffice to say that contrary to some early interpretations of these political changes and the propaganda of single-party advocates, the return to multi-partyism was not imposed by the international community and did not materialise as a spill-over effect of the changes that took place in eastern Europe.

The pressure that forced Daniel arap Moi and KANU to grant the opening of the political landscape came as much from the 'third wave' of global democratisation of the early 1990s as from the specific push of the international community at the end of 1991, as well as from the victims of the *Saba Saba* riots and Kamukunji demonstrations of 1990 and 1991 who paid the price of what they hoped would become their second liberation. As Samuel Decalo once put it: 'The spill-over effect, though it definitely crystallised and catalysed pro-democracy demonstrations in Africa, does not tell the whole story. The continent was already more than ripe for upheaval, and there was already additional internal and external factors that played a crucial role in leading the democratic pressures to successful fruition' (Decalo 1992:9).

Observing and analysing elections: which methodology?

Since the early 1990s, the field of electoral studies on Africa has slowly developed. After a few courageous research efforts had opened the way and showed that even under single-party regimes African elections were worth studying (CEAN/CERI 1978; Hermet et al 1978; Chazan 1979; Hayward 1987), more and more studies have been published, following the rhythm of electoral contagion that spread to almost all African countries. Yet, despite this renewed interest for African elections, few new perspectives seem to have emerged. As several bibliographical assessments of this literature revealed, most analysis focuses on the role of elections in the democratisation processes of Africa, but are usually pessimistic or doubtful about their usefulness or relevance for that matter (Buijtenhuijs and Thiriot 1995; Cowen and Laakso 1997; Otayek 1998). Moreover, these election studies rarely dwell with attempts to develop a comprehensive electoral sociology. Most of them are chronicles, short presentations and analysis of the results or developments on the prerequisites of genuine democratisation.

Few elections are studied in their own right, for what they reveal about the renewed patterns of domination in African countries, what voting really means, and what they say about the political socialisation of African electors. To a great extent, the results of the few scholars who have been working on the meaning of the 'elections without choice' have not been retained, and the diagnosis Fred Hayward made about the situation of the scientific literature almost fifteen years ago still applies today: 'Conventional wisdom about the importance, success, and meaning of elections in Africa in the 1970s and 1980s increasingly became negative and pessimistic . . . Some concluded that the misuse and abuse of electoral institutions demonstrated that the process was ill-suited to Africa' (Hayward 1987: 1). Moreover, despite the general emphasis on the consequences of the return to a multi-party system, no real sociology of political parties is ever attempted. The recycling of the political establishment in a multitude of small and inconsequential organisations as well as their lack of political programmes or ideology is usually emphasised. Why such a gloomy appraisal? Have political scientists become too cynical or intellectually disenchanted about the possibility of any significant change in Africa?

As Mike Cowen and Lisa Laakso stress, elections in Africa raise issues which are not new (Cowen and Laakso 1997). They raise the problem of political domination and regime legitimacy, the articulation between the local and national levels of politics, and the perennial problem of the lack of institutionalisation of legal procedures and techniques imported from European countries. In any case, even if almost a decade of pluralism has clearly shown its limits, few would seriously disagree about the assessment Samuel Decalo made in 1992: 'whatever the ultimate verdict – that, as with all social changes, is likely to be mixed – the political atmosphere is radically different: exhilarating, ebullient, optimistic. Former awe-inspiring leaders have without ceremony been cut down to size' (Decalo 1992:9). The return to multi-partyism and pluralist politics definitely brought a significant change to African polities, and as such the study of elections is crucial to understanding the nature of this change. Elections are indeed a very privileged moment of political interaction in any country and reveal a lot about its political culture. Yet, there are some significant theoretical and methodological issues which have to be dealt with in order to show and understand this culture.

Electoral studies: a Kenyan tradition
Kenya has held regular general elections since independence and has benefited from a regular and very rich flow of electoral studies. From the early 1960s up to now, a number of publications have attempted to decipher the different logics behind electoral politics and, as this volume again illustrates, some of this excellent work has been produced by Kenyan scholars, most of them trained at the Department of Government of the University of Nairobi, e.g., Engholm 1960; Bennet and Rosberg 1961; Sanger and Nottingham 1963; Gertzel 1970; Hyden and Leys 1972; Lamb 1974; Barkan 1976; Barkan and

Okumu 1978; Chege 1981; Mulaa 1981; Nzomo 1983; Oyugi 1983; Alila 1984a and 1984b; Barkan 1984; Khadiagala 1984; Orwa 1984; Wanjohi 1984a and 1984b; Bourmaud 1985; Barkan 1987; Hornsby, 1989; Hornsby and Throup 1992 and Throup 1993.

As the early work of the 1960s mainly described the electoral processes that lead to independence and the installation of single-party regimes, most of the studies conducted by Joel Barkan and John Okumu in the 1970s emphasised the role of elections for the regulation of political competition during the Kenyatta era and the acute understanding that Kenyan electors could have of this political game. A heavy blow was sent to the developmentalist school and its theory of the passivity of the African masses entrenched in their traditions.

In the 1980s, the complexity of Kenyan politics was revealed a step further, thanks to the perspective brought by the different works showing the conflicting patterns taking place among rural and urban constituencies. The stimulating work on the 1983 elections by the staff members of the Department of Government of the University of Nairobi (Chege, Mulaa, Alila, Nzomo, Orwa, Oyugi, Wanjohi) illustrated how the study of local politics contributed to the understanding of Kenya's complex polity. This work greatly influenced many of the contributors of this volume. From the mid-1980s, the increased authoritarianism of the Kenyan regime and the forced exile of many Kenyan scholars limited the possibility of extensive fieldwork and independent research. Fortunately, since the early 1990s, and the reopening of the country to free speech and free thinking, the flow has of course resumed.

Following this renewal, a debate has risen on the assessment of the changes that took place in Kenya as in other parts of Africa. This debate rose from the disappointments of the democratisation flops in the wake of the first pluralist elections of the early 1990s. To many hopefuls, the absence of government change over despite heavily contested pluralist elections (Cameroon, Côte'Ivoire, Gabon, Mali, Ghana, Zimbabwe, Kenya) and the authoritarian patterns shown by the new rulers of the liberalised polities (Zambia, Niger, Burkina-Faso, Congo) illustrated the illusory belief in the democratisation of African societies. To summarise their argument, the undifferentiated social structures of African countries and the accumulated experience of 30 years of authoritarian rule combined with the legacy of almost untouched colonial structures of government could not allow fast and genuine rooting of the democratic experience. No genuine democratisation then, but what was the real impact of political liberalisation? Interpretations can differ tremendously in this respect.

For some, considering the current state of political development of African countries, multi-partyism does not make any difference. Patronage and ethnicity are the key entries for understanding politics and the study of the new elite's behaviour definitely illustrates that nothing is really going to change (Daloz 1999). Worse still, multi-partyism could even lead to the break-up of the fragile post-colonial polities where ethnic identities are much stronger than any national or class consciousness. It has led to the expression of ethnic nationalism which often supersedes the past politics of development or clanism. Through the presidential contest, the rivalries between individuals have now become a competition between ethnic groups. Among the analysts of Kenyan politics, David Throup and Charles Hornsby illustrated this trend to the extreme. They concluded their encyclopaedia on the return to multi-party politics and the 1992 general elections in the following way:

> The election clearly demonstrated the primacy of ethnicity over ideology. Of all the myriad sources for internal divisions within the opposition between compromisers and purists, old and young, politicians and professionals, conservatives and radicals – it was the division between Kikuyu and Luo which eclipsed all else. Communal solidarity did not have to be enforced but was clearly voluntary in the homelands of the four major presidential candidates. As President Moi warned, multi-party democracy has intensified ethnic rivalries and completed the isolation of the Kikuyu who, even more than the Luos in the 1960s, are totally identified with the opposition. Thus, although single party states are unlikely to sustain accountability, they may create an effective political order in Africa's ethnically divided societies. They provide some controls on centrifugal tendencies that threaten to fragment the still comparatively insecure and weakly institutionalised state structures. Even single-party rule may provide a more attractive alternative to multi-partyism in the form of single-party states, in which each party is all powerful in its own ethnic stronghold, but where one group controls the centre and the distribution of patronage and development. . . . The events of 1992-4 clearly demonstrated the primacy of individuals and ethnicity over policy, ideology and class, though the ethnic identification revealed was more a rational reflection of economic self-interest than some 'traditional' pattern of political orientation. . . . Multi-party competition also starkly revealed the lack of political principle within the Kenyan élite. The primary objective of most political leaders seemed to be personal gain and financial advantage. Kenya proved to have few statesmen or citizens of political principle. Many were open to the highest bidder, which inevitably, given its control of the State, was KANU (Throup and Hornsby 1998: 590-92).

This assessment of the Kenyan political changes may be harsh but it has been substantiated by very high quality data from primary and secondary sources and the most extensive and comprehensive analysis of Kenyan politics that has ever been published. The authors have displayed an intimacy with the contradictions of Kenyan politics which is as challenging as it is striking. To their credit, Throup and Hornsby have written a 'loud and clear' in-depth study that many Western commentators and analysts of African politics believe, but would never publish for fear of jeopardising their careers. So, in the end, is there anything wrong with their conclusions?

To a great extent, the chapters in this book proceed from the same approach as Throup and Hornsby. Many have tried, more or less successfully, to display the same mastery and talent in revealing the intricacies of Kenyan politics, articulating the consequences of local politics on national power relations and vice-versa. Yet, they are also very different. Indeed, many of them are extremely different, especially in their interpretation of the facts, in so far as they try to understand the Kenyan political culture and its internal changes for what they are and not for what they should be (see also in the same vein Haugerud 1995; Grignon 1998c and 1998d). They attempt to reveal the potentials and prospects of Kenyan politics as elements of an historical trajectory which will never be similar to the European one. As Sindjoun (1997:89), has convincingly demonstrated in the case of Cameroon which is very similar to Kenya: 'it is highly questionable to minimise the changes induced by pluralist electoral competition even if they prove to be tainted by numerous irregularities . . . pluralism, however imperfect, produces new beliefs, new patterns of representations and new types of actions which affect political competition despite the possible stability of the leadership.' We should not be blinded by 'the illusion of continuity'. Before proceeding to a rapid presentation of the chain of events that led to the 1997 general elections, it is necessary to dwell briefly on the theoretical and methodological background which is at the heart of the analysis and understanding of electoral processes in Africa, and which can lead to contradicting interpretations of their meaning.

Some theoretical clarifications: how developmentalism re-enters through the backdoor

The conclusions presented above by Throup and Hornsby have a strange similarity with the words of their developmentalist peers, published in the 1960s, just after independence. Developmentalism is indeed re-entering through the backdoor, in the shadow of strategic analysis and especially its neo-Weberian variation (see also Otayek 1997). The perception of African politics has changed, of course. Political development is not addressed directly as the main focus and scholars do not talk anymore about the penetration of the state in rural societies, the 'backwardness' of rural masses or the necessity of national integration. The analysis has gained a great deal of empirical strength and the epistemological turnaround of the early 1980s has been partly integrated: no more grand theories, no more general model. The main focus is not on the political system or on its functions but on the political actors and their strategies. Yet, the absence of clearly stated theoretical reference does not mean that it is not included in the analysis, quietly shaping the interpretation of the facts presented and the methodology that led to the collection of these facts.

In the sociological jargon, the theoretical framework we are dealing with here is one of the variations of what is usually called strategic analysis. Strategic analysis was a reaction against the theoretical approaches of the 1960s and the 1970s when developmentalism and the neo-Marxist dependency theory had shown their limits. It led to a healthy methodological return to the primacy of empirical data over theoretical models, the need to consider African history in order to understand contemporary society, and the absolute necessity to focus on the actors in this history, and on their strategies, since they were considered instrumental in determining historical forces (Deloye 1996). Strategic analyses resulted in different variations, with differences expressed over the methodology used, the type of actors considered and the interpretation of the role of culture in the analysis. These differences are important as they raise two patterns of interpretation at the heart of the debate we are interested in: neo-Weberian analogies and cultural analysis.

The main interpretation trend in political science is usually inspired by Weberian sociological theory. It focuses mainly on state capacity, elite politics, factional rivalries, political and economic networks of power. This theory built the concept of neo-patrimonialism to characterise contemporary African polities and identified the behaviour of the 'big man' as its main embodiment (Médard 1982, 1991 and 1992). Implicitly using the ideal-type methodology, African states are analysed in reference to the rational-legal model of bureaucratic domination characteristic of the European pattern of political development. The Weberian typology is solicited to identify a type of domination which corresponds to a mixture of tradition and modernity. From one of the ideal-types of traditional domination, the patrimonial one, the concept of neo-patrimonialism is built as an hybrid form of legal-rational domination perverted by patrimonial patterns of behaviour such as the confusion between the public and private spheres and, especially, varying degrees of institutionalisation. The big man manages his political career as an entrepreneur, investing his different kinds of capital (economic, political, social, symbolic) to enable him consolidate and gain more power. The analysis and interpretation of electoral processes and election results presented above proceeds from the same school of thought and suffers from a number of serious drawbacks.

First, the focus is often exclusively centred on the politics of the elite, even local elite, considering the common man's understanding of it all as irrelevant. Second, it assumes that because there is no exclusive class-consciousness in Africa there is no conflict with socio-economic dimensions. Then, it perpetuates a reification of ethnicity to explain the nature and dynamics of African politics.

It argues that this 'vertical' link refrains any 'horizontal' social stratification. It leaves aside the fact that identities are never exclusive, and that ethnicity might well be the principal idiom of expression of contemporary socio-economic conflicts and political ideologies. But more dangerously, the neo-Weberian methodology is always riddled with ethno-centrism, and often opens the backdoor for the return of developmentalists' assumptions. If many authors have managed to control efficiently that risk, others have kept in their minds the 'model' of the European-bureaucratic entity built up by Weber as an ideal-type. This is clear in the Jackson and Rosberg typologies of personal rule (Jackson and Rosberg 1982), in Richard Sandbrook's famous book, *The politics of Africa's economic stagnation* (Sandbrook 1985), and in the work of Throup and Hornsby. In his analysis, Sandbrook implied, as did Goran Hyden in his *No shortcuts to progress* (Hyden 1985), that ultimately the only way to get peasants out of the 'economy of affection', to get at last a 'real' state with a 'real' bourgeoisie and a 'real' working class[1] stimulating 'real' ideological debates for a 'real' democratic election to take place, was either to use state-sponsored coercive means and develop capitalism by force for a good number of years or, recently, in a more IMF/governance-inspired approach, to let the 'miracle of the market' do its work by destructuring bit after bit the colonial inherited and overdeveloped state machinery.

The apologists of the governance/free-market/civil society triptic dream, to a certain extent, about the same African future as the neo-developmentalists or neo-Weberian adepts. It is a future which looks very much like the Western one. They just differ on the ways to achieve it. They cannot conceive an African future which will be the product of its own historicity, and they sometimes give unsolicited opinions and judgements on what is best for African countries and what their history should be. Our criticism is based on two different grounds: the interpretation of the data offered to the analyst in his quest to understand African contemporary societies and his role as a Western social scientist dealing with a foreign society where he will always remain a guest and a non-actor. Many 'foreign experts', usually Western, are nowadays involved in the observation of African elections. This book is partly the product of such an involvement. Moreover, since the participation of foreign academics in the election observation exercise in Kenya has been considered to be a new model for this type of activity, it is important to reflect on its limits. Whether presented in academic journals or in semi-confidential reports handed-over to their diplomatic contractors, the interpretation of African politics by social scientists should proceed from the same approach, largely inspired by historical and cultural sociology.

Historical and cultural sociology: some principles

The definition of area studies might be a convenient way to organise departments of scientific institutions but it has no scientific relevance. Politics in Africa, Europe, America or Asia proceed from the same logic, the same ambitions, the same aspirations for power and domination by human beings. The forms, the expression of these political relations, are of course different, but none of them is unique. Although they are the result of different historical trajectories which have shaped the way people think and the way they talk, none of them is fundamentally or substantially different (see for the different dimensions of this school of thought Coulon and Martin 1991). Therefore, the Western historical trajectory is not a model but most definitely the non-exportable product of its own specificities. Moreover, considered on a world scale, it was shared only by a small minority. However dominant in the past, political scientists have nothing to do with the reproduction and the perpetuation of its hegemony. As Tom Young once put it: 'Africans should be left alone with the only right worth having ... the right to construct their own future in their own way' (Young 1993: 309). And no Western social scientist has any business telling Africans what they should do with their own lives or what kind of government they deserve. What they are here to do is to contribute to the proper understanding of African societies and, as much as they can, inform their own governments about the right course of action.

In order to do so, the first principle is definitely to apply humility and analyse to what extent the scientific knowledge and debates that take place for the interpretation of European or American polities are relevant to understand the African ones. The understanding of the so-called 'exotic' polities requires the same scientific rigour, the same methodological safeguards and the same theoretical thinking as any other one. In this respect, the historical sociology of European polities and the interpretative debates on the 'rationality' of the European elector are highly relevant for the study of African elections. The act of voting, as it is performed now in Western societies, is the product of a political socialisation intimately linked to the changes of the relation between the European state and society after the First World War. Bribery, violence, vote buying, communal voting, or the absence of secret ballot were critical characteristics of the European polling scenes not so long ago and still remain prevalent in some regions (Bacot 1993). The European trend has been marked by a progressive learning and mass internalisation from the late nineteenth century onwards of an 'electoral civility' which sanctifies the vote as the individual expression of one's opinion through the secret ballot (Garrigou 1992; Deloye 1993; Ihl 1993). Yet, this domestication of the citizenry through the social institutionalisation of strict electoral techniques, implementing slowly a ritualised and pacified form of political expression, does not mean that voting has become what the democratic theory wanted it to be.

Other works of electoral sociology have clearly demonstrated that voting had very little to do with a rational choice based on the arguments presented by parties with different ideological inclinations. Such a conception of Western politics is a dream or, worse still, a blinding and patronising belief in superiority. It confuses democratic theory with actual situations. Sociological investigations have shown that the majority of the electorate was not intellectually equipped or even interested in assessing the political programmes of parties (Gaxie 1977). Voting in Europe is often an internalised call for duty to which the electorate answers through the mediation of their positioning in society, and according to the electoral offers from political parties. Voting is, therefore, as much a predisposition as a transaction. It is through the exchange (social, symbolic, economic) with political entrepreneurs that latent socio-political predispositions crystallise in opinions and votes:

> Voting is the result of the more or less stable conjunction between how a candidate or a party is perceived (comparatively with his/its competitors) and the beliefs of the voters as they have been shaped by their personal primary and secondary socialisation and the history of the specific political arena within which it is taking place . . . electoral predispositions and orientations are reactivated though the networks of interactions that constitute the primary groups of socialisation, among which associations, religious institutions, political parties or unions play as much a role as families, neighbourhood groups or other communities (Gaxie 1985:20-24).

Three dimensions are therefore systematically entrenched in the act of voting: a transaction, an expression of belonging or an identity, and a conviction. The analytical differentiation between exchange voting, communal voting and opinion voting which is often presented to reveal the social intricacies of electoral politics (Ihl 1996) should nevertheless not be taken as three different empirical situations corresponding to different stages of political development. Whatever the level of pacification of the electoral process and whatever the internalisation of the electoral discipline by the voters, those three dimensions are always empirically entrenched in the voting behaviour of the electorate.

What can we learn from the European experience and the scientific debates that surround its interpretation then? First, Europe is not the embodiment of democratic theory and Africa is not its distorted image, reflecting a mismatch between an exported political machinery imposed on an hostile culture. Electoral sociology tells us that the European voter is not always rational. He is often politically illiterate and does not operate according to a calculated choice balancing his interests as the democratic theory implies. His voting behaviour is the product of his belonging to society and of the given state of the political arena.

Voting is, therefore, as much the expression of identity as an opinion and an exchange. It is the product of the three rhythms of history. Long-time history shapes the representations and beliefs associated with the social positions and family experiences of the electorate, through several generations. Medium-time history produces the structure of the political offer and the ways and means of electoral politics. Short-time history determines the actual political offer itself leading to the specific choices of the electorate. The respective histories of each country shape the respective structure of their polities, the respective socialisation of their populations and the respective offer which will be available on voting day. Each country is the product of its own specificities but every polity – African, European, American or Asian – is shaped by the same logic. It would be ridiculous to expect European ways of doing politics and class-related ideological references in African polities where they only have a very remote significance. The same way the social and institutional history of the past two centuries have shaped current European polities, the specific historicity of African countries must be taken into account to understand the recent trends in Africa. While in France and Britain two industrial revolutions gave birth to class-based political parties and while confessional belonging has proved to be one of the heaviest long term factors influencing electoral behaviours, in Kenya the socio-economic differentiation relevant for its politics is, to a great extent, regional in character – a result of colonial and post-colonial government policies together with discrepancies in access to power and wealth due to age, lineage or gender.

Ethnicity is, therefore, one of the languages used to express other socio-economic or political aspirations. As any other identity, it has no substance in itself. Often underlying the seemingly formidable force of ethnic consciousness are issues of political representation and resource distribution. Furthermore, even when voting behaviour appears to reflect membership in a particular ethnic group – suggesting the now popular notion of ethnic voting blocs – rather than adherence to a particular ideology, it must be seen as no more than a component of an otherwise dynamic and multifaceted identity. Kenyan voters do indeed carry the ethnic labels of Kamba, Kikuyu, Luo, Kalenjin etc. but their civic identities are by no means limited to these labels. Kenyan voters, in other words, are also influenced by even more subtle identities such as age group or (sub) clan as well as their socio-economic location in society as taxpayers, as employed or unemployed persons, as city or rural dwellers. There is ample evidence in the contributions to this book, that these multiple aspects of identity above and beyond ethnicity, in the common yet narrow sense of the word, constitute particular interests which, in combination, come to influence the political and voting behaviour of individuals.

In the end, the specific historical trajectory of Kenya, articulated around its long-time, medium-time and short-time dimensions, produced specific political languages or what Angelique Haugerud and John Lonsdale have identified as a specific culture of politics (Lonsdale 1992; Haugerud 1997). Yet, the social mechanisms that lead to these specificities are neither unique nor exotic. They are pretty banal and common, similar to what can be identified in other parts of the world. Therefore, as for any other European or American polity, the aspirations for democracy, human rights protection, consumerism or welfare expressed by different corners of Kenyan society are genuine demands which deserve international consideration and recognition despite the discrepancies between them and the actual situation of the economy and polity of the country. Such contradictions are a common social phenomenon and do not invalidate in any way the relevance of the democratic claims. This is why there is absolutely no reason for Western analysts or diplomats to treat African polities differently from their own. Kenyan citizens deserve 'free and fair' elections and a democratic government as much as any other voters. It is not because they are Africans that: 'a bit rigging is acceptable, considering the political development of the country' as a Western diplomat shamelessly commented after the 1997 results were announced. Moreover, whichever the route taken by Kenya, whatever the failures and the actual result of the past ten years of democratisation, every single issue of the free press which has been published, every single political prisoner who has come out of jail, every single rape, beating, killing which has been avoided, because its possible perpetrator knew that impunity was not anymore totally guaranteed, makes a difference. And this difference shows that the return to multi-partyism was not in vain and that it brought a significant change to the daily lives of the Kenyan population.

This is the methodological and theoretical background which was, to great extent, adopted in this volume. Before proceeding to the actual analysis of the electoral process, we still need to introduce the context in which the polls and their observation took place.

General background of the 1997 polls

Election observation: towards a new model
The Kenya 1992 elections were characterised by widespread allegations of irregularities, such as stuffing of ballot boxes, destroying opposition votes and count rigging (see e.g., Barkan 1993; NEMU 1993; Throup and Hornsby 1998). Local observer groups had united in the National Electoral Monitoring Unit (NEMU). They trained and deployed some 8,000 domestic observers throughout the country. The international community observed the elections in the usual way: election observers from all over the world were flown in some days before election day (29 December) and left shortly afterwards. The

two most important outside teams were the Washington-based International Republican Institute (IRI) and the Commonwealth Secretariat team. In addition, national delegations from Denmark, Egypt, Germany, Japan and Switzerland were sent. Still, there were fewer than 200 international observers for 7,000 polling stations. The co-ordination of election observation efforts by the foreign missions was minimal and neither the foreign nor the local observer groups had the capacity or resources comprehensively to investigate rigging allegations. Consequently, they reported only the most blatant and easily verifiable irregularities.

Having learnt their lessons from their 1992 experience and eager to prevent any similar criticism of inefficiency and sometimes 'election observation tourism', local observer groups and the international community embarked on a new model for election observation. From the earliest stages in 1997, Western embassies devised various observation methods to obtain a more comprehensive and in-depth insight into the electoral process, not just limited to election day. Domestic observer groups, including the churches, received financial support to train and deploy almost 30,000 local observers while the international community employed diplomats stationed at the embassies and guided by a small election observation centre of specialists of Kenyan politics and election observation. Its major purpose was to provide information to 22 Western missions concerning election rules, constituencies to be visited, and what to observe as well as co-ordinating the travel plans of the missions.

The main bottleneck the observers faced was the uncertainty regarding the date of the elections. In principle they should have been held in 1997, five years after the 1992 elections and at the end of President Moi's term. The elections could be held within a period of some three months after the president decided to dissolve parliament. As a result, the donor group needed to prepare itself for observing the elections somewhere between August 1997 and April 1998. By December 1997 the international community at large had, therefore, set up an original combination of direct involvement in the observation exercise, which would be greatly reinforced by the mobilisation of embassies' staff on polling day, and support to the local observers, aiming at being present in every single polling station of the country. It finally demonstrated a genuine commitment to the support of 'free and fair' polls in Kenya.

For the ruling party KANU, the main political goal of these elections was not only the re-election of President Moi and the reconduction of a majority in parliament which could form a government, it was also to determine the scenario through which the head of state would happily retire from active national politics and devote his time to the resolution of the regional conflicts tearing apart Kenya's neighbours. As the 'Mzee' of eastern African politics, Daniel arap Moi, had on several occasions expressed his wish to pass over the

Kenyan mantle, and had proposed his services to facilitate peace processes in the Sudan and Somalia. KANU was, therefore, supposed to deliver a comfortable victory to its leader in order to peacefully solve the succession issue within its ranks and safeguard the security of the outgoing regime's members accumulated wealth. For all purposes, KANU, especially the close associates of the president among its ranks, had necessarily to win and seemed ready to deploy, once again, all means to do so.

By January 1997, President Moi had organised a major reshuffle of his cabinet for the preparation of the elections. The main result of this reshuffle was the full reinstatement of Nicholas Kipyatur Biwott, his long-time aide, who had been suspended from the government since December 1991 after his alleged involvement in the Ouko murder saga. This reshuffle also implemented the demise of several opponents of Biwott, including heavyweight cabinet ministers such as Kipkalya Kones (Internal Security), William ole Ntimama (Local Government) and Simeon Nyachae (Agriculture) KANU-A faction to junior ministries. As Daniel arap Moi started to systematically hit the campaign trail, it was not only a vigorous election campaign which was offered to the Kenyan electorate, it was also a succession scenario. The Kenyan voters were not only asked to decide whether they wanted to give a final term to their long-time leader, but also to endorse his choices for the succession which was to be orchestrated mainly by cabinet ministers Joseph Kamotho, Nicholas Biwott and Vice-President George Saitoti. This grand alliance, reintroducing the 'Kikuyu element' at the heart of the succession, was identified as KANU-B and nicknamed 'KABISA' by the popular press (from Kamotho, Biwott, Saitoti), a word meaning 'total' in Kiswahili, as a sign of its total control of state power and total determination to keep the presidency. In order to better understand the answer of the Kenyan electorate, and more broadly the 'total' rejection of the succession scenario advertised by Daniel arap Moi, whatever the tricks, tactics and strategies which allowed him to be re-elected and KANU to regain a tiny majority in parliament, it is highly necessary to recall the economic and social basis that informed the electorate's decision, and equally to evaluate the political alternatives offered by the opposition parties as well as the proofs they provided of their capacity to rule the country if they won the elections.

The 1992-1997 years
The bitterly fought 1992 general elections left the country's economic, social and political landscape in disarray. The opposition parties were devastated by their defeat. They felt strongly that they were cheated and, more generally, never really recovered from it or learnt the lessons of their mistakes (see Throup and Hornsby 1998). But, on the KANU side, there was no reason to triumph.

The personal humiliation suffered by President Moi in Luo Nyanza and Central Province where not a single KANU MP was elected and where he obtained less than 5 per cent of the votes, and the somehow mitigated results he made in Eastern (37 per cent) and Western provinces (41 per cent) blatantly confirmed the main outcome of the 1992 contest. A huge majority of Kenyans (63 per cent of the voters but most probably 75 per cent of the entire 1992 electorate if we account all those who could not register) wanted him out of office. Some communities might come back to him as a second best bet to avoid the return of a Kikuyu president (Matiba, Kibaki) or the coming of a Luo one (Oginga Odinga), but Moi was not a first choice for the majority of Kenyans. The turnout of the 1992 elections had been the highest since 1963: 67.9 per cent of registered voters. Daniel arap Moi did not really win these elections, a divided opposition lost them.

In addition, the 1992 general elections had been costly. A minimalist economic assessment estimated that between 300-500 million US dollars were diverted from the state coffers by the ruling party during 1992, depriving the country of at least 2 per cent of GDP growth and bringing the inflation rate to more than 40 per cent (Barkan 1993: 89). Moreover, the improvement of the situation seemed extremely fragile. Throughout the 1993-97 years, a frightening contrast developed within the government between the efforts of a few technocrats to keep the economy afloat by tightening the spending belt and improving relations with the international community, and the systematic looting and waste KANU politicians kept committing with an amazing consistency on the meagre government revenues (the Controller and Auditor General's Report for the financial year 1995/1996 estimated the unaccounted expenditures of the government at Ksh.107.5 billion! An increase of 300 per cent compared to the Ksh.34.7 billion of 1993/1994 (CGD 1998). From 1993, both the new Central Bank director, Micah Cheserem, and the minister for Finance, Musalia Mudavadi, were credited with some success in putting back the country on the right track. Following the implementation of a tight monetary policy and the resumption of the support to the balance of payments after the long-awaited first implementation of structural adjustment measures in 1993, macro-economic indicators showed some improvement.

The overall GDP growth rate which had gone down to 0.4 per cent in 1993 rose to 4.3 per cent in 1995 and remained at an encouraging 4.6 per cent in 1996 before suffering again from election anxiety (2.3 per cent in 1997). As a result, the Kenyan GDP per capita figure stood at around US$270 in the 1990s. Inflation which had risen to 46 per cent in 1993 came down to 28.8 per cent in 1994, before falling to 1.8 per cent in 1995 and coming back to roughly 10 per cent in 1996. The depreciation of the Kenyan shilling was a good stimulation for national exports which rose by 20 per cent between 1995 and 1996, and the exceptionally high international prices of tea and coffee guaranteed high reserves of foreign currencies to settle the import bill. Yet, the financing of this macro-economic recovery, which also included a reduction of the total external debt from US$4,687 million to US$3,900 million in 1997, was done mainly by issuing treasury bills and bonds which almost brought the country to a financial crisis – the three-months bills reached interest rates of 27 per cent at some point. The internal debt consequently skyrocketed to Ksh.140 billion in 1997 (US$2.3 billion) bringing its service to roughly US$450 million, more than twice the amount of the Enhanced Structural Adjustment Facility (ESAF) disbursement agreed for the same year – which was in fact frozen.

The apparent recovery of some macro-economic indicators, moreover, hardly hid the worrying signs coming from the production and employment sides. Foreign direct investments (FDI) almost disappeared from Kenya in 1993 and 1994 and remained at miserable levels even in 1996 and 1997 (US$33 million, 37 million, 100 million and 101 million, respectively). Comparatively, Uganda and Tanzania benefited from US$851 million and 684 million of FDI in 1996 and US$1.6 and 4.9 billion in 1997, respectively (EAC 1998). Whereas these FDI contributed to the creation of 12,000 jobs in Kenya in 1996 and 1997, they created over the same period of time 48,500 jobs in Uganda and 57,000 jobs in mainland Tanzania. Indeed, the times when Kenya inspired confidence in international investors are long gone and the international financial transfers that could be accounted for were only attracted by speculative short-term investments in the government's 91 days treasury bills. Even more worrying, the agricultural sector, which still represents 28 per cent of the GDP, remained depressed throughout the period. Coffee, once the black gold of the country, still earned more than Ksh.16 billion in 1996 and 1997, but this was due to exceptional high international prices. The national output remained depressed (70,000-100,000 tonnes whereas it had reached constant outputs of 120,000-130,000 tonnes in the late 1970s and early 1980s), smallholder producers of the Central Province being the first to abandon their production, suffering from the mismanagement and politicking of their co-operatives. The milk, tea, sugar, rice and cereals sectors, suffering equally from politicking, half-baked implementation of structural adjustment programmes, lack of competitiveness on the now opened national market and the dumping of foreign goods imported by 'politically correct' businessmen, were also tremendously threatened. Maize and wheat producers suffered most from the ethnic violence. Hectarage and production of maize, the most important food crop in the country, which had decreased between 1990 and 1994, never recovered their levels of 1989 (IEA 1998: 308) and Kenya has now become a net structural importer of maize, incapable of meeting its population's needs.

Illegal dumping of imported goods eased by political connections also became a threat to the local manufacturers. The quantity of tyres, clothes, edible oils, etc., entering Kenya in transit to Uganda, Tanzania, Burundi and Rwanda but being 'lost' en route, reached such proportions between 1993 and 1997 that several foreign investors complained bitterly to the government about this unfair competition. Firestone East Africa Ltd warned the government that this dumping was seriously threatening their operations in the country. At least 20,000 jobs were lost in the textile industry between 1993 and 1995 due to unfair competition from clothes and shoes of South-East Asia origin and the reduction of the American import quota from 1 million to 380,000 shirts a year (EIU 1996). Imports from India reached US$250 million in 1995 compared to US$12.5 million in 1990. Consequently, whereas the trade deficit consistently worsened and reached an all-time high of Ksh.760 billion in 1997, the manufacturing sector created only a meagre 23,000 jobs between 1993 and 1997 and more than 1.5 million Kenyans had no other choice than to adopt survival strategies within the informal sector. By 1997, with a total workforce of approximately 10 million people, Kenya had only 4.7 million workers employed either in the private, public or informal sector (EIU 1999). With such a crippled economy, the impoverishment of the great majority of Kenyans worsened tremendously and the disparities between the rich and the poor increased dramatically.

By 1994 the bottom 20 per cent of the rural population received only 3.5 per cent of the rural income and in urban areas, the bottom 20 per cent received only 5.4 per cent. On the other hand, the top 20 per cent of the population controlled 61 per cent of the rural and 51 per cent of urban incomes. These disparities only increased with the decline of education standards. Less than half of those who enrolled for primary education in the 1990s completed it. The increase of university fees to resorb their public debts, as recommended under SAPs agreements, provoked a direct decrease in national enrolment (-5.2 per cent in 1996/97). Yet, the demand by Kenyans for secondary and university education remains very high. More than 200,000 of the children who qualified for enrolment in secondary education in 1997 could not get places. In 1995-96, the proportion of those qualifying for post-secondary education but failing to get a place reached 75-80 per cent (EIU 1999:18).

On the political side, the kleptocratic nature of the Kenyan state was bluntly revealed. Far from seeking to serve effectively a variety of politico-economic and social interests on behalf of its citizens, or even as a useful mediator between them, the Kenyan state has historically been seen as an unending source for private accumulation. One year after the 1997 general elections an editorial of a Kenyan weekly echoed the views of Frantz Fanon in the following words: 'We do not have capitalists in this economy. Nor do we have what Marxists refer to as a national bourgeoisie. What we have are a group of parasites who depend on the patronage of the state to stay in business, and who depend on money borrowed from banks to live opulent and ostentatious lives' (*Weekly Review* 04/12/98). It is quite fitting, then, that in 1998 Transparency International rated Kenya as the eleventh most corrupt nation among those surveyed (*Business Day* 03/12/98). Confronted with a rapidly diminishing supply of international financial resources to plunder, increasing political pressure from unionised workers and other sections of the civil society, and mounting sanctions from the Bretton Woods institutions, the regime resorted to all sorts of desperate measures to ensure its material and political survival – from violence to natural and public resources thievery. And it is partly against this backdrop that the notorious 'Goldenberg' scandal must be seen.

The 1993-97 years in Kenya were, to a great extent, the 'Goldenberg years'. Kamlesh Pattni, the director of Goldenberg International Ltd, the firm which benefited from unjustified compensation from the central bank for illusionary gold exports recently re-evaluated at US$ 600 million, not only bankrolled KANU's political activities during and after the 1992 general elections but succeeded in ruining the credibility of the most formidable parliamentary opposition to the government: FORD-Kenya. Soon after the elections, the revelations that Jaramogi Oginga Odinga had received 'gifts' from Pattni for a by-election campaign provoked the first break within the party, as a group of 'Young Turks', including Paul Muite, Kiraitu Murungi and Gitobu Imanyara, decided to resign from their leadership positions.

But two years later, following Kijana Wamalwa's succession after Jaramogi's death in January 1994, Pattni managed again to completely discredit FORD-Kenya's leadersnip. This time allegations of bribery were made against Kijana Wamalwa. It was stated Wamalwa, as the head of the Public Accounts Committee, had recommended that more money should be given to Goldenberg International by the Central Bank. It was Musalia Mudavadi, the KANU minister for Finance, who had to battle and have the recommendation struck out from the report before its approval by parliament. This episode irremediably led to an increase of the battle between Raila Odinga and Kijana Wamalwa for the leadership of FORD-Kenya and subsequently provoked its break-up when Raila Odinga left for the National Development Party (NDP), taking with him most of the Luo following.

FORD-Asili and the Democratic Party (DP) suffered a different fate from that of FORD-Kenya but neither of them gave a testimony of their capability to rule with some efficiency. The divisive strategy followed by KANU and its government towards both formations was to promote anti-Kikuyu feelings among them and lead to the isolation of their leaders, Kenneth Matiba and Mwai Kibaki. This strategy was not even needed to tame FORD-Asili, since the illness and uncompromising attitude of Kenneth Matiba in rejecting the election results and his quarrelling with his secretary general, Martin Shikuku, led to the slow but certain collapse of the party. Moreover, if Matiba retained some popularity in Central Province and FORD-Asili did not lose a single by-election among the Kikuyu, Martin Shikuku faced defeat after defeat, losing all his fellow FORD-Asili Luhya MPs to KANU and their seats in the subsequent by-elections.

The DP suffered most from the divisive strategies of KANU. Propagating the prejudice that Kikuyu political leaders could not be trusted, KANU put pressure on the DP Kamba MPs and tried at the same time to prop up agreements with the GEMA (Gikuyu, Embu, Meru Association) old-guard of the party to substantiate the prejudice. This led to the GEMA-KAMATUSA (Kalenjin, Maasai, Turkana Samburu) talks of 1995, around table of ethnic negotiation opened by Nicholas Biwott and Njenga Karume with the proclaimed agenda of resettling the victims of the Rift Valley clashes. The talks aborted abruptly due to the uncompromising and hostile stance taken by KANU hawks notably William ole Ntimama and Kipkalya Kones, but the DP lost a lot of credibility and suffered afterwards from the defection of John Keen and Agnes Ndetei to KANU, respectively the secretary general and second vice-president of the party.

For those who could not be bought or compromised in any scandal, and who kept a tough stand against the government in parliament or through their publications, KANU had kept the heavy stick of its provincial administration, General Service Unit (GSU) and other branches of its political police. Cases of police harassment, beatings, and political thuggery against uncompromised opposition leaders such as James Orengo (FORD-Kenya), Peter Anyang' Nyong'o (FORD-Kenya), Mukhisa Kituyi (FORD-Kenya), Kiraitu Murungi (DP), Charity Ngilu (DP) among others, against the journalists of the free press (e.g., *Daily Nation*, *Society*, *Finance*), and against the leaders of human rights and civic awareness organisations, (e.g., Willy Mutunga, Kivutha Kibwana), became a constant feature of the 1993-97 years. The Mwangaza Trust and CLARION, two civic organisations created to prepare a political alternative for the country and shed light on malpractices were deregistered in 1994 and 1996. Safina, 'the ark' in Kiswahili, a would-be political party formed in 1995 and led by the internationally known white Kenyan archaeologist Richard Leakey and the outgoing FORD-Kenya leader Paul Muite, did not get its official registration until November 1997, one month before the elections. Leakey, Muite, and Njeri Kabeberi, another Safina representative, moreover, were heavily clobbered and physically assaulted by KANU youths when they attempted to visit Koigi wa Wamwere in September 1995 in Nakuru. Wa Wamwere had been arrested on charges of 'treason' two years before and his political trial was internationally described as 'a mockery of justice'.

At the game of 'divide, beat and rule', Daniel arap Moi has been a winner for almost 40 years and could not be expected to lose, having kept all the major cards in his hands. His constant 'give and take' tactics with the international community offered another example of the prowess of the self-proclaimed 'professor of politics'. After the resumption of international support to the balance of payments in July 1994, following the implementation of the first measures of structural adjustment, President Moi gave in his new year message of January 1995 the impression of a willingness to amend the constitution and somehow level the political field before the 1997 contest. He first announced the establishment of a constitutional review commission. Eighteen months later, in June 1996, when the irritation of the international community started to be expressed publicly regarding the total absence of any progress on this matter, he requested parliament to take charge of the process since it had the mandate and the possibility to do so. However, by early 1997, two years after his initial declarations and as he was starting his re-election campaign, nothing had been done. By July 1997, the cabinet had recovered so much leverage to handle the international community– the country had the highest level of foreign exchange reserves for almost ten years – that it decided it could do away with the safeguards and technocrats that had been put in place at the head of the Kenya Revenue Authority and Customs Department to refrain tax evasion and the illegal dumping of goods. This led to a second aid freeze by the IMF and the World Bank.

Of particular significance throughout this pre-election period was the growing prominence of the so-called 'civil society' in the continuing struggle against autocratic rule. A section of this amorphous category came under the organisational umbrella of the National Convention Assembly (NCA) and its executive arm, the National Convention Executive Committee (NCEC). With its leadership drawn largely from the ranks of the middle class, the NCA had become so effective in mobilising the energies of a broad range of interest groups that it became a constant source of worry and concern to the KANU government. The political 'confusion' resulting from the sudden upsurge of the pro-democracy momentum prompted the active resurgence of social groupings (both old and new) and social mechanisms that gave voice to the public in new ways. Decades of authoritarian rule which quashed any semblance of effective structures of collective organisation had created a void that now came to be filled by a multiplicity of dynamic informal groupings seemingly established along the lines of sex, gender, religion, etc., each seeking to articulate the concerns and interests of its members. In the struggle to inscribe their members as stake-holders in the political arena, these groups served as important fora for galvanising communal anger in the quest for democratic change.

But the hitherto vibrant 'civil society' soon became hostage to the personal and factional ambitions of the political elite, ambitions that were sometimes rationalised along ethnic and nationalist lines. The political elite – including many of those who had been at the forefront of the crusade for political reform – acquiesced to KANU's political manoeuvres, craftily engineered through the formation of the Inter-Parties Parliamentary Group (IPPG). The coalition of human and women's rights activists, university teachers, lawyers, students, clerics and other pro-democracy forces from within the civil society who insisted on genuine and thorough-going political and legal restructuring before elections, suddenly saw themselves abandoned by politicians who were now busy dusting off their campaign wares. In the final analysis, therefore, it is difficult to determine how much influence these civil society groups ended up exercising over the voting behaviour of their members at election time.

This is, broadly framed, the political, economic and social environment that surrounded the December 1997 general elections in Kenya. This context must be kept in mind when trying to understand the Kenyan electoral process. Elections in Africa are often a war for political and economic survival; losing an election is often losing everything. The control of the state is the central concern of politicians partly because the state has been, since the beginning of the continent's postcolonial history, the engine of kleptocratic accumulation and the essential generator of both patronage and resources. This context justifies the general approach of this book which was designed not only to give an account of the general results of these elections and to illustrate how the electoral commission, the local observers and the international community tried to ensure that it respected international standards of decency; but it also attempts to show how Kenyans relate to the electoral process, how they use it, benefit from it and, occasionally, put their faith in it.

The book is, therefore, organised in four parts, presenting successively: the direct pre-electoral background of the polling exercise (Chapters 2-4), the technical and national analysis of the general elections (Chapters 5-9); regional studies focusing on 'the grassroots level' of Kenyan politics (Chapters 10-19); and finally a review of the violent election aftermath, political developments in 1998 and 1999 and some conclusions on the meaning of electoral politics in Kenya (Chapters 20-22).

In a preview to the 1997 elections, *African Business* journalists Milan Vesely and Anver Versi earmarked the 29 December polls as perhaps the most important in the history of the country. They questioned whether Kenya would enter an era of full democracy and a renewed period of stability or whether it would, following the sad examples of Congo, Somalia and the Sudan, be ripped apart by tribal politics. Vesely and Versi referred to the worries, especially in Britain and the United States about what would happen to KANU, and who will be Kenya's leader after Moi, after the 2002 elections. One of the interviewed insiders claimed that there was no reason to worry because 'Kenya is heading for a higher level of democracy, political maturity, and with it, renewed economic progress. It won't be after this election, which Moi will steal, but it will be after the one in 2002' (*African Business*, No 227: 19). The journalists concluded that it seemed almost certain that both KANU and President Moi would win the elections 'although perhaps not as comfortably as they might have liked'. This book demonstrates how comfortably KANU and President Moi won the 1997 elections.

Note

1. See the shift from Hyden 1980, to Hyden 1985 and finally Hyden 1992.

References

Alila, P.O. 1984a, 'Kenya General Elections in Bondo and Gem: the origin of Luo ethnic factor in modern politics', Institute for Development Studies, *Working Paper No.403*, University of Nairobi.

Alila, P.O. 1984b, 'Luo ethnic factor in the 1979 and 1983 elections in Bondo and Gem - Kenya', Institute for Development Studies, *Working Paper No.408*, University of Nairobi.

Andreassen, B.A., Geisler, G., and Tostensen, A. 1992, *Setting a Standard for Africa*, Bergen: Chr. Michelsen Institute.

Bacot, P. 1993, 'Conflictualité sociale et geste électoral. Les formes de politisation dans les lieux de vote', *Revue Française de Science Politique*, 43(1): 107-35.

Barkan, J.D. 1976, 'Comment: Further reassessment of conventional wisdom: political knowledge and voting behaviour in rural Kenya', *The American Political Science Review*, 70(2): 452-55.

_____ 1984, 'Legislators, elections and political linkage', in Barkan, J.D. (ed.), *Politics and public policy in Kenya and Tanzania*, New York: Praeger: 71-101.

_____ 1987, 'The electoral process and peasant-state relations in Kenya', in Hayward, F.M. (ed.), *Elections in independent Africa*, Boulder: Westview Press: 213-38.

_____ 1992, 'The rise and fall of a governance realm in Kenya' in Hyden G. and Bratton M. (eds), *Governance and Politics in Africa*, Boulder and London: Lynne Rienner: 167-92.

_____ 1993, 'Kenya: Lessons from a Flawed Election', *Journal of Democracy*, 4: 85-99.

Barkan, J.D. and Okumu, J.J. 1978, 'Patrons, Machines et Elections au Kenya', in CEAN/CERI, *Aux Urnes l'Afrique! Elections et pouvoirs en Afrique noire,* Paris: Pédone: 119-48.

Bayart, J.-F. 1986, 'Populist political action. Historical understanding and political analysis in Africa', in Jewsiewicki, B. and Newbury, C. (eds), *African historiographies. What history for which Africa,* Berverley Hills: Sage Publications: 261-68.

Bennet, G. and Rosberg, C. 1961, *The Kenyatta election: Kenya 1960-1961,* Oxford: Institute of Commonwealth Studies.

Bourmaud, D. 1985, 'Elections et autoritarisme: la crise de la régulation politique au Kenya', *Revue Française de Science-Politique,* Vol. XXXV, No.2, avril: 206-31.

Buijtenhuijs, R. and Thiriot, C. 1995, *Démocratisation en Afrique au Sud du Sahara. Un bilan de la littérature,* Bordeaux/Leiden: CEAN/IEP de Bordeaux/Afrika Studie Centrum.

CEAN/CERI 1978, *Aux Urnes l'Afrique! Elections et pouvoirs en Afrique noire,* Paris: Pédone.

CGD 1998, Policy Briefs June 1998, Nairobi: Centre for Governance and Democracy.

Chabal, P. 1992, Power in Africa. *An essay in political interpretation,* London: Macmillan.

Chazan, N. 1979, 'African Voters at the Polls: A Re-examination of the Role of Elections in African Politics', *Journal of Commonwealth and Comparative Politics,* 17(1): 137-58.

Chege, M. 1981, 'A tale of two slums: Electoral politics in Mathare and Dagoretti', *Review of African Political Economy,* 20, January-April: 74-88.

_____ 1994, 'The Return to Multi-Party Politics', in Barkan J.D. (ed.), *Beyond Capitalism vs Socialism in Kenya and Tanzania,* Boulder, Lynne Rienner: 47-74.

Coulon, C. and Martin, D.-C. (sld) 1991, *Les Afriques politiques,* Paris: La Découverte.

Cowen, M. and Laakso, L. 1997, 'An overview of election studies in Africa', *The Journal of Modern African Studies,* 35(4): 717-44.

Daloz, J.P. 1999, 'Les approches élitaires comme nécessaire antidote', in Daloz J.P. (sld), *Le (non)-renouvellement des élites en Afrique sub-saharienne,* Bordeaux: CEAN/IEP de Bordeaux: 13-31.

Decalo, S. 1992, 'The Process, Prospects and Constraints of Democratization in Africa', *African Affairs,* 91: 7-35.

Deloye, Y. 1993, 'L'élection au village. Le geste électoral à l'occasion des scrutins cantonaux et régionaux de mars 1992', *Revue Française de Science Politique,* 43(1): 83-106.

_____ 1996, *Sociologie historique du politique*, Paris: La Découverte.

EAC 1998, Database August 1998, Arusha: East African Co-operation Secretariat.

EIU 1996, Kenya Country report 1995, London: Economist Intelligence Unit.

____ 1999, Kenya Country report 1999, London: Economist Intelligence Unit.

Engholm, F. 1960, 'African elections in Kenya, March 1957', in Mackenzie W.J.M. and Robinson K. (eds), *Five elections in Africa,* Oxford: Clarendon Press: 391-461.

Garrigou, A. 1992, *Le vote et la vertu. Comment les Français sont devenus électeurs*, Paris: Presses de la FNSP.

Gaxie, D. 1977, *Le cens caché*, Paris: le Seuil.

_____ 1985, 'Le vote comme disposition et comme transaction', in Gaxie D. (sld), *Explication du vote. Un bilan des études électorales en France*, Paris: Presses de la FNSP: 11-34.

Gertzel, C. 1970, *The politics of independent Kenya 1963-1968*, Nairobi: East African Publishing House.

Grignon F. 1994, Understanding multi-partyism in Kenya: the 1990-1992 years', IFRA *Working Papers* No.19, Nairobi: French Institute for Research in Africa.

_____ 1998a, 'Les années Nyayo. Racines de l'autoritarisme et graines de démocratie dans le Kenya Contemporain' in Grignon F. and Prunier G. (eds), *Le Kenya Contemporain*, Paris: Karthala: 315-48.

_____ 1998b, 'La démocratisation et le multipartisme en question', in Grignon F. and Prunier G. (eds), *Le Kenya Contemporain*, Paris: Karthala: 363-82.

_____ 1998c, 'Espace public, démocratisation et imaginaires politiques : remarques théoriques et méthodologiques à propos d'une recherche sur le Kenya' in Martin D.-C. (sld), *Nouveaux langages du politique en Afrique orientale*, Paris: Karthala: 15-28.

_____ 1998d, 'La démocratie au risque du débat? Territoires de la critique et imaginaires politiques au Kenya (1990-1995)', in Martin D.-C. (sld), *Nouveaux langages du politique en Afrique orientale*, Paris: Karthala: 28-112.

_____ 1999, Une situation de "multi-parti uniques"? Le renouvellement paradoxal des parlementaires au Kenya (1992-1997)' in Daloz J.-P. (sld), *Le (non-)renouvellement des élites en Afrique noire*, Bordeaux: CEAN/ Institut d'Etudes politiques: 57-75.

Grignon, F. and Maupeu, H. 1998, 'Les aléas du contrat social kényan', *Politique Africaine*, No.70: 3-21.

Hayward, F.M. (ed.) 1987, *Elections in independent Africa*, Boulder: Westview Press.

Haugerud, A. 1995, *The culture of politics in modern Kenya*, Cambridge University Press.

Hermet, G., Rose, R. and Rouquié, A. 1998, *Elections without choice*, London: Macmillan.

Hornsby, C. 1989, 'The social structure of the National Assembly in Kenya 1963-1983', *The Journal of Modern African Studies*, 27(2): 275-98.

Hornsby, C. and Throup, D. 1992, 'Elections and political change in Kenya', *Journal of Commonwealth and comparative politics*, Vol. 30, No.2: 172-99.

Hyden, G. 1980, *Beyond Ujamaa in Tanzania. Underdevelopment and an Uncaptured Peasantry*, London: Heinemann.

_____ 1985, *No Shortcuts to Progress: African Development Management in Perspective*, London: Heinemann.

_____ 1985, 'Governance and the study of politics', in Hyden G. and Bratton M., (eds), *Governance and politics in Africa*, Boulder: Lynne Rienner: 1-26.

Hyden, G. and Leys, C. 1972, 'Elections and politics in single party systems: the case of Kenya and Tanzania', *British Journal of Political Science*, 2(4): 389-420.

IEA 1998, *Our Problems, Our Solutions: an economic and public policy agenda for Kenya*, Nairobi: Institute of Economic Affairs.

Ihl, O. 1993, 'L'urne électorale: forme et usage d'une technique de vote', *Revue Française de Science Politique*, 43(1): 30-59.

_____ 1996, *Le vote*, Paris: Montchrestien.

Jackson, R.H. and Rosberg, C.G. 1982, *Personal rule in Black Africa*, Berkeley: University of California Press.

Khadiagala, G.M. 1984, 'Electoral politics in Busia central: a study in the dynamics of rural politics', Dept. of Government seminar series on the General Elections in Kenya, *Seminar Paper* No.6.

Lafargue J. 1996, *Contestations démocratiques en Afrique. Sociologie de la protestation au Kenya et en Zambie*, Paris: IFRA/Karthala.

Lamb, G. 1974, *Peasant politics. Conflict and Development in Murang'a*, London: Jullien Friedman.

Lonsdale, J. 1992, 'The political culture of Kenya', *Centre for African Studies*, Edinburgh University, *Occasional Papers* No.37.

Médard, J.-F. 1982, 'Underdeveloped State in tropical Africa: political clientelism or neo-patrimonialism?', in Clapham C., (ed.) *Private patronage and public power. Political clientelism in the modern State*, London: Pinter: 103-34.

_____ 1991, 'L'Etat néo-patrimonial en Afrique noire', in Médard J.-F. (é.r.p.), *Etats d'Afrique noire*, Paris: Karthala: 323-54.

_____ 1992, 'Le 'big man' en Afrique: esquisse d'analyse du politicien entrepreneur', *L'année sociologique*, No.42: 167-92.

Muigai, G. 1993, 'Kenya's opposition and the crisis of Governance', *Issue*, 21, Nos.1-2: 26-34.

Mulaa, J. 1981, 'The politics of a changing society: Mumias', *Review of African Political Economy*, 20, January-April: 89-120.

Nzomo, M. 1983, 'The 1983 General Election in Mombasa', Dept. of Government seminar series on the General Elections in Kenya, *Seminar Paper No.2*.

NEMU 1993, *The Multi-Party General Elections Kenya, 29 December 1992*, Nairobi: National Election Monitoring Unit.

Orwa, K. 1984, 'Political recruitment in Mbita constituency: a study in electoral politics', Dept. of Government seminar series on the General Elections in Kenya, Seminar Paper No.3.

Otayek, R. 1991, 'Organisations et competitions politiques' in Coulon C. and Martin D.-C., *Les Afriques politiques*, Paris: La Découverte: 186-99.

_____ 1997, 'Démocratie, culture politique sociétés plurales: un approche comparative à partir de situations africaines', *Revue Française de Science Politique*, 47(6): 798-822.

_____ 1998, 'Les élections en Afrique sont-elles un objet scientifique pertinent?', *Politique Africaine*, No. 69: 3-11.

Oyugi, W.O. 1983, 'Electoral politics in Kenya: lessons from a constituency (Karachonyo)', Dept. of Government seminar series on the General Elections in Kenya, *Seminar Paper* No.1.

Sandbrook, R. 1985, *The politics of Africa's economic stagnation,* Cambridge University Press.

Sanger, C. and Nottingham, J. 1964, 'The Kenya general election of 1963', *Journal of Modern African Studies*, 2(1): 1-40.

Sindjoun, L. 1997, 'Elections et politique au Cameroun: concurrence déloyale, coalitions de stabilité hégémonique et politique d'affection', *African Journal of Political Science*, 2(1): 89-121.

Thomas, C. 1998, 'L'économie politique d'une succession annoncée', *Politique Africaine*, No.70: 40-53.

Throup, D.W. 1993, 'Elections and political legitimacy in Kenya', *Africa*, 63(3): 371-96.

Throup, D. and Hornsby, C. 1998, *Multi-Party Politics in Kenya. The Kenyatta & Moi States & the Triumph of the System in the 1992 Election*, Oxford: James Currey.

Wanjohi, N.G. 1984a, 'The politics of ideology and personality. Rivalry in Murang'a district, Kenya', Institute for Development Studies, *Working Paper* No.411, University of Nairobi.

_____ 1984b, 'The politics of Land, Elections and Democratic Performance in Kenya', Institute for Development Studies, *Working Paper* No.412, University of Nairobi.

_____ 1997, *Political parties in Kenya*, Nairobi: Lengo Press.

Waruhiu, S.N. 1994, *From autocracy to democracy in Kenya*, Nairobi: Expert Printers Ltd.

Young, T. 1993, 'Elections and electoral politics in Africa', *Africa*, 63(3): 299-312.

PART 1

THE ELECTORAL BACKGROUND

2

Civil Society and the Election Year 1997 in Kenya

Ralph-Michael Peters

The Kenyan general elections of 29 December 1997 fell short of universal standards for 'free and fair' elections. The elections and the campaigns in the preceding two months, however, showed improvements compared to the elections of 1992, the first full multi-party elections since 1963. At the beginning of 1997 hardly anybody considered this progress possible. Although parliamentarians from the ruling party KANU and the opposition negotiated the enabling reforms, the pioneering work to this end came from a large number of national civic organisations and the mainstream Christian churches. It was basically their pressure for constitutional and legal reforms which forced the government into a reform dialogue with the opposition – a dialogue the government had long resisted.

In this chapter the focus will be on the political role of civil society and its umbrella organisation, the National Convention Executive Council (NCEC), that paved the way for this important though still limited change of the Kenyan political landscape. Foremost, the period that ended with the reform proposals of the Inter-Parties Parliamentary Group (IPPG) will be discussed as this eventually restored calm and redefined the relation between civil society organisations, the political parties and the Kenyan government.

Civil and political society

The political role of the NGOs and the churches cannot be analysed without taking into consideration their relationship with the political parties. Therefore, we need to differentiate between civil and political society as both spheres of society are determined by different values, principles and sets of rules which shape their strategic choices in the political arena (Peters 1996: 2-5). A functional relationship between civil society and democracy is presumed. This implies that only those organisations and groups which have a 'creative tension' (Streeten 1993: 1287) with the state qualify for civil society. Thus, these groups must be distinct from the state. While criticising the state and trying to influence its decisions, they do accept the monopoly of power held by the state. They insist on political accountability of the government, on the rule of law and adherence to human rights (Chazan 1992). Civil society organisations are generally more guided by universally accepted values than by considerations of power. This is what partly distinguishes them from political parties which are primarily driven by the desire to gain or retain power in political society.

In a transitional or democratic regime, political society is conceived as the realm in which power over the state apparatus is competed for, contested and negotiated (Bratton 1994; Linz and Stepan 1996). The taking over or prolongation of power is generally the guiding principle of all actors in political society. The mechanisms to win (or maintain) power in a transforming or in a democratic regime may, however, differ substantially. When neo-patrimonial regimes with strong patronage networks, as in sub-Saharan Africa, become multi-party systems, the fight for power is usually centred upon the politicisation of ethnicity. In order to direct social issues into ethnic channels, political leaders try to reinforce latent ethnic tensions or even to create ethnic cleavages. This alone, however, would not necessarily complicate or threaten the democratisation process. It is rather the 'winner-takes-it-all' syndrome often resulting in fierce determination by groups and parties fighting for their success under conditions of economic scarcity that poses a severe danger for transition processes. In contrast, in consolidated democracies power struggles tend to be less intense as the main political players accept basic democratic rules and no longer perceive success and defeat in existential terms. Ethnic affiliations may still influence politics, but their impact has certainly decreased. In the immediate transition period, actors of civil society often try to soften the ethnic-political polarisation and to direct the political debate to issues like governance, social justice and democratic reforms. Although their influence depends ultimately on the political situation in a particular country, the influence of civil society generally tends to decline once the political system has been opened. This has to do with the second distinction between political and civil society.

This distinction concerns the political role of the actors in the two realms at different periods of the democratic transition. Civil society usually becomes the torchbearer for a democratic opening of the political system when authoritarian rule still prevails. At this stage political society is a closed shop dominated by single party or military rule. No opposition to the government is tolerated from within political society. Though threatened by repression, civil society organisations become the only source of non-violent opposition to the government. Once the breakthrough is achieved and a multi-party system is put in place, the initiative within the opposition passes from civil society organisations to opposition parties which are now legal and legitimate alternatives to the ruling party. Ideally, civil society and the opposition forces within political society tend to co-operate (Linz and Stepan 1996: 8). This, however, only rarely happens due to the different political approaches of the actors of the two spheres.

What distinguishes political from civil society is the different rationale and principles that guide the two realms. In reality, however, the differences are fluid. Two possible deviations from this path are of particular interest in our context.

First, some of the people who head and direct civic organisations may enter political society to seek political mandates. Any of their efforts to advance values and norms of civil society organisations into political society is not only a challenge to the incumbent regime but – almost even more importantly – amounts to an attempt to change the rules of the political game as it implies demands for the adherence of the rule of law and calls into question the arbitrary nature of power under neo-patrimonial rule. Although the democratisation processes in sub-Saharan Africa are also results of the crisis of these neo-patrimonial systems, its institutions certainly possess varying degrees of inertia.[1] Thus, the struggle for political power is complicated by the struggle over the defining powers of the rules and mechanisms of the game. And those informal institutions like 'patronage' may prove more durable than the governments which used them. This in turn means that entrants from civil society may be able to influence these institutions to some degree but will find it very difficult to survive in political society if they do not adjust to some extent to the informal rules of the system. As a result, it is a very challenging exercise to sustain a fragile balance between reform commitment and institutionalised requirements of the game.

Second, there are basically two exceptions to the rule that civil society organisations do not become involved in immediate power struggles. The first exception may occur in the early stages of a transition process, when opposition parties are not yet organised, the second at later stages, when opposition parties prove too weak to offer a credible alternative to the government. If the government can at the same time not withstand intense pressure to concede reform talks, it may give way to negotiations, in which, for lack of alternatives, civil society organisations assume the role of a major political player. With regard to the initial transition stages this was the case in several Francophone African countries in the early 1990s where the process led to the holding of national conferences. In some instances, national conferences assumed successfully the powers of the sovereign, thereby abrogating the constitution, dissolving parliament and establishing an interim-government. A failure of opposition parties during the transition can again catapult civic organisations into the first line of political actors. Possibly these events also culminate in a national conference. However, even if civic associations take over government capacities, they do so only in trust and temporarily. In co-operation with other political, social, cultural and economic groups and organisations, they would then prepare the ground for elections and the final transfer of power into the hands of an elected government.

Civil society and constitutional reform up to 1997

When Kenya approached the 1997 election year, the KANU government seemed to be heading for a safe victory. This was less due to its own strength than to the weaknesses of the opposition parties. All the three main opposition parties were at different stages of disintegration and thus paralysed. Due to the personal ambitions of the party leaders and ethno-political animosities between different communities (especially between the Kikuyu and the Luo), the opposition parties had been preoccupied with internal leadership quarrels ever since the 1992 elections. Even as the 1997 elections drew closer, they proved neither capable of settling these quarrels nor of agreeing on a common and single presidential candidate, the only realistic approach to unseat Moi. As the opposition parties did not dispose of any strategy on how to win the forthcoming elections, they could not exploit the rifts and power struggles within the ruling party, where two strong factions were fighting for the Moi succession, constitutionally due after the next legislative period. The resources of all actors of political society were tied up with internal problems and none of the leaders was taking the government to task over burning issues like mass unemployment, the deteriorating social living conditions, the declining infrastructure or massive corruption.

Against this background nothing seemed to hint at the events that eventually forced the government with its back to the wall. The events and the campaign for constitutional and legal reform, however, had quite a long pre-run.

The prologue: the model constitution and the reform debate 1994-95

Constitutional and legal change has been an issue of public debate since the first calls for a return to multi-party politics in the early 1990s. The demands by the opposition for a democratic overhaul of the constitution were countered with proposals for the introduction of a *majimbo*-constitution favoured by KANU hawks.[2] Although the debate did not fade out completely after the 1992 election campaign, it was reduced to a more academic debate without real significance for the political arena. The starting point for the reform debate that eventually culminated in the events of 1997 can be ascribed to 3 November 1994. On that day three national civic organisations, the Law Society of Kenya, the International Commission of Jurists (Kenyan Chapter) and the Kenya Human Rights Commission publicly presented the draft of a model constitution

('The Kenya We Want'), in which they proposed a more adequate framework for a democratic multi-party system. Up to then only section 2(A) of the constitution, which had made Kenya a *de jure* one-party state, had been repealed in December 1991. Without any consultation from the opposition, minor amendments were made in August 1992 (*Weekly Review* 14/08/92:14f). Neither the president's wide ranging powers nor the numerous repressive laws, which mainly originate from the colonial era, were touched.

With their demand for constitutional reform, these organisations had the moral support of the Catholic church and of the NCCK, the umbrella organisation of the Protestant churches. On several occasions and in pastoral letters both institutions had emphasised the need for a comprehensive overhaul of the constitution. At a first caucus in Nairobi's Ufungamano House in mid-December 1994, the model constitution was discussed by representatives of a wide range of civic and religious organisations. Although politicians of all parties had also been invited, only a few attended the conference, Raila Odinga (then member of parliament for FORD-Kenya) being the only one from the leadership level. Nevertheless, the debate gained momentum and became the central public issue in the last two months of that year.[3] Sensing the potential dynamic of the debate, Moi in his New Year's message promised a constitutional review to the people. If the debate was unavoidable then he wanted to be at the top of the movement to determine its direction and speed. In order to get an operational base, the steering committee of the conference transformed itself into the Citizen's Coalition for Constitutional Change (4Cs).[4]

In the following weeks and months, however, it became clear that the 4Cs did not yet have a strategy on how to sustain the debate. There were basically two main problems. The first problem had to do with the relation between civil and political society. The actors within civil society wanted to avoid a mistake they had made in 1991-92. After the repeal of section 2(A) and the opening of political society, civil society organisations had found themselves and their agenda sidelined by former KANU dissidents, who were now running the opposition parties. Legal and constitutional reforms had been top priorities before the return to multi-party politics, but were now pushed aside by the new party leaders. In the hope of winning the elections, against Moi and their opposition competitors, none of the party leaders wanted to restrict the legal powers they expected to enjoy themselves. Against this background, the 4Cs signalled that civil society organisations were ready to take the political centre stage in order to overcome the reform deadlock. This time the 4Cs did not want the political parties to become too much and too prominently involved. They feared that the party leaders would either try to slow down the campaign as the politicians did not want another competing power centre to emerge or use the debate as a forum to distinguish themselves from their colleagues.[5] In any case, they did not expect the political leaders to be genuinely interested in the issue. Still, the 4Cs needed the politicians because they had to reach the grassroots and it was the parties which commanded a mass following. Thus, the 4Cs depended on the parties' support to transform the rather urban-based demand for constitutional change into a mass movement. The question then was how to involve the party leaders without surrendering the whole initiative to them. The following two years were characterised by heavy wrangling between the 4Cs and the opposition parties over supremacy over the campaign.

The second problem had to do with the 4Cs' approach to the campaign. They wanted to initiate a nation-wide enlightened debate on the need for constitutional reform. Therefore, it was necessary to popularise the issue, to show how the constitution and laws affect the daily lives of the ordinary *wananchi* (Kiswahili for citizen, literally 'children of the soil'). Actually, *wananchi* tend to blame 'bad leadership' for harassment or lack of economic progress. Thus, a sensitising campaign was to be a time-consuming exercise and would have to precede a nation-wide campaign. A first step to this end was the translation of 'The Summary and Highlights of the Model Constitution' into ten different local languages, including Kiswahili. A number of foreign foundations sponsored the initiative.

With the pressure for reform easing, Moi saw no reason to uphold his promise for constitutional reform. In his Madaraka Day speech on 1 June 1995, he ruled out any major changes of the constitution (*Economic Review* 05/06/95:6).

Delays and renewal of the reform initiative, June 1995 to April 1997

From June 1995 to April 1997 the issue of constitutional reform did not feature prominently in the news. It was an issue of debate among the political elite occasionally, but it did not grow into a new campaign. Quietly, however, progress was made with regard to civic education, in which the need for constitutional reform was one of the central issues. At the end of a three day workshop on civic education in February 1996 about 60 NGOs proclaimed 1996 as the year of civic education.[6] Although the goals, in terms of organisational set-up, range and co-ordination of activities, proved too ambitious, still a relatively large number of civic education workshops and seminars was carried out by NGOs over the year. The workshops were always in danger of being cancelled by the district administration allegedly for creating disorder. Therefore, the NGOs had to operate carefully and sometimes to disguise their intentions. They could operate more easily on the so called opposition territory than in the KANU strongholds.[7] As the events of 1997 showed, they made progress in raising the awareness of the relevance of the legal framework for the people's living conditions.

The reason the first caucus for the constitutional convention did not take place earlier than April 1997 was the result rather of the quarrels between civil and political society over the leadership of the initiative than the outcome of any strategy by the 4Cs. The 4Cs, however, masterminded the initiative. It was basically the skilful and hard bargaining of Willy Mutunga, one of the four co-chairpersons of the 4Cs and a former chairman of the Law Society of Kenya, that prevented the initiative from being at the mercy of two competing alliances of the opposition parties.[8] After the caucus planned for the end of May 1996 was aborted, the 4Cs created a new steering-committee, the National Convention Planning Committee (NCPC), in which political parties – though part of the whole set-up – were not represented. It was chaired by Bishop Zablon Nthamburi of the Methodist church as the representative of the NCCK and co-chaired by the widely respected Bishop Ndingi Mwana a'Nzeki for the Catholic church, Professor Maria Nzomo for the National Commission on the Status of Women, Willy Mutunga for the 4Cs and Davinder Lamba for the National Council of NGOs, the NGO umbrella organisation (*Weekly Review* 02/08/96:9).

The opposition parties finally gave in to this set-up for two reasons; first, they were too much involved in their internal power struggles and second, they did not dispose of the necessary financial resources needed for organising and staging a national convention. The NGOs, on the other hand, were well connected with foreign NGOs willing to financially support the phases up to the convention. The opposition parties, however, did not abandon their involvement altogether. Both opposition blocs kept contact with the NCPC and accepted for the time being a sort of junior partnership. They were too suspicious that the rival group could get an upper hand through co-operation with the NCPC, finally succeed in championing the reform movement and, by that, earn the credit for the reform progress.

Whereas the reform forces feared that the delay of the caucus would make the run up period to the elections too short for meaningful reforms to be realised, it later appeared that from their perspective the delay also had its advantages. One advantage was that the delay made it possible for civic and voter education seminars to yield positive results. The second advantage was that the NCCK was able to complete its internal restructuring. Energies, which had been tied to that exercise, were now free. A first manifestation of this renewed commitment to the reform was the statement of the NCCK after its 53rd General Assembly in August 1996. Its general secretary, Mutava Musyimi, and its chairman, Church of the Province of Kenya Bishop Joseph Wasonga demanded minimum reforms before the next elections. Although this option had been internally discussed by leading figures of civic organisations, the NCCK was the first to publicly come out with this demand. Thus, the NCCK set the tone and direction for the next stage of the initiative. The writing of a completely new constitution before the elections or a postponement of the elections for that purpose was not envisaged any longer. The objective was now to try to force the government to concede reforms before the elections that allowed for a more even, if not level, playing field. So far the conditions for political competition between the ruling party KANU and the opposition parties had been distorted in KANU's favour (*Weekly Review* 09/08/96: 9-10).

If the elections were to be at least more 'free and fair' than the elections in 1992, these distortions had to be corrected well in advance. A constitutional convention was to take place after the elections. With this change of the agenda, NGOs and churches also wanted to counter the government's argument that there was not enough time for a comprehensive constitutional review before the elections. Even more moral weight was lent to the cause as the Catholic bishops released a pastoral letter simultaneously with the NCCK's statement, in which their demands were similiar to those of the NCCK (*Weekly Review* 09/08/96: 9). Without the whole-hearted support of the opposition parties, the support of the churches was even more vital and essential for developing the initiative into a campaign. The Christian churches are well rooted in the Kenyan society. They possess a moral authority especially at the grassroots that is derived from their concrete social work within the local communities. It is this community work in particular that gives the gospel and the sermons of the bishops and reverends a real meaning – in stark contrast to the government's and opposition parties' rhetoric on the improvement of the living conditions of the poor. This way the churches have become a source of alternative legitimacy and, thereby, an indispensable pillar of the reform movement.

By the end of 1996, civil society actors had been able to outmanoeuvre the opposition parties in the leadership of the reform initiative. Preparations for another caucus were underway. In demanding at least minimal reforms before the elections, the NCPC did not abandon its long-time aim of organising a constitutional convention. They rather graded the steps up to that point. However, nothing seemed to suggest that the still rather small reform-movement would grow into a force that could bring the government almost down onto its knees.

At this point, it may be helpful to highlight the different motives of the civil society actors, on the one hand, and of the opposition party leaders, on the other hand. The latter had basically an instrumentalist approach to democracy. With the exception of Raila Odinga and Charity Ngilu, all leaders and main presidential candidates of the opposition had been members of the ruling party before. For all of them, ethnicity was the main organising principle of political and social interest. This had been reinforced by the Moi regime, as the sidelining of political heavyweights always implied the marginalisation of their respective ethnic communities. This resulted from the rationale behind the patronage and neo-patrimonial system: when the politicians no longer had a voice in the centre of power, they could no longer secure funds for development projects in their constituencies. To be sure, only a few of these projects materialised to the extent politicians had promised before, but, as long as these politicians were part of the government, they could nourish the hope of their followers for improvements. That former KANU-dissidents were now on the opposition side was thus due, to a large extent, to the fact that they and their ethnic communities had been sidelined by the Moi regime during the 1980s. This applies to politicians from the Kikuyu (Kenneth Matiba, Mwai Kibaki) and from the Luo (Raila Odinga) in particular. Under the one-party system, their political career had come to an end (Matiba, Martin Shikuku, Michael Wamalwa) or had reached a dead end (Kibaki). They needed multi-party politics to challenge the Moi regime. Their main concern was – not unusual for political society – to get back into power. As all of them, however, had been socialised in the neo-patrimonial KANU system, to them power meant rather the ability to 'eat' than to initiate wide ranging reforms. They primarily wanted to alter the regional patterns of distribution in favour of their regions, but not to change the overall parameters of distribution and leadership. They were not concerned with empowering the *wananchi*. For all of that, their interest in reform was limited. The legal and constitutional reforms they wanted concerned the removal of obstacles on the way to a more even playing field so that they could compete with the ruling party on a more equal basis (Peters 1996:15-17, 48-49).

Civil society forces, on the other hand, were more genuinely interested in wide ranging democratic reforms. It was no accident that lawyers and church leaders had been the first outspoken critics of the government in the eighties and now again played a leading role in the quest for reform. Most of the critical jurists either obtained their law degrees in Dar es Salaam or at one of the prestigious universities in Great Britain or in North America.[9] They felt bound to the principles of the separation of powers and of the rule of law which were taught there. Also inspired by their studies, they subscribed to a more comprehensive understanding of law that encompasses explicit social and political considerations. This position stood in stark contrast to the narrow and positivistic approach of the majority of lawyers and jurists in Kenya in the 1960s and 1970s, a time during which the bar was still dominated by lawyers from Great Britain and India. Church leaders, like the CPK Bishops David Gitari and the late Henry Okullu or Timothy Njoya, Reverend of the Presbyterian Church of East Africa (PCEA), have always pointed out that the church had a concrete and worldly responsibility for the less privileged. They used to speak out on behalf of the poor on issues like land-grabbing, corruption etc. Thus, there is a clear moral guideline that can be discerned in the lawyers' and church leaders' political activities, through which they gained moral authority among the modern urban middle class and the poor as well as among the rural people. It was, for these reasons, only a matter of time before they clashed with the authoritarian Moi regime. The institutions they represented or which provided shelter for them were, however, not interested in power (Peters 1996: 28-39).

There is a third group that can be identified. This group is basically made up of lawyers and academics. They stood in the forefront of the reform movement in the early 1990s and then – after the return to a multi-party system – decided to join political society, and to seek mandates. Lawyers like Paul Muite and Gitobu Imanyara had worked closely with Matiba and the late Oginga Odinga. They had tried to convince the political establishment of the necessity of a broad reform strategy which should be based on a coalition of the ethnically heterogeneous opposition forces, and which should be committed to substantial democratic reforms. As the political landscape unfolded and ethnicity crystallised as the rallying point for organising political parties, their influence decreased. Some of these so-called 'Young Turks', like Muite, Kiraitu Murungi and Peter Anyang' Nyong'o, were elected in 1992 due to a combination of factors such as efficient local networks, a development-oriented agenda for the particular constituency, and being in the right party in the right province.[10] But despite efforts, especially by Muite, to create the image of a national or at least communal leader none of them was able to do so. Their impact on their parties' political moves was clearly limited.[11] This had to do with the inertia of informal institutions like the patronage networks which are the transmission belts for the politicisation of ethnicity. The reintroduction of the multi-party system had even more reinforcing effects on the patronage networks because it provided KANU dissidents like Odinga and Matiba with the perspective of assuming power. In contrast to the one-party system, from which they had been excluded, they now could offer their followers a return to the pork barrel. Against this background, Muite and Co. barely had a chance of winning the hegemony over the political discourse by pursuing a genuine reform agenda. In order to maintain influence within the opposition spectrum, Muite and the others kept close contact with some of their former colleagues in civic organisations and actively supported the initiative for constitutional reform. Their emphasis on the need for reform was also to serve as a particular resource in the internal party quarrels over influence and power. In case the fragile opposition parties collapsed and the annoyance at the patronage networks grew, they could appear as a credible alternative and profit from the disappointment over the old-style politics. In other words, what prevented Muite and the like from rising to the leadership level within political society at the moment could prove an advantage in the long run.

The election year 1997 and the impact of civil society

The first plenary session for the National Convention and its signals

At the beginning of the election year, the short-term goals of the opposition parties, the 'Young Turks' and the civil society organisations converged. For different reasons all were now interested in minimal reforms before the elections. That allowed for more efficient co-operation, especially as the campaign got into higher gear.

The first plenary session of the National Convention finally took place in Limuru in Central Province from 3 to 6 April 1997. A wide range of representatives from NGOs, statutory and professional bodies, opposition parties and churches attended the meeting; altogether over 600 people. While the three leaders of the slowly melting 'Opposition Alliance', i.e., Kibaki, Wamalwa and Shikuku, turned up with strong delegations, its rival group, Matiba's and Odinga's 'Opposition Solidarity', endorsed the meeting but only sent junior representatives. The session was given some international recognition through the presence of the German ambassador and of representatives from the Canadian High Commission and the US and Dutch embassies. The convenors wanted to appear non-partisan and so they had invited KANU as well. Nobody was surprised that no single KANU representative showed up *(Economic Review* 07/04/96; *Weekly Review* 11/04/97; 25/07/97).

In the highly polarised political climate every attempt to reduce the powers of the government was perceived by KANU bigwigs as a personal attack on Moi. This was even more so as the leadership of the reform group consisted of almost lifetime critics and opponents of the regime like Mutunga, Kamau Kuria and Kibwana. This unavoidable partisan character of the initiative seemed to have moved the mainstream Christian churches to take a back seat in the new organisational arrangements. The churches were eager to appear as a neutral force in the struggle. They were committed to the reform cause, but – almost trying to square the circle – did not want to antagonise the government. In order to be in a position where the government was still willing to meet them, they tried to run their own reform project. Thus, they did not want to become too closely associated with the civic activists. As the NCPC transformed itself into the National Convention Assembly (NCA) and appointed a new steering committee, i.e., the National Convention Executive Council (NCEC), the churches kept a close distance. Musyimi and Mwana a'Nzeki did not participate any longer in any capacity. Willy Mutunga (representing the 4Cs), Davinder Lamba (Mazingira Institute) and Bishop Zablon Nthamburi (Methodist Church) chaired the NCEC.

The NCA approved a list of minimal legal and constitutional reforms to be put in place before the elections. They gave Moi an ultimatum until the beginning of May to initiate the necessary reform steps or otherwise face civic action. As ultimatums given by opposition leaders were usually not followed by any consequences, KANU's secretary general Joseph Kamotho and other KANU hawks dismissed it as the usual inconsequential radical straw fire. In contrast to the normal situation, however, the NCA was very specific in its plan of action. It outlined a slowly escalating set of measures to force the government to negotiate reforms. As expected, the government let the ultimatum elapse without any further reaction.

To the surprise of almost everybody who has followed Kenyan politics during the last years, the opposition showed a new seriousness and readiness to challenge the government. That became evident when the NCEC called the first in a series of rallies at Nairobi's famous and historic Kamukunji grounds. Deliberately they disregarded the Public Order Act, according to which every group that wanted to hold a public meeting must obtain a licence from the provincial administration. By neglecting the legal requirements, the opposition for the first time since 1991 acted, consequently, as if the Public Order Act was one of the contentious acts it wanted to have scrapped. On 3 May 1997 opposition politicians and activists turned up in large numbers at Kamukunji, among them Kibaki, Wamalwa, Shikuku, Muite (FORD-Kenya/Safina), Rev. Timothy Njoya, Gibson Kamau Kuria, Willy Mutunga, Kivutha Kibwana and the former chairman of the Law Society of Kenya (LSK), Paul Wamae. They all succeeded in entering the grounds but were then fenced off from the arriving crowds by the police and units of the notorious General Service Unit (GSU). Though there were some tussles between security forces and youths, the police had chosen an effective de-escalating tactic to prevent the rally from taking off. Thus, the event was no doubt a first success for the opposition, but it did not lead to a real showdown with the government yet (*Weekly Review* 09/05/97: 10-12).

In the meantime, the Catholic church and the NCCK finally became disillusioned with the government. Bishop Ndingi Mwana a'Nzeki, the designated new leader of the Catholic church, Archbishop David Gitari for the CPK, the chairman of the Episcopal Conference, John Njue, and the general secretary of the NCCK, Mutava Musyimi, had held private meetings with Moi in April and on 5 May. They tried in vain to convince the president that reforms were desirable for the benefit of all Kenyans. After the unsuccessful meetings, the Catholic church and the NCCK in an unprecedented move convened a common press conference by the middle of May at which they, too, gave the government an ultimatum, however unspecified, to allow minimum legal changes (*Weekly Review* 30/05/97:8,10). This gave a major moral boost to the NCEC's next action.

The situation escalates – the decisive steps

Again, without applying for permission, the NCEC called for the next rally at Nairobi's Central Park on 31 May. The organisers cleverly chose Madaraka Day (1 June), the day Kenya obtained its internal self-administration, and that guaranteed a wider media coverage. It was attended by almost the same politicians and activists as the first rally. The security forces were almost as restrained as they had been four weeks before. It was a far cry from the brutal and ruthless use of force that Kenyans were used to in the early 1990s, and that students still suffer from when the police is called on campus. While the police offered help and shelter for journalists, they were determined, at the same time, to prevent the rally from taking off and thus allowed neither the opposition leaders nor the crowds into the park, occasionally using tear gas but no stronger means. Even opposition leaders conceded that the police used only the force necessary to stop the rally.

Later on, however, the situation escalated as groups of youth, hawkers and criminal gangs started rioting and ransacking shops in the city centre. The police now used stronger force, but was unable to get the situation under control. Meanwhile, parts of the dispersed crowds moved to the city as well and there they met another huge crowd that was accompanying Matiba and Odinga. They had not participated in the Central Park rally, but had just addressed their own press conference, where they had demanded the same constitutional changes and had announced their own rally in Mombasa later that month. All of them were not spared by the police either. Though Matiba and Odinga pursued their own strategy and were criticised by NCEC members for trying to aggrandise themselves, it was apparent that all important opposition forces now subscribed to the reform agenda. And despite the quarrels about who supported whom, in the eyes of the public the opposition found a common ground for agitation not known since 1991 (*Weekly Review* 06/06/97: 7-8). Under the impression of the aborted rally and the subsequent chaos in Nairobi, Moi offered to replace the Public Order Act with a less restrictive new law in his Madaraka Day speech. The offer was turned down unanimously by all reform forces on the ground that it was not sufficient to guarantee 'free and fair' elections (*Weekly Review* 06/06/97:9).

With the clamour 'No Reforms, No Budget', the opposition went a step further. The public and the authorities had expected attempts to disrupt the usual proceedings of the Budget Day through demonstrations outside parliament. Therefore, strong security forces around parliament, and in town, ensured that no opposition demonstration took place. In addition, KANU chairmen and representatives of Nairobi sub-branches reportedly received Ksh. 50,000 each to organise counter demonstrations. There were even rumours that Moi himself dished out money to certain key parliamentarians on the morning of Budget Day to make sure that they did not participate in any demonstrations.

Nevertheless, they were all in for a big surprise as the opposition parliamentarians tried to prevent the Finance Minister Musalia Mudavadi from reading out his budget speech. James Orengo, a lawyer, vice-chairman of FORD-Kenya and the most ingenious member of parliament, rose on a point of order and argued that the discussion of legal and constitutional change had precedence as a matter of national urgency over the budget speech. No sooner had parliament speaker Francis ole Kaparo (KANU) rejected the motion of adjournment, all hell broke loose. In the presence of Moi and transmitted live by Kenya Broadcasting Corporation (KBC), the opposition displayed placards and interrupted Mudavadi constantly on points of order which were dismissed by Kaparo. Three parliamentarians, among them Paul Muite, then tried to grab the mace, the symbol of the constitutional authority of the House. They engaged in almost physical quarrels with Cabinet Minister Nicholas Biwott and others who defended the mace. Until KBC abruptly stopped the transmission, the public witnessed an unprecedented face off between the opposition parties and the government *(Economic Review* 23/06/97: 6-10).

It became apparent that the government's refusal to institute reforms not only incapacitated parliament, but was also driving the country to the verge of being ungovernable. A further proof was to be witnessed on 7 July. This day, in Kiswahili called *Saba Saba*, is reminiscent of the first, historic, and groundbreaking rally for a multi-party system in 1990. On 7 July 1997 demonstrations took place not only in Nairobi but also in several other towns in the country. In the countryside the massive turnout was to varying degrees the result of the NGOs' civic education workshops, the inspiration of the congregations through the pastors and fathers, and the mobilisation of the people through the opposition parties. The police exercised no restraint this time. Chaos and terror by security forces reigned in Nairobi and other parts of the country for most of the day. At least 14 people were killed and an unknown number injured, including several politicians and reform activists. One of the most serious incidents happened at Nairobi's famous All Saints Cathedral. Members of the GSU entered the compound and even the cathedral and started beating up people who had come for prayers and to seek refuge from the police violence on the streets. PCEA Reverend Timothy Njoya was beaten thoroughly and he later disclosed that it was foreign journalists that helped him escape alive *(Economic Review* 14/07/97: 6-8). By using brutal force, the government put itself in the wrong. It supplied the reform lobby with the best arguments for urgent legal change. The government was losing the remains of its moral authority.

In addition, tactical failures by the government contributed to the growth of the reform movement. In the middle of the fight for constitutional change, the government passed a new restrictive bill for the universities. The death of the student leader Solomon Muruli in February 1997, under very suspicious circumstances, reinforced university students' traditional critical attitude towards the government. Now they felt even more incited to protest. In the aftermath of *Saba Saba*, students clashed several times with the police. Finally, Joseph Kamotho, the minister of Education, closed the University of Nairobi on 9 July and sent the students back home.

At this stage Moi could no longer be sure of regaining the control of the political process if he continued his line. However, owing to the still ongoing disintegration of opposition parties, he was quite confident of winning the forthcoming elections even if he conceded a minimum set of reforms. The suddenness of Moi's turnabout and his announcement that he was now willing to initiate reforms surprised many observers and marked the beginning of the end of the co-operation between civil and political society forces.

Moi's U-turn and its implications for the reform lobby

With unexpected speed Moi started his bargaining offensive. He first declared his readiness for reforms on 11 July, only four days after the *Saba Saba* terror. He then met separately with Wamalwa who as chairman of the strongest opposition party in parliament was the official leader of the opposition. Wamalwa was not known for an uncompromising, principled stance. One day later, on 15 July, he received 17 church leaders to discuss the issue of reform. Wamalwa's meeting with Moi was especially controversial as all reform campaigners had agreed before that it was the NCEC which would negotiate with the government. Wamalwa's disregard of the NCEC guideline signalled a new crack in the uneasy alliance between civil and political society (*Economic Review* 21/07/97: 4-7).

Now with the prospect of reform talks, the tension in the country eased and the opposition front started to disintegrate. This first became evident, when the NCEC's planned nation-wide strike on 8 August (*Nane Nane* in Kiswahili), received only a lukewarm response and was only partly successful in Nairobi. The NCEC even lost some moral ground as a plain-clothed police officer was identified at an undisrupted public opposition meeting in Nairobi and killed by demonstrators.[12] Towards the end of July, the Kibaki - Wamalwa wing tried to get their approach to negotiations with the president endorsed at a meeting between the NCEC and opposition parliamentarians, but were turned down. The majority agreed that a selected group of the NCA would present reform proposals to the president personally.

However, Moi declined to meet any NGO representative, claiming that they did not have the mandate of the public to speak on anybody's behalf. These sentiments were silently shared by the Kibaki - Wamalwa group and loudly supported by Matiba and some parts of the media, especially the *Weekly*

Review. This way they all disclosed, once again, a narrow understanding of democracy and of a democratic culture. It is a constituent ingredient of civil society that NGOs intervene in the public discourse and that they derive the right to do so from their professional competence. They cannot substitute any decision-making institution, but their function is to challenge its members and the government on certain issues. By excluding the NGOs, Moi exploited the rifts between civil and political society that had been covered so far for the sake of the reform campaign. As in the past, Moi once again staged his *divide-et-impera* game successfully. As he insisted that talks should be held by elected politicians, he indirectly supported the Kibaki-Wamalwa wing in reasserting their leadership role within the opposition. They eagerly accepted this assistance. Through the negotiations with the government each of them additionally hoped to improve his chances of getting endorsed as the single opposition presidential candidate should one of them emerge as the leader of the movement.

By mid-August the churches were emerging again as the broker between the conflicting factions. Within a couple of days, they held meetings with the president, the NCEC, the opposition parties, a newly appointed constitutional committee of KANU chaired by Vice-President George Saitoti, with the diplomatic community and the press. Only the president, however, endorsed the churches' role, less so did the NCEC or the parties. This way Moi brought in certain churches, known for being close to the government which had not raised their voices on the issue of reform so far. The mediation committee that was finally set up was comprised of two representatives each of the NCCK, the Kenya Episcopal Conference (KEC), the Evangelical Fellowship of Kenya (EFK) and the Supreme Council of Kenya Muslims (Supkem). Musyimi of the NCCK was its speaker. With the silent support of the government the EFK had been founded in the early 1990s as a rival body to the NCCK which in the eyes of the government was acting as an opposition force. Supkem too had the reputation of being government friendly. Thus, even though the reform lobby of the churches was not neutralised by the integration of the government-friendly bodies their influence was at least balanced (*Weekly Review* 15/08/97: 4-6; *Economic Review* 18/08/97: 24).

Despite high expectations, the mediation committee did not get anywhere. The first official meeting between KANU and the opposition brokered by the churches was aborted. Arguing along the same line as Moi, the KANU delegation, led by Saitoti, refused to accept the civic organisations as equal partners as they did not have any mandate. The KANU team of 37 parliamentarians insisted that these organisations could only participate in the talks in an advisory capacity and that they were not eligible to vote. Thus, they rejected the 60-strong NCEC team which consisted of a mix of members of parliament and representatives of civic groups. Up to that point, the coherence of the reform alliance was still officially maintained (*Economic Review* 25/08/97: 24; *Weekly Review* 05/09/97: 5-7).

The events of the last week of August, however, marked the final parting of the ways between the NCEC and the opposition parties with the NCEC becoming more radical and the opposition parties becoming softer and more moderate. The NCEC was convinced that the government was not seriously committed to reforms and only wanted to play a waiting game with the opposition. Parliamentarians, though not convinced of Moi's seriousness either, opted for negotiations with KANU. They did so for basically two reasons: first to avoid further violent escalations and second to regain the leadership role in the opposition.

Radicalisation and compromise: two answers to the government's reform offer

In its second plenary session the NCA went ahead with its plans for a National Convention. In Nairobi's Ufungamano House it was hotly discussed whether the NCA should transform itself into a Citizens Constituent Assembly if the government did not respond to their reform demands. There were different interpretations of what was meant by Constituent Assembly. Some participants, like the former LSK chairman Paul Wamae, warned the audience that the term implied that the NCA would transform itself into an alternative or parallel government although it did not have any means to enforce the resolution. Gibson Kamau Kuria, Willy Mutunga and Kivutha Kibwana tried to ease the tension by pointing out that it was clarified in the resolution that the assembly would only collect and discuss proposals for constitutional reform. That, however, was something that could also be done under the roof of the NCA. The resolution was finally endorsed. It made it clear that the NCA would transform itself into a Constituent Assembly in case Moi called elections before any meaningful reforms were initiated (*Weekly Review* 05/09/97: 7-9; *Economic Review* 01/09/97: 6-11).

The message that the NCA sent to the public and to the government was ambiguous. It seemed that it wanted to challenge the government substantially but was indecisive about the appropriate means. The second plenary session was a radicalisation of the civil society forces without any decisive leverage. By threatening to become a sort of parallel government, the NCA clearly overestimated its capacities and resources.

The NCEC might only have been able to regain its strength if the negotiations between KANU and the opposition parties had failed. This, however, was not to be the case. The opposition members of parliament met their KANU counterparts with caution. Wamalwa, Kibaki and the SDP presidential candidate, Charity Ngilu, among other politicians kept an observing distance. At the first meeting, attended by approximately 54 MPs (37 from KANU and 17 from the opposition, among them Martin Shikuku and George Anyona of the KSC), the KANU delegation assured their colleagues that no elections would be called as long as the reform process was underway. Within a week the informal group became the Inter-Parties Parliamentary Group (IPPG) and started negotiating seriously. With 36 opposition and some 70 KANU parliamentarians involved, the IPPG agreed on a wide range of reforms that hardly any observer had expected. It recommended inter alia that the electoral commission should be expanded and de-linked from the Executive, that several repressive laws (Preservation of Public Order Act, Public Order Act, Chief's Authority Act) be scrapped, that KBC be bound by law to ensure fair coverage of all political forces and that provisions for a coalition government be introduced. With the success of the IPPG all further plans of the NCEC for mass action became waste paper. The NCEC stuck to its critique of the IPPG, and maintained that a level playing field was far from being achieved. However, many Kenyans were pleased and relieved as the reform consensus materialised.

Conclusion

The co-operation between the divergent opposition forces in 1997 led to the most serious challenge of the Moi regime since 1991. It showed that a united, determined and reform-committed opposition front is able to force the government, however reluctant it is, to institute democratic reforms. For the first time since 1991, the opposition was willing to enter into direct conflict with the government and did not shy at mass action with unpredictable outcomes. The broad positive response of the public which turned up in huge numbers at demonstrations and meetings indicated, on the one hand, the depth of the discontent of the *wananchi* with the Moi regime and, on the other hand, their readiness to become mobilised if the opposition offered a convincing political agenda and strategy. During the election year, the opposition parties and civil society organisations had a common interest: to remove restrictive and repressive laws from the political playing field so that the elections could be more 'free and fair' than in 1992. Having achieved this, however, there was the prospect that the democratic transition might be closed by political society as both KANU and the opposition parties were not interested in permanently opening up the political decision-making process to other social and political forces.

Stephen Ndegwa's stand (1998: 196) that the IPPG-package was foremost an elite pact can be supported. It is, however, remarkable that due to the pressure of the NCEC and the churches the reforms exceeded the degree which political society would have been content with. One may conclude that minimal democratic reforms do not necessarily need to be negotiated by genuine democratic forces as long as those forces can be kept under pressure by a determined civil society that does not avoid severe and open conflicts with either the government or the opposition parties.

With the exception of Matiba and possibly Raila Odinga, the leaders of the opposition parties appeared to be rather self-content with their opposition role. Their main concern seemed to be securing the leadership within their respective ethnic community and through that holding a stake in the political arena without risking too much. During the period between the elections, however, the discontent of their followers with their inactivity had grown. And it was at this point that civil society forces could capitalise on these disillusions and fill the vacuum within the opposition. By taking on the opposition leadership role the NCEC was prepared to exceed the borderline between civil and political society, at least for a limited period of time. The challenge by the NCEC was one major reason for the party leaders to become more determined.

To conclude, however, that Kenya possesses a strong civil society from the flourishing of the NGO sector, basically concerned with human rights, women issues and civic education, may be rather misleading. Taking a closer look, it appears that the strength of civil society rests on a small group of committed persons rather than on well-entrenched institutions. Ironically, a Kenyan jurist once maintained that Kenya's civil society consists of 30 people in 60 organisations. Church leaders, jurists and economists basically carry the burden, and they establish new organisations whenever deemed fit or demanded by a particular situation. Over a medium or longer period of time, however, the tasks of civil society can only be carried out by institutions that have built capacities that are to a certain extent independent of the people who work in them. In Kenya so far this criterion is only matched by the NCCK and the Catholic church and, to some degree, by the LSK.

Notes

1. Following Bratton and van de Walle (1997: 40) a relatively broad definition of institutions, including informal customs like 'patronage', 'clientelism' or 'seniority principles' is used here.
2. Kenya had a *majimbo*-constitution (*jimbo* = region in Kiswahili) for a brief period of time right after independence. It provided for a semi-autonomy of the different regions of the country; for a discussion of the early *majimbo*-constitution, its renaissance since the early 1990s and its significance for the democratisation process see Ngunyi (1996).
3. The two leading daily newspapers (*Daily Nation* and *East African Standard*), for example, carried serials about the purposes and significance of a constitution, in general and for

Kenya in particular, printed excerpts of the draft constitution and provided discussion forums for constitutional experts and politicians. Almost every day, politicians from the opposition and the ruling party exchanged arguments for and against a reform of the constitution. Informal political groups started strategising and preparing their own kind of model constitution.

4.   The steering committee communicated this decision to the public in a long advert in the daily newspapers. See, for example *Daily Nation* 10/01/95.

5.   Interviews with Professor Kivutha Kibwana (12/12/94, Nairobi), Gibson Kamau Kuria (02/04/96, Nairobi), Willy Mutunga (24/06/96, Bonn).

6.   Interview with Reverend Jephthah K. Gathaka (03/03/96, Nairobi), Executive Director of the Ecumenical Centre for Justice and Peace; formerly, i.e. before the restructuring of the NCCK, the Centre was part of the NCCK as the Commission for Justice, Peace and Reconciliation.

7.   Interview with Alfred Ndambiri (10/04/96, Nairobi) of the Legal Resource Foundation, a small NGO, that carries out civic education programmes, partly in co-operation with other NGOs and church organisations.

8.   The opposition parties were internally divided. With the formation of the 'Opposition Alliance' in December 1995 the chairman of the DP, Mwai Kibaki, the chairman of FORD-Kenya, Michael Kijana Wamalwa, and the general secretary of FORD-Asili, Martin Shikuku tried to gain advantages over their internal rivals, Kenneth Matiba (FORD-Asili chairman) and Raila Odinga (FORD-Kenya), who in turn formed their 'Opposition Solidarity' in order to hold a similar strong bloc. All opposition leaders maintained they sought alliances in order to find a solution to the most pressing problem of the opposition, i.e., the procedure how to select a single presidential candidate. In reality, however, it was a struggle by each opposition leader against the other as no one was willing to back down in favour of the other aspirants.

9.   Willy Mutunga and Gibson Kamau Kuria graduated in Dar es Salaam in the 1960s and obtained their doctorate degrees in Oxford and Canada. Kivutha Kibwana studied in Nairobi, London and Harvard while Pheroze Nowrojee did so in Yale.

10.   The term 'Young Turks' originates from a political reform movement in the Ottoman Empire in the 1860s. It pursued liberal constitutional objectives. In the African context it had been first applied in the 1940s to a group of young men around Nelson Mandela, Walter Sisulu and Oliver Tambo who were, at that time, members of the South African 'Youth League' (Hastings 1979:29).

11.   They temporarily held important positions within one party, FORD-Kenya, but many (e.g. Muite, Imanyara, Murungi, Robert Shaw) resigned their party posts over the internal conflict of the Ksh. 2 million donation of Kamlesh Pattni, the proprietor of the scandalous Goldenberg enterprise, to party chairman Oginga Odinga in May 1993 (see, e.g., Throup and Hornsby 1998: 548, 562). When founding Safina in 1995 Muite and comrades failed to seize the moment of public support and euphoria around the time of its launching. This may have been Muite's only chance so far to rise to the status of a national leader. Thus, to avoid losing the parliamentary seats, Muite, Murungi, Anyang' Nyong'o and Mohammed Farrah remained officially in FORD-Kenya until the elections of 1997, but were fairly isolated within the party.

12.   According to information from Kivutha Kibwana, one of the NCEC organisers, the meeting at which the policeman was killed was a gathering of supporters of Raila Odinga who addressed a crowd near the Kenyatta memorial in Central Park. NCEC officials, Kibwana among them, had just discussed and assessed the outcome of the strike at All Saints Cathedral which is not far away from the memorial. They were just approaching the gathering when the policeman was attacked. They intervened and were taking the police officer to a taxi to drive him to hospital when he collapsed and died on the spot.

Though the gathering may not have been convened by the NCEC, the media attributed the events to its activities and in the public eye the NCEC came to be seen as responsible for the death of the policeman.

References

Bratton, M. 1994, "Civil Society and Political Transition in Africa', in Harbeson, J., Rothchild, D. and Chazan, N. (eds), *Civil Society and the State in Africa*, Boulder/London: Lynne Rienner Publishers: 51-81.

Bratton, M. and Walle, N. van de 1997, *Democratic Experiments in Africa*, Cambridge University Press.

Chazan, N. 1992, 'Africa's Democratic Challenge', *World Policy Journal*, Vol.9, No.2: 279-307.

Hastings, A. 1979, *A History of African Christianity 1950-1975*, Cambridge University Press.

Linz, J. and Stepan, A. 1996, *Problems of democratic transition and consolidation—southern Europe, South America, and post-communist Europe*, Baltimore/London: Johns Hopkins University Press.

Ndegwa, S. 1998, 'The Incomplete Transition: The Constitutional and Electoral Context in Kenya', *Africa Today*, Vol. 45, No.2: 193-212.

Ngunyi, M. 1996, 'Resuscitating the Majimbo-Project: The Politics of Deconstructing the Unitary State in Africa', in Olukoshi, A. and Laasko, L. (eds), *Challenges to the nation-State in Africa*, Uppsala: Nordiska Afrika Institutet: 183-212.

Peters, R.-M. 1996, 'Zivile und politische Gesellschaft in Kenya', *Focus Afrika. IAK Diskussionsbeitrage 5*, Hamburg: Institut für Afrika-Kunde.

_____ 1998, 'Die Präsidentschafts- und Parlamentswahlen in Kenya 1997 – Hintergründe, Verlauf, Resultate und politische Folgen', *Focus Afrika. IAK Diskussionsbeitrage 10*, Hamburg: Institut für Afrika-Kunde.

Streeten, P. 1993, 'Markets and States: Against Minimalism', *World Development*, Vol.21, No.8:1281-98.

Throup, D. and Hornsby, C. 1998, *Multi-Party Politics in Kenya. The Kenyatta & Moi States & the Triumph of the System in the 1992 Election*, Oxford: James Currey.

3

The Churches and the Polls

Hervé Maupeu

Unlike many other African citizens, Kenyans have been voting regularly for the past 40 years. Elections therefore play a vital role in the country's regulation of political competition. The advent of multi-partyism in 1992, however, changed the form and methods of electoral competition. Many new political actors such as the Christian churches, which are far more involved in the public domain in Kenya than in the other East African countries, emerged. While the clergy in Uganda or Tanzania have always criticised their respective authoritarian regimes, in Kenya they have actively got involved in the democratisation process.

This political commitment is not universally shared and usually remains the characteristic of only a few religious organisations. Out of Kenya's thousands of churches, less than a dozen really politicise their activities. The churches contributed to the early christianisation of the country and are most strongly rooted in the rural areas. They assemble, therefore, a great majority of the Christians. For the past 10 years, the Catholics, the Anglicans (formerly Church of the Province of Kenya (CPK) which became the Anglican Church of Kenya (ACK) in 1998), the Presbyterians (Presbyterian Church of East Africa, PCEA) and the Methodists (Methodist Church of Kenya, MCK) have been at the forefront of the fight against the authoritarian practices of the Moi regime and contributed a lot to the return to multi-party rule in 1990. On the other hand, the African Inland Church (AIC), with the support of some other evangelical churches, devotedly supported the head of state[1]. Yet, this general outline of the political involvement of the Kenyan churches is not definitive. Whatever the official position of these religious institutions, in every one of them there are interpretative trends, factions and determined individuals with specific representations of their own mission who do not share the same conception of their secular commitments. In 1992 and 1997, prelates of the same church could support different presidential candidates. Furthermore, a religious leader could be an avowed rival of the national leadership of the country, but still work closely with the provincial administration and with elected leaders of the same party at the local level.

In Kenya, religion and politics interact in many different ways and at different levels. This can be seen clearly at the time of elections when most of the ways and means of the politics of the country are revealed. The study of the involvement of the churches in politics during the 1997 general elections therefore requires an analysis of the collective, individual and institutional relations between these religious groups and Kenyan politicians. We need to assess how religion shapes political issues and to what extent churches as institutions, social groups and individual voices get involved in designing the electoral landscape. It is equally important to identify the role of christianity in the political culture of Kenyans and also to understand how religious forces intervene in politics. If it is true that belonging to a church can shape the political attitude of followers, to what extent is this possible? This chapter will proceed therefore in four steps. First, we will recall how Kenyan churches entered the political arena and became one of the strongest opposition forces of the country. Second, we shall present the general theological background that made this entry possible. Third, we will see how churches behaved during the 1997 elections and, lastly, we will attempt to measure the influence of christianity on the political behaviour of Kenyans.

The slow formation of a Christian opposition (1960-92)

The churches in Kenya did not just wake up one day and join the opposition forces. Their conversion to politics has been a long process which followed specific dynamics studied by several scholars (Benson 1995; Ngunyi 1995; Sabar-Friedmann 1995; Throup 1995; Maupeu 1991, 1995 and 1997; Grignon 1998; Throup and Hornsby 1998). A recollection of their observations and analyses is necessary here as it illustrates the webs of constraints which conditioned the scope of actions of the churches during the 1997 election campaigns.

Indeed, political behaviour stems from the social structure of a society. The memory of institutions and the socialisation of the actors limit the possibilities of creation of alliances, shape the type of political interventions and constrain the capacity of mobilisation. Such processes have shaped the formation of a Christian opposition in Kenya, which reached its peak with the rigging of the 1988 general elections.

Before 1988
The involvement of churches in politics is a relatively recent phenomenon. It is directly linked to the democratisation process, which owes a lot to them. Religious activity during President Kenyatta's regime was restricted to the private sphere only. In the 1960s, churches were mainly pre-occupied with freeing themselves from their colonial missionary origin to become national and independent religious organisations. Among the Protestants, this meant

the observance of a safe dissociation from politics. The Western clergy tried to make people forget their acquaintance with the colonial powers and African pastors, who were members of the East African Revival Fellowship, were still traumatised with the trying experience of the Mau Mau movement. The revivalists had paid heavily for their refusal to declare their stand, either as loyalists or guerrillas, and suffered from the violence of both parties. This cleavage, being still strong in the early years of the young republic, Protestants found themselves locked out of the public sphere. As for the Catholics, their history in the country could not enable them to get involved. Since most of the missionaries were not British, they took a low profile during the entire colonial period. When the reservation of certain areas of influence for particular denominations was done away with at independence, the Catholics concentrated on a systematic evangelisation mission, seizing opportunities to expand their influence. In this context, the churches could have been satisfied with the fulfilment of some supplementary secular and social responsibilities, even though the government had reduced them and assumed full charge of the education and health sectors throughout the country. Politically, they could have embodied a vague moral reference or a cultural filter assisting the citizenry to make sense of national politics since the Bible had become the main book of reference for political mobilisation during colonial times (Lonsdale 1992). They, however, became full political actors in the 1980s.

The increasing influence of the churches in politics came first from President Moi who needed them to play a political role in order to gain independence from the inheritors of the Kenyatta state. In 1978, at the beginning of his first term in office, President Moi decided to modify to his advantage the ideology in place as well as the network of political exchange. He replaced the *Harambee* spirit (literally 'pulling together' i.e., towards development and welfare) with the Nyayo ideology (literally the 'footsteps' meaning that he was following the footsteps of Jomo Kenyatta, the founder of the nation, and that the rest of the country was to follow his, those of the new guide), a populism riddled with Christianism which he regarded as an important medium for ideological integration. This religious reference was meant to make him appear like a divinely inspired guide, another Moses leading his people to the shores of Canaan, the 'land of milk and honey', and a national leader not driven by ethnicity and factional differences but by the interest of the entire population of the country (Benson 1995; Grignon 1998).

Unlike his predecessor, President Moi chose at that time to rely less on sources of legitimacy linked to the loyalty of regional power brokers, but to create a direct relation of trust, religious communality and understanding with the population. Daniel arap Moi, therefore, engaged in a form of neo-Constantinism, where churches actively supported and were responsible for the spread of presidential propaganda in the secular circles where they were in charge of creating a nation of docile Nyayo followers. Unfortunately for him, his good relationship with the churches did not last long. The churches were seduced into promoting the ideology of this hegemonic project but they did not want to serve as an obedient link between the state and civil society or maybe only at the local level through the various development projects they started in the 1980s (Maupeu 1991; 1995).

Agitation for multi-partyism

The divorce between the state and the Kenyan churches was reached quite early in 1983 with the exclusion of Charles Njonjo from the political scene. The eviction from the government and the ruling party KANU of this very influential lay leader of the Church of the Province of Kenya (the Anglican church) illustrated the beginning of a constant policy to weaken the Kikuyu politico-economic establishment. Some analysts have argued that the involvement of churches in politics can be seen as a sign of solidarity from Protestant prelates who are mainly from the wealthy Kikuyu families at war with the regime. Most of the Protestant bishops were indeed, at that time, Kikuyu, and the religious revolt came mainly from their churches as the Catholics maintained a very low profile. This kind of explanation is, however, not enough. The increase in authoritarianism is what progressively led to the establishment of a Christian opposition to the regime of Daniel arap Moi. The radicalisation of the churches and their involvement in politics can be traced through several steps and emanated from three or four different regions of the country, reaching a climax in 1988 (for a detailed account see Throup 1995). The Kikuyu Presbyterian, Methodist or Anglican prelates, Timothy Njoya, Samuel Kobia and David Gitari, were not the only ones to oppose the state. The actions of the Anglican Bishops Henry Okullu and Alexander Muge, respectively of Luo and Nandi origins, are very significant in this respect.

In the 1988 contest, the government modified the election procedure and implemented queue voting instead of the secret ballot. Queue voting required the voter to stand in a queue behind his or her candidate or picture. This new pattern of voting was violently opposed by the churches and the Law Society of Kenya. As a result, the voter turnout in these elections was lower than it had ever been before, thus putting into question their legitimacy. Not only had the churches obtained assurances from the government that members of the clergy would be allowed to vote through secret ballot, thus invalidating the whole legitimacy of this latest Nyayo dictum, but they also illustrated the strong influence they could have on the politics of the country. The clergy, moreover, brought to light the extensive rigging that took place through the queuing system. The Anglican Bishop David Gitari filmed the queues in his diocese, contradicting the official election results and thus proving how fraudulent they were. The 1988 mobilisation against queue-voting was still limited to a number of prelates strongly rooted in their dioceses and benefiting from international connections. These were: Bishop Henry Okullu whose articles in the Christian media had shaken the relationship between the church and state since the 1970s; Bishops David Gitari and Alexander Muge who took every opportunity to denounce the excesses of the government in power and criticised the members of parliament in their dioceses; and Rev. Timothy Njoya whose critical sermons became a common feature of the political columns of newspapers. But through these individuals' utterances and actions, the political conversion of the clergy as a social group and the mobilisation of the church as an institution slowly took place. The mainstream Christian churches began to realise that Kenya was slowly turning into a closed society where the single party was determined to control the citizenry. Only the church remained as an independent institution that could position itself between the state and civil society. As a matter of fact, only churches had the financial independence (through international aid), the ideological independence (through their theology of power) and a social foundation that could oppose the state. With the assistance of a group of jurists, the churches started in 1990 the agitation for the return to multi-partyism.

During their sermons, prelates systematically criticised the actual abuses of power that had characterised Kenyan politics since independence—the excessive powers of the president and of the members of the ruling party, neo-patrimonialism, corruption and their effects such as illegal political imprisonment, police violence, harassment and profound economic crisis. These discourses broke the univocal Nyayo tune that the government tried to maintain through authoritarianism and regular renewal of the political elite. It also questioned some of the Kenyan taboos by claiming loudly that the single-party system was not a Kenyan fatality and was not necessarily the best solution for the country. Political heavyweights excluded from the regime such as Oginga Odinga, Kenneth Matiba and Charles Rubia followed this move and a new generation of politicians, who were independent professionals, joined in the fray in agitating for the return to multi-partyism (for the most detailed account of this period see Throup and Hornsby 1998).

The 1992 general elections

After the legalisation of multi-party politics in December 1991, the churches had to review their political stands. They could have promoted the creation of religious political parties given that they had played the role of parties in the years before. This, however, could never become a genuine possibility as the clergy as a group at no time shared the same political convictions. Churches, therefore, played the role of 'facilitators', as the National Council of Churches of Kenya (NCCK) secretary general, Rev. Kobia, once described it. They participated in the organisation of meetings between the leaders of opposition parties, trying to unite the front against KANU, and promoted the establishment of a common platform of action (about electoral procedures, political prisoners and the ethnic clashes, among other issues). Yet, not a single church was considered to be neutral. The Anglican church was one of the most divided. Its Archbishop, Manasses Kuria, openly campaigned for FORD-Asili, whereas Bishop Henry Okullu campaigned for FORD-Kenya. Catholics mainly supported Kibaki's Democratic Party and only the NCCK, an organisation that unites the Protestant churches and handles several of their social activities, embarked on an attempt to unify the opposition, but without much success. Churches also played the role of facilitators by undertaking extensive civic education for the masses in order to explain the modalities of voting and the new stakes that accompanied the return to pluralism. They participated in the observation of elections through a joint effort led concurrently with several human rights NGOs within the board of the National Election Monitoring Unit (NEMU). In the end, some church leaders who had opposed President Moi for months and tried to level the ground of the political competition took his victory as their own failure. The results of these elections served as a lesson for the churches and their failure to promote successfully political change in the country partly shaped their behaviour in the 1997 contest.

The churches and the production of electoral stakes

The doctrines of the major churches do not differ much on secular issues. Yet, a distinction must be made between the approaches of the Protestants and the Catholics. They both reach similar conclusions but use different patterns and rhythms to arrive at those conclusions. After the general elections of 1992, some administrative staff of the Protestant organisations put forward the analysis of their institutions' secular strategies. According to Agnes Abuom (CPK), the absence of a stable Protestant theology about power in Kenya has rendered it impossible for churches to adopt a common political course. She states: 'the church's theological and philosophical conceptual frameworks have been poorly articulated within its involvement in social change processes. Consequently, it has only managed to provide knee-jerk comments on questions of governance and has been caught up in various conflicts that beset the nation' (Abuom 1996:98).

Originally these churches shared a conservative evangelical doctrine obsessed with individual salvation, sexual morality and very little concern with other social issues. For a long time, they had some doubt about the human rights ideology which was considered to be too liberal and whose inspiration was judged to be atheist. Since the 1970s, African Protestantism has, nevertheless, changed greatly. It has become polarised between an ecumenical trend, opened to the changes of the world and busy finding the best strategies to support development, thus embodying a Christianity freeing its members from poverty and ignorance, and an evangelical trend, oriented towards rigorous fundamentalism, exclusively interested in conversion and salvation of its members, and refusing the idea of development and, especially, the knowledge brought by the social sciences. In the Lausanne Covenant (1974) that ratified the divorce between the main denominations and the evangelists, the latter displayed their deep-rooted anti-communism and the rejection of the approach displayed by other churches which they judged too political. Kenya could not remain foreign to this separation, Nairobi being one of the capitals of African Christianism.

In 1976 Nairobi hosted the first Pan African Christian Leadership Assembly. Soon thereafter, the Association of Evangelicals of Africa and Madagascar established their headquarters in the city, in order to compete with the All African Conference of Churches (AACC), who also had their headquarters there and represented the African ecumenical churches. This decade-long rivalry clearly puts into focus the crisis faced by the NCCK in the mid-1980s. When the NCCK started criticising the government, some evangelical churches immediately quit the umbrella body to form their own national organisation. The African Inland Church, closely associated with the head of state, easily convinced several religious groups to quit the NCCK. This split should not be over-emphasised as numerous exercises of reconciliation have taken place since the mid-eighties, but it always remains latent. During the second Pan African Christian Leadership Assembly held in Nairobi in 1994, the reconciliation between these two forces was indeed ratified.

What could be viewed as an exercise of theological acrobatics is not necessarily the case. Mugambi (1997) reminds us that prelates in Kenya are not necessarily embarrassed by this situation. Leaders of the ecumenical movement regularly contribute to the evangelical conferences and to interdenominational crusades. Furthermore, the East African Revival Fellowship, dubbed 'grassroots theology' by Kwame Bediako, reflects to a large extent the mentality of the Protestant clergy and presents some doctrinal aspect that brings them close to evangelism: born again Christianity, insistence on the power of the holy spirit, etc. The revivalists insist on individual salvation but this does not prevent political awakening. As such, D.M. Gitari reports that towards the end of 1980, his congregation threw out of his church KANU youths trying to disturb his preaching by singing revivalists hymns. The same church burst into the same songs when it welcomed the 'mothers of political prisoners' who were demonstrating for the release of their sons (Gitari 1996:87). The revival can serve as a source of mobilisation and can lead to the emergence of communal feeling during difficult times. Certainly, most of the evangelical churches avoid active participation in politics but once their freedom of action is hampered, their attitude changes. The Religious Bodies Registration Bill of 1996 was aimed at giving the government some means to control street churches which are rapidly increasing in the big towns. Bishop J. K. Kimani, FORD-Asili MP for Nakuru North and leader of Kenya National Evangelical Fellowship, started a 'holy war' against the passing of this bill by parliament (*Finance* 10/12/96).

Yet, the intellectual context of Kenyan Protestantism did not really ease the emergence of a political theology. In the 1980s, pastors of the ecumenical churches, such as Okullu, Gitari and Njoya, developed the main guidelines for the establishment of a theology of secular power. But these were the work of isolated individuals who never found their way into seminaries where the principal author to be studied remained Rev. J.S. Mbiti, the promoter of inculturation who categorically rejected all forms of theology of liberation. It is only in the 1990s that ecumenical theologians from the All Africa Churches Conference developed 'a theology of reconstruction' which was aimed at bringing to light the depth of the crisis of Kenyan society and, therefore, proposed a number of social principles to guide the secular commitment of the church. However, as Professor Mugambi, one of its promoters, recognises, this theology of reconstruction has only supported a prospective vision up to now, and has not influenced the political agenda of the churches.

If the Protestants suffer from the consequences of the weaknesses of their political theology and the lack of doctrinal training of their top staff, the Catholics suffer from the opposite. Many pastors dream about the quality of training given to future priests. They leave the seminaries with a solid intellectual background which makes it possible for them to analyse the political situation in view of their Catholic beliefs. Two doctrines nurture their political theology: the theology of liberation and the social doctrine of the church. The former has not been developed in Kenya, as in Tanzania and South Africa. Since the Catholic church in Kenya mainly supports the Roman orthodox tradition, the theology of liberation is not popular. The presence of several South American missionaries in East Africa has made it possible for this theology to be discussed. It is worth noting that one of the editors of the pastoral letters in the 1990s was a South American Jesuit. Most of the Catholic clergy, therefore, adopted an option of this theology in favour of the poor which is not based on the criticism of the distribution of wealth among socio-economic categories, but includes the defence of women and persecuted groups. Furthermore, the concept of 'oppression' was broadened not only to include economic but also cultural, ecological and religious oppression. Under these circumstances, the numerous development activities of the Catholic church would logically give rise to political conscientisation of the Christians. It would be important to see whether this social action of the church will be politicised and if it will be used to mobilise the Christians.

Moreover, within the hierarchy of the Catholic church, the changes since the *Rerum Novarum* encyclical (1891) have been such that the social doctrine of the church has indeed become unanimous. Pope John Paul II has proved to be extremely conservative in the moral domain, but he has been committed to encouraging the discussion on social issues as per his encyclical letter *Sollicitudo Rei Socialis* (1987) which he addressed to the Catholics in the South and the encyclical letter for the hundredth anniversary of *Rerum Novarum*. The synod of the African bishops specifically emphasised this subject (of the 211 points raised during the synod, 40 were directly about justice and peace). The clergy found it necessary to undertake an objective analysis of reality which takes into account the contributions of human sciences and the quest for 'integral development' which respects human rights, the state of law, and democratic principles and which requires certain economic reforms. This approach appeals to the Christians' conscience, a conscience that forms the basis for the taking of moral decisions. But, this also demands that church leaders take clear and courageous positions.

The programmatic axes

The political demands of the churches have hardly changed from one election to the other. The same themes are repeated over again, sometimes discussed in more depth and detail. However, participants in this debate have clearly changed and have thus created new presentations and types of mobilisation linked to these requests.

Two critical questions emerge from the list of these religious demands; the churches want to be the custodians of human rights and thus insist on broad constitutional reform. In the human rights realm, instances of indignation are common in Kenya. Protestants in particular denounced the evictions taking place in some of the major slums of Nairobi in 1996. Surprisingly, the Protestant churches were least concerned about the plight of refugees in East Africa whereas Catholics have always focused on this issue. However, the two Christian groups united to jointly condemn the ethnic massacres which took place between 1991 and 1997. The ethnic cleansing in 1992/93 convinced the main churches of the harmfulness of the Moi regime and of the necessity to denounce clearly and loudly what appeared to be state-inspired violence. In their numerous official declarations on these events, the churches linked them directly to the machinations and authoritarianism of the government. They condemned the behaviour of certain ministers for inciting their constituents towards ethnic violence, and highlighted the role of the political elite in organising and arranging these murders.

In the first half of the 1990s, the Protestants were especially active in condemning these activities. The NCCK publications greatly inspired the parliamentary reports on the massacres. But in the middle and late eighties, the radical position taken by the Catholic church on ethnic clashes progressively changed the less favourable perception many Kenyans had about the Catholics. The ethnic clashes occurred in predominantly Catholic areas, and the Catholic church hosted the refugees for a long period.[2] It received and broadcast most of the reliable information about the murderers. Nakuru Bishop Ndingi Mwana a'Nzeki courageously embodied this position in his sermons, so much that he was regularly attacked by KANU politicians, especially in 1996 when he announced that new killings were being arranged in his diocese. The Catholic church strongly defended its prelate and since 1991 at least eight pastoral letters (official messages from all the bishops in the country) have been issued to denounce the ethnic clashes and the responsibilities of the government in their organisation.

The need for constitutional reform has been the other theme at the centre of almost all of the pastoral letters written in the 1990s. This issue has generally been approached at two levels: first, a criticism of the institutional set up and of the current constitutional practices, and second, suggestions to remedy this situation. The clergy's stand on the constitutional debate has enhanced its influence on the Kenyan political system. Church leaders have become legitimate political actors, maintaining that they are empowered to discuss the human rights and welfare record of the country which gives them the authority to address those issues together with politicians. The precision of the suggestions, orientations, and propositions of the churches on the constitutional debate significantly illustrates the input they can have in determining the future of the country and of the seriousness they attribute to this task.

The clergy derives its approach to judicial matters from Anglo-Saxon and, in particular, American concepts of a constitutional state where emphasis is put on respect for the law and human rights as a moral responsibility which goes hand in hand with respect for religion. Respect for human rights and the law from a religious point of view gives the clergy the legitimacy and *locus standi* to comment on the constitution. Moreover, they view the law, justice and human rights as instruments to achieve social change; they should become instruments to regulate democracy and control the state. This concept of the law is very popular among Kenyans who have a passion for judicial procedures, despite the limitations encountered in the administration of justice.

Compared with programmes of other groups that have a political vocation, this form of constitutionalism might seem to be less original. Still, we need to stress again that none of the players on the political scene necessarily share the same idea about the concept of juridical rights. For example, the ruling elite does not believe in the capacity of the law to bring solutions to social and political conflicts; rights here are considered to be a mere cover-up of the interests of a specific group. They consider first and foremost that the law is a protection for the state over civil society. One could as well state that, for the ruling class, what is supreme is politics and they do take the judiciary as a way to score and win political conflicts. Consequently, in the debate on constitutional reform, the parties involved do not necessarily speak about the same issues and have divergent views on the relevance of the law in society.

There are evidently several schools of thought guiding the churches in their analysis of the constitution. They, however, realise that they need to speak with one voice in order to be considered credible on the political scene. The Catholics are responsible for the majority of views and proposals discussed on the legislature and judiciary in the co-ordinating meetings. On the other hand, the Protestants are foremost involved in suggestions concerning matters of the executive and central government. The churches have conducted their political agitation in a good ecumenical spirit. Still, it is hard to deny the impression that, towards the end of the 1990s, Protestant leaders have displayed themselves as a discreet lot aiming to keep a low profile among the rest of the Kikuyu elite as if they expected nothing much from the elections. The Anglicans were at the centre of the debate on the involvement of the church in politics during the first multi-party elections[3]. In 1997, the Catholics spearheaded the debate. Since 1992, Catholics have issued about 20 pastoral letters and bishops' messages. At their own cost, they managed to reach a wide audience since these messages were published in the leading newspapers in the country. At the same time, the Protestants were preoccupied with their own internal problems. The NCCK became less militant with the departure of Rev. Samuel Kobia from the helm of their organisation. KANU politicians who are used to games of destabilisation had vilified him very much. After some churches fell out of favour with the NCCK, in 1995 John Wycliffe Wanga announced from Eldoret the formation of the Regional Council of Churches of Kenya to accommodate these splinter churches. Wanga was capitalising on the troubles the NCCK faced about its source of funding from the West (see *Economic Review* 17-23/04/95: 27). Corruption and fraudulent activities in the NCCK were denounced in the opposition newspaper *Finance* (15/01/97) in 1997. As much as NCCK was able to absolve itself, in a way it admitted its delicate financial position.

The Anglican church, on its part, was involved in sex scandals. Rev. Simon Muting'ole Okech of the Maseno North Diocese was in 1993 accused of adultery. In 1995 the Archbishop of Mt Kenya South Diocese was suspected of being unfaithful with an employee of the political party FORD-Asili. In addition, the CPK has been involved in factional fights which have taken an ethnic dimension. Following the death of Alexander Muge[4] in 1990, Rev. Kewasis (a Pokot) won the CPK elections in the politically sensitive Diocese of Eldoret. Christians led by Rev. Elijah Yego opposed Rev. Kewasis' leadership arguing that the diocese is highly populated by the Nandi and should thus be led by a Nandi. Four years later, new elections were conducted which confirmed the leadership of Rev. Kewasis. Similarly, since 1992, the new Anglican Diocese of Kajiado has been headed by the archbishop, because the elected bishop Rev. Bernard Njoroge, a Kikuyu who supported the opposition, was prevented from performing his duties by the pro-KANU Maasai faithful. The same problems existed in western Kenya where some factions demanded the creation of a new River Nzoia Diocese out of the Maseno North Diocese. In other words, even within its own circles, the Anglican church is occupied with addressing the issue of ethnicity. This is understandable given the way Christian organisations contributed in shaping and reshaping colonial and post-colonial identities. This problem is amplified amongst the Protestants who operate a presbytero-synodal mode, by which the local church embraces the faithful and operates almost in a closed circuit. These centrifugal forces seem to operate foremost in times of transition.

Archbishop Manasses Kuria, who was at the helm of the Anglican church from 1980, retired at the end of 1994 following a one-year sabbatical leave spent in the USA. Dr David Gitari was the acting archbishop during church summits until he was officially elected to succeed Manasses Kuria at the end of 1996. He found a rival in the Rt Rev. Joseph Wasonga, Bishop of Maseno West Diocese. The latter is a prelate of the new generation and is considered to be close to the regime. This is an indicator that there exists amongst the CPK a group of people keen on having good relations with the state. This division could have served as a good excuse for some members of the clergy to join the opposition. During this impasse and for the rest of 1997, it was only Dr Gitari who raised his voice. His utterances did not have much effect due to the reduced influence of the central organs of the Anglican church (provincial synods, Bishops' Council, arbitration role of the archbishop). During 1996 and at the start of 1997, several changes were made in the top leadership of other churches. The Presbyterians elected three new leaders. None of them belonged to the church's faction that was advocating direct involvement in politics in favour of the opposition. On the evangelical side, Rt. Rev. Titus Kivunzi replaced Archbishop Ezekiel Birech as the head of the African Inland Church, and maintained the church's pro-KANU stand. Another church associated with the political leadership, the Nairobi Pentecostal Church at Valley Road, saw the departure of Rev. White, replaced by Pastor Boniface

Adoyo. During the same period, Peter Gatabaki Mundati, one of the founding fathers of the African Independent Pentecostal Church, passed away. During his funeral, this independent church's proximity to KANU was manifested by the presence of about 20 members of parliament, several former ministers and leaders of political parties.

In short, the new leaders of the major churches were unaccustomed or unwilling to handle the political tension of the general elections. This was a very important indicator on how the churches would behave during the political campaign.

The church and the election campaign

Electoral studies have generally emphasised long-term factors (e.g., party identification, attitude changes) and overlooked the study of electoral campaigns. Yet, inquiries on political communication have underlined the importance of these moments, of their strategies and the mobilisation that takes place before the elections. In brief, the electoral campaign is a moment of very specific political action. It has a clear dynamic that has to be evaluated and interpreted. Finally, it is not usually a real reflection of the socio-economic reality. Thus, the campaign logic works first and foremost to the benefit of institutional political actors, in the process enabling them to marginalise the actors of the civil society without any difficulty, their representativity not withstanding. This is particularly the case with the churches which have displayed a certain level of angelism regarding the methods of campaigning and the current political practices in Kenya. To understand this situation, the major steps of the campaign must be retraced.

Electoral campaigns can be seen as a well-structured interplay made up of several protagonists. They produce composition effects that none of the actors involved can completely control. Nevertheless, some of them possess more resources than others. This is the case with the head of state. Being in the presidential regime, he can turn to a powerful administration through which he can get information on the opinion and strategy of the opposition. This administration equally enjoys immense power to authorise or stop electoral meetings from taking place and to mobilise the numerous and disciplined police forces. President Moi has played several games to substitute his weaknesses with a defensive and counter-attack type of campaign. Despite these games, in 1997, the head of state had neither the initiative of the campaign nor the capacity to set its themes. As such, right from the beginning of the year, he made known his electoral programme, but this neither interested the media nor elicited debate. The campaign began in April 1997 during a meeting in Limuru (headquarters of the main Protestant seminary) which saw the birth of the National Convention Executive Council (NCEC). This council brought together various civil society actors under a common objective: to obtain an in-depth constitutional review before the polls. NCEC was from the beginning a heterogeneous body, with representatives from NGOs and churches. Its governing staff preached pluralism: the three leaders were Dr Willy Mutunga (of the Citizens' Coalition for Constitutional Change (4Cs), Davinder Lamba (of Mazingira Institute) and Bishop Zablon Nthamburi (of the Methodist church). Another group falling within this realm were leaders from different opposition parties, who participated in the public meetings of the NCEC, with the aim of benefiting from the media coverage enjoyed by the NCEC. These leaders were political professionals considered by political analysts as 'moderates' in that they claimed to be ready to negotiate with those in power. On the contrary, journalists classified NGOs and churches as 'radicals', because they were not ready to compromise electoral discussions prior to negotiation. These discussions entailed solid constitutional reforms, 'No Reforms - No Elections' which all year round was the NCEC motto.

President Moi's tactic consisted in imposing his own style and rhythm on the campaign by inciting some factions against others, thus deepening the divisions in the opposition while acquiring a relative majority. Before re-examining the different stages of his schemes, we must state clearly that only one group of actors seems not to have been influenced by the approach of the government: these were the NGO representatives. This can be explained by the behaviour of some 'political' NGOs. From the late 1980s onwards, human rights NGOs were at the forefront of the democratisation process. This small social environment has, however changed, a lot in the past ten years. Leaders of the early 1990s have been leaving these organisations to join factional ones. Some NGOs have become rich and more professional and are now seeking contracts and subsidies from the West rather than political mobilisation. The evolution of these pioneers of democratisation can also be interpreted in terms of social stratification. Thus, the actions of the Law Society of Kenya in the early 1990s revealed the political frustrations of the bourgeoisie and of a Kikuyu middle-upper class who were particularly marginalised by the regime of the time. From 1995, the Kikuyu-Kalenjin elite talks saw the revival of dialogue through the creation of the Central Province Development Support Group (CPDSG), whereas the LSK lost its political virulence.

On the contrary, the emergence of NCEC in 1997 reflected the ambitions of a middle class less linked to the state elite and whom the government found more difficult to discuss with. That major change of the environment among the NGOs equally brought about changes in their relationship with the churches. While they were still very individualised, they were getting rooted in a real 'Juridical-Christian public sphere'. Many contacts were developed over the past years between these two sectors. The attempt of the government to control the NGOs made them create structures to defend their common interests; consequently, development NGOs, mainly those sponsored by churches, worked together with human rights NGOs. Legal advice NGOs, such as *Kituo Cha Sheria*, were given cases by church-sponsored NGOs, dealing in social aid in the parishes. Contacts between churches and politicised NGOs became regular and are not just linked to the coming of elections. They have developed organic links. However, the organisations do not overlap at the political level. Even if these two segments of the civil society make the same analysis of the socio-political situation and recommend the same solutions, they do not agree as far as the means used to attain the objectives are concerned. Both camps recommend the exclusive use of peaceful means , but churches generally refuse to accept some types of mobilisation such as general strikes or civil disobedience.

This disagreement enabled the government to incite the churches against the NGOs. During the electoral game, President Moi always acted like a *Deus ex Machina*, resolving conflict situations in his favour by taking advantage of the naivety of the prelates. From the first quarter of 1997, NCEC focused attention on the necessity of constitutional reforms before elections, something the government could not listen to. A major election boycott was looming. Opposition parties could not involve the electorate in their election programmes; they strove to mobilise and to find an audience within NCEC whose meetings were moreover getting more successful. The government reacted with violent repression both at Kamukunji (early May) and Central Park (early June) NCEC meetings. This momentarily neutralised the stand of political actors, but in June Moi sorted out the deadlock when, during the ordaining of the new Catholic archbishop, he pretended that he wanted to meet the bishops to discuss constitutional reforms.

This call for dialogue with the churches was not surprising in so far as they constituted the usual representatives of the civil society from the urban and, especially, the rural areas. Moreover, dialogue proved to be much easier since the top leaders in both the church and the government shared similar conservative ideologies despite their differences on constitutional matters. In 1997, as in 1994, the religious hierarchy denounced the effects of strikes such as the mobilisation of the medical staff. Similarly, mobilisations of teachers (in September 1997) attracted their criticism. Some churches found it difficult to adapt to the changes of Kenyan society and tended to reject the position of the middle class which was, for them, synonymous with secularism and a morally dangerous cosmopolitanism. Hence, in a bid to end the mass movements and strikes, President Moi invited representatives of religious organisations to State House, including the most conservative ones. This well calculated dialogue did not solve the problem, but enabled the president to open the political game and gain time. It blurred the political image of the churches and compromised their leaders.

The beating of clergymen and NCEC leaders in the compound of the Anglican cathedral in Nairobi caused divisions among the church leaders between the moderates (who preferred dialogue with the government and questioned mass action) and the radicals. Six months before the elections, it was clear that churches and NGOs were no longer co-operating and they had even cut their links. In July and August, shortly before the *Saba Saba* (07/07/ 97) and *Nane Nane* (08/08/97) riots, the Catholic archbishop and the NCCK asked the NCEC to cancel their rallies. Following the death of four people, during the general strike of 8 August 1997, NCEC action was officially condemned. In August, once again, the churches helped the government out of the situation by establishing a mediation committee devoted to finding solutions to constitutional questions. The committee was mainly composed of clergymen and headed by the virulent Archbishop Gitari. Muslim and evangelical Protestant representatives were also included. This committee never worked, but it enabled the government to buy time and organise its last manoeuvre. This led to the creation of the Inter-Parties Parliamentary Group (IPPG) in charge of negotiating cosmetic constitutional changes as well as some renovations in the rules of the coming elections. Politicians held discussions to the exclusion of NCEC and religious groups that had activated election campaigns in 1997. The political space is usually non-expansive and disputed and political professionals colluded to exclude amateurs and to prevent the civil society from encroaching on their zone of action and competition.

Finally, the last episode of the church's marginalisation during these elections came after the polls. Without proper reports from the observers, the Catholic church recognised the validity of the elections and accepted the results. The archbishop was then accused of having been bought by the government. Rumours spread about his recent acquisition of a Mercedes Benz and his desire to become a cardinal for which he could not be seen as a radical. This anticipated action was not well received by the Protestants and, especially, the opposition leaders. Mwai Kibaki, former vice-president and leader of the Democratic Party, termed religious leaders as 'Agents of Satan'. At the same time, disagreements existed within the Catholic hierarchy, as Archbishop Ndingi Mwana a'Nzeki only feebly condemned the ethnic massacres that began in the Rift Valley at the beginning of 1998. The Anglicans also accepted the election results but after particular discussions. In his sermon on the first anniversary of his election in office, Archbishop Gitari dwelt on the outcome of the elections. According to him, it was better to accept rigged elections than to risk chaos. Moreover, he emphasised that the results reflected the wish of the majority of Kenyans and, from then on, it was up to them to repent and face the consequences of their behaviour. Still, some preachers reacted in a different way. *Vision Magazine* (03/02/98) reported that the pastors of the Tabernacle Church, in Nairobi South B, suggested that elections should induce the church to examine its internal behaviour: 'How can a corrupted Church pray for the government?', asked one of the pastors. The church's political interventions during the electoral campaign were, therefore, far from straightforward. One wonders what effect they had on the election behaviour of the Christians.

The political behaviour of Kenyan Christians

Based on the current knowledge of electoral sociology of Kenya, it is still hard to define and give a definite explanation of Christians' political conduct. In 1992 as well as in 1997 a relative majority of the electorate supported politicians not supported by the churches. Voting for the opposition was definitely not backed by religious motives. More generally, there is certainly no christian vote. Yet, the clergy is still politically influential. It is capable of mobilising its followers on certain issues (see previous section); more importantly, it participates actively in the political socialisation of Kenyans.

The non-existence of a christian vote
Despite the hostility of the big churches towards the government, Christians voted for the ruling party. There is a legitimist vote in Kenya which favours the status quo inspired partly by religious conservatism. Moreover, with the exception of the unregistered Islamic Party of Kenya, opposition parties were never formed with an open or even covert religious basis. They certainly socialise with religious media and christian associations that can represent effective electoral communication tools[5], but official affiliation to one church would be suicidal. Some parties would wish to have strong religious identity. In 1992, DP's presidential candidate Mwai Kibaki, who was strongly supported by the Kikuyu living in the north of Central Province, wanted to seduce the Kikuyu in the south and Christians from other parts of the country by appealing to the support of the Catholic church. Yet, the church leaders did not actively support the idea and the electorate did not respond to the party's strategist hopes. In 1997, the party wanted the Catholic church's support again. According to some close friends of the archbishop in Nairobi, the prelate attended the rally during which Kibaki declared his candidature but had not been clearly informed of the real motive of this public meeting. The prelate refused to publicly endorse Mwai Kibaki's candidature. Some members of the Catholic clergy urged Christians to vote for the Democratic Party while others opted to vote for other parties. The majority did not state their position. In brief, there

is no denominational party in Kenya. It is also observable that religious pluralism did not create political divisions in the society.

In order to apprehend Christianity's political influence, it is also important to consider regional variations. There are regions where religious tendencies could be viewed in political terms. Most Nandi Anglicans suffered during the 1980s from political domination under the political elite from another church: the AIC. In order to maintain the support of this particularly strategic region for President Moi, the leaders co-opted John Sambu, an Anglican (a close friend of the famous Bishop Muge) and dropped the politicians elected in 1988. In other regions, on the contrary, the religion criteria did not affect their political orientation. Grignon (1997) observed that for the Kamba, divisions along Christian/non-Christian lines as well as the beliefs in the legitimacy of traditional oath taking persist till now, but religious speeches have no direct political motives. Globally, it seems that clergy mobilisations did not considerably affect the voting trends. Instead, they urged Christians to vote for candidates of their choice, to be courageous enough to vote for opposition candidates, and to finally accept the elections outcome. The role churches play in helping to accept and implement constitutional rules and principles among social classes that are politically marginalised (middle class) and those which are not socially and economically integrated (labourers and rural people) cannot be ignored. Moreover, while religious personnel seem to posses the ability to spread political messages, their status does not provide them with sufficient resources to make good electoral candidates out of them. In the 1992 elections, four members of the clergy together with a young woman purporting to be a prophetess joined parliament. During the same elections, three other pastors and one bishop lost their seats. In 1997, even fewer joined parliament and out of the five elected in 1992, only one retained his seat. The clergy also influence electoral campaigns through provision of logistical support to candidates. Some priests and pastors take advantage of their positions to promote a candidate but, again, the extent of their influence seems to be limited. The AIC Rev. Silas Yego[6] actively supported John Kittony, former KANU' 92 Youth leader and son of Ms Zipporah Kittony – chairperson of the *Maendeleo ya Wanawake* women's organisation, nominated MP and a relative to President Moi – yet he lost bitterly.

The real new pattern could be the changes in the level of perception through which the churches themselves view the exchange between politics and religion. The Catholics, for instance, think that they no longer have the vocation to inspire the individual's total existence and his social life. As the results of interviews conducted among clergymen indicated, the majority admitted that there is a big gap between private and public sector and they no longer view themselves as an organic and hierarchical counter-model. Indeed, the Catholic church is no longer one single block or an unquestionable unit. Currently, there are several religious trends and several Catholic identities leading to different political inclinations. Active small Christian communities (SCCs), developed at the grassroots level by the church, are capable of socialising their congregation into active citizens. However, that is not the case among all Catholic groups: the charismatic movement, which is quite influential among the middle classes, is far less active politically. In conclusion, if churches cannot determine the behaviour of the electorate (such attempts are, moreover, more and more strongly discouraged), they certainly have influence on the people. They provide a social and moral matrix for political behaviour.

The political socialisation of Christians

Political socialisation begins with civic education. In 1992, two Christian organisations developed programmes: NECEP (National Ecumenical Civic Education Programme) born from the collaboration between the Catholics and the NCCK and Education for Participatory Democracy, financed by the Anglicans. Their goal was to publish books for the voters and to organise mass seminars to popularise democracy principles in the church at grassroots level. Large sums of money were, consequently, allotted for this project. Journalists of the *Weekly Review* (07/02/92:13) estimated the sum spent by NCCK to be 15 million shillings. However, some observers pointed out some setbacks. Hezekiah Oyugi, in his evaluation study of the NECEP, complained about the diversity of programmes proposed by Christians and the divisions occasioned by this process.

In 1997, civic education run by Christians once again brought about diffuse initiatives. Methods used in previous elections were still applied. Meanwhile, the Catholic Justice and Peace Commission organises a 'Lenten Campaign' every spring which emphasises socio-political issues. The theme of 1998 was, 'Kenya: A people in Pain'. Observers found that civic education was less emphasised than in 1992 with information needs being less urgent. This demobilisation, however, did not prevent the clergy from displaying their political aspirations during their sermons. Furthermore, during the last general elections, churches emphasised the observation of elections. The observers were many, well trained and consisted of many church followers who were sensitised and well informed of their role. A form of civic education was apparent. Some parishes propagated political information by inviting theatre groups to perform plays with democracy themes. Borrowing from the Latino-American models, organisations were established to transmit socio-political messages, for instance about how AIDS is transmitted and on methods of contraception (Ogolla 1997). These organisations are however not legally registered and prefer to keep a low profile. They engage in little advertising and survive on temporary jobs offered through religious channels.

The top-down diffusion of ideas and active participation of Christians in many parish organisations constitutes a form of civic education. The laity (including the Catholics) has always been involved in church activities. Burgman (1990) explained that in western Kenya, the Diocesan Pastoral Council had as many laymen as clergymen by 1969. To him, the laity movements, such as youth, co-operatives, and trade unions, were developed mostly in the 1970s. Ten years later, these traditional tendencies of the Catholics seem to have been exhausted. However, rural development activities and small Christian communities are multiplying. These two phenomena are often interrelated. Faced with an acute shortage of clergymen – in 1969 one priest for 2,600 followers; in 1989 one for 5,200 – the conference for East African bishops decided to encourage the formation and growth of small Christian communities. Without losing grip with prayer groups, these communities initiated co-operation activities for mutual assistance and development. For many, this was an opportunity to evaluate the practicability of democracy in small communities. Several people took up responsibilities and benefited from the training offered by the diocese or the National Council of Churches. In the 1980s, they were confronted by development activists from the Catholic church who introduced the Development Education Programme which endeavoured to sensitise the rural poor to assume full responsibility over their own destiny within the framework of their cultural and socio-economic realities (see Mulwa 1987). This model of participatory development gave birth to a multitude of initiatives, which affected the daily life of Christians. It is clear that the local influence of the church benefited greatly from this development. Church organisations supplemented government capacity to provide services not necessarily by providing them themselves, but by involving interested parties. While demanding real commitment from Christians, this religious framework can be a proper forum for freedom of speech, particularly at SCC level. This is also often the case at parish level where monthly bulletins are true yardsticks of the community. At the diocesan level newspapers in local languages are sometimes released: the bulletin in Kikuyu language for the Diocese of Murang'a, *Inooro*, was banned from 20 February 1995 due to its radical political stance.

However, one should not overvalue the impact of religious socialisation on politics, given the fact that secularism is on the increase and participation in activities of the big churches in towns has reduced significantly (see Shorter and Onyancha 1997). More and more Kenyans are breaking away from the religious matrix that got them socialised. The political influence of the churches has therefore weakened. Equally, the Christian universe is moving away from the mainstream churches as some religious institutions find it sometimes difficult to accommodate the democratisation of society and are not exempt from what Bayart (1993) calls 'The politics of the belly'. As this author argues, far more radical commitment will, therefore, be necessary from the mainstream churches to provoke a significant change.

Indeed, the marginalisation of the churches brought about during the 1997 elections is a much better indicator of the actual political system in Kenya than of the strength of religious organisations. This imbalanced relationship between the public sector and civil society shows that there is a serious crisis of representation which the advent of multipartyism has not been able to solve. The Kenyan social contract, if it ever existed, is now dead and little has been done to revive it in the past years, whatever the efforts of the religious actors.

Notes

1. Evangelical churches remained silent during the 1997 elections. In this chapter we concentrate on those religious organisations that contested the regime.
2. At this level, Protestants were implicated, the massacres having taken place mostly in their new dioceses.
3. Radio Trottoir renamed *The Church of the Province of Kenya, The Church of the Politics of Kenya.*
4. Muge was killed in a bizarre road accident in August 1990 when coming from a tour of Busia district after having been warned by the then minister of Labour and MP for Bunyala, the late Peter Okondo that he would not come out alive if he dared to set foot in Busia (*Weekly Review* 20/06/97).
5. See the examples from the study of Maria Maas (1986) on the association of Anglican women, in 'Women's Groups in Kiambu, Kenya: it is always a good thing to have land', *Research Report* No. 26, Leiden: African Studies Centre.
6. In 1999, it was revealed that AIC Bishop Silas Yego, who admitted the allegation and who had been leading in the Kitale Pokot region of Trans Nzoia district, was involved in a land scandal. Among a group of other top-ranking personalities – Minister Lotodo, PC Mberia, AG Wako, MP Ewaton, DC Chelagoi, PS Kimalat, ex-MPs Ekidor and Moiben among others – he was allocated illegally 20 acres of land belonging to the Kenya Agricultural Research Institute (KARI) in Kitale (*Daily Nation* 22/06/99; 23/06/99).

References

Abuom, A.C. 1996, 'The Church's involvement in Democratization process in Kenya', in Assefa, H. and Wachira, G. (eds), *Peacemaking & Democratization in Africa*, Nairobi: EAEP: 81-104.

Bayart, J.F. 1993, *Religion et Modernité Politique en Afrique noire*, Paris: Karthala.

Benson, G.P. 1995, 'Ideological politics versus biblical hermeneutics, Kenyan Protestant Churches and the Nyayo State', in Hansen, H.B. and Twaddle, M. (eds), *Religion and Politics in East Africa*, London: James Currey: 177-99

Burgman, H. 1990, *The way the Catholic Church started in West Kenya*, Nairobi: Mission Book Service.

Gitari, D. 1996, *In Season and out of Season, Sermons to a Nation*, Carlisle: Regnum.

Grignon, F. 1997, *Le politicien entrepreneur en son terroir: Paul Ngei à Kangundo, 1945-1990*, these pour le Doctorat en science politique, Université Montesquieu-Bordeaux IV, mimeo.

_____ 1998, 'La democratisation au risque du debat? Territoires de la critique et imaginaires politiques au Kenya (1990-1995)', in Martin, D.-C. (ed.), *Nouveaux langages du politique en Afrique orientale*, Paris: Karthala: 29-112.

Lonsdale, J. 1992, 'The political culture of Kenya', Centre for African Studies *Occasional Papers* 37, Edinburgh University: 1-19.

Maupeu, H. 1991, 'Une Opposition en régime Autoritaire: L'exemple du Réveil Est-Africain au Kenya', *Canadian Journal of African Studies*, Vol.25, No.2: 257-72.

_____ 1995, 'Les Eglises et la transition démocratique au Kenya', in Esoavelomandraso, M. and Feltz, G. (eds), *Démocratie et développement-Mirage ou espoir raisonnable?*, Paris: Karthala: 299-326.

_____ 1997, 'Les Eglises chrétiennes au Kenya: des influences contradictoires', in Constantin, F. and Coulon, C. (eds) *Religion et transition démocratique en Afrique*, Paris: Karthala: 81-113.

Mugambi, J. 1997, 'African Churches in Social Transformation', in Mugambi, J. (ed.), *Democracy & Development in Africa, The Role of Churches*, Nairobi: AACC: 12-28.

Mulwa, F.W. 1987, 'Enabling Rural Poor through Participation', *Spearhead* No.132-33: 88-97.

Ngunyi, M. 1995, 'Religious Institutions and Political Liberalisation in Kenya', in Gibbon, P. (ed.) *Markets, Civil Society and Democracy in Kenya*, Uppsala, Nordiska Afrikainstitutet: 121-77.

Ogolla, L. 1997, *Towards Behaviour Change. Participatory Theatre in Education Development*, Nairobi: PETAD Publication.

Sabar-Friedman, G. 1995, '"Politics" and "Power" in the Kenyan Public Discourse and Recent Events. The Church of the Province of Kenya (CPK)', *Canadian Journal of African Studies*, Vol.29, No.3: 429-53.

Shorter, A. and Onyancha, E. 1997, *Secularism in Africa. A case study: Nairobi City*, Nairobi: Paulines Publications Africa.

Throup, D. 1995, 'Render unto Caesar the Things that are Caesar's. The Politics of Church-State Conflict in Kenya, 1978-1990', in Hansen, H.B. and Twaddle, M. (eds), *Religion and Politics in East Africa*, London: James Currey: 143-76.

Throup, D. and Hornsby, C. 1998, *Multi-Party Politics in Kenya – The Kenyatta & Moi States & the Triumph of the System in the 1992 Election*, Oxford: James Currey.

4

Politics of Marionettes: Extra-legal Violence and the 1997 Elections in Kenya

Peter Mwangi Kagwanja

The road to the second multi-party elections that were held on 29 December 1997 was a dangerous minefield of vigilante violence. This was a continuation of the orgy of 'ethnic cleansing' that engulfed parts of rural Kenya from late 1991 and which was partly responsible for the flawed elections of December 1992. Shattering the euphoric celebration of Kenya's return to pluralism in December 1991, human rights organisations began to draw attention to what has since become the most profound threat to democracy and the rule of law – extra-legal violence (see Human Rights Watch/Africa Watch 1993; Human Rights Watch/Africa Watch 1995a). Vigilante violence – that went under the epithets of 'ethnic', 'land clashes', 'cattle-rustling', 'border dispute', or simply 'gangsterism' – was state-sponsored. Evidently, President Daniel arap Moi's regime ended political monism and reverted to a multi-party system only after unrelenting domestic and international pressure. In subsequent years, it remained recalcitrant and passionately opposed to pluralist ideals. Accordingly, it was accused of sponsoring vigilantism as a tool of 'informal repression' in its desperate bid to derail multi-partyism and to hold on to power.

It is difficult to situate this discussion of extra-legal violence in multi-party Kenya within the mainstream discourse on vigilantism – the tendency to take the law into one's hand or to deal with socio-political problems without recourse to lawful procedures. In the first place, academic literature in Africa on the subject is not as developed as in the West. As Kelly Hine (1998) has recently shown, vigilantism in western society, especially in the United States, rose in response to the failure of the law enforcement system to provide full protection to citizens and their property. Hence, such vigilantes laid a legitimate claim to a moral high ground for their work in the preservation and betterment of the existing system. They had no connection with the state or its functionaries. On the contrary, the vigilantes of multi-party Kenya were 'deadly marionettes', to use the apt title of the London-based press freedom watchdog, Article 19, in the service of the elite at the helm of the state (Article 19 1997). Evidently, they were sponsored by the state to stem the tide of the multi-party challenge and to help sustain the hegemonic elite of the one-party era in power.

Vigilantism assumed several characteristics. First, it was portrayed as a product of 'ancient animosities' or long-standing 'communal hatreds'. Second, it relied on ethnic warriors, often identified with traditional ethnic symbols and attire, and wielding traditional weapons such as spears, swords, bows and arrows. In some cases, however, 'warriors' wielded modern firearms. Thirdly, sometimes, security forces provided training, protection and worked hand in hand with ethnic vigilantes during attacks. Without exception, attacks were made against groups associated with the opposition or pro-democracy movement.

'Communal' and the 'primordial' cultural images that were attached to vigilantism were intended to conceal the involvement of the government – itself perceived to be in the realm of the 'modern' – in instigating violence. In the same vein, vigilante violence was depicted as a logical consequence of the collapse of the authoritarian structures that previously kept centrifugal forces at bay. As such, the state presented itself as a victim of forces beyond its control and of externally imposed alien structures and ideologies. Nevertheless, vigilantism seemed consistent with the political agenda of the Kenya African National Union (KANU) in the multi-party era. Internally, vigilantism enabled the government to pursue a wide plethora of political goals with astounding success. These goals included repressing and preventing the nascent opposition from building a nation-wide political base and networks, stemming the tide of constitutional reforms and forestalling the emergence of a genuine democratic culture, and manipulating, compromising and predetermining the outcome of multi-party elections by displacing and disenfranchising groups associated with the opposition. In addition, violence was employed to create divisions within the ranks of the opposition groups by instigating border clashes or cattle rustling between pro-democracy groups and thus preventing the solidification of inter-ethnic political alliances, and to punish those sections of society that did not vote for the government in elections.

In the same vein, violence served as a form of mobilising support for the hegemonic elite within its own ethnic constituency. Thus, it used property, especially land, illegally acquired from the displaced communities, to buy support from its ethnic constituency, and to reward it for voting for the ruling party during the elections. Moreover, extra-legal violence had an external and more ambitious purpose. First, in a world that was increasingly stressing the primacy of human rights in citizen-state relations, vigilantism enabled the government to violate the rights of its critics and, simultaneously, to shield itself from international censure for such violations. Diligently, the elite employed this form of violence to manipulate the deep-seated predisposition towards 'stability' and the fear among its Western financiers that ethnic violence might 'rock the boat' to wring endorsement for compromised elections and, thus, to get a flawed mandate to remain in power. This is the long and short of marionette politics in multi-party Kenya whose impact on the 1997 elections this chapter seeks to examine.

Honing the tools of violence: vigilantism and the road to 1997

Before 1997, ethnic violence focused on the Rift Valley and its border with Nyanza and Western provinces. From mid-1997, however, there occurred a spatial expansion of ethnic violence into virtually all provinces. Certainly, the Moi state was reacting to a determined challenge by a pro-democracy alliance – the National Convention Executive Council (NCEC) – that demanded far-reaching constitutional and structural reforms ahead of the 1997 elections (see Chapter 2). In the run up to the elections, the culture of vigilantism reached a fever pitch. A month to the elections, Kenya was a cesspool of all genres of communal violence. In the Rift Valley, the regime used violence to intimidate and disenfranchise rival communities, and to suppress resistance within its own ethnic constituency.

At the coast, it employed vigilantes to displace and disenfranchise inhabitants in such opposition strongholds with the aim to eliminate the demographic basis of a nation-wide political alliance between up-country and coastal groups. Moreover, reprisals by security forces against the Mijikenda enabled the state to undermine an emerging political alliance between the latter and their Arab-Swahili neighbours on the basis of an Islamic or 'coastal' identity. In Nyanza Province, ethnic violence ensured that existing ethnic groups did not unite under one opposition party and thus locking KANU out of the province. Finally, in the traditionally insecure northern Kenya, violence escalated, making it impossible for the opposition to penetrate the area. A combination of vigilantism, the legal coercive force from security forces and the structural vestiges of the one-party state enabled the ruling elite to compromise the election and to wring out yet another 'flawed mandate' (see Southall 1998).

Ethnic violence first broke out in Kenya in November 1991 at Miteitei, a small settlement on the border between Western, Nyanza, and Rift Valley provinces.[1] The rise of vigilantism occurred against the background of mounting pressure on President Moi and KANU to legalise pluralism. The regime capitulated and Kenya became a multi-party state in December 1991. Simultaneously, violence escalated and spread to all multi-ethnic districts in the Rift Valley and western Kenya. This brought two questions to the fore. Was this violence a spontaneous opening up of the Pandora's box of ethnic animosities as a result of the collapse of the authoritarian structures of the one-party state that contained them? Or was the government presiding over it for political gains? In its careful and exhaustive study of the violence in November 1993, Human Rights Watch/Africa Watch arrived at the latter conclusion. It noted that:

> President Daniel arap Moi of Kenya confidently predicted that the return of his country to multiparty system would result in an outbreak of tribal violence that would destroy the nation. His prediction has been alarmingly fulfilled. One of the most disturbing developments in Kenya over the last two years has been the eruption of violent clashes between different ethnic groups. However, far from being the spontaneous result of a return to political pluralism, there is clear evidence that the government was involved in provoking this ethnic violence for political purposes and has taken no adequate steps to prevent it from spiralling out of control (Human Rights Watch/Africa Watch 1993:1).

At a *prima facie* level, the violence, it appears, was partly meant to fulfil President Moi's prediction. At a deeper level, the architects of the violence sought to transform the Rift Valley into an ethnic enclave where one ethnic group, the Kalenjin, were politically, if not legally dominant, for two reasons.[2] First, it was to ensure that the 44 parliamentary seats reserved for the province went exclusively to KANU. The Rift Valley Province had the highest number of constituencies accounting for nearly a quarter of the 188 seats in the National Assembly. Second, it was to use this parliamentary clout to bargain for regional autonomy and to shield itself from possible prosecution for alleged misdeeds such as corruption and abuse of power in case Moi lost power.

In this context, the Kalenjin elite invoked *majimboism* – a Kenyan-style federal system based on the notion of exclusive ethnic territorial claims – in the Rift Valley Province.[3] Citizenship in the province was redefined. The Kalenjin, Maasai, Turkana and Samburu – who collectively went under a new acronym of KAMATUSA – were defined as the *bona fide* citizens or 'indigenous' people of the province (*Finance* 15/10/94: 18-22). Non-Kalenjin, including the Kikuyu, Luo, Luhya and Gusii, were categorised and demonised as non-citizens or 'aliens' (*Daily Nation* 30/06/93; *Kenya Times* 20/05/93; 21/05/93). In this sense, *majimboism* was not only used to reassert the ethnic political and economic rights of the Kalenjin but also to strip non-Kalenjin of their citizenship and the rights that go with it. Finally, *majimboism* metamorphosed into an ideological justification for indiscriminate and violent expulsion of 'non-citizens' and the consequent 'ethnic cleansing'.

Systematic attacks were carried out by 'warriors' who embraced Kalenjin traditional symbols, used traditional weapons – bows and arrows – and painted their faces with clay marks used during the Kalenjin rite of initiation. They burned down houses and crop fields and stole livestock from their target groups, raped their women and forced hundreds of thousands to flee their homes for safety. The Human Rights Watch/Africa Watch study cited:

> . . . the government has relied on different tactics, such as extra-legal intimidation and violence, to silence and disempower critics. The change in tactics appears to be a deliberate move on the part of the government to avoid international censure. A growing culture of state-sponsored harassment and vigilante violence against opposition leaders and other critics is being encouraged and fostered by the government. The chilling aspect of the violence is that the government usually denies any knowledge of or responsibility to it, attributing it instead to unknown vigilantes (Human Rights Watch/Africa Watch 1993:11).

Between November 1991 and April 1992 Kalenjin 'warriors' targeted the Luo, Gusii, Luhya and, to a lesser extent, Kikuyu in Kericho and Nandi districts and their environs. Predictably, this initial attack had three broad aims. First, the violence was meant to 'silence the ruling elite's critics within the Kalenjin community, especially among the Nandi and Kipsigis' (Throup and Hornsby 1998: 198). Second, it was intended to provoke a mass reaction in support of President Moi and KANU within the group and thus prevent the populous Nandi and Kipsigis, in particular, from joining the opposition.[4] Finally, it was designed to drive away thousands of non-Kalenjin workers, thought to be associated with the opposition, in Kericho district's tea plantations.

Next, the guns were turned on the Kikuyu in Molo, Rongai, Narok North, Eldoret North, South and East constituencies, and the Luhya in Eldoret South, Trans Nzoia and Bungoma. This was the most violent and horrifying phase that generated the most profound humanitarian crisis in independent Kenya. Here, the promise of land after evicting non-Kalenjin proved a powerful incentive for violence. But a total displacement of the Kikuyu was to prove an impossible mission. The Kikuyu comprised nearly 20 per cent of the population of the Rift Valley and were the second largest single group after the Kalenjin. Out of an estimated total of 240,975 internal refugees generated before the 1992 elections, 82,000 and 40,700 came from Uasin Gishu and Nakuru districts, respectively (NEMU 1993: 96-104; GoK/UNDO 1993:8).

In the 1992 elections, KANU had a field day. First, it countenanced fraudulent transfers, pressured sales and illegal occupation of land left by fleeing victims as a reward to the Kalenjin for political loyalty. Ethnicisation of politics ensured that the Kalenjin voted almost as one for KANU and President Moi. But, it also increased ethnic animosity and polarisation with the displaced groups voting overwhelmingly for opposition parties. The clashes guaranteed KANU victories in constituencies where the party's chances of winning the seat were slim or at risk. As the international Commonwealth Monitoring Group noted, as many as 1.5 million eligible voters in clash-torn areas did not register to vote in the 1992 elections as a result of discrimination, harassment and intimidation (Commonwealth Secretariat 1993:20). The National Election Monitoring Unit (NEMU) reported that as a result of intimidation and harassment by both the security forces and KANU vigilantes, a total of 54 opposition parliamentary candidates were unable to reach nomination centres, 30 of them in the Rift Valley alone. Consequently, 16 KANU MPs were returned unopposed (NEMU 1993:18).

The volatile political environment created by the violence enabled the government to amplify the theme that Kenya was poised for a disaster and thus to get Western governments to accept the flawed elections as a *fait accompli* and to endorse it for the sake of 'stability' (*Weekly Review* 13/03/92: 18-19). In this context, the two principle international election monitoring groups – the American International Republican Institute (IRI) and the Commonwealth Observer Group – quickly declared the elections 'a significant and early step in Kenya's road back to democracy.' While it was widely acknowledged that the elections were muddled with violence, harassment and blatant manipulations, it was, nevertheless, awarded what the *Daily Nation* (03/01/93: 6) dubbed a 'C-minus pass'. More damning, however, is the legacy of vigilante violence as a tool of legitimising flawed elections. In the run-up to the 1997 elections, this type of violence was stepped up once again and it has since become a keystone of marionette politics.

Nevertheless, in 1992 KANU failed to capture 8 out of the 44 seats in the Rift Valley for two reasons. First, the Luhya in Trans Nzoia and the neighbouring Bungoma voted for FORD-Kenya. Secondly, the Kikuyu in Nakuru, Uasin Gishu and other parts of the province overwhelmingly supported the Kikuyu-based FORD-Asili and Democratic Party of Kenya (NEMU 1993a: 21). Consequently, clashes continued in order to punish the two groups, prevent those displaced among them from returning to their farms, open new fronts of displacement and make more land available to reward the constituent ethnic groups. In turn, this ensured that the displaced people did not go back to reclaim their land and that the favourable electoral demographic order that enabled KANU to win a number of seats was not interfered with by externally-induced resettlement programmes.

The vigilante war to punish groups associated with the opposition entered the streets of the main towns in the Rift Valley. For instance, in May 1993, administration police and KANU youth squads demolished 600 kiosks in Nakuru town overwhelmingly belonging to Kikuyu hawkers. Some of the voters were sheltering victims of displacement from the rural areas (*Daily Nation* 11/05/93). The Kikuyu, in particular, were singled out for special retribution throughout the Rift Valley. Their farms in Rukini, Kondoo, Lokwania and Ya Mumbi in the Burnt Forest area were constantly invaded to intimidate and prevent them from returning and reclaiming their farms (NEMU 1993a: 14). It was reported that some of the farms had even been given new Kalenjin names signifying new ownership (*Daily Nation* 26/08/93). There were frequent reports of fraudulent land transfers, illegal occupation and pressured sales to the Kalenjin in Olenguruone, Nakuru, dubbed 'Kenya's West Bank' – referring to the contested Israeli/Palestinian area (Human Rights Watch/Africa Watch 1997:72).

On 2 September 1993, President Moi declared a 'Security Operation Zone' in the clash-torn areas of Molo, Burnt Forest and Londiani. Rather than bringing the vigilante war to a close, this move opened a new chapter in human rights abuses against the displaced, as well as members of the press, civil society, church leaders and foreigners who attempted to visit the areas (Human Rights Watch/Africa Watch 1993: 38-42). Hence, in March 1994, for instance, a vicious attack in Burnt Forest left 18 dead and displaced nearly 25,000 people, most of them Kikuyu (Human Rights Watch/Africa Watch 1995a: 104). Ripples of anti-Kikuyu backlash were felt as far as West Pokot. Here, Francis Lotodo, a cabinet minister, demanded that the Kikuyu should leave and instructed fellow Pokot to deal with the Kikuyu 'mercilessly'. Consequently, over 10,000 traders and farmers, mostly Kikuyu, were evicted from the district, their houses, farms and businesses set on fire and their animals stolen (*Weekly Review* 05/11/93: 16-18).

The most brutal assault on a Kikuyu settlement occurred in Narok North. On the night of 15 October 1993, Maasai moran, security forces and Narok County Council game rangers attacked Kikuyu settlers in Enoosupukia, killing at least 30 people and displacing 30,000 others. When the area MP, William ole Ntimama, was named in parliament as the instigator of the violence, he declared that he 'had no regrets about the events in Enoosupukia because the Maasai were fighting for their rights.' He further charged that the Kikuyu 'had suppressed the Maasai, taken their land and degraded the environment. [W]e had to say enough is enough. I had to lead the Maasai in protecting their rights' (*Daily Nation* 20/10/93). KANU backed the minister lock, stock and barrel and defeated an opposition motion calling for his dismissal from the cabinet (KBC 20/10/93). The motive was to punish the Kikuyu for voting for the opposition in the 1992 elections; second, to reward the local Maasai elite with some of the most fertile land and, third, to change the electoral demography in the area ahead of the 1997 elections.

Another group that was targeted for punishment was the Bukusu sub-group of the Luhya because it overwhelmingly voted for FORD-Kenya and its presidential candidate, Jaramogi Oginga Odinga. In January and February 1993, for instance, vigilante attacks aimed at intimidating and preventing Luhya refugees from returning to their farms in Saboti and Chwele areas in Bungoma left 14 people dead (*Daily Nation* 08/05/93). Church sources described scenes of terror at Kolongolo area in Trans Nzoia where over 200 Luhya families had fled Pokot raiders. Here 'It [is] really death for many families along the Trans Nzoia/West Pokot border as they could hardly stay for a week without a person being killed, animals stolen or a woman raped or a man sodomized' (*The Update* 31/03/97:4).

At the end of 1993, it was estimated that vigilante violence in the Rift Valley and parts of western Kenya had claimed over 1,500 lives, and driven over 300,000 people associated with the opposition from their homes and communities (Human Rights Watch/Africa Watch 1993: 71). In the intervening period, the KANU elite moved to ensure that most of the displaced people in camps did not return to their homes if the political gains that accrued to the party from displacement were to be sustained. Hence, it trained its guns against the displaced in the camps.

On 3 June 1993, for instance, the government forcibly dispersed over 2,000 Luhya and Teso refugees from Endebess camp in Trans Nzoia district (Human Rights Watch/Africa Watch 1993: 67-71). In January 1994, security forces and KANU youths flattened the makeshift shelters of the displaced people at Maela camp and closed down a medical clinic and a makeshift school. At the time, the camp was sheltering nearly 10,000 refugees among the 30,000 who were evicted from their homes in Enoosupukia, Narok. In a final assault on 24 December 1994, government officials and KANU youths razed the entire camp to the ground, herded over 2,000 victims into government trucks and dumped them in separate spots in Central Province considered the 'traditional' homeland of the Kikuyu. Three days later the police raided and demolished a makeshift camp the displaced people had made at Kirigiti Stadium in Kiambu, leaving the twice displaced without shelter (Kenya National Council of NGOs 1995: 10). Only 200 displaced people, who were defined by the government as 'genuine', were settled in 2-acre plots in a government land called Moi-Ndabi (Entapipi). This sealed their fate as citizens, voters and farmers of Enoosupukia.

The government dispersed and expelled the refugees for a variety of reasons. First, refugee camps were eyesores to the government because they drew the attention of domestic and international humanitarian organisations, UN officials, and leaders of Western governments. Second, it was politically expedient to disperse the refugees and force them to 'assimilate' into society without the obligation of resettling or providing for them. Third, it sought to terminate the UNDP's Displaced Persons Programme. From mid-1993 the government was receiving funds from the UNDP under a Ksh. 1.4 billion (US$ 2.3 million) agreement to resettle all victims of ethnic clashes throughout the country. However, for almost a year, it had successfully managed to keep the UNDP at bay and the programme in a cold storage. It is charged that the government scandalously used the UNDP programme's resources to bolster its ethnic constituency ahead of the 1997 elections by 'resettling' the Kalenjin and Maasai in Molo and Narok rather than the *bona fide* refugees. Moreover, it used the same funds to underwrite the demolition of Maela camp and the dumping of some of the refugees in Central Province (Human Rights Watch/ Africa Watch 1997: 71-77). Fourth, it forestalled a situation where it would have to retrieve the land it had culpably allowed its ethnic constituency to occupy, a real political danger in the run up to the 1997 elections. In relation to the Kikuyu, the question of resettlement was to linger on into the elections and after.

Nonetheless, in the run up to the 1997 elections, the KANU elite played the 'resettlement card' to woe Kikuyu voters back to KANU. In November, the government, in collaboration with the Catholic church in Nakuru, resettled over 700 Kikuyu families displaced from Chapakundi in Olenguruone at new lands in Kapsita in Elburgon (*The Update* 30/06/97). President Moi personally handed over the title deeds to the families. The maverick MP for Molo, Njenga Mungai, whose stand on the clashes had hitherto made him KANU's arch-enemy and the most influential Kikuyu leader in the Rift Valley, defected to KANU. The 'resettlement-for-vote' strategy, however, failed to attract the mass of the Kikuyu voters for several reasons. First, coming too late in the election year, the Kikuyu viewed it as a transient vote-catching device rather than a genuine change of heart on the part of KANU. Second, the resettlement process was not as comprehensive as the displacements were. In fact, by the time the elections were held, at least 100,000 people were not resettled. Thirdly, and more damning, even the 700 families were not resettled in their own homes but in new government land.

Koigi wa Wamwere, a presidential candidate in the 1997 elections, argued that by not resettling the displaced Kikuyu population back to their land, 'KANU had formalised "ethnic cleansing" in Nakuru by letting the culprits occupy the land left by victims.' He posed the question: 'If the government can annul legally issued title deeds and let an army of ethnic killers occupy the land, what will stop the army from chasing away the resettled victims?' (*Daily Nation* 03/12/97). Henceforth, Kikuyu politics in the Rift Valley, and Nakuru specifically, took a hard-line course. Mungai and those who favoured the idea of a détente with KANU fell out of favour as opinion in Molo shifted in favour of the fiery politician and long-standing Moi foe, Kihika Kimani. Hence, in 1997, as in 1992, Nakuru and Laikipia districts where the Kikuyu were the majority went to the opposition. Consequently, fierce clashes erupted in the two districts in January-February 1998 with the aim of punishing the Kikuyu for voting for the opposition (see Chapter 20).

The displaced people in other parts of the Rift Valley entered the 1997 elections as a traumatised and intimidated group. For instance, in Moi-Ndabi – where the 200 families from Maela camp were resettled – terrified residents were apprehensive about talking to Human Rights Watch/Africa Watch researchers on 'the ground that they might get into trouble with the local government authorities, or perhaps even lose the land they had been given' (Human Rights Watch/Africa Watch 1997: 79). In Burnt Forest, the Kikuyu considered silence the safest ship home. As one expatriate worker evinced: 'It is better for them to keep quiet. By talking or identifying with the opposition, they will be digging their own graves. They can vote for candidates of their choice quietly without arousing the anger of the Kalenjin. They have learned their own lesson.'[5]

The eviction of non-Maasai in October 1993, and their subsequent dispersal from the Maela camp in December 1994, wiped out the opposition as a political factor in Narok North. Here, William ole Ntimama, the architect of the violence, was elected unopposed while President Moi's vote catapulted from 62 to 77 per cent. Narok North also recorded a significant decline in the number of registered voters from 50,927 in 1992 to 46,866 by 1997, thanks largely to the clashes (NEMU 1993:109, 212; *Daily Nation* 04/01/98: 18-20). Vigilante violence had increased the ethnicisation of politics in the Rift Valley and largely accounted for the ethnic pattern of voting in the 1997 elections.

Dealing with ethnic renegades

In 1997, KANU employed vigilantism to deal with dissent within its own ranks. This was largely responsible for the clashes in Marakwet, West Pokot and Trans Mara districts. In West Pokot, Cabinet Minister Francis Lotodo relied on armed agents to confront the challenge by Pokot rivals. Non-Pokot, suspected of supporting his challengers, were targeted for intimidation and eviction. In Trans Mara district, political rivalry among the Maasai elite and clans triggered communal violence. In the context of unfolding national and local political events, the problem snowballed and affected the whole Gucha/ Trans Mara border area. And in Marakwet district the elite of the Marakwet sub-group of the Kalenjin boldly challenged KANU. Retribution against them took the form of the traditional practice of cattle rustling in the Marakwet/ West Pokot border area.

President Moi's Kalenjin power base was never entirely solid either during the one-party or the multi-party epochs. Hence, he remained apprehensive of the two most populous, most politically mobilised and most economically developed Kalenjin sub-groups, the Nandi and the Kipsigis. Yet, in 1997, political challenge to KANU came from the Marakwet who, together with the Keiyo and Tugen, were hitherto considered as part of the core of the KANU's ethnic constituency. From early 1997, the Marakwet were targets of forays of cattle raids from their Pokot neighbours. Violence between the Pokot and the Marakwet began effectively in early 1997. In April, for instance, raids and counter-raids between the two Kalenjin sub-groups left 20 people dead, as well as 500 Pokot and between 400 and 500 Marakwet families displaced. It is estimated that 4,000-5,000 goats, 104 sheep and 400 head of cattle were stolen from the Marakwet side during the mayhem (*The Update* 30/04/97). By November, continuing violence displaced at least 10,000 families from both sides (*The Update* 31/12/97: 12).[6]

Marakwet politicians accused the government of laxity in defending the community against the well-armed Pokot while others even charged that the government was siding with the activities of Pokot. For instance, Frederick Cheserek, the member of parliament for Kerio West, charged that President Moi was 'treating the crisis between the Marakwet and the Pokot as if it is not a major issue, and yet he knows that the consequences could be serious' (*The Update* 30/04/97: 3). What is not crystal clear is whether the government was using the Pokot as a club to punish the Marakwet for their rebellion or whether it was simply unable to control the Pokot as was the case with other marginal frontier areas. Be that as it may, the Marakwet dissent had strong political links. On the one hand, it was part of the mounting challenge to the party from within its Kalenjin power base over its failure to deliver on its electoral promise of development. On the other hand, the Marakwet protest was viewed as a court rebellion. A group of outspoken Marakwet leaders locked horns with Nicholas Kiprono Biwott, a Keiyo, one of the men believed to be the power behind President Moi's throne, on the questions of equal development and security.

But what may have specifically incensed the KANU leadership was the political inclination of the Marakwet leaders towards the opposition. For example, in March 1997 they hosted the then leader of the opposition, Michael Kijana Wamalwa, who used the occasion to throw salvos at the government for its laxity in quelling the Pokot-Marakwet violence. President Moi, in turn, blamed the opposition for the problem, prompting Wamalwa to dare the government to arrest and charge him (*The Update* 30/04/97: 3). However, on 4 June, the government arrested and charged Philip Rotino, a Pokot, the Sigor member of parliament for allegedly instigating the violence, and declared the area a 'Security Operation Zone'. The MP was barred from visiting the area, but was later acquitted (*The Update* 30/06/97:3). As the Marakwet politics radicalised, intimidation and attacks against the community increased. Against the good advice of the core Kalenjin elite, the Marakwet fielded their out-spoken leaders like Cheserek during the KANU primaries. They were defeated or, as informants alleged, rigged and bundled out of the elections. Thus, they sought election on opposition tickets, further alienating themselves from and provoking the wrath of the Keiyo-Tugen axis. The security situation in Marakwet district dropped to its nadir as the elections approached. A concerned

Marakwet from Tot division lucidly captured the dismal security situation as follows:

> Every time the general election is called, the [Marakwet] community is a target of attack by trigger-happy Pokot. At present, the security situation in the area is deplorable and tense. Residents claim that if security is not restored in time before then (general election), attacks similar to the ones that occurred in 1992 and April this year could occur. Pokots who believe in the sanctity of human life have sent emissaries warning the community of an impending attack during the voting day [29 December]. The attack, as they allege, is meant to be a lesson to Marakwets due to their overwhelming resolve to re-elect their outspoken MPs on a Kanu ticket and as well vote as a bloc to an opposition president of their choice instead of Moi who over the years did not want to hear anything from the community however pressing and reasonable it was. At the time of writing this letter, word is going round the villages to the effect that the dreaded General Service [GSU] personnel stationed in the area would be relegated to duties outside the district in order to pave the way for the raiders. Already, fear has gripped villagers who have moved the elderly and children to the hilly caves of Elgeyo escarpment for protection against the anticipated attacks. As a matter of urgency, the hunger-stricken Marakwets are crying for both land and air security during the voting day so that they exercise their democratic right (*The People* 05-11/12/97:VI).

On Christmas eve 1997, the Pokot eventually attacked the Marakwet. In Tot division, they killed 12 people, injured scores of others and set property and homesteads ablaze. One source surmised that the attack 'was aimed at destabilising the Marakwet community, especially in the valley where the opposition was gaining ground' (*The Update* 31/12/97: 12). In the end, the outspoken Marakwet leaders, including Cheserek lost in the elections. But profound political changes had occurred in the area. In 1992, this was an exclusive KANU zone 'from which the opposition was ruthlessly excluded throughout the campaign, and from where opposition candidates were prevented from standing in all . . . seats' (Throup and Hornsby 1998: 464). In 1997, opposition parties were a formidable force; prompting the decline of President Moi's vote from 99.8 per cent in 1992 to 72.8 per cent in the 1997 elections.

In West Pokot district, non-Pokot communities were targets of harassment and intimidation by Cabinet Minister Francis Lotodo's agents. Allegedly Lotodo had a well-equipped private army that he consolidated using illegal arms acquired from troubled Uganda and southern Sudan in the 1980s and 1990s. In 1997 Lotodo instigated his supporters against non-Pokot alleged to be allied to his Pokot rivals. During the KANU primaries his agents barred non-Pokot from participating in the exercise. Since 'Pokot is not their Motherland', it was argued, non-Pokot had no right to vote. Hence, they were warned never to set foot in the nomination ground while those who defied the warning and appeared for nomination, especially at Chepareria and Sok polling stations, were flushed out of the lines while many left without casting their votes because of intimidation (*Daily Nation* 30/01/98). Civic candidates in the rival political camp withdrew from the KANU nomination process in fear of harsh retribution, leaving Lotodo and his allies unopposed. Intimidation against non-Pokot voters intensified as the 1997 elections got under way. On 15 December, for instance, Lotodo's agents shot at houses of non-Pokot at Makutano and later in other towns, forcing many to flee for safety outside West Pokot (*Daily Nation* 17/12/97). Church leaders accused Lotodo of employing violence and intimidation to disenfranchise non-Pokot voters. In the final analysis, all KANU civic and parliamentary candidates in West Pokot were unopposed and Daniel arap Moi's presidential vote in West Pokot shot from 88.1 per cent in 1992 to 95.4 per cent in 1997, a testimony to the dividends of violence (*Sunday Nation* 04/01/98).

Violence in Trans Mara district began around March 1997 (see also Chapter 15). While it was largely attributed to intra-Maasai political rivalries, it was the Gusii in Trans Mara and the neighbouring Gucha district who bore its blunt. Maasai *moran* are said to have made raiding forays into Gucha, provoking counter-raids from the Gusii. On 17 August, amidst escalating violence and public outcry, the government deployed the GSU and the regular police in the border between the two districts. In spite of this, no less than 100 cattle raids and counter-raids occurred in the region in 1997. In October alone 15 people died in different incident of violence (*The Update* 31/10/97: 1-2). An attack on non-Maasai residents at Kilgoris town on 21 November, for example, killed 12 people, destroyed property and displaced many non-Maasai in Trans Mara. Cattle rustling and land disputes were the professed reasons for the clashes. The violence, however, had a deep pedigree in the electoral agenda of the local and national KANU elite in 1997. Gusii elders, for instance, laid the blame for the escalation of violence at the door of a well-connected Maasai businessman in the area who the government declined to apprehend (*The Update* 31/10/97:7).

However, the root cause of the violence was a struggle between the various Maasai elite for the control of the new Trans Mara district. This feud pitted Julius ole Sunkuli, a powerful assistant minister in the Office of the President, against a Maasai rival, Gideon Konchela. Non-Maasai backed Konchela against Sunkuli, a KANU hard-liner. Following a defeat in the KANU primaries, Konchela vied for election on a DP ticket, subsequently importing the KANU-opposition hostility into the intra-Maasai feud. This political crisis was compounded by the fact that the neighbouring Gusii constituencies of Bonchari and South Mugirango had been opposition strongholds since 1992. Another political rationale for the violence was to harass, intimidate and prevent opposition presidential candidates from making inroads into the area. On 21 November, for instance, Raila Odinga, the presidential candidate on the National Development Party (NDP) ticket, was beaten, his car stoned and his aide severely injured by Maasai *moran* when he toured Kilgoris town to console the victims of a recent attack (*Sunday Nation* 23/11/97). Finally, on 18 December, President Moi declared Trans Mara, among other troubled spots in the area, a 'Security Operation Zone'. This effectively outlawed his rivals from entering and campaigning in the area.[7]

'Jeshi la Mzee': vigilante war on reformers

Continued state repression and restriction of the space of the civil society left grave doubts as to whether 'free and fair' multi-party elections were possible. From early 1997, an amalgam of civic groups and individual opposition politicians coalesced around the newly constituted National Convention Assembly (NCA) and its executive, the National Convention Executive Council (NCEC). This pro-democracy alliance rallied around the platform of far-reaching constitutional, legal and administrative reforms ahead of the general elections scheduled for 29 December 1997. The NCEC set its agenda around the clarion cry 'No reform, no elections' (Southall 1998:103). It held its first constitutional conference in Limuru on 3 April 1997 and resolved to convene nation-wide public rallies and to use non-violent methods to get the Moi state to initiate fundamental reforms that would create a level playing field for all parties in the 1997 elections (*Nairobi Law Monthly* Aug/Sep 1997).

KANU panicked. In the ensuing hiatus, it even lost initiative in the reform process. Hence, it honed its tools of coercion, both legal and extra-legal, to confront the NCEC and reclaim its political initiative. This resulted in the spread of vigilantism in urban areas and the spatial expansion of violence to virtually all parts of rural Kenya. The police and the paramilitary GSU on the one hand, and state-sponsored vigilantes on the other, joined hands in one of the most violent onslaughts against civil society in the multi-party era.

Against this background, a new vigilante force called *Jeshi la Mzee* (the old man's army), purportedly President Moi's army that is not part of the officially recognised state security system, surfaced in Kenya's main towns at the end of April (KHRC 1997: 51). The force brought together some members of the notorious KANU Youth Wing and fresh recruits drawn from the burgeoning *lumpen*, the unemployed, impoverished and disillusioned youth who thronged Kenya's main cities. The former was created in the 1980s to hunt down 'anti-party' elements, monitor and punish public dissent through indiscriminate violence, thuggery and extortion.[8]

In the multi-party era, the presence of vigilantes in Kenya's urban space was only witnessed immediately after the 1992 elections. During the opening ceremony of the first multi-party parliament in April 1993, Maasai *moran* clad in traditional attire (*shukas*) and wielding clubs, machetes and whips terrorised opposition supporters in Nairobi. William ole Ntimama claimed that the *moran* had acted in self-defence (*Weekly Review* 09/04/93). Barely one month later, KANU's secretary general, Joseph Kamotho, admitted that the *moran* were part of a 3,000-strong youth squad hired by the government to deal with opposition supporters (*Daily Nation* 02/02/93). In an even more astonishing attack, Maasai warriors broke up an exhibition of photographs of the Rift Valley violence by a prominent environmentalist, Prof. Wangari Maathai, during the World Conference on Human Rights held in Vienna, Austria in June 1993 (KHRC 1993). The *moran* were part of Ntimama's entourage to the Vienna conference. In 1997, squads of *Jeshi la Mzee* stalked the main towns of Nairobi, Mombasa, Nakuru, Kisumu, Eldoret as well as smaller ones like Wundanyi, Machakos and Murang'a. Private militias of some KANU bigwigs also went under the rubric of *Jeshi la Mzee*. For instance, Joseph Kamotho was reported to have a hit squad in his Mathioya constituency in Murang'a district (*Finance* 08/12/97:3).[9] Similarly, another KANU leader, Darius Mbela, was reported to have a private militia, *Jeshi la Mbela* (Mbela's army) in Taita-Taveta, Coast Province (KHRC 1997:51).

Working in cahoots with the police, *Jeshi la Mzee* militias disrupted the nation-wide rallies that the NCEC convened. For example, *Jeshi la Mzee* vigilantes, supported by squadrons of the GSU, violently broke the first constitutional reform rally convened by the NCEC at Kamukunji grounds in Nairobi on 31 May 1997. Observers were puzzled by the high level of co-ordination between the vigilantes and the GSU during the operation. The police brutally dispersed NCEC rallies on 7 July, 8 August, and 10 October in which 13 pro-democracy protesters were killed by police using teargas, bullets and batons and 500 people arrested (Human Rights Watch 1998: 41). It is reported that in the course of dispersing the protesters, police shot people at point-blank range. In one instance, they even stormed the Anglican cathedral, tear-gassing and clubbing parishioners. On 26 July, a NCEC rally in Mombasa was marred by violence between pro-reform youths and *Jeshi la Mzee* squads. During the mayhem, Karisa Maitha, a KANU activist, is reported to have drawn a pistol and threatened some of the rally organisers. He was never charged for the crime (*The Star* 09-11/12/97).

Jeshi la Mzee militias also harassed presidential hopefuls and disrupted their campaign programmes. A KANU councillor at Masinga in Machakos district disclosed that KANU had mobilised 6,000 youths under the aegis of the *Jeshi la Mzee* to flush out opposition elements in the area that he claimed was a 'KANU zone'. Consequently, on 12 July, Charity Kaluki Ngilu, the leader of the Social Democratic Party (SDP) and a leading contender for the presidency, was attacked and injured by 'thugs' after addressing a political rally at the small town of Mutito Andei along the Nairobi-Mombasa highway (KHRC 1997a: 44). She was targeted for attacks because of her growing support in Kambaland, considered a KANU stronghold.

Another target group were university students most of whom joined the pro-democracy movement. Here, the role of vigilantes was less visible but not absent all the same. Police shot dead four students in three different university campuses in 1997. One fatal incident is remarkable largely because it involved secret attackers. On 23 February, Solomon Muruli, a student leader at the University of Nairobi, was killed after a mysterious explosion and fire gutted his dormitory room (Human Rights Watch 1998:42).

Explaining this spatial spread and intensity of violence in 1997, Mazrui argues that violence was meant to create a justification for the KANU elite to declare a state of emergency – as the British did in 1952 following the outbreak of the Mau Mau movement – and, therefore, rule by decree. He writes: 'The [KANU] hawks hoped to precipitate conditions of crisis which would justify a declaration of a State of Emergency nation-wide under the provision of chapter 57 of the laws of Kenya titled "The Preservation of Public Security Act"' (KHRC 1997:51). While this may be true for the period before November, the political rationale for the escalation of violence in the latter months of 1997 was meant to compromise the elections and to ensure a victory for the incumbents.

In November, President Moi succumbed to national and international pressure and ordered the police to stop breaking up the non-violent rallies. But the activities of vigilantes took over the centre-stage simultaneously with the reform process later in the year. The NCEC succeeded in galvanising opinion in favour of reforms, but KANU hijacked the process in order to forestall sweeping changes that would undercut its structural leverage. As Ndegwa (1998: 202-03) has rightly observed:

> Succumbing to the NCEC's strident demands for reforms and threats to derail the elections, KANU chose to pursue reforms within parliament, where it was assured of control at two levels. First, it maintained a majority, though not a supermajority, in the House. Second, by creating a parliamentary platform for negotiation KANU was able to reconstitute the agenda more to its liking.

While the stymied reform process failed to ensure a level playing field for all actors in the election, vigilante violence that flared up in many parts of the country compromised and sealed the fate of the 1997 election process.

In September, christened by one source as 'the month of violence', there were over a dozen clash-torn spots throughout the country ranging from Likoni, Kwale, Mombasa, Kilifi, Tharaka/Nithi, Nyambene, Igembe, Isiolo, Kuria, Gucha, Migori, to Bungoma (*Expression Today* 1997:2). Violence escalated in traditionally bandit-prone northern Kenya. In the damning words of one report, in this region 'the government is spoken in past tense, mocking its claim to be in charge' (*Expression Today* 1997:2). Another report by the Catholic Diocese of Marsabit in northern Kenya said that 200 people had been killed, 6,000 displaced; over 25,000 heads of cattle, 21,000 goats, 1,000 camels and 127 donkeys stolen by October 1997 (*Expression Today* 1997:2). The phenomenal spread, intensity and range of political objectives of vigilante violence were also clearly evident in Coast and Nyanza provinces.

'Killing' the vote: violence at the coast

A few days after the NCEC rally in Mombasa on 26 July 1997, 'ethnic' violence erupted at the coast. On 13 August between 200 to 500 Mijikenda 'warriors' dressed in short pants, red headbands and traditional *kanzu* (cotton robe) attacked and burned down the Likoni Police Station, a nearby tourist police booth and a block that housed the Likoni District Officer and the area chief, killing six police officers and making away with 30-50 guns and 3,000-5,000 rounds of live ammunition (African Rights 1997). The whole administrative and security infrastructure was wiped out. The target of the violence, however, were up-country people – mainly the Luo, Luhya, Kikuyu and Kamba. Armed gangs attacked and razed businesses and houses belonging to up-country people in Ukunda, Matuga and Msambweni in Kwale district. Although on a lesser scale, gangs also attacked up-country groups in Kaloleni and Malindi in Kilifi district. Leaflets warned the people from up-country to leave the area or face attacks: 'The time has come for us the original people of the coast to claim what is rightly ours. We must remove these invaders from the land.' This is reminiscent of the reconstruction of citizenship and group rights in the Rift Valley. Indeed, '[t]he warnings and attacks were strikingly similar to the ethnic violence which had taken place prior to the 1992 elections in the Rift Valley, and targeted some of the same groups' (Human Rights Watch 1998:42).

The distinct feature of the vigilantes at the coast is that these appeared to be well-trained guerrillas rather than uncoordinated gangs. Studies by the Kenya Human Rights Commission indicate that these men were trained in Shimba hills, Kaya Bombo, Kaya Waa and Similani caves in Kwale district by ex-servicemen, Kiswahili-speaking Hutu refugees from Rwanda and a few Ugandans. So well-trained and armed were the attackers that a force of over 5,000 security personnel was unable to trace them. It is reported that the attackers were able to withstand heavy operations carried out by 'crack' security units, including the GSU, the Anti-Stock Theft Unit, the Flying Police Squad and regular police (Kenya National Council of NGOs 1997:8). At one stage, they had a three-hour pitched battle at Kaya Bombo area in which three police officers were killed (African Rights 1997:15). When they were recruited, the warriors were told that they were 'part of the security arrangement for Mzee [as Kenyans respectfully refer to President Moi] during the forthcoming elections' (African Rights 1997:15). Leaflets distributed in Likoni identified key actors in the government and KANU machinery as the underwriters of the violence. These were code-named the 'five-stars'.[11] According to the London-based body, African Rights, that carried out an extensive study of the violence at the coast, nearly a 100 people were killed and over 100,000 forced to flee their homes for safety.

The government denied any involvement in the sponsorship or knowledge of the origin of the violence; it even claimed to have been a victim. Articulating this point, President Moi told a press conference on 27 December:

> I must remind you that the first victim of the [Coast] violence were my policemen. It is, therefore, absurd and senseless to claim . . . that the Government instigated the confrontation to make political gain. My belief is that politicians on both sides [of the political divide] instigated the violence as a means of making political capital and embarrassing my Government, especially with regard to tourism. . . . I must admit that we have not yet found the root cause of the violence (*Sunday Nation* 28/12/97:8).

The government made some 300 arrests, including KANU supporters. But, as it will be shown later, the reprisal was part of the larger plan to regain control over Mombasa and Kwale politics. Instructively, the violence at the coast followed shortly after voter registration ended. Hence, it is widely surmised that the government instigated the violence after voter registration data indicated that it was going to lose the crucial Mombasa and Kwale seats (Human Rights Watch 1998:42).

Violence at the coast in 1997 seemed to revolve around three inter-related political objectives. First, the KANU elite sought to break the political dominance of the unregistered Islamic Party of Kenya (IPK) in Mombasa. Second, it was designed to undermine the unfolding regional political alliance at the coast between large sections of the Swahili-Arab and Mijikenda elite. Finally, it intended to displace and disenfranchise up-country people in Mombasa and Kwale in order to undermine the electoral demographic basis of the IPK alliance with other opposition parties.[12]

In 1992, KANU lost much of its power in Mombasa to a coalition of intellectuals and Islamic teachers who formed the Islamic Party of Kenya. The Kenyan authorities refused to register the IPK. In a successful strategy to circumvent the political constraints imposed on it by denial of registration, the IPK entered into an informal political pact with FORD Kenya led by Jaramogi Oginga Odinga. The IPK's part of the deal was to back Odinga's presidential bid. As a *quid pro quo*, FORD-Kenya gave the IPK a free rein to nominate parliamentary candidates for Mombasa on a FORD-Kenya ticket (*The People* 05-11/12/97). The pact was based on a solid demographic force provided by Luo and Luhya migrant workers and settlers from Nyanza and western Kenya who backed FORD-Kenya. As Table 4.1 shows, the target up-country population (Luo, Luhya, Kamba and Kikuyu) was about 42 per cent in Mombasa and 12 per cent in Kwale. The Luo and Luhya, the major FORD-Kenya supporters at the time, comprised over 23 per cent of the total population of Mombasa.

Table 4.1: The proportion of the main up-country groups in Mombasa and Kwale districts, 1989

Group	Mombasa	% of total	Kwale	% of total
Luo	64,088	13.88	4,445	1.16
Kamba	54,842	12.53	34,143	8.91
Luhya	42,790	9.27	3.060	0.80
Kikuyu	29,099	6.30	4,013	1.05
Mijikenda	128,860	27.91	316,240	82.56
Taita	31,041	6.72	3,288	0.86
Others*	111,033	23.39	17,964	4.66
Total	461,753	100.00	383,053	100.00

Source: Republic of Kenya Population Census 1989 Vol.1, March 1994.

*Mostly smaller up-country groups (Kisii, Embu, Maasai), Europeans, Swahili (Kwale) Bajun, Kenyan Arab, Kenyan Asians (Mombasa).

The IPK/FORD-Kenya pact captured the Kisauni and Likoni seats in 1992. The Democratic Party of Kenya captured the Changamwe seat, leaving KANU with the Mvita constituency. Much to KANU's displeasure, the IPK renewed its pact with the late Odinga's son, Raila Odinga, now in the National Development Party of Kenya (NDP) in 1997. Some IPK members, including Munir Mazrui of the NCEC and Supkem, Omar Bwana (a former Director of National Museums) and Khelef Khalifa, a founding member of the IPK, were actively negotiating an alliance with the Safina party which the government registered belatedly after great local and international pressure. The IPK, through its Mijikenda activists, was also forging a pan-coastal and pan-Islamic alliance with the predominantly Muslim Digo. This alliance was potentially a threat to KANU's political future in Kwale and Mombasa. Hence, the violence at the coast was a dual pronged attack on both the up-country allies of the IPK as well as its supporters among the Digo. As will be demonstrated later, vigilantes focused on the up-country people while security forces zeroed in on the Digo in a division of labour meant to safeguard KANU's political future.

The total number of registered voters for Mombasa was 256,165, while 130,765 registered in Kwale. The presence of up-country people largely contributed to the high numbers of registered voters in Likoni (40,414), Changamwe (76,567), Kisauni (74,246), Mvita (64,638) and Msambweni (59,922). The average voter registration in the entire Coast Province was 37,238 people per constituency (ECK 1999: 138). It is estimated that the rate of displacement ranged from 75 to 100 per cent in some areas (KHRC 1997: 49). Villages where up-country people lived such as Shoda-Maweni and Ujamaa were emptied.[13] Almost a third of the displaced lost their identity cards, voter cards, passports, drivers' licenses, title deeds and birth certificates during the clashes. Electoral regulations require that a voter must have an identity card or passport, in addition to a voter's card in order to be eligible to vote.[14]

Even the church refuge was invaded. Terrorist gangs continued to intimidate those inside the Likoni Catholic church compound. In a daring move on 22 August, raiders attacked the displaced within the church compound, killing two people and injuring a policeman (African Rights 1997: 6-7). Gangs also invaded and intimidated internal refugees at the Baptist High School asylum. They climbed over the wall of the compound, threatened and intimidated the displaced, telling them to disperse.[16] In a shocking move, the government gave the Likoni Catholic church an ultimatum to force the refugees out of the church. Archbishop John Njenga rejected the ultimatum saying the refugees' security had not been insured (KHRC 1997a).[17] Continued low-key violence in November through December scared away up-country voters. The vigilantes were determined to ensure that the displaced did not come back to vote.

Six days to the elections, people were 'still being killed in such villages as Ujamaa [in Likoni]. We are living in fear. As the election day approached, most houses are empty.'[18] And African Rights concluded that 'Even if voters are able to return eventually to their constituency in order to cast their vote, political terror makes a farce of "democratic elections" as people have good reasons to fear expressing any sort of political preference' (African Rights 1997: 24). Once again, vigilantism triumphed and disenfranchised opposition voters at the coast.

While the up-country people were tortured, raped, mutilated and murdered by marauding gangs, it was the Mijikenda, particularly the Digo, who faced the full barrage of reprisal by enraged security forces (KHRC 1998:74). Over 800 Digo fled their homes and camped in Markaz, Ridhiwani, Nuru and

Sarkina mosques. Hundreds of others fled to Lunga Lunga in Tanzania, the first crop of refugees to flee Kenya. An estimated 218 Digo men and women were arrested, incarcerated and subjected to all manner of torture in Shimo la Tewa prison. Among those arrested were Digo Muslim clerics and scholars such as Sheikh Hamisi Amir Banda, Imam Ali Chizondo, Jumbe Rashid Tosha and Khelef Khalifa and other intellectuals from the coast such as Alamin Mazrui. They were charged with instigating the violence at Likoni. The GSU intimidated and harassed government critics among the Digo, especially those suspected of radicalism and connected with the IPK or up-country opposition parties. Apparently, this was also a veiled warning to the Digo not to join these parties.

KANU also encouraged the intensive ethnicisation of Digo politics, arguably to counteract religious or regional alliances that would undermine KANU's influence. In November, the government registered the Shirikisho Party of Kenya (SPK) with its political base among the Digo, particularly in Likoni. This was the first coastal party to be registered. Since the onset of pluralism in 1992, the KANU regime refused to legalise all Mijikenda parties, including the National Democratic Union (NADU) and the United Muslims of Africa (UMA).

There are two possible reasons for the registration of Shirikisho. First, reprisals by security forces had profoundly weakened KANU's political support in the Likoni and Matuga areas. The late legalisation of Shirikisho seemed like a strategy to ensure that the Digo did not vote for the opposition. Secondly, the registration of Shirikisho sealed the fate of coastal unity on the basis of religion and regionalism. In a sense, KANU benefited from the political effects of the new party. While it fielded civic and parliamentary candidates, it did not sponsor a presidential candidate. The government's behind-the-scenes control of Shirikisho came into the open in November. When the intellectual militants within its ranks articulated an independent position relating to the violence that seemed to undermine KANU's image in Digoland, the Registrar of Societies threatened to de-register the party (*Daily Nation* 27/12/97). Thus, the threat of de-registration hung over the head of SPK throughout the election period, keeping it on an even keel to KANU's advantage. There were speculations that some of the party's officials were working closely with KANU, especially in Likoni where they supported Moi's presidential bid. Like the KANU militants in the Rift Valley, the SPK activists espoused *majimboism* in Coast Province. On the countdown to the election in December, it was charged that the party's activists were threatening the few up-country people who held on that 'if you don't vote for our party, you will not stay here after the elections.'[19] In the end, only some 8,000 people displaced in the run up to the 1997 elections who took refuge in the Likoni Catholic church managed to go back and vote (Kenya National Council of NGOs 1997:8).

The outcome of the violence was that KANU's parliamentary strength in Mombasa grew from one seat in 1992 to two in 1997. But the sweetest victory was the virtual demise of its formidable foe in coastal politics, the IPK, that lost both the Likoni and Kisauni seats. The IPK-NDP axis lost the Likoni seat to SPK's Suleiman Shakombo, a KANU old-timer who was instrumental in organising the Likoni violence (KHRC 1998a). The alliance also lost the Kisauni seat to yet another long-standing KANU stalwart, Emmanuel Karisa Maitha, who defected to DP after losing in the KANU primaries. KANU was more prepared to do business with its estranged activists than with its arch enemies in the IPK. President Moi's vote also improved tremendously from an average of 34 per cent in 1992 to 42 per cent in 1997 in the four constituencies of Mombasa – Mvita, Kisauni, Likoni and Changamwe. The rise was even more dramatic in Likoni, the scene of the worst violence. It increased from 31 per cent in 1992 to nearly 42 per cent in 1997.

Voter turnout in Coast Province was 56.3 per cent only. Mombasa scored bottom. In Mvita, a pathetic 44.3 per cent turned out while in Likoni only 36.2 per cent of the registered voters turned out to vote in the presidential elections, a nation-wide low. For the parliamentary elections, the turnout scores for Mvita and Likoni were 44.5 and 39.7 per cent respectively. In the three Kwale district constituencies, turnout was in the range of 60-66 per cent, with all three seats going to KANU. The impact of the violence at the coast is that KANU successfully reclaimed its authority in the urban space at the coast and crippled its enemies in the IPK-NDP alliance. Simultaneously, it was pushing the war into NDP's Nyanza turf.

Nyanza: the mission to divide-and-win

In late October 1997 violence erupted in Nyanza Province. This wave of violence had deep roots, not in any pre-existing political rivalry between the ethnic groups involved, but in the changing national political scene. Although different from the Rift Valley or Coast provinces, Nyanza is multi-ethnic. While migrant communities and Asian business communities play a negligible role in the politics of the region, the three resident communities; namely, the Luo, Gusii and Kuria, occupy distinct territories. More importantly, these communities enter the arena of national politics on their own terms with little or no loyalty to a territorial or provincial identity. It is the Luo, however, more than the Gusii or Kuria who have played a more influential role in the national political arena for both historical and demographic reasons. The Luo, Kenya's third largest and most politically mobilised group, did not only play a leading role in the anti-colonial struggle, but bitterly resisted the tyranny of the Kenyatta and the Moi regimes. In the 1990s, they entered the multi-party era as a hub of opposition through the leadership of Jaramogi Oginga Odinga. On their part, the Gusii and the Kuria were part of what in multi-party politics has come to be called 'swing communities', who could tilt to either side of the political divide depending on the prevailing circumstances.

While ethnic clashes in Nyakach and Muhoroni in 1991 severed the last cords of the client-patron relation with a section of Luo leadership, violence in the Rift Valley and in the Trans Mara/Gucha area in 1997 alienated large sections of the Gusii community from KANU. In 1992 all the 18 seats in Luo Nyanza went to the opposition; in Kisii, 6 out of 10 constituencies voted for KANU; while the single Kuria constituency voted in majority for KANU. Thus, by 1997, the three communities were politically divided, though some Gusii constituencies were won by the opposition.

In 1997, the scenario that provided the backdrop to the violence in Nyanza was unsavoury for KANU for two reasons. First, Jaramogi Odinga's fiery son did not only inherit his father's mantle in Nyanza, but his take-over and revitalisation of the National Development Party (NDP) at the end of December 1996 injected new vigour into Nyanza politics. As pointed out earlier, Raila Odinga moved to consolidate the nation-wide pacts that his late father had made, especially with the IPK at the coast, and moved to undercut KANU in non-Luo Nyanza. Second, and related to the first factor, with nearly 50 Gusii killed in the Trans Mara clashes, relations with KANU reached their lowest ebb. Even Gusii KANU aspirants had come to believe that it was politically unwise to campaign for President Moi in Kisii while a senior Gusii politician, in reference to Moi, was reportedly overheard saying that everyone should carry his own cross (*Tazama* 24/12/97: 8). Indisputably, the KANU elite had a stake in the 'swing communities' in Nyanza. Moreover, the meteoric rise of Charity Ngilu in Kamba politics as well as her growing popularity in parts of Kisii destabilised KANU's scheme in the 'swing communities', of which the Kamba and the Gusii are the most populous groups. This must have forced KANU to belatedly adopt new strategies if President Moi was to get 25 per cent of the presidential vote in five provinces and avoid a run-off with the closest contender as required by the electoral laws. Nyanza Province, and Gusiiland in particular, where he had scored 14.5 per cent of the presidential vote in 1992, was a prime target.

Apparently, KANU adopted a double-barrelled strategy in dealing with the challenge in Nyanza. It sought to widen the political gap between the Luo on the one hand and the Kuria and Gusii on the other. Simultaneously, it prevented other opposition parties from entering the area. The spread of vigilantism in the Migori, Gucha and Kuria areas related to the first part of the strategy. Clashes in Migori/Gucha area focused on the Ochadororo, Nyabera and Cham-Gi-Wadu border areas (*Daily Nation* 15/11/97). In the initial attack on 20 October, five people were killed, several injured, over 30 houses razed and several hundred villagers, overwhelmingly Luo, forced to flee their homes. In another attack on 22 October, 13 houses belonging to Luo farmers were burned down in Ochadororo area and hundreds of people displaced from their farms (*The Update* 31/10/97: 3).

The Luo-Kuria clashes also began in October and focused on the border areas of Remo, Sageki and Ogwedhi. In October alone 20 people were killed, several herds of cattle stolen and 200 Luo families displaced from Ogwedhi, Sageki and Remo villages. In one attack at Remo village, 14 houses were razed to the ground. It is estimated that by December at least 600 families had fled their homes and sought shelter in schools and churches. The clashes affected the Luo. This is because the Kuria and Gusii had traditional militia called the *Chinkororo*, who engaged in raids and counter-raids in the area. Indeed, Kuria *Chinkororo* possessed guns which turned the clashes in Nyanza bloody and greatly affected the unarmed Luo.

Expectedly, government sources attributed the violence to cattle raids and disputes over land. The Kuria-Luo clash, for instance, was attributed to a dispute over a 100-acre strip of land at Remo and Sageki. Another view is that the clash began when the Kuria raided the Luo and took three heads of cattle. When the latter pursued the Kuria raiders, this culminated in open ethnic conflict. Luo elders blamed government laxity for the escalation of violence and called on it to disarm the Kuria who used guns during their attacks. While blaming government laxity for the continued conflict, most victims of the violence read a sinister political ring in the clashes. As one Luo victim stated, 'the Luo and Gusii have lived along the border in harmony since time immemorial. Now, they live in fear and apprehension' (*Daily Nation* 23/11/97). Besides land disputes and cattle rustling, there are two political reasons to which the violence was attributed both of which revolved around the political role of the NDP in Nyanza politics. The first is the euphoria generated by the NDP among its Luo adherents and the latter's tendency to turn violent, especially in relation to those belonging to other parties. One Gusii informant blamed the NDP youths for forcing the Gusii to join the party and to use force to penetrate KANU strongholds in Kisii and Kuria. Other Gusii informants attributed the violence to KANU's manoeuvres to divide the Luo and their Gusii and Kuria neighbours for political gains.

The perpetrators of the violence in Nyanza drew upon the popular image of ruffianism associated with Raila and the Luo-dominated NDP. The bloodletting political fight between Raila and his father's successor, Kijana Wamalwa, over the leadership of FORD-Kenya in 1995-96 bequeathed to him an image of a political ruffian, perhaps rivalled only by KANU. As Throup and Hornsby (1998: 571-2) observe:

[S]ince mid-1995 Raila Odinga has repeatedly challenged Wamalwa and James Orengo, his main Luo backer, mobilising the support of the unemployed youths in Kisumu and other Luo towns to intimidate his opponents in FORD-Kenya as much as KANU. . . . Even in Nyanza Province, Odinga encountered strong opposition from Luo MPs who resented his confrontational tactics and unpredictable behaviour, while older people, business leaders and well-educated professionals deplored his reliance on hired ruffians and intimidation to enforce his views. . . . While the softly spoken *Jaramogi* Oginga Odinga had been widely revered, his son has become almost as widely feared.

The second strand of KANU's strategy was to lock out opposition politicians from the areas to ensure that they did not make political capital from its woes. On 18 December, following his campaign trip in the area, President Moi declared the clash-torn areas in Gucha, Kuria, Migori and Trans Mara districts a 'Security Operation Zone'. In plain political language, this meant that all (opposition) civic, parliamentary and presidential candidates were *persona non grata* in the affected districts. Constitutional lawyers declared the order illegal and unconstitutional. They argued that section 88 of the Kenya constitution that empowered the president to declare an area a 'Security Operation Zone' also required the government to publish the order in the gazette, which the president had not done. Two Nairobi-based constitutional lawyers, Kamau Kuria and Kathurima M'Inoti, charged that the timing and the selective nature of the declaration made the president's motive suspect. They asked: 'Why didn't he take action when parts of Likoni and Kwale were hit by insecurity recently?' (*Daily Nation* 19/12/97). As such it was widely felt that the 'Security Operation Zone' was designed to disrupt the campaign programmes of other presidential hopefuls. The Electoral Commission itself was not comfortable with the declaration of the 'Security Operation Zone'. The president neither sought the commission's counsel nor informed it of his intentions and reasons before or after the act. It was rightly pointed out that Moi, himself a candidate, was out to arrogate to himself the power to determine the rules of the game which was the prerogative of the commission. Confronted with the reality of despotism in the middle of an election campaign, the commission could only lament: 'It will be sad if the candidates will be denied access to such places. Once we get the details, arrangements will have to be made so that when they go there chances of violence are minimised by having security provisions to ensure that the people don't clash' (*Sunday Nation* 21/12/97: 2).

This never came to be for KANU was determined to ensure that opposition candidates did not enter the area. Those who never read the signs on the wall and ventured into the area behind the iron curtain lived to regret their experiences in the hands of security forces and vigilantes. When Charity

Kaluki Ngilu, the SDP presidential candidate, attempted to enter the area on 19 December, she was confronted by police who cocked their guns and proceeded to disperse her supporters with tear-gas (*Daily Nation* 20/12/97: 2). The police also prevented another presidential candidate, Mwai Kibaki, from entering the area. And in response, President Moi bitterly indicted his opponents for defying his declaration and seeking to enter the 'Security Operation Zone' (*Daily Nation* 21/12/97). Shielded from public spotlight by the curtain created by the zoning order, vigilantes and security forces had a field day as they intimidated and harassed opposition candidates and their agents in the area. On 19 December, armed youths shot dead four DP supporters who had accompanied the party's parliamentary candidate for Bobasi, Oguta Daniel Matoke in a campaign trail to Nyangusi town. Around the same time, vigilantes attacked SDP candidates in Nyaribari Masaba constituency (*Daily Nation* 21/12/97: 1). And on the eve of the elections, Maasai *moran* shot and killed three brothers at their home in Bomachoge Borabu location, Gucha district (*Daily Nation* 29/12/97).

The NDP was the immediate casualty of the violence in that it was a non-factor in the Gusii-Kuria areas. In fact, it is opposition parties from outside the province such as FORD-Kenya and the DP that gave KANU a run for its money. It is estimated that over 40 per cent of the registered voters in the clash-torn area never cast their votes for reasons related to the violence (*Daily Nation* 04/01/98). Vigilantism and the zoning of the area brought to KANU enormous political dividends. The party won 10 out of a total of 12 seats in the areas directly hit by violence in Nyanza and Trans Mara. President Moi's vote in Nyanza Province shot from 14.5 per cent in 1992 to 23.5 per cent in 1997, narrowly short of the target 25 per cent. Once more, violence had brought political gains to KANU while killing, maiming and disenfranchising tens of thousands of innocent Kenyans.

Notes

1. Kenya is divided into eight administrative provinces, namely, Coast, North Eastern, Eastern, Central, Rift Valley, Western, Nyanza and Nairobi.
2. The Kalenjin, who belong to the Highland Nilotic cluster consist of 11 distinct ethnic groups that share linguistic and cultural traditions: Elgeyo, Dorobo, Kipsigis (Lumbwa), Nandi, Pokot (Suk), Keiyo, Marakwet, Tugen, Saboat, Sebei, Terik.
3. *Majimboism* first appeared in the late 1950s as the nationalist movement disintegrated into ethnic alliances on the eve of independence. The Kalenjin, Maasai and the Mijikenda elite espoused it ostensibly to protect the political rights of the smaller groups against the domination of the larger ones, i.e., Kikuyu, Luo, Kamba. The white settlers, whose future was uncertain, also backed the system to the hilt as a response of the fiery nationalism of the latter groups. The system, which was safeguarded by the independent constitution, was abolished in 1964 and its principle architects,

Daniel arap Moi and Ronald Ngala, rejoined President Kenyatta's government. Subsequently, Moi was appointed Kenyatta's deputy and *de facto* heir.

4.   In a wider sense, the Kalenjin elite refers to a larger coterie of leaders from the eleven Kalenjin groups. However, membership of this coterie changed over the years with the ebb and tide of client-patron politics within the Kalenjin group. As such, it is the more consistent and enduring inner circle of President Moi's inner court, consisting of a small but powerful clique drawn from the president's Tugen group and the neighboring Keiyo that wielded state power. Indeed, in or out of the cabinet, the power behind Moi's throne was Nicholas Kiprono Biwott, a Keiyo, and a long time business and political ally of President Moi who, in glory or in disgrace, never pretended to be more than the president's 'backroom boy'.

5.   Interview with Wilfred Schasfoort, Technical Adviser, National Council of Kenya, Displaced People's Programme, Eldoret, 25/11/97.

6.   Ibid.

7.   Section 85 of the Kenya constitution gives the president the power to invoke part III of the 'Preservation of the Public Security Act' by an order published in the Kenya Gazette. The specific part of the Act allows the president to regulate, restrict the movement of persons, censure the press and abridge the freedom of assembly in the affected area(s). In all cases, the government did not publish the order in the Gazette before imposing it. It was also selectively applied in those areas where stakes were high and utterly ignored where continued violence favored the government's electoral agenda.

8.   A detailed exposition of the evolution of the KANU youth group is given by the Human Rights Watch, *Taking Liberties*, New York: Human Rights Watch, July, 1991.

9.   Interview with Joseph Mutua, field researcher with the Kenya Human Rights Commission's Violence Monitoring Group, 16/01/98.

10. The Mijikenda literally means nine houses. It refers to the nine Bantu ethnic groups that inhabit the coast, namely, the Chonyi, Digo, Duruma, Giriama, Jibana, Kambe, Kauma, Rabai and Ribe. The violence at the coast occurred in Kwale that is dominantly Digo. Besides the fact that the warriors were recruited from among the Digo youths, it was also the Digo population that bore the brunt of police reprisals.

11. These included President Moi's principal adviser and then minister for Home Affairs, Nicholas Biwott, Rashid Sajjad – both of whom were named in parliament in connection with the violence – and Karisa Maitha, Suleiman Shakombo and Omar Masumbuko.

12. President Daniel Moi's interview with Bernard Nderitu appeared in the *Sunday Nation* of 28/12/97.

13. KANU's determination to vanquish the IPK was illustrated by its treatment of the fiery Islamic preacher Sheikh Khalid Balala, a founder member of the party. Balala was arbitrarily stripped of his citizenship and prevented from entering Kenya, although his parents and children, all bona fide Kenyan citizens, were in Kenya. The government insisted that he was an Yemeni Arab while the Yemeni government denied this. By the time the government restored Balala's citizenship and allowed him to come back to the country in late 1997, he was already disenfranchised since registration was long past and, by law, he was not eligible for election to any position. Moreover, long absence had weakened his influence in the IPK.

14. Interview with Athanasius Muga, Chair (Bishop) Mombasa Baptist Association, 23/12/97.

15. interview with Agnes Mailu, in charge of the Displaced Persons in the Catholic Secretariat, Mombasa, 22/12/97.

16. Interview with Pastor Earnest Ombava, in charge of refugees in the Baptist High School, 23/12/97.

17. Kenya Human Rights Commission, *Quarterly Repression Report, July-September, 1997.* The Catholic Church, however, took the threat seriously and resettled the refugees on a temporary basis in privately rented housing for two months. By 22 November 1997, 600 families had been resettled through this humanitarian effort to salvage the right to vote.
18. Interview with Bishop Athanasius Muga, 23/12/97.
19. Ibid.

References

African Rights 1997, 'Violence at the Coast: The Human Consequences of Kenya's Crumbling Political Institutions', *Witness* No.2, October-November 1997.

Article 19, 1997, *Deadly Marionettes: State-Sponsored Violence in Africa*, London: Article 19.

Commonwealth Secretariat 1993, *The Presidential, Parliamentary and Civic Elections in Kenya: The Report of the Commonwealth Observer Group, December 29, 1992.* London: Commonwealth Secretariat.

ECK 1999, *1997 General Election Report*, Nairobi: Electoral Commission of Kenya.

Government of Kenya/UNDP 1993, *Program for Displaced Persons, Inter-Agency Joint Programming.*

Hine, K.D. 1998 'Vigilantism Revisited: An Economic Analysis of the Law of Extra-Judicial Self-Help or Why Can't Dick Shoot Henry for Stealing Jane's Truck,' *The American University Law Review*, Vol.47, No.5, June 1998: 1221-53.

Human Rights Watch, 1998, *Kenya: World Report 1998*, New York: Human Rights Watch.

Human Rights Watch/Africa Watch 1993, *Divide and Rule: State-Sponsored Ethnic Violence in Kenya,* New York: Human Rights Watch.

Human Rights Watch/Africa Watch 1995, *Playing the "Communal Card": Communal Violence and Human Rights*, New York: Human Rights Watch.

Human Rights Watch/Africa Watch 1995a, *Multi-party Betrayed in Kenya: Continuing Rural Violence and Restrictions on Freedom of Speech and Assembly,* New York: Human Rights Watch.

Human Rights Watch/Africa Watch 1997, *Failing the Displaced: The UNDP Displaced Person's Program in Kenya*, New York: Human Rights Watch.

KBC 1993, 'Opposition Ultimatum for Dismissal of Local Government Minister Rejected', Nairobi: Kenya Broadcasting Corporation.

Kenya National Council of NGOs 1995, *Deception, Dispersal and Abandonment: A Narrative Account on the Displacement of Kenyans from Enoosupukia and Maela Based upon Witness, Church/NGO and Media Accounts*, Nairobi: National Council of NGOs.

Kenya National Council of NGOs 1997, *Investigation Report on Violence Mombasa, Kwale and Kilifi Districts*, Nairobi: National Council of NGOs.

KHRC 1993, *The State of Human Rights in Kenya: A Year of Political Harassment*, Nairobi: Kenya Human Rights Commission.

KHRC 1997, *Kayas of Deprivation, Kayas of Blood: Violence, Ethnicity and the State in Coastal Kenya*, Nairobi: Kenya Human Rights Commission.

KHRC 1997a, *Quarterly Repression Report, July-September 1997*, Nairobi: Kenya Human Rights Commission.

KHRC 1998, *Killing the Vote, State-Sponsored Violence and the Flawed Elections in Kenya*, Nairobi: Kenya Human Rights Commission.

KHRC 1998a, *Kayas Revisited*, Nairobi: Kenya Human Rights Commission.

Ndegwa, S.N. 1998, 'The Incomplete Transition: The Constitutional and Electoral Context in Kenya', *Africa Today*, Vol.45, No.2: 193-211.

NEMU 1993, *The Multi-party General Elections in Kenya December 29, 1992*, Nairobi: National Election Monitoring Unit (NEMU).

NEMU 1993a, *Courting Disaster: A Report on the Continuing Terror, Violence and Destruction in the Rift Valley, Nyanza and Western Kenya*, Nairobi: National Election Monitoring Unit (NEMU).

Southall, R. 1998, 'Moi's Flawed Mandate: The Crisis Continues in Kenya', *Review of African Political Economy*, 75 (1998): 101-11.

Throup, D. and Hornsby, C. 1998, *Multi-party Politics in Kenya. The Kenyatta & Moi States & the Triumph of the System in the 1992 Election*, Oxford: James Currey.

PART 2

THE NATIONAL PROCESS

5

As Biased as Ever?
The Electoral Commission's Performance
Prior to Polling Day

Francis Ang'ila Aywa, François Grignon

A sound and fair assessment of the performance of the Electoral Commission of Kenya (ECK) prior to the 1997 polls is not an easy task.[1] Never, since its creation after independence and the return to multi-party politics, has the ECK benefited from a reputation of competence and impartiality, two of the very important characteristics that such institutions need to acquire to operate outside the political debate. To many, the ECK is just like the General Service Unit or the provincial administration, one of the executive's arms, participating in the political schemes aimed at salvaging Daniel arap Moi's regime. Indeed, up to the 1997 polls, the credibility and legitimacy of the ECK to organise free and fair elections, could not be established. The 1992 commission was solely composed of President Moi's appointees. Its chair, Justice Richard Zachaeus Chesoni, carried with him a dubious reputation. Moreover, in 1996, just before starting the constituency review process, four of the commissioners whose mandate had expired – they last five years – were not re-appointed, and among them was commissioner Habel Nyamu, who was known for his criticism of the chair's dictatorial and pro-KANU stands.

By September 1996, as the electoral process was getting into its first steps, the ECK seemed, therefore, even less independent from the government than it had been in 1992 and lacked both the credibility and the legitimacy to organise a free and fair contest. Moreover, there is no evidence that the changes made in the composition of the ECK following the minimal constitutional review package voted in November 1997 after the Inter-Parties Parliamentary Group (IPPG) negotiations, reduced the politicisation of the electoral administration. The expansion of the ECK to 22 commissioners including ten new ones representing the views of the opposition is not necessarily a sign of its increased independence.

It is first an implicit acknowledgement that the chair, the vice-chair and the first ten commissioners had been all this time working for KANU. Second, there is a strong probability that the ten new commissioners proposed by the opposition parties would attempt to favour their own party throughout the remaining stages of the electoral process. Neither of these scenarios leads to the assumption that the ECK became more independent after the implementation of the IPPG reforms. The primary objective of an electoral administration must be to deliver free and fair election services to the electorate. As such, it must undertake its functions in an impartial and efficient manner. It must ensure that the integrity of the electoral process is adequately safeguarded from incompetent election officials and fraudulent manipulations. Its most important attributes, therefore, should be:

(a) independence and impartiality
(b) efficiency
(c) professionalism
(d) impartial and speedy adjudication of disputes
(e) stability
(f) transparency.

In reality, there is often a very thin line between political scheming, lack of administrative capacity and sheer incompetence. As any other under-funded Kenyan administration, the ECK is desperately in need of well-trained and motivated personnel, modern equipment and basic institutional capacity. Its employees are as prone to corruption as any other members of the civil service, from the central Nairobi office to the constituency or polling station level, where its clerks and agents are often under various pressures from politicians and their supporters, whether in KANU or in opposition dominated areas. Some of the ECK failures could, therefore, reasonably be attributed to pure administrative incapacity and have nothing to do with any 'grand plan' to rig the opposition out or even the president (!), as he himself claimed after one day of electoral chaos.

In this chapter, our efforts must also be oriented towards giving the ECK the benefit of doubt, despite its dismal performance in 1992 and the renewal of a leadership totally unfit for the job. There are enough conspiracy theories circulating in Kenya and we would not want to add any to the flow. The different activities of the ECK need to be closely scrutinised in order to determine whether it contributed to a grand rigging scheme, as was sometimes argued by the opposition. Yet, there is no doubt that the liabilities carried by the ECK in the rigging of the 1992 contest are very heavy.

As pointed by David Throup and Charles Hornsby, two major factors dramatically impaired the credibility of the ECK in 1992. First, there was no precise definition of its duties and responsibilities. The commission restricted its role to the technical aspects of the electoral process, it always denied being a guarantor of its fairness, and it rejected the duty of regulating political competition. A vacuum was, therefore, conveniently left open on such crucial issues as the control of the media and the use of violence during political campaigning, giving total leverage to the ruling party and the provincial administrations for all sorts of abuses. The Election Laws Amendment Act No.1 of 1992 had given back to the ECK the responsibilities transferred to the director of elections at the end of the 1960s, but the new legal provisions were vague and they were not immediately fully implemented. The new section 42.A of the constitution provided that 'The Electoral Commission shall be responsible for:

(a)   the registration of voters and the maintenance and revision of the register of voters;

(b)   directing and supervising the Presidential, National Assembly and Local Government elections, and

(c)   such other functions as maybe prescribed by law.'

The new positions of director and deputy director of elections were created within the commission, but the late Justice Richard Chesoni appointed these officials just one month before election day. Moreover, in addition to his personal lack of credibility linked to past financial misdeeds that had him declared bankrupt and barred from the judiciary, his high-handedness over all the electoral processes as well as his secretive and authoritarian behaviour became a genuine problem. It was criticised as much by opposition parties and foreign diplomats as from within the commission itself. Disputes over the accomplishment of their respective duties regularly erupted between the chair and some of the eight other commissioners in charge of supervising the electoral process in the provinces of the country. Justice Chesoni's behaviour became, therefore, highly detrimental to the credibility of an institution that, moreover, never evinced any attempt to seek independence from the executive. On the contrary, the strategic collusion between the Attorney-General and the ECK to call for early elections on 7 December and take the opposition by surprise, giving them less than one month to campaign after nomination day, which had been scheduled for 11 November, was a genuine proof of its allegiance to the regime (Throup and Hornsby 1998: 245-8). The plot was defeated as the opposition obtained from the High Court an injunction barring the ECK from proceeding with the elections before their case against the AG's change of the electoral rules could be heard, but proof had been given that anything could be expected from Chesoni and his team.[2] Their liability in favouring the ruling party through the manipulation of the registration exercise was also very heavy.

In 1992, the registration exercise had been probably the worst attempt at blatant manipulation ever experienced in Kenyan electoral history, even worse than the 1988 queue counting exercise where the results were announced by the returning officers regardless of the actual length of the queues of voters. In total 7.95 million Kenyans were registered out of an estimated 11 million voters, a figure barely higher than for the 1983 contest, almost ten years earlier!

The Office of the President, by refusing or delaying the issuance of ID cards to young voters who had turned 18 in the previous few months or years preceding the registration exercise, contributed a lot to this disenfranchisement. The National Assembly & Presidential Elections Act (Chapter 7 of the Laws of Kenya) provides that a citizen has to show proof of having reached the age of majority by showing a national identity card to be registered (section 4). The Presidential and Parliamentary Elections Regulations also required the production of an ID card before issuance of a ballot paper to the voter[3]: no ID, no chance to vote.

But the Office of the President was not the only one to blame for the disenfranchisement of voters. Evidence of clerks deliberately making incorrect entries and, therefore, invalidating future attempts to vote were collected throughout the country, and especially in areas where the fight between KANU and the opposition was thought to be very close. Transporting voters from one constituency to another and their valid registration even though they would not qualify (through residence, ownership of land or work), double registration, and change of registration figures after the event, were some of the other irregularities which were also heavily documented by the international and local observers (NEMU 1993: 45-7; Throup and Hornsby 1998: 257-64). Finally, the employment of easily bullied civil servants from all quarters of the para-public administration as returning and presiding officers with the duty to supervise the voting and vote counting was the ultimate push given by the ECK to the ruling party prior to polling day. Indeed, in 1992, everything had been prepared to guarantee that President Moi and KANU would get a smooth ride despite the general hostility of the great majority of the electorate.

When the same ECK team, which had presided over more than 25 by-elections from 1993 to 1996 without correcting the anomalies contained in its books, announced in September 1996 that it would review some boundaries and create 22 new constituencies, the fear that a scenario similar to the 1992 experience was being prepared seemed realistic and genuine. Our objective is, therefore, to assess whether or not the ECK unfairly contributed to President Moi and KANU's disputed victory, and if it did, how this happened. The three stages of its preparation of the 1997 contest will, therefore, be considered here: constituency creation and border modifications; registration of voters; nomination of candidates and preparation of the polls.

Constituency creation and gerrymandering

Elections in Kenya, which has a first-past-the-post electoral system, are won and lost by a simple majority, regardless of the number of registered voters in a constituency who turn out on polling day to cast their ballots. It is the least complicated system. Individual candidates are nominated and voters invited to place a mark against one name on the ballot paper. The candidate who gets the most votes is the winner even if he or she obtains less than 50 per cent of the total valid votes. The delineation of electoral areas is, therefore, one of the most sensitive and politically controversial issues in the electoral process. In Kenya, this is even more so owing to the potentially conflictual nature of the existing boundaries and the ethnic distributions they underline.

The demarcation of constituencies in Kenya was first done in 1962 immediately before independence when the then Regional Boundaries Commission divided Kenya into 8 provinces and 41 districts. At independence, Kenya had a bicameral legislature. There were 113 seats in the House of Representatives and 38 in the Senate. By the time the 1969 elections were held, Kenya had reverted to a single chamber parliament with 158 seats, created in 1966 (Preparative Review No.2 Order 1966 of 19 December, Legal Notice No.344). This remained in place until 1987 when the number of seats was increased to a minimum of 188 and a maximum of 210 (Kenya Parliamentary Constituencies Review Order, 1987 of 11 November 1987, Legal Notice No.309). In 1992, there were 188 seats which were increased to the constitutional maximum of 210 in 1996 (Kenya Parliamentary Constituencies Review Order 1986 of 23 September 1996, Legal Notice No.298 and amended by Legal Notice No.320 of 1996). The constitution also states that all constituencies shall contain as nearly an equal number of inhabitants as appears reasonable. This has proved to be the source of controversies that have surrounded constituency making over the years. There have been claims that the practice seriously deviated from the laid down criteria.

The constitution (section 42(1)) states that the electoral commission may divide Kenya into such number of constituencies having such boundaries and names as it may prescribe. In subsection (2), however, it provides that parliament may prescribe the minimum number of constituencies into which Kenya shall be divided. It goes further to set a minimum of 188 and a maximum of 210. To the extent that both provisions appear to bestow the same power in different – and potentially conflicting – bodies, it has been accepted that the intention of parliament was to reserve the ultimate power of determining the numbers to itself. After all – at least in theory – if the electoral commission went ahead to determine its own number, parliament (as the watchdog of public expenditure) could refuse to approve the salaries of the extra MPs elected to the extra constituencies.

More importantly though, the constitution states that all constituencies should contain 'as nearly equal numbers of inhabitants as appears to the Electoral Commission to be reasonably practicable'. It then allows the commission to depart from this principle to the extent that it considers expedient in order to take account of the following:

(a) population density, in particular, the need to ensure adequate representation of urban and sparsely-populated rural areas;
(b) population trends;
(c) means of communication;
(d) geographical features;
(e) community of interest; and
(g) boundaries of existing administrative areas

The concern of the constitution here is the principle of equality of citizenship – or one person, one vote. This means, therefore, that the cardinal consideration in the creation of a constituency is the number of inhabitants as determined by the prevailing population of eligible voters. However, there are two problems here. First, exceptions are quite broad so that the interpretation of how to apply the underlying factors is equally broad. In any event, there has been no consistency in the practice so that in certain areas, the purpose at hand was gerrymandering[4]. Moreover, in every election since 1963, the members of Kenya's smallest, poorest and most geographically dispersed ethnic communities have been systematically over-represented by allocating more parliamentary constituencies to them than to Kenya's larger and wealthier groups (Fox 1997; Throup and Hornsby 1998; Barkan and Ngethe 1998). A situation has emerged in Kenya where the remote and underdeveloped areas are the ones ruling the country (by virtue of their electoral might). As one commentator put it, this is akin to 'the most advanced parts of the US being ruled from the Nevada deserts and not the Iowa cornfields. Or in UK terms, the wealth creating area of the British heartland are in perpetual political slavery to political bosses from the remote Welsh valleys' (K. Wales in a letter to the Editor, *Daily Nation* 04/01/98).

As a result of the distribution of voters and seats, it has been possible for a political group with a minority of the vote, concentrated in semi-arid areas, to win a majority of the National Assembly. The disparity became even more apparent (and significant) with the advent of multi-party politics because the average size of a secure KANU constituency was only 28,350 voters while seats in the opposition areas were on average 80 per cent larger with 52,169 voters. In 1992, as in 1997, the discrepancy in parliamentary constituency sizes destroyed the opposition's chances of converting a numerical majority among the urban population and sedentary cultivators into coterminous majority parliamentary seats.

Removing the cobwebs: the nexus between the creation of districts and constituencies in Kenya

Kenya is administratively divided into eight provinces: Nairobi, Rift Valley, Coast, Nyanza, Western, Central, Eastern and North-Eastern. These are further divided into districts. Each district has divisions, which are in turn divided into locations and sub-locations. But it is the districts that have attracted a lot of attention as far as the country's politics is concerned. In theory, the process of drawing district boundaries is bureaucratically distinct and separate from that of drawing constituency boundaries.

First, there are no express criteria in law to guide the creation of districts. Secondly, they are the preserve (at least before the courts decide otherwise) of the executive branch of government, with all the political considerations that this engenders. It can, therefore, be argued that there is no connection between the creation of districts and the creation of constituencies. Yet, the constitution allows for consideration of 'the boundaries of the administrative areas' as a factor to be taken into account for constituency creation. Moreover, in practice, there has been a tendency, since independence, to make divisional and constituency boundaries coincide. This eased the delivery of development projects to constituents of members of the government. Consequently, the administrative factor has often been given priority to create new constituencies and more recently to generate extra seats in pro-KANU areas which had just been awarded a new district or a new administrative division. This is the background against which we should view some of the recent single constituency districts like Mt Elgon, Kuria, Trans Mara, Suba or some others like Mwingi, which were allocated a second constituency on the grounds of discrepancy between administrative and electoral demarcations (2 divisions versus 1 constituency).

Between the 1992 elections and the time the commission started reviewing constituencies for purposes of the 1997 general elections, there was a frenzy in creating new districts that left many suspicious of what was afoot (*Sunday Standard* 21/04/96). From 41 districts that went to the polls in 1992, the country was suddenly talking of over 15 new districts created hurriedly in a fashion that left easy guesses as to the intentions. Where population density has often been thought to be the key indicator as to which new areas would need new administrative units, the new districts did not seem to conform much to this logic. Looked at from an economic point of view, the rush to create new districts at a time when economic growth barely matched population increase defied common sense. The financial costs involved in the creation of new districts are immense. It includes not only the costs of putting up office blocks – *wananchi* have to, besides paying tax, also raise money through harambees for these 'developments' – but also salaries for the extra staff to work in the new district, electricity, telephones, etc. In the 1996 budget speech, for example, the minister for Finance revealed that the government would spend Ksh. 97 million to build six new district headquarters for Makueni, Trans Nzoia, Uasin Gishu, Nandi and Vihiga. Lower administrative units were not included. The speed at which new districts have been created makes it difficult to keep count, nearly 30 over the last 10 years! (*Sunday Nation* 07/04/96). In early 1998 an official list from the Office of the President had the number at 67.

Initially, the creation of new districts, achieved by hiving off parts of existing districts like in the case of Kisii, Kakamega, Machakos, South Nyanza, Meru and Kericho, appeared motivated by rational decisions meant to ease the administrative burden in populous and unwieldy districts. But subsequent creations have prompted what Kenyans are seeing as a crudely political balkanisation that fits snugly with KANU's agenda for promoting certain political interests. It is out of the newer districts (Kuria, Mt Elgon, Migori, Nyambene, Mwingi, Marakwet, Trans Mara, etc.) that a political agenda is most discernible. Trans Mara, Suba, Mt Elgon, and Kuria districts, for example, were created as the first districts in the country to comprise single parliamentary constituencies and their inauguration as districts came amid clearly political and ethnic moves designed to benefit the ruling party. The mere creation of new districts – be it in Marakwet, Trans Mara or Suba – is not in itself supposed to have any bearing on the matter of constituency review. The reality, however, is different.

The case of Mt Elgon merits elaboration here. It was formerly a division of Bungoma district whose dominant community, the Bukusu, voted solidly for the opposition in 1992. Mt Elgon also happens to be inhabited by the Sabaot, a sub-group of the Kalenjin community that solidly backed KANU and was the only one of the five constituencies in Bungoma district to elect a KANU MP both in 1992 and 1997. The same calculations apply to Kuria. In fact, it was rumoured that Kisii, together with Kuria and Basuba, may be hived from Nyanza into an entirely new pro-KANU province which would give President Moi another chance to reach 25 per cent of the votes in five provinces of the country. As a result, we now have a situation where whole districts like Mt Elgon, Kuria, or Suba are represented by one parliamentarian, almost an absurdity. What is generally believed is that the new districts were created, first and foremost, to push the ECK to fix things to suit KANU.

On 25 September 1996, the ECK announced the creation of 22 new constituencies bringing the total to the constitutional maximum of 210. Out of these, Rift Valley got 5; Western 4; Central 4; Eastern 4, Nyanza 3; Coast 1; North-Eastern 1. Nairobi got none. The new constituencies were Bura,Wajir North, Tigania East, Manyatta, Mwingi South, Kaiti, Ol Kalou, Kerugoya/ Kutus, Mathioya, Gatundu North, Emgwen, Eldama Ravine, Kuresoi, Sotik, Ainamoi, Matungu, Khwisero, Bumula, Butula, Kisumu Town East, Uriri and Gwasi. The commission further recommended to parliament to legislate for a further review that would create an additional 48 constituencies to raise the total to 258 constituencies. The reason why certain provinces, like Nairobi, got no new constituency was not explained. Most of the constituencies in Nairobi, when compared to constituencies in the Rift Valley, for example, are apt candidates for splitting. Similarly, the basis for the creation of a constituency like Mathioya in Central Province was thought to be mainly political. It was said to consist of areas in Kangema that had traditionally voted for Joseph Kamotho, KANU's secretary general, and by extension KANU.

Balancing the criteria for constituency creation

The ECK and others in government defend the variation in constituency size on the ground that there is wide variation in Kenya's population density. Some constituencies, while geographically large, are so sparsely populated that their population is still below average. This is how it should be, according to some. Constituency size must take into account ease (or difficulty) of representation as well as equality of representation. Constituencies should be kept to a reasonable geographical size – no matter how small the population – so that the members of parliament can visit all areas within the constituency without undue difficulty. Constituencies in North-Eastern Province with small populations are defended on this ground. With regard to Nairobi, the argument goes that constituencies here are relatively 'easy' to represent owing to their small geographical size. Thus, their large population size is legitimate. Others even argue that only one MP rather than its current eight should represent Nairobi.

Clearly the creation of 22 new constituencies was not oriented towards enforcing the principle of equality of representation between voters. The extreme variance in the population sizes violates the Kenyan constitution's first principle of determining constituency boundaries. This variance has significant political ramifications as well, given the current political/partisan map of Kenya, in which there is a strong correlation between region and party affiliation. There is also a correlation between over-representation (or under-representation) and a region's voting behaviour. For example, the relatively over-represented provinces of Coast and North-Eastern voted overwhelmingly for KANU in 1992 and again in 1997. The under-represented provinces of Nairobi, Central and Nyanza cast a majority of their votes for opposition political parties.

Table 5.1: Location and political affiliation of 22 alternative new constituencies chosen on the basis of population density only

No.	Constituency	District	Pol. affiliation	Reg. voters (1992)
1	Mathare	Nairobi	Opposition	116,630
2	Molo	Nakuru	Opposition	111,679
3	Nakuru Town	Nakuru	Opposition	105,729
4	Lang'ata	Nairobi	Opposition	102,840
5	Embakasi	Nairobi	Opposition	91,688
6	Nakuru East	Nakuru	Opposition	85,101
7	Eldoret North	Uasin Gishu	KANU	84,738
8	Starehe	Nairobi	Opposition	84,180
9	Kisauni	Mombasa	Opposition	78,590
10	Mvita	Mombasa	KANU	75,731
11	Kamukunji	Nairobi	Opposition	74,466
12	Juja	Kiambu	Opposition	74,408
13	Runyenjes	Embu	Opposition	73,639
14	Kipkelion	Kericho	KANU	73,258
15	Dagoretti	Nairobi	Opposition	70,654
16	Kanduyi	Bungoma	Opposition	69,931
17	Gatundu	Kiambu	Opposition	69,908
18	North Imenti	Meru	Opposition	68,596
19	Kiharu	Murang'a	Opposition	68,272
20	Nithi	Tharaka/Nithi	Opposition	67,411
21	Ndia	Kirinyaga	Opposition	65,399
22	Belgut	Kericho	KANU	65,230

If the population criteria had been the only one taken into account to create the 22 new constituencies, the distribution would have been largely a compensation of the urban/rural imbalance in the political representation of the country, giving a total of ten seats to urban areas: five extra seats to Nairobi, two to Nakuru, two to Mombasa, and one to Eldoret. But since highly densely populated areas were also mostly supporters of the opposition in 1992, it's not difficult to figure out why such a split, based on population density alone, did not happen. It would most probably have given 18 seats to the opposition and only four to the ruling party (see Table 5.1).

On the other hand, using the population criteria only, we can say that seven of the 22 newly created constituencies had indeed to be created. They were carved out of some of the 22 most populated constituencies of the country and their creation is totally legitimate. These are Tigania East (from Tigania and North Imenti), Manyatta (from Runyenjes), Kuresoi (from Molo and

Nakuru Town), Ainamoi (from Kipkelion and Belgut), Bumula (from Kanduyi), Gatundu North (from Gatundu), and Kerugoya/Kutus (from Ndia). This does not necessarily nullify the political considerations behind their creation. There is a high probability that three of theses constituencies were indeed created because they were thought to become KANU seats thanks to the combination of pro-KANU areas within their boundaries (Tigania East, Kuresoi), or because of the personality of the KANU candidate (Uhuru Kenyatta in Gatundu South). But at least these seven constituencies had legitimate population grounds to be created.

Yet, population size is not necessarily the only factor leading to the creation of a constituency. The Electoral Commission of Kenya can indeed argue that other considerations, such as the size of the constituency and the need to represent small communities, need to be taken into account. This could lead, therefore, to the creation of constituencies less populated than the national average, with a legitimate variation compared to the average national size. In 1997, the average number of registered electors for a constituency was 42,994. If we apply a variation of 50 per cent to this figure, aiming at ensuring fair representation of sparsely populated areas peopled with pastoral communities, all Kenyan constituencies should have between 60,000 and 21,500 voters. Most existing constituencies from Maasai, Samburu, Pokot, Tugen and Turkana districts easily fit into this bracket. Regarding our fifteen remaining new constituencies, thirteen qualify in this respect. But, there is no question that the creation of Bura (15,300 registered voters) and Wajir North (7,631 registered voters) were totally unjustified. These two creations were only geared to give KANU two easy extra seats.

Finally, if the thirteen remaining constituencies definitely qualified under the balanced population criteria that we have proposed, many others did too. We are bound to wonder why they were created in the specific areas where it happened and whether these creations served or did not a specific political purpose. Prior to the creation of new constituencies, the Electoral Commission usually tours the country to receive the opinions of interested parties. In 1996, this process took place between September and December, when the ECK received the memoranda and recommendations from politicians of all parties, NGOs, individuals and from each district development committee (DDC). Run by the district commissioner, the DDC usually centralises the information on the development needs of the area under its jurisdiction and recommends the different departments of the central administration to channel the proper investments through appropriate planification. Why were the thirteen last constituencies created in the areas they were and not somewhere else? Definitely one reason is the creation of new districts in electoral areas targeted by KANU.

Before the review started, President Moi had not only announced that there would be a review – something that necessarily brought him out as influencing the process – but he also went round the country announcing the creation of new districts. Soon thereafter, Justice Chesoni said he did not think that the newly created districts of Suba, Teso, Mt Elgon, and Mbeere would automatically get new constituencies. Yet, they did. To counteract this abuse of power, Raila Odinga of NDP (then in FORD-Kenya) filed a suit in the High Court seeking to bar further creation of districts and the nullification of prior districts established by the president. He argued that only parliament had such powers. The lawsuit was later withdrawn and the president continued announcing the creation of these districts even after the creation of the new constituencies. In all, 24 new districts were created. It was very difficult, therefore, for the commission to defend itself against accusations of allegiance to the executive. Of the 22 constituencies, 8 are in the new districts: Tigania East (Nyambene), Mwingi South (Mwingi), Kaiti (Makueni), Gwasi (Suba), Uriri (Migori), Eldama Ravine (Koibatek), Gatundu North (Thika) (See Table 5.2).

If, as we have seen, the creation of Gatundu and Tigania East were based on genuine population grounds, there is no reason to believe that six others were not for political reasons, i.e. the will of President Moi to reward some of his supporters before the elections by the creation of a new district or to attempt the capture of an opposition area's weak position. In this respect, the creation of Mwingi South was due to the lobbying of the minister for Foreign Affairs, Kalonzo Musyoka, and Kaiti was destined to a long time aide of Nicholas Biwott, Gideon Ndambuki (see Chapter 12 in this volume). Gwasi was an attempt to seduce the minority Suba in the opposition stronghold of Nyanza, and Uriri, where a strong minority of Luyha workers settled, could have helped KANU capture a second seat in Luo Nyanza (NCCK 1996). As for Eldama Ravine, carved out of Baringo South, it was a very safe KANU seat offered to Musa Sirma, brother to the coast provincial commissioner. Out of the remaining eleven new constituencies which satisfy the population criteria, eight seem indeed to have been created without any direct political intentions: these are Kerugoya/Kutus, Ol Kalou, Matungu, Bumula, Butula, Ainamoi, Emgwen and Kisumu Town East. Four went to the opposition and four went to KANU.

The other three, although not linked to the creation of any districts are obvious products of KANU's scheming. Khwisero was created to weaken and capture a seat from Martin Shikuku's stronghold of Butere; Mathioya is the brainchild of Joseph Kamotho, fearing to be once again defeated by his long time opponent John Michuki; and Kuresoi, which was carved out of the opposition strongholds of Molo and Nakuru Town, is largely populated by the clients of hawkish Minister Kipkalya Kones, who bought the 200 acre

Sirikwa ADC farm and settled a number of Kipsigis families around it in the locations of Likia, Sululu and Teret (NCCK 1996:8). The creation of 22 new constituencies was not, therefore, as politically neutral as the ECK or even the election results might imply.

Indeed, it is arguable that because the election results in the newly created constituencies did not show any clear benefit for KANU, the exercise was acceptable. Of the 22 new constituencies, 13 were won by KANU and 9 by the opposition. This was a politically very significant gain, as these new constituencies alone arguably gave KANU their majority in parliament. Yet, in absolute terms, this was not a striking advantage given to the ruling party, which roughly shared the new seats with the opposition. Moreover, the effect of the creation of the new constituencies on the neighbouring constituencies remains equally mitigated. In some cases, a constituency was simply split (e.g., Gatundu in Gatundu South and North), in others, two or three constituencies were redrawn to become three or four respectively (e.g., Mosop, Aldai, Tinderet were changed in Mosop, Aldai, Tinderet and Emgwen), which means that some locations might have been redistributed in order to protect a KANU seat from any opposition threat.

The creation of a new constituency won by the opposition might also save a seat in the 'old' constituency that might otherwise have been lost altogether. Thus, the hiving out of opposition areas might protect the original seat for KANU (e.g. Wajir West). Yet, in 35 of the constituencies which were modified through new creations for the 1997 contest, KANU, which had won 18 in 1992, won only 16 in 1997 (see Table 5.2). Therefore, the creation of the 22 new constituencies does not seem to have given a significant advantage to KANU over its competitor in the neighbouring 35 constituencies. Similarly, out of the other 29 constituencies which had their boundaries modified after the constituency review process without leading to any new creation[5], KANU, which had won 17 of them in 1992, won only 14 back in 1997.

Table 5.2: Origin and political effect of the creation of 22 new constituencies

New Constituency (Distr.) Reg. voters, 1997 winner	Constituencies of origin (1992)	Parliam. 1992	Parliam. 1997
Bura (Tana River)	Galole	KANU	KANU
15,300, KANU	Garsen	KANU	KANU
Tigania East (Nyambene)	Tigania (Tigania West)	DP	DP
35,679, KANU	North Imenti	DP	DP
Manyatta (Embu)	Runyenjes	DP	FORD-A
52,542, DP			
Mwingi South (Mwingi)	Kitui North (Mwingi N.)	KANU	KANU
43,836, KANU	Mutito	KANU	SDP
Kaiti (Makueni)	Machakos Town	KANU	SDP
34,569, KANU	Kilome	KANU	KANU
Wajir North (Wajir)	Wajir East	KANU	KANU
7,631, KANU	Wajir West	KANU	Safina
Kisumu Town East (Kisumu)	Kisimu Town (Kisumu Town West)	FORD-K	NDP
36,810, NDP			
Gwasi (Suba)	Mbita	FORD-K	NDP
23,662, NDP			
Uriri (Migori)	Migori	FORD-K	NDP
28,683, NDP			
Emgwen (Nandi)	Mosop	KANU	KANU
50,040, KANU	Aldai	KANU	KANU
	Tinderet	KANU	KANU
Eldama Ravine (Koibatek)	Baringo South (Mogotio)	KANU	KANU
31,181, KANU			
Kuresoi (Nakuru)	Molo	FORD-A	DP
54,819, KANU	Nakuru Town	FORD-A	DP
Ainamoi (Kericho)	Kipkelion	KANU	KANU
53,900, KANU	Belgut	KANU	KANU
Sotik (Bomet)	Chepalungu	KANU	KANU
44,128, KANU	Bomet	KANU	KANU
Butula (Busia)	Nambale	KANU	KANU
28,598, KANU			
Bumula (Bungoma)	Kanduyi	FORD-K	FORD-K
39,820, FORD-Kenya			
Matungu (Kakamega)	Mumias	KANU	KANU
33,657, KANU			

Table 5.2 continued

Khwisero (Kakamega) 27,534, KANU	Butere	FORD-A	KANU
Ol Kalou (Nyandarua) 48,589, DP	Ndaragwa	DP	DP
	Kipipiri	FORD-A	DP
Mathioya (Murang'a) 26,747, FORD-P	Kangema	FORD-A	FORD-P
Gatundu South 43,209, SDP	(Gatundu N.)*	FORD-A	SDP
Kerugoya/Kutus (Kirinyaga) 43,595, DP	Ndia	DP	DP
Total: 22 KANU: 13 DP: 3 FORD-K: 1 SDP: 1 NDP: 3 FORD-K: 1	Total: 35	KANU: 18 DP: 5 FORD-A: 8 FORD-K: 4	KANU: 16 DP: 8 FORD-A: 1 FORD-P: 1 FORD-P: 1 SDP: 4 NDP: 3 Safina: 1

* Gatundu North was officially earmarked as the new constituency but the polictical effect was to come from Gatundu South

Do these results contradict our prior evaluation on the political schemes attached to the 22 new constituency creations? The analyst cannot seriously base his assessment of the ECK's work on the results of the elections *a-posteriori*. Indeed, there would be a fundamental methodological flaw in doing so. It would be neglecting all the other factors which balance the outcome of an electoral contest, i.e. the candidates failure to present their nomination papers, their inability to campaign because of financial problems, the wrong assumptions and calculations of the political schemers or, of course, the volatility of the Kenyan electorate who usually like to contradict the most secure predictions. Uhuru Kenyatta knows it well.

Our aim here is to understand whether the electoral commission fulfilled its duty towards Kenyans not to favour any of the parties before the polls and to organise a contest that would guarantee the principle of equal representation for all. Regarding constituency creation, our assessment shows clearly that it failed. At least 12 of the new constituencies (Mwingi, Kaiti, Kuresoi, Eldama Ravine, Gwasi, Uriri, Gatundu North, Mathioya, Khwisero, Sotik, Bura and Wajir North) were created with clear political intentions to increase the number of the ruling party's representation chances in parliament and, moreover, their creation did not counterbalance the existing situation of unequal representation in the country, contrary to the principles expressed in the constitution.

Voter registration in 1997

The voter registration exercise organised by the ECK from 19 May to 20 June 1997 (later extended to 30 June) offered as many grounds for controversy as the process of creating new constituencies. As can be expected, the opposition feared greatly that the same scenario as 1992 was going to be repeated and that, through the manipulation of election registers, they would be rigged out, six months before the polls. Scathing attacks were, therefore, systematically made against the ECK at every opportunity. Yet, the reports issued by local and international observers give generally a non-alarmist overview of the voter registration process. Correct, the period opened for registration, which was extended twice and had lasted in the end slightly less than six weeks, was still far shorter than the usual time given in the past exercises. In 1969, 1974, 1978 and 1983, the average period opened for voter registration lasted roughly three months. True also, the exercise was marred by serious administrative disorganisation. Maybe as a prelude to what was going to happen on polling day, the ECK gave a first clear testimony of its incapacity to perform. Registration centres often opened several days late, there was a constant shortage of forms in almost all areas, laminating machines used to produce the voting cards were too few and overused, so many broke down rapidly, etc.

Nevertheless, the blame for possible discrepancies or anomalies in registration figures does not have necessarily to be put on the electoral commission alone. The Office of the President, in charge of issuing ID cards to potential new voters, holds a powerful means to disenfranchise thousands of young Kenyans. Without an ID card, one cannot register. More than ever, sources and methodology are crucial to establish a firm and reasoned assessment of the ECK's work. We will, therefore, proceed by presenting the data collected in the press and from the international and local observers before counter-checking them by analysing the credibility of the figures themselves.

The registration process and the second-generation ID card saga, as reported in the press and surveyed by observers

The Institute for Education in Democracy conducted an extensive survey on the registration process through the interview of 30,000 respondents throughout the country, out of which 6,000 were randomly sampled for analysis (IED 1997). The conclusions of this survey are clearly in favour of the ECK. It states that 'over 90% of those who went to register as voters were actually registered'. This means more precisely that there was almost no disenfranchisement on the registration sites themselves. Nine out of ten of those who presented themselves to register actually did so although there were some districts and specific areas where lack of stationery, confusion along the new constituency boundaries, slowness of the process and the contestation of ID cards became problematic. But these problems were marginal compared to the overall success of the exercise. An overview of some press reports balances the good impression left by the IED survey. Indeed, the disorganisation, lack of training and mistakes made by the ECK staff amounted to a genuine risk of disenfranchisement for maybe 10 or 20 per cent of the electorate.

In early May, Justice Chesoni explained to the press how the registration would take place. The opening of 12,600 registration centres, compared to 6,000 in 1992, was given as a justification for the restrictive time frame. The opening of more than double the number of locations and recruitment of twice the staff was to guarantee the success of the 35 day-process. Moreover, the new computerised and centralised system of handling the registers would completely stop the problem of double registration, as a scan was to be applied on all entries, and similar numbers would, therefore, be automatically revealed. Unfortunately, the logistics did not match this ambition and no action was systematically taken against the culprits.

Right from the start, the organisers looked incompetent. In the evening of the opening day, the centres in Wajir district had to close down as they had received only 100 forms from the Nairobi (ECK) central office and no other till the beginning of June (*Daily Nation* 02/06/97). In most semi-arid areas of Eastern, North-Eastern and Coast provinces, lack of materials and transport for the officers endangered the take off of the whole exercise. Similar problems were equally felt in more accessible and densely populated areas such as Machakos, Vihiga, Hamisi, Nyandarua, Kisii, Gucha, Mt Elgon and Migori districts (*Daily Nation* 04/06/97; *East African Standard* 23/06/97 and 24/06/97). As late as 21 June, the issue of shortage of materials was again reported as very acute in Nyandarua and Lagdera (*East African Standard* 22/06/97).

The strongest outcry, though, came from Nyanza Province. More than 100,000 voters' cards were issued in the province after three weeks of registration with only four identification digits. The supervisors of the clerks had called them back in Tom Mboya Teachers' College in Kisumu after a few days of registration to tell their subordinates that the ten digit entries required would actually not fit on the small laminated cards and that they were, therefore, to enter only four digits. On 9 June, 12 opposition MPs from Nyanza demanded the nullification of the whole exercise and called for fresh voter registration. On 11 June, Nyanza ECK Commissioner Jura confronted the

MPs and assured them that only errors had taken place and that there was no conspiracy to disenfranchise the Luo community. He apologised to the Nyanza electorate and promised to replace the faulty cards. He also announced that all complaints would be examined by the commission on 20 June to assess the legitimacy of the grounds for an extension of the registration period (*Daily Nation* 12/06/97). Even after it had done so and one day before the first closing date of the registration process, on 21 June, James Orengo, nevertheless, filed a suit in the High Court on behalf of 26 other opposition and KANU MPs seeking the cancellation of the entire exercise. In addition to the issuance of faulty cards, he claimed that the forms used for registration were not the right ones and Nyanza had been hit by a dramatic shortage of materials (*East African Standard* 21/06/97).

Yet Nyanza was not an isolated case. In Mombasa, thousands of faulty cards had also been issued with missing digits. Yet, there, the ECK officials apologised quickly for their mistake and announced that they would replace all the faulty cards once returned. The registration process had been almost equally slow and muddled in the Rift Valley. In Bomet district, only 60,000 voters had registered out of the expected 200,000 by 2 June (*Daily Nation* 03/06/97). At the close of 15 June, reports indicated that security operations in Turkana and West Pokot districts had paralysed the registration of voters, and a number of centres had been abandoned. Jullu, Lorogon, Kaptir, Nakwamoru, Lorengipi, Kotaruk and Loye centres had been closed down while the inhabitants had to run away and escape the violence of cattle rustlers. By 18 June, West Pokot, Nandi and Uasin Gishu had only registered one third of their potential voters (*Daily Nation* 19/06/97). In Trans Mara, only 25,156 of the 60,000 expected voters had registered by the week before closure (*East African Standard* 22/06/97). In total, Rift Valley Province had registered only 1.4 million voters by 20 June, 700,000 short of what was expected (*Daily Nation* 21/06/97). President Moi himself raised the alarm on the issue of invalid electors' cards circulating in the country. He reported that a syndicate was producing such cards and that 5,000 fake cards were circulating in his Baringo Central constituency alone. However, after the joint investigation by the Criminal Investigation Department (CID) and the ECK, it was revealed that the suspicious cards were those the commission had declared invalid but had not destroyed (ECK 1999:53).

A number of genuine irregularities were also reported, confirming that localised attempts at rigging through transporting voters or registration of ineligible applicants were taking place in some constituencies. In the Londiani area of Molo, mischief was suspected against the Kikuyu voters as electors' cards had been issued with eight identification digits instead of ten and without apology from the local officials of the ECK (*Daily Nation* 03/06/97). On 6

June, *The People* opposition newspaper alleged that KANU was registering Ugandans in Kwanza division in order to tame the fiery FORD-Kenya MP, George Kapten. The Sabei people from Uganda, cousins of the Kenyan Sabaot, had been given ID cards and were registering in the border centres of Suai, Kaibai, Morlem and Testaboi. The Ugandans were promised land, jobs and business ventures and Sam Moiben, a KANU nominated MP, was accused of organising this rigging scheme. The same process was denounced in Budalanga'i of Busia district, but this time by a KANU candidate, James Osogo (*Daily Nation* 03/06/97). In Webuye, KANU officials equally condemned their branch secretary, John Sambu, for importing voters from neighbouring Lugari (*Daily Nation* 14/06/97). In Mathioya, suspicions were high that voters imported from Embakasi and Kangemi in Nairobi were registering with fake ID cards (*Daily Nation* 06/06/97). On the coast, the fear of illegal transport of voters was running high. In Kwale, vigilante youth groups were formed to prevent politicians from doing so. Two illegal voter registration centres were, nevertheless, reported to have been opened in Mwawesa location of Kaloleni by local KANU leader Japhet Baya (*Daily Nation* 04/06/97). The youth vigilante groups later complained that clerks were going round Likoni at night accompanied by politicians to illegally register voters from their home (*Daily Nation* 10/06/97).

The process was, therefore, far from flawless. Yet, the attitude of the ECK was radically different from that of 1992. The holding of press conferences every two or three days, the release of some provisional results, the apology made twice by commissioners in charge of Nyanza and Coast provinces regarding their most widespread mistakes and their promise of quick rectification, seemed to indicate a genuine good will from the commissioners and their wish to reduce the grounds for easy accusations of mischief. In addition to this public relations exercise, the ECK agreed as promised to review the grievances of the public on 20 June and to assess the extent of its performance two days before the deadline. Finally, on the eve of the closing day, Justice Chesoni gave in to pressures from political parties, the press and the public at large and granted two more days which were, later on, extended to 30 June.

The progression of the registration exercise provided by the provisional reports of the ECK revealed that the extension was compelling: 3.9 million (08/06/97); 4 million (14/06/97); 5.1 million (18/06/97); 8 million (22/06/97); 9 million (30/06/97). Almost three million voters registered at the last minute, between 19-22 June, and one extra million benefited from the extension period of the deadline to 30 June. Nairobi, Coast, Eastern, Rift Valley and Nyanza provinces benefited most in that order.

The breakdown of the figures per province also shows that the ECK kept its promise to correct the initial mistakes made in the first three weeks. Nyanza and the Rift Valley were just 10 per cent from their final roll on 22 June, but Coast and Nairobi provinces were really behind (16 and 22 per cent respectively see Table 5.3). After the closure of the registration exercise, the commission took fourteen days to compile the voters' register and then opened them for one month for inspection. Despite its claims that registers were open to public scrutiny in all public venues (markets, schools, churches) throughout the country (ECK 1999:51), the possibility of inspection was poorly advertised and the actual level of inspection was very low (IED/CJPC/NCCK 1998:48).

Table 5.3: The 1997 registration figures per province

Province	Provisional figures (24/06/97)	Final figures (30/06/97)	Per cent of voters registered in last week
Rift Valley	1,940,793	2,155,504	10
Eastern	1,259,121	1,464,152	14
Central	1,242,894	1,344,612	8
Nyanza	1,207,685	1,345,602	10
Western	964,681	1,024,252	6
Coast	671,812	797,378	16
Nairobi	567,293	725,620	22
NEP	159,525	171,669	7
Total	8,015,804	9,028,789	11

More allegations of rigging were also made after the registration process had closed. *The People* newspaper reported again that voter registration was going on in Nairobi, Mathioya, parts of Kericho district, Bomet, Wajir and Nakuru. At Siongiroi shopping centre in Chepalungu, the exercise took place till 4 July. Registration in Mathioya and Wajir South was alleged to be taking place within the capital city. Kirinyaga clerks, ferried by KANU officials, were also reported to be based in one of the posh hotels in Nairobi, to register voters for Kerugoya/Kutus, two weeks after the deadline (*The People* 18/07/97). On 22 August, the same newspaper published pictures showing the circulation of two sets of ID cards, some of them fake. All these irregularities were possible. As with the earlier reports of transporting voters and illegal registration in a few constituencies, these might have been eased by the corruption of some ECK officials and the pressure of some powerful KANU politicians, such as Joseph Kamotho for the incidents related to Mathioya.

Moreover, did the ECK really have the culprits of electoral offences such as double registration prosecuted and barred from voting? The commission reported that it found a total of 61,696 people who had registered more than once. Of these 15,363 were in Coast Province alone, 10,411 in Nyanza, 9,921 in Rift Valley and 5,941 in Western Province. An assistant chief was found guilty of double registration in Migori and a voter seems to have gone through the process twenty times in Mvita constituency, Mombasa (ECK1999:52). No independent report has confirmed that these voters were actually erased from the books.

Yet, despite all these problems, no huge rigging scheme can be documented and the irregularities mentioned previously here cannot invalidate the general satisfaction that IED expressed about the whole process, even though the double registration problem might have had a crucial impact on the results of certain highly contested constituencies. The initial disorganisation put the ECK on the verge of catastrophe but, progressively, the registration exercise was under control and the target of 10 million registered voters was almost reached. The only fundamental problem indeed might have been this target of 10 million registered voters. Who established it as the figure to be reached?

The ECK, the local observers and the press endorsed it as a revealed truth. In its 1999 official report, the ECK declared that this target figure was provided by the Registrar of Persons Bureau based within the Office of the President. The bureau had announced that it had issued 10.9 million ID cards. The announcement did not specify whether or not this figure totals the old and new ID cards (ECK 1999: 49). But whatever the case may be, the ECK surprisingly established its target at a figure 900,000 lower than the official figure of the Registrar of Persons Bureau. Moreover, official estimations of the Central Bureau of Statistics from the Ministry of Planning published in 1996 do not put the total population eligible to vote at 10 million. They estimate it at 14 million (CBS 1996). Therefore, whereas three million young voters had been disenfranchised in 1992, there are reasonable grounds to wonder whether in 1997 this figure did not reach the figure of 5 million, thanks again to the control of the issuance of the ID cards by the Office of the President.

The ID card confusion

From 1995, fear had spread among politicians regarding the issuance of the so-called second-generation ID cards. These cards, benefiting from a centralised and computerised data base, became quickly controversial as, in addition to the usual residential and age information, they were to indicate the name of the constituency of the applicant (*Economic Review* 13/11/95). It was indeed unclear whether, come registration time, people would be able to register in a different area than the one indicated on their ID card or whether they would even be able to indicate on these cards a constituency different from their location of birth. These two uncertainties led to great fears of illegal abuse of the capacity of voters to register where they are allowed to, which according to the law is determined by residence, ownership of land or work, and has nothing to do with location of birth. Initially, every citizen was mandated to acquire his new ID by 29 February 1997. However, this deadline was lifted in due time and the applications proceeded. Controversy on the issue of ID cards, nevertheless, arose when members of the government and the electoral commission differed publicly on whether the old ID cards would be valid for registering and voting. President Moi himself, followed by Jackson Kalweo, his minister of state in the Office of the President in charge of Internal Security, stated that the old IDs would not be accepted for registration. Then, after Justice Chesoni announced that the holding of second-generation IDs would, in fact, not be compulsory, Attorney General Amos Wako confirmed a week before registration started that, 'as far as he knew', the old IDs could be used to register just like the new ones. Jackson Kalweo again raised fears of interference from the Office of the President when he stated soon thereafter that, even if they could be used for registration, the old IDs would be invalidated and the new cards would be the only ones acceptable for voting (*Weekly Review* 16/06/97). In the end, both old and new IDs were allowed to be used for registration and voting.

The only questions remaining to be answered regarding this specific issue are whether or not there was a discrimination against the young voters, as in 1992, and whether people managed to get ID cards upon their first-time application as easily as when simply applying for a renewal. The NCCK report on the issuance of second-generation ID cards provides some insights on what actually happened in this respect. The main complaint registered by the team during their investigation is about the delays taken for processing and delivery of the new ID cards. It quotes cases from all over the country where ten months after the application, the new ID cards had not yet been delivered. The blame here was not put on the local offices of the provincial administration but on the central office in Nairobi and the data base management of the process. Either the Office of the President did not provide enough qualified personnel to do the job or Thomson, the French company contracted to supply the equipment, training and technical assistance, was not up to the task. Corruption was also a problem. As for any other service, the chiefs regularly asked for 'lunch' or 'Harambee contributions', fuel or camera batteries, when applicants presented their forms to be signed.

More worrying was perhaps the hostility of the provincial administration towards the NCCK investigation team. The DC's office systematically refused to issue the provisional figures on the number of applications and, in Migori, Nandi, Nakuru and Mombasa, the process was particularly secretive (NCCK

1996). The secrecy about the whole exercise necessarily fuels all kinds of speculations. Moreover, there was a genuine concern that the Office of the President could have deliberately delayed the issuance of their ID cards to first time applicants in a number of key constituencies where KANU could benefit from the disenfranchisement of the pro-opposition youth. As for the issue of truly registered voters, it is possible to speculate on whether the ECK did or did not cook the books after the exercise was closed, and whether this was organised on a large scale or concerned just a few constituencies where the corruption of some officials gave room for such practices. Irregularities have been noted but no grand scheme unveiled. Five million potential voters seem to be missing from the voters' roll, but no information has been collected to substantiate the hypothesis of planned and organised rigging. We have, therefore, to turn to the credibility of the actual registration figures to evaluate whether the process was fair.

The figures: passing the credibility test?

The registration figures by themselves cannot tell us anything about what happened in May/June 1997. To have an indication on how many voters might have been disenfranchised, these figures have to be compared with an evaluation of the actual number of eligible voters (population of 18 years old and over), and the comparison of this ratio (registered voters/eligible voters) has to be matched with levels of voter registration for previous elections. Indeed, there is always among the Kenyan electorate a number of potential voters who do not go to register at the time they could. They might be sick, they might be travelling, they might not know about it or they might even think that Kenyan politicians do not deserve their attention and time. Whatever the reasons, no serious assessment of the voter registration rolls can assume that the entire eligible population is actually going to register. To evaluate the proportion of these regular disenfranchised voters, all chances of registration being equal through time, we can use an average figure calculated from the registration levels of the 1969, 1974, 1979 and 1983 general elections compared with the eligible population of these times. Table 5.4 presents this data.

The percentages of registration levels for each election year have been calculated using official census data. The population of 18 years old and over was determined as a percentage of the entire population, different for each district. The percentage of the 1979 census has been used for the calculations of the eligible voter population in 1969, 1974, 1979, and 1983. For the 1992 and 1997 elections, the district percentages of the population of 18 and over have been calculated from the figures of the 1989 census, using official population projections for the year 1992 and 1997 (CBS 1996). To compare figures from the 1992 and 1997 registration exercises with those of previous

Table 5.4: Comparison through time of the 1997 level of voter registration

1969 District	1974 Rg.El. (%)	1979 Rg.El. (%)	1983 Rg.El. (%)	Rg.El. (%)	Average Rg.El. (%)	1992 Rg.El. (%)	1997 Rg.El. (%)	Diff. (97-Av.)	1997 Elig. Voters	1997 Reg. Voters
Nairobi	78.5	71.3	79.2	78.4	76.8	65.0	56.9	20.0	1,276,117	725,620
Mombasa	63.5	78.6	83.5	Na	75.2	81.2	74.6	0.6	359,520	268,333
Kwale	72.1	88.2	80.8	85.3	81.6	48.7	58.8	22.9	223,798	131,482
Kilifi	72.2	65.8	80.1	76.2	73.6	52.7	65.8	7.7	345,227	227,267
Tana River	67.6	60.4	73.1	67.0	67.0	73.6	69.8	-2.7	77,105	53,797
Lamu	89.8	85.9	99.0	Na	91.5	88.2	85.7	5.8	37,232	31,923
Taita Tav.	82.4	Na	84.2	91.0	85.9	65.1	75.6	10.3	111,898	84,576
Garissa	70.1	41.9	56.1	79.1	61.8	58.6	55.0	6.9	105,059	57,732
Wajir	68.1	28.0	46.4	73.1	53.9	48.6	60.2	-6.3	98,964	59,610
Mandera	36.6	63.3	77.9	82.6	65.1	47.9	49.9	15.2	108,888	54,327
Marsabit	70.6	67.6	70.0	80.4	72.1	75.0	75.7	-3.5	77,785	58,845
Isiolo	93.6	Na	80.7	Na	87.1	84.4	72.3	14.9	-46,638	33,699
Meru	82.4	Na	84.5	87.7	84.9	62.7	67.3	17.5	671,879	452,334
Embu	75.8	93.7	88.2	91.0	87.2	75.4	75.1	12.1	209,221	157,154
Kitui	84.0	73.5	80.6	89.6	81.9	66.1	69.4	12.6	357,414	247,903
Machakos	77.1	74.4	89.5	82.3	80.8	63.9	67.7	13.1	759,285	514,217
Nyandarua	92.3	Na	72.2	77.7	80.7	81.3	85.3	-4.6	175,390	149,656
Nyeri	89.1	71.2	87.0	Na	82.4	78.3	75.1	7.3	341,481	256,378
Kirinyaga	89.5	90.1	86.1	90.4	89.0	72.5	77.0	12.0	219,727	169,256
Murang'a	93.1	Na	89.3	92.4	91.6	75.3	74.6	17.0	437,639	326,663

Table 5.4 continued

Kiambu	97.6	66.2	82.5	95.6	85.5	74.0	74.3	11.2	596,037	442,659
Turkana	30.9	65.1	57.2	80.5	58.4	61.4	80.4	-21.9	97,859	78,632
West Pokot	34.7	65.2	78.1	82.0	65.0	58.9	61.2	3.8	134,185	82,146
Samburu	86.6	Na	83.2	Na	84.9	78.7	65.3	19.6	64,105	41,847
Trs. Nzoia	76.9	80.9	66.4	75.4	74.9	69.3	73.8	1.1	228,885	168,820
Uas.Gishu	76.4	62.7	88.1	95.2	80.6	76.0	69.3	11.3	281,845	195,327
Elg-Marak	87.2	Na	86.4	97.8	89.7	79.7	82.5	7.2	126,113	103,986
Nandi	85.8	Na	84.0	82.4	84.1	65.3	71.9	12.2	255,505	183,613
Baringo	98.5	81.4	78.3	83.6	85.4	84.2	82.5	2.9	165,636	136,684
Laikipia	Na	Na	93.6	Na	93.6	88.2	80.0	13.6	140,474	112,326
Nakuru	92.4	63.8	88.5	94.7	84.9	64.1	74.0	10.9	540,831	399,996
Narok	71.8	90.4	74.2	70.7	76.8	68.1	59.6	17.2	239,501	142,708
Kajiado	Na	50.1	74.1	96.2	73.5	81.0	74.7	-1.2	167,774	125,348
Kericho	72.7	85.2	86.6	91.0	83.9	72.3	70.8	13.1	542,795	384,071
Kakamega	90.1	97.6	90.8	96.8	93.8	66.9	72.1	21.7	783,482	565,247
Bungoma	Na	88.7	92.5	94.1	91.7	61.9	62.7	29.0	456,908	286,612
Busia	Na	Na	94.2	86.2	90.2	75.3	75.1	15.0	229,464	172,393
Siaya	74.3	Na	84.9	92.0	59.0	64.5	65.2	-6.2	346,784	225,972
Kisumu	91.5	99.3	82.1	89.1	90.5	38.4	58.5	32.1	428,622	250,591
S.Nyanza	74.2	76.1	72.4	87.2	77.5	58.2	58.7	18.7	745,155	437,543
Kisii	78.4	57.3	76.7	97.1	77.4	65.8	64.1	13.3	673,209	431,496
Aver./Total					79.8	68.7	70.0		13,285,436	9,028,789

Source: Kenya Population Census, 1969, 1979 and 1989; CBS 1996; IED 1997; IED 1998.

elections, they have been re-aggregated according to their pre-1990 administrative units (e.g., in Table 5.4 Machakos 1997 = Machakos 1997 + Makueni 1997). When the tabulations presented surrealistic results due to unreliable census data (especially from the 1969 volumes) or to equally unreliable registration figures which could not be confirmed from any other official source, they have been ignored. What does Table 5.4 tell us? First of all, it confirms that roughly 4.25 million Kenyans who were eligible to register for the 1997 general elections did not. The general level of registration of the electorate is barely higher than it was in 1992. Yet, based on the average level of non-registration in the country (20 per cent of the electorate), we can reasonably argue that out of these 4.25 million Kenyans, 2.68 millions would not have gone to register, whatever the role of the ECK or the Office of the President in this respect. This figure, 2.68 million eligible voters, is the average level, equal through time, of people who cannot be expected to register.

On the other hand, it is possible to argue that the remaining 1.57 million eligible voters were clearly disenfranchised. Where do these disenfranchised voters come from? Interestingly, they are mainly from opposition areas. Even if traditional KANU voting districts such as Kericho (10.9 per cent of electorate unusually missing), Nandi (12.2), Uasin Gishu (11.3), Kisii (13.3), Taita Taveta (10.3) and Samburu (19.6) have recorded unusually low levels of voter registration, the worst hit areas are pro-opposition. They are: Nairobi (20.0), Meru (17.5), Embu (12.1), Kitui (12.6), Machakos (13.1), Kirinyaga (12.0), Murang'a (17.0), Kiambu (11.2), Laikipia (13.6), Nakuru (10.9), Kakamega (21.7), Bungoma (29.0), Busia (15.0), Kisumu (32.0) and South Nyanza (18.7). The low level of registration in Narok (17.2 missing) is most probably significant of the ethnic cleansing which took place in the district against the Kikuyu migrants after the 1989 census, as in Kwale (22.9 missing) where the upcountry people must have feared to register, remembering the 1993 violence. In total, the disenfranchised voters coming from opposition areas or generally identified as being opposition supporters count for 92 per cent of the total number of disenfranchised voters: 1.44 million. The figures are striking. There is no doubt that, once again, disenfranchisement among the Kenyan electorate was overwhelmingly detrimental to the opposition and largely beneficial to the ruling party KANU.

These tabulations, of course, only illustrate general and approximate trends. Moreover, they do not necessarily point accusingly at the electoral commission. The Office of the President can be blamed for not allocating enough ID cards to the 2.44 million young Kenyans who had turned 18 since 1992 (CBS 1996), and it is arguable that both in Nairobi and Murang'a, the low levels of registration are either due to the anti-registration call of Kenneth Matiba or to a general lack of interest for the 1997 contest, from an electorate tired with politics and deprived of its champion. Especially in urban areas, the interest of the poorest for electoral politics is bound to diminish, considering its total irrelevance in their daily lives. Yet, the main trend revealed here remains equally unchallenged: once again, almost one and a half million Kenyans eligible to vote have been illegally disenfranchised and almost all of them come from opposition dominated areas of the country.

From IPPG to the polls: new faces, no power, too late

Two months before the polls, a number of significant legal and political changes affected the work of the ECK. First, the enforcement of the Inter-Parties Parliamentary Group (IPPG) minimal reform package dealt with a number of abnormalities and tried to empower the ECK to become the true regulator of the electoral contest. The law had first been changed to increase the number of commissioners to 'no more than twenty-one and a Chairman'. Opposition parties proposed the names of the ten new commissioners who would be nominated by President Moi. The National Development Party, which did not participate in the IPPG talks, was not allocated any commissioner. The composition of the ECK, therefore, became the following (see Table 5.5).

Table 5.5: Composition of the ECK prior to the polls

Initial commissioners	New commissioners with party affiliations
1. Mr Samuel M. Kivuitu (Chairman)**	12. Mr Stephenson Mageto (KSC)
2. Mr Gabriel K. Mukele (Vice-Chairman)**	13. Mr Abuya Abuya (FORD-Kenya)
3. Ambassador Ms. Margaret W. Kenyatta*	14. Mr John Habel Nyamu (DP)
4. Mr Isaiah Cheluget*	15. Justice (Rt.) William Mbaya (DP)
5. Ambassador Francis Karugu Nganatha*	16. Mr Kihara Muttu (DP)
6. Mr Bashir Sheikh Ali*	17. Ambassador Jack B. Tumwa
7. Mr Silas Buko Tunu***	(FORD-Kenya)
8. Mr Eliphelet Njiru M'Thambu***	18. Ambassador Brig. (Rtd) Reuben
9. Mr Edward Chemoiwo Cherono***	Musonye (FORD-Asili)
10. Mr Henry Jura***	19. Mr Philip Gachoka (FORD-Asili)
11. Mr Nicholas Ng'ang'a***	20. Mr Samuel M. Manyunza (SDP)
	21. Mrs Rachel Mzera (FORD-Kenya)

Source: ECK 1999: 30-31;

 * re-appointed in 1996; ** re-appointed in 1997; *** appointed for
 the first time in 1996

As we stated earlier, this expansion of the number of electoral commissioners could not be a guarantee of an increased independence of the commission.

Whereas the press celebrated the return or the appointment of highly competent former civil servants such as Habel Nyamu, Jack Tumwa, William Mbaya or Reuben Musonye, who could have brought some credibility to the administrative management of the commission, it was far too late for any significant internal changes to take place. All the election officials had already been recruited and supposedly trained. Once again, retired civil servants and mainly teachers had been recruited among the 64 election co-ordinators, 210 returning officers, 286 deputy returning-officers, 12,778 presiding officers and 14,804 deputy presiding officers, and it was at this stage absolutely impossible to check whether or not this recruitment had been done independently, and whether or not special branch personnel had been positioned among the ECK staff to favour the ruling party, as it was often alleged.

On 10 November parliament was finally dissolved and all seats were declared vacant by the Speaker of the National Assembly. Two days later, the election timetable was announced by the chairman of the ECK. After the presidential, civic and parliamentary nominations (3-9 December), election campaigns were to take place officially between 10 and 28 December, and finish just one day before the polls. Justice Zachaeus Chesoni, the controversial figure embodying the institution's lack of credibility, was also moved back to the judiciary and appointed chief justice on 2 December 1997. He took with him the spontaneous feeling of suspicion and distrust that had marred the reputation of the ECK and brought it to the judiciary. The political interpretation of this appointment was, of course, that President Moi was taking no chances. With Justice Chesoni having a final say on the result of electoral petitions against Moi and any other KANU MPs, their failure was guaranteed. Samuel Kivuitu, the vice-chairman, an advocate of the High Court of Kenya and a former MP for Nairobi and a largely unknown figure to the public, took over the mantle of ECK chair. He presided over the nomination of 15 presidential candidates and 883 parliamentary ones. The period devoted to the presentation of the candidates' nomination papers had been extended from half-a-day to two days. This time, no kidnapping, beating or other forms of brutal intimidation disturbed the exercise. KANU, nevertheless, proceeded with 11 unopposed candidates who were, accordingly, declared duly elected[6].

The Constitution of Kenya (Amendment) Act No.9 of 1997 had added the following powers to the commission:

(a)   To promote free and fair elections
(b)   To promote voter education throughout the country.

Regarding voter education, a self-explanatory statement of the official 1999 ECK report summarises what happened: 'The Commission was eager to take up this role, but due to the then existing financial constraints and the lateness of the legislation nothing much could be done in 1997' (ECK 1999: 32). More generally, the IPPG reform package did not significantly empower the commission to de-link itself from the government and arose too late for it to have any genuine impact on the remaining stages of the electoral process. Two dramatic examples illustrate the incapacity of the commission 'to promote free and fair elections': its relation with the Kenya Broadcasting Corporation (KBC), and its failure to react to breaches of the newly endorsed Electoral Code of Conduct.

It was a mandatory requirement for the Kenya Broadcasting Corporation to consult the ECK before allocating airtime to the different parties. Yet, the commission had no real power to ensure a fair allocation of broadcasting time to all the parties by the KBC. The Kenya Broadcasting Corporation Act (Cap. 221), section 8 had been amended to require KBC to 'keep a fair balance in all aspects in the allocation of broadcasting hours as between different political viewpoints; . . . in consultation with the Electoral Commission, during the campaign period preceding any presidential, parliamentary, or local government election, allocate free airtime to registered political parties participating in the election to expound their policies'.

Respecting the spirit of the new law, the KBC, the ECK and the parties prepared a common schedule 'giving each of these parties the day, time and hours each party was to expound its policies. The Commission even did more than that – it drew out guidelines for KBC which, if complied with would lead to equitable balancing of the opposing or concurrent political views' (ECK 1999: 95). Yet, the ECK had no power to monitor how the guidelines were to be implemented. After an initial minimal share between parties, the airwaves were once again overwhelmingly devoted to KANU propaganda (KHRC 1998). The ECK claimed, legitimately, that it could not do anything about it. It had been given no powers to do so.

Moreover, following the IPPG package recommendations implemented in section 34. A of the National Assembly and Presidential Elections Act, an Electoral Code of Conduct had also become law on 7 November, and was to be ratified by each party. One week before the official start of the campaigns, no party had made any attempt to endorse the new code. Finally, on 28 November, 18 parties, including all the main ones except KANU, endorsed it. After a few days of humming, Joseph Kamotho, the ruling party's secretary general, finally agreed to comply, and joined his colleagues to commit his party to respect the Electoral Code of Conduct just before the campaigns started. The code forbids the use or threat of violence, the disruption of political rallies, carrying of weapons, and, among other provisions, the use of foul language. None of the registered political parties which signed the code respected it. Even though the campaigns were far less violent than they had been in 1992, especially from the KANU ranks, all parties were involved in the open abuse of their opponents (see regional chapters for a detailed account). Yet, this time, despite the creation of a Code of Conduct Committee within its ranks led by commissioners Reuben Musonye, Edward Cherono and William Mbaya (ECK 1999:92), the ECK did not react accordingly. It merely came forward in the press to warn inciters and youth wingers to refrain from engaging in violent activities, but the arrest, prosecution and control of party activities remained solely the monopoly of the Kenya police and provincial administration. The ECK did not initiate, request or demand the arrest of any politician for breaching the Electoral Code of Conduct their party had endorsed. It did not regulate the abusive campaign activities of parties and failed again to honour its duties in this respect. Its claims that it did not have the financial means to monitor the parties' activities (ECK 1999: 93) is most definitely an excuse for not antagonising the ruling party. Reported cases of violence should have been brought to court. The commission was never asked to try the culprits themselves. Based on local observers, international observers and published press reports, it could have easily requested the police to investigate a number of cases and then let the public prosecutor take action.

Conclusion

The overall assessment of the electoral commission's performance prior to the 1997 polls might not appear as damning as it was in 1992, but the end result is undoubtedly the same. Whether we consider the creation of new constituencies, the registration of voters or the regulation of the party activities, the ECK failed to provide a 'free and fair' environment and, therefore, failed to honour its duties towards the Kenyan electorate. Regarding the creation of new constituencies, at least 12 of them (Mwingi South, Kaiti, Kuresoi, Eldama Ravine, Gwasi, Uriri, Gatundu North, Mathioya, Khwisero, Sotik, Bura and Wajir North) were carved out with clear political intentions to increase the number of the ruling party's representation chances in parliament. Moreover, their creation did not counterbalance the existing situation of unequal representation in the country, contrary to the principles expressed in the constitution. Regarding the registration exercise, almost one and a half million Kenyans eligible to vote were intentionally disenfranchised with the tacit agreement of the commission, and the great majority of them were from opposition areas. Finally, regarding the regulation of political party activities, the ECK never called for the prosecution of politicians or activists guilty of violence.

Such a failure can be explained in at least two ways. First, there is the commission's lack of independence. Indeed, since all commissioners were political appointees, it is not surprising that their allegiance was with their respective promoters and not with the Kenyan electorate. As long as the membership of the ECK is considered as a political reward for long-serving and KANU-compliant civil servants, the ECK will continue to lack credibility. The appointment of truly independent electoral commissioners, competent professionals free from political affiliations, remains one of the most important factors that would improve the efficiency, accountability and general performance of the ECK. In this respect, the IPPG-negotiated expansion measures were totally inadequate. Secondly, there is, of course, the legal framework which does not fully empower the commission to rise up to its task. The ECK does not have any power to implement its various recommendations on political fairness. Moreover, in its official report on the 1997 general elections, the ECK reveals another reason why it failed in its duty. The financial constraints under which the commission was working were clearly an impediment. As it stated in its report:

> When it was set up, the Constitution did not grant the Commission a free hand in the procurement and utilisation of funds. The Accounting Officer, appointed by the Minister for Finance under the Exchequer and Audit Act, was the Clerk of the National Assembly. The money spent by the Commission was a vote to the National Assembly, so that as far as money matters is concerned, that remains under the control of the Clerk. Moreover, there is no provision in law for the Commission to negotiate and receive donations, or grants or bequests from any source . . . Once the money had been voted for as part of the annual recurrent expenditure, the actual procurement was subject to the usual bureaucracy in government offices, with the result that money urgently needed for important tasks was sometimes not available or sometimes took too long to be disbursed . . . In fact the staff of the National Assembly ran with complete freedom the Commission's accounting, the supplies and personnel services. This should tell the clout that the Clerk of the National Assembly had over the way the Commission performed its functions (ECK 1999: 32-3).

After the removal of Justice Chesoni, time and financial constraints became probably the most important impediments preventing the commission from fulfilling its new duties. As biased as ever, then? Maybe not, but biased enough to once again betray the Kenyan electorate. There is no middle ground here. Either the electoral administration succeeded in offering the eligible electorate a genuinely non-partisan service, or it did not. And whatever the reasons, Kenyans deserve better than *mitumba* (second-hand) elections. They are no lesser voters and they have no fewer rights than the British, French, Dutch or American electorate. If the principle of equal rights is to stand whatever the country and the principle of 'one man, one vote' is to be universally supported, there should be zero tolerance of electoral malpractice. A hopeful sign of change within the commission could be the transparency and desire expressed in its official report on the 1997 general elections to gain a fully independent status from the government. We can only hope that genuine constitutional reform will one day give the electoral commissioners the opportunity to show their commitment to the organisation of free and fair elections.

Notes

1. Some parts of this chapter dealing with the creation of new constituencies are the result of an investigation conducted by the Institute for Education in Democracy (IED) which was published in 1998 (IED 1998). We wish to thank the executive director of IED for allowing us to use this text in the present volume and we wish to acknowledge the support of this organisation for documenting this chapter. Yet, the opinions presented here, except as they appear in IED's book, remain solely and entirely those of the authors.
2. The Attorney General's office, in its Legal Notice No.276/1992, had amended the section 13(3)(b)(i) of the National Assembly and Presidential Elections Act, providing that the day(s) upon which each political party shall nominate candidates shall be not more than twenty-one days after the date of publication of such notice. This modification is still valid (cf. Statute Law & Miscellaneous (Amendment) Act No.10 of 1997) and means that the AG may give only one day to the parties to present their candidates for nomination. Provided that KANU would be informed in advance of the date of publication of this Legal Notice and that its candidates would be ready to present their nomination papers one day after, it would give the ruling party a decisive advantage over its opponents.
3. This rule was amended by Act No.10 of 1997 to include Kenyan passports.
4. The term originates from the practice of Elbridge Gerry, a politician who, as the governor of Massachusetts, reshaped an electoral district in a salamander-like outline in 1812 for political purposes.
5. These are: Magarini, Malindi, Kasarani, Starehe, Westlands, Lang'ata, Dagoretti, Ntonyiri, Igembe, Kitui Central, Mutomo, Makueni, Kibwezi, Rangwe, Rachunyo, Turkana North, Turkana Central, Kapenguria, Sigor, Nakuru East, Konoin, Narok South, Narok West, Kajiado Central, Kajiado South, Amagoro, Dujis, Lagdera, and Gatanga.
6. They are Robert Kochalle (Laisamis), Francis Lotodo (Kapenguria), Christopher Lomada (Sigor), Francis K. Lagat (Eldoret East), Joseph Lotodo (Baringo East), Andrew Kiptoon (Baringo North), William ole Ntimama (Narok North), Kipkalya Kones (Bomet), Isaac Ruto (Chepalungu), Charles arap Kirui (Belgut), Samuel arap Rotich (Kipkelion).

References

Barkan, J. and Ngethe, N. 1998, 'Kenya Tries Again', *Journal of Democracy*, April: 208-26.

CBS 1996, *Kenya Population Census 1989: Analytical Report Volume VII, Population Projections*, Nairobi: Government Printers.

ECK 1999a, *Report on the 1997 General Elections*, Nairobi: Electoral Commission of Kenya.

ECK 1999b, *1998 Annual Report*, Nairobi: Electoral Commission of Kenya.

Fox, R. 1997, 'Bleak Future for Multi-Party Elections in Kenya', *The Journal of Modern African Studies*, Vol.34, No.4: 597-607.

IED 1997a, *National Elections Data Book Kenya 1963-997*, Nairobi: Institute for Education in Democracy.

IED 1997b, 'Voter Registration for the 1997 General Elections in Kenya: a survey', mimeo, Nairobi: Institute for Education in Democracy.

IED 1998, *Understanding elections in Kenya. A constituency profile approach*, Nairobi: Institute for Education in Democracy.

IED/CJPC/NCCK 1998, *Report on the 1997 General Elections in Kenya, 29-30 December, 1997*, Nairobi: Institute for Education in Democracy/Catholic Justice and Peace Commission/National Council of Churches of Kenya.

NCCK 1996, 'Study on the creation of the 22 new constituencies in Kenya and an overview of the on-going issuance of second-generation ID cards', mimeo, Nairobi: National Council of Churches of Kenya.

NEMU 1993, *The Multi-Party General Elections in Kenya, 29 December 1992*, Nairobi: National Election Monitoring Unit.

Throup, D. and Hornsby, C. 1998, *Multi-Party Politics in Kenya—The Kenyatta & Moi States & the Triumph of the System in the 1992 Election*, Oxford: James Currey.

6

Election Day and the Results

Charles Hornsby

Polling day, Monday 29 December 1997, and the count that followed were less 'rigged' than the 1992 polls, but were far more chaotic administratively. Although there were many incidents of electoral malpractice in the run-up to the polls, the delinking of the administration from the conduct of the election reduced administrative intervention and abuses. As in 1992, despite a majority of hostile voters, President Daniel arap Moi and his Kenya African National Union party (KANU) managed to emerge victorious although their parliamentary victory was narrow. The political coalition around the president proved more fragile than in 1992 in some peripheral areas of the Rift Valley such as Maasailand and Turkana. Moi's position was also distinctly weaker in the Kamba and Luhya communities, both with serious candidates of their own for the presidency for the first time. Nonetheless, the patterns of regional voting followed very similar lines to those of 1992. The three core 'homeland' areas monolithically voted for 'their man'; the coast, the semi-arid and the peripheral areas generally following the government; and the main undecided areas were the swing communities, the cities and the 'ethnic borderlands' where different communities coexisted.

Polling day and the count

Polling day proved to be a nightmare for the Electoral Commission of Kenya (ECK). Inadequate preparation, bad luck and appalling weather conditions caused disaster throughout much of the country. In some seats, ballot papers did not arrive at all. Where they did, election staff did not. There was a shortage of vehicles everywhere to transport boxes, papers and election officials on election day morning. Some ballot papers, particularly those for civic seats, were sent to the wrong constituency, in many cases to completely wrong areas of the country, so that the Kasipul Kabondo papers from Nyanza were found in Kitui in Eastern Province. Other papers had incorrect candidate information on them, and several Safina and Social Democratic Party (SDP) civic candidates had their names omitted from the ballot papers entirely (see IED/CJPC/NCCK 1998: 67-79).

In contrast to 1992, voters did not arrive at first light to queue. This was lucky, since the majority of the 12,750 polling stations opened late, even in areas where the materials required were adequate, and opening times of 8 to 9 am were common. There were shortages of presidential, parliamentary or civic ballot papers in polling stations in almost every constituency. The lack of ballots particularly affected some pro-government areas such as Sotik, Bomet, Ainamoi, and Konoin in the Kalenjin 'KANU zones' of the Rift Valley, but everywhere angry voters queued and argued with election officials while desperate attempts were made to find excess ballots from neighbouring polling stations, or to recover ballots sent elsewhere in the country. Vice-President Saitoti himself was unable to vote on 29 December, due to a lack of ballot papers in his home location in Kajiado North. Meanwhile, bad weather also prevented voting from commencing over much of the Coast and North-Eastern provinces, also pro-government areas. The situation was particularly bad in Garissa and Tana River, where most roads were impassable and only the few helicopters and small aeroplanes could transport election materials to isolated locations.

Polling station security in general was adequate and there was little open favouritism by police or security officers, or by most poll officials towards any party. However, accusations of election rigging became almost irrelevant in the face of the logistical chaos. While little could have been done about the bad weather, a product of El Niño, the appalling distribution of ballot papers was evidence of either incompetence or malice. The DDDG observer group took the view that 'The distribution of ballot papers was flawed at three stages: first from the printers in Britain; secondly, from central stores of the Electoral Commission of Kenya, and finally by the Returning Officers in many constituencies.' (DDDG 1998).

The way in which the papers were packed by Smith and Ouzman Ltd, of the UK, may have contributed to the problems, exacerbated by the way in which they were split by the ECK between polling stations. Extraordinarily, the commission claimed that it had not even bothered to open the boxes of papers to check whether the ballots were correctly packed. The printers denied any responsibility, describing the accusations of the ECK as 'face-saving nonsense' (*East African Standard* 31/12/97:3).

Following the chaos of the first day, at about 7 pm that night, the electoral commission announced that polling would continue for a second day (30 December) in areas where voters had been unable to cast their ballots.[1] This applied to at least 30 per cent of constituencies, including Wajir and Garissa districts in the North-East; Lamu district, Ganze, Msambweni and Magarini on Coast Povince and in the Rift Valley most of Kajiado, Kericho and Bomet districts, Kilgoris, parts of Nakuru, Narok South, Turkana Central and Samburu

West. In Nyanza Province polling continued into day two in Kisumu Rural, Alego, Rarieda, and most of Rachuonyo district. In the Eastern Province, polling continued over most of Central Imenti, Nithi and North Horr. Western, Central and Nairobi fared much better, with only a few seats, such as Kandara and Juja in Central, and Funyula in Western Province forced into a complete repeat. Elsewhere, some constituencies reopened those specific polling stations that had seen a lack of papers. ECK Chairman Samuel Kivuitu claimed 28 seats were affected by the mix-ups and 24 did not get enough papers. Adding those where weather was the determining factor, a third or more of the country was forced into a second day of voting.

The KANU reaction to these events was extraordinary. For almost the first time in history, a ruling party in power for 35 years accused its own state-nominated and funded electoral commission of rigging it out of office. The bad weather and administrative confusion were concentrated in the less developed and semi-arid areas, all of which were KANU strongholds, and KANU was extremely worried that the elections might be aborted entirely in seats they relied upon for electoral victory. On polling day, KANU officials attacked the ECK for not '. . . explaining the reasons and circumstances leading to the malfunctioning of the electoral process in this election.' and accused the ECK of 'flawed and corrupt machinations' (*East African Standard* 30/12/97:24). The same day, Vice-President George Saitoti also accused the ECK of rigging and said he was 'scandalised and horrified' by the evidence of incompetence he witnessed. Fellow minister William ole Ntimama alleged that the fact that most polling irregularities were experienced in KANU areas was '. . sabotage by an ethnic community out to seize the leadership of the country' (*Daily Nation* 30/12/97:9). This was a comment on the recent expansion of the ECK's membership to include several opposition nominees.

On Tuesday 30 December, the situation became even more ludicrous as the results began to be reported in a sequence which indicated that the Democratic Party's (DP) Mwai Kibaki was likely to enter the lead. The *East African Standard* splashed a story with a photo of a furious President Moi and a full page headline 'They're Rigging Me Out', following Moi's accusations in a press statement that the ECK 'was pro-opposition and was deliberately disrupting the polls in government areas' (*East African Standard* 31/12/97:1). KANU's national executive officer Geoffrey Kathurima and Jeremiah Nyagah who spoke later in the day at a press conference made similar claims, describing events as '. . . an obvious scheme by the EC to rig the elections in favour of the opposition.' Opposition leaders and other politicians also attacked the ECK, and some, such as the SDP, demanded the annulment of the results. The ECK meanwhile was silent, refusing to hold a press conference until Moi's allegations were published on 31 December, after which Chairman Kivuitu went public for the first time, admitting many shortcomings in the process, but refusing to resign, commenting 'Nobody ever resigns in Kenya!' (*East African Standard* 01/01/98).

Meanwhile, 'voting by instalments' had proved almost as chaotic as the original day had been. It was completely unclear to returning officers and polling clerks which stations were supposed to re-open on Tuesday and which ones were not. In some constituencies, all stations re-opened, in some none, and in some only certain stations. Voters queued to vote in some stations only to be told that they would not re-open. The instruction to continue polling was in fact given so late that in many cases the ballot boxes had already been sealed awaiting transportation to the count. Thousands of voters nationally were thereby unable to vote.

The issue of overnight security for the ballot boxes, completely unplanned, was solved in different ways in different areas. In most constituencies, the officials, observers and police simply stayed at the counting centre or polling station all night, sleeping in snatches and guarding the boxes against stuffing or theft. In a few, they were taken to police headquarters or a similar 'secure' place for guarding and were returned the next morning.

To permit voting to continue in the affected areas, Tuesday 30 December was also declared a public holiday. However, by the end of Tuesday, voting had still not begun in polling stations in Magarini, where helicopters were being used to transport materials upcountry, nor parts of Central Imenti, Narok South, Lamu East and Msambweni. In these and other areas, voting continued through 31 December (Wednesday). In parts of Garsen and Bura in Tana River they had not yet voted on 1 January (Thursday) and in Galole, on Friday 2 January voting had not commenced. Others had not voted in Ijara, Fafi and Lagdera by Saturday 3 January. In nine stations in Fafi, polling never took place at all.

At 7 pm, the same time as voting was extended, the count in constituencies which had polled satisfactorily was also postponed by Kivuitu until 7 am on 30 December. The reasons for this were unclear, but it was widely seen as a method to avoid early presidential polling figures giving huge majorities for the opposition since the smaller, more central and better developed constituencies had experienced the fewest problems. Kibaki and other opposition leaders complained, but to no effect, although a few constituencies took no notice and counted on Monday night anyway. By midday on 30 December, counting had started in many urban and more developed constituencies though it was unclear which constituencies were counting and which polling; some constituencies were both polling and counting at the same time.

The 1997 poll was the first time that ballots were counted at the constituency centre rather than all being transported to the district headquarters.

Nonetheless, as in 1992, the count continued agonisingly slowly. It was made even worse by the late start, and was again affected in some areas by counting agents demanding the payment of their salaries for the work in advance. As the results trickled in, it was quickly clear that President Moi was going to win the presidential election again, against a divided opposition, though how easily was uncertain.

It was far from clear, however, whether KANU would win parliament. The last few seats in parliament were extremely closely contested, and the delayed polling in Tana River and elsewhere meant that the final results were long-delayed. On Friday 2 January, at 9 pm for example, the *Kenya Times* reported that KANU and the opposition were 'neck and neck', with 99 KANU wins to 97 for the opposition. The gap widened slightly with the last few seats to 107-103.

Following their recognition of defeat, as in 1992, opposition leaders then denounced the elections as rigged. On this occasion, Mwai Kibaki and Raila Odinga were the most vociferous, issuing a joint statement on 2 January 1998, accusing KANU of direct rigging. Safina and FORD-Kenya, however, accepted the results as legitimate though still objecting to the inefficiencies and problems experienced in the process, as did the local poll observers.

The overall results

The presidential results

Incumbent President Daniel arap Moi was re-elected with considerably greater ease than in 1992. He won 25 per cent or more of the vote in the same five provinces as in 1992, with an increased percentage of the total vote (up from less than 37 per cent to over 40 per cent). Facing 14 opposition candidates, he remained the sole candidate with a truly national constituency.[2]

President Moi easily won the tiny North-Eastern Province (with 73 per cent of the vote), Rift Valley (70 per cent), and Coast (63 per cent), narrowly beat Charity Ngilu of the SDP in Eastern (35 per cent) and came second in Western to Kijana Wamalwa of FORD-Kenya (44 per cent). He nearly took 25 per cent in Nyanza this time round, polling just under 24 per cent of the vote.

Mwai Kibaki ran Moi a good second, with 31 per cent of the vote, a dramatic improvement on his 1992 performance of only 19 per cent. Kibaki emerged from these elections as the only existing opposition presidential candidate with a real national constituency, and for the first time emerged as a potential future president. This was a decisive development for a man written off one year before as weak and out of touch.

With Kenneth Matiba out of the picture, and the boycott of little relevance, he won Nairobi (44 per cent) and Central (89 per cent) and came third in

Eastern (28 per cent). He came close in the Rift Valley with 21 per cent. He received almost all the Kikuyu votes, but also polled creditably in other areas such as Kisii. He out-polled his parliamentary candidates in most seats.

Raila Odinga decimated FORD-Kenya in Luo Nyanza, taking almost all the votes his deceased father had won in 1992 on his old party and winning Nyanza Province with 57 per cent of the vote (84 per cent of the vote in Luo Nyanza). Outside Nyanza, he performed appallingly badly, receiving less than 3 per cent of the vote in the other seven provinces.

Kijana Wamalwa did well in Western Province, but he had little success outside his Luhya community. He won his home province with 48 per cent of the vote, but passed the 25 per cent hurdle in no other area and again polled only 3 per cent of the vote outside Western. He was less popular than his candidates in the majority of seats.

Table 6.1: 1997 presidential results by candidate[3]

	Moi	Kibaki	Odinga	Wamalwa	Ngilu	others	Total
Nairobi	75,270	160,124	63,086	24,971	39,707	6,560	369,718
Central	57,029	892,260	6,556	3,414	30,058	18,114	1,007,431
Eastern	363,027	298,850	7,787	7,017	360,492	16,179	1,053,352
North-Eastern	70,506	20,404	307	4,411	440	544	96,612
Coast	257,065	52,489	27,844	11,306	38,264	25,957	412,925
Rift Valley	1,140,231	343,529	34,738	102,178	11,345	10,233	1,642,254
Western	315,772	10,119	13,497	339,122	3,445	25,248	707,205
Nyanza	215,054	138,202	520,550	14,623	15,301	14,774	918,504
Total	2,493,954	1,915,977	664,825	507,623	499,052	117,609	6,208,001
Per cent	40.2	30.9	10.9	8.2	8.0	1.9	100.0

Source: ECK, 1999; IED 1998; author's calculations

Figure 6.1: Overall presidential results by candidate

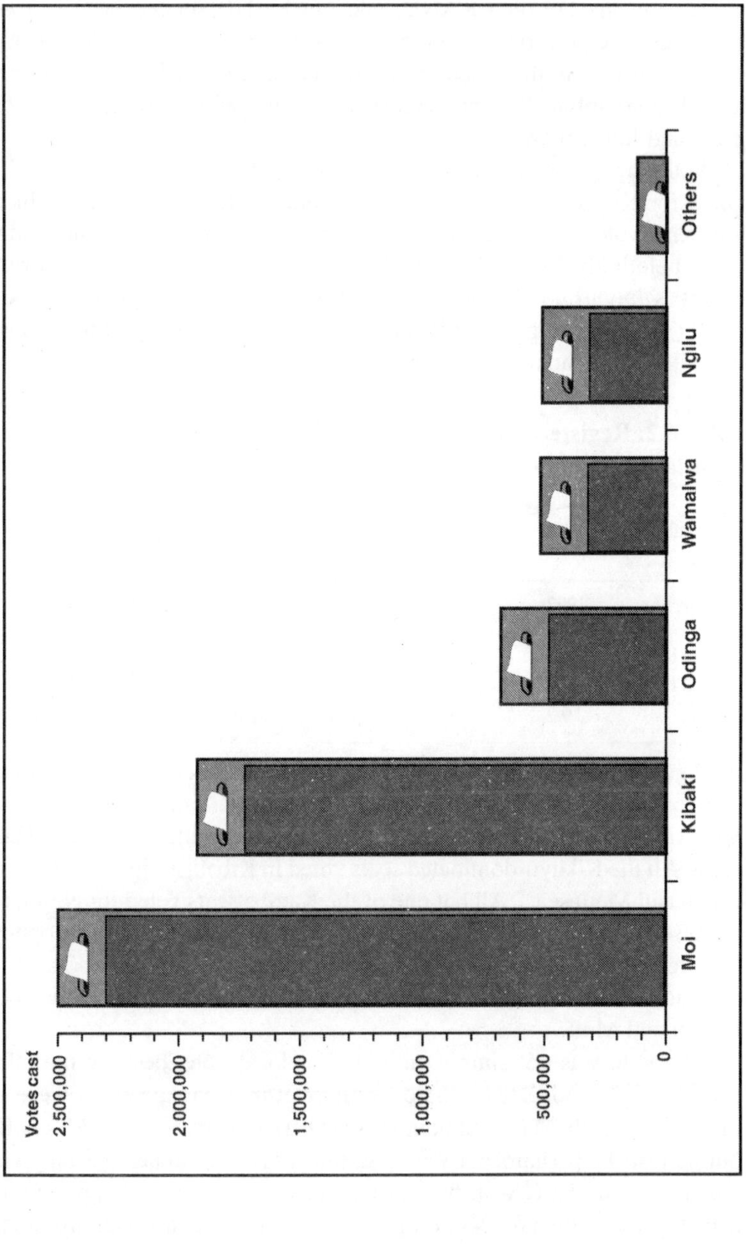

Charity Ngilu won as expected much of her home region of Ukambani, weakening KANU's position in Eastern Province, but probably took more votes from the DP than KANU, and ran KANU second even in Eastern. Elsewhere she performed more poorly than expected, polling less than 4 per cent of the vote in the other seven provinces. Ngilu proved to be more of a local leader 'inflated' to national scale by her gender, ethnicity, and by the press and international interest.

Voters again voted as a 'bloc' over a big chunk of the country. The Kikuyu voted for Kibaki, the Luo for Odinga, and the Kalenjin for Moi. In 1992, registered voters in the electoral regions with presidential candidates had voted overwhelmingly for 'their man'. They did so again, although to a reduced extent. Kikuyu/Luo antipathy in voting preferences proved the most extreme of all (Table 6.2). Ngilu and Wamalwa also won a majority of their kinsmen, but without the monolithic voting seen above.

Table 6.2: Registered voters supporting the local man in ethnic homelands (in per cent)

Electoral region	Moi	Moi	Kibaki	Kibaki /Matiba	R. Odinga	O. Odinga
	1997	1992	1997	1992	1997	1992
Central Rift	78.3	81.0	3.1	3.0	1.1	1.3
Central Province	5.7	1.8	66.1	80.0	0.7	1.0
Nyanza	9.2	4.5	0.3	0.6	58.1	70.0

As Figure 6.4 shows, the presidential voting reveals a consistent pattern which was confused by local issues and alliances at the parliamentary level. Moi and KANU continued to represent the pastoral, semi-arid, coastal and Kalenjin areas. All the Kikuyu-dominated seats voted in Kibaki as did all but one of the Embu and Meru seats. All but one of the Kamba seats voted for Ngilu, but no one else did. Kajiado South was the only 'minority tribe' seat to vote opposition for president. All the Luo-dominated seats voted for Raila. The Luhya-dominated seats split between Wamalwa and Moi while the Kisii voted for Kibaki and Moi.

The vote was not simply an ethnic or local vote, because the other 11 presidential candidates, whatever their ethnic background, were of no importance. Only Martin Shikuku (FORD-Asili) narrowly beat Moi in Butere but he lost the parliamentary vote to the KANU candiate, and only George Anyana of the KSC won his parliamentary seat. One, Stephen Oluodhe, actually stood down for Moi on the eve of poll, and conservationist and civic society activist Wangari Maathai was reported in the press as having stood

Figure 6.2: Presidential results by province

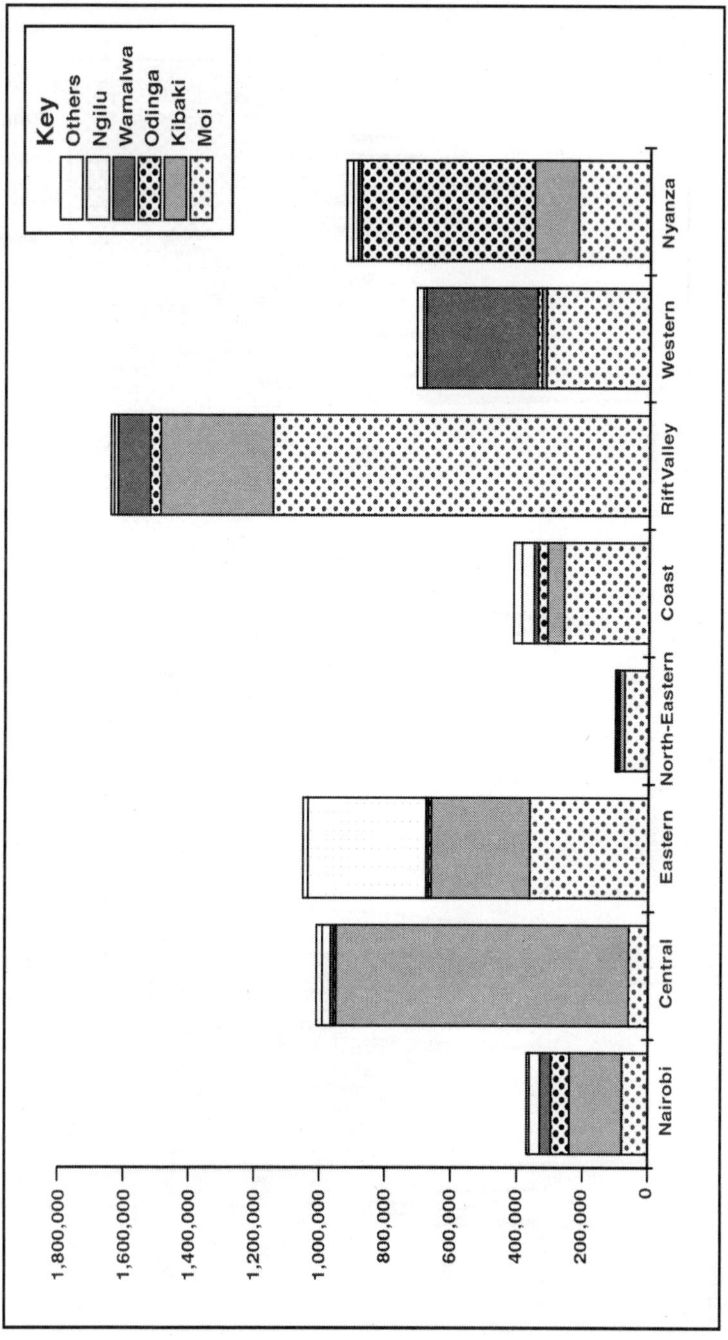

Figure 6.3: 1997 presidential results by constituency

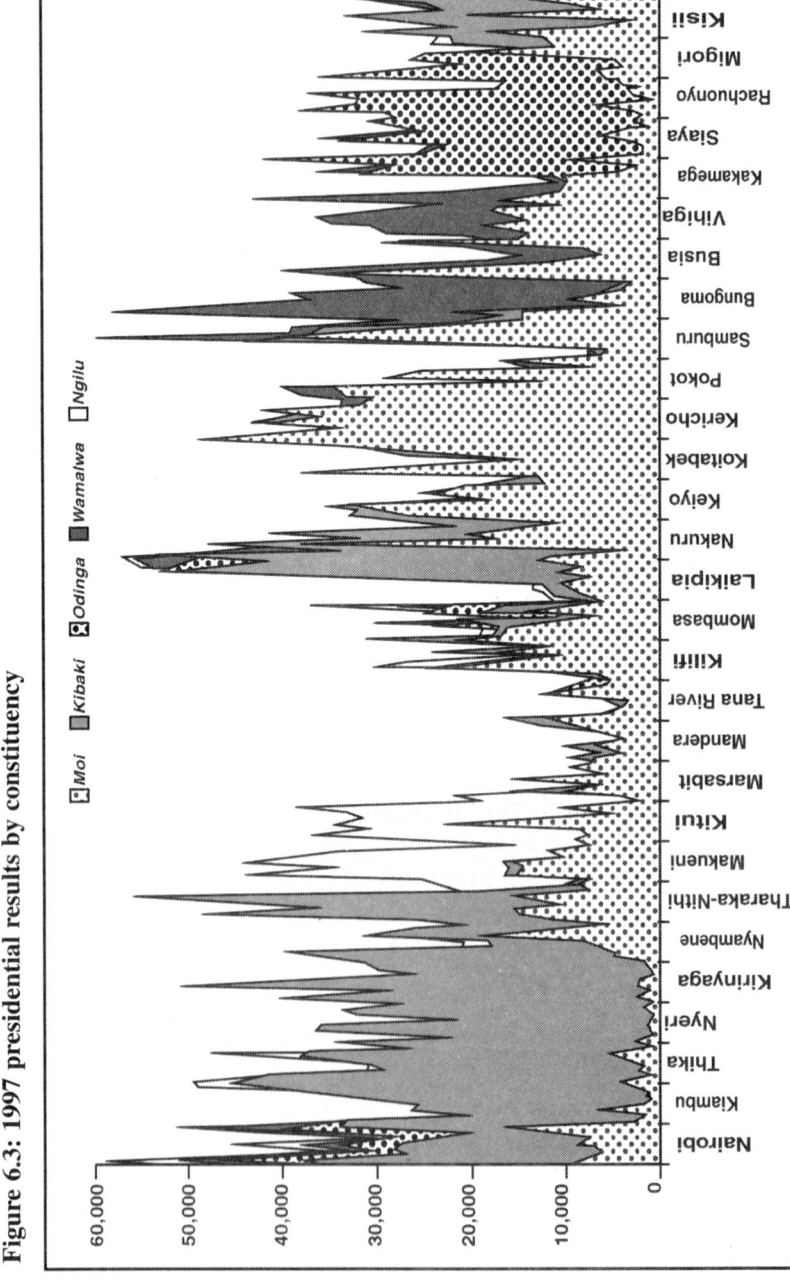

Figure 6.4: Presidential results 1997

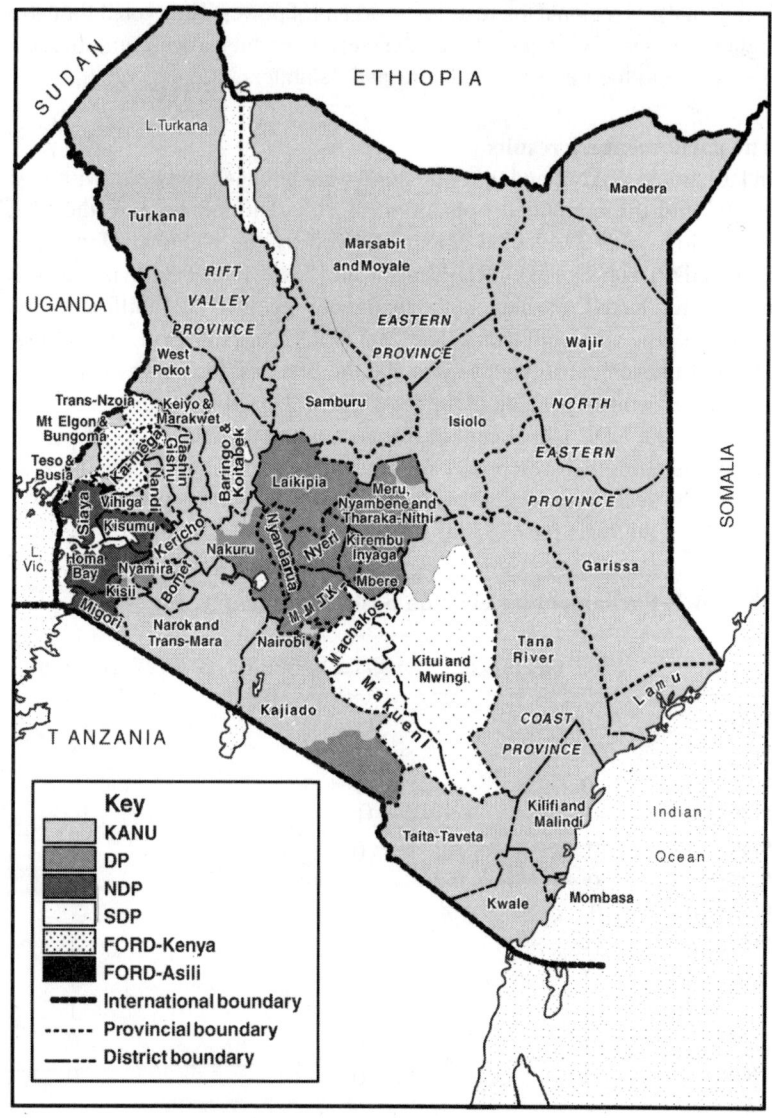

down, but denied actually doing so. It made no difference anyway. Voters clearly saw that their interests lay in voting for a presidential candidate with a chance of winning, who would best represent their particular economic, communal and regional interests in the organs of power. They voted for national figures (preferably though not exclusively from their own communities) in preference to their eleven local sons and daughters.

The parliamentary results
In Parliament, KANU and the opposition were left neck and neck, with KANU at 107 and the combined opposition at 103. The DP became the official opposition, with 39 elected MPs, followed by the National Development Party (NDP) with 21 and FORD-Kenya with 17 (see Table 6.3). In parliamentary party votes, KANU parliamentary candidates received 2.24 million votes (38 per cent of the vote), but won 51 per cent of the seats, due to the multiplicative effect of uneven constituency sizes and the first past the post system.[4]

The DP won 19 per cent of the seats with 1.27 million votes (22 per cent of the vote), the NDP 10 per cent of the seats with 634,000 votes (11 per cent), benefiting from their regionally focused Luo vote. FORD-Kenya took 8 per cent of the seats with 593,000 votes (10 per cent of the vote), and the SDP 7 per cent of the seats for 476,000 votes (8 per cent of the vote).

Table 6.3: Parliamentary election positions by party, 1992-97

Party	1992 elections	1997 dissolution	1997 elections
KANU	100	111	107
DP	23	21	39
NDP	0	1	21
FORD-K	31	31	17
SDP	0	0	15
Safina	0	0	5
FORD-P	0	0	3
FORD-A	31	23	1
KSC	1	1	1
Shirikisho	0	0	1
KNC	1	0	0
PICK	1	0	0
Total	188	188[5]	210

Note: Two seats were technically vacant due to deaths, but the incumbent party is recorded here

Table 6.4: Distribution of parliamentary seats by province (1992 results in brackets)

Province	KANU	DP	NDP	FORD-K	SDP	Safina	FORD-A	Others
Nairobi	1 (1)	5 (0)	1(-)	0 (1)	1(-)	0(-)	0 (6)	0(0)
Central	0 (0)	17(10)	1(-)	0 (1)	5(-)	3(-)	0(14)	3(0)
Eastern	17(21)	8 (9)	0(-)	1 (1)	9(-)	0(-)	1 (0)	0(1)
North-Eastern	9 (8)	0 (0)	0(-)	0 (1)	0(-)	2(-)	0 (0)	0(1)
Coast	18(17)	2 (1)	0(-)	0 (2)	0(-)	0(-)	0 (0)	1(0)
Rift Valley	39(36)	7 (2)	0(-)	3 (2)	0(-)	0(-)	0 (4)	0(0)
Western	15(10)	0 (0)	0(-)	9 (3)	0(-)	0(-)	0 (7)	0(0)
Nyanza	8 (7)	0 (1)	19(-)	4(20)	0(-)	0(-)	0 (0)	1(1)
Total	107(100)	39(23)	21(-)	17(31)	15(-)	5(-)	1(31)	5(3)

The most obvious losers were FORD-Asili (not a single one of their incumbents won re-election on the same party) and FORD-Kenya (losing all but two of the Luo seats). However, the most significant loser was actually the governing party. From the dissolution, at a time of their choice and at a time when the opposition remained as divided and fractious as ever, they declined from 59 per cent to 51 per cent of the house. In by-elections between 1992 and 1997, their ability to focus money, promises of development and intimidatory tactics on one small region had gained them eleven seats. They had lost none. Yet with the assembly enlarged, they won even fewer seats than they had held before. For the first time, voters elected opposition MPs from the Rift Valley periphery (Turkana in the north and Kajiado in the south), and Taita/Taveta, indicating a softening in the pro-KANU stance of these semi-arid regions.

There were many reasons for this poor performance (though, of course, KANU still had a narrow overall majority). The most important was the most obvious: KANU was either the first or second party in 190 of 210 constituencies (almost everywhere outside Central Province), competing with regionally strong ethnically-based parties that could not seize power nationally, but which could defeat KANU in their home areas. The opposition (sometimes involuntarily) showed a greater degree of cohesion and cases of opposition split-vote wins for KANU were fewer.[6] The election was effectively 'KANU versus the strongest local opposition party'. The individual opposition parties did not even attempt to create a national ticket in the parliamentary polls, and saved their time and money to focus on winnable constituencies, having learned their lesson from 1992.

Another reason for KANU's weak parliamentary performance was that unlike in 1992, the 1997 results showed far more split ticketing. The 'three-piece suit' of 1992 (voting the party ticket for president, parliament and civic elections) was weakened substantially, with Kibaki being the main beneficiary. For example, in Kisii voters supported KANU and FORD-Kenya parliamentary candidates, but voted KANU or DP for the presidency. In fact, Kibaki won Kisii without winning a single parliamentary seat there.[7] Similarly, in Matiba's old heartlands of southern Central Province, voters backed specific wealthy or outspoken individuals from any opposition party (DP, SDP, Safina, FORD-People, even NDP), but unanimously voted for Kibaki in the presidential race. The looser coupling between levels in the hierarchy also allowed voters to support Moi, but elect a non-KANU MP or councillor. Despite this, it was still the main parties, with their publicity, money, political support and ethnic constituency that dominated the polls. As in 1992, fringe candidates and defectors standing on 'ragtag' parties like PICK (the Party of Independent Candidates of Kenya) performed poorly.

As in 1992, though to a lesser extent, there are serious concerns about the conduct of the count in the last few results to declare, in the light of the government's determination to secure a parliamentary majority. Nonetheless, despite the electoral abuses that occurred (see below), KANU remained the party with the broadest national constituency. They combined unquestioned support in the Kalenjin areas with strong local alliances in Coast Province, in Western and Kisii, and relied upon the power of the state in the less-developed and semi-arid areas which will vote for whichever candidate is supported by the administration and the state machinery.

KANU again put up a candidate in every constituency, and improved its performance in the opposition areas of Central Province and South Nyanza although it still polled very poorly in these areas, in Wamalwa's Bungoma and in Kikuyu-dominated Nakuru and Laikipia (see Figure 6.5).

The only other party to exhibit a real national constituency was the DP (see Figure 6.6). Dominant in the Kikuyu areas of Central Province, Nakuru and Laikipia, their candidates also managed to do well at the coast, a few seats in Ukambani, the North and North-East, Kisii and a few Kalenjin seats with significant settler communities. Nonetheless, with only 133 candidates, they had virtually no candidates this time in the Central Rift, few in Western and none in Luo Nyanza. They voluntarily gave up fielding candidates in Mathioya, Gatundu South and Kangema (seats KANU saw as potential victories, or where 'allied' candidates were standing) to avoid split voting.

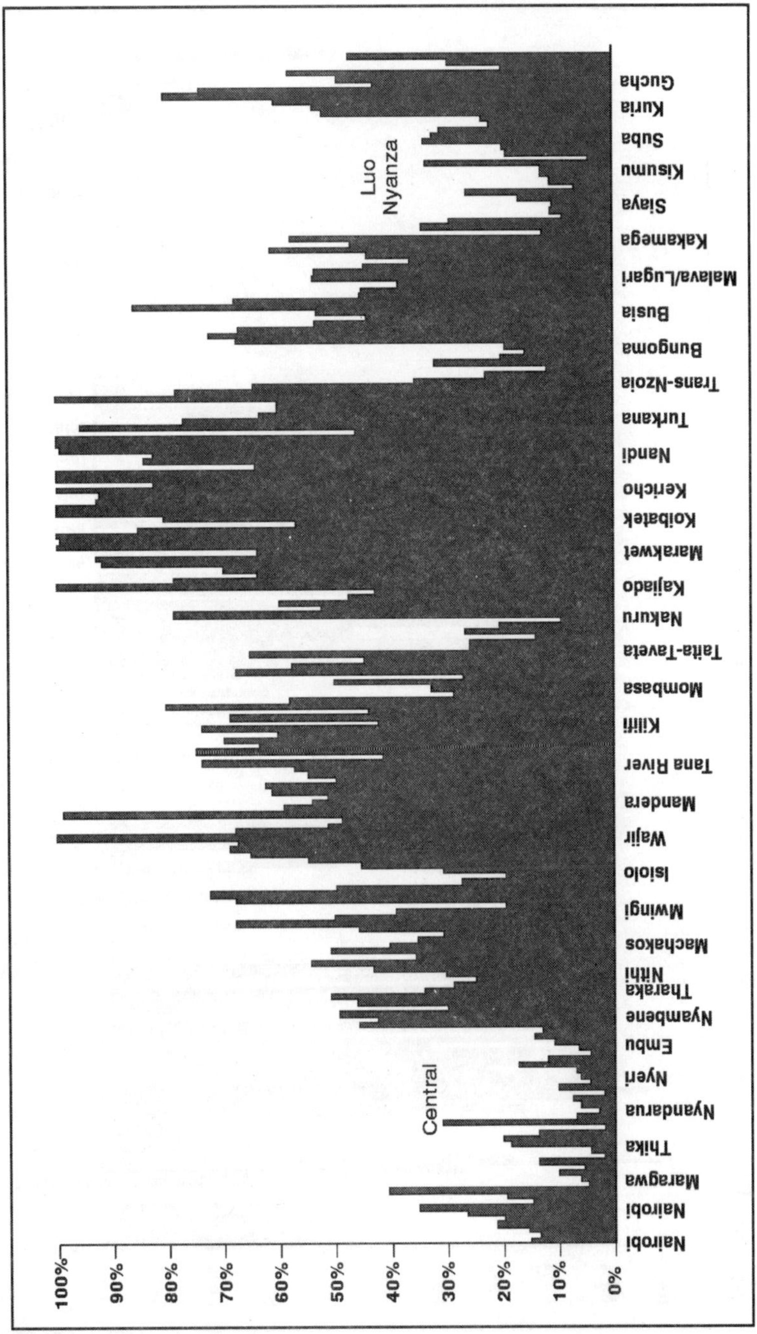

Figure 6.5: KANU parliamentary candidates' percentage of the vote by seat

Figure 6.6: DP parliamentary candidates' percentage of the vote by seat

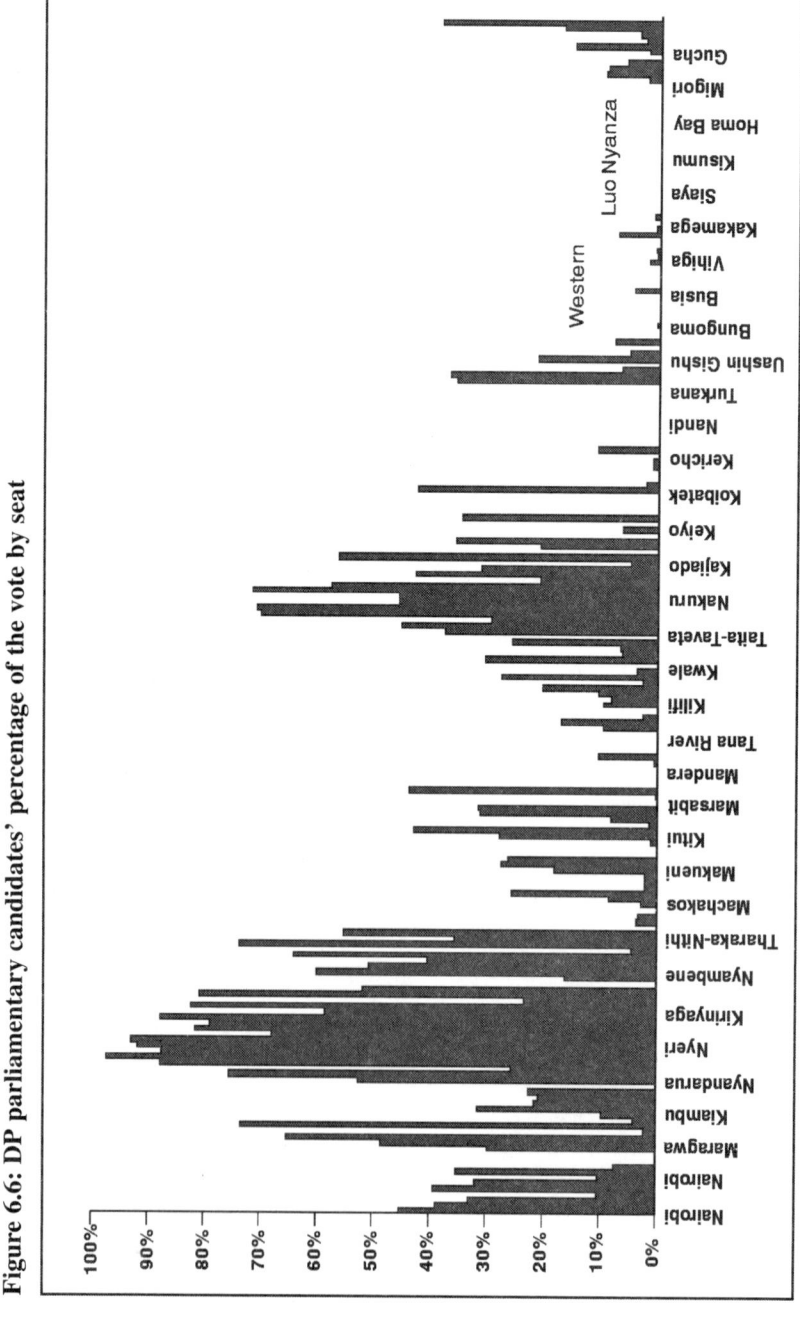

Figure 6.7: FORD-Kenya parliamentary candidates' percentage of the vote by seat

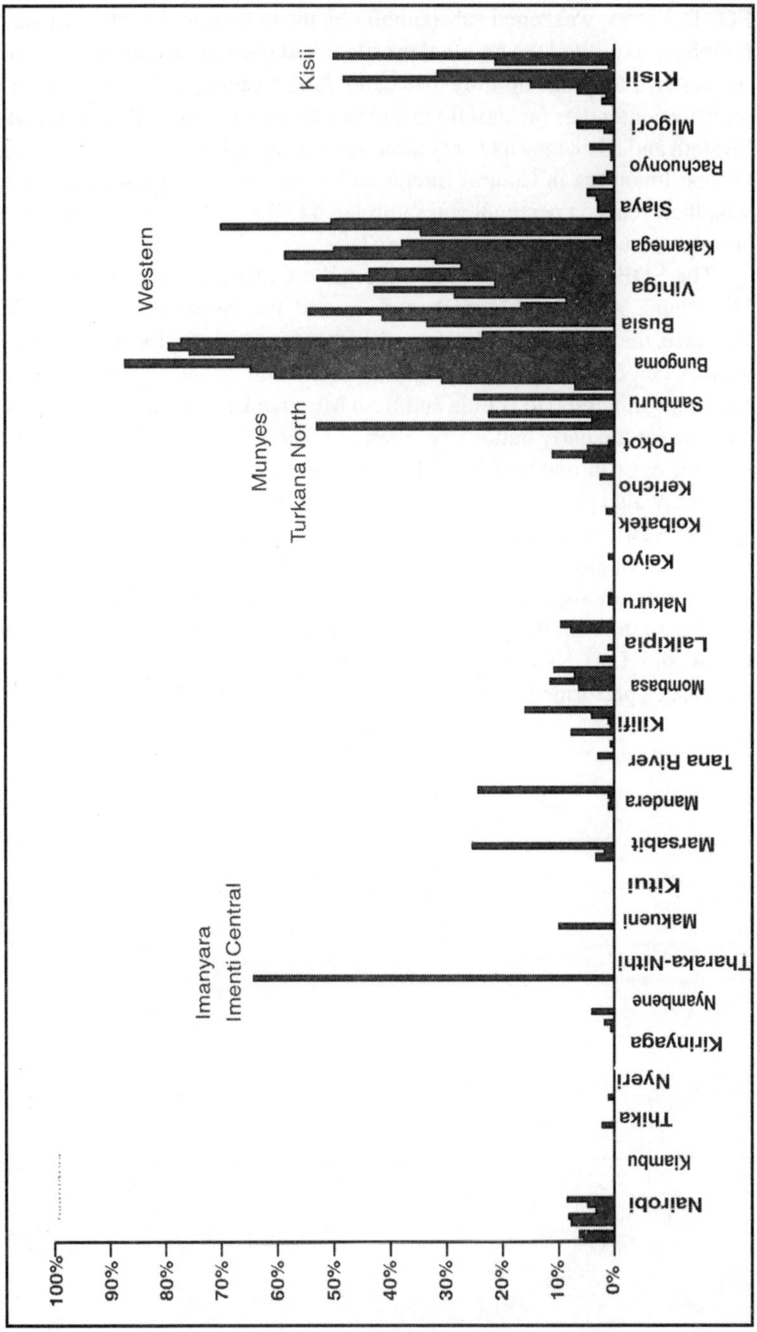

FORD-Kenya, weakened substantially by the mass Luo defection to the NDP, no longer exhibited the national profile it had tried to display in 1992. Strong in Western, they put up only 104 candidates in total, and few of these were realistic contenders (at least three had stood down before polling day). Outside Western and Kisii, they had only three serious figures, James Orengo in Ugenya, Gitobu Imanyara in Central Imenti and John Munyes in Turkana North. All won their seats on personal votes unrelated to their party. Elsewhere, the party simply ceased to exist (see Figure 6.7).

The SDP also proved weak nationally. Outside their new stronghold of Ukambani, a reasonable poll in Kisii and the confused southern Central Province, they benefited from personal votes for respected local political figures such as Peter Anyang' Nyong'o in Kisumu Rural, Mwacharo Kubo in Taveta, Clement Odhiambo in Butula and Beth Mugo in Dagoretti, but there was little support for the party nationally. Even in Ukambani, votes decided not to 'put all their eggs in one basket' and split their voters between KANU and SDP. The party also put up only 104 candidates (see Figure 6.8).

The NDP performed equally badly outside its home area of Nyanza (Figure 6.9). With roughly the same number of candidates (107), again they had a few strong individuals, who swung local voters towards them, but it had little or nothing to do with the party they represented. Outside Raila's Lang'ata, the Coast and Luo Nyanza, they had only four constituencies where their candidates performed creditably, in Kasarani, Limuru, Igembe and Amagoro.

Figure 6.8: SDP parliamentary candidates' percentage of the vote by seat

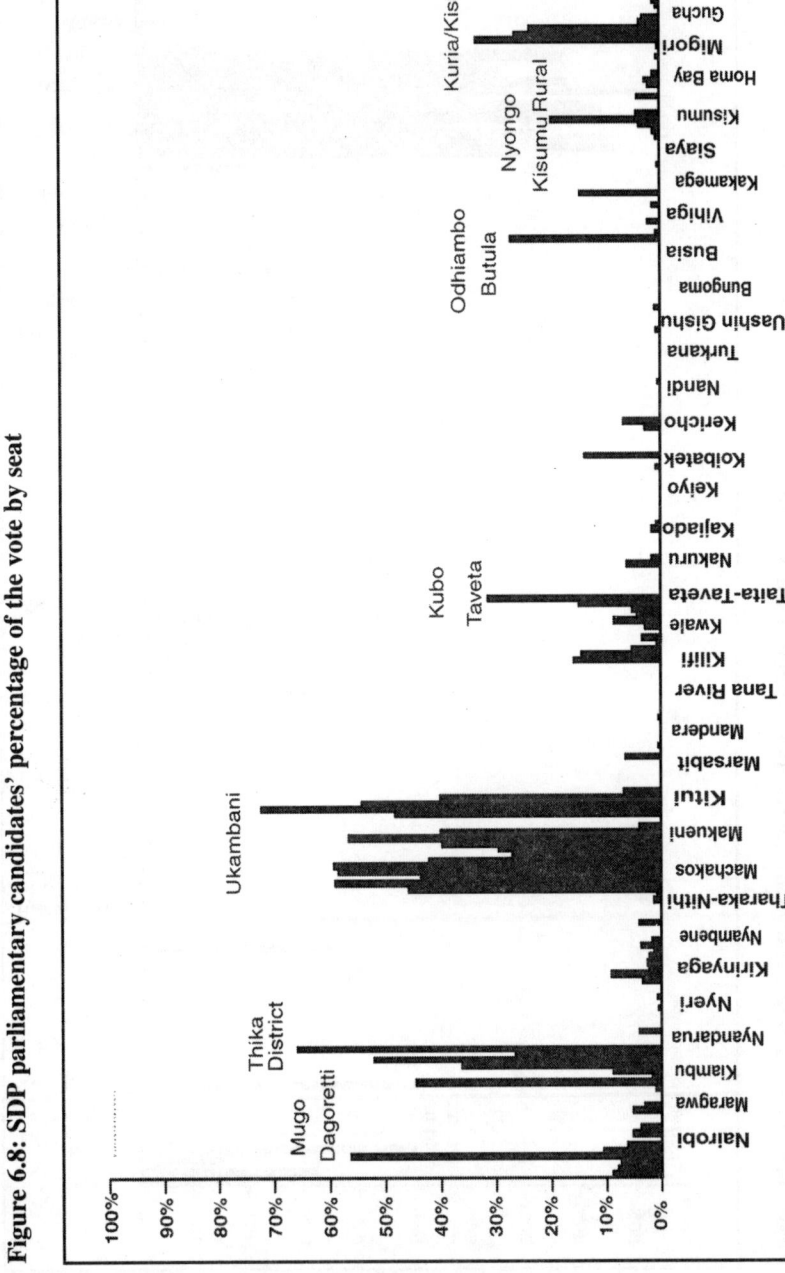

Figure 6.9: NDP parliamentary candidates' percentage of the vote by seat

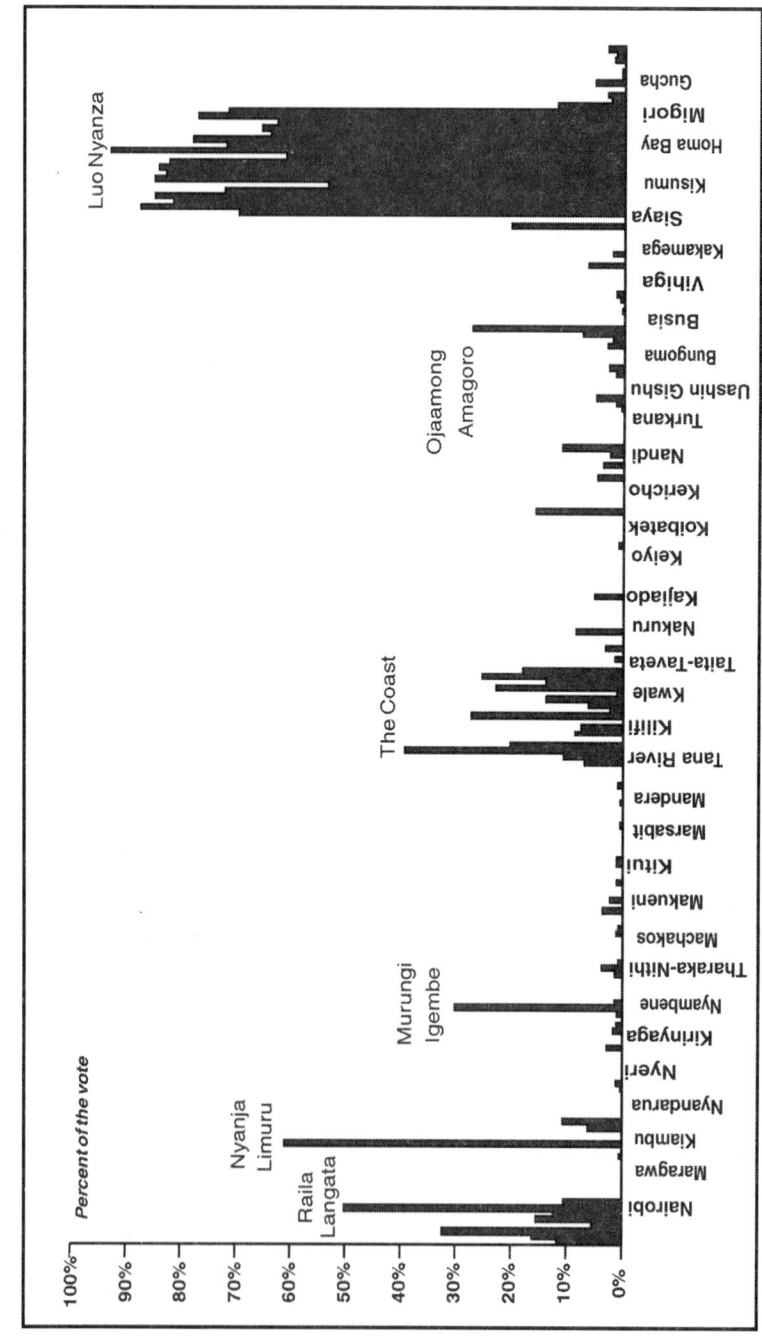

The late-registered Safina, with only 47 parliamentary candidates (11 of which were last minute KANU defectors, hardly an indication of extreme radicalism) and no presidential candidate, won only 5 seats. They took three seats in Central (including Kenneth Matiba's home seat of Kiharu) and two in the North-East, where they polled very well on a clan basis, having picked up most of the major KANU defectors.

The civic polls

The civic results followed the same patterns as the parliamentary and presidential votes, but with more room for local manoeuvre. According to the IED/CJPC/NCCK report, KANU won 60 per cent of the civil seats, the DP 14.6 per cent and the NDP 10.1 per cent. This better KANU performance at civic level was partly due to civic gerrymandering, and partly due to KANU having deeper organisational and financial resources at lower levels. More work, however, is needed to reach a final conclusion on this. (See, for example, the useful work of Southall and Wood (1996)). Civic ticket voting seemed weaker than in 1992, with the DP, for example, winning civic seats in Samburu West, the NDP in Sotik and Bahari, and KANU winning seats in Luo Alego and Gem. There were some examples of cross-party tickets being campaigned and voted. In the main, though, the civic results followed the parliamentary ones. In many cases there were tighter links between the civic and parliamentary teams than to the national stage.

Turnout

Despite the administrative and weather-related problems, the turnout at 68.8 per cent was much the same as in 1992 (69.0 per cent). Again, the main combatants (the Kikuyu and Kalenjin) showed the highest turnouts, but the picture became healthier than in 1992, with turnouts falling in the regions most politicised in 1992 and rising in the least politicised areas. There were certain constituencies where the turnouts were suspiciously high, including Baringo North, which reported a wholly implausible 96.4 per cent turnout, as it had in 1992. In general, however, the second day of voting compensated for some of the worst problems, and seats where day one had seen a fiasco reported turnouts not dissimilar from those of their neighbours.

Figure 6.10: Presidential turnout by seat

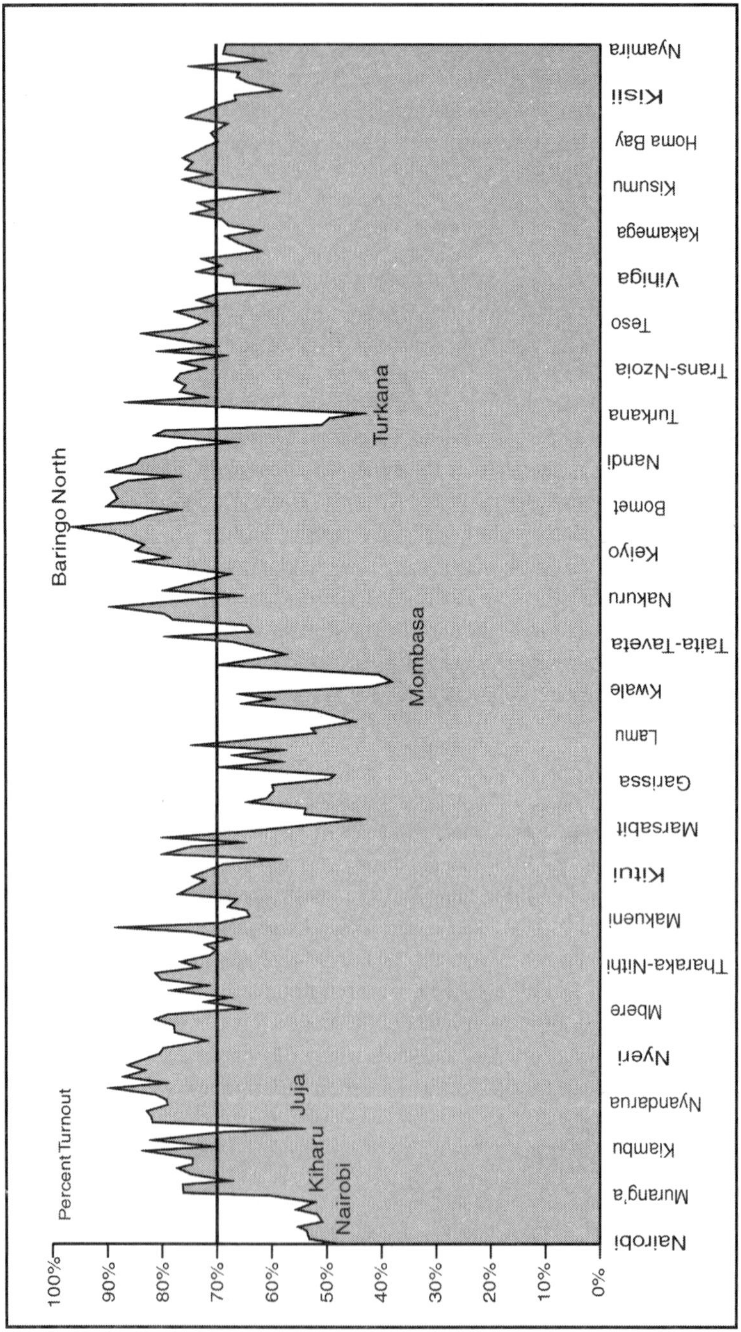

The turnout was higher across much of the country, particularly in Kisii and in Ukambani, which now had a presidential candidate of its own (see Figure 6.11). It fell dramatically in Luoland (66 per cent against 73 per cent in 1992) and in the old Matiba areas (from 85 per cent to only 70 per cent), reflecting that the boycott did have some effect in seats such as Juja and Matiba's own Kiharu. The boycott had little effect, however, outside Murang'a and Nairobi. In the Central Rift, the turnout was also down, from 87 per cent to 84 per cent, although turnouts rose dramatically, a rather odd result, in the northern periphery (Northern, North-Eastern, Turkana, Samburu and Pokot).

The lowest turnouts again, as in 1992, were in urban Mombasa where the combination of the Likoni clashes (which drove out upcountry voters) and double registration by rural voters out of town during the Christmas season saw turnouts as low as 42 per cent in Kisauni, though like Nairobi, Mombasa has always seen poor turnouts.[8] Areas of the Coast Province such as Ganze and Malindi also saw poor turnouts (50 per cent or less) caused by the weather and logistics difficulties.

The illusion of change

An interesting feature of 1997 was the stability of the voting patterns thereby revealed. Although the parties themselves had fragmented, realigned and boycotted, changing dramatically the party position, the ethnic and regional factional blocks underlying them continued to behave in a consistent fashion. In 1992, for example, KANU won parliament and also won the presidential vote in every seat in Isiolo, Marsabit/Moyale, Samburu, West Pokot, Baringo/Koibatek, Uasin Gishu, Keiyo, Marakwet, Nandi, Kericho, Bomet, Narok/Trans Mara, Kilifi/Malindi, Kwale, Tana River and Lamu. They did the same in 1997. In 1992 KANU lost every Luo seat in Siaya, Kisumu, Migori and Homa Bay to a Luo-dominated party led by an Odinga. They did almost the same in 1997. In 1992, Kibaki and Matiba took the presidential poll in every Kikuyu-dominated seat. In 1997, Kibaki did this alone.

Of 210 parliamentary constituencies, 130 were represented in January 1998 by the same party as before the elections. The main changes were in southern Central Province, Nyanza and Ukambani. KANU won seats from the opposition in Mombasa, Machakos, Meru, Western, Kisii and North-Eastern, but their position as a national party, facing a series of strong regional leaders, left them more vulnerable than in 1992 in the parliamentary polls. The DP gained seats in Meru, Kajiado, Taita/Taveta and Mombasa, and spread down to seize additional Kikuyu seats in Kiambu, Murang'a/Maragwa, Thika and Nakuru. Charity Ngilu hit both the DP and KANU hard in Ukambani and Wamalwa also won seats from KANU in Western though several were actually won by FORD-Asili in 1992 and had been lost in by-elections in the meantime.

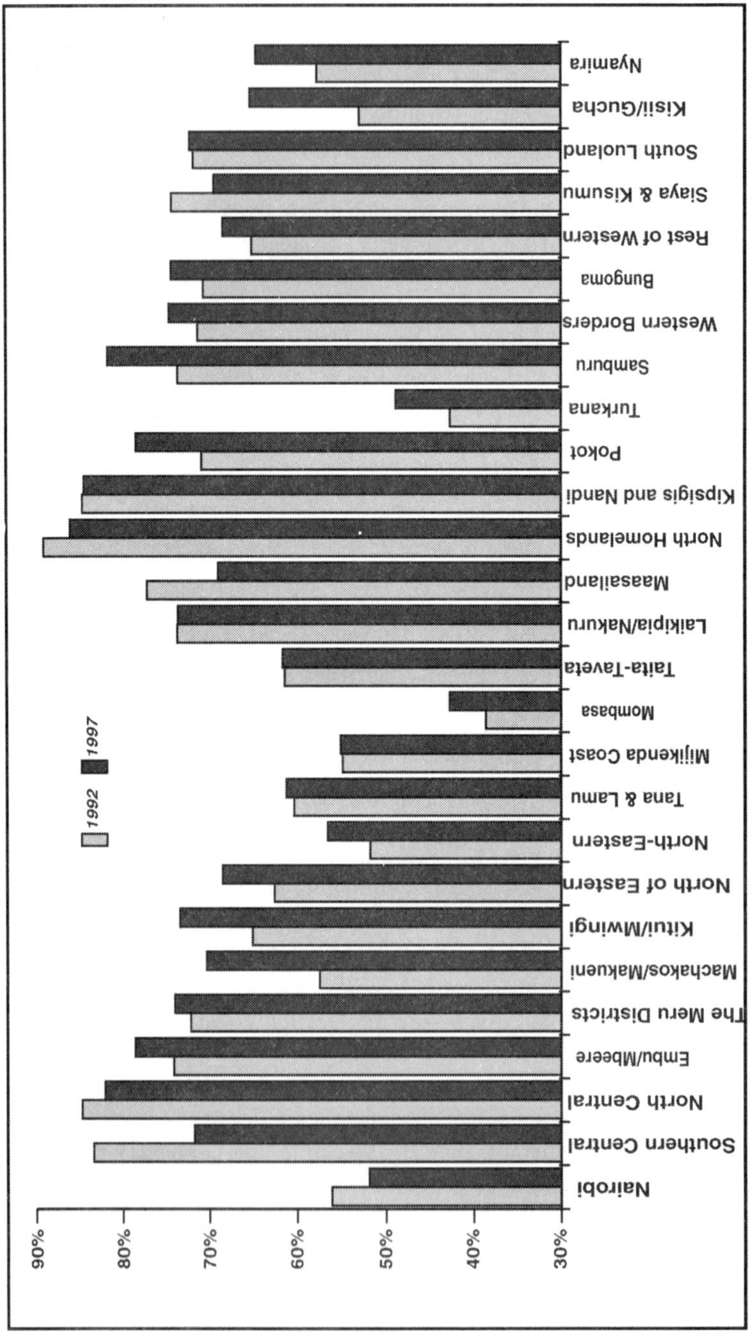

Figure 6.11: Presidential turnouts by region, 1992 and 1997

How fair were polling day and the count?

The issue of whether an election can be deemed fair or not is usually determined long before by such issues as media access, gerrymandering of constituency boundaries and access to state funds for the governing party. The issue of whether it is free is generally settled at the polling station and the count by whether the result reported reflects solely and completely votes intended to be cast by actual voters. By these standards, the 1997 elections were both freer and fairer than in 1992 though far less competently conducted.

There is still evidence of deliberate state-sanctioned malpractice, but it appears to have been more limited in scope and to have been focused in the Kalenjin homelands and in certain key marginals. The appalling abuses of 1992 nomination day were completely absent and there were fewer well-documented cases of ballot box stuffing although they did still occur. Nonetheless, the preferences of the voters as expressed in party voting on polling day were not precisely reflected in the composition of the National Assembly. Concerns relate to relatively few seats, but in a situation where the governing party has a majority of only four, malpractice in two or more seats effectively determined whether the government was a majority or minority one. KANU seems to have tolerated a far closer run than in 1992, but at the last minute, facing the prospect of becoming a minority in parliament for the first time since independence, some results were altered to ensure their victory.

Election day allegations and abuses

In some constituencies, as ever, polling day witnessed fighting, bribery and election abuses as had occurred at every previous Kenyan election. There were the same claims of 'assisted' public voting for illiterates, pre-marked ballots being smuggled into polling stations, campaigning in polling stations, payment for votes and pressure by local officials. In general, the administration was far more neutral than in 1992. Police and security officials were rarely directly involved in polling day abuses in contrast to previous polls. Nonetheless, as the voting patterns and anecdotal evidence showed, covert pressure continued to be an important weapon in mobilising support for each candidate in his or her home areas at the presidential level.

One of the seats in which there were allegations of systematic abuses was Kitui Central, home seat of Charity Ngilu, who was forced to abandon her eve-of-poll rally in Nairobi to travel to Kitui to shore up waning support and to investigate reports of massive vote card-buying and destruction by KANU. A lack of ballot papers on polling day also led her and her supporters to force their way into the returning officer's office where 20 books of unused papers were found. It was also reported that, 'Some of the documents and papers she confiscated indicated that voter registration in Kitui Central continued in secret until 2 December' (*Daily Nation* 30/12/97:3). It had already been clear that KANU was doing everything it could to defeat her in her home seat, whatever happened elsewhere in Ukambani, to ensure she could not participate in a presidential runoff.

Unfortunately, electoral violence was more common than in 1992, partly inspired by the frustration of voters at the slow pace of polling and then of the results. Unlike in 1992, it was more directed at KANU than the opposition. In several cases, the incidents involved assaults by opposition youth on houses allegedly being used for voters bribery by local KANU agents. People were injured in Shinyalu, Vihiga and Malava in Western Province in clashes involving KANU and FORD-Kenya supporters. There was fighting in Lagdera, Nyamira district and Central Imenti between KANU and opposition supporters. Chaotic scenes in Saitoti's Kajiado North led to the burning of nine ballot boxes on polling day. In Nakuru Town, voting in one station was prevented on the second day by pro-DP crowds. They claimed a vehicle had brought in KANU-supervised ballot boxes on Monday night and, therefore, sealed off the station. Indeed, there were several scuffles and fights associated with suspicious and angry crowds attacking trucks and individuals suspected of poll rigging.

In some seats, the violence was more premeditated. In Ndia in Kirinyaga district, one candidate supporter's car was involved in a fierce fight which ended with the pick-up in the ditch. It was photographed full of stones and whips to be used to attack rival supporters. Three were killed in Alego constituency in Siaya district in incidents of violence between KANU and NDP supporters on polling day. The next day, a Tuesday, two more people were burned to death in the same constituency after a fight between rival youths at a polling station, bringing the death toll to five. The KANU candidate's house in Ol Kalou was burnt to the ground on polling day, and the FORD-People candidate for Mathioya also had his car torched and others damaged. The KANU-supporting ex-DP MP for Mwea was injured by DP youth, as was a KANU civic candidate in Meru.

Threats were also made against opposition supporters in KANU-dominated areas although they were less pervasive than in 1992. In Samburu on the eve of the poll, for example, the local KANU assistant minister Peter Lenges threatened that, 'Outsiders who are not ready to sing the Samburu song and are out to provoke them would be ejected from the district.' (*Daily Nation* 29/12/97:4). Domestic poll watchers reported instances of campaigning in polling stations and threats by KANU agents '. . . that they will not be given guns and maize by the government if they vote for the opposition' (see NCCK/ IED/CJPC-Samburu 1997). The *Sunday Nation* reported on 28 December that unnamed 'Nandi leaders' were demanding that non-Kalenjin either vote in

Moi and KANU or quit the district by polling day and leaflets demanding that the Luo leave Kericho district were also circulated over Christmas. In West Pokot, non-Pokot were driven by a series of threats and attacks out of the area before polling day (KHRC 1998). Upcountry voters were already gone from some coastal areas.

On polling day itself, threats were reportedly made by KANU agents in a few polling stations, as in Kuria for example. Interestingly, they were not alone. In Dujis, for example, five different polling stations reported threats by Safina and DP agents against voters, plus the distribution of small photos of Mwai Kibaki to voters inside the stations (see NCCK/IED/CJPC-Dujis 1997). Campaigning by agents in and around the stations was reported in hundreds of stations, although, depending on the proclivities of the presiding officers (POs), it was either swiftly quashed, allowed to flourish or driven round the corners and out of sight of the stations themselves. Presiding officers themselves on occasion showed their preferences. In Kuria, for example, one PO was saying to illiterate voters 'Here we have a tractor symbol for the Luo tribal party and Jogoo for our own leaders' party (KANU). So where do you want me to mark for you?' (NCCK/IED/CJPC-Kuria 1997).

There were widespread and well-documented allegations of election day bribery. There were reports of KANU bribery, mainly by agents or campaigners just outside the polling stations, in Kajiado North and Central, Tinderet, Kwanza, Turkana Central, Kuria, Isiolo North, Tigania East and West, Ikolomani, Malava, Butere, Lurambi and elsewhere. In Igembe in Nyambene district, local observers reported bribery and campaigning by KANU campaigners and agents in 14 stations, including illiterate voters being asked the loaded question by the presiding officer, 'Who is your President?' (NCCK/IED/CJPC-Igembe 1997). In Kiambaa, the KANU campaign team similarly alleged bribery by the opposition (*Kenya Times* 31/12/97:19). Safina activists similarly protested at DP bribery in Mukurweini (Ksh. 20 a vote). Two people were arrested for vote buying in a Lamu polling station and there were other Lamu West bribery claims (*East African Standard* 31/12/97:7). The DP victor for Nithi later had his election nullified, partly due to bribery (*Daily Nation* 24/04/99:1). Changamwe in Mombasa saw bribery and/or campaigning by KANU agents outside the polls in at least nine polling stations (Ksh. 100 to Ksh. 200 a vote was the going rate in stations 14 and 25) (NCCK/IED/CJPC-Changamwe 1997). Many voters were demanding cash payments to vote in Lagdera, a KANU target to recapture as the only opposition-held North-Eastern Province seat. Safina activist and FORD-Kenya MP Farrah Maalim claimed that senior civil servants, including the Eastern deputy provincial commissioner, were going round the area bribing people to vote him out. Anecdotal evidence suggests that, with the reduction in political ferment and fervour compared to 1992, financial incentives proved a more important determinant of voting preferences.

The level of multiple voting, voting by minors, impersonation and vote card buying and destruction appeared lower than in 1992. As usual, there were a few cases of voters unable to find their names due to misspellings or other errors. The new computerised register in general proved adequate, but recourse was regularly made to the 'black book' (the original paper register) to resolve disputes.

Actual ballot box stuffing and multiple voting on polling day was alleged, but far less often although there were some polling stations, such as one in Likoni, where the count later revealed more votes than voters. In multi-ethnic Nakuru Town, three ballot boxes full of papers were allegedly found stuffed when polling began. In Ntonyiri, police arrested one presiding officer after he was reported to be marking ballot papers in a bar (*East African Standard* 31/12/97:2). There were claims of KANU agents with numbers of ballot papers in Kangundo. A DP supporter was arrested after being found with ballot books in South Mugirango, which were allegedly being stamped and smuggled in through the window and given to the PO (*Kenya Times* 01/01/98).[9] In Baringo North, under pressure to turn out a huge vote for Moi in a 'KANU zone', some presiding officers simply filled in the missing votes when the polls closed. In the words of an NCCK/IED/CJPC observer in station 015, '. . . the presiding officer say that the voting now is finished, so there were 36 voters remain [sic] the presiding officer and the clerks vote [sic] for these voters.' (NCCK/IED/CJPC-Baringo North 1997).

In a new development, KANU attacked domestic election observers in some areas following unwise comments from polling station observers that their job was to ensure KANU did not win. In Nakuru Town, KANU, SDP, NDP and FORD-Kenya all accused the NCCK and Catholic Secretariat of openly campaigning for the DP (*Kenya Times* 03/01/98:4). Indeed, the polls revealed an obvious tension between the roles of observer and 'anti-government' activist, both of which have been roles played by some churches in recent years.

The ink used for marking voters' thumbs again proved to be completely inadequate. In one station in Nyeri, for example, each voter had their finger marked, voted, then left the station and moved over to a nearby water tank, where they scrubbed the ink off again with water and pumice stone, leaving no mark at all.[10]

The practice of bribing or threatening voters to vote for a particular party, then ensuring they delivered by demanding that they declare themselves illiterate and, therefore, voted publicly in front of the party agents continued to compromise fairness in many areas.[11] New legislation which made it an election offence for a presiding officer to mark a ballot for a voter who was capable of marking it for himself was not enforced.

The count and its problems

In 1992, many of the worst electoral abuses had occurred during the count. Again, 1997 was better although some abuses may have been concealed by the chaos associated with the second day of polling and overnight storage, plus the movement of ballot papers between stations. Again, there were votes for the presidential candidates found in parliamentary boxes and vice versa. This time, the rules were better understood and they were not counted in most places.

The count saw as much violence as the polling itself, again associated with frustration and fears of rigging. One person was shot dead and others injured during scuffles outside Homa Bay County Hall where the Rangwe seat's votes were being counted. Two people were killed and dozens more injured during riots outside the counting centre in Nakuru Town when pro-DP voters tried to prevent three civic boxes from being taken to the station for counting. The boxes were later checked, found to be correct and counted. There were numerous beatings and car-burnings caused by angry and bored youth. There was fighting between groups of supporters in Kisumu, and various constituencies in Luoland saw rowdy NDP youth involved in fights and confrontations with KANU and government officials. There was also fighting in Kitale when youth tried to storm the counting hall, and fighting inside the counting hall in Malava in Western and Bobasi in Kisii.

Some seats saw problems indicative of pre-planned abuses. Somehow, unmarked ballots got out of the ECK machinery and into the hands of individuals in some seats. Some were then re-introduced. Some seats also saw attempts to introduce ballot boxes acquired from unknown sources (test-boxes, boxes left over from the last elections or over-ordered boxes).[12] Some constituencies saw counting clerks mixing the votes of one candidate with votes of another, thereby over-counting one and under-counting the other.[13] Most problems reported, however, appear to have either been misunderstandings by observers or agents, or the result of makeshift procedures (e.g. sealing the boxes with the wrong materials where the right ones were not available). Some attempts to modify voter preferences were detected and prevented. Others, even where they were eventually accepted by returning officers, could not have modified the parliamentary results since the final margin was very substantial.

In Dagoretti, Nairobi, a PO was arrested after being found tampering with the ballot boxes. An NDP agent in Kasarani was arrested in possession of ballot papers outside the counting hall (*Kenya Times* 03/01/98). KANU's Fred

Gumo 'won' wealthy Westlands in a violent election that was marred by blatant rigging during the last moments of the count. Following a visit from two State House officials (which it is alleged offered the returning officer Mary Moraa one million shillings to change the result), the returning officer on live TV announced a different result from that collated from the individual boxes, refused the statutory recount and left the hall surrounded by security police. The last few results were coming in, and KANU knew it was close to losing majority control of the House. They needed representation in Nairobi and Gumo was their last chance.[14]

In Central Province, the count was smooth and clean. The only exception was a claim that three stuffed ballot boxes full of unused pro-KANU papers were found in the home of a school teacher in Kibaki's home seat of Othaya (*Sunday Nation* 04/01/98:3). In Eastern Province, the Tigania East DP loser claimed bribery on polling day in polling stations and the introduction of unsealed boxes. The IED count certifiers concurred, reporting folded ballots in sequence and no seals on some parliamentary boxes. KANU won by 3,000 votes (*Sunday Nation* 04/01/98:4; NCKK/IED/CJPC-Tigania East 1997b).

In Nithi, the DP MP's election was nullified, partly due to the seals being broken on ballot boxes and other boxes dumped. Blank ballot papers were found hidden under a seat in the counting hall for an Embu seat before counting began (*East African Standard* 31/12/97:5). In Igembe, there were also claims of ballots in boxes not matching the booklets of counterfoils.

The worst problems, however, were in the marginal Kamba areas. SDP candidate Joseph Mulusya in Kangundo in Machakos district insisted he had been rigged out, claiming one ballot box had 'neatly stacked' votes in it (*Kenya Times* 03/01/98:5). There were anomalies in Kilome with claims of fraudulent counting and introduced ballots. One box was not counted as a result. In Mwingi North, Minister Musyoka's seat, nine ballot boxes were left uncounted until the end of the count due to disputes over their validity. The IED reported that eight boxes were improperly sealed and some serial numbers had been interfered with. Boxes arrived without security; there was fraudulent counting and stuffing and ballots introduced. Requests to view the counterfoils for the disputed ballots were refused (NCCK/IED/CJPC-Mwingi North 1997b). Nonetheless, KANU's margin was so huge at 14,000 for parliament it probably did not change the result. The EOC were also very critical of Kitui West, as were the local observers. In one station during the night, when boxes were being stored awaiting transport to the count, men dressed in police uniform arrived and attempted to seize the ballot boxes. They were resisted and vanished (NCCK/IED/CJPC-Kitui West/Kangungi station 034/062 1997). In the count itself, the domestic observers reported boxes arriving unaccompanied by agents, substitution of returns, stuffing, fraudulent counting, and substituted boxes

(NCCK/IED/CJPC-Kitui West 1997b). The final parliamentary result announced by the returning officer (a narrow KANU victory of 17,572 to 17,009) did not match the box-by-box totals recorded by the observers (SDP 17,401 versus KANU 16,892). The SDP won the presidency vote by 28,000 to 4,500.

In the Rift, in Uasin Gishu, there were riots in Eldoret town after a ballot box from Eldoret South was allegedly found stocked with counterfeit votes at the house of a presiding officer. In Eldama Ravine, there were claims of pre-marked pro-KANU ballot papers though whether any were actually introduced is unclear. Domestic observers reported theft of parliamentary ballot papers and a mixing up of DP ballots with KANU's by counting clerks (NCCK/IED/CJPC-Eldama Ravine 1997b). In Samburu West, six ballot boxes arrived with the seals broken, the returning officer was partial to KANU and the KANU agents were pressurising clerks to count opposition as KANU votes (NCCK/IED/CJPC-Samburu West 1997b). There were boxes whose seals did not match the presiding officers' in Laikipia East. Cherangani in Trans Nzoia also saw fraudulent counting, substitution of election returns and new ballot boxes introduced although KANU's Kirwa won a decisive victory anyway.

As in 1992, Nakuru saw some serious problems. There were claims of fraudulent counting in Rongai and one station's boxes were accompanied by KANU agents only. Nakuru Town also reported fraudulent counting and introduced boxes. In Molo, some boxes arrived with seals broken, and the count saw a theft and destruction of ballots and fraudulent counting (NCCK/IED/CJPC-Molo 1997b).[15] It is unlikely that any results were modified in the process. In Konoin, observers reported other candidates' votes being counted for KANU and an innovative new counting technique used, whereby the ". . . total votes casted [sic] was subtracted from spoiled on[sic] and remain[sic] was said for Jogoo.' (NCCK/IED/CJPC-Konoin 1997a). There were other more minor reports of possible stuffing, fraudulent counting or destruction of ballots by observers in Kilgoris, Turkana North, Baringo North, Kajiado Central, Narok South and Emgwen.

At the coast, in Magarini, all opposition candidates boycotted the count claiming pro-KANU favouritism and alleging that ballot papers from two polling stations had been tampered with. In Minister Ngala's Ganze, there were complaints of unstamped ballot papers being counted (*Daily Nation* 03/01/98:5). An IED observer reported that police retrieved a ballot box from a private individual's house, where it was apparently being filled with ballots (NCCK/IED/CJPC-Ganze 1997b).[16] In Kaloleni, some boxes had had their seals tampered with and the KANU parliamentary candidate's car was allegedly somehow used to carry some boxes (NCCK/IED/CJPC-Kaloleni 1997b). Count certifiers reported minor questionable activities in Msambweni and Bahari.

Nonetheless, in no case (even if the claims were true) was the result changed. The only possible exception was Changamwe in Mombasa where seven boxes arrived without agents and with only the presiding officers' seal. There were protests, but the boxes were eventually counted (*Kenya Times* 31/12/97:4). KANU won by 500 votes with 1,000 spoilt, and there were furious allegations that the presiding officer had added up the totals differently on a second tally and, thereby, given the seat to KANU. There were no major issues reported in North-Eastern where the polls and counts seem to have been reasonably fair despite the chaos, bar Wajir West, where there were some indications of box stuffing.

In Western Province, in Amagoro in Teso district, a presiding officer was reported beaten up after bringing in three boxes irregularly. Police also arrested a clerk in possession of 200 blank papers at the counting hall (*East African Standard* 31/12/97:6). This was a safe KANU seat. An assistant chief in Bungoma was beaten up then arrested after being found with Bumula ballot papers. Nambale reported a fraudulent counting and theft of ballot papers, and a FORD-Kenya agent was allegedly found counting the votes with the clerks though observers felt the result was not affected. Elsewhere, things went well.

In Nyanza, in controversial Rangwe constituency, seven ballot boxes were rejected from the count after being found open, and a counting clerk was sacked after being found mixing votes for KANU with the NDP bundles (see e.g., *East African Standard* 01/01/98:5). In Kisii seats, there were serious allegations of malpractices in Kitutu Chache, including destruction of papers and stuffing, with new boxes introduced during the count (NCCK/IED/CJPC-Kitutu Chache 1997b).[17] There were some irregularities in Bonchari and Bobasi, while South Mugirango saw a clear incident of stuffing in one station, with ballots all stuffed in sequence and folded together (NCCK/IED/CJPC-South Mugirango 1997b).

Strange days
There are some useful statistical methods that can be applied to assess the validity of these results. One is to compare the presidential results for the candidate with the polls for his parliamentary candidate. There were some unusual events that require explanation. This is very clear in the case of KANU and President Moi.

Figure 6.12: Moi and his candidates

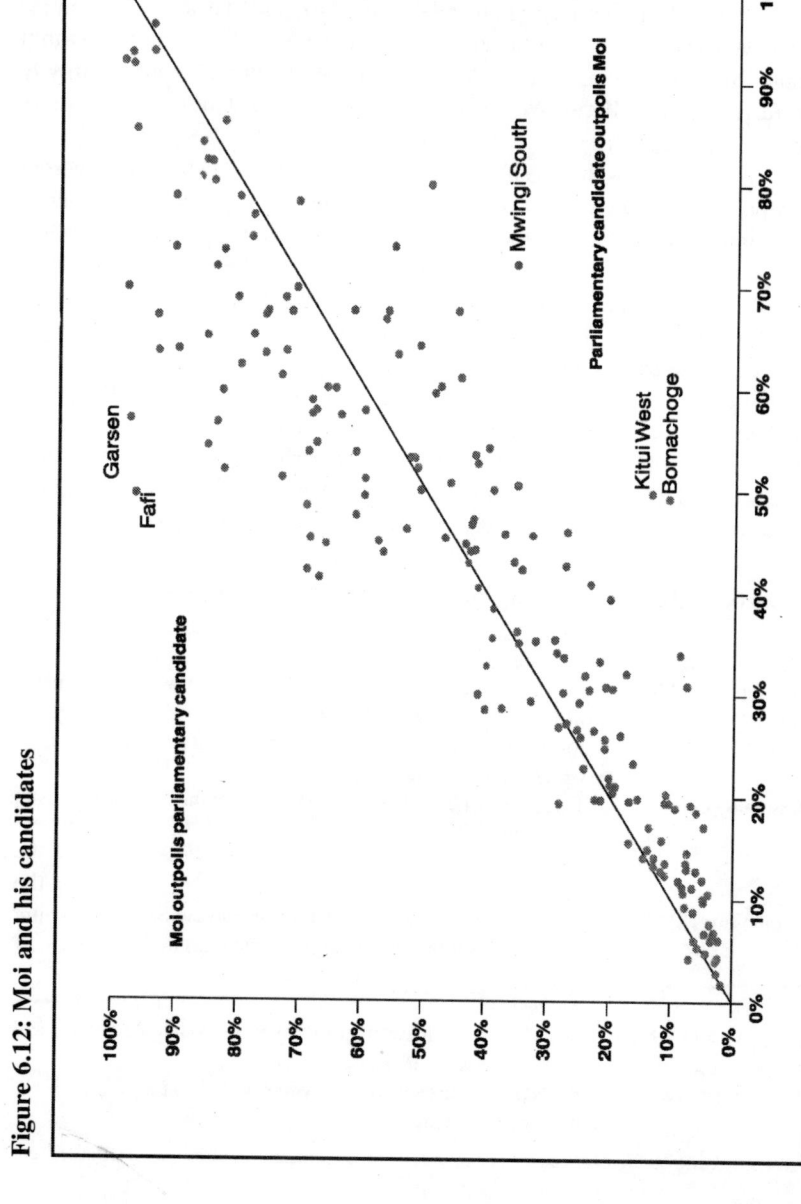

Figure 6.12 shows the characteristic 'S' curve which Moi's results also showed in 1992; where he was popular, he was more popular than his candidates, mainly due to local support for KANU-nomination defectors. Where he was unpopular, he was even more unpopular than his candidates who pick up some local clan or factional support independent of their party (Throup and Hornsby 1998: 453-533). In semi-arid Fafi and Garsen, Moi polled nearly 100 per cent of the vote, but voters split ticketed for Safina ex-KANU defectors. Mwingi South stood out as a massive victory for the local MP, though voters narrowly preferred Ngilu. Kitui West and Bomachoge stood out as extremely questionable results.

We can also view the presidential and parliamentary statistics from another viewpoint. There were 13 closely fought parliamentary constituencies where the number of parliamentary ballots was either far too many or too few compared to the number of presidential ballots, and/or the number of missing, lost, disallowed or miscounted ballots were greater than the majority of the winning candidate. These are strong indicators of a high-risk situation. In most cases, an exact count (always an unlikely situation in the confusion of a counting hall, even without malpractices) should have revealed slightly more presidential than parliamentary ballots, since a few voters voted for the presidency but refused to vote for the civic or parliamentary polls. Errors in counting and totalling should normally have cancelled each other out if they were accidental.[18] Table 6.5 lists the statistically strange results.

Table 6. 5: Questionable parliamentary results statistically

	Nairobi
Westlands (KANU)	This seat, rigged during the count, shows up well by this metric with 1,600 more votes for president than parliament, 1,400 spoilt and a majority of 5, 1,000 or nothing at all depending on which version of the results is used.
Kasarani (DP)	This narrow DP victory of 255 votes over the NDP was assisted by 1,700 spoilt ballots
	Central
Githunguri (SDP)	Arthur Magugu narrowly lost the seat to the SDP by only 435 votes, with more spoilt votes than the margin.
	Eastern
Kitui West (KANU)	KANU won a narrow majority of 563 in a disputed count with 1,900 too many parliamentary ballots.
Isiolo North (KANU)	KANU won this seat by 380 votes with 866 too many parliamentary ballots.

	Coast
Kisauni (DP)	The DP's narrow win here by 534 votes was overshadowed by 716 spoilt votes and 1,145 more parliamentary ballots in the count than presidential.
Changamwe (KANU)	The DP's narrow loss here by 511 with 1,400 more presidential than parliamentary ballots and 1,000 spoilt is certainly odd.
Bura (KANU)	KANU won Bura from the NDP by only 127 votes, with 1,700 too few parliamentary votes reported.
Voi (DP)	The DP narrowly won this seat by only 34 votes with 324 votes difference between president and parliament.
	Rift Valley
Kajiado Central (KANU)	This narrow KANU win by 431 votes, with 1,100 more parliamentary than presidential ballots was extremely closely contested.
	Western
Emuhaya (KANU)	KANU narrowly won this seat from FORD-Kenya by only 786 votes, with over 2,700 more parliamentary ballots than presidential. Their victory was assisted by split voting for the liberal candidate, a FORD-Kenya defector.
Butere (KANU)	In Shikuku's home seat, he narrowly won the presidential election by 200 votes, but then lost his own parliamentary seat by 550 votes, with 1,600 parliamentary votes spoilt and 2,000 more parliamentary than presidential votes.
	Nyanza
Gem (FORD-K)	Massive failures to vote for parliament caused by an injunction against the NDP candidate allowed the FORD-Kenya candidate to win by 3,210 votes, with over 9,000 voters declining to vote for either candidate and 3,137 spoilt votes.

Despite the catalogue of issues in Table 6.5, this was distinctly less blatant 'rigging' than that unearthed in 1992 (Throup and Hornsby 1998: 453-533). In contrast to 1992, some losers were happy to report that they lost fair and square. Radical presidential candidate Koigi wa Wamwere, for example, reported that 'I did not see any direct rigging in my constituency.' (*Sunday Nation* 04/04/98:4). Generally, there seemed to be more experience and understanding of procedural norms, and greater pressure on officials who did not follow them. There were several cases of POs being arrested for failing to follow election regulations regarding the control of papers and boxes. Three presiding officers were arrested in Kitutu Masaba for transporting ballot boxes to the count without party agents, for example, and in Narok South, a deputy PO was arrested for cheering when the KANU parliamentary candidate was declared the winner.

The elections were certainly not fair, but were generally free in that most voters were able to cast their ballots for their preferred candidates and the results were not dramatically 'rigged' in the vast majority of seats. The overall conduct of the polls, despite the chaos, was both better than 1992 and better than expected. Nonetheless, the result was so close that the pro-KANU malpractice that did occur almost certainly changed the result from a minority to a majority government. Such malpractice in tight contests in Changamwe, Westlands, Kitui West, and possibly in Butere, Tigania East and Bomachoge gave KANU an overall majority that was not earned by votes cast.

ECK Chairman Kivuitu was unsurprised at foreign observers' complaints about the results in eight constituencies, but indicated that electoral petitions by the losers were the sole legal method of dealing with such issues. Just as in 1992, the post-1997 petitions were completely unsuccessful. Of 50 anti-KANU petitions submitted in 1992, zero were successful. Of 40 petitions against opposition winners, 5 were successful.[19] These figures are not entirely by coincidence. By June 1999, again, no KANU winners had had their election nullified, as a result of the 26 parliamentary petitions filed, but already one opposition MP had lost his seat. Many of the key petitions had been voided on technicalities, such as that against Gumo in Westlands.

The results by electoral region

Nairobi

The Nairobi results were a reversal of the DP's crushing defeat of 1992. With Kenneth Matiba's overwhelming support fragmented, Kikuyu voters backed Mwai Kibaki everywhere, and Kibaki won seven of the eight Nairobi seats in the presidential polls.

Five of the eight seats ended up in the DP's hands, including Norman Nyagah, who moved from Gachoka to Nairobi's Kamukunji to make way for his brother Joe, the KANU candidate. Dagoretti went to the SDP's Beth Mugo, Kenyatta's niece and one of the few successful female candidates. Raila Odinga triumphed in his Lang'ata stronghold both in parliament and the presidential polls and, as discussed earlier, KANU narrowly 'won' Westlands.

In general, KANU's vote improved by between one and five percentage points, a reflection of the reduced level of polarisation compared with 1992. Examining the changes in voting patterns by seat, we can make an estimation,

Figure 6.13: Nairobi presidential results

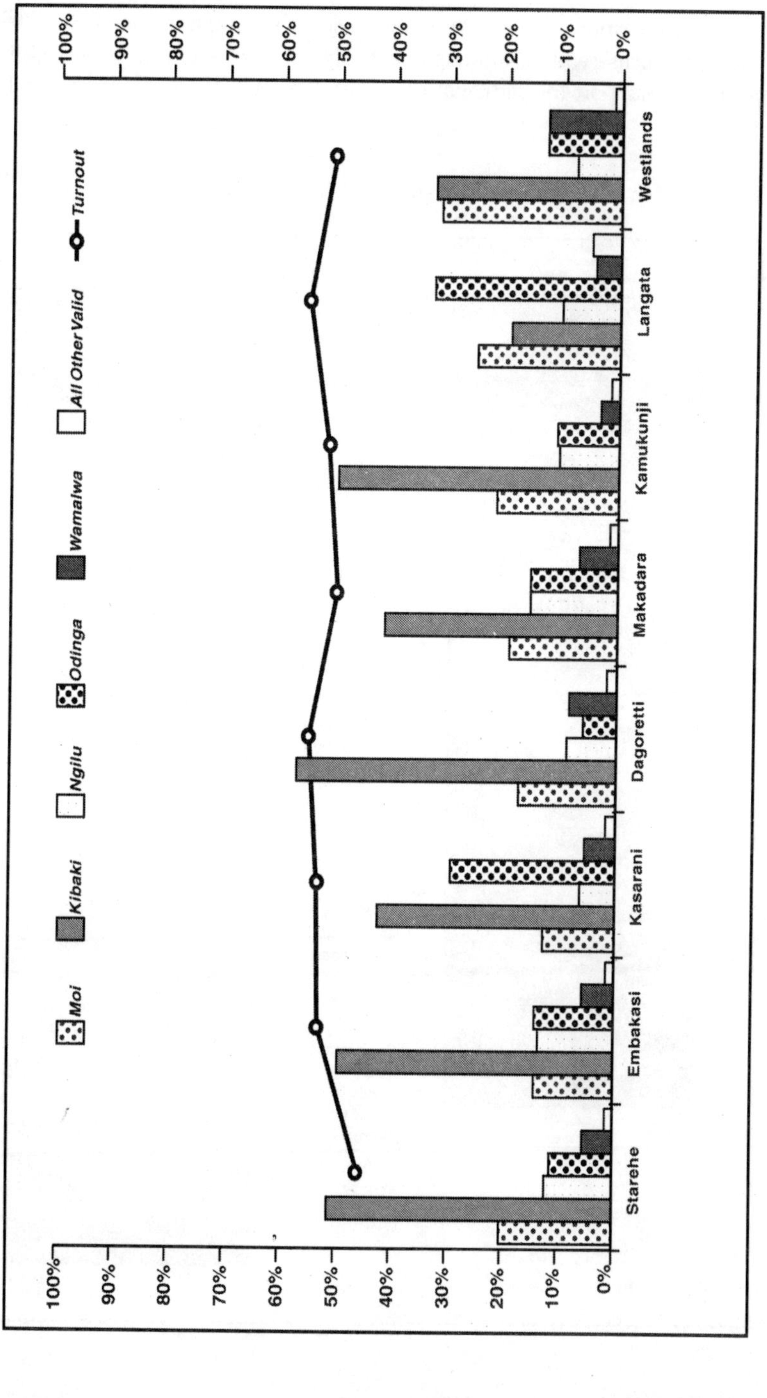

by nature approximate and based on some assumptions about stability of voting patterns (which, although probably true, are far from proven), of the changes in support for particular candidates/trends in the region between 1992 and 1997.

Figure 6.14: Changing voting patterns in Nairobi

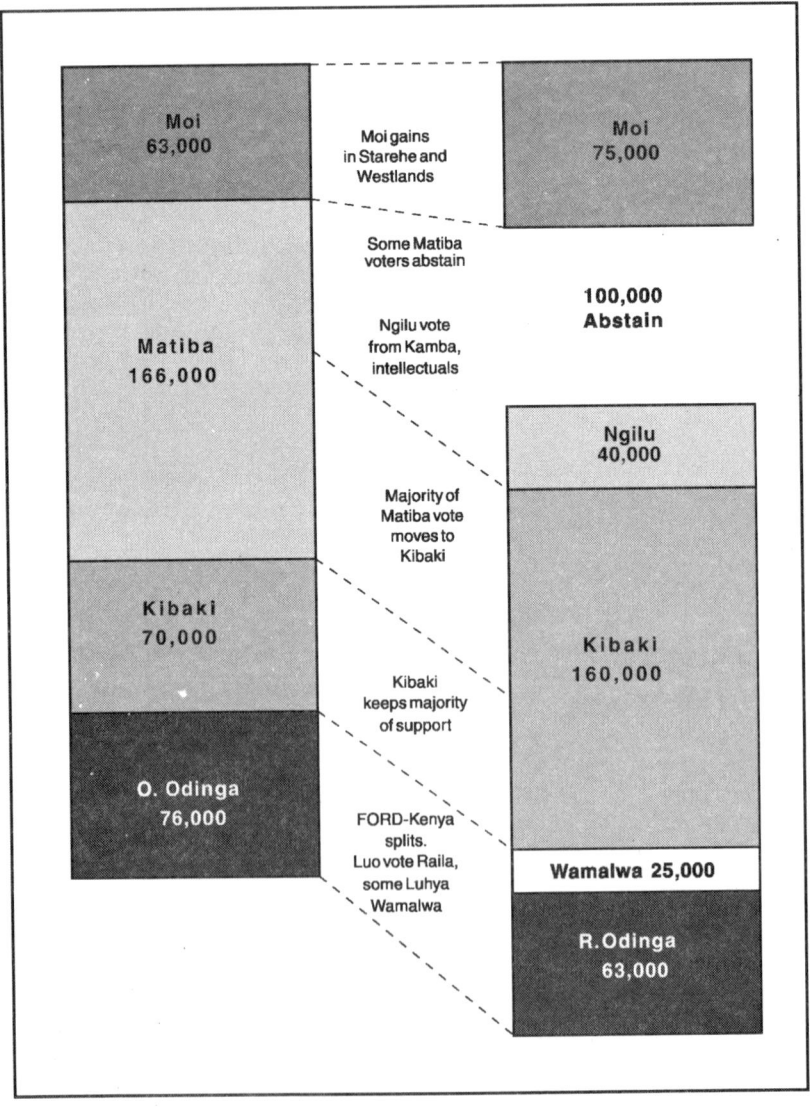

Many Nairobi voters abstained. The average nation-wide increase in actual votes cast from 1992 to 1997 was nearly 10 per cent and in Nairobi the population grew much faster than that; yet Nairobi saw a fall, indicating that at least 100,000 and probably more new or migrated voters did not bother to vote.

Central Province

The Central Province results were the most interesting, unpredictable and confused of any region. With Matiba glowering from the sidelines, his southern Central Province heartlands were divided between boycotters and participants, and among participants between those who believed Kikuyu solidarity mean their votes should now lie with the DP and those looking for more radical alternatives in Safina, the SDP and FORD-People (the new participationist rump of FORD-Asili).

Kibaki won the presidential ballot in every single Central Province constituency, quite easily. The minor Kikuyu candidates (Wangari Maathai, Kimani wa Nyoike, Koigi wa Wamwere) had no impact at all and all easily lost their parliamentary seats. Many SDP and Safina parliamentary candidates openly campaigned for Kibaki. His victory in his homeland of northern Central Province (Nyeri, Nyandarua and Kirinyaga) was complete (see Figure 6.16), and nearly so in the southern areas (Figure 6.17).

Turnouts were lower in the ex-Matiba 'homelands' of 1992, and a few voters switched to Charity Ngilu. Joseph Kamotho, a KANU man, turned out a good vote for Moi in the gerrymandered Mathioya seat. Otherwise, Kibaki still dominated. Nonetheless, the depth of confusion and resentment at the DP as a party showed in Kikuyu voters' support for candidates of five different parties in the parliamentary polls. Voters backed local 'big men' – either wealthy and influential or politically active and confrontational. The DP retained all the northern Kikuyu strongholds, won the new Maragwa district, and DP-financier Njenga Karume won a sole victory in Kiambaa, but the southern Kikuyu continued to reject the DP. Kikuyu 'leader without a party' Paul Muite (Safina) won another massive endorsement (the largest vote for any candidate in the election) in Kabete whilst SDP candidates won all the seats in Thika and the aggressive and controversial George Nyanza, sacked from several parties as unelectable, defied all predictions and seized Limuru for the otherwise irrelevant NDP.

Figure 6.15: Central Province

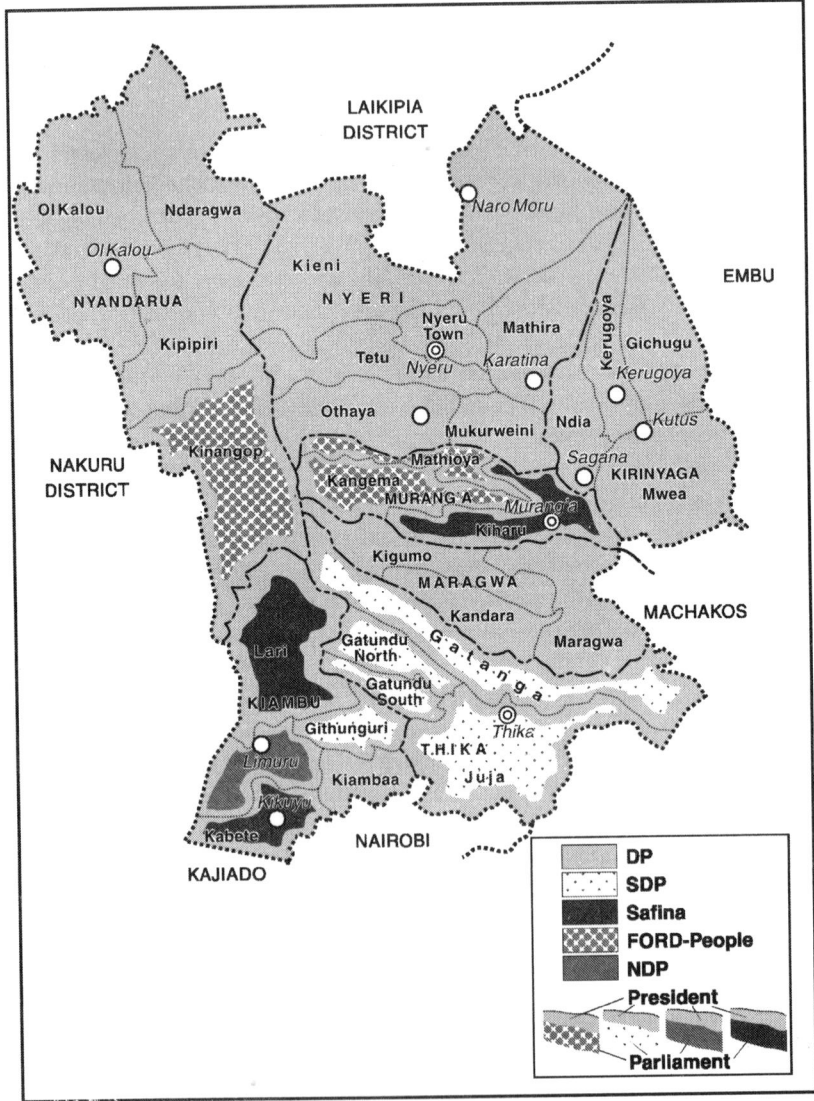

Figure 6.16: Presidential results in Kibaki's 'homeland'

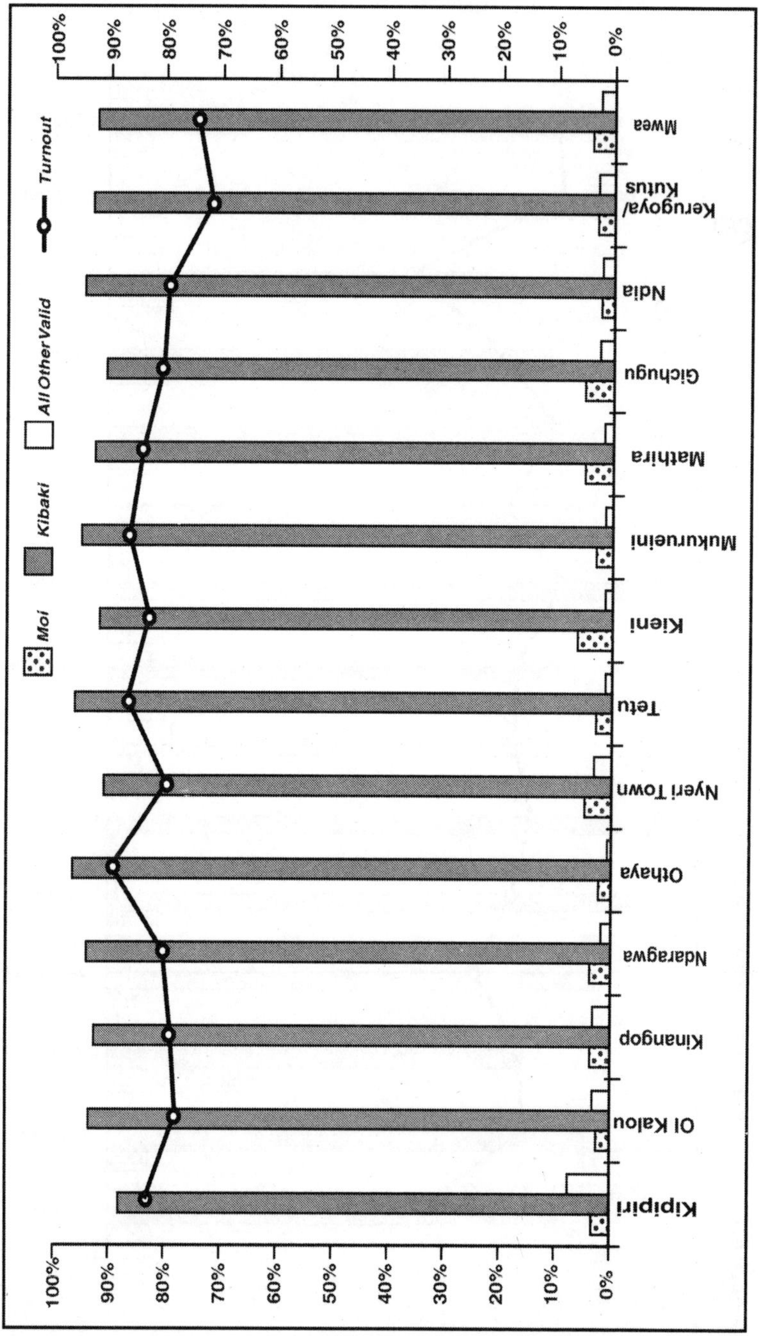

Figure 6.17: Presidential results in southern Central Province

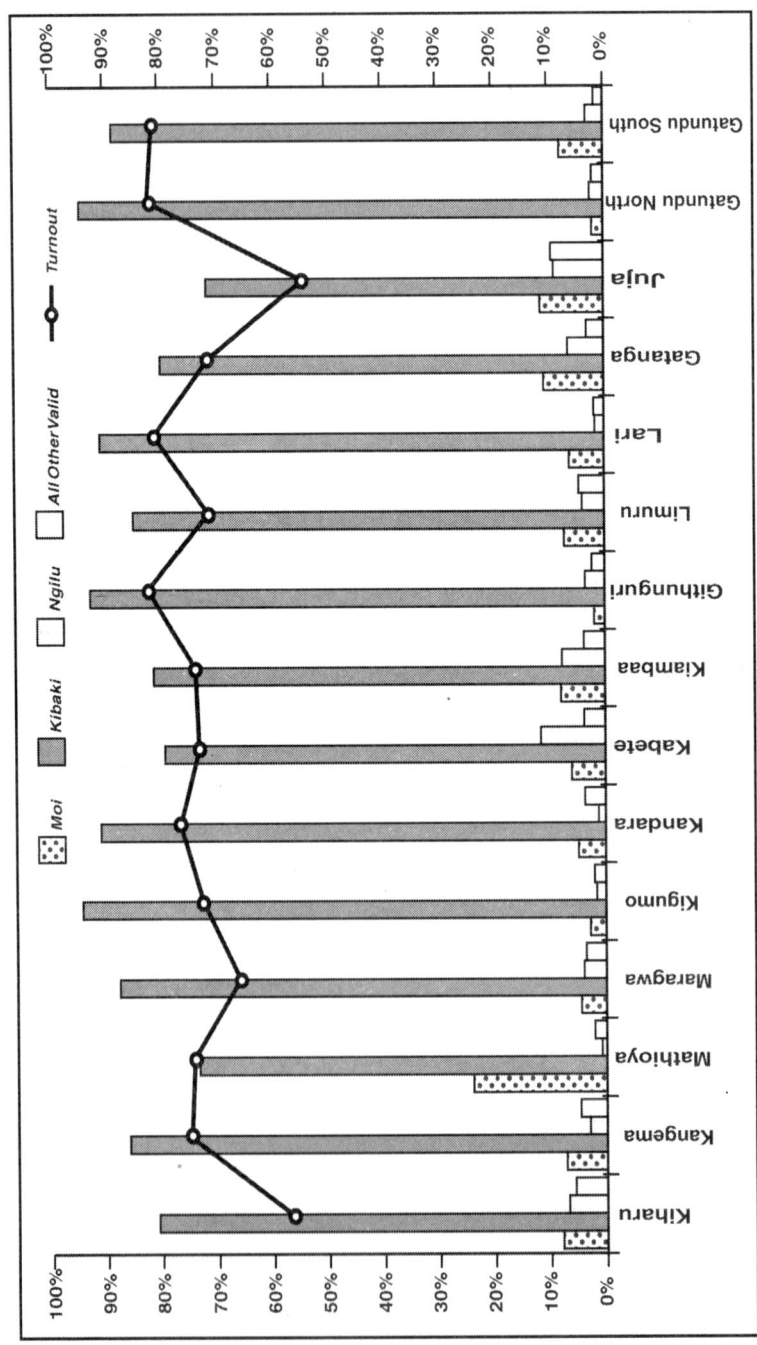

Moi and KANU's desperate attempts to woo the Kikuyu through Uhuru Kenyatta in Gatundu South and the widely disliked but loyal Minister Joseph Kamotho in the new Maragwa district were again unsuccessful, though the KANU vote increased in parts of the province with most seats seeing a rise of between two and eight per cent (see Figure 6.18). The Central Province Development Support Group team (KANU's secret weapon of rich Kikuyu elites) was eliminated without a whimper. Voters were so open that they treated their campaigns as 'hotels' at which they could 'eat' until 29 December, but without any intention to vote for them.

Again, a substantial chunk of southern Kikuyu voters boycotted, particularly in Murang'a and Maragwa. Perhaps 150,000 opposition votes were lost as a consequence.

Embu, Meru, Nyambene and Tharaka/Nithi

The DP 'allied territories' of Embu, Mbeere (a new district), Meru, Nyambene (another new district) and Tharaka/Nithi continued to return strong DP majorities, though KANU succeeded in winning new seats in Gachoka and Tigania East.

Figure 6.18: Central Province presidential vote changes 1992-97

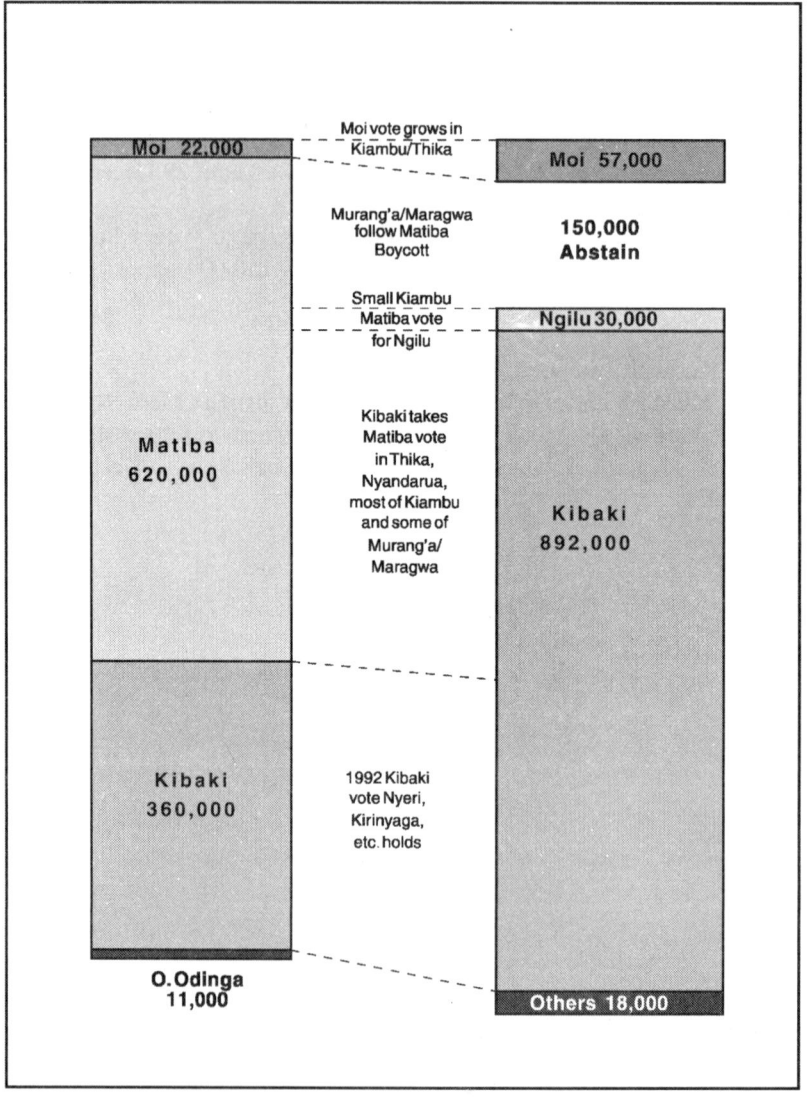

Figure 6.19: The Meru, Embu and Mbeere districts

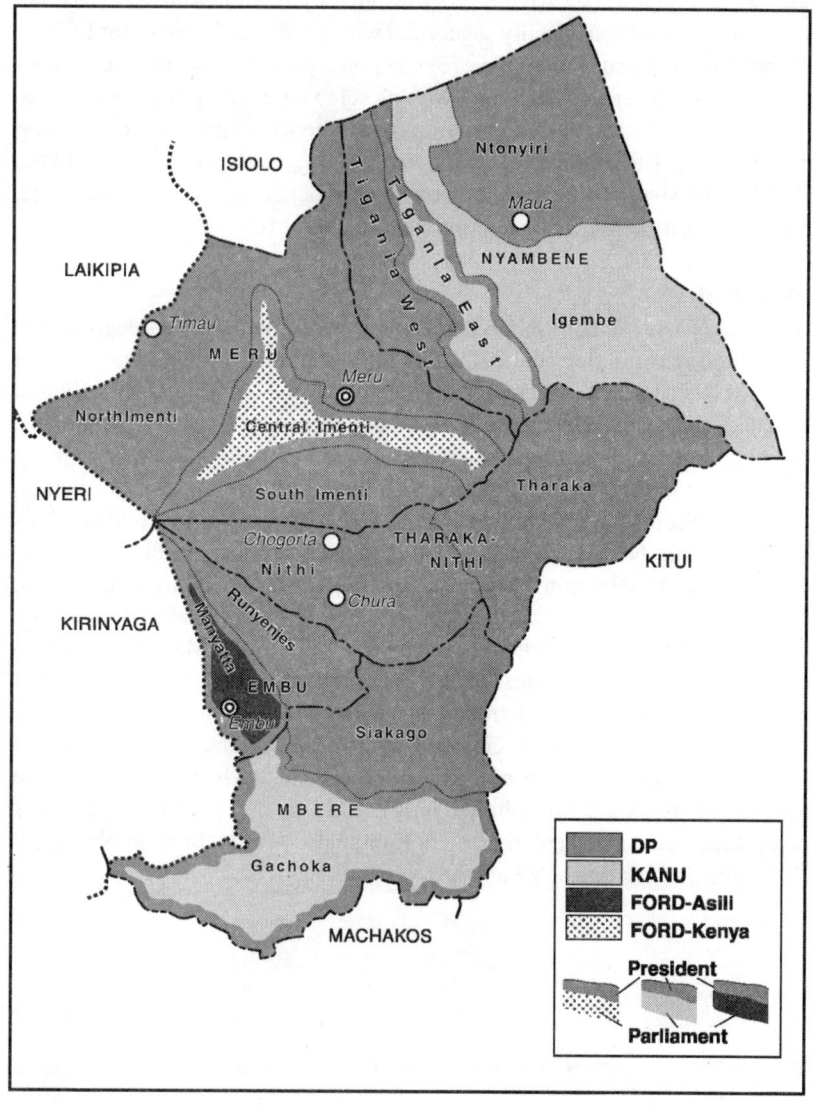

The DP gained seats in Embu and Tharaka/Nithi, and Kibaki improved his position throughout, winning the majority of the presidential vote in every seat save for Igembe (a KANU victory inspired by Jackson Kalweo's personal vote). Gitobu Imanyara finally succeeded winning Central Imenti for FORD-Kenya, their only success in the province, on a purely personal vote.

In Embu/Mbeere, FORD-Asili won its sole victory, Augustine Kathangu, an ex-detainee colleague of George Anyona, who won Runyenjes on a strong personal vote. The DP took two seats, and KANU's Joe Nyagah, brother of the DP MP who switched to Nairobi, won on split ticketing and a personal vote, plus support from the Kamba community in the area.

Ukambani

A DP/KANU swing zone in 1992, Ukambani remained a key battleground in 1997 although this time the nature of the confrontation had changed to a SDP-KANU choice, a consequence of the groundswell of support for a Kamba candidate for the presidency at last. With numerous KANU and DP candidates defecting to Charity Ngilu during mid-1997, it was clear than she was going to dominate the region and, in the event, the party won most of the region. Ngilu won the presidential poll in every seat, bar Minister Kilonzo Musyoka's Mwingi North; but KANU won seven parliamentary seats where Ngilu outpolled Moi, a reflection either of split ticket voting or, in some cases, malpractice. KANU's percentage of the vote fell precipitously in Machakos by an average of 19 per cent compared with 1992. Their Makueni vote was reduced by less. Nonetheless, KANU continued to poll solidly and Moi received 30 per cent of the Kamba vote (with 64 per cent for Ngilu), assisted by local political alliances, clannism and the advantages of incumbency (including the greater wealth of the KANU team and the distribution of famine relief to pro-KANU households only). Indeed, the KANU candidate's percentage of the vote actually rose in Kangundo, Mwala, Mwingi North and Kitui West (all bar one of which they won).

Figure 6.20: Presidential results in the DP 'allied territories' of Eastern Province

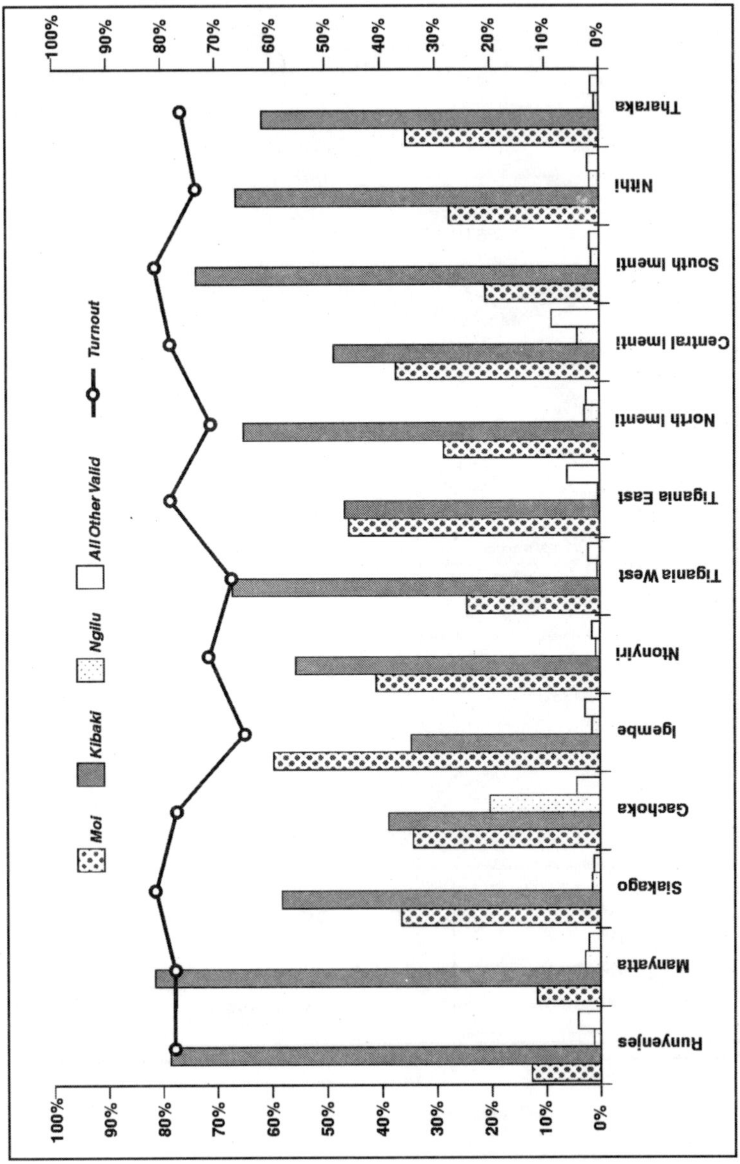

Figure 6.21: Ukambani

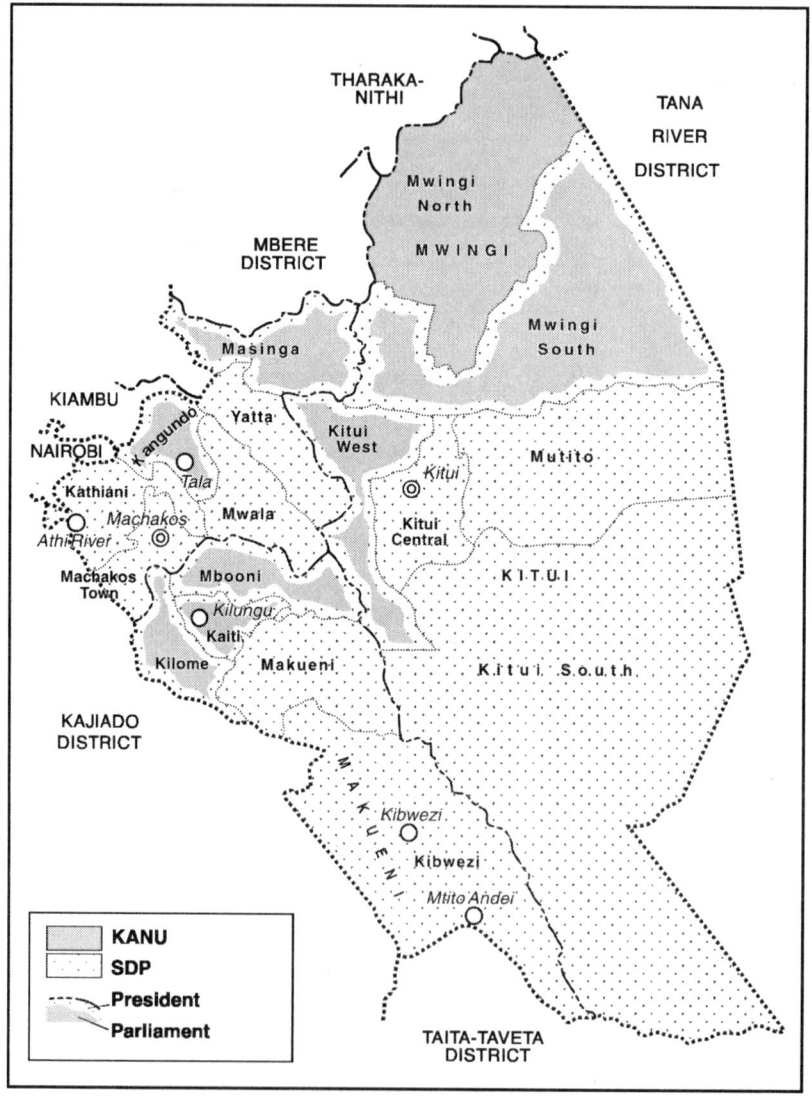

The DP campaign organisation defected en masse to Ngilu in Kitui and the DP also lost far more than KANU did from her advent in Machakos, their vote falling by an average of 30 percentage points. They were nearly eliminated everywhere, falling by between 7 and 50 percentage points in Makueni and Kitui, once their strongholds. Only in Mwala did the DP perform creditably, in the person of the secretary general, Joseph Munyao, who still came in third, but was rewarded with one of the DP's two nominations to parliament after the polls.

North-Eastern Province and the north of Eastern Province

President Moi won massive victories in every northern and North-Eastern seat, even more decisively than he had in 1992. Poor communications, state authority and weak party allegiances combined with electoral malpractice have generally led the Somali and other pastoral communities to vote for the presidential incumbent. Kibaki was the main opponent, but the presidential vote was still driven by local issues, with Raila Odinga being the major opponent to Moi in North Horr and the Safina candidates in Mandera apparently campaigning for Wamalwa.

However, at the parliamentary level KANU's hold on the Somali remained shaky and local clan, locational and personal factional voting lost them two of 11 seats, as in 1992. Safina won both, but both winners were KANU nomination losers who had defected and then won their seats. They had little ideological sympathy for the opposition.

Figure 6.22: The Northern Rift, North and North-East of Kenya

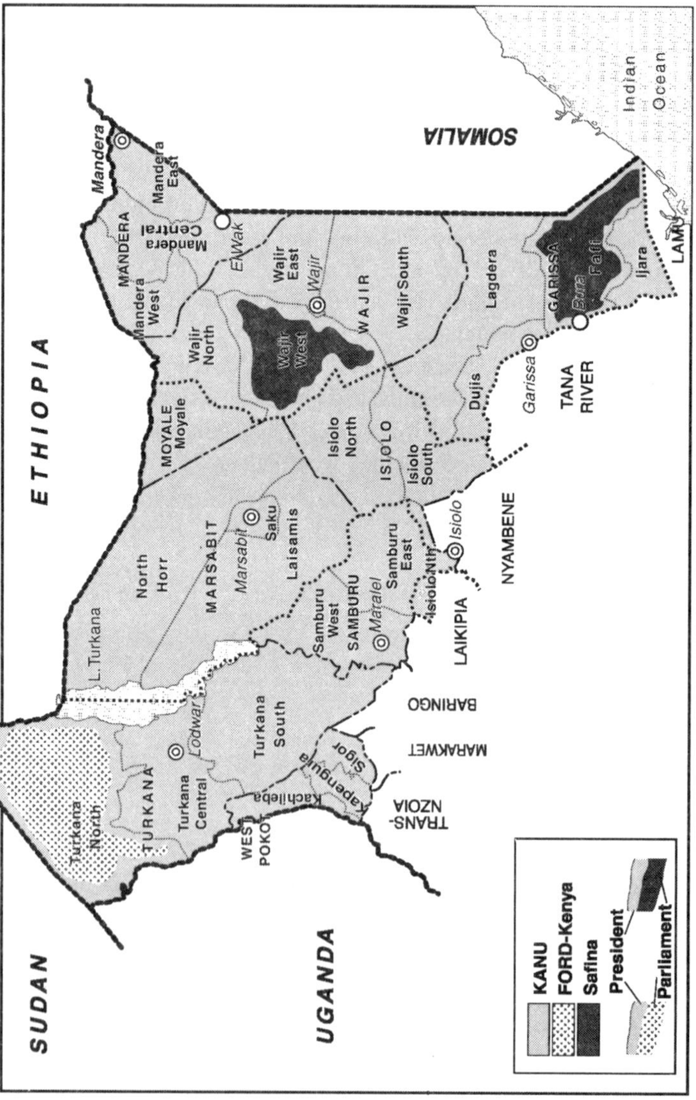

Figure 6.23: North and North-Eastern presidential results

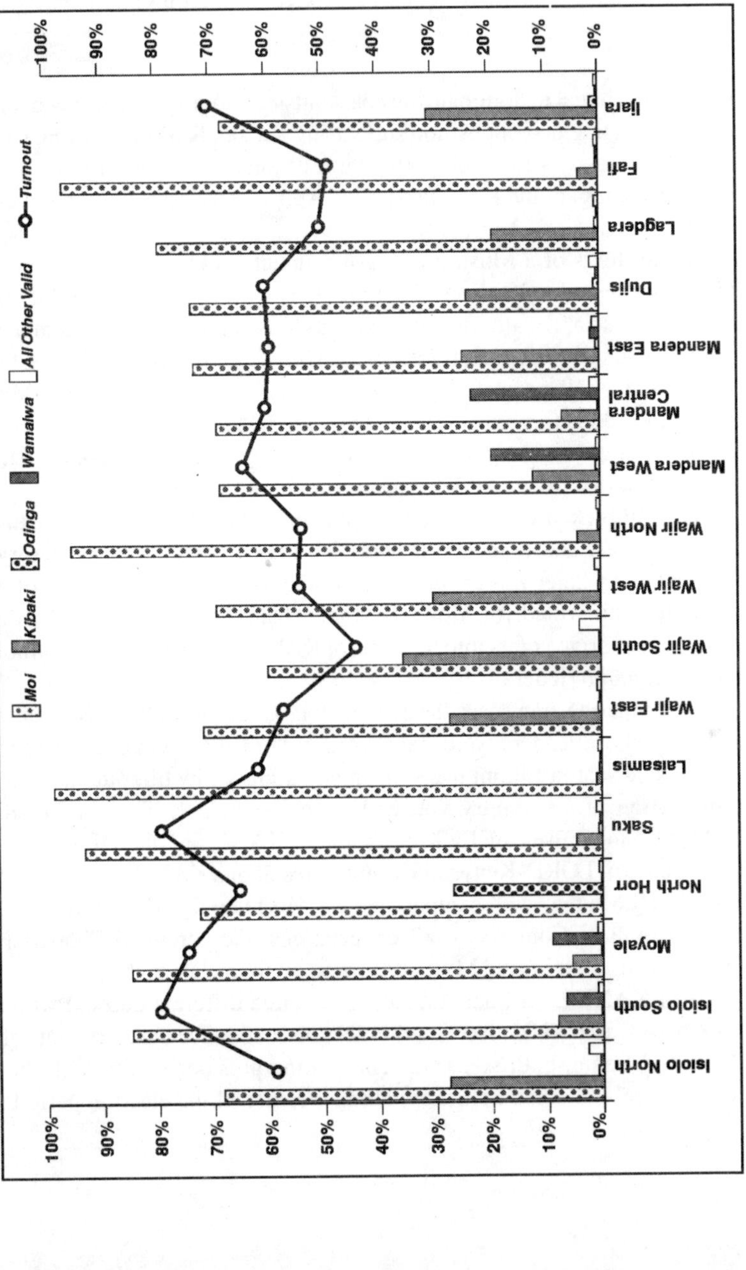

KANU was even more successful in the isolated pastoralist Boran, Rendille and Somali of Marsabit and Moyale districts, where they took all four seats with little difficulty. Isiolo North again nearly went to the DP, influenced by the Meru settlers in the urban areas and bordering Meru and Laikipia, but KANU remained narrowly in charge. KANU won Isiolo South easily.

The Coast

KANU continued to dominate the coast outside Mombasa, winning decisively against a fragmented opposition supporting Kibaki, Ngilu and Odinga, though Kibaki emerged as the main opposition candidate in these areas also. Prof. Katama Mkangi of the KNC also polled well in three seats though not enough to win.

Again, fears of a Muslim anti-government backlash did not materialise. The violence and repression of the previous months at the coast did not lose KANU seats in Kwale, despite expectations, and Minister Katana Ngala continued to rally KANU's forces successfully against Muslim Safina, FORD-Kenya and NDP protest votes in Kilifi and the new district of Malindi. Opposition defectors won several seats for KANU, helping to secure their victory, despite local fury over the abuses of the government crackdown against the Mijikenda following the Likoni clashes.

The DP picked up increased support in Taita/Taveta in three of the four constituencies, and managed to win Voi, their first rural coast victory ever although the winner was another last-minute KANU defector, many of whose supporters still voted for Moi. Elsewhere, fears of 'up-country' domination continued to drive voters into the arms of KANU – the 'party of the minorities' and of *majimbo* [federalism].

In Mombasa's four seats, the new hardline Coast federalist party, Shirikisho, some of whose leaders were implicated in the Likoni violence, managed to win its sole seat in Likoni itself on an appallingly low turnout and extensive intimidation of up-country voters. Joseph Kennedy Kiliku, the DP Kamba MP for Changamwe, finally lost his seat to KANU and the DP triumphed at the expense of FORD-Kenya in Kisauni, a result of a KANU hard-line defector Emmanuel Maitha (who campaigned for Moi) having adopted their party at the last minute. Contrary to all expectations, the perennial Sharriff Nassir managed an easier win in Mvita. Moi won all four seats in the presidency and in effect KANU hard-liners (standing for three different parties) won every Mombasa seat. KANU also won the elections in the five northern seats of Tana River and Lamu, both in parliament and the presidency although the polls were severely affected by the appalling weather of the election period.

Figure 6.24: **Coast presidential results**

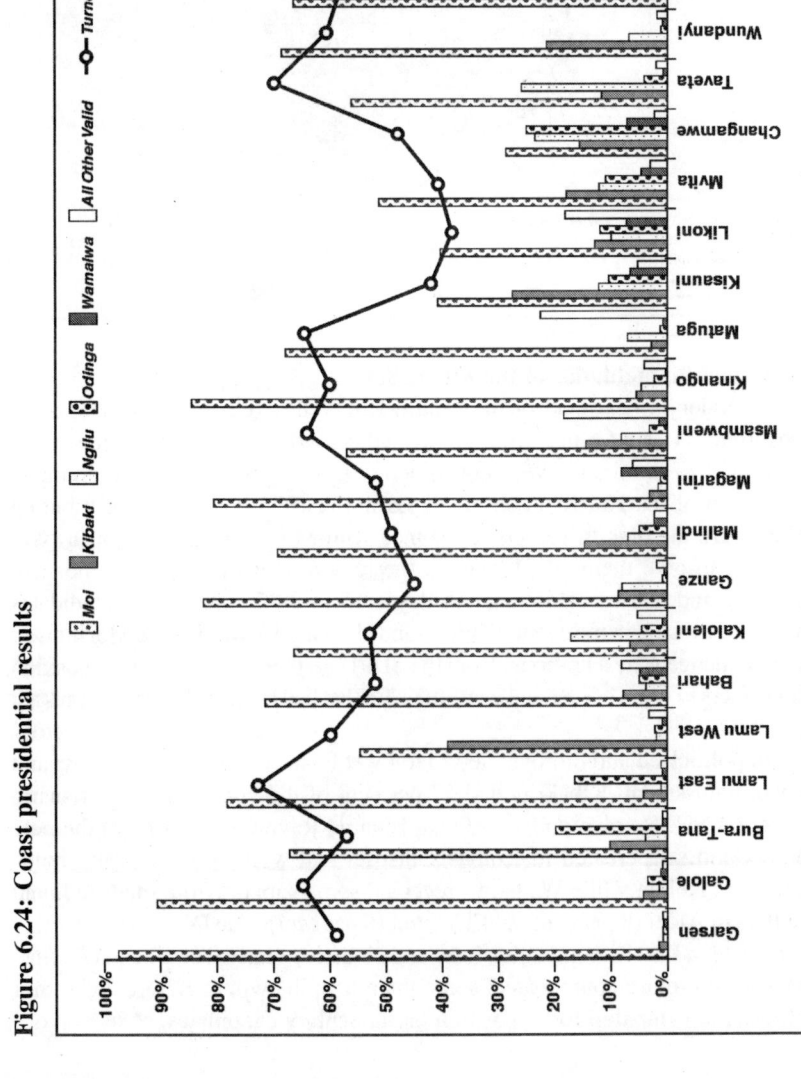

Figure 6.25: The southern Coast

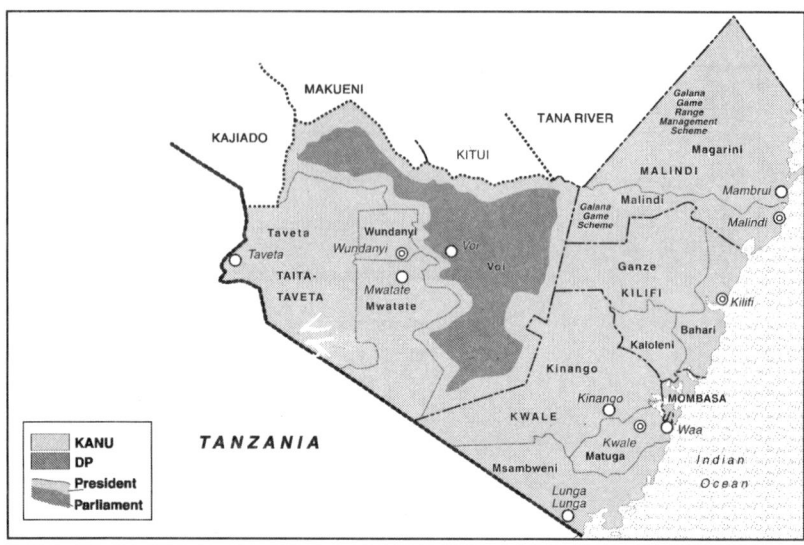

The Kalenjin highlands of the Rift Valley

In the Kalenjin heartland of the central Rift Valley (excluding Trans Nzoia, Nakuru and Uasin Gishu, which are treated below), KANU and President Moi continued to dominate every constituency (see Figure 6.26). The dramatic expansion of the Kalenjin constituencies in the 1996 boundary redistribution (they were the biggest gainers) combined with Moi's continued popularity in the area to give them all 21 seats in the region. However, without the state pressure and abuses of nomination day seen in 1992, opposition candidates managed to stand in most seats (Throup and Hornsby 1998: 389-98). Moi himself was challenged (by a no-hoper from the SDP) and there were serious opposition contenders in some borderland constituencies that had been too severely repressed to vote in 1992.

In politicised and discontented Marakwet East, suffering from famine and Pokot harassment, Kibaki polled 27 per cent of the vote in a straight swing from KANU. He also polled votes in Eldama Ravine (14 per cent) the new borderland seat created in Koibatek district and won 12 per cent in multi-ethnic Kipkelion while Wamalwa received some support from the Nandi and settlers in Aldai (8 per cent) and Tinderet (6 per cent). The DP's parliamentary candidate (a KANU nomination loser and defector) nearly won Eldama Ravine. Making life more complicated, some internal splits within KANU led senior officials to campaign for opposition parliamentary candidates, as in Keiyo

North, where the KANU nomination loser had defected to Safina, and was backed by Biwott and senior local figures (and obtained 30 per cent of the vote).

Figure 6.26: The Central Rift Valley - Kalenjin heartlands and ethnic borderlands

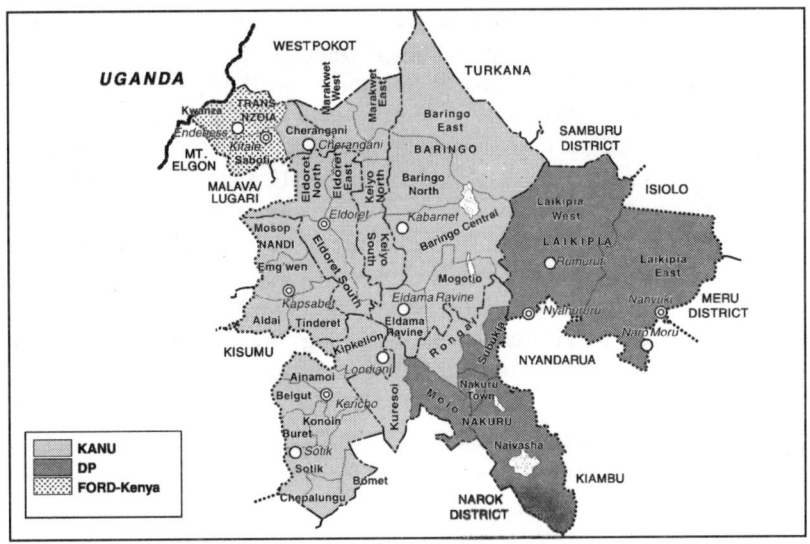

The ethnic borderlands

The borderlands between Kalenjin and Kikuyu and Luhya settlement in Nakuru, Uasin Gishu and Trans Nzoia followed a voting pattern very similar to 1992 (see Figure 6.26). Wamalwa's FORD-Kenya again won Kwanza and Saboti and again lost Cherangani in Trans Nzoia to KANU's popular Kipruto arap Kirwa. In Uasin Gishu, Moi won clear victories in every seat against an opposition split between the DP and FORD-Kenya. KANU's share of the vote improved everywhere.

The DP again dominated Laikipia as an extension of Nyeri settlement. The Nakuru situation changed with the collapse of Matiba and the DP swept up most of the Kikuyu vote. However, boundary changes had created another pro-KANU seat in Kuresoi, covering the region of Molo where ethnic clashes had led to the ousting of Kikuyu farmers and a new dominance of Kalenjin. KANU, therefore, took two seats to the DP's four. Kihika Kimani, the old 'Change the Constitution' leader moved from his old seat of Laikipia West to Molo specifically in order to take on and defeat, Njenga Mungai, a defector to

KANU, which he decisively succeeded in doing, thereby establishing himself as the only MP ever to represent three different seats in parliament.

The Rift periphery

In the southern Rift periphery of Kajiado and Narok, intra-KANU factionalism led to a unique DP victory in both presidency and parliament in Kajiado South, a rejection of electoral abuses during the KANU nominations by pro-Saitoti forces. Elsewhere, KANU won the remaining five seats in both parliament and presidency with little problem although voting patterns indicate that people were voting more for individuals than for parties. Vice-President George Saitoti performed far better than in 1992 in peri-urban Kajiado North by winning easily against a single serious opposition candidate Philip Odupoy, now in the DP, with John Keen having defected back to KANU. Saitoti was supported by Kikuyu as well as Maasai, having defended them during the clashes. Ntimama was unopposed in Narok North. The violence of the pre-poll period in Trans Mara between Maasai and Kisii did not lose KANU the poll although the hard-line DP candidate, Col. Konchela, came close to success in Kilgoris. Kibaki polled very well in Maasailand, increasing his vote by more than 30,000 taking most of the Matiba vote and 10,000 votes from KANU.

Figure 6.27: Maasailand

In the northern Rift of Turkana and Samburu, KANU lost Turkana North to FORD-Kenya, and an independent liberal KANU member also won the nomination and poll in Turkana Central, significantly weakening KANU's overall hold on this isolated semi-arid area (see Figure 6.22). Samburu remained pro-KANU, but Moi and KANU's share of the vote fell by over 30 per cent. The Kalenjin-related Pokot of West Pokot (led by hardline Minister Francis Lotodo) remained solid, and two of the three seats were unopposed in parliament.

Western Province
Western Province was effectively contested by only two parties, FORD-Kenya under their Luhya presidential candidate leader Wamalwa and KANU, led by Minister Musalia Mudavadi and others.

Figure 6.28: Western Province

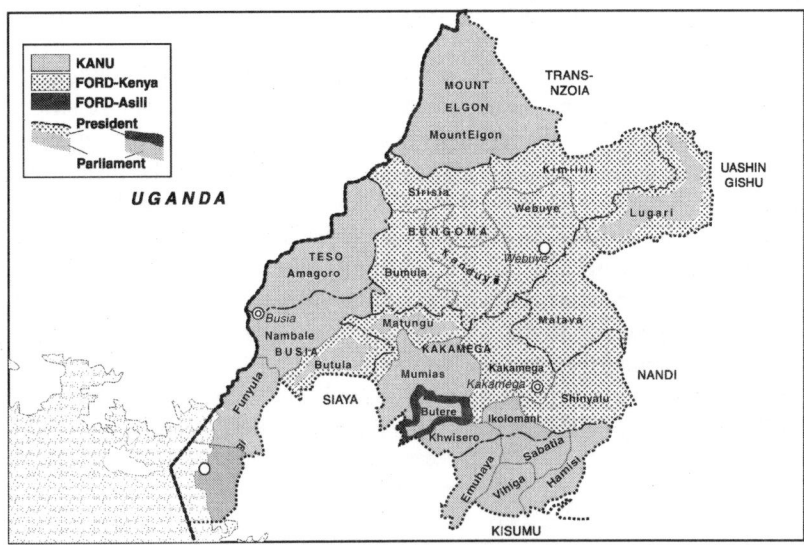

FORD-Kenya took all of the Bukusu area of Bungoma and did well in Kakamega and Malava/Lugari. KANU again won the pastoralist minority communities of Mount Elgon (the Sabaot) and Teso districts (the Iteso) and took all of Mudavadi's Vihiga district in the south and the rest of the Kakamega and Malava/Lugari seats. Wamalwa won four seats that his candidates lost, a slightly odd result, indicating weak local candidates or electoral malpractice. Martin Shikuku, the 'people's watchman' finally lost his Butere parliamentary seat, a victim of electoral boundary changes that split his seat into two, the implosion of FORD-Asili and Wamalwa's inheritance of FORD-Kenya, but somehow he managed to win the presidential poll in his seat. Cyrus Jirongo, the ex-YK'92 leader, won his Lugari seat for KANU with some cross voting amongst FORD-Kenya supporters. Minister and ex-dissident Joshua Angatia lost Malava, however. The DP was near-eliminated throughout. Much of the voting in Kakamega and Malava/Lugari in the final polls was clan-based.

Luo Nyanza

Luo Nyanza voted overwhelmingly for Raila Odinga and the NDP, as they had for his father Oginga Odinga. The Luo 'cultural identity' continued to focus around the Odinga dynasty and the confrontational anti-government politics they have represented. Only two of FORD-Kenya's 18 seats at the dissolution remained in their hands, namely James Orengo in Ugenya with a strong personal endorsement although it left him in an untenable long-term position; the neighbouring Gem, where the NDP candidate was barred from standing by an injunction, leading NDP supporters to vote FORD-Kenya to keep KANU out.

KANU won only Kuria, in the new Kuria district, as in 1992. Attempts to create more Maragoli and Basuba constituencies in Migori and Suba districts and to promote the Basuba identity (an ethnic group who had ceased to be recorded as such since the 1969 census) in order to 'disentangle' them from the Luo had little success. Nonetheless, KANU's vote increased throughout Luo Nyanza, by between 2 and 35 percentage points. They polled 25 per cent of the vote in Alego and did well in multi-ethnic Kisumu Town West, Karachuonyo (22 per cent), Gwasi (28 per cent), Migori (21 per cent), Uriri (20 per cent), Nyatike and Rongo showing that multi-ethnic South Nyanza still remained softer than the hard-line North. Raila, with 19 of 21 Luo MPs firmly behind him, most elected purely on his coattails and with little local support, was left in a strong collective bargaining position in the up-coming post-Moi settlement.

Figure 6.29: Luo Nyanza

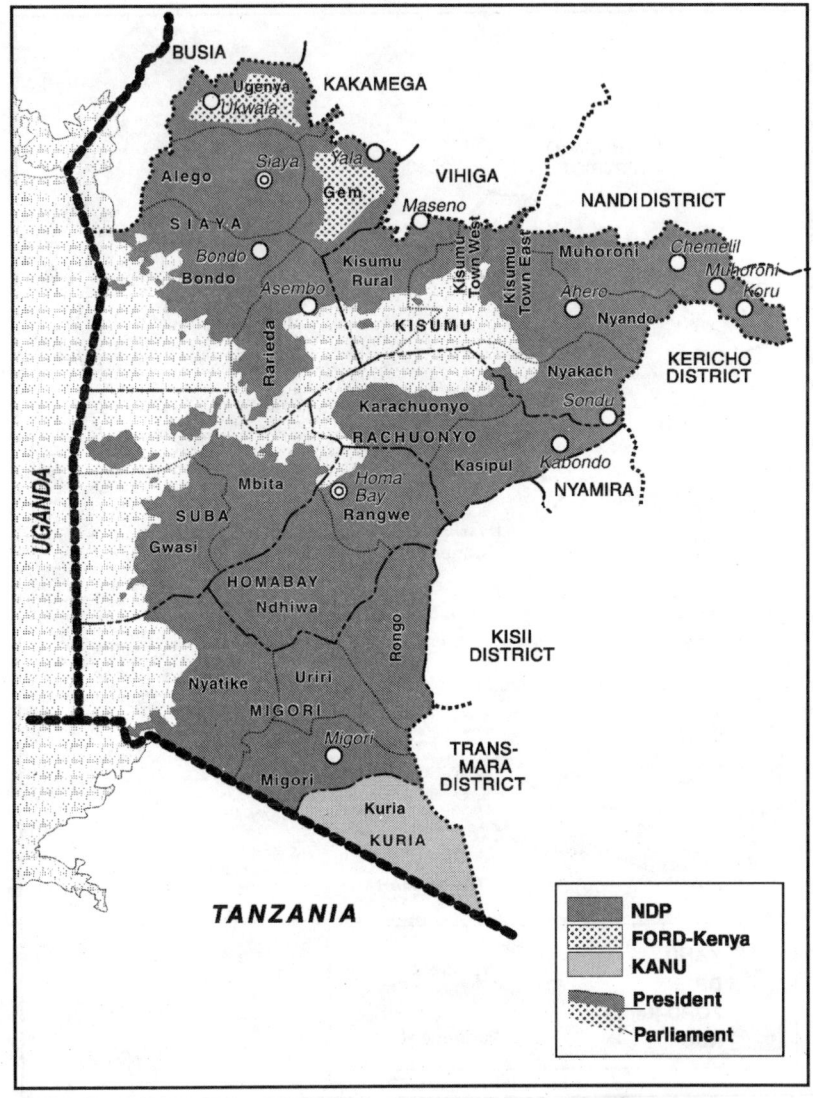

Figure 6.30: Kisii

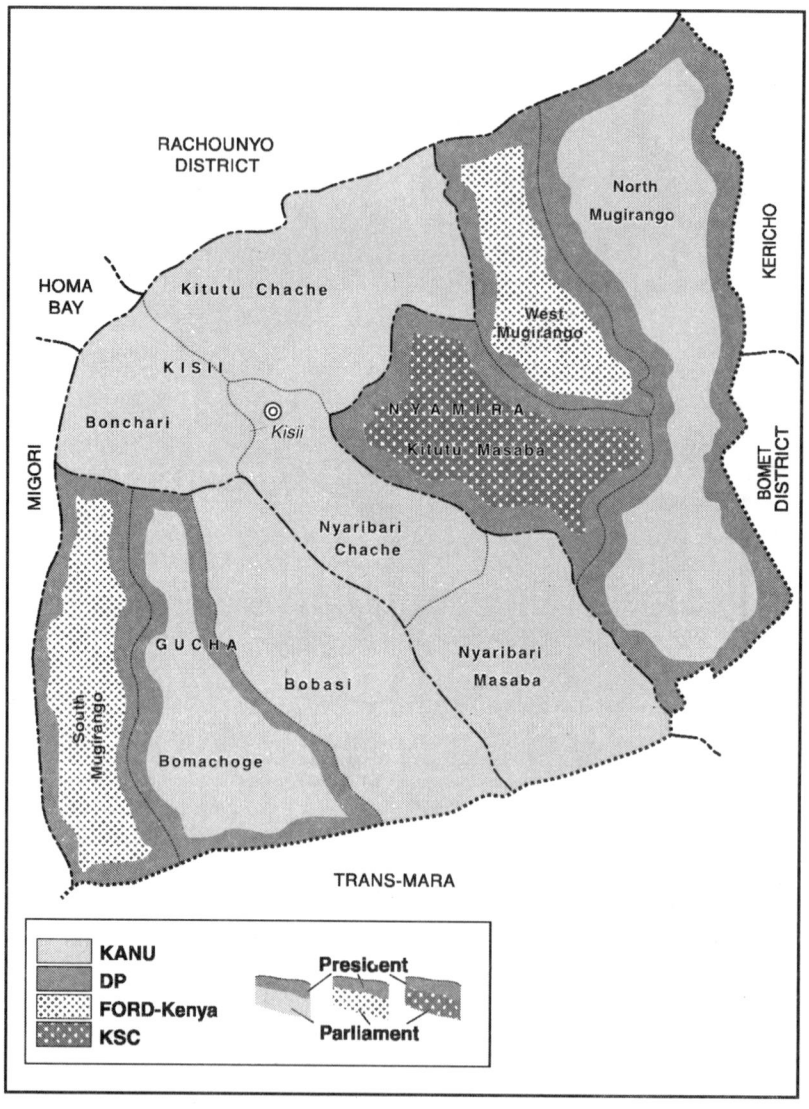

Kisii

The Kisii results were more varied and more surprising. Mwai Kibaki won five of the 10 presidential votes personally without his candidates taking a single parliamentary seat, a near-unique result, and a strong personal endorsement for him, with his percentage of the vote rising from 21 per cent to 48 per cent. Moi won almost all the remainder. KANU did better than in 1992, winning seven of ten parliamentary seats, with George Anyona hanging on as the sole Kenya Social Congress (KSC) member. FORD-Kenya held onto West Mugirango and won South Mugirango to compensate for their loss of Bomachoge to KANU. There appeared strong support for Minister Simeon Nyachae in Kisii district proper (up between 11 and 42 percentage points), but, partly as a result of the pre-poll violence, this did not universally translate into votes for Moi. The pro-Nyachae 'slate' in fact crossed three parties and his opponents, led from within KANU by Sam Ongeri and Chris Obure, also had allies outside. Little changed in the new southern Gucha district-in-waiting or in pro-opposition Nyamira. The border clashes between Kisii and Maasai in the run-up to the poll certainly did not help KANU's parliamentary candidates, but they still won three of the four border seats.

The new parliament and government

The new parliament of 210 elected members, up from 188 in 1992, saw further changes in composition, completing the process of change initiated in 1992. More of the old guard went out, including Martin Shikuku and several ministers, more eliminated in the KANU party primaries than in the final poll. In came a second tranche of new-comers, many educated or even born after independence. By 1998, only four of the original independence politicians elected in 1963 and 1964 were still in the House: Moi and Kibaki (both members continually since independence), Sayid Mohamed Amin in Mandera West and Simon arap Choge (who had served some years in jail in the meantime) in Aldai in Nandi. By contrast, more than ten MPs were not born until after independence, and the majority of MPs for whom data is available had reached adulthood after 1963.

As usual, most candidates and most winners were middle-aged, relatively well educated men. Despite their assertive 'solidarity' stance before and during the polls, women performed poorly, reflecting the continued reluctance of Kenyans to see women in positions of leadership unless 'sponsored' by men. Some civil society and NGO individuals now began the move into active politics, a trend that is expected to continue.

The new government

Moi was sworn in for his sixth and constitutionally final term on 5 January 1998, as the last results trickled in from the constituencies most affected by the rains. As in 1992, he did not form a coalition government.

This time, Moi was more constrained in his choice of ministers as KANU now had only 6 of 12 nominated members of parliament to select, following the IPPG's new system of proportional allocations. The president appointed the nominated MPs from a list submitted by the parties according to their size. KANU received six, taking their total to 113, the DP two, and the NDP, SDP, FORD-Kenya and Safina one each (a total of 109). Joseph Kamotho was the only re-nominated government minister and Moi brought in a surprising new set of nominees, including Mark arap Too, the moderate Nandi/Eldoret power-broker; Rashid Sajjad, a wealthy coast financier and Mohamed Yussuf Haji, previously the Rift Valley provincial commissioner. The opposition used the occasion to nominate some heavyweight politicians. Safina nominated its front man, Richard Leakey, while the DP chose its secretary general, Joseph Munyao, and Tabitha Seii, a loser to Biwott in the elections. The SDP used the opportunity to return Kisumu loser and *eminence grise* Peter Anyang' Nyong'o, while FORD-Kenya rewarded Mohammed Galgalo from Moyale for his last minute defection.

The biggest surprise of the new government was that George Saitoti was not initially re-appointed vice-president. With the succession crisis looming, Saitoti represented no clear national or ethnic constituency and only one wing of the party. Moi was forced to leave the position open in order to reconcile the conflicting claims, and to use the post as a lure for co-operation with some opposition parties in order to secure a working majority in parliament. Simeon Nyachae, only a year ago humiliated and demoted, rose again to replace Musalia Mudavadi at Finance, while Mudavadi moved to Agriculture. Moi demoted Nicholas Biwott from the Office of the President to East African Co-operation. Musyoka was also demoted from Foreign Affairs to Education, being replaced by a surprise appointment for the northern Borana, Bonaya Godana, the first Boran, Rendille or Gabbra minister ever. One re-elected minister, Darius Mbela, was dropped and replaced by another Taita representative, Marsden Madoka.

Table 6.6: The ethnic composition of the new government, 1998

Community	% of population[20]	1998 cabinet	1993 cabinet
Kikuyu	20.8	1 (Kamotho)	1 (Kamotho)
Luhya	14.4	5 (Mudavadi, Masakhalia, Anangwe, Okemo, Wako)	4 (Mudavadi, Masinde, Angatia, Wako)
Luo and Basuba	12.9	-	1 (Otieno)
Kalenjin	11.5	7 (Moi, Biwott, Lotodo, Kones, Kiptoon, Ng'eny, Kosgey)	5 (Moi, Biwott, Lotodo, Ng'eno, Sambu)
Kamba	11.4	4 (Musyoka, Ngutu, Ndambuki, Nyenze)	4 (Musyoka, Mulinge, Kyalo, Makau)
Kisii	6.1	2 (Nyachae, Ongeri)	2 (Nyachae, Onyonka)
Meru and Tharaka	5.5	1 (Kalweo)	2 (Kalweo, M'Mukindia)
Mijikenda	4.7	1 (Ngala)	1 (Ngala)
Somalis	2.0	1 (Maalim)	1 (Maalim)
Maasai	1.8	2 (Ntimama, Saitoti)	2 (Ntimama, Saitoti)
Embu and Mbeere	1.7	1 (Nyagah)	1 (Munyi)
Turkana	1.3	-	-
Taita	0.9	1 (Madoka)	1 (Mbela)
Teso	0.8	-	-
Kuria	0.5		
Samburu	0.5	-	-
Borana	0.4	1 (Godana)	-
Arab	0.2	1 (Nassir)	-
Others	2.6	-	-
Total	100	28	25

The new government, therefore, included no Luo representatives at all, and only Kamotho for the Kikuyu (if you exclude George Saitoti who now, as part of calculated KANU-B strategy to reach out to the Kikuyu, for the first time began to proclaim his Kikuyu origins). The coast was represented by three ministers not two as before, while the Kalenjin's share increased from five to seven ministers (see Table 6.6).

How the incumbents fared

With the dramatic changes of the previous elections over, incumbents performed better than they had done in 1992. Government ministers did particularly well, simply as a consequence of the fact that the zonal pattern of the 1992 results had meant there were few potential Luo or Kikuyu ministerial candidates any more. Defeated ministers were the nominated Luo and Kikuyu ministerial representatives Ndolo Ayah and Joseph Kamotho, respectively, plus Jackson Mulinge in Ukambani, Kirugi M'Mukindia in Meru and Joshua Angatia in Western.

Table 6.7: Performance of elected incumbents by status

	Won		Lost		Did not stand or lost primary		Total	
Election	'92	'97	'92	'97	'92	'97	'92	'97
Ministers	10	12	16	3	5	6	31	21
Asst. Ministers**	18	16	18	9	30	24	66	49
Backbenchers	21	50	31	32	37	34	89	116
Total	49	78	65	44	72	64	186*	186*

* two seats were vacant in both elections at the dissolution
** KANU chief whip, deputy chief whip, and deputy speaker have been classed as assistant ministers.

Eighty per cent of the ministers left after the primaries won the final poll, 64 per cent of assistant ministers and 61 per cent of backbenchers, but there was little here related to ministerial performance. The results were dominated by the party divide and by the fact that popular and powerful local figures (more likely to win re-election) were also more likely to be appointed as assistant ministers and ministers. It was also a reflection of the clearout of the primaries. Of the 186 incumbents at the dissolution, 60 (32 per cent) ended the nomination season without a party. Assistant ministers (generally viewed as a political reward with little real function) were particularly seriously purged.

Elite formation, circulation and incorporation
There were major changes in the level of previous political experience of the active political elites. The vast majority of candidates who competed in 1997 were either new candidates or were standing for different parties compared to 1992. Less than half of KANU's 210 candidates had even been nominated to stand in 1992. Again, a new elite group emerged into the local leadership. KANU and the DP, the two best-established parties, had the lowest number of new entrants (around 50 per cent). The three FORDs (-Asili, -Kenya and -People) fielded around 66 per cent new candidates while the new SDP, LPK and Safina parties contained over 75 per cent newcomers.

Table 6.8: Election characteristics of 1997 parliamentary candidates (per cent in brackets)

	KANU	DP	FORD-K	FORD-P	SDP	NDP	Safina	Others
Stood before 1992, but not in 1992[21]	15	9	6	0	4	7	3	7
Stood in 1992	94 (45)	55 (42)	32 (32)	12 (32)	24 (23)	14 (13)	8 (18)	44 (26)
- same party	69	36	25	0	0	0	0	14
- different party	25	19	7	12	24	14	8	30
By-elections 1992-97	3	0	0	0	1	7	0	0
Newcomers	98 (47)	68 (52)	63 (63)	25 (68)	75 (72)	79 (74)	34 (76)	111 (68)
Total	210	132	101	37	104	107	45	162

One of the reasons KANU won, albeit narrowly, was that in key marginals it co-opted back into the party popular local figures who had given them a scare in 1992. Of the 94 previous contestants among the KANU candidates, 25 had actually stood for the opposition in the 1992 elections. KANU candidates in Embakasi, Dagoretti and Kamukunji in Nairobi; in Kigumo, Limuru, Kieni and Mukurweini in Central Province, Mbooni and Kitui West in Eastern; Garsen, Bura, Lamu East, Bahari and Msambweni on the Coast, Molo, Sigor and Turkana Central in the Rift, Webuye, Kanduyi, Nambale and Shinyalu in Western, and Ndhiwa, Migori and South Mugirango in Nyanza had all stood for the opposition in 1992.

Some of these 'turncoats' were opposition MPs who had defected to KANU during 1993-97. Others were KANU primary losers in 1992 who had defected to PICK or a similar minority party, but who were natural KANU supporters. Such politicians as David Kombo in South Mugirango come to mind. The majority, however, had simply crossed the floor at some point in the preceding five years, and now served as useful assets for KANU. These included Chris Okemo, Alfred Sambu and Joseph Khaoya in Bungoma, Molu Shambaro and Sheikh Mohamed Abdi Galgallo in Tana River, Mohamed Hasim in Lamu, David Ethuru in Turkana, Jembe Mwakalu in Kilifi and Marere wa Machai in Kwale. FORD-Kenya, ravaged by splits and with several strong candidates in the 'wrong party' back in 1992, was a particular victim. KANU might well have lost Msambweni, Bahari, Nambale, Kitui West, and Turkana Central (and therefore their parliamentary majority) if they had not achieved this over the preceding period.

Again, the conduct of the candidates before the polls showed the irrelevance of party as an ideological entity. Candidates picked parties and parties picked candidates on the basis of their perceived chances of victory. Where a social, cultural or ethnic 'slate' was clearly going to win, all candidates competed for this party's nominations unless paid handsomely to do otherwise. The losers then defected to the second most popular party and the process continued. Where there was no clear dominant 'social consensus' on party, the parties competed for the popular candidates (those with wealth, oratorical ability, good political connections, a history of development -consciousness, etc.) who in turn could pick the national or regional group best able to provide them with their material or organisational needs.

Again, numerous candidates moved from KANU to the opposition and vice versa during and just after the nomination season. In the words of the *East African Standard* on a seat in Kwale district, '. . . the Opposition had no known candidate before the ruling party held their nominations which seemed to tear the party and create room for the Opposition' (*East African Standard* 22/12/97:E4). More than 190 (and probably more than 25 per cent in total) of the final 880 or so parliamentary candidates are known to have changed parties between mid-1997 and nomination day. Indeed, 34 of the resulting 103 opposition MPs had started the political season with a different partner. As in 1992, a substantial chunk of the opposition's candidates were KANU defectors – more than 100 defected before or during the primaries. The DP MPs for Embakasi in Nairobi, Siakago, Tharaka, Kisauni in Mombasa, and Kajiado South were all KANU-supporters in mid-1997. Nine NDP MPs came from FORD-Kenya and two from KANU. The two North-Eastern Safina winners were both KANU defectors, storing up trouble for the future of Safina. FORD-Asili's implosion provided the SDP, FORD-People and FORD-Kenya with eight MPs and many candidates.

KANU's newcomers to parliamentary politics included several of the YK'92 leadership who had acted with such enthusiasm during the 1992 campaign and had used their experience and financial resources gained as a result to springboard themselves into national politics. These included chairman Cyrus Jirongo (Lugari), Rajab Wailula (defeated in Kimilili), William Ruto (Eldoret North) and Joe Kimkung (Mount Elgon).

There were several well-known parastatal organisation figures who, as has become the norm, made the move from 'political' state or parastatal positions into full time politics after retirement. These included Simeon Mkalla from the Kenya Ports Authority (KPA) in Kinango, who was disgraced during the KPA scandal, but unaffected locally since he was seen as having acted to prefer coast businesses and workers over up-country people. Kipngeno arap Ng'eny, the controversial managing director of Kenya Posts and Telecommunications Corporation for many years and then head of the Kerio Valley Development Authority, who had again been implicated in several KANU funding scandals, became the new MP for Ainamoi in Kericho. The ex-head of the civil service, Joseph arap Leting, won Emgwen in the Kalenjin heartlands of Nandi.

The DP also introduced new faces. Of their 132 candidates, only 41 per cent had stood in 1992 and of these, 18 actually stood in a different constituency or for a different party. They acquired some hard-line KANU defectors, including winners David Mwenje in Embakasi and Emmanuel Maitha in Kisauni, but also took candidates from FORD-Asili, the KNC (John Keriri in Ndia and Henry Kinyua in Central Imenti) and FORD-Kenya (notably Kiraitu Murungi in South Imenti).

Safina was virtually unrepresented outside the Kikuyu areas of Central Province, Nairobi, Laikipia and Nakuru and the North-East, where many of their candidates were ex-KANU defectors. Apart from Paul Muite himself and a few weak FORD-Asili last-minute defectors (Ruhio, Icharia, Gitau), they were almost entirely new to parliamentary politics.

Conclusion

The 1997 elections were another significant step along the road to parliamentary democracy. KANU won, but the opposition was close to control of the house and, theoretically, facing a 'lame duck' president. Since 1997, KANU has begun to transform itself in the absence of a clear succession and without clear leadership. Dissident KANU members are making common cause with the opposition in a way that has never occurred before. Nonetheless, Kenya is still nowhere near the end of the democracy road. Multi-party democracy continues to fragment the nation along ethnic lines, and ethnic bloc voting is clearly the dominant force among the majority communities, fighting with promises and money for the support of the uncommitted and less developed regions and their politicians.

The 1997 elections were far freer than those in 1992, when the government blatantly abused a fledgling political system for its own ends. The 1997 polling was chaotic and the count was slow, but favouritism was reduced as were the more blatant manipulations of the electoral process. In the words of the local observers, the elections despite their flaws were 'acceptable' in that voters turned up and could vote on the whole freely and the counts were open and properly monitored and conducted in the main (IED/CJPC/NCCK 1998: 109).

Nonetheless, KANU still cheated, bribed, intimidated and finally rigged its way into an overall majority of the House by manipulation of a few key results. The original 1963 over-representation of the semi-arid and arid areas in population terms, reinforced and refined in three boundary redistributions, continued to deliver more parliamentary seats to a governing party (KANU) than would normally be considered acceptable (51 per cent of the seats for 40 per cent of the votes).

In the presidency, Moi won 'fair and square', in that no other candidate came close to beating him. Although some vote counts were inflated, it did not change the result, and it is pretty clear that he achieved 25 per cent of the votes cast on the day (for whatever reason) in Eastern and Western, the two most marginal regions under the 25 per cent rule. Nonetheless, the majority of Kenyans still felt cheated. The generalised expectation of electoral fraud among the people was little changed and though it appears there was less actual malpractice this time round, there would still be little that the opposition could do about it if it were to occur. As 1992 and 1997 showed, returning officers can still be manipulated. Observers can still be ejected. Boxes and papers can be acquired clandestinely. Results can be falsified. Following the election petitions of 1993-5, not one single KANU candidate lost his seat as a result of the serious abuses of the 1992 elections. Thus, although the changes of the NCEC and IPPG period were a great step forward in creating legitimate space for political and civil activity, it is unclear that the institutional and cultural systems have advanced enough to prevent a rollback in different circumstances.

The election results also showed how, despite 35 years of authoritarian government, KANU the party (still near indistinguishable from the government) could reinvent itself as a populist party in key marginal areas and incorporate the opposition who themselves revealed a near universal preference for power over principle. The new KANU of 1997 was, despite its 'old guard' leadership, a very different beast from that of 1992. Seventy per cent of the 1997 KANU MPs had never sat in the single party house. In 1997 KANU was more of an 'umbrella movement' of widely differing views although still controlled by a small group of 'old guard' politicians, closely allied with commercial and civil service interests.

Democracy in Kenya remains a collective, not an individual phenomenon. Outside the elites of the urban areas, the vast majority of individuals who made political choices did so as part of a public, collective, consensus-driven process. This was particularly obvious in the ethnic homelands of the party leaders, but even in tightly contested constituencies individual candidates gained strong support from particular locations, most of which voted clearly for one candidate or the other.

The widespread bribery and selling of votes reinforced the obvious fact that even in a multi-party democracy, control and access to money and other benefits remains the key issue for both peasants and politicians. Politics in Kenya (as in many other places) is inherently a 'dirty business'. It is about representation, but it is also about the use of office for personal and collective gain. A truly clean politician may survive one term, but is unlikely to win re-election. Politics and elections need money, lots of it, and unless the candidate is already immensely wealthy, something must give in order to acquire the required assets. An elite which through cash and promises buys its support from a poverty-stricken and cynical electorate is unlikely to initiate fundamental change.

In many ways, 1997 was a repeat of 1992, with some new actors and new movements, but with much the same results. The near-hung parliament and the imminent departure of the incumbent president began, following the elections, to break a political logjam which had lasted for 20 years. The elections of 2002 will be very different from those of 1992 and 1997, and may well for the first time usher in a genuinely new government in Kenya. Whether it will be primarily a rotation of faces or will initiate a genuine period of economic and social change remains to be seen.

Notes

1. The *Daily Nation* headlined that evening 'Chaos forces poll extension' (see *Daily Nation* 30/12/97:1).
2. Outside Central Province and Nakuru district, Moi still improved his position, from 45 to 47 per cent of the total vote.
3. This table presents corrected official ECK results. The official totals are very similar to but not identical to the sum of the detailed constituency by constituency results which have been collated from numerous sources and which are used in the analysis henceforth. These subsequent figures are based on a parallel count, carried out initially during the polls, then supplemented and corrected by newspaper reports, official results where published, and independent parallel counts carried out by IED/NCCK/CJPC count certifiers. The majority of these results match very closely those reported in the IED/CJPC/NCCK Report on the 1997 general elections, and those reported by the ECK, but have been corrected for some results, which were incorrectly reported, such as Kigumo and Lugari (see Appendix I).
4. Adding in the 11 unopposed seats, they would have polled about 2.4 million if these seats had been contested.
5. KANU had gained Bonchari, Mandera East, Machakos Town, Shinyalu, Ikolomani, Hamisi, Siakago, Kibwezi, Lugari, Lurambi and Starehe. The DP had won Kipipiri, but lost Machakos Town, Kibwezi and Bonchari. FORD-Kenya had won Mathare but lost Lang'ata. FORD-Asili had lost Kipipiri, Mathare, Ikolomani, Starehe, Shinyalu, Hamisi, Lurambi and Lugari.
6. There were some informal agreements between NDP, DP and FORD-Kenya in specific constituencies not to compete against each others' candidates. The DP fielded no candidates in Luo Nyanza and few in Western. The NDP fielded only seven candidates in Central Province.
7. There are still rumours that the Nyachae team in the region may have been lukewarm in their campaigning for Moi.
8. There seems little doubt that KANU gained from these low turnouts since many upcountry voters who registered successfully were unable or afraid to vote in the polls.
9. This was clearly of little electoral impact, as the DP performed very poorly here.
10. As witnessed by the author.
11. The IED/CJPC/NCCK 1997 Report (page 76) identifies that this was occurring in 5 per cent of constituencies, but it could well have been more.

12. The IED/CJPC/NCCK 1997 report identified that according to their records, 8.2 per cent of constituencies observed for the count reported attempts to introduce alien boxes and 4 per cent reported stuffing.
13. It is, therefore, always a key issue whether a party can get their own supporters introduced as counting officials.
14. This was the subject of a detailed note from the Election Observation Centre and extensive protests by donors to Kivuitu.
15. Molo had been a rigging centre in 1992.
16. This was prevented and the observers were finally happy with the result.
17. The same thing happened in 1992.
18. A number of blatant errors in the reported results were found and corrected in these figures before presentation by recourse to box-by-box counts in some situations. Spoilt ballots have been included.
19. For statistics, see Throup and Hornsby (1998: 556-58). The losers were Mzee in Kisauni, Kombo in Webuye, Kiliku in Changamwe, Ahmed in Mandera East and Macharia in Mathare.
20. According to the disputed 1989 census, as reported in *Kenya Factbook*, 15th Edition, 1997-98, Kul Bhushan, Newspread International.
21. Those from KANU who had stood before 1992, but not in '92 included Choge, Gumo, S.M. Amin, Obure, Ongeri, Angwenyi, Hemed, Joseph Mutisya, Kiano, Samwel Moiben, Tarar, Anthony Kimeto, Raphael Kitur, and Andrew Kiptoon. The DP's candidates included Isaac Muchiri, Maina Kamanda, Wanyiri Kihoro, Silas Ita, Joshua Musyoka, John Kavali, Job Lalalampaa, Davidson Mairura, David Onyancha. FORD-Kenya's were Ms Kemoli, Jael Mbogo, Timothy Lewa, Joseph Yeri, Anton Etheri, Livingstone Ombete, the SDP's Francis Wambua, Peter Katu, Augustus Momanyi, and A.K. Soi. The LPK fielded John Muthamia, the NDP Ratib Hussein, Hosea Gakondu, Justin Cingano, Japhet Kase, Frederick Diwani, Ali Mwakileo, Joseph Waudi and Safina Nduati Kariuki, Stephen ole Leken, and Sammy Choge. Others included Toweett (PICK), three Shirikisho (Mboja, Juma, Mwachiro), Koigi and Mirugi.

References

DDDG 1998, Executive Summary Final Statement of 26 January 1998, submitted 2 February to the ECK.

IED/CJPC/NCCK 1998, *Report on the 1997 General Elections in Kenya*, Nairobi: Institute for Education in Democracy, Catholic Justice and Peace Commission, National Council of Churches in Kenya.

KHRC 1998, *Killing the Vote, State Sponsored Violence and Flawed Elections in Kenya*, Nairobi: Kenya Human Rights Commission.

NCCK/IED/CJPC 1997, Observers/Poll Watchers Checklists, December 1997.

NCCK/IED/CJPC 1997a, Rapid Count Reports, December 1997.

NCCK/IED/CJPC 1997b, Count Certifier Reports, December 1997.

Southall, R. and Wood, G. 1996, 'Local Government and the Return to Multi-Partyism in Kenya', *African Affairs*, Vol.95, No.381: 501-27.

Throup, D. and Hornsby, C. 1998, *Multi-party Politics in Kenya. The Kenyatta & Moi States & the Triumph of the System in the 1992 Election*, Oxford: James Currey.

7

Domesticating Election Observation: Experiences from the 1997 General Elections

Marren Akatsa-Bukachi

This chapter seeks to outline the work of Kenyan domestic observers in the 1997 general elections that saw the mounting of the largest observation exercise ever conducted in this part of the world. The Domestic Observation Project was a joint project of the Institute for Education in Democracy (IED), the National Council of Churches of Kenya (NCCK) and the Catholic Justice and Peace Commission (CJPC), under the banner *Together for Peaceful Elections*.

The project consisted of all the three different strands in election observation, i.e., short term observation on election day; long term observation throughout the pre election period including the campaign; and the analysis and presentation of the results. It is recognised that observation of elections by non-partisan domestic organisations is becoming increasingly important in Kenya. The presence of domestic observers in almost every polling station and their detailed knowledge of the contesting candidates and key aspects of local politics made their contribution unique. The IED/NCCK/CJPC observation project is to date the largest joint election observation exercise undertaken in Kenya.

As the limitations of now established international election observation are realised, domestic observation is seen as a way of overcoming these limitations by offering opportunities to observe the whole electoral process in more detail, provide for greater coverage on election day itself and increase the confidence and participation of voters in the electoral process. Besides, domestic observation will enhance and strengthen the capacity and professionalism of domestic organisations involved in this process. This will contribute to the further enhancement of civil society and civic participation. Domestic election observation also strengthens the credibility and transparency of the elected government which, in theory at least, is likely to lead to a government that is more responsive and transparent in meeting the development priorities of its citizens.

An obvious advantage of domestic election observers vis à vis traditional international observers is their permanent presence before and after the elections. They live with the elections' outcome long after the event. However, in the case of the 1997 Kenyan general elections, an interesting factor was that this time around the international observers were mainly resident diplomats. This group had reasonable knowledge of the country, its people and politics and continued to reside and work in the country after the elections, thus rendering a level of continuity in the post election period and maintaining a longer-term interest (see Chapter 8). This was more advantageous in comparison to what has been the norm in traditional international election observation where a delegation arrives a few days prior to the election, observes polling day activities in a few polling stations, makes a verdict on whether the elections were free and fair immediately at the end of counting and departs to await the next elections.

Observing the 1997 general elections was, therefore, very important as the country was going into its second transitional elections and, at the same time, witnessing the dawn of a new era. The elections were held in an atmosphere wrought with clamour for comprehensive reforms which people had hoped would be instituted early enough to produce a less tilted playing field. Citizens wanted to see the establishment of a constitutional order that would conform to the demands, needs, and challenges of political pluralism.

In response, the government enacted a number of constitutional, legal and administrative reforms prior to the elections (see Chapter 2). The applicability of these reforms given the proximity to the general elections and the inadequate time for their implementation was raised. Besides this, the role of the media, political parties, the provincial administration, the security forces as well as the Electoral Commission of Kenya (ECK) were subjected to closer scrutiny than ever before. Particular attention was paid to the accuracy of the voter registration list, to electoral laws as well as campaign rules. These were subjected to greater detail of evaluation (see Chapter 5). A critique of the Election Observation Project must begin with the introduction of the three organisations that carried out the exercise in more detail: IED, CJPC and NCCK.

Characteristics of the collaborating organisations

The Institute for Education in Democracy (IED)

IED was established in 1993 as a public non-profit organisation committed to the promotion of democracy in Kenya. It came about to fill the void that was left by National Election Monitoring Unit (NEMU) after the 1992 general elections. It was realised that citizens were not sufficiently aware of their rights in a democratic dispensation. IED is non-partisan and is not affiliated to any political party, pressure group, or religious body. IED's vision is of an informed and democratic society where all citizens participate effectively in the social, political, and economic affairs of their country and live in prosperity through justice. To achieve this vision, IED strives to:

- promote and influence the evolution of a democratic ethic and culture in the management of national affairs;
- provide information and skills for positive political behaviour;
- promote positive attitudes about the electorate's ability to participate in developing the policies and forms of government it considers desirable;
- support the evolution and growth of an institutional framework that will motivate people to participate in the election of their political leaders and the formulation of public policy.

Since its inception in 1993, IED has conducted numerous successful activities in the field of civic and voter education, and election observation. IED is a relatively small outfit whose secretariat consists of a core team of eleven staff members made up of sociologists, lawyers, political scientists and supporting staff. Temporarily contracted employees work as trainers, data entry assistants etc, whenever there is a need to supplement the core team. IED is funded by a number of international and bilateral donors.

Catholic Justice and Peace Commission (CJPC)

The Catholic Justice and Peace Commission was established in 1988 as an arm of the Kenya Episcopal Conference (KEC). CJPC's mandate is to study all issues connected with justice and peace in Kenya. The objectives of the commission are to:

- develop programmes of education in the principles and practices of justice;
- guide and co-ordinate pastoral action to make justice known through the social teachings of the church;
- work for the eradication of injustice in concrete situations; and
- provide information, advice and encouragement to all those involved in the promotion of justice.

Of the 22 Catholic dioceses in Kenya, 20 have a Justice and Peace office with a diocesan team drawn from the area covered by the diocese and a network extending down to the basic Christian community level. Operations at diocesan level involve working with the 630 Catholic parishes and approximately 7,000 prayer houses under the parishes.

National Council of Churches of Kenya (NCCK)

The National Council of Churches of Kenya (NCCK) is one of the largest umbrella church organisations in Kenya. Formed in 1913 as the alliance of Protestant missions, it brings together 30 Protestant denominations with the aim of facilitating their common Christian mission. The focus of the NCCK is ecumenicism and human welfare.

NCCK is one of the leading development organisations in Kenya and works with nine regional offices. The NCCK has been deeply involved in the democratisation process in Kenya well before the reintroduction of political pluralism in 1991. Prior to the repeal of section 2(A) of the constitution, which saw Kenya revert to a multi-party system, NCCK consistently advocated democracy, social justice and the restoration of a multi-party system. Between 1992 and 1997, NCCK was at the centre stage in the constitutional review debate and in civic affairs generally in Kenya.

Historical background and objectives of the 1997 Domestic Observation Project

The year 1992 marked the first time election observers were deployed to observe the electoral process in Kenya. Several civil society organisations came together under an umbrella organisation, the National Election Monitoring Unit (NEMU) to observe the election process. NEMU comprised a loose coalition of organisations namely, the International Federation of Women Lawyers (FIDA Kenya), the Professional Committee for Democratic Change (PCDC), The International Commission of Jurists (ICJ Kenya) and the National Ecumenical Civic Education Programme (NECEP). NEMU put out 5,000 poll watchers while other organisations such as the Catholic church also deployed poll watchers. In the end there were between 7,500-10,000 poll watchers observing polling day, 29 December 1992.

This effort was reasonably successful although greater co-ordination between the various organisations could have made the programme more effective. There remained a lack of clear delineation of roles between the organisations so that accountability was left to only one organisation, FIDA, while the church-based organisation (NECEP) struck out on its own in the end.

For the 1997 elections, organisations wanted to avoid similar mistakes and there was a clear delineation of roles, accountability and management structures. However, it needed outside intervention to bring the groups together. By early 1997, the IED, CJPC and NCCK presented separately almost similar proposals to observe the 1997 general elections to various donors. This presented a dilemma to the donors who saw possible overlap and potential competition among the three organisations. It was, therefore, considered necessary to bring the three initiatives together in a collaborative effort to avoid duplication. Discussions were started in July 1997 to check the willingness of the three organisations to collaborate. Upon a positive response from the three organisations, the London-based Electoral Reform International

Services (ERIS) investigated the feasibility of combining the three proposals into a joint project.

ERIS provided support services in designing the overall observation project and the subsequent follow-up. After extended negotiations between the organisations and the donors, agreements were signed in the third week of October 1997. In addition to preventing duplication, it was realised that each organisation had different strengths and comparative advantages that could be fused to form an effective observation unit. Each organisation was, therefore, assigned a different role and responsibility in order to optimise the quality of the election observation exercise. For example, it was considered that CJPC had the greatest structural capacity and access to the largest number of poll watchers. IED, on the other hand, offered the greatest technical knowledge of elections and election observation, while the NCCK was considered to have the best understanding of the electoral and political context and the ability to deal with publicity and the media. Within the Election Observation Project, each organisation was responsible for its own funds and activities. This way the three organisations were able to avoid the problems experienced by NEMU and to maintain organisational autonomy.

The following indicators were identified:
- successful completion of an effective election observation programme by the three partner organisations;
- full observation reports on the role of electoral authorities and state institutions, the voting and counting process, and the media campaign to be available by February 1998;
- joint press statements within 48 hours of poll closure; and
- final report available within 8 weeks of the poll closure.

The joint effort involved the deployment of 840 nomination and campaign process observers, 28,126 poll watchers, 420 count certifiers and 19 regional officers. Teams were able to observe party primaries, the nomination exercise on 8 and 9 December, the campaign period, election day and the subsequent count. The poll watchers worked in teams of two in almost all of the 13,500 polling stations spread over the 210 electoral constituencies across the country. For the campaign monitoring and count observation, between two and four domestic observers were present. It was believed that a comprehensive, cascade approach to observation would have important voter education spin-offs through encouraging the public to vote and to shun electoral violence.

The three organisations also individually examined various aspects of the electoral process as part of their mandates. For example, apart from the survey of the voter registration exercise the IED also conducted research on the electoral environment in Kenya with an aim of advocating minimum electoral reform prior to the 1997 general elections. CJPC had an on-going activity involving the training of poll observers while the NCCK's advocacy programme had been active in election-related public awareness projects for some time. This election observation exercise thus involved harnessing each organisation's strengths and wide ranging experiences.

On election day, teams covered the whole country and completed checklists which were collated and entered into a central database. From this database a preliminary statement was produced on 31 December, i.e. within 48 hours after the close of the elections. A final statement was released four days later. The whole election observation project lasted a mere six months. The elections report was produced in June 1998. The project marked the beginning of a partnership between donors and local NGOs in promoting domestic election observation on a scale not witnessed before in this country.

The deployment of observers during the campaign period and at polling stations on election day and during the following count was the most crucial aspect of the observation effort. The domestic observers evaluated the adequacy of a wide range of polling day activities, including the opening and closing of polling stations on time; the performance of electoral commission officials and party agents; procedures for securing ballot boxes; voter identification procedures; as well as the procedures for counting and announcing the results. Greater precision in the documentation of violations was achieved through the deployment of more refined tools provided to the observers. In short, observers had at their disposal instruments that were more wide ranging and discriminating than ever before.

A number of other local organisations were also involved in the observation process and their roles served to add further to the confidence amongst voters regarding the exercise. Notable among these were the Federation of Kenya Women Lawyers (FIDA Kenya), the National Council of Women of Kenya (NCWK), the Bureau of Education in Electoral Research and Observation (BEERAM) and the Kenya Human Rights Commission (KHRC). Many ordinary Kenyan citizens across the country also observed the elections in their own unique and innovative ways. FIDA and the NCWK were mainly interested in the gender dimensions, BEERAM concentrated on observing electoral violence while KHRC mounted a media monitoring exercise of both the electronic and print media. However, none of these organisations mounted a nation-wide observation but restricted their movements to specific areas of constituencies that were of interest to them.

The roles of the three organisations in joint collaboration

As mentioned before, it was realised that in addition to avoiding duplication, joining forces would have another advantage in that different tasks could be linked to the best suited performer. In the collaboration exercise, IED was responsible for:

1. design and production of the checklists to vet the nominations, campaign events, polling and counting;
2. analysis of the individual checklists;
3. design and procurement of identification clothing for all observers;
4. training of trainers (TOTs) of the other joint collaborators;
5. production of the election observation manual;
6. production of the accompanying trainers' guide;
7. recruitment of 19 regional officers; and
8. taking the lead in writing the final election observation report.

IED also acted as the secretariat for the joint observation exercise and was responsible for taking the minutes and calling the meetings.

CJPC's role in the joint election observation exercise included:

1. logistics development and deployment of the 28,126 poll watchers;
2. recruiting and training poll observers;
3. distributing materials to observers;
4. training constituency organisers to whom the poll watchers reported;
5. deploying of election observers on election day;
6. recruitment, training and deploying 420 count certifiers; and
7. collecting completed checklists and onward transmission to IED.

The role of NCCK in the joint collaboration exercise was to:

1. select, recruit and train 840 constituency campaign observers;
2. co-ordinate the observation of nominations;
3. collate and analyse campaign report forms;
4. establish a public information office to publicise the observation project through the media, produce a newsletter, *Tazama* (Kiswahili for 'observe') based on field reports received during the campaign, and organise press conferences to release the project's statements and updates. As the elections neared, this office disseminated information on the joint collaborative activities in both the print and electronic media. Six issues of this publication were produced.

Management framework

To ensure the smooth operation of the joint election-observation project, two management organs were established: The Strategic Management Board (SMB) and the Project Steering Committee (PSC). The SMB consisted of senior board members from the three organisations while the PSC consisted of senior operations staff from each of the three organisations and was responsible for the day to day implementation issues. It reported to the SMB. The three organisations offered each other analytical and methodological sophistication, competent staff, well-organised structures and comprehensive coverage.

The management of the project was designed in such a manner as to allow for maximum flexibility and communication at the national level. Weekly meetings that dealt with everyday practical issues were held at the level of the PSC, while the SMB held monthly meetings mainly to resolve conflicts and closer to the election period for decision making on urgent electoral matters. Technical working groups were appointed and appropriate terms of reference developed. These working groups were concerned with recruitment and training, logistics, deployment and communication, and media and publicity. All the working groups were required to report to the larger PSC and had membership from all three organisations.

Financing was managed through M/S Price Waterhouse, an accounting firm that pooled and disbursed the funds for implementation to the three organisations on an imprest basis. They also advised each organisation on suitable accounting procedures compatible with their existing systems and provided ongoing assistance during the project life period. The use of a disbursement agent enabled the donors to dispense with their normal financial accounting procedures and reduced the amount of time donors would have otherwise put into administering the project.

Finally, the donors established a Donor Steering Group (DSG) to co-ordinate their involvement and refine the time frames or budgets as required, in consultation with the PSC.

The different components of the project were managed through the internal mechanisms of the respective organisations. This entailed the designation of particular responsibilities to existing regional NCCK and CJPC diocesan offices. In the case of IED, this involved the appointment of the 19 regional officers mentioned above. The NCCK regional offices co-ordinated the activities of their 63 district co-ordinators, who in turn recruited and trained 840 constituency campaign observers. The CJPC diocesan offices co-ordinated the activities of their parishes which recruited, together with IED and the NCCK, 28,126 poll watchers and 630 count certifiers. In addition, the CJPC recruited constituency organisers, and the NCCK recruited district organisers. These latter two groups were important for the management of the poll watchers and campaign monitors which was done through the two organisations' internal mechanisms.

Consultants from ERIS participated in the PSC for the period that they were in the country for follow up and liaised closely with the DSG, providing ongoing assistance during the life of the project. They visited the country at least four times, initially to help put together the proposal, the second time in October to follow up on the project's progress and the third time in December during the elections and, finally, in April-May 1998 to participate in the evaluation process.

The collaboration

Materials development
The immediate task for the organisations was the preparation of materials that were to be used as information gathering tools during the electoral process. IED had begun the process in August even before the grant agreement was signed in October. This was in recognition of the fact that the process of materials development would be an inclusive process involving all partners. They were designed by IED as the technical experts and pre-tested with national and regional personnel from the CJPC and the NCCK. Care was taken to ensure synergy between different instruments and to avoid duplication. In addition to this, checklists were colour-coded and letter referenced for recognition and ease of identification. The checklists ranged from A to G and also had a 'rapid response' one-page form, which was to be remitted to the hub at IED.

The one-page form was designed to enable the project to issue a statement within 48 hours of the poll, based on information received from a sample of poll watchers. A critical incidents form was also designed for use in case of serious violations such as rigging, electoral violence or gross interference with the electoral process. There was a checklist to observe the campaigns, another for polling day activities, a separate one for the count, the rapid report form and the critical incident checklist. It was considered important that a separate form accompany each stage of the election.

Training
Training was conducted at various levels. The first level consisted of 'Training of Trainers' (TOTs) and was conducted by IED. The trainees were NCCK regional and district co-ordinators, IED's regional officers and CJPC constituency organisers. This training was conducted in November at both national and regional levels.

The second level consisted of training of poll watchers and count certifiers by the CJPC constituency organisers and training of campaign monitors by the NCCK. This training took place at the local level and as close as possible to the final deployment unit. An attempt was made by the Washington-based National Democratic Institute (NDI) to introduce parallel voter tabulation (PVT). However, this came too late in the day and was therefore discarded. NDI had assisted CJPC in conducting poll watcher training and also organised training on logistics and communication with the three organisations in August 1997.

Poll watchers were trained to:

- record whether procedures were adhered to by the electoral commission of Kenya personnel in the administration of the polling station (according to stated electoral law);
- record the performance of all returning officers.

The count certifiers were trained to:

- monitor the transportation of ballot papers from the polling station to the count centre;
- ensure that all procedures were followed at each count centre in accordance with the electoral law.

Special observation and training manuals designed as part of the project were used. Participants were introduced to various checklists and the anticipated logistics and communication processes. Training was conducted mainly in Catholic pastoral centres in various dioceses; and constituencies falling within every diocese were grouped together for ease of co-ordination. The selection of poll watchers was based on the following criteria:

1. a minimum of 'O' level of education;
2. ability to communicate in English and/or Kiswahili;
3. be aged 18 years and above; and
4. be a registered voter.

It was stated that preference would be given to those who had previous experience in election observation. However, only a few of these persons were used, mostly people employed by church organisations in 1992. Those who had worked for NEMU could not be traced, as the NEMU records were inaccessible. A majority of IED's by-election personnel missed an opportunity to be recruited due to some confusion among the three organisations on the appropriate list to be used.

Publicity

Publicity for the project was the responsibility of the NCCK which set up a Public Information Office for the period. This office produced a weekly newsletter, *Tazama*, made press statements and advertisements, and arranged for press conferences. *Tazama* was the joint newsletter produced on behalf of the organisations by the NCCK. Reports from campaign monitors were used as a source of information for the newsletter as well as the articles submitted by the reporters. In this way, it was possible to verify the articles submitted for publication.

Representatives of the three organisations sat on the media and publicity working group of the Project Steering Committee (PSC). These meetings were used as a forum to discuss the content of *Tazama* and approve articles selected by the technical team for publication. Ten thousand copies of each of the six editions of *Tazama* were printed and distributed chiefly through the nine NCCK district organisers, through IED and the CJPC. The balance was distributed from Nairobi. It was considered that the 10,000 copies would be adequate due to the multiplier effect, whereby more than one person would read the same copy. The office worked through various reporters in different parts of the country who were employed from 27 November 1997 to 8 January 1998, and worked for a period of six weeks. Their brief was to report on the project as well as observe the elections.

The Public Information Office also worked on advertisements and publicity. These included full-page newspaper adverts with information on the project and its role in election observation, radio spots and television adverts. An animated civic awareness programme that encouraged people to come out and vote was also broadcast on the Kenya Television network. The Public Information Office also organised three press conferences. The first was for the launch of the joint project, the second for the preliminary statement and the third for the final statement.

Procurement
A procurement officer was locally contracted to work on the project for a period of four months. He was to liaise with each organisation in order to:
1.   provide advice on sourcing of required materials and equipment;
2.   provide advice on relative costs of hire or purchase;
3.   negotiate bulk prices with suppliers;
4.   validate tenders for key materials and items of equipment;
5.   assist organisations to procure and arrange for delivery of materials and equipment; and
6.   ensure delivery and installation of all equipment in the Nairobi offices of the three organisations (delivery and installation of all field based equipment was the responsibility of the two church organisations in the field establishments once it had been delivered to their headquarters).

Enhancement of organisational capacity
The project not only aimed to observe the 1997 general elections but also to enhance the capacity of the organisations to carry out work of a similar nature in future. In this regard, various equipment was given as grants to the organisations according to their needs. The NCCK received nine fax machines for the regional offices to speed up communication, especially with regard to the *Tazama* newsletter, and a powerful high-speed computer as well as a printer for the Public Information Office. In addition, a computer and two fax machines

were rented for use during the project period. The CJPC received two computers, a printer and two fax machines. The IED was granted two computers, a printer, and four fax machines to speed up data reception. A further two computers and a printer were rented closer to the polling day to speed up data input and analysis. These were connected through a common network.

One week before the elections three more computers, a photocopier and a further printer were rented for use by IED. A KVA generator was also loaned to IED by the Royal Netherlands Embassy for that period as a back up in case of power failure. This would allow data input to continue on a twenty-four hour basis without hindrance. The NCCK rented a laptop computer for the period. Additional telephone lines were also installed for this period. IED further received office furniture for the additional staff that would be working on the project.

Accreditation

As part of the agreement to maintain individual organisational autonomy, accreditation from the Electoral Commission of Kenya was sought on an individual basis. IED and CJPC were easily accredited but the NCCK had to negotiate for their accreditation after it was initially denied on the grounds that their previous work on constitutional reform and conflict resolution in the Rift Valley clash areas portrayed them as a partisan organisation. In the end they were accredited.

What domestic observers looked out for

The objective of the 1997 domestic observation exercise was two-fold: first, to deter fraud through the presence of observers inside polling stations and counting centres, and second, to make an assessment of all aspects of the electoral process. By so doing, observers intended to contribute to the integrity of the process and to further democratic development in Kenya.

The observers identified a list of critical constituencies that were of particular interest. These were constituencies that:
1.   were strongly pro-opposition;
2.   were strongly pro-KANU;
3.   were newly created;
4.   were hit by pre-election clashes;
5.   were hit by clashes after the 1992 general elections;
6.   had a history of violence;
7.   were affected by the El Niño phenomenon;
8.   had presidential candidates;
9.   had women candidates.

Checklists from these constituencies were given special treatment in the data analysis.

Data capturing

A Swedish consultant was contracted to provide training and assist with application. Prior to her arrival, however, IED had started developing a system using SPSS and it was decided to continue with this rather than confuse the situation by introducing a new computer programme. It should be recognised that SPSS is not necessarily the most appropriate or user friendly software. The information collected during the life of the project was entered into a database for analysis. IED organised a highly efficient system of collecting, coding and entering data. This included a 24-hour shift system for staff and the training of additional temporary data entry staff engaged specifically for this task.

Problems experienced

Where three organisations are working on a project of this nature and magnitude for the first time, there are bound to be areas of conflict. Issues of organisational identity, personalities and financial concerns arose. These were compounded by the fact that there was inadequate time to identify and work on issues requiring pre-agreements such as the format and content of the final report or the structure and content of the statements.

The main issues were in the recruitment of poll watchers. Having prepared to observe elections as a sole entity, each organisation had made preparations to have their team of poll watchers in the field. However, the collaboration introduced unforeseen complications as the poll watchers were more than the allocated number. CJPC, for example, had already received funding from the Agency for International Development (USAID) to train 20,000 poll watchers whereas IED was expecting to work with 7,000 while NCCK had a list of 5,000. A compromise was reached whereby CJPC agreed to work with 15,000 to allow IED and NCCK to retain their original number.

However, when it came to the actual recruitment and deployment, new problems arose. CJPC complained of inadequate lists from IED and NCCK in which the information provided could not enable its field personnel to easily identify the poll watchers. IED and NCCK, on the other hand, complained that their people were not recruited by CJPC field personnel who, because of their structural autonomy from their headquarters, felt at liberty to recruit their own people. This allowed them to recruit freely as they so wished without resorting to instructions from their national office. Moreover, the collaboration did not take into consideration prior arrangements made by individual organisations and commitments to their poll watchers. But there were also cases where everything went well and there were few complaints on the recruitment process.

Other problems were experienced in transmitting information back to IED. Some individuals from the church-based organisations felt more confident in transmitting information through their headquarters, but ended up creating another tier of communication in the collection of results. However, IED had put in place a reasonable logistical process where courier vehicles were to be used to forward constituency checklists and this was reasonably successful as was hand delivery and telephone calls to IED.

Statements and final report

The three statements produced by the project explained in detail the context in which the elections took place as well as specific instances of administrative and other shortcomings. Effort was made to ensure that they were balanced and gave a fair reflection of the situation. On 27 December, the Strategic Management Board issued a press statement giving details of several irregularities during the pre-election period which had come to its attention. A preliminary statement was issued on 30 December, focusing on the administration of the elections and calling for a commission of enquiry to establish the reasons for the logistical chaos that had marred them.

On 4 January 1998, the project issued the final statement, based on the reports submitted by the poll watchers, campaign monitors and count certifiers. This statement was issued after over 10,000 checklists had been received and analysed. Representatives from all the three organisations and the ERIS consultants were present to agree on the tenor of the final statement. The statement was drafted jointly at the initiative of the ERIS consultants and IED. At the end of the day, all those present were asked to contribute to and agree on the wording of the statement. While there may have been reservations, these were not expressed and the statement was released as a consensual statement of the project. The statement was fairly critical of the electoral process, but the media gave the impression that the verdict of the project on the 1997 general elections was favourable. It is arguable that the project's statements played an important role in calming the situation immediately after the elections when a number of political parties suggested calling for a boycott of the results.

The statement said that, as a whole, the elections reflected the will of the Kenyan people, but detailed the concerns observed and suggested remedial measures that should be taken to improve the electoral environment. It turned out that CJPC had reservations about the content of the statement but did not voice them at the time. The structure of CJPC is that it falls under the Kenya Episcopal Conference (KEC) which had the mandate, on behalf of the Catholic church, to comment on such issues. On this occasion, KEC had divergent views from that of the joint collaboration team and this posed a dilemma to CJPC. It was later recognised that such structural complications could have been dealt with more easily had this problem been posed earlier at the conception stage. The wider membership of the NCCK and CJPC also felt that the statement did not reflect their feelings about the elections. This poses the question as to how exactly consensus could have been gathered from the church community as religious people belong to various political parties and, therefore, may be of completely opposite views.

Evaluation of the *Together for Peaceful Elections Project*

Two external evaluators from Frontier Consultants of South Africa conducted the project evaluation (Frontier Consultants 1998). Five regional workshops were held during the evaluation so as to get the perspective of all the players. Poll watchers, count certifiers, regional officers, constituency organisers, campaign observers and members of the PSC attended the workshops. The areas covered in the discussions were:

1. *Organisation of the observation of the electoral process*
   It was felt that this would have been more successful if the idea had come from the three organisations and not from the donors.

2. *Training, selection and recruitment*
   It was felt that involvement of personnel at the regional level would have enabled the smooth flow of communication between the three organisations rather than the instructions that were issued centrally and at times did not take into consideration issues at the lower level such as diocesan independence and autonomy. Training had to be given to a large number of people over a relatively short period. It was undertaken by the different organisations at different times, and given to different groups. This resulted in a lack of coherence between the various workshops. This rush could be attributed to the short period given for implementation. A longer time frame could have resulted in a more co-ordinated planning.

3. *Liaison between and within co-operating organisations*
   The central structure of the liaison was a barrier to effective communication at the lower level. At the upper level, an organisations with a hierarchical structure such as CJPC was not upfront with this information so that complications later arose as to who had the power to speak for CJPC.

4.   *Reporting and information*
     Information was relayed from the central planning unit in Nairobi to the regions by individual organisations. In some cases, this information may have been contradictory or diluted as it trickled downwards since there was no uniformity in the delivery. This should be remedied in future.
5.   *Analysis and documentation*
     It was felt that data reports could have been pre-designed in a format known and agreed upon by the project partners and with a view to easily and graphically assessing the predetermined benchmarks. In the case of the joint observation group, no predetermined benchmarks were set.

Recommendations and lessons learned

These workshops provided valuable insights into the way the project functioned and made the following recommendations for any future collaboration:

1.   In future, similar projects should have a longer time frame and should be planned well in advance.
2.   In particular, the identification of issues which require pre-agreements, and agreement on the process to be followed when dealing with these issues, would prevent difficulties that may arise during the life of the project.
3.   Proper planning, possibly in the form of an intensive weekend seminar to establish the responsibilities of the different organisations, would have assisted in the implementation of the project.
4.   Planning and management should not be centralised but should include regional and district level role players to ensure regional ownership and to iron out difficulties presented by the nature and structure of the three separate entities. Participants at the evaluation workshops agreed that the centralised planning system adopted by the organisations did not allow them to participate effectively in the implementation of the project and created confusion as individual organisations sent conflicting messages to their people. Joint structures at a regional level would facilitate smooth implementation and more effective delivery.
5.   The particular constraints facing each organisation need to be made clear upfront and to be understood by all project partners.
6.   Funds need to be released in a timely manner to avoid a rush in project implementation.
7.   The donors should also be conscious of the time frame and expedite payment faster. In this particular project, the time taken for funds to be released impacted negatively on the implementation of the project.

8.   Joint training at a regional level of personnel from all three organisations would ensure that they were sufficiently aware of each other's roles and responsibilities, and promote teamwork on the ground. The development of a common ethos would facilitate the smooth and effective running of the project.

Even though it is evident that there were constraints brought about by different organisational structures, management and decision-making processes, over-all the collaboration was considered a large success worth emulating. The project was later on criticised for the exclusion of Muslim organisations in the observation exercise. The issue of inclusion of Muslim organisations arose earlier during the project inception process, but the three organisations felt that rather than involve Muslim organisations per se, they would work with individual Muslim observers. This was successfully done in the predominantly Muslim areas of north-eastern and coastal regions of Kenya. The justification given for not involving the Muslim community at an organisational level was that its existing structures would conflict with those of the Christian organisations. The decision not to include them was, therefore, taken to avoid any structural conflict.

The final report was launched in June 1998 at a ceremony attended by the chairman Electoral Commission of Kenya, the diplomatic community, political party leaders and members of the civil society. The report concluded that despite some attempts, Kenya still does not have a fully functional electoral system. However, despite lacunae in the electoral legal regime, the electoral process in Kenya is premised on solid democratic principles. Even when there have been highly irregular elections, there has never been an overtly expressed intention to abandon the basic rules of free and democratic elections. The report not only covered the more visible aspects of the electoral process – the nomination of candidates, the campaigns, the polling, and the counting of votes – it also gave an account and evaluation of what happened in the run up to the elections.

It made the following recommendations:

Civic education
1.   Immediate steps should be taken to create effective civic education programmes nation-wide. Public resources such as the government run Kenya Broadcasting Corporation (KBC) should be engaged for this purpose.
2.   The Electoral Commission of Kenya should promote civic and voter education.

Gerrymandering

An Act of Parliament should be passed to empower the ECK to undertake an immediate review of all the parliamentary constituency boundaries in order to recover the basic tenet of one person, one (equal) vote.

The electoral code

There is need for a comprehensive code which should be a single legislation covering all aspects of the electoral process. The electoral code should deal with the following areas that affect the freedom, fairness, and integrity of the electoral process:

1. registration of political parties and enforcement of the code of ethics by the ECK.
2. financing of political parties through state subsidies.
3. financial ceilings on how much political parties and candidates can spend on elections.
4. disclosure of sources of funding of political parties and candidates ensuring accountability for these funds.
5. provision for independent candidates.
6. counting of votes at polling stations.
7. use of other forms of identification other than the national identity card and passport during both voting and registration.
8. provision for special voting arrangements, for example, through the Kenyan embassies and high commissions or by post for non-resident Kenyans.
9. method of voting in which illiterate voters are able to vote without the assistance from the presiding officer so as to ensure the secrecy of the ballot and preserve illiterate voters' dignity.
10. provision for declaring an election petitioner the winner without having to subject the constituency to a by-election in cases where a recount shows clearly that the petitioner won the majority of votes.

Institutional capacity of the ECK

Most of the logistical flaws in the 1997 general elections were attributable to the lack of an effective secretariat at the ECK. Therefore, as soon as possible, there should be an evaluation exercise to determine the human resource needs of the ECK, followed by a recruitment and deployment programme for both the national secretariat and field level offices (IED/CJPC/NCCK 1998).

Conclusion

Though there is still room for improvement of the election observation exercise, in general, the domestic election observation met the ambitious expectations set at the start. The Kenyan people welcomed and accepted the observers. Their presence boosted the confidence of the electorate. The project as a whole achieved its major objectives. Over 28,000 poll watchers, 840 campaign observers and 630 count certifiers were recruited and trained to observe the elections. Communication and data capturing systems were put in place and operated efficiently. The local organisations involved in the project, IED, CJPC and NCCK, have been able to gain considerably in terms of the ability to manage large projects and capacity-building of local staff. The project was arguably the most comprehensive and sophisticated domestic election observation operation ever to be mounted in Africa and stands to provide an exciting and innovative model for other countries to follow.

References

Frontier Consultants 1998, *Evaluation of the 1997 Kenyan General Election Domestic Monitoring Project,* Frontier Consultants.

IED/CJPC/NCCK 1998, *Report on the 1997 General Elections in Kenya, 29-30 December, 1997*, Nairobi: Institute for Education in Democracy, Catholic Justice and Peace Commission, National Council of Churches of Kenya.

8

International Election Observation during the 1997 Kenya Elections

Norbert Braakhuis

The time frame of election observation is often seen as covering only elections themselves and a short period running up to them, but not, or insufficiently, including the broader political context and longer-term process of which elections form part. As a result, international election observation exercises have given way to serious criticism. The way the international community decided to approach the 1997 general elections in Kenya stemmed to a large extent from reflections on the deficiencies of the 1992 international election observation as well as of similar exercises elsewhere.

This chapter attempts to give an accurate description of the way the 1997 elections in Kenya were approached by a majority of the Western diplomatic and donor missions represented in the country, united in the Donors for Development and Democracy Group (DDDG – re-baptised Democratic Development Group or DDG in early 1998).[1] In doing so, it tries to identify elements for an approach that relies more on long-term, in-depth knowledge and accompaniment of democratisation processes of which elections are an important part and expression, than on short-term, relatively ad-hoc exercises.

International election observation in Kenya: The 1992 experience

The 1992 elections had been the culmination of a tense and at moments violent process of democratisation that ended a 23-year period of single party rule. Many Western embassies had been closely following and stimulating a process that started at the beginning of 1990 through a church leaders' campaign for the return of a multi-party system, soon to be joined by broad sectors of Kenyan society including politicians and NGOs. At the time, the international donor community which insisted not only on political changes but equally on major economic reforms to stop the decline of Kenya's economy and halt corruption, had threatened to withhold further donor support.

When President Daniel arap Moi gave in to the pressure in December 1992 and withdrew section 2(A) of the constitution that had transformed Kenya into a one-party state, the way to redemocratisation lay open. New political parties were launched, heavily manned by transfugees from the former single party – Kenya African National Union (KANU). Elections, which were held on 29 December 1992, were generally expected to lead to a change of president and government; they became the subject of an important observation effort locally and internationally. The local observers had united in an ad hoc organisation, the National Election Monitoring Unit (NEMU). The organisation trained and deployed about 8,000 domestic observers throughout the country with financial assistance from several Western countries (see Chapter 7).

International observers were flown in from all over the world just before election day and left the country almost collectively in the aftermath of that day. Of particular importance were the delegations from the Commonwealth and from the Washington-based International Republican Institute (IRI). There were also teams from Denmark, Egypt, Germany, Japan and Switzerland.

Although important – besides the 8,000 local observers, some 200 international observers scrutinised the elections – the deployment of the international observers covered only a limited number of the over 7,000 polling stations, many of which were moreover subdivided and could not be simultaneously covered by a single observer.

Worse, many of the irregularities that biased the results took place in the run up to the elections and were, therefore, out of the realm of the foreign observers. Most seriously in this respect, the limitation of the observation to the election day only had left out of the observers' notice any possible manipulation taking place earlier on in the electoral process. The manipulation of the electoral process included the obstruction of public meetings of the opposition; the forceful or otherwise impediment of opposition representatives to register as candidates; the campaigning in favour of the ruling party by members of the civil service; the utilisation of public means such as vehicles for the KANU campaign; police brutality and the restriction of territorial access to the opposition. As a consequence, the playing field was tilted to favour the ruling party. National and international observers, embassies and the like were simply not prepared to oppose the salami tactics that increasingly reduced the chances of the opposition to win the elections by introducing uneven electoral conditions.

The elections themselves produced widespread allegations of fraud and irregularities, including the stuffing of ballot boxes, the destruction of opposition votes and other means of count rigging. As *Africa Confidential* put it in 1993, 'Neither the foreign nor the local observer groups had the capacity or resources to investigate comprehensively rigging allegations. Consequently, they reported only the most blatant and easily verifiable irregularities.'

Further limitations in the quality of the observation stemmed from what Geisler has called (1993: 615) the phenomenon of 'election tourism'. Finally, comments from different groups of observers tended to be made hastily, without collective overall assessment. As a result, the international observation exercise lost credibility as post evaluation of the elections showed that many of the manipulations that had characterised the whole election period had not been taken into consideration.

All these elements contributed to a feeling of extreme caution amongst the Western embassies in Kenya concerning a repeat of the international observation effort of 1992 along the same lines. Already at an early stage in 1997, Western embassies - united in the DDDG, which included the European Union embassies - decided that different ways of observation had to be defined to reach a more comprehensive and in-depth observation of the electoral process, not to be limited to the election day only. This led to a more balanced and objective judgement of the validity of the election results.

International observation: if and how

The if question: risk assessment

Although the possibility of international observation of the elections was envisaged at an early stage in 1997, no decision was taken until later that year. From 1995 onwards, the European Union member states present in Kenya, but also other Western members of the DDDG, had met regularly between themselves, and on several occasions with high government representatives. The purpose was to identify or communicate the basic principles to be respected in the electoral process and corresponding measures to be executed by the government if elections were to be considered 'free and fair'. The central element was: levelling the playing field between opposition parties and KANU. If the steps taken by the government to guarantee the application of these principles made substantive progress in this respect, international election observation could be decided upon.

The DDDG members wanted to avoid the impression that, through participation in the observation process, the international community would be endorsing an election result that, as a consequence of serious distortions in the process preceding election day, could no longer be considered acceptably 'free and fair'– even if the elections themselves would have been conducted in a reasonably 'free and fair' way. A continuous evaluation by the DDDG members of steps taken by the Kenyan authorities would conclude if those could be considered sufficient. In addition to the DDDG-evaluation, the EU members would conduct their separate assessment.

On several occasions, ambassadors of e.g. the Netherlands, the UK and the USA touched upon those principles in public speeches, provoking some harsh reactions from Kenyan government officials. Included in the list of principles were freedom of opinion, of expression, of organisation (including registration of political parties), of the press, of access without restriction to the whole Kenyan territory for candidates of all parties, and the freedom to hold meetings. In order to guarantee the application of those principles, more concrete bench marks were defined. Concerning, for example, the freedom of expression – which in a democracy includes the right to vote for a candidate of one's own choice – particular attention was given to equal opportunities for all Kenyan citizens aged 18 or above to obtain in due time an identity card, which was a prerequisite to be registered as a voter, and second, equal opportunities to register.

Through the system of continuous evaluation, it proved possible to avoid falling victim to the aforementioned 'salami tactics' as had happened in 1992. Divide and rule strategies did not work: the collective effort made it difficult for the Kenyan government to silence DDDG members through singling out one or two more vocal or outspoken countries for heavy criticism, thereby expecting others to abstain from public statements, pressure on the government or support to those subjected to government attacks. Although interpretation of government steps towards the implementation of the basic principles could differ between DDDG members, a common denominator was in general easily agreed upon.

Crucial to the decision to observe the elections were the events of *Saba Saba* day (7 July 1997) and of *Nane Nane* day (8 August 1997). A lethal confrontation between opposition supporters and the police, together with international pressure, fragilised a hitherto inflexible government position on reforms and led to an accelerated implementation of measures designed to create a more level playing field. This in turn was expected to create more even conditions for reasonably 'free and fair' elections. Many of the demands for respect of basic principles in democracy building were met by concrete and in part immediate measures elaborated by a hastily organised Inter-Parties Parliamentary Group (IPPG), in which part of the parliamentary opposition participated. Although late, and on some occasions partial or half-hearted, these measures nevertheless represented serious changes in the playing field and improved the possibilities for elections freer and fairer than in 1992. Apart from immediate measures, the government accepted the principle of constitutional reforms within a two-year period after the general elections. Calm returned to the streets.

Largely on the basis of the IPPG reforms, the DDDG decided to go ahead with the international observation exercise. Talks about the creation of an observation unit had already started in May-June 1997 and different forms of observation had been considered, but the final decision to proceed was seriously delayed – not least because of uncertainty about the election date. The final assessment by the DDDG members of progress made in levelling the playing field came at a late stage, just as President Moi announced the election date of 29 December 1997. This left relatively little time to prepare for the start of the observation exercise.

In contrast, the local observation process had made more progress. Started in May 1997, in a concerted effort between some DDDG-members and three major non governmental organisations – the Institute for Education in Democracy (IED), the Protestant National Council of Churches of Kenya (NCCK), and the Catholic Justice and Peace Commission (CJPC) – local NGO observation was not submitted to the same risk of endorsing a possibly flawed electoral process. Major players within the nation-wide local observation effort had over time expressed serious criticism about the government's position on democratisation and could hardly be expected to rubber-stamp the outcome of the electoral process.

The 'how' question: defining the model
The form in which to organise the election observation exercise had been the subject of debate earlier in 1997 between the DDDG members. In essence, three possibilities were considered:
- a more loosely co-ordinated observation by incoming missions through the DDDG;
- an international observation exercise headed by the UN (i.e. UNDP) like in 1992;
- an observation exercise consisting essentially of local diplomats and other persons related to diplomatic missions, co-ordinated by means of a separate co-ordination unit operating under the DDDG.

The first option had some implicit inconveniences. The DDDG structure was not designed to do a major, time-consuming co-ordination and harmonisation effort. Moreover, a loosely co-ordinated effort would almost certainly lead to discrepancies in the comments from the different incoming observers and observer groups.

Furthermore most, if not all, observers would only stay in Kenya for the elections themselves, not covering the whole range of previous stages that were equally important to reach a balanced conclusion. Experience in 1992 and in other countries had moreover shown that external observers tended to plan their departure shortly after the officially planned closure of the ballot boxes, with events often still unfolding and voting time expanded.

The UNDP option did not generate much enthusiasm, mainly for two reasons. On the one hand, experience had shown that a UN-led unit would have difficulties avoiding contradictory comments from different participating observation missions and in reaching a harmonised verdict on the election process and outcome. In past years, UNDP had seemed to lack firmness, e.g., in co-ordinating the assistance to ethnic clash victims in Kenya, and questions were raised whether it would show total independence from the Kenyan authorities and so avoid serious criticism of the electoral process observation. Also, UNDP did not manifest a strong interest in running an observation unit.

The third option, therefore, looked the most promising. It allowed for a longer lasting coverage of the electoral process. It profit from the accumulated knowledge of local diplomatic missions and offered many possibilities for a more systematic follow up of possible recommendations, using the network of contacts with national and local authorities, NGOs, civil society movements, etc.

An election observation unit would potentially represent a central unit for all incoming experts from the DDDG member states and, therefore, seriously reduce the risks of duplication of effort. Even if experts from DDDG member states would prefer to operate outside the co-ordination mechanism of a central unit, it would be easy for such a unit to establish contacts through their respective member states. This would enable monitors to cover as many polling stations as possible and to reach a harmonised final opinion or at least to avoid contradictory observations.

On 28 May 1997 an initial meeting to discuss the creation of an observation unit brought together a number of like-minded parties (Denmark, the Netherlands, UK, USA, the European Commission) and showed that genuine interest to combine efforts and make available the necessary funds and personnel existed. It showed, at the same time, that the definition of such a unit needed to be looked at carefully clarifying the legal implications of its creation, its internal structure and the relationship between an observation unit, those funding it and the DDDG. Moreover, it was necessary to make an assessment of its needs in terms of personnel, finance and equipment.

In July 1997, two consultants (Marguerite Garling for the EU, Judith Geist for USAID), in close consultation with DDDG members, looked into the three different alternatives for election observation. They spoke out in favour of the third model: a small and flexible secretariat, linked to the DDDG, allowing for rapid information exchange and analysis, optimising available resources and harmonising positions. The model employed in the 1995 Ethiopian elections (though distinct) had given valuable inputs for developing the innovative model for the Kenyan election observation. Garling and Geist (1997) outlined the structure, functioning and financial set up of the secretariat as follows:

- The secretariat would be staffed by a co-ordinator in charge of overall supervision, liaison with the DDDG/donors and public relations; an information and analysis officer; three to four research assistants; and an office manager;

- The secretariat would take care of the production of observation forms, news summaries, briefing material and a deployment strategy, assist in actual field observation and analyse and comment on the observation results for the diplomatic missions;
- Individual diplomatic missions would ensure the availability of funds.

The UN informed the DDDG by early July that it had no intention of setting up its own election observation unit for the coming general elections. The UN representative underlined the need to support local observers, and welcomed the announcement that several donors had already taken the lead to do so.

In that same meeting, the DDDG endorsed the recommendations of the consultant to set up an Election Observation Centre (EOC) with one notable exception: instead of a hierarchical structure, they opted for a division of responsibilities between at least three or four co-ordinators. They considered that establishing a hierarchical relationship between 'Kenya experts' flown in from different DDDG member states might create some tension.

The terms of reference established by the DDDG for the co-ordinators stipulated the following main tasks for the EOC:

- Collect and analyse material concerning election rules and regulations, constituencies and the location of polling stations;
- Monitor the local press;
- Liaise with the diplomatic missions of the DDDG;
- Provide advice to the DDDG missions on which constituencies would merit visits, and guidance on what to observe;
- Produce checklists for diplomatic observers for each phase of the election period;
- Co-ordinate travel plans of observers, including DDDG missions;
- Maintain and distribute records of observer reports;
- Maintain close contact with domestic observer organisations, possible other international observation teams and the political parties;
- Maintain close contact with the electoral commission.

Legally speaking, the EOC was not to be established as an entity in its own right. It would not have a legal status of its own or enter into contracts with third parties (and could, therefore, not be held liable for any problems that might occur). Its members would be drawn temporarily from collaborating diplomatic missions or from experts brought in from abroad by individual DDDG members and attached to the EOC. If the EOC would have operated with a proper legal identity, a problem of work permits for the EOC staff, for example, could have occurred. EOC members were supposed to refrain from making public or press statements and external contacts would be assured through the DDDG presidency, in this case Canada.

General agreement existed, however, about the need for transparency towards the Electoral Commission of Kenya, political parties, domestic observation organisations and civil society actors at large with regard to the EOC structure, objectives and working methods.

The EOC at work

Operationalisation of the EOC

As soon as the British co-ordinator and his Canadian DDDG counterpart arrived in Kenya by the end of October 1997, the EOC entered its operational phase. They paved the way for the proper functioning of the centre, without tryouts. Their first actions were threefold: establishing essential contacts with major actors in the electoral field (electoral commission, political parties, domestic observer groups, NGOs, civil society organisations and the DDDG members); arranging for the necessary logistics (housing for the EOC, equipment, administrative support) and developing information flows (input such as subscription to press publications, output such as election profiles). Of particular importance was the mobilisation of the financial contributions. With some exceptions, donors proved slower than anticipated in providing the promised, financial contributions even though they came in part from 'quick disbursement funds' available at diplomatic mission level. The Australian High Commission showed great flexibility when it put its diplomatic mission at the disposition of the EOC. By the second half of November, the EOC was fully operational with the arrival of the last co-ordinators and full funding and equipment.[2]

The co-ordinators and their support staff, some of them volunteers, reached agreement on a division of labour, attributing specific responsibilities to each of them for geographical regions, political parties and organisations such as DDDG, the electoral commission and the media. The function of the head of administrative operations (assigned to a volunteer) proved essential to the donor community. The importance of some logistical functions, e.g., drivers, had initially been underestimated.

EOC in operation

The EOC had to cover six distinct phases:
(a) Registration of voters (conducted from 19 May to 30 June 1997);
(b) Designation of candidates within the political parties (party primaries late November, early December);
(c) Official nomination of candidates (presidential 2-3 December, local and parliamentary 8-9 December);
(d) Campaign period;

(e)   Election day including vote counting (29 December plus extension);
(f)   The election aftermath.

(a) *Registration of voters (19 May - 30 June)*
The voters' registration process had taken place earlier in 1997, from 19 May to 20 June, but under heavy pressure extended to 30 June 1997, before the EOC was established. However, some of the eventual co-ordinators were present during the process. The Institute for Education in Democracy (IED), under donor funding, also observed this process. Surrounded by controversy over the use of new and old identity cards, over allegations of ethnic exclusion and excessive registration in some constituencies, and by confusion over cards containing errors and their late availability, the overall assessment was nevertheless that in the registration process irregularities had stayed relatively limited. An estimated 2 million overwhelmingly young voters had, however, not been issued with new generation identity cards, which had to be applied for in a limited period running from the end of 1996 to the beginning of 1997. This excluded them from the voting process. The final number of registered voters (9 million) did not reflect adequately the increase in the number of potential voters as a result of Kenya's population growth.

(b) *Party primaries (late November – early December)*
The EOC staff had collected through the press, interviews and domestic observation groups the necessary information on each constituency in order to identify priority 'hot spots' where observation by diplomatic observers would be necessary. In addition, deployment plans and checklists for the observation of the party primaries had been prepared.

An instruction meeting for the diplomatic observers of this phase took place on 24 November with the participation of representatives of domestic observation groups.

The bulk of the actual observation work was done by the EOC team and British, Canadian and Dutch diplomats in 24 districts, covering KANU, DP, NDP and FORD-Kenya primaries (Rutten 2000). The ensuing EOC report presented to the DDDG concluded that the primaries had been conducted in ways similar to 1992, but with notably less interference from the provincial and local authorities. Serious problems had occurred, especially in urban areas, but ethnic violence, although present in the Trans Mara-Kisii border, played a lesser role than in 1992. It had been subdued in the Likoni south coast area, but not before having chased away numerous opposition voters from two coastal constituencies, depriving them of ultimate access to the ballot.

(c) *Nomination of parliamentary and civic candidates (8-9 December)*

Following the primaries, the EOC finalised a detailed plan of action, rationalising its activities and division of labour. Similar to the previous phase, the EOC produced and distributed to the observers nomination observation forms, constituency profiles and additional information, and singled out the new 'hot spots'. Over 50 observers from 11 diplomatic missions visited a similar number of constituencies, with again the British, Canadians and Dutch forming the core group. Like in the previous and coming phases, an important deployment of local observers assured a high observer presence in the nomination exercise.

Instructions were given to report serious incidents directly to the EOC for transmission to the electoral commission to allow for possible remedial action. After complaints from political parties in Nandi and Siaya, observers and EOC experts were dispatched to those areas. Subsequently, the DDDG chair transmitted concerns on districts to the Electoral Commission of Kenya for Nandi where opposition candidates had been denied clearance of their nomination papers. At the closure of the nomination period, however, there were no reports of candidates having been prevented from presenting their papers.

Although not without some serious irregularities, the nomination process had been conducted with greater respect for regulations and in a more peaceful environment than the 1992 nominations. One of the IPPG reforms, namely the extension of nomination time from half a day to two days, was a major factor in this. The efficient organisation and timely opening and closure of most of the nomination centres deserved praise. Some of the more notorious problems found their origin in party headquarters, where attempts were made to replace some winners of the internal party nominations by candidates from opposed factions.

(d) *The campaign period (10-27 December)*

Although the EOC was well prepared at the start of the campaign period on 10 December, it was facing difficulties in accessing information on election campaigning. This was mainly due to the fact that the political parties operated in a fairly disorganised manner, often deciding only at the last moment when and where venues would take place. If available, information was generally limited to presidential candidates. The diplomatic missions were briefed at the start of the campaign period, receiving campaign rally checklists and information packages.

The EOC indicated which meetings deserved priority, but sometimes observers arrived at the place chosen only to discover that the party at the latest moment had cancelled or rescheduled the meeting. With some notable exceptions, police and provincial administration abstained from interfering with gatherings, a huge improvement over 1992.

Throughout the election period, however, observers witnessed acts of bribery, harassment or provocation from parties operating in their respective strongholds. Some of those acts were of particular concern, such as those directed against one Kandie, a candidate for parliament against President Moi, or the imposition by the authorities of severe restrictions on campaigning along the Trans Mara-Kisii border where party supporters were ambushed and killed.

Special mention should be made of complaints made by non-diplomatic sources to the DDDG and EOC relating intimidation, harassment and aggression against female candidates, which started even before the internal party nomination process. Some cases could be checked. The discrimination took place at least partly within the candidates' own parties and on one occasion a candidate had to go underground.

Compared to 1992, the campaign period was nevertheless more peaceful and open. Opposition politicians were in general free to move throughout the territory. Notwithstanding an agreement within the IPPG package on balanced radio and television coverage between ruling party and opposition, the electronic media dedicated a disproportionate amount of time to KANU and President Moi, primarily with negative reporting on the opposition. The written press reported more evenhandedly and as far as observers could witness, the press was not seriously interfered with during the election period (see also Chapter 9).

(e) *Election day and subsequent counting*
The EOC moved into its highest gear in the two weeks running up to the elections themselves. So far, the co-ordinators had been able to combine fieldwork and work at the centre, partially relying on the support staff for the necessary logistics and servicing the diplomatic missions. Some understaffing (in particular of aides and local service staff) had at times put strains on the co-ordinators, which became increasingly critical in the last pre-electoral period. Diplomatic deployment would concern some 150 persons; paperwork intensified.

The EOC called for a preparatory meeting on 19 December, distributing the Diplomatic Election Observers Field Guidance, a self-prepared documentation containing guidelines for observers (e.g. code of ethics, instructions for press contacts and security), election observation forms, investigation and reporting guidelines and an observation kit which included constituency profiles, area maps, lists of Kenyan electoral officials (returning officers, electoral commissioners, district electoral co-ordinators), polling stations and deployment details, diplomatic observers' T-shirts and external material such as IED observers training manuals, the official Electoral Commission of Kenya election manuals, vehicle badges and observer badges, as well as letters of observer accreditation to the elections.

As in earlier phases, observers were advised to contact the EOC in case of serious incidents. Apparently, anodyne tasks like maintaining contact with the Electoral Commission of Kenya and local observers, checking if embassies had asked for accreditation or permanent rescheduling of the observers deployment represented a more complicated and time consuming operation than foreseen, without mentioning basic work such as photocopying and preparing the field activities of the EOC staff itself. Moreover, each co-ordinator had to dedicate special attention to the observers of his or her own country.

On 19 December, the EOC – in conjunction with the DDDG – informed the international press of their observation efforts. As far as possible, in particular for the outer regions, diplomats went to the field one or two days before election day in order to be present at the opening of the polling stations (6 am on 29 December).

The start of the elections turned out to be chaotic. In the middle of the preparatory process President Moi had transferred the electoral commission chairman, Justice Chesoni, to the High Court, a decision which proved to have a very negative impact on the supervision of electoral logistics. The problems were aggravated by errors in the ballot distribution at all levels: the British printer, the central stores of the electoral commission and returning officers in many constituencies. Opening and closing hours of the polling stations varied erratically, with voting extended in some places to more than 48 hours. As a result, the counting process became equally erratic, sometimes taking almost a week, creating major problems for international as well as local observers. Many international observers had to return home before the counting was finalised, some of them in order to participate in the first assessment meetings of the European Union and, subsequently, the DDDG. Co-ordination in the post-election days was considered of critical importance to avoid the 1992 diverging comments and to give swift reactions in case of major problems.

The counting process took place at constituency level. Earlier demands to count at the polling stations themselves in order to avoid transport of ballot boxes, a process feared to open the doors to fraud, were not met by the electoral commission. Logistical problems abounded. Late closure of polling stations, late delivery of the ballot boxes from distant polling stations, and lack of counting officials prolonged the count in some places for over a week. Surprisingly enough, under those adverse circumstances, the count was generally conducted in a fair and transparent way. The exceptions gained all the more notoriety.

Serious incidents were reported in about 15 constituencies. They varied from outright rigging to intimidation and included attempts to add ballot papers to the boxes or spoil correct ones, introduction after closing hours of unsealed ballot boxes, kidnapping of returning officers, and improper handling of ballot papers by election officials. Irregularities in three constituencies were so serious that they led to the inversion of the results. The most telling case was Westlands in Nairobi, as witnessed by several EOC co-ordinators. In this case, openly executed irregularities turned an opposition win into a KANU victory.

(f) The election aftermath: reports and reactions
The reports from the 115 constituencies (500 polling stations) covered by the international observers were all received by 2 January 1998. Although, the coverage of the constituencies was partly done at random as a result of preferences of individual embassies, it was mainly based upon choices and suggestions of the EOC, including consideration of geographical coverage and conflict potential. Parts of Kenya's central, eastern and northern territory had however been rendered inaccessible as a result of heavy El Niño rains. Voting itself was severely hampered in these regions.

Overall, the reports presented a fairly broad spectrum of Kenya's regional, political and ethnic diversity. After quantitative and qualitative analyses – the latter including the results of internal discussions between the observers per region – the EOC finalised its report to the DDDG on the electoral process on 4 January 1998. As stipulated in its terms of reference, the EOC itself had no right to go public on its own.

Although there had been irregularities, the election of Daniel arap Moi as president was accepted. With respect to the interpretation of the parliamentary elections, the DDDG did not want to rely on anything else but the information coming exclusively from international observers, leaving the use of information generated through the network of local observers to the responsible non-governmental organisations. The EOC had to a limited extent based its initial analysis on data from outside the network of international observers, but adjusted this later on. Furthermore, in its one-page draft summary, written by the EOC on request of the DDDG, subsequent deductions leading to outspoken, critical conclusions were reached. On request by some of the DDDG members the statement, without losing the basic findings, was adjusted in this respect.

The DDDG and the EOC opted, therefore, for a two-stage approach: the EOC would present its own findings, including deductive analysis, to the DDDG in the form of a confidential report. The DDDG subsequently would take responsibility for a partially redrafted (although still critical) report which was to be presented confidentially in the name of the DDDG to the chairman of the electoral commission. The DDDG restricted itself to a short public statement on 9 January 1998 in which it referred to the domestic observers' statement and stressed foremost the main improvements of the 1997 general elections as compared to those of 1992 although it also pointed at bribery, intimidation and the troublesome distribution of ballot papers undermining the fairness of the poll (*Daily Nation* 11/01/98).

A number of DDDG members preferred not to go public with the main report in order not to prejudice, as a consequence of the sub judice rule, election petitions that might be brought to court by losing candidates. After some debate, this position was accepted by the DDDG as a whole. A subsequent legal opinion showed, however, that the sub judice rule did not apply here. After some debate, the DDDG still decided not to go public but to engage in a confidential dialogue with the Kenyan electoral authorities.

One of the report's main conclusions stated that three constituencies (Westlands, Kitui West and Changamwe) had been incorrectly attributed to KANU; if corrected, the 107-103 KANU majority would have turned to a 104-106 minority. A final chapter of the report contained recommendations to the commission for improvements in the electoral process. An analysis of irregularities encountered in eight constituencies was equally annexed to the report. On 2 February 1998, the report was presented to the electoral commission.

The press managed to get access to the report and to elements of the internal DDDG debate with respect to its preparation. Comments were critical, among others, regarding the DDDG conclusions, as had to be expected considering the issues at stake (see e.g., *Daily Nation* 20/01/98; *Economic Review* 26/01-01/02/98; 23/02/03/98). The DDDG, however, stuck to its position and did not engage in public debate.

Pros and cons of the new model

In terms of advantages over the short run, external observation efforts merit the following special observations:

1. Continuity
In-country experience of diplomatic missions and foreign expertise gives the election observation a longer-term perspective. Observers stay in the country. This allows for maximum use of knowledge about the strengths and weaknesses of the electoral process; early liaising with the authorities and major actors about steps to deepen democratic principles and level the playing field; assessment of progress made in this respect; identification of possible tricks in and manipulations of the electoral process; assessment of the risk that

international observation legitimises a faulty process or an outcome considered to be seriously flawed; and optimal co-ordination in evaluating the election results.

Last but not least, it makes possible a continuous dialogue with the authorities, the electoral commission in particular, to further the implementation of recommendations stemming from the election observation process. While in general international support for democratisation processes tends to seriously diminish in between elections, the alternative model allows for more continuity in this respect.

2. Common strategy and outcome
The harmonisation of the positions of international observers, obtained through long-term co-operation, will be based on common principles underlying a common interpretative framework and strategy, and lead to unified statements, conclusions, recommendations and follow up. It will be difficult for authorities reluctant to start or deepen democratisation processes to create dissension between foreign missions and observers exercising pressure for democratic change.

3. Liaising with local observers
Mutual trust generated through long-lasting relations will lead to optimisation of the complementarity between local and international observers, e.g., in the fields of information, contacts and training. In the case of deployment of observers, international observers can be directed to critical spots where their presence represents the highest added value. Long-term in-country presence makes it possible to assess NGO partners according to their capabilities. Co-ordinated efforts heighten the impact of conclusions about the electoral process and of recommendations for future improvements.

4. Value for money
Cost effectiveness of international observation was high in the Kenyan case. Estimates for the whole exercise added up to about US$ 250,000. This included the cost of running the office, domestic travel and accommodation of the participating diplomats, salaries, travel and accommodation of the EOC collaborators. The entire electoral process was covered, not just a short election period.

The effectiveness of the model depends, however, on the fulfilment of several conditions:

1. Co-ordination

Paramount is the existence of strong co-ordination among the major diplomatic missions involved in the democratisation process. In Kenya, international organisations were not represented in the co-ordinating group, which was limited to diplomatic missions representing countries. One of the reasons was the feeling that international organisations, of which Kenya is member, might find it difficult to withstand possible Kenyan pressure to soften critical analysis.

Such co-ordination among missions, as materialised in the DDDG set up, must be long-term and must be based upon commonly agreed principles and a common strategy. Moreover, the rules of the game of an election observation unit must be clearly defined, such as the respective responsibilities of diplomatic missions and the staff of the unit, agreements on confidentiality of information, analysis and reports, and the attribution of first line responsibilities between diplomatic missions, e.g. for the daily work in the observation unit, contacts with the press or authorities, etc. Of particular importance is the unequivocal, ex-ante definition of criteria for the treatment of information and how this translates in the reports of experts and diplomatic missions.

Co-ordination efforts can only be successful if a core group of personally committed diplomats and experts engages itself in the process. Part of the co-ordination and election observation activities demand an engagement beyond the regular professional activities of those involved. The added value of these activities will in general largely justify the efforts undertaken. For experts it can, for example, materialise in field research and material for publications. For diplomatic missions, it could translate into better in-depth knowledge of and influence upon democratisation processes and the advancement of human rights.

2. Planning

Financially and logistically planning must be engaged in early on. Financial commitments, although for relatively limited amounts, must be received well in time. This is particularly important if more than one donor participates. In such a case, common arrangements for disbursement, monitoring and evaluation must be agreed upon in order to harmonise or make compatible procedures that may vary greatly between contributors. Flexibility must be maintained as changes in events may call for adjustments at short notice. For example, sudden changes in election dates should be anticipated and accommodated. Timely staffing and a commonly agreed division of labour in an election observation unit are critical to its functioning.

3. Linking national and international observation
Collaboration with local observers (and those financing them) will amplify the impact of international observation and vice versa. Access to local knowledge is one of the essential ingredients for success of international observation. So is the division of labour to direct international observers, more limited in number than their local counterparts, to the spots where their presence makes the biggest difference.

4. Liasing with authorities
Liasing with authorities, especially electoral authorities, is a pre-requisite for smooth operating as well as implementation of, for example, observation recommendations. The same applies to the relationship with political parties and civil society organisations. It is important to search constantly for common ground and to keep communication lines as open as possible.

5. 'In-flying' observers
It is important to persuade any group of international non-resident observers to associate themselves as close as possible with the locally organised co-ordination activities in order to avoid as much as possible conflicting conclusions based on insufficient exchange of information or knowledge.

Conclusion

Western countries represented in Kenya and united in the DDDG have tried to overcome the limitations inherent in short-term international election observation, by linking it to the broader political and democratisation processes in which elections are embedded.

An alternative model of international election observation emerged – with clear advantages, but operational only under certain conditions. The main characteristics of the model are: strong co-ordination between missions of democratic (in general, Western) countries through the establishment of a low-cost, flexible co-ordination unit; agreement on a list of basic principles to be applied to any democratisation process, in order to obtain higher levels of openness and fairness; in-country presence of election observers over a longer period of time; assistance of country experts, associated with or united in the co-ordination unit for the period of the election process; association of possible in-flying observers to the co-ordination unit; and open communication between international observers, authorities and civil society organisations before, during but also after the elections.

For diplomats, the EOC-experts and Kenyans alike, the observation exercise represented a win-win situation. The diplomatic community benefited from the added knowledge the experts brought, a professionally co-ordinated observation exercise, and analytical and reporting capacity. Through their participation in the EOC the experts also got unique access to information they would not have got otherwise. Added to this was the possibility to study an electoral process not only from the outside, but from within, including the opportunity to combine positive action and research.

Kenyans profited in more than one way: improved international observation; a more regular and better informed post-election follow up from the side of the international community; reinforcement of the position of local observers; a better understanding by all the DDDG missions of the pro-democracy movement; and longer term attention and support for local initiatives and civil society organisations.

Notes

1. The Donors for Development and Democracy Group (DDDG) consisted of 22 Western diplomatic missions and the representation of the European Commission. DDDG members at the time of the Kenya 1997 general elections were Australia, Austria, Belgium, Canada, Czech Republic, Denmark, Finland, France, Germany, Greece, Hungary, Italy, Japan, The Netherlands, Norway, Poland, Portugal, Spain, Sweden, Switzerland, United Kingdom and the United States of America.
2. The staff members of the EOC consisted of four co-ordinators: Dr Judith Geist (USAID), Prof. Palle Svensson (Denmark-Aarhus University), Dr David Throup (British Foreign Office) and Dr Marcel Rutten (Netherlands-African Studies Centre).

References

Africa Confidential 1993, 'Kenya: Failing the Democracy Test', Vol.34, No.1.

Garling, M. and Geist, J. (1997) 'Diplomatic Election Observation Secretariat – Proposed Structure and Operation', Nairobi.

Geisler, G. 1993, 'Fair? What has fairness got to do with it? Vagaries of Election Observations and Democratic Standards', *Journal of Modern African Studies* 31, 4: 613-37.

Rutten, M. 2000, 'The Kenyan General Elections of 1997: Implementing a New Model for International Election Observation in Africa', in Abbink, J. and Hesseling, G. *Election Observation and Democratization in Africa*, London: Macmillan Press: 295-320.

9

The Kenyan Media in the 1997 General Elections: A Look at the Watchdogs

Joe Kadhi, Marcel Rutten

In his book, *I accuse the Press* (1992: 189-92), Philip Ochieng argues that freedom of expression and the freedom of the press are possible only in situations where as many people as possible in any given society take part in the creation, analysis, synthesis and dissemination of the ideas, especially through the media. Ochieng, a former editor of a number of newspapers in Kenya, Uganda and Tanzania, continues that it is only when a society reaches a level of culture, economics, technology, art and intellect to free enough members of the society from the daily chores of producing their own subsistence needs that it can devote efforts to engage in abstract thoughts that have nothing to do with subsistence production. Until then the production of the material needs should be the basis and target of all the ideas expressed. It is only then that Africans can produce sharper ideas and thus guarantee the freedom of expression itself in the secondary level of law, politics, ideology and human rights.

Ochieng's comments should be placed against the trend in Africa where since the 1980s an independent press has mushroomed. According to Kussendrager and Meulenberg (1996:13-4) this began in Senegal and Benin, spread throughout the continent and now, they claim, there are independent newspapers in almost every African country, even if governments in countries like Kenya, Nigeria, Zimbabwe and Zambia try to muzzle their journalists by intimidation or refined legal tactics. As opposed to Ochieng's view, others claim that the press should not wait for economic wellbeing but must blow the whistle on violators of human rights, on corruption and on unjust regimes (KHRC 1997). The Kenyan Union of Journalists and the Kenya Media Institute concluded on World Press Freedom Day in 1999 that freedom of the press in Kenya had improved in the past ten years. Yet they accused politicians of suppressing the press and undermining the 'hard-won gains of the struggle for democracy and human rights' (*Daily Nation* 3/5/99).

In the following analysis, an overview will be presented of the Kenyan media as it stands today. Ownership, policies and the role of the media in the process of democracy building will be looked at. The performance of the press during the Kenya 1997 elections in particular will be reviewed in detail. Our central question will be: How did the watchdogs play their role?' We will examine how the press covered the elections in the framework of the changing legal and power base of the Kenyan media. For a clear understanding of the latter, we will start with sketching the Kenyan media landscape as it developed during this century.

History and landscape of the Kenyan media until 1992

In 1902 A.M. Jevanjee started Kenya's first newspaper, the *African Standard* (a monthly) in the then British headquarters for East Africa, the town of Mombasa. Within six years, the embarrassment of critical statements by his British editor made him sell the paper to the more white settler-friendly Anderson and Mayer, who changed the name to the *East African Standard*. The daily is still alive and is Kenya's second largest selling newspaper (about 55,000 copies) in the hands of influential Kenyans who are close to Kenya African National Union (KANU), the ruling party. They bought the newspaper in 1996 from the Lonrho conglomerate.

Kenya's leading newspaper today is the *Daily Nation*. Started in 1960 with the help of 'Fleet Street journalists', and financed by the Aga Khan[1], the paper now leads with 185,000 copies sold everyday. To this group also belongs the *Taifa Leo*, a Kiswahili daily started in 1958. The *Kenya Times* became Kenya's third largest newspaper (10,000 copies). Started as the *Nairobi Times* in 1977 as a weekly, it was bought in 1983 by KANU from Hilary Ng'weno. The Kenya Times Media Trust, the current publisher, also publishes *The Herald* pamphlet. The former *Nairobi Times* owner, Hilary Ng'weno, has been a major player in the Kenyan media landscape. In 1975 he founded the *Weekly Review*. For a long time, it was Kenya's only weekly magazine addressing economic and political issues. The magazine stopped appearing in May 1999 due to financial problems. In the mid-1980s it sold 25,000 copies. In the end, this had dropped to a meagre 5,000. By the end of 1978, Ng'weno urged Kenya's newspapers to dispense with foreign ownership as this would limit editors and reporters in their freedom of speech and choice for covering local news. How 'journalistic freedom' would be ensured, though, was a question not addressed.

Actually, before 1992, those who dared to air too critical a voice on local issues were soon silenced. *Beyond,* a National Council of Churches of Kenya (NCCK) publication, was banned for exposing fraud in the 1988 elections. Its editor was jailed for failure to remit returns to the registrar of books and newspapers. The *Financial Review* published since the middle of 1986, initially as a sister publication to the *Weekly Review*, but later bought by its managing editor Peter Kareithi, one of the founders of the Kenya Human Rights

Commission, was also banned in 1989 after it revealed fraud by powerful government officials. Kareithi was forced into exile (KHRC 1997:3). A number of publications have faced legal suits, confiscation of issues, bans, harassment or detention of its journalists and editors. These included *Target* and its Kiswahili sister *Lengo*, run in the 1970s by the Anglican Church, notably the late Bishop Henry Okullu; *Jitegemea* and *The Watchman*, Kikuyu Christian publications; and *The Nairobi Law Monthly*, started in 1987 by lawyer and member of parliament Gitobu Imanyara. His magazine led the fight for multi-party democracy in 1990. Another one is *Society* of Pius Nyamora, started January 1992. While praised abroad and among human rights, pro-democracy and press freedom organisations, in a British Broadcasting Corporation (BBC) interview in Zimbabwe President Moi stated, 'I will say this: if you read *The Nairobi Law Monthly* or *Society*, you will ask yourself what government, even in Britain itself, would allow such publications to exist' (*The Nairobi Law Monthly* January 1995).

To prevent a similar fate as the papers mentioned above, other media groups chose the safer option of self-censorship. The early 1980s saw the country caught in political rivalry that ended in a coup attempt and witnessed a growing tension between the press and the authorities. Even the mainstream press, despite its self-censorship, was at times attacked by leaders who felt they were not respected, misreported or totally ignored. In the latter half of the 1980s, criticism was mainly targeted at the foreign (mostly British) press allegedly for misinforming the world about events in Kenya, even leading to the deportation of a British journalist in December 1988.

The Kenyan broadcasting scene is even less independent. The country's two broadcasting stations, the Kenya Broadcasting Corporation (KBC) and the Kenya Television Network (KTN) are owned by the government and KANU (until 1998) respectively. In February 1989, the Kenya Broadcasting Corporation Act came into effect, creating a broadcasting authority that replaced the Voice of Kenya (VoK) which had hitherto operated under the Kenya Broadcasting Corporation (Nationalisation) Act of 1967. VoK was a product of the nationalisation of the colonial Kenya Broadcasting Service (KBS), and operated as a government department under the Ministry of Information and Broadcasting. The 1989 Act made KBC largely a commercial enterprise but with certain powers in law derived primarily from its link with the political establishment. This relationship was illustrated by the opening signal tune for the station's radio news bulletins, which was an adaptation of KANU *Yajenga Nchi* (KANU is building the nation), the party's anthem. This preceded almost all news bulletins. The content of these programmes underlined the tight connection between the party and the station. In the pre-1992 days, presidential events took as much as 15 minutes in a 25-minute bulletin. The clips for the presidential news came directly from the State House-based Presidential Press Unit (these days known as the Presidential Press Service), and the editors at Broadcasting House were obliged to run it in its entirety.[2] Afterwards came a chronology of ministers' utterances and a dreary account of routine work by administration officials.

The second broadcaster and first private station, the Kenya Television Network (KTN), came into operation only in April 1990. It was launched by the Kenya Times Media Trust, which had been established in 1987 by KANU and Robert Maxwell. Yet until now it has not been fully clear who really owned the company during this time.[3] KTN was portrayed to be independent but was obviously sympathetic to the ruling party.

According to David Makali, head of the Nairobi-based Media Institute, 'Liberalisation of the airwaves in Kenya started when the country's leadership realised that broadcasting stations were being established in the region to compete with Radio Uganda and Radio Tanzania' (*Media Review* May 1999: 13). Television is a potentially influential medium especially for most developing countries where low literacy levels make the broadcast media, and radio in particular, rather than the press, the most accessible source of information. Some 80 per cent of the Kenyan population listens to radio according to a KBC survey. Moreover, it has been estimated that only about 3 per cent of Kenya's 30 million people can afford to buy a newspaper daily, with the percentage of those who can afford periodicals dwindling even further (*Media Review* May 1999:37). During the 1980s a number of radio stations such as BBC, Radio Cologne, Radio Deutsche Welle, Voice of America, and nearer home Radio Tanzania Dar es Salaam became the respected sources of news alternatives for a growing number of Kenyan listeners.

The impact of the 1992 'liberalisation' of the Kenyan media

On the threshold of the return to multi-party politics in 1991, 20 publications stood officially banned (KHRC 1997:4). Yet in the run up to the first multi-party elections in 1992, Kenya witnessed an unprecedented explosion of press freedom. A proliferation of opposition magazines and newspapers were suddenly publishing reports about sensitive issues that were unthinkable only a year earlier (see Waruru 1996: 26). Politicians almost alone funded a large number of the new pamphlets, newspapers and weeklies. When the novelty of an open press wore off after the elections, however, sales began to drop. This same phenomenon could be witnessed during the 1997 elections. Lack of advertisers and a lost of interest in politics in the end meant the disappearance of most of these publications.

Among the most popular and lasting newspapers, however, is *The People*. This weekly tabloid first appeared on 14 February 1993. Initial copies were confiscated by the police. The magazine is owned by 1992 opposition presidential contender Kenneth Matiba, a wealthy businessman, who stood and lost in 1992 and refused to vie for the presidency in 1997, claiming that the elections were pre-rigged. He called upon voters to burn their voter's cards. By 1 December 1998, *The People* turned itself into a daily newspaper, *The People Daily*, a move the owners had been announcing as early as mid-1994. The daily appearance (an impressive 100,000 copies) will certainly have worried the ruling party KANU as *The People* practise investigative journalism and reveal regularly stories about fraud, corruption and the behind-the-scenes power struggles at State House. The main question will be whether daily reporting will allow the paper to keep up this standard. In this line, biweekly, *The Star*, became a popular player in the field of 'revealing' stories at the time of the elections. Said to be a Kibaki-friendly paper, *The Star* was especially favoured among the Kikuyu of Central Province where Kibaki comes from. *The Star* collapsed when the editor, Magayu Magayu, was accused of stealing funds and its main financier passed away.

Pamphlets are a new feature on Kenya's press scene. In line with the London-based *Africa Confidential*, Kenya witnessed the appearance of *Kenya Confidential,* a weekly. It is printed on the same kind of paper, has the same layout, including the pointers on the backside of its eight pages of A4-size. It presents itself as a 'political and economic awareness newsletter'. It is thought to be financed by people close to the Democratic Party of Mwai Kibaki.[4] Another paper in this line is *The Dispatch*. In its subtitle it calls itself 'The Conscience of the Nation'. It is published by Seronga Communication Services and was started in January 1998. In August 1998 it turned itself from an eight-paged pamphlet into a 16-page weekly. It now also addresses sports, leisure and arts. Yet it soon had to return to the eight-page pamphlet outfit.

The most poorly edited of all publications to emerge on the local scene, according to, among others, the Media Institute, is *The Weekly Sun* (see for example, *Expression Today*, July 1998:8). It is an eight-page pamphlet-like paper thought to belong to MP and Assistant Minister Gumo, a KANU hawk of renown.[5] A majority of the stories published in *The Weekly Sun* are baseless and aimed at maligning certain individuals. Allegations are made that the paper is not just used to hurt the opposition, but is also instrumental in the infighting going on within KANU. To make matters more complicated, it also involves leading Asian businessmen, because some power barons are in discord over business deals that went sour. At one time, it released two editions (No. 5 of 18 July and 20 July 1998 respectively) to please both camps (see *The Dispatch* 27/07/98:16). *Dunia* and *Exposure* are a similar kind of tabloid and pamphlet-like papers, airing pro-government views. *Dunia* was started after President Moi complained that the ruling party did not have a paper like *Kenya Confidential* or *The Star.* By the middle of 1999, some of these pamphlets were still operative.[6]

Just before the 1992 elections The *Weekly Review* got a serious competitor. In October 1992, the *Economic Review* appeared on the streets of Nairobi. Its founding fathers were former *Daily Nation* business editors Peter Warutere and Nixon Kariithi. From the start, it dealt with economic as well as political issues. It addressed Kenyan, African and other international issues. It soon became a major competitor to the *Weekly Review.* The *Economic Review* gained more popularity when the *Weekly Review* seemed to have lost its teeth in addressing issues regarding corruption. Initially, the magazine influenced the decisions of foreign countries on Kenya, which earned the *Weekly Review* constant attacks from government offices (*Media Review* May 1999:7). By the late 1980s, however, the *Weekly Review* had turned itself into KANU's mouthpiece. It became the eccentric apologist of the system and propagated profoundly pro-government views.

The much-praised *Economic Review* magazine, however, disappeared from the streets shortly after the 1997 elections. In April 1998, it ran into trouble with the Kenya Revenue Authority, the body in charge of tax collection and at that time headed by Hilary Ng'weno, which charged the *Economic Review* a crushing Ksh10 million. The paper could not meet its financial obligations such as staff salaries after its accounts were frozen. It was bought by an Asian businessman linked to the KANU establishment. He said the journal was too political and wanted to turn it into a more economic-oriented magazine. However, the magazine never re-appeared under the same name. By December 1998 *The Analyst* rose from the ashes of the *Economic Review*, i.e., having the same editor, Macharia Gaitho. It appears monthly, is more business-oriented and at Ksh 200 a copy is too costly for most Kenyans.

A more critical stand is taken by weekly magazines such as *The Post on Sunday* and *Finance.* The publications have attracted mixed reactions from media analysts and practitioners. Critics argue that the publications have crossed the limits of ethical journalism by publishing wanton claims without proof. But many observers approved of their role in keeping the government on its toes and exposing the excesses that the mainstream conservative media will not dare touch.

Finance, started in March 1984, is owned by Njehu Gatabaki, a member of parliament, while *The Post* appeared only in 1997 after Tony Gachoka broke away from *Finance* to start *The Post on Sunday.*[7] Shortly after the 1997 elections were over, these magazines ran into trouble with the government. In a press release dated 10 July 1998, Registrar General Omondi Mbago said his office had rejected applications for the registration by three publications, *The Star*, *The Post on Sunday* and *Finance*. The statement did not give any reasons or cite the legal basis for rejection other than to quote an entire Act. The following day, the mainstream press splashed stories with screaming headlines purporting that the three publications had been banned. The wave of harassment started at a time when a number of key personalities in power were out of the country. The three magazines protested and stated that Kenyan law did not give the Registrar General powers to ban any publication. *The Star* published as scheduled on 14 July 1998, simultaneously with a suit filed in the High Court. The court granted an interim injunction setting aside the registrar's confusing order until its legality was disposed of. The registrar's action came in the wake of failure by various litigants to close the publications. Over a dozen libel suits had been filed against the three magazines and *The Star* and *The Post on Sunday* had been dogged by a myriad court injunctions since its inception in December 1997.

The Dispatch was spared the ban.[8] In its editorial, *The Dispatch* condemned the illegitimisation of *Kenya Confidential* and the banning of *Finance*, *The Post on Sunday* and *The Star*. It reasoned that in a free market, the simple rule of demand and supply had shown that the four papers were able to sustain themselves without advertising. There is simply a need for bold reporting, the exposition of corruption and hypocrisy among government officials and Kenyan society at large (*The Dispatch* 20-26/07/98:2).

Like the press, the broadcasting media also showed a rise in numbers after the 1991 return to a multi-party political system. However, in February 1995, Aurelia Brazeal, the American ambassador to Kenya, stated that her country was in favour of the enactment of a law by the Kenyan parliament freeing the airwaves before June 1995. However, despite promises to liberalise the airwaves, the government continued to exercise a monopolistic control over the broadcast media. This is clear when one analyses the ownership and programme content of the new channels. For example, KBC started music channels Metro 1 (Western music) and Metro East FM (Asian music) for Nairobi only.

The first commercial entry in the broadcast media was Capital FM, owned by Magnet Media Service, which broadcasts a menu of almost solely foreign music within the capital's confines.[9] Royal Media Services has been licensed to run a Nairobi-based radio station called Citizen FM, which went on air by April 1999, and also first and foremost broadcasts music. A glimpse of freshness is its current affairs programme *Yaliotendeka*. With powerful frequencies, Citizen FM is only second to the KBC in its reach. It is estimated that the station could reach 70 per cent of Kenya's population (*Media Review* May 1999). Ownership is once again vested in the hands of ruling party affiliates.[10]

The BBC has been licensed to broadcast on an FM frequency throughout Kenya, but there is no thorough local news content available on this station.

Similar shortcomings are manifest in the area of television. KTN is now owned by The Standard Ltd, which in turn is owned by Mark Too a close ally of Moi. The deal was signed in December 1997. Again it was not clear who were the original owners of KTN, yet is thought to include KANU personalities, including President Moi himself, Nicholas Biwott, and Abraham Kiptanui (see KHRC 1997:28). KTN is still facing a Ksh 117 million civil suit filed by founder chairman Jared Kangwana. It lost its star reporter Linus Kakai, who won the CNN Africa-Journalist-of-the-Year Award in 1998, to the South African Broadcasting Corporation to become their East African bureau chief (*Media Review* May 1991:4).

TV channel Stellavision (STV) owned by Hilary Ng'weno's Stellagraphic Ltd solely carries foreign material content (e.g soaps such as *The Bold and the Beautiful*). It is the local partner of Sky Television of England. In early 1999 the company entered into a partnership with the Mauritius-based African Broadcasting Network for a 26 per cent stake and management. That might save STV falling into the fangs of the well-known 'vendors' from State House (*Media Review* May 1999: 7). South Africa's M-Net satellite package is commercially oriented, carries no local content and is relatively expensive. On 1 May 1999 Royal Media Services' Citizen Television started, amid evidence that they were still trying to overcome starters' problems. The station mainly broadcasts cartoons, old movies and CNN programmes. It is still a far cry from what its owners promised. Yet, the station has so far not shown itself supportive of the government or KANU. It seems to be mostly Kikuyu-oriented and as such the pro-government owners might show their full agenda, if allowed to do so, towards the 2002 general elections.

Broadcast companies which have been issued with frequencies but are not yet on air include Kitambo Communications Ltd. and Cable TV, owned by the Cable Television Network. Nicholas Biwott, the minister for Trade and Tourism, again, is named as one of the owners. The East African Television Network (EATN) was also allowed a frequency that was, however, withdrawn following the purchase of a majority share by the Nation Group. The ensuing heated debate on this withdrawal resulted in the Nation Group being given a television licence in its own right. Still, court battles had to be fought to implement the licence to its full potential as the Nation Group licence was restricted to Nairobi only. By early 1999, there was still a case in court challenging the authorities for denying a countrywide licence. Events so far show that until this move, the opening up of the airwaves has been an issue of increasing the number of stations on air under ownership deemed supportive of the ruling party. Those who are on air are aware of their limits. The government's allergy to criticism means that unless laws guaranteeing press freedom are legislated, there will continue to be adverse court orders issued against critical publications.

In addition to growth in the number of publications and broadcast stations, a qualitative change in content is evident, particularly in the print media. The existing daily newspapers have become somewhat bolder in their hard news coverage and editorial news analyses of Kenya's political and economic environment. Also cartoonists nowadays dare to draw pictures which were unthinkable a decade ago. During 1997 journalists could be seen arguing with state security officers during unlicensed reform rallies stating they were simply doing their job and wanted to continue doing so. However, the Kenyan press has yet to convince itself that it can truly be free. At KTN, editors are careful not to overstep the boundaries that KANU expects the station to operate within. Individual journalists who have broken this code of silence have been ruthlessly dealt with. So far, several have been sacked for airing items apparently sympathetic to the opposition.[11] This trend of self-censorship is induced by what the Kenyan Union of Journalists (KUJ) termed a system of reward and punishment: 'Many editors in the mainstream press own plots and other properties as a reward for their favourable coverage of politicians. Corruption in our newsrooms has reached alarming rates. Media owners who have also been compromised are another reason newspapers ignore certain news' (KHRC 1997:24).

Another interesting change is the rise of independent content providers filling the gap left by the state-controlled Kenya News Agency (KNA). These content providers include local information and communication businesses and NGOs such as the African Women and Child Information Network (ACWIN), with a focus on gender reporting; IRIS (Interlink Rural Information Services) which mainly reports on development issues in the rural areas. Also the formation of new, local, freedom of expression NGOs, such as the Media Institute and the Network for the Defence of Independent Media in Africa (NDIMA) testify to the increased willingness of the profession to address state hindrances to journalistic practice by organising, in solidarity, the legal defence of journalists facing state charges for merely carrying out their work.

In spite of these improvements in press freedom, Kenyan journalists are still facing government hostility in times of political anxiety. For example, on 18 March 1994 two journalists were charged with subversion for reporting that nine people were killed and hundreds replaced in ethnic clashes in the Molo area. In June 1994 *The People* newspaper was fined Ksh.1.7 million after being found guilty of contempt of court. An editor and reporter were for some time jailed for failing to apologise and pay fines. That same year the *Daily Nation* complained about political harassment of its Kisumu correspondent (*Media Review* May 1999: 124). Also at this time hitting at foreign journalists, especially Americans mainly, was intensified once again.

Apparently, the increased bravery employed by journalists enraged the ruling elite and increased in the number of libel suits against the media and banning of journalists from public meetings.

Characteristics and legal aspects of the Kenyan media

According to the Institute for Economic Affairs (1998: 38-40), the following are the weaknesses of the Kenyan media:

(a) limited press coverage (lack of correspondents and high levels of illiteracy among the public);
(b) limited scope of languages (*Taifa Leo* is the only Kiswahili daily);
(c) limited variance in the political-economic orientation of the dailies;
(d) limited diversity in broadcasting content (mainly foreign music);
(e) insecure financial position of Kenyan languages papers;
(f) harassment of journalists (especially photographers);
(g) partial liberalisation of the broadcasting sector (KBC is a ruling party broadcaster);
(h) cumbersome licensing procedures (as many as 39 radio and 103 television and satellite broadcast license applications are pending at the Ministry of Information and Broadcasting);
(i) lack of diversity of media ownership; and
(j) urban bias in media content

The strengthening of a democratic society is fostered by the existence of an informed citizenry. The freedoms of expression and information and the right to communicate must, therefore, underlie all regulatory and policy proposals for society in general and the media in particular.

In 1995 the government mandated a task force on press laws to develop a new legal and policy regime for all forms of media in line with the government's expressed commitment to and civil agitation for full media pluralism. A Press Council Bill was proposed which provided for the formation of a council to oversee the registration of journalists. The Kenya Union of Journalists (KUJ), among others, criticised another bill drafted by the task force i.e., the Kenya Media Commission (draft) Bill. This bill provided for the jailing of journalists who flout a government mandated code of conduct.

Also the recommendation that the president should be the appointing authority of the proposed Kenya Media Commission was generally objected, too. It was stated that parliament would be a better body to appoint members of the commission. The membership of a Media Commission should be from the major stakeholders in the industry and consist of persons of known ability and integrity, the Media Owners Association has said (see *Daily Nation* 27/11/97). The bill was shelved by President Moi after protests by local journalists, politicians, NGOs and foreign diplomatic missions. Also, questions were raised regarding the sincerity of the government as the task force's work had been pre-empted three times by the Attorney General's office by the latter's release of the press bills in 1996, the Kenya Communications Bills of 1997 and 1998.

The Institute for Economic Affairs (1998: 42-55) recently called for a number of legislative repeals, reforms and innovations.

In the short term:

1. The fundamental right to freedoms of expression, information and communication should be guaranteed constitutionally.
2. Specific legislation should be enacted to support the freedom of information, i.e., easier access to public and privately held information deemed to be of public interest.

In the medium term:

1. Establish an independent statutory media council run by elected representatives of various stakeholder groups within the media sector to deal with registration, complaints, and code of conduct.
2. Conduct a review of all content-neutral legislation to simplify processes of establishing and running the print media.
3. Formulate and enact a regulatory framework to ensure the equitable, efficient and development-oriented allocation and management of frequencies for both commercial and non-profit community broadcasters, according to plans submitted, to start broadcasting on a short term and with clear goals which meet national information and communication needs and ensuring media pluralism.
4. Reform the public radio and television-broadcasting sector to make it more responsible and accountable to ensure that the country is reached with independent news reporting. Independent, community-based, participatory press and broadcasters need to be created.
5. Reform the Kenya Posts and Telecommunications Act. This act is an impediment to the objectives laid out above. It grants the minister of internal security the power to interfere with transmission.
6. Amend the second draft of the proposed Kenya Communications Bill, 1998, to do away with a complicated five-step licensing procedure, lacking criteria on issuing such licenses and transparency.
7. Establish an independent public broadcasting authority.
8. Review the role of the Ministry of Information and Broadcasting KBC should become an independent public broadcaster and the KNA autonomous, but privatised.

In retrospect, although press freedom has improved, regulatory and policy efforts on the media in Kenya to date should still be characterised as restrictive:

witness the foiled Kenya Mass Media Commission Bill, 1995, and the Press Council of Kenya Bill, 1995.[12] Underlying these press bills was the assumption that more regulation was better than less, to control rather than facilitate the developing profession and media content. Laws relating to the establishment of media are multi-fold and pose impediments to potential new owners. Also, a broad range of laws was applied to control day-to-day management of the media, e.g. failure to make import duty payments are used to punish publishers. Even more important are the content-based laws on subversion, treason, criminal libel and alarming publications and reports. Finally, civil laws, such as contempt of court, defamation and ordinary libel, are increasingly used to limit the freedoms of expression and information. Against this general background, how did the Kenyan press play its role in the 1997 general elections?

Role of the media in the process of democratisation: the 1997 Kenyan elections

Studies of the media in election coverage have found two patterns of fundamental importance. Alger (1990) established that journalists covering elections concern themselves with two distinct election events: first, they are concerned with the 'game of strategy'. The second concern of election journalists is what could be termed as the 'substance of elections'.

Most journalists covering the 1997 Kenyan elections were more interested in the 'game of strategy' rather than the 'substance of elections'. They found the first one to be of greater interest to both editors and the readers because it concerned itself with election. It is called 'game of strategy' because, like in any other game, it has a winner as well as a loser. The exciting story of how the race was taking place and how one contestant was struggling to take over the leadership from another was always of great interest to Kenyan readers, viewers and listeners. People enjoy competition and they take chances in backing winners or losers. Many journalism scholars have compared election competition with horse racing and the excitement of the two is more or less the same.

When journalists get carried away with the competition element of the elections they tend to forget a much more important aspect of the process which concerns the 'issues' involved. According to Alger (1990), 70 per cent of all the news of elections is about the 'game' rather than the 'issues'. The coverage of at least four elections (1974, 1979, 1983 and 1988) in the country and the stories which were then used on the front pages of the time were more or less based on the 'game of strategy' rather than the 'substance of elections'. In the 1997 elections, however, both these two patterns played an important role in the coverage of the event bearing in mind the fact that voters were more educated and enlightened than at any other time in Kenya's political history. To examine what the coverage of the elections was like, it is important to separate the two aspects and look at them in greater details.

The game of strategy

During the 1997 elections journalists in Kenya tended to pay greater attention to: (a) the candidate's style and (b) the candidate's image. They wrote long articles about the various styles adapted by candidates to win parliamentary and civic seats. The styles varied from addressing public rallies to meeting the voters in various places which included church organised gatherings and even funeral ceremonies.

Long stories were also written about candidates' images including the important positions they held in society. By and large the 1997 elections, whether they were contests between political parties or within political parties, were normally centred around personalities, and the press, on the basis of their style and image, highlighted the rivalry between them. When the coverage was based on the 'game of strategy' alone, however, voters were not given the opportunity to understand what various candidates had to offer if and when they ended up as representatives of the people.

The situation was made worse by the so-called youth wingers of all the political parties who went round the constituencies advertising the images of various candidates through songs and sometimes offering bribes. When all this happened, reporters covering the elections were, more or less, only concerned with the strategy and logistics of winning elections and so all they wrote about was what Alger (1990) would call 'appearance and hoopla'. In other words, the reporters were only concerned about how much popularity various candidates were gathering as they conducted their campaigns.

Substance of elections

Given the fact that the Kenyan voters who happened to be both regular newspaper readers and customary TV viewers or constant radio listeners were among the elite in our society, the 1997 elections coverage became more demanding than the provision of stories based on mere 'games of strategy'. These were the people who wanted to know from the media a little bit of background information about the candidates such as their qualifications and their leadership abilities.

Journalists interested in the substance of elections became serious writers who provided their readers with backgrounders, news analysis and commentaries about policies of political parties and what was contained in their manifestos. The 'race horse' drama of who was winning the elections and who was losing was brought about in their reports in the form of letting the people know what they stood to gain or lose by their choice. This kind of analytical coverage of elections in 1997 tended to be the exception rather than the rule and was mainly confined to a handful of the up-market media such as the *East African* and to a lesser extent the *Sunday Nation*.

Although not uncharacteristic of other election writers, what was most noticeable among Kenyan journalists in 1997 was their preference to concentrate on issues concerning disagreements among the candidates so that the stories they wrote tended to be rather sensational. This was in keeping with the journalists' desire to highlight issues concerning conflict as human-interest stories. Another aspect of concern for reporters interested in the substance of elections was the candidates' traits and record. In a minority of cases, serious journalists reviewed all the candidates' past positive and negative contributions to the society and predicted what was likely to happen when the electorate gave them positions of responsibility.

This kind of analysis was not done adequately in the 1997 elections; yet it was clear that, if used effectively, it could rid Kenya of the culture of electing candidates whose only qualification was the tribe they belonged to or the support they got from bigger godfathers. It was the kind of journalism that would have made sure candidates were elected on merit rather than other parochial considerations, including membership of a clan or accumulation of vast wealth. The notion that journalists would always highlight human interest issues caused by odd incidents was proved right in 1997 elections coverage when even the most serious among them pegged their otherwise unprejudiced analysis to petty incidents of conflict, adventure and self interest.

This meant that no matter how much journalists wanted to dwell with the 'substance of elections' in 1997, the factors and orientations of news production pushed them to see policy statements as quickly losing their 'newsworthiness' whereas campaign missteps and the bizarre events of the electoral process were 'fresh occurrences', which adequately answered the journalist news value requirement of timeliness. Unfortunately, once a candidate made his position on an issue known, further statements concerning that issue declined in news value sense. Therefore, journalists covering the 1997 elections had to have a good nose for news to produce a good story after sitting through innumerable repetitions of speeches by the same people talking about the same issues in different parts of constituencies.

One area that totally failed in Kenyan journalism during the coverage of the 1997 elections was the little attempt made by the practitioners to get exclusive stories from candidates on significant policy issues that would have led to real assistance to the voters by laying bare at least two aspects of the candidates:

(a)   Whether they had adequate knowledge about the matters highlighted in their manifestos; and
(b)   Whether their general proposals on such important issues as the country's budget were actually reasonable and not mere election wishful thinking.

Despite the fact that Kenya's economic, social, political problems were so well known, serious journalists did little to pose relevant questions to all the candidates from all the parties in order to give those candidates an opportunity to tell the people what actions would be taken to solve these problems once elected to parliament or to the local authorities. These issues should have been at the centre of the campaigns with constant efforts to get answers on solutions from candidates of all parties. What the public got from the media was mostly the game. Kenyan voters would also have benefited a lot if newspapers had started a trend of running a special series of articles on the major party candidates, including synopses of background, education, career, qualities as public figures and a fair amount of material on policy positions. This way, the media would have played an important role in agenda setting.

Patterson's belief that the media could be instrumental in the formation of images was clearly seen in the coverage of the 1997 elections in Kenya.[13] By writing in-depth profiles of certain well chosen leaders and their tribalistic power structure, the Kenyan press *(Daily Nation, East African Standard* and *Kenya Times)* and almost all the magazines helped to create favourable images of the selected politicians who by and large were party leaders. The fact that many of the party leaders held the top positions in their political organisations, without even being elected legitimately, did not seem to bother the journalists.

If newspapers succeeded in conveying the fullness of the images of candidates, television made an even more effective attempt in giving the voter a proper impression about certain favoured candidates' personalities and leadership capacity. The KANU-controlled TV stations (both KBC and KTN) selectively covered certain campaign events with the aim of promoting the political image of President Moi and his closest KANU contestants.

The notion by Arterton[14] that interpretations placed upon campaign events could frequently be more important than the events themselves became true in the coverage by TV of the 1997 election campaigns. In other words, the political contests were shaped primarily by the perceptual environment within which candidates conducted their campaigns. This was particularly common in the early nomination stages when perceptions about party leaders outweighed reality in terms of their political impact.

TV journalists communicated these perceptions to voters and party activists and their main job was to make the viewers, who were the voters, believe that campaigns by Moi and his party were succeeding. The perception by TV journalists put President Moi as the front runner and candidates like Koigi wa

Wamwere among the last ones. One of the most important interpretations made by Kenyan journalists during campaign time was to predict the winners. In some developed countries this is done by the use of survey projections. Competition between the networks and the use of various survey sampling techniques have made media men in these countries announce election winners well before the polls have closed in some parts of the country.

During the 1997 general elections in Kenya, a number of print media and other institutions tried to conduct some kind of polls. None was actually right, which meant that the kind of polls they conducted were either faulty or things changed drastically after their predictions. The ability to highlight issues and to force politicians to respond to them is more powerful than trying to predict the winner or loser of any election. Journalists could and should challenge politicians to air their views on foreign policy, housing, health, education, employment, agriculture, environment and the gender issue in an intellectual, demandingly rigorous format and make them address the topics in a way they might not in a mere campaign speech.

A number of journalists were trained by one of the authors, among others. Journalists were advised to make a thorough examination of the constitution and encourage public debate about its amendments in order to create a conducive atmosphere that would allow free and fair elections. Reporters in 1997 were, therefore, particularly asked to look for instances where the law was used during the campaign period to extinguish, suppress or dilute the individual's free enjoyment of these rights. Four freedoms were particularly important for the journalists to bear in mind while observing the elections. These were freedom of conscience; freedom of expression; freedom of movement; and freedom of assembly and association. Also journalists were instructed to critically examine the shape and structure as well as the behaviour of the electoral commission as the country prepared for the 1997 elections.

According to Tom Maliti, no democratic government in the world would ever want to go to an election with the kind of record the Moi administration had when it was preparing for the 1997 general elections.[15] Yet, it managed to remain in power despite claims of rigging and the absence of a level playing field. To what extent, one may ask, did the media in Kenya help educate the voters on their electoral rights and how far did they succeed in bringing to light issues that helped the voters cast their votes wisely?

Journalists and constitutional changes

The preparations for the 1997 general elections began with a national debate on the need to change the constitution in order to make future elections in Kenya free and fair. The debate was initiated by various institutions within the civil society led by the National Convention Assembly and its executive wing, the National Convention Executive Council (NCEC) (see Chapter 2). The argument put forward by constitutional reformists was that the 1992 elections were conducted on a playing field which tended to favour President Moi's ruling party KANU. Without a level playing field, it was argued that the national elections in 1997 would end up as an exercise in futility that would only hoodwink the people and deny them their democratic right to elect leaders and parties of their choice.

If there was any time when Kenyan journalism neared excellence in its interpretative presentation of events, then it was in the reporting of the NCEC demands and the conditions set by the people for constitutional reform. NCEC representative Prof. Kibwana's press conferences were not only well attended, but they were also well covered by both the national and the alternative press. His own organisation, Centre for Law and Research International (CLARION) came up with a publication, *The Citizen*, which set new standards of analytical journalism in Kenya. Never before has the work of so few journalists been so useful in mobilising so many in the struggle for true democracy in Kenya.

Obviously, the proponents of constitutional reform met with vehement opposition from Moi's government and his party which accused Prof. Kibwana and his supporters of attempting to grab political power unconstitutionally. Moi's stand was also backed by his supporters in the media circles who made futile attempts to dampen NCEC's demands. Despite the suggestions made by the enlightened members of civil society, President Moi's government took great advantage of the unchanged constitution to tilt the playing field in favour of the ruling party long before the date for the new elections was known. In 1996, for example, the KANU-controlled electoral commission started reviewing constituency boundaries and ended up with creating 22 new ones. This aspect did not get the kind of publicity NCEC's strike threats captured. It was obvious that strikes made better headlines as human-interest stories than constituency boundary changes. Once again journalists abdicated their watchdog role at the altar of headline-catching stories without being guided by consequences as an important news value.

As the democratic forces led by NCEC were championing meaningful constitutional reforms, KANU managed to get some members of parliament from the opposition to work together with the Inter-Parties Parliamentary Group (IPPG) and produce some changes in the constitution. Since the IPPG had the blessings of both KANU and President Moi, the KBC gave its deliberations maximum positive publicity and any suggestions made by the NCEC received condemnation by both the KBC radio and television. When the KANU-IPPG campaign to popularise the constitutional changes suggested by the group was in full swing the attorney general published two bills: the Constitution of Kenya Review Commission Bill and the Kenya Statute Law Repeal and (Miscellaneous) Amendment Bill.

The IPPG suggestions, which were eventually adopted by parliament, were not entirely undemocratic. Certain progressive changes were made by the IPPG which had also managed to get support of the private national print media including the *Daily Nation* and the *East African Standard*. The IPPG also managed to get the backing of some powerful international organisations, including the United States Agency for International Development (USAID). Locally, it had the support of the Centre for Governance and Democracy which produced widely circulated pamphlets telling the voters the advantages of the changes introduced by the IPPG.

Maybe the greatest achievement of the IPPG proposals was to make it illegal for all civil servants, including those in provincial administration, to engage in the functions of any political party. The sub-chiefs, chiefs, district officers, district commissioners and provincial commissioners, who previously openly campaigned for KANU, were banned by the new laws from acting as agents or supporters of any political party which meant that civil servants were not allowed to express public support for any party or any candidate; were not allowed to preside over campaigns and other political meetings; were not allowed to participate in nomination exercises of any political party; and were also not allowed to give preferential treatment to any candidate, party or supporters. The new law required that all candidates should be served equally and it received massive support of the media. By 1999, after President Moi had directed that the constitutional review should be brought back to parliament and away from civil society, the same media showed their hypocritical stand. For example, the *Daily Nation's* columnists stated that 'Moi never had the intention to have the constitution changed' and, 'Moi all along intended to perpetuate his rule beyond 2003' and phrases along those lines. When the NCEC uttered these words in 1997, the *Daily Nation* 'made them veritable lepers in their own land while preaching the virtues of IPPG, which, . . . marked the "dawn of a new era in Kenyan politics", no less.' (*Expression Today* May-June 1999: 3).[16]

The press did not take this criticism seriously when, in November 1999, the NCEC launched 'A vision for national renewal', a 37-page booklet containing suggestions to break the constitutional deadlock by implementing six steps to democratic renewal. In the proposal, it suggested (step 2) the formation of a transitional caretaker 'government of national unity' of all stakeholders, including KANU, opposition political parties, religious organisations, NGOs, the private sector and the armed forces. At the launching gathering, attended by one of the authors, the booklet was presented and discussed. The next day the *Daily Nation* headline screamed that the NCEC wanted the military to join a reform government (*Daily Nation* 05/11/99). The *East African Standard* likewise solely focused on the military involvement.

Also, in their editorials the papers tried to finish the NCEC initiative by highlighting only the military inclusion proposal. As a result, a bizarre circus was set in motion by cabinet ministers and MPs from both sides of the floor all hastily seeking the limelight as they condemned the NCEC for trying to repudiate the legally elected government of President Moi. They also accused the NCEC of forming a parallel government and wanted its officials to be charged with treason. At best, the NCEC proposals were naive, dangerous, unfortunate or impractical (see *Daily Nation* 06/11/99). The Kenyan press once again seriously misbehaved and deserved to be accused of misleading the public or worse.

The Media Watch project

Throughout the campaign period from about August to December of 1997, both the international and Kenyan human rights organisations were keen to see how the media could influence the electoral process. Backed by Article 19, the Kenya Human Rights Commission produced a special publication, *Media Watch*, which specifically focused on the 1997 elections. The project sought to take advantage of the pre-election mood and energy to 'invigorate the nation with an on-going campaign for a level playing field' (KHRC and Article 19, 1997).

Although the publishers of *Media Watch* were concerned with raising public awareness to generate national support and activism for constitutional reforms and to ensure that the elections took place on a level playing field, the main objective of the publication was to monitor the state-owned Kenya Broadcasting Corporation (KBC) radio and television. This was an effort to document and release timely, accurate, and reliable data together with analysis on the coverage of news, commentaries, and press conferences. The data was widely distributed locally and internationally in monthly reports, with a view to pressurising KBC to maintain impartial and independent broadcasts.[17]

Using 15 media monitors who worked in four-hour daily shifts, the project managed to monitor 16 hours of broadcasts daily from 7 am to 10 pm. The broadcasts on KBC's radio and television covered both the national service in Kiswahili and the English services.

Among the most important observations made at the beginning of campaigning was the fact that the KANU government wanted to maintain its monopoly on broadcasts during the crucial period. The team observed that critical and independent individuals or establishments that had applied for licences to operate either radio or television stations found it difficult to have their applications reviewed. Secondly, they noted that the government had used its control by selectively granting to pro-KANU licences but denying licenses to opposition applicants. Thirdly, even when licences were issued to the opposition, they typically contained restrictions that prohibited the licence holder covering news.

Given the fact that the majority of Kenyans depended almost entirely on the KBC, the 1997 election campaigns started with that corporation as the most accessible source of information. This meant that whoever controlled KBC had the unchallenged power to reach the people of Kenya with whatever message he wanted. From the very beginning KBC openly supported KANU and hit at the opposition. If the authorities had good reasons for not licensing private radio and television stations, then the journalists did not provoke the government enough to reveal that reason. The issuance of broadcasting licences to private institutions was viewed by journalists as a private campaign by individual applicants and, therefore, not good enough a subject for a national debate. Likewise, the KBC monopoly during the 1997 elections was never discussed by journalists as a national issue.

Despite the IPPG reforms the *Media Watch* reports of August 1997 indicated that the KBC coverage of 'meet-the-people' tours was biased in favour of KANU. Most of the airtime went to presidential ceremonies and KANU events. The opposition received 3 per cent and 4 per cent radio and TV news airtime, respectively, while KANU and presidential public events combined received 91 per cent and 83 per cent, respectively. Also, news commentaries were geared at endearing KANU and the President to the public. The *Media Watch* August report showed that KBC ignored certain stories of critical national importance while misreporting others. The KBC, for example, made no mention of the nationwide pro-reform strikes. The independent media did. Thus, on 7 August, the KBC stated that workers in Nairobi had ignored the strike and that 'most business premises except banks remained closed' in the city's central areas, and in Kisumu, Nyeri, Nyahururu, Murang'a, and Thika out of 'fear of looting'.

Figure 9.1: KBC airtime devoted to the president, KANU, the opposition and other news items

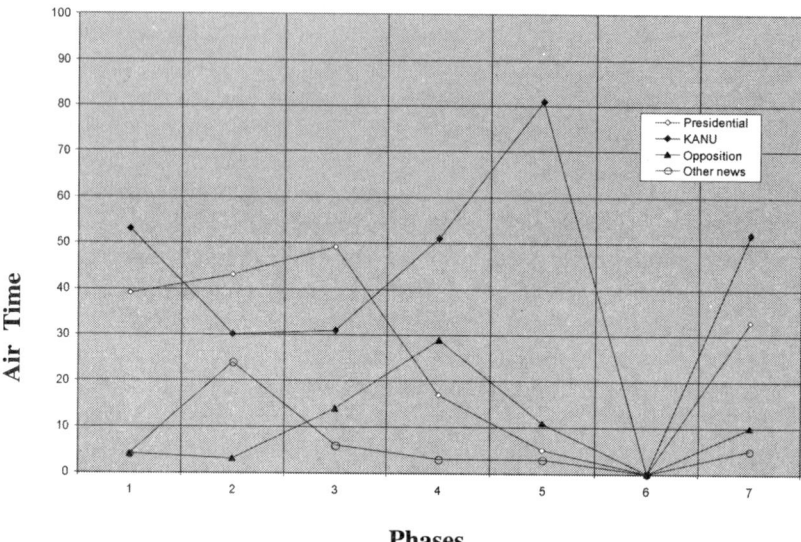

Phases

Source: KHRC & Article 19 (1998)

Phase 1: The pre-IPPG agreement phase (7 July-29 August)
Phase 2: The IPPG negotiation phase (30 August - 12 September)
Phase 3: The IPPG implementation phase (13 September - 2 December)
Phase 4: The nomination phase (3-9 December)
Phase 5: The campaign period (10-28 December)
Phase 6: The polling period (29-31 December)
Phase 7: The post-polling period (1 January - 3 February)

Figure 9.1 provides an overview of the recorded airtime devoted to the president, KANU, the opposition and other news items in seven political phases related to the 1997 general elections that Kenya went through. The *Media Watch* recording exercise shows that in spite of the IPPG agreement calling for a balanced and as much as possible impartial coverage of the players in the election period, the KBC continued to bias its reporting to the benefit of KANU and President Moi. The initial improvements recorded in phase 3 and continued in phase 4 were soon lost with the onset of the official campaigning period (phase 5). KBC again acted as a mouth-piece of the ruling party. It tried to improve its behaviour during the actual polling days (phase 6). According to

Media Watch this was due the fact that during these days the fate of the elections was in the hands of the voters. Thus KBC could afford to be completely impartial, except for some few omissions that would have potentially been negative for President Moi and the ruling party. But in the post-polling phase the curve rose again rapidly to its pre-IPPG levels in favour of KANU and Moi (see KHRC & Article 19 1998:25).

Ethics, accusations, impartiality and corruption in election journalism
No matter what the critics of President Moi's regime say about the freedom of expression in Kenya, the 1997 general election campaign was accompanied by the emergence of an increasing number of all sorts of political periodicals airing all manner of political opinions which made Nairobi one of the most free cities in Africa at least in the print media. However, since 1991 when Kenya adopted a multi-party political system, the government has had an inconsistent relationship with the press. Last year, Kenya's rating fell from 'partially free' to 'not free' according to the Freedom House, a New York-based organisation that evaluates social, political, and economic rights in all countries.

At a conference for African editors in South Africa in May 1996, Dr Doyin Abiola, managing director of Concord Press of Nigeria Ltd, stated that a free press is characterised as the 'last bastion of hope'. Abiola argued that 'it is, perhaps, more desirable now than ever to have a press with an open agenda, seeking to do the greatest good for the greatest number; a press that is untiring in looking for feasible alternatives; a press dedicated to providing a true market place of ideas. . . . To put it another way, a press which is daring enough to be a people-oriented medium with unalloyed faith in the ordinary people; a press that is not a cohort with any government or business elite; a press without a vested interest in the status quo' *(Nairobi Law Monthly* Nov. 1996: 34-35).

Some questioners have asked whether the press in Kenya is playing this role. For example, Pheroze Nowrojee, a Kenyan lawyer and constitutional reform activist, accuses the press of helping to distort post-election reality. By questioning the steps made in the reform process as it develops in Kenya these days, steps that upon close scrutiny seem to be directed mainly by a handful of powerful individuals, he points out that the press needs to ask itself whether it is a participant in 'this process of manipulated amnesia and disempowerment? Is the media a conscious or unconscious vehicle of this forgetting and uncaring process?' *(Expression Today* July 1998: 32). Instead, Nowrojee continues,

> Kenyans must first look at their problems frankly and openly. We must harness the real demand for peace we see. But we must also be prepared to face our real fears. We must examine our ethnic differences and distrust. . . . We need a Government of National Unity in substance. . . Those in power now must resist that temptation to tailor the changes to personal

benefit. And the media must realize that forgetting all the time amounts in the end to participating in the distortion of reality?' (*Expression Today* July 1998: 32).

If the alternative press in Kenya appeared to be rather weak on the ethical requirements of impartiality during the campaigns, they are even weaker on the principle of fair play. Hardly ever were readers of the alternative publications, which made scathing attacks against KANU leaders, given the opinion of the people they pounded upon. Yet professional ethics demand that that voice should be heard too. Ethically, any accusation made by a newspaper outside a court of law should have been balanced by opinions of those being accused. The alternative press in Kenya was full of serious accusations of leaders in the government and the ruling party KANU. Very often the accusations were legitimate since the papers publishing them were only playing their watchdog role of the Fourth Estate. However, the manner in which the stories were presented to the people was unprofessional as it failed to observe the important ethical requirement of fair play. Stories accusing the government of all manner of things would have sounded more authentic if the accusations were balanced by comments of the accused, even if that comment was simply saying 'no comment!'.

It was easy for journalists in the alternative press to be biased during the election time, because they rubbed shoulders more often with opinionated politicians. It was also possible many of them did not even know that being publicly biased was being unprofessional. The thrill of chasing an exposé on a major corrupt practice within the government easily blinded them to the fact that as professionals they had to always make an attempt to see the other side of the coin.

In Kenya, the survival of the alternative press during the 1997 general elections appeared to depend heavily on exposés obtained from freelance writers who were not necessarily reliable news gatherers. Numerous were the times when the use of stories from such reporters landed an editor in serious legal problems, yet when all is said and done it was only natural for the independent newspapers to have a professionally healthy hunger for exposés. That hunger was always nurtured by the use of stories which did not withstand the scrutiny of editors in search of authenticity.

A close examination of the Kenyan press (both mainstream and the alternative) during the 1997 general elections revealed that falsehoods could and did slip through editors' fingers, thus making it difficult to erect an airtight defence against lying reporters. The need for editors to check and check all the facts before they published them seemed to have been considerably relaxed during the 1997 campaign.

Both the alternative and the mainstream press in Kenya had little problem with decency which is an important pillar of journalistic ethics. Indecent presentation of stories of prurient nature exposing extramarital activities of certain candidates was used in Kenya during the 1992 general elections. In an infamous daily pull-out in the *Kenya Times* known as *KANU Briefs*, pseudo journalists produced stories hitting below the belt against opposition candidates. The practice of writing indecent articles against candidates did not show its ugly head so much in the 1997 general elections.

Although journalism in Kenya is among the most admirable in Africa, it faced a serious problem of inaccurate reporting during the 1997 general elections. Accuracy became a major professional concern among editors during the campaign period owing to the short supply of reliable news and sources even among official circles. Yet, a lot of what was published in Kenyan newspapers at the time was second-hand information. MacDougall (1968) admits that most news gathered by reporters is second-hand, but warns journalists to remember that news sources are unquestionably responsible for as many if not more news story errors than reporters. He even suggests that mistakes made by those giving out news may be intentional.

The reporters' weapons against inaccuracy, as a result of news sources' inability or unwillingness to give reliable information, are verification and honesty of purpose. If a reporter approaches the task of both reporting and writing his story without prejudice, whatever error he makes at least will be unintentional. Fairness and caution both require that when two persons interviewed differ greatly as to the truth, the statement of both should be included in the news story. However, Kenyan journalists trying to reach accuracy during the 1997 campaign were often dealing with people capable of making public statements and totally denying ever making them when they were in political or legal hot soup the next day.

A good example came from the then FORD-Asili chairman Kenneth Matiba who told journalists that he had resigned his Kiharu parliamentary seat and promised to communicate his resignation to the speaker of the National Assembly the next day (*East African Standard* 31/05/97). But the next day Matiba disowned the story scapegoating the journalists who had written it. Reporters in Kenya had to be extra careful because they were not only dealing with inaccurate, misleading and sometimes outright lying sources of information but with extremely ruthless laws that dealt cruelly with journalists who published falsehoods. The only answer for the true professionals was to be truly responsible journalists ready to publish the truth and be damned for it. This leads to the next most important pillar of journalistic ethics: responsibility.

Whenever the Kenyan despotic leaders talk about 'responsible' journalism or press they mean the journalism and press they have in their pockets and, therefore, under their total control. Their repeated calls for 'responsible journalism' are usually louder at election time and the 1997 period was no exception. A number of newspapers, magazines and all the radio and television stations in Kenya are usually systematically manipulated by various interested parties to influence voters' opinion during election time. A good number of them were subjected to that predicament during the 1997 elections. Little did some of the editors concerned seem to realise that they were actually being used to perpetuate the misrule of dictatorship. Journalism scholars felt that Kenyan practitioners had, therefore, a much harder obligation of upholding journalistic principles of responsibility at the risk of not only being labelled traitors by the dictators but of endangering their jobs and, in some cases, even their lives during the 1997 election time.

One famous Kenyan journalist, Kwendo Opanga, a former political commentator of the *Sunday Nation*, in his column 'The week that was' of 28 September 1996 wrote: 'Kenya's newspeople now have to decide whether they will be society's headlamps or its mirror. . . If newspeople want to be mirrors of society, they will be corrupt. If, however, they want to be headlamps, then they must shun corruption.' In July 1998 Opanga resigned from the *Daily Nation* after allegations were made by the *Kenya Times* and *The Weekly Sun* of him taking bribes from KANU in 1992. Apparently, the action against Opanga was started after he suggested in a recent commentary that Kipruto arap Kirwa, a junior in the KANU ranks, was more competent than Moi. Opanga admitted he had worked for KANU as a consultant. He was under pressure to help the party and made the mistake of attending some meetings of a KANU 'Think Tank' and accepting some money offered before quitting the job. Opanga later on became managing editor of the *Sunday Standard* in December 1998. KANU had successfully forfeited a popular journalist known and trusted by the ordinary Kenyans for his independent opinions and for making critical remarks towards the ruling party and the Kenyan government.

George Krimsky in *Finance*, 9 August 1998, questioned the relevance of all this to the emerging democracies around the world. Certainly, the Western experience, for all its messiness, provides a useful precedent, if not always a model. For example, when one talks about an independent media, it is necessary to include financial independence as a prerequisite, in addition to political independence. The Western revenue-earning model of heavy reliance on advertising is highly suspect in many former Communist countries but one has to weigh the alternatives. Are government and party subsidies less imprisoning? If journalists are fearful of contamination by advertisers' pressure, they can build internal walls between news and business functions, similar to those that Western newspapers erected earlier in this century. If they are fearful of political contamination of the information gathering process, they can build another wall separating the newsroom from the editorial department – another important concept in modern Western journalism. The problem in many new democracies is that journalists who once had to toe the single-party line equate independence with opposition. Because they speak out against the government, they say they are independent. But haven't they just traded one affiliation for another?

There is little room for unvarnished truth in a partisan press. Is objectivity a luxury in societies that have only recently begun to enjoy the freedom to voice their opinions? The watchdog role of the press can only appear as mean-spirited. How do the government and public protect themselves from its excesses? In the West, it is done in a variety of ways. One, for example, is the use of the 'ombudsman'. In this case, news organisations employ an in-house critic to hear public complaints and either publish or broadcast their judgements. Another one is the creation of citizens' councils, which sit to hear public complaints about the press and then issue verdicts which, although not carrying the force of law, are aired widely. Last, and most effective, is libel law.

There is still a need today, perhaps more than ever, for distinguishing sense from nonsense, for sifting the important from the trivial and, yes, for telling the truth. Those goals still constitute the best mandate for a free press in a democracy. Kenya still has a long way to go in both respects. It will be a road with ups and downs as the Kenya Union of Journalists observed recently. When the elections were over, a rise in cases of open violence against journalists by state agents and gangs on the payroll of powerful individuals was witnessed. For example, in July 1998 Patrick Mayayo, a *Daily Nation* reporter, broke a story on kickbacks in the customs department that led to the arrest of high-ranking officials. He later on received threats and was followed. On 8 November 1998 Bernard Liru, a correspondent with the *East African Standard,* died from injuries sustained in a suspicious automobile crash after he published a report on graft and malfeasance involving the Mumias Sugar Company. On 15 February 1999, *Expression Today* executive editor David Makali was seized at the Stanley Hotel in Nairobi by a gang of 12 unidentified men who beat and tortured him before abandoning him in Karura forest in Nairobi's outskirts. Makali had shortly before published a report in the February issue which gave details of the involvement of prominent politicians and businessmen in a major drug network in Kenya.

Attacking journalists is one way to silence the press, but more effective is the winding up of the hardware, i.e., the printing industry. The setting ablaze of printing press and magazine offices are part of the intimidation of press freedom in Kenya. For example, on 28 April 1995 a police squad disabled Colourprint Ltd, which prints *Finance* magazine and *The People,* and arrested its director (*Media Review* May 1999:125). Once again, on 4 May 1998, Colourprint Ltd was attacked by a gang of seven arsonists who destroyed property worth over Ksh. 20 million. Another premise of the company had been attacked shortly before the general elections. The company also prints leaflets, posters and magazines that the government views with suspicion (see *Daily Nation* 05/05/98). Finally, there is a need to address informal repression within the media, in the form of proprietorial interference, corruption and a deteriorating working environment for journalists (see *Daily Nation* 03/05/99). For this reason the press should by all means try to overcome the obstacles mentioned by Philip Ochieng. Kenya's reality does not allow the postponement of a high standard press until material wellbeing has been uplifted.

Conclusion

A close look at how journalists performed their duty during the 1997 elections reveals many ethical and professional transgressions which were not only confined to the largely inexperienced alternative press, but also the accomplished mainstream press in Kenya. There was considerable evidence that in the 1997 Kenyan elections, editors and media proprietors determined the important issues that formulated the main agenda of the polls namely ethnic loyalty. In other words, the media did set some form of agenda in Kenya before, during and after the elections. Whether the media were distinctly professional in selecting the national topic to highlight is another matter altogether. Their Fourth Estate role was obviously minimised by their parochial approach to issues. It is also obvious that during the 1997 elections journalists in Kenya faced a professional problem, which was developing into an art form: the perennial dilemma over getting too close to the people in politics who made news. When too close a relationship was struck up between the two parties it became rather difficult to play the Fourth Estate role.

The other lesson learnt from the coverage of the 1997 elections was the fact that whenever a journalist succumbed to tribal loyalty, life became extremely difficult for the legitimate seekers of truth. The upkeep of professional ethics for journalists was essential if they were to embark on the road to real democracy; but to do so more effectively would have entailed a greater concern with what was happening in their own back yard where bribes exchanged hands with impunity.

With corruption in journalism swept under the carpet, exposure of other forms of dishonesty within society during the elections had to be done with considerable care lest it boomeranged. Maybe the most important lesson learned during the 1997 elections was the importance of journalists getting involved in unearthing the truth about candidates and their parties, their policies and capabilities, right from the very beginning of the electoral process for the delectation, or otherwise, of the voter. It was important for journalists to realise that the battle ground in the electoral exercise was not only between parties but also within the parties themselves.

Out of the 1997 elections came the realisation that the role played by the watchdogs of the watchdogs contributed to the adherence to professionalism in at least as far as the print media was concerned. When they knew their work was being closely scrutinised by experts, journalists always performed better even though that made the undertaking akin to walking on eggshells for fear of earning the wrath of the likes of KHRC and the Article 19 Media Watch project. This exercise showed clearly the partiality of the Kenya Broadcast Corporation during the 1997 elections in Kenya. These organisations should also play their part in the much needed reform of the media landscape in Kenya.

The role of the press in the coverage of free and fair elections required journalists to be courageous enough to expose evils, which probably made those journalists popular with the entire community. Internal despotism in political parties, for example, was popular with tribalists, but in some journalistic quarters it aroused dismay and the writers, few as they were, openly emerged as principal spokesmen and women for the dismayed.

For a long time journalists believed that no one else should examine the manner in which they observed their own ethics. Many believed that rules restricting their behaviour as journalists amounted to control. They thought the non-existence of such rules was good and even noble in its goals. After seeing how some of them violated their own ethics in the 1997 election coverage, many would agree that there was a need to expose corruption within the profession. Non-existence of any guidelines for writers may be good for them, but what is good for Kenyan journalists during elections might turn out to be disastrous for the readers and voters. Hence, another lesson learnt is the need for strict methods to ensure journalists would be ethically upright throughout campaign periods.

It must be accepted that during the 1997 elections there were many editors in the country who operated in newsrooms as political commissars for various parties or tribal unions. Their biased presentation of news made the readers' trust in their credibility badly shattered. Looked at in this manner, the 1997 elections made many journalists lose their credibility as people's watchdogs and, for them to regain public trust, they must in future prove to be morally and professionally more upright than the politicians. That way their credentials as people's watchdogs and occupants of the Fourth Estate will always be reassured.

Notes

1. The Aga Khan is the inherited title of the leader of the Shiite sect of the Ismaili Muslims who can be found mainly in Pakistan, India, Yemen, Iran and Eastern Africa. The current Aga Khan IV was born in 1936 in Geneva. His real name is Karim Al Hussaini Shah. He inherited the title from his grandfather and was educated in Switzerland and at Harvard University.

2. Very often regular programmes were postponed to allow live telecasts of the president at the Nairobi International Show or at the University of Nairobi graduation ceremony. Few things epitomised the folly of the preoccupation with the person, rather than the event, as the determinant of an item's value than KBC's treatment of Nelson Mandela's release from prison. The world had waited with bated breath for days on end to see how Mandela would look after 27 years behind bars, years when no photographs of the man had been seen by the outside world. So what was KBC TV's lead item in their news bulletin that day? President Moi at church, the perennial opening item, with nothing more happening than the singing of hymns and the sermon from a regular preacher. And that historic moment of Mandela walking out of prison was delayed in Kenya for 10 minutes (KHRC and Article 19 1998:15).

3. Among the previous directors of KTN were Mwakai Sio, who was also chairman of Transnational Bank, Wilson Kibet (also chairman of *Kenya Times*), Philip Murgor (former KTN chairman), Sham Solei (deputy general manager of Transnational Bank) and Charles Field-Marsham (son-in-law of Cabinet Minister Nicholas Biwott). In 1993 Minister Kamotho said it was owned by KANU. At the time Jared Kangwana, initial investor in KTN, one-time chairman of Transnational Bank and Kenya Times Media Trust, and owner of The Mall, a shopping centre in Nairobi's Westlands suburb, was removed from the station. By early 1996 Kangwana filed a case against KTN claiming Ksh. 212 million. Sidney Quantai appointed KTN's editor-in-chief, later fired for reporting on issues not welcomed by KANU, at one time stated it was private individuals owning KTN. *The Star* also concludes its investigations that KANU never owned KTN (see *The Star* 12-15/12/97:20).

4. The late David Munene Kairu, a close friend to Mwai Kibaki, who passed away soon after winning the elections for parliament in Kieni constituency, is said to be the financier of both *Kenya Confidential* and *The Star.*

5. The international observers indicated that according to their observations, Gumo is believed to have fraudulently acquired his seat in parliament for the Westlands constituency in the Kenya 1997 elections (see also Chapter 14). *The Weekly Sun* is published by Scallatti Communications Services in Mombasa.

6. It is believed that the power struggle over the vice-presidency was the main reason why politicians continued to support some of the pamphlets. These publications have increased in number with a new one called *The Weekly Citizen* coming out regularly and always supporting Simeon Nyachae, the ex-minister for Finance, who resigned from the government in March 1999 after being demoted to the Ministry of Trade and Industry. The other new pamphlet-like publication is *The Metropolitan*, which campaigned (unsuccessfully) against the appointment of Prof. George Saitoti as the new vice-president. The paper is generally against the Kikuyu and appears to support Musalia Mudavadi. Minister Kalonzo Musyoka, another potential candidate, is said to be linked to *The Kenyan* magazine that stopped appearing after only four issues when Musyoka's bid for the VP post seemed without hope after the reappointment of Saitoti (*Media Review* May 1999:6). There is a big racket concerning the publications of the pamphlets. Journalists producing them are literally for sale and can be bought by individual politicians to attack

their enemies in the most dangerous manner without caring about the truth, professional ethics or laws of libel.

7. The example of Gachoka is interesting in that it shows the interconnections between media, business, politics and harassment rather clearly. The Gachoka family owns a 110-acre farm in Thika. While Tony Gachoka was having a fight with an influential billionaire banker the farm was unprocedurally transferred in broad daylight and yet neither the Minstry of Lands nor the police could unearth the truth. Tony Gachoka went to see President Moi to solve the problem and this enraged Gatabaki, his former employer at *Finance* (see *Daily Nation* 14/12/97). Rumours are that one of the financiers of *The Post on Sunday* is one of the five sons of Moi who wants to politically kill his brother Gideon Moi.

8. Some speculated that the four publications were banned because of propagating a tribal agenda (i.e., in favour of the Kikuyu community), whereas *The Dispatch* is not. This does not mean that *The Dispatch* is free from harassment. On 21 April 1998, *The Dispatch* editor Maneno Mwikwabe was charged with 'publishing an alarming report' after he published a report about a mysterious disease outbreak and 'restlessness' in the army following reports of a government plan to stage manage a coup (see *Expression Today* July 1998: 34). Also people claiming to be policemen were confiscating *The Dispatch* while others resold the copies to the vendors at Ksh. 5 each). According to the editor, this was worse than banning since it was costing the investors in *The Dispatch* money in production and salaries while earnings were taken by thugs (see *The Dispatch* 27/07/98:2).

9. Magnet Media Services received its licence a month before it was incorporated as a company. Mark Too, a key Moi ally, belongs to the group of owners.

10. The case of Royal Media Services is instructive. Royal Media first applied for a licence for radio and TV in 1992. Its proprietor, S.K. Macharia, was then regarded as an opposition sympathiser and an opponent of the government, having pleaded many cases against the state on business related matters. When the Ministry of Information and Broadcasting did not respond to Royal Media's application in a reasonable time, Macharia went to court seeking to force the government to make a decision. At one time he even sought Minister Makau to be sent to jail for contempt of court. In 1996, Macharia re-emerged in public life as the chairman of a shadowy group of Kikuyu elite, senior civil servants, and businessmen who were organising strategies of luring the Kikuyu people to KANU under the patronage of Education Minister Joseph Kamotho. As chairman of this group, which is now known as the Central Province Development Support Group (CPDSG), Macharia has taken a high profile convening of meetings supporters and fund-raisers for KANU. On 29 April 1997, minister Makau announced that Royal Media Services had been granted a licence to operate a radio and television station (KHRC 1997:27).

11. For instance, Rose Lukalo was fired after airing the launch of the Democratic Party in 1992. Vitalis Musebe and Isaiya Kabira, head of news and deputy head of news respectively were suspended for covering the 7 July 1997 indiscriminate police brutality in Nairobi and other parts of the country. The two were accused of giving the government bad publicity. Before they were suspended they were grilled at State House, at a meeting attended by ministers Saitoti and Kamotho among others (*Daily Nation* 10/07/97; KHRC 1997:24).

12. In January 1996, news about the two proposed media bills leaked out. The bills sought to restrict the practice of journalism through requirements that journalists be licensed and have formal training in journalism to qualify for the licence. They established mechanisms for registration and de-registration of newspapers by government appointees without recourse to an appellate authority in case of de-registration. After fierce opposition, they were hastily shelved by the Attorney General.

13. Thomas E. Patterson is a professor of Political Science at Syracuse University and in his *The Mass Media Election* (New York: Praeger, 1980) he talks about creating winner and loser images, something which actually happened in Kenya's 1997 general elections.
14. F. Christopher Arterton has served as a policy maker for various American candidates and is the author of *Race for the Presidency: The Media and the Nomination Process* edited by James David Barber Englewood Cliffs, NJ: Prentice -Hall,1978).
15. In an article published in the December/January double issue of *Executive Magazine,* journalist Maliti suggested Moi's administration was seeking the people's mandate to remain in power when it had the worst record of economic mismanagement and political unpopularity.
16. In mid-1999, after a one-year stalemate in the constitutional review process, *Expression Today* (May-June 1999: 1) admitted that the 'independent' press had failed in providing information on the constitutional review process to the public. 'Our failing in this particular duty was illustrated by a recent proposal by President Moi that the entire constitutional review be left to parliament. In its skewed view of objectivity the Press simply reported the proposal as it was, without making any intellectual response to it in the reports.'
17. The joint effort between the KHRC and Article 19 monitored and documented KBC coverage of news, news commentaries, documentaries and press conferences for about nine months leading up to the 1997 general election. The initiative successfully assessed the impartiality and independence of KBC coverage of various political parties.

References

Abiola, D. 1996, 'A Free Press as the Last Bastion of Hope', *The Nairobi Law Monthly* No.64, November 1996: 34-5.

Alger, D.E. (1990) 'The Media in Elections: Evidence on the Role and Impact' in Graber, D.A. (ed.) *Media Power in Politics*, Washington, DC: Congressional Quarterly Inc.: 147-60.

IEA 1998, 'Media and policy regulation' in Institute of Economic Affairs *Our Problems, Our Solutions-An Economic and Public Policy Agenda for Kenya*, Nairobi: Institute for Economic Affairs: 34-46.

KHRC 1997, *Shackled Messengers - the media in multiparty Kenya*, Nairobi: Kenya Human Rights Commission.

KHRC and Article 19 1997, *Elections '97. Media Monitoring in Kenya, August 1997*, Nairobi: Kenya Human Rights Commission and Article 19.

KHRC and Article 19 1998, *Media Censorship in a Plural Context—A Report on the Kenya Broadcasting Corporation*, Nairobi: Kenya Human Rights Commission and Article 19.

Kussendrager, M. and Meulenberg, M. 1996, 'African Journalism in Transition – new Dilemmas in a Changing Society', *Cahier journalistiek en communicatie 14*, Culemborg: Hogeschool van Utrecht.

MacDougall, C. 1968, *Interpretative Reporting*, New York: The Macmillan Company.

Ochieng, P. 1992, *I Accuse the Press- An Insider's View of the Media and Politics in Africa*, Nairobi: Acts Press.

Rutten, M.M.E.M.1998, Kenya General Elections 1997 - Implementing a new model for international election observation in Africa - Report submitted to Royal Netherlands Embassy, Nairobi, Leiden: African Studies Centre.

Waruru, W. 1996, 'The Press in Kenya', *The Courier*, No.157, May—June 1996: 26.

PART 3

REGIONAL ANALYSIS OF THE RESULTS

10

Ethnic Voices and Trans-ethnic Voting: The 1997 Elections at the Kenya Coast

Alamin Mazrui

As the 1997 general elections were approaching, it was widely expected that the Kenya African National Union (KANU) and its presidential candidate, Daniel arap Moi, would experience a severe blow at the polls in various parts of the Coast Province (See map on p. 188) due to a number of factors. Primary among these was the alleged persecution of the local Digo community by the security forces which the government had sent to quell the ethnicised violence in Likoni in August 1997. The violence had quickly spread to other sections of Mombasa, parts of Kwale and, to a much lesser extent, Kilifi and Malindi districts. So strong were the anti-KANU sentiments, that KANU MPs for Matuga and Msambweni, Boy Juma Boy and Kassim Mwamzandi, respectively, found it politically expedient to condemn the KANU government for the suffering of the local people and even threatened to quit the ruling party. Ironically, both lost during the party's primaries.

In Taita/Taveta district, tensions had escalated after KANU decided to nominate the Minister for Agriculture, Livestock Development and Marketing, Darius Mbela, to defend his Wundanyi parliamentary seat following reports that he had lost to Patrick Mwangola in the primaries. This seeming imposition of a leader that the people had rejected at the ballot box is said to have generated much anti-KANU resentment which became a major cause of worry for the ruling party. Opposition parties were able to capitalise on this political moment to make deep in roads into the district and, in some cases, nominated strong candidates (some of whom had defected from KANU) to challenge the KANU incumbents.

Elsewhere in the Coast Province, there was widespread discontent due to insecurity in some parts, especially in Tana River and Lamu districts, and to the general state of under-development and neglect in areas such as education, the infrastructure, agriculture and the environment. And the issue of so-called 'grabbing' of prime agricultural land and beach plots by 'outsiders', encouraged as it was by the increasing entrenchment of plutocracy in Kenyan society, took an ominously political dimension in many parts of the province. These 'outsiders' included upcountry people, some well-connected to the corridors of power, who sometimes entered into shady land transactions with non-Kenyans, in the process aggravating the already explosive squatter problem in the province.[1]

It is the accumulation of these and other factors that created a strong impression in the run-up to the general elections that KANU and Moi were likely to face their greatest challenge in the province since the return of the multi-party era. For a while, political awareness seemed sufficiently aroused to make KANU jittery about its own election prospects.

The results of the 1997 general elections, however, demonstrated once again that the Coast was indeed a Moi-KANU zone, whether by default or by design. Moi himself garnered a massive 63.1 per cent of the total presidential vote. The Coast was second only to the North-Eastern (72.9) and Rift Valley (69.4) Provinces as Moi's most devoted constituencies. KANU, on the other hand, won 18 of the total 21 parliamentary seats in the Coast Province (*Weekly Review* 09/01/98). Two of the three seats taken by the opposition, the Likoni and Kisauni seats, went to candidates who were considered KANU stalwarts in opposition garments, candidates who, though nominally in opposition, were known to have campaigned openly for KANU's presidential candidate, Daniel arap Moi. These were Suleiman Rashid Shakombo of the Shirikisho Party of Kenya (SPK) and Emmanuel Karisa Maitha of the Democratic Party of Kenya (DP), respectively. And the Voi seat, the third that KANU lost to the opposition, went to yet another KANU defector to the DP, namely Basil Mwakiringo. So strong has been KANU's influence, in fact, that even popular opposition candidates in the 1992 elections, like Marere wa Mwachai of Msambweni and Jembe Mwakalu of Bahari, decided that KANU was the only ship to parliament.

What factors, then, beyond rigging and electoral irregularities, can explain this seemingly continuing hold of KANU and Moi on the coastal political imagination?

The provincial level

The more general causes of the Moi-KANU success story in the Coast Province are probably twofold. There is first the widespread belief that much of the province has remained in the margins of 'civil society', a formation which, in Kenya, has tended to be predominantly an urban phenomenon. The appalling state of economic and infrastructural underdevelopment has relegated many coastal groups to the periphery of the ongoing struggle for political reform in the country and rendered them, in the process, 'uncaptured' as communities by the political opposition. In the final analysis, then, the less integrated into the civil society a community is, the more pro-establishment it is likely to be, everything else being equal. And a large proportion of the Coast is probably second only to the North-Eastern Province in its marginalisation vis-à-vis the civil society in Kenya.

It is against this geopolitical backdrop that we must understand the statement by the Institute for Education in Democracy that, 'What has been noticeable since independence . . . is an attempt by KANU to over-represent the members of Kenya's smaller, marginal and more dispersed communities . . . 'by apportioning them more parliamentary constituencies than the larger and more populous ones like the Kikuyu, Luo and Kisii' who are deemed 'more progressive' (IED 1998: 4-5). The term 'progressive' here probably alludes to comparative political awareness, with the core of civil society being at the higher end and the more marginal communities at the lower end of the scale. What we witness here, then, is not only the fact of marginality of provinces like the Coast and North-Eastern but also, and perhaps more importantly, a political motive on the part of the KANU government to maintain that state of marginality. For it is through their underdevelopment and lack of integration into the civil society, as well as disproportionate representation in parliament, that KANU continues to rule the country.

The local administration, especially at the district and sub-district levels, plays a crucial role in perpetuating this state of marginality. It is the government structure that cordons off the people, especially in the rural areas and, through coercive and despotic measures, isolates them from the centre of national political life. In this way, only KANU and Moi become sufficiently institutionalised to have a real and tangible existence in the political consciousness of the electorate.

The second factor for KANU's and Moi's triumph at the Coast had to do with the ethnicisation of politics in Kenya. As a region characterised by relatively small ethnic groups, there has been the latent fear of domination by larger ethnic groups from other parts of the country. Such sentiments almost automatically put at a disadvantage the four leading opposition contenders for the presidency, namely Mwai Kibaki of DP, Charity Ngilu of the Social Democratic Party (SDP), Raila Odinga of the National Development Party (NDP) and Kijana Wamalwa of the Forum for the Restoration of Democracy (FORD-Kenya). They are all from ethnic groups – the Kikuyu, Kamba, Luo and Luhya, respectively – which are numerically large enough to be considered as potentially hegemonic. KADU-type of politics and political alliances, therefore, continued to hold sway in much of the province, with Moi's KANU emerging as the more probable protector of minorities and minority interests.

Related to the issue of ethnic hegemony is the fact that the Kalenjin group's presence, to which Moi is associated, is far less visible at the coast than that of some other ethnic groups. According to the 1989 population census report, for example, 31.5 per cent of the immigrants at the coast come from the Eastern

Province, 22.5 per cent from Nyanza, 14.8 per cent from Western Province, 12.5 per cent from Central Province and 19.8 per cent from other provinces (RoK/CBS 1991a). Immigrants from the Kalenjin homeland of Rift Valley Province appear not to have been numerous enough to warrant independent categorisation. This ethnic configuration thus tended to influence coastal responses to national candidates: presidential candidates from upcountry areas with a stronger ethnic constituency at the coast generally fared more poorly than Daniel arap Moi.

These two factors, marginal civil society status on the one hand, and the politics of ethnicity, on the other, came to express themselves in various ways and to varying degrees in different parts of the Coast Province. But in general, the fear of 'internal colonialism' was more noticeably a factor in the electoral political calculations in districts and constituencies with a substantial presence of people of upcountry origin who are generally identified with the opposition, as in Mombasa, Malindi, Kwale, Wundanyi, and Lamu West, than in areas such as Tana River district where such a presence is more limited.

The district level

In addition to the two overarching issues discussed above, however, election results at the Coast were also influenced by more local, sub-provincial considerations. In Lamu district, for example, there was a massive injection of monies by the Mombasa tycoon, Twahir Sheikh Said (or TSS as he is widely known) in support of 'his' two candidates: Fahim Yasin Twaha in Lamu West, a newcomer who was not even a resident of Lamu at the time of his candidature, and Mohamed Hashim Salim (who stood and lost on a FORD-Kenya ticket in 1992) in Lamu East. Important issues affecting the region, from banditry to poverty, were relegated to the periphery as TSS continued to call the shots and the two candidates proceeded to score landslide victories in their respective constituencies. Even the political force of the fast-growing population of the opposition-inclined Kikuyu of the Kenyatta Settlement Scheme at Mpeketoni, estimated at over ten thousand people, could not prevent TSS from achieving his objective (*Weekly Review* 30/10/97).

In contrast to neighbouring Lamu, Tana River district has various political currents that revolve around differences in economic cultures. These have assumed the form of the ethnic divide between the predominantly pastoral Orma and the mainly agricultural Pokomo. Each of these communities has been determined to prevent the other from gaining a political edge for fear that such an advantage would eventually translate into a loss of grazing land, on the part of the Orma, or agricultural land, on the part of the Pokomo, and their associated water points. The activities of the Kenya Wildlife Society that have tended to enclose more and more land, naturally exacerbates the competition for these dwindling resources between the two groups and heightens tensions between them.

In this ethnic-cum-economic struggle, politicians have sought to strengthen their positions by playing on the insecurities of the minority Somali communities, precipitated over the years by government hostility towards them. Expectedly, these have so far tended to align themselves with fellow pastoral Orma, leading to the victory of the pro-establishment Molu Galogalo Shambaro of KANU in Garsen. With over 70 per cent of its population being of Pokomo origin, Galole voted for Tolla Koffa Mugava of KANU, himself a Pokomo, while Mohamed Abdi Galgallo, an Orma, captured the seat in the newly created and predominantly Orma constituency of Bura.

There is, however, a sectarian dimension in Tana River, which sometimes encourages trans-ethnic voting. While the Orma are predominantly Muslim, the Pokomo population comprises a substantial proportion of Christians. The latter are seen as the more privileged ones in terms of access to the state and state resources. This politicised religious divide within the Pokomo community leads sections of the Muslim Pokomo to vote with fellow Muslim Orma for Muslim candidates, irrespective of their ethnic affiliation. In this case, a trans-ethnic religious consciousness comes to override ethnic allegiance.

In Malindi, on the other hand, there has been a rapid increase in the population of people of upcountry origin, which has become a significant pro-opposition factor in the politics of the district. There has also been the more traditional tension between the Mijikenda and members of the Arab-Swahili community which goes back to pre-colonial times and which continues to manifest itself, especially in the struggle for land, with a large proportion of the Mijikenda having been reduced to squatters. In addition to these more indigenous economic dynamics of ethnic politics have been controversial land questions involving 'outsiders'. Very many land allottees in the area are upcountry people who often end up selling their plots to German and Italian investors for huge profits, all contributing further to the dispossession and displacement of the Mijikenda. In spite of these burning issues, however, the political marginality of the district ensured the return of the KANU incumbent, Abubakar A. Badawy, in Malindi, and the victory of a KANU newcomer, David Noti Kombe, in Magarini. Katana Ndzai who garnered over 87 per cent of the vote on a KANU ticket in the 1992 general elections, acquired less than three per cent of the votes on a DP ticket in 1997.

As for Kilifi district, this is one of the least developed areas in the country with the highest concentration of squatters in the whole of the Coast Province. Although it is near Mombasa town, it is a severely marginalised zone of Kenya's growing civil society. As expected, KANU had a landslide victory in all its three constituencies of Bahari, Kaloleni and Ganze. The latter two went to KANU incumbents Mathias Keah and Noah Katana Ngala, respectively.

The most dramatic development in the electoral politics of Kilifi, however, was the landslide victory of Jembe Mwakalu. A politician of radical ideological inclination, Jembe Mwakalu has a long history of harassment and persecution by the KANU establishment that goes back to the early 1980s. His 1992 bid for the Bahari parliamentary seat on a FORD-Kenya ticket was an orgy of harassment and frustration, threats and intimidation by the local administration (Throup and Hornsby 1998: 405-07). His defection to KANU, however, ensured his success in the 1997 elections, and he went on to be rewarded with an assistant ministerial portfolio in spite of the fact that there is little evidence of an ideological change or capitulation on Mwakalu's part. Mwakalu's triumph, then, may yet be another indication of KANU's capacity to change from within in response to the dictates of the local place and time.

Not unlike Kilifi, there is a large number of squatters in Taita/Taveta district resulting mainly from the expansive national parks and large holdings of sisal estates and ranches, many illegally acquired, especially when Darius Mbela, the MP for Wundanyi, was the minister for lands. He has access to the district's natural resources and benefits from wildlife resources. Therefore, land and squatters have been twin issues at the core of electoral politics in the area.

Mbela, arguably the most pre-eminent figure in Taita/Taveta politics, was initially confirmed by KANU headquarters as having lost to Patrick Mwangola in the party's primaries. But in a repeat election exercise ordered by KANU for no obvious reasons of fairness, Mbela was declared the party's candidate for Wundanyi. Widely believed to be a close ally of George Saitoti, Mbela is expected to be a key player in the struggle to succeed President Moi. More notorious, however, is Mbela's alleged sponsorship of *Jeshi la Mbela* (a private militia or vigilante gangs bearing his name) which is mobilised around election periods to intimidate his opponents and their allies (*Daily Nation* 05/08/97).

In 1992, the opposition did not make much of an impact in the district despite fielding such big names as Mwashengu wa Mwachofi (DP) in Wundanyi, Norman Lukindo (DP) in Taveta, Eliud Mwamunga (DP) in Voi and Baldwin Mwangaji (FORD-Asili) in Mwatate. In 1997, however, KANU's fortunes were more mixed, having lost to a DP candidate, Basil Mwakiringo, by a very narrow margin in Voi, and with Mwachofi having significantly reduced the margin of difference between himself and Mbela in Wundanyi. On the other hand, Basil Criticos of Taveta and Marsen Madoka of Mwatate emerged from the race with impressive victories for KANU. Criticos is himself an owner of a large sisal estate and his own employees are said to have constituted a significant proportion of the electorate in his constituency (Throup and Hornsby 1998:479).

Mombasa and Kwale

The 1997 electoral politics in much of the province, however, were overshadowed by Mombasa and Kwale districts, the location of the pre-election violence that began on 13 August 1997, which left hundreds of people killed or maimed for life, thousands of others displaced and millions of dollars in property and revenue lost through arson and the resulting decline of the tourist industry. By all indications, the tragedy belonged to the political aberration of ethnicised violence intended to undermine democratic choice. There is now considerable evidence, even if much of it is still circumstantial in nature, incriminating some prominent coastal politicians of the ruling Kenya African National Union (KANU) with easy access to the corridors of power of involvement in the violence by way of providing organisational and logistical support to the 'raiders' (see KHRC 1997). Almost invariably the main targets of this tragic orgy of violence were the upcountry people (the so-called *wabara*) most of who had come to settle in the area in search of economic opportunities and whose political allegiances have often been associated with the opposition. Evidence also suggests that one of the explicit objectives of the violence was to sufficiently alter the demographic profile of the area to guarantee KANU's chances of obtaining a winning vote in the elections.

Setting the pre-election stage
Like the rest of the Coast Province, Mombasa and its adjoining district of Kwale had long been considered integral parts of the so-called 'KANU zone', one of the many such declared zones supposedly impenetrable by the opposition. But the growing influx of people of upcountry origin into the area was seemingly threatening this political status quo. During the 1992 general elections, for example, KANU lost three (Kisauni, Likoni and Changamwe) of the four Mombasa parliamentary seats to the opposition and almost lost the fourth (Mvita) to FORD-Kenya. In all these instances, the strength of the opposition rested, in no small measure, on the 'upcountry' vote. By 1989, the population that could be classified as upcountry in ethnic origin in Mombasa district was already above 40 per cent (RoK/CBS 1991).

In Kwale district, of course, KANU captured all the three seats (Kinango, Matuga and Msambweni). In spite of its limited size, the district's population of upcountry origin, estimated at about 10 per cent, was significant enough to pose some threat to KANU in Msambweni and, to a much lesser extent, in Matuga (RoK/MPND). Five years later, the pitfalls and lessons of the 1992 general elections were still fresh in KANU's mind as it began to prepare for the next round of elections.

While it was difficult to establish the ethnic distribution of registered voters in Mombasa and Kwale districts, one could speculate that, relative to their respective numbers, there was a higher proportion of registered voters among the *wabara* than among the *wapwani* (coastal people). This prediction is based on the impressionistic observation that, on the average, in respect to local politics the upcountry population is more politicised than the coastal one. Even where the population of upcountry origin was relatively small, therefore, it had the potential of translating into a significant show of electoral might in terms of the registration figures and the eventual casting of votes. The records of the 1997 voters' register, therefore, may themselves have sent a red signal to local KANU politicians of what was lying in wait for them in the general elections.

This possibility was affirmed by Emmanuel Karisa Maitha, who claimed that the actual planning of the violence started soon after the 1997 voter registration exercise (i.e., 30 June 1997), when it dawned on the KANU power brokers that the upcountry vote in Mombasa and Kwale that was expected to go to the opposition at polling time was quite sizeable and threatened KANU's chances of capturing the parliamentary seats in the respective constituencies.[2] Maitha's suggestion, then, was in conformity with the popular belief that one of the central objectives of the violence was to downsize the upcountry vote in the area in favour of KANU.

Eyewitness accounts of the violence also described the mercilessness of the attacks, the seeming vengeful cruelty of the attackers, seeking to maim in the very process of murdering. Underlying this horrific brutality was a determination, perhaps, that the displacement resulting from the threat to personal security would be permanent or at least long lasting enough to amount to disenfranchisement during the elections. It is estimated that the displacement of upcountry people ranged between 75 per cent and 100 per cent in those spots directly hit by the violence, and some sub-locations of Likoni, like Maweni and Ujamaa, which had hitherto been populated predominantly by people from the upcountry, continued to look like semi-ghost villages well after the polling exercise (KHRC 1997:49).

Churches within the Likoni-Kwale area, which provided refuge to those fleeing from the violence, had the potential of reducing the degree of disenfranchisement caused by the violence. But soon, these sites too became targets of terror desperate to transform displacement into disenfranchisement. According to Father Raphael Lombardo of the Likoni Catholic church, which hosted over 6,000 displaced people, for example, terror gangs continued to intimidate those inside the compound. In a daring move on 22 August 1997, for example, raiders attacked the church refugees, killing at least two people in the process (African Rights 1997: 6-7). The pressure on the displaced to leave the Likoni-Kwale area altogether was further aggravated by a government order that the refugees evacuate the church compound even before security was restored in the affected region (KHRC 1997a: 17). Fearing further attacks against the refugees as the elections approached, the church itself began to encourage them to return to their upcountry 'homes', providing what assistance it could from its limited resources.

Outside the 'refugee camps', it was not only the fear of the raiders but also of the security forces and of police-raider confrontation that forced people to abandon their homes and seek refuge elsewhere. For the upcountry people, this fear of double victimisation was particularly true during the 10 days' government moratorium to the raiders to surrender their arms. This is the period when the police reportedly engaged in wanton acts of coercion and brute force against people of upcountry origin designed to intensify and expedite their departure from the Likoni-Kwale area. In the process, many displaced people lost their identity cards, having been forced to surrender them either to the police or to the raiders, and without which they could now no longer cast their votes.[3]

There were also reports that, fearing yet another wave of violence during and immediately before election day, more upcountry people fled from the area within days of the polling exercise. Rumours were rife that new pamphlets had been distributed, ordering people of upcountry origin to leave the area, to go and cast their votes in their own upcountry 'homes'. Many of those who resettled in safer areas of Mombasa, after being displaced from Likoni-Kwale, chose to abstain from voting altogether rather than return to the area, even briefly, for this electoral exercise for fear of their personal security.[4]

By the time of the elections, therefore, raiders and police actions, and real and imagined fears, had combined to create a mass exodus of potential voters from the Mombasa-Kwale area, and to ensure that the displaced would also, in fact, be disenfranchised. Furthermore, the outflow of this pro-opposition population was complemented by an influx of pro-KANU and pro-Moi voters from outside Mombasa and Kilifi districts. Reports were rife that a massive number of voters had been 'smuggled' in from Kilifi and Malindi districts to augment the size of the electorate in favour of KANU and Moi. Against this demographic reconfiguration, then, KANU seemed poised to win by a large majority.

But the violence also precipitated an unforeseen dynamic, in the form of the response of the security forces that threatened the electoral agenda of the architects of the tragedy. If the upcountry people were the primary victims of the raiders, it was now the local population that became the main target of police brutality. Victim and eyewitness accounts indicated an alarming degree of arbitrary arrest and police torture of the Digo people and the violation of virtually all the rights of the arrested persons. There were also reports of Digo victims of police and the General Service Unit torture, the injured and the dead among them, being dumped at night at Magandia in Kwale district. Like the raiders, security officers also engaged in extensive looting and plunder, with the Digo as the main target. But even more frequently than the raiders, the security forces were reported to have used rape as an instrument of terror and intimidation (KHRC 1997: 37-48). It is important to note that the members of the security forces accused of these crimes against the local population were predominantly of upcountry origin.

The end result of this oppressive response of the armed forces to the tragedy and plight of the residents of the area was to alienate the local population and gradually turn it against KANU. By mid-December 1997, barely two weeks before polling day, the anti-government sentiments in the Mombasa and Kwale areas appeared strong enough to easily make up for the opposition's demographic loss. KANU's and Moi's defeat now seemed virtually imminent. As we now know, of course, and to the surprise of many analysts and the disappointment of others, the outcome of the elections was decidedly in favour of KANU. Later on in this discussion, we shall explore some of the possible reasons for the 'unexpected' election results in Mombasa and Kwale districts.

The violence as a campaign issue

The 1997 general elections confirmed once again the power of ethnicity and ethnic consciousness in the exercise of the freedom of political association and in multi-party electioneering in Kenya. The DP made a spectacular performance in areas dominated by the GEMA communities (of Gikuyu, Embu and Meru); the NDP dominated the whole of Nyanza and little else outside it. In spite of the split vote in the Western Province, it is there that FORD-Kenya was most successful.

This ethnic pattern of voting was even more glaring in the presidential race. The presidential runner-up, Mwai Kibaki of DP, met the 25 per cent provincial requirement in the three Central, Eastern and Nairobi provinces where his GEMA community is well represented. Raila Odinga, who came third, passed the 25 per cent test only in his own home province of Nyanza. The same applied to Kijana Wamalwa of FORD-Kenya and Charity Ngilu of the SDP, in their Western and Eastern provinces, respectively. And if KANU appeared any less ethnic-bound than the opposition, it was largely because of the image it has acquired under Moi's rule as a representative of the collective fears of 'minority' groups of political and economic domination by larger groups. Against this backdrop, it was to be anticipated that the *wapwani-wabara* (coastal-upcountry) divide that constituted such an essential structural condition of the Mombasa-Kwale violence would also manifest itself in the pronouncements of the various political parties in their campaign activities in and around the affected areas of the Coast Province.

As expected, of course, virtually all the coast campaigns of the opposition parties were united in laying the blame for the Mombasa-Kwale tragedy at the doorstep of KANU, its President Daniel arap Moi and his government. But between the upcountry-based parties and the coast-based parties, the focus of the blame was radically different. Campaigners of SDP, NDP, DP and of other upcountry-based parties put heavy emphasis on the violence as a product of KANU's political agenda, seeking to turn one Kenyan sibling against another for the sole purpose of undermining and weakening the opposition.[5] As a result, there were repeated calls for a resolute stand against KANU's 'divisive tactics' and for trans-ethnic unity as the only means of 'sweeping away' KANU and Moi from the arena of political control through the ballot. These are the parties that supposedly recognised from among the victims of the violence compatriots from their own ethnic strongholds in the upcountry. And, on the average, presidential candidates from these parties had little to say about the suffering of innocent Digo victims at the hands of government security operations during the period of the violence.

Candidates from coast-based opposition parties, on the other hand, tended to highlight a different dimension of the violence. There are only two political parties, of course, that can be described as coast-based in the demographic sense used here: the Kenya National Congress (KNC) and the Shirikisho Party of Kenya (SPK). As is widely known, the KNC originated as an upcountry-based party. Formed in 1992 by Onesmus Mbali and others, it was once described as one of the diversionary parties 'from the Kamba area' (Wanjohi 1996: 97). But once it attracted some prominent coast politicians like Dr Chibule wa Tsuma and Professor Katama Mkangi, the party increasingly assumed a coastal garb in ideological orientation and electorate strength. This 'coastalisation' of the KNC was later consolidated by the tacit father-figure support it received from the veteran coast politicians Robert Matano and the eloquent Sheikh Abdillahi Nassir, once the leader of the now defunct Coast Peoples Party (CPP).

The Shirikisho Party of Kenya, on the other hand, is of more recent origin. It was officially launched on 20 November 1997, barely a month before the 29 December general elections, with Hamisi Jeffa as the national chairperson and Mbwana Warrakah as its secretary general. It had initially sought registration under the name of the Kenya Federal Democratic Party-Shirikisho in 1994, but its application was turned down almost three years later on the ridiculously flimsy ground that another party with a similar name, the Federal Party of Kenya, had just been registered.[6] It was soon after this communication that the party reapplied for and was granted registration under the new name, Shirikisho Party of Kenya.

What is perhaps most significant about SPK is that it was even more narrowly founded in its ethno-regional catchment base than KNC: it actually began as a Digo party, a party of the indigenous population of the area of the coast most affected by the 1997 violence. Ardent supporters of SPK continue, in fact, to discount the KNC as just another upcountry party while referring to theirs as the *kaya* party, the only party that genuinely reflects the sentiments and represents the interests of the people of the coast.

Whether KANU had a hand in the establishment of SPK, as is widely suspected, is difficult to establish. But given the timing of its registration, it may well have been a reflection of KANU's own fears of losing the elections, following the successive blunders of its government's security operations in the area. Under the circumstances, it may have calculated that it was 'better' to lose to an extremely weak and localised party like SPK and one that had no presidential candidate to field than to any of the more established opposition parties.

Whatever the case, as the only two coast-based opposition parties, KNC and SPK paid greater attention, throughout their political campaigning, to the suffering of the local Digo population during and after the period of the Likoni-Kwale violence than did any of the upcountry-based parties. While espousing the popular view that the violence was state sponsored, opposition candidates from KNC and SPK focused almost exclusively on the anguish and agony of the local people in the hands of the police and the General Service Unit. There were constant attempts to recount in graphic detail instances of maltreatment, looting, arbitrary arrest and torture, with the frequency of rape as a metaphor for the collective violation of the entire Digo community being a subject of recurrent description. Reference to the plight of upcountry victims of the violent tragedy, on the other hand, was conspicuously absent in KNC's and SPK's campaigning forays.

There was also a strong inclination among KNC and SPK candidates to make direct or indirect allusions to the marginalisation of the people of the coast, especially in the economic sphere. The upcountry domination of the lucrative tourist industry and the Kilindini harbour establishment was a popular theme that was quick to ignite the political passions of large sections of the audience. The collapse of the Ramisi Sugar Factory in Kwale, the Kenya Cashewnut Factory in Kilifi, the Kenya Cooperative Creameries venture in Mazeras, and the Kenya Meat Commission in Mombasa was often described as part of the wider KANU government silent policy of neglect that continued to disempower the local population economically and politically. Directly or indirectly, therefore, problems and regionalist solutions were foremost in the minds of KNC and SPK candidates.

This alleged state of marginalisation of the people of the coast was used to explain why the two parties proffered *majimbo* as the only constitutional arrangement capable of accommodating the interests of 'minorities' in the country. This was SPK's and KNC's galvanising message virtually throughout the campaign period. Opposition parties that attempted to discredit *majimbo* were often accused of hypocrisy that they should advocate American-style democracy while holding it anathema to consider a modified form of American-style federalism. At the same time, however, SPK's and KNC's candidates went to great lengths to distance themselves from the 'distortion' of *majimbo* that equated it with ethnic cleansing.[7]

Between the KNC and SPK, however, it is the latter that is more unequivocal in its advocacy of a federal system of government. Article I of SPK's manifesto, for example, states: 'SHIRIKISHO seeks to re-introduce regional governance, under a federal system of government, for the benefit of residents of those regions. The unitary system of government is no longer feasible and has failed in many ways.'

The preamble to the party's constitution also alludes to the alleged state of internal colonisation at the coast in the following words: 'Let all men of goodwill and understanding know that the dignity of man lies in the struggle for liberation of the body, mind and soul from any form of domination, be it political, economic or social'. The constitution then goes on to declare its objectives among which are 'to strive for the creation of a Kenya Federal State with a view of giving the various communities an equitable access to their natural resources and other economic facilities for the purpose of creating wealth for the people and the regions' and 'to work towards Federal Unity on the basis of equality in the distribution of opportunities.'

This *majimboist* thrust of the SPK, and to a lesser extent of the KNC, introduced a different dimension to the violence as a campaign issue to the extent that the violence was considered to have been engineered by the state and KANU hawks, SPK and KNC also understood why it had to happen. A people dominated will sooner or later rise and take-up arms in quest for liberation, with or without an 'external' spark. This 'double message' from SPK and KNC on the violence in Mombasa and Kwale also explains why the two parties never came out openly to condemn the terror and mayhem directed against Kenyan compatriots of upcountry origin.

Different from all opposition parties in the campaign trail was the position of KANU. In as much as the opposition was somewhat united in condemning KANU and its government for the violence, the ruling party in its turn placed the blame squarely on the shoulders of the opposition. The violence was thus projected as a product of cheap political machinations of the opposition in its bid to discredit KANU in one of its strongest zones. In organising the orgy of violence and counter-violence, therefore, the opposition was supposedly seeking to pre-empt another KANU victory in the area, especially in Kwale district.

In sum, then, the campaign exercise, in and around the Mombasa-Kwale area in particular, was a competitive attempt by various political parties to exploit different dimensions of the tragedy, real as well as imagined, to win the support of the electorate. But, as we shall see in a moment, the electorate was perhaps swayed by considerations that went beyond the immediate reality of the violence that bedevilled the area barely a couple of months before the 1997 general elections.

The polling exercise and the results

The depopulation, apathy and fear precipitated by the violence was bound to have an impact on the voter turnout in Mombasa and Kwale where it was mostly concentrated. The voter turnout in the two adjacent districts fell below the national average. In Likoni, the constituency hardest hit by the violence, the (parliamentary) voter turnout was 39.7 per cent, by far the lowest in the country. The Mvita constituency (which also holds a sizeable population of upcountry people) followed closely with a turnout of only 44.5 per cent (ECK 1999: 124). While the political nature of the violence made some people, both local and from upcountry, even more determined to cast their votes, it seems to have had the reverse effect on many others.

But even those people who chose to exercise their right to vote on the polling day did not always manage to do so. In addition to the many and widely reported election irregularities that afflicted various parts of the country, there was a rigging in Likoni and parts of Kwale specifically targeted at voters of upcountry origin. There were instances, for example, in which people of upcountry origin were denied the opportunity to cast their votes because, supposedly, their names did not appear in the register of voters in spite of the fact that it was in those same constituencies that they had, in fact, registered as voters (see e.g., KHRC 1998: 39-41).

Of particular significance in the polling exercise in Likoni, specifically, were the repeated threats directed at people of upcountry origin by both KANU and SPK stalwarts and activists. As some of the voters were hounded away from the polling stations, others were warned not to set foot in Likoni ever again if they dared vote for a party other than SPK. In some cases, SPK 'trouble-shooters' reportedly walked right into the polling rooms with the explicit intention of intimidating voters of upcountry origin (see e.g., KHRC 1998: 39-41).

The camaraderie reported by many eyewitnesses between local KANU and SPK functionaries around the polling stations on the polling day was perhaps a good indicator of how much local sentiments towards KANU had changed within a span of less than a month. The hostility towards KANU as a result of the harassment of the local people by its security forces during the period of the violence now seemed to have given way to empathy and support. This change of political attitude was soon to be confirmed by the election results.

In terms of the number of parliamentary seats, KANU performed better in Mombasa in the 1997 elections than it had in 1992, taking Mvita and Changamwe two of the four seats and, as in 1992, it won all of the three Kwale seats (Kinango, Matuga and Msambweni). Furthermore, the 1992 FORD-Kenya win of the Likoni and Kisauni seats was more decisively anti-KANU than the 1997 win of the Likoni seat by SPK and the Kisauni seat by the DP. After all, both the successful SPK candidate for Likoni, Suleiman Rashid Shakombo[8] and the DP candidate for Kisauni, Emmanuel Karisa Maitha, were zealous KANU supporters and candidates and crossed over to their respective opposition parties only after they had lost to Hisham Mwidau and Said Hemed respectively in the party's primary elections. And indeed there are indications that both candidates crossed over with the explicit permission of President Moi. Ironically, both campaigned for Moi as president.[9]

With regard to the presidential elections, the percentage of votes cast in favour of Moi in 1997 in the Coast Province, in general, was similar to the 1992 general elections. Moi garnered 63.1 per cent of the coastal vote in 1997 as compared to 63.2 per cent in 1992. Moi's average score for the four constituencies of Mombasa, however, rose from 36.3 per cent in 1992 to 40.9 per cent in 1997, just as it dropped dramatically from 77.6 per cent in 1992 to 66.5 per cent in 1997 for the three constituencies of Kwale (IED 1997; IED/CJPC/NCCK 1998). There is a possibility that the anti-Moi vote in most constituencies of Mombasa was essentially an abstention vote since the influence of the civic lobby, the National Convention Assembly, with its mixed call for an election boycott, was seemingly more pronounced in urban Mombasa than in the more rural Kwale district. On the other hand, the outcome in Kwale may also have been the result of residual anti-government sentiments that were initially triggered by the suffering of the local population during the violent pre-election period.

Most surprising of all, however, was the presidential election outcome in Likoni, the constituency most drastically affected by the violence. In 1992 KANU's Daniel arap Moi lost to FORD-Kenya's Jaramogi Oginga Odinga. Moi garnered 26.4 per cent of the votes while Odinga, partly benefiting from his party's alliance with the unregistered Islamic Party of Kenya (IPK), scored 32.6 per cent. The 1997 results, however, demonstrate a Moi win with an impressive vote. Moi scored 44.5 per cent and beat his closest rival in the constituency, Mwai Kibaki, by a margin of over 30 per cent.[10] The demographic effects of the violence, then, clearly seemed to have had their toll on the strength of the opposition presidential candidates in this particular constituency.

How, then, does one explain the overwhelming support that KANU and Moi received in the Mombasa-Kwale area, contrary to popular expectations? Was it all a product of the massive irregularities in the electoral process and rigging in the exercise? No doubt these flaws had their effects on the election results in Mombasa and Kwale districts as they did in many other parts of the country. But our investigations also suggest that there were other more local political factors at play, which may have re-directed the potential flow of votes from the opposition to KANU in the last few days before polling. These included the following:

1. The registration of the Digo-based Shirikisho Party of Kenya in the immediate aftermath of the violence was reassuring to many local residents of the area as it seemed to herald an end of the denial of their own particular expression of citizenship in the form of a political party based on 'coastal values'. The move was regarded by many as the first sign of a political will on the part of the Moi-KANU regime to create a more inclusive space for the freedom of association, allowing the Digo people, in particular, and the coastal people, in general, a long desired platform of political organisation and expression.

As it turned out, more people still opted to vote for KANU and DP candidates, for example, than SPK candidates. Of the nine parliamentary candidates that SPK fielded during the 1997 general elections only one, the candidate for Likoni, managed to capture a winning vote. But for the brief pre-election period in which it was allowed to operate, SPK served well as a platform for the expression of local political aspirations and grievances and, in the process, it assisted, perhaps, in diffusing an otherwise tense situation and, paradoxically, in reducing the antagonism towards Moi and his party, KANU.

These results also bring to focus a fundamental distinction between allegiance to particular political parties and allegiance to particular political leaders. There was tremendous support, at least in sentiment, for the SPK and its political ideals throughout the Mombasa-Kwale area. This allegiance to the party, however, did not amount to votes for the preponderant majority of SPK candidates. Political leaders like Marere wa Mwachai, the KANU member of parliament for Msambweni and an assistant minister in the Ministry of Local Government, on the other hand, would probably have emerged triumphant on any party ticket in a free and fair election. Likewise, many supporters of the opposition opted to cast their votes in favour of Moi, a KANU candidate, in the presidential race. The coastal electorate, therefore, continued to manifest paradoxical conflicts and contradictions in their political allegiances.

2. A few days before the elections word was widespread that KANU had entered into dialogue with some local leaders of the area and promised to make significant social and economic amends in favour of the Digo community within a year of its new tenure of office. According to Juma Bugu, the chief of

Waa location, the alleged spiritual leader of the raiders, Mzee Swalehe Khalfani and some of his followers even met the president during his campaign tour of the coast. The president supposedly made certain assurances to 'deliver' if he won another presidential term.[11] In spite of the fact that there was no independent verification of these rumours, they were strong enough to have assisted in turning the local campaign tide in favour of Moi and KANU within a matter of days before the polling exercise.

3. In as much as the local population was not particularly pleased with Moi and KANU, it was equally disappointed with the opposition. Feelings abounded that while virtually all the opposition candidates came out strongly to condemn the killings of people of upcountry origin, none of them seemed in the least to be sympathetic to the plight of the Digo at the hands of the predominantly upcountry police and the GSU in their public pronouncements. The Kibakis and the Railas, therefore, were seen as leaders who were unlikely to treat the Digo any better than the Mois. There was thus a sense of resignation to settle for the *zimwi likujualo* (the ogre that knows you, that is, KANU and Moi) which, in popular imagination, never quite devours you to the finish.

The context of the violence

But underlying the reasons behind KANU's success story in Mombasa and Kwale in the 1997 general elections are the social and economic conditions which explain how it was possible for politicians with selfish political agendas to instigate the violence in the first place in this area once regarded as a 'haven of peace and co-existence'. These conditions are two-fold: structural and systemic.

1. The structural factor is related to population dynamics. The area in question is often regarded as a Digo and Duruma 'homeland'. These groups together constitute about 80 per cent of the population. But migrations from other parts of the country have introduced a population of upcountry origin comprising mainly, in order of diminishing numerical strength, Kamba, Luo, Kikuyu and Luhya – which, according to the Kwale district *Development Plan of 1994-96*, is close to 10 per cent of the residents of the area. In addition to this ethnic distribution, there is a sectarian dimension, which is equally important in comprehending the demographic politics of the area. This is the divide between the predominantly Muslim Digo and Duruma, and the predominantly Christian population of upcountry origin. What we get, in other words, is the superimposition of cultural variations over an ethno-regional matrix.

In the context of Kenya's ethnocratic and, especially under the presidency of Daniel arap Moi, christocentric politics and economics, the up-country presence at the coast has precipitated a growing local reaction along the dangerous axis of 'we' (the insiders) versus 'they' (the outsiders). Though both sides of the axis are ethnically heterogeneous, the developing polity has been regionally and religiously dual: predominantly Muslim *wapwani* versus predominantly Christian *wabara*. As Ali Mazrui argues, dual settings, like the one that prevails in Likoni and Kwale, can be potentially more volatile than more plural situations if they remain unmediated by other potentially neutralising forces (Mazrui 1995).[12] Had the coastal and upcountry people been more religiously mixed, allowing for the existence of sectarian empathy across the *wapwani-wabara* regional divide, for example, the situation is likely to have been less prone to a violent eruption.

2. The systemic factor, on the other hand, is tied to considerations of politics and the economy. Juxtaposed on the demographic duality of the area is a politico-economic dispensation that has tended to privilege the upcountry leg of the Likoni-Kwale population at the expense of the more local component. While the specific socio-economic data on the region is not readily available, there is a good deal of general information that seems to support the sentiments of the local people that they are, in fact, systemically disadvantaged vis-à-vis the 'other'. These politics of relative treatment naturally exacerbated the tensions, latent as they may have been, in the relationship between the coastal and upcountry people of Mombasa and Kwale districts.

Conclusion

The underlying conditions of the violence outlined above are also the ones that explain why *majimbo* came to be such an important rallying point for the electorate in Mombasa, Kwale and in many of the other districts of the Coast. *Majimbo* became a response-call of a marginalised people confronted by the 'spectre' of an upcountry population that is seemingly growing in numerical size, and economic and political strength. And as long as KANU, in its present configuration, can gain political advantage from the marginality of the Coast and exploit its fears of internal colonialism, it is likely to continue having an upper hand in many of the constituencies in the province.

Above and beyond the question of marginality and the fear of ethnic hegemony as factors that provide part of the explanation for the Coast's tilt towards KANU and Moi, however, there is the coastal arm of plutocracy in Kenya. As indicated earlier KANU, through the government machinery under its control, is able to exploit the marginality of provinces like the Coast and North-Eastern to strengthen its own position in the struggle for power. This role of marginal constituencies has led the Institute for Education in Democracy to claim that '. . . a situation has emerged in Kenya over this period where the remote and underdeveloped areas are the ones ruling the country (by virtue of their electoral might).' The Institute for Education in Democracy then continues to quote another commentator to the effect that the Kenyan situation is now '. . . akin to the most advanced parts of the US being ruled from the Nevada desert and not from the Iowa cornfields.' And this, Kenya's 'Nevada desert', is said to include the Coast Province (IED 1998:5).

In reality, however, the marginalised poor of the coast have been no more than pawns in a political dispensation that has turned increasingly plutocratic. The balance in Kenya has shifted towards a political system that prospers on the wings of wealth and flourishes on the credentials of avarice. In the process, ethics, morals and the rule of law have been set aside as the rich compete in pursuing all manner of corruption to get richer and richer. It is the rule of this corrupt class of people that Kenyans are now experiencing – especially in the Moi era.

At the coast, the class of plutocrats has included the likes of Rashid Sajjad, A. Bawazir and Twahir Sheikh Said (TSS). In their efforts to cushion the plutocratic state against the onslaught from the opposition, they constantly seek to influence and control political developments and processes in the region. They aim to determine for the people who their mayor should be, who should represent them in parliament, and who should have access to whom and to what. They not only sponsor individual candidates to parliament and councils but, if need be, they also organise communal violence and bloodletting if, by so doing, they will position, within the political establishment, those people of their preference who can best safeguard their plutocratic and kleptocratic interests.[13]

In the final analysis, then, the 1997 general elections at the Coast raised a number of issues that are of critical importance to the ongoing struggle for political reform. These include:

(a) the need to empower ethnic minorities in a way that will minimise the exploitability of ethnicity in national and local politics by political self-seekers of all shades;

(b) the need to democratise local authorities and reduce their capacity to turn communities of Kenyans into 'enclosures', thereby deepening their marginalisation, and

(c) the need to retrench the plutocratic regime and harness the roots of a more social democratic order.

Naturally, these are challenges that require, in part, creative engineering in the constitution-making process as Kenya enters the next millennium.

Notes

1. 'Upcountry' is, of course, the popular Kenyan term for the hinterland. But, in general, 'upcountry' is more appropriate in an uplands-versus-lowlands political configuration that characterizes countries like the Malagasy Republic, than the coast-versus-hinterland configuration.
2. Maitha was notorious as KANU's 'trouble-shooter' at the coast and has been mentioned in various reports as a key player in the Mombasa-Kwale violence. He defected to the Democratic Party of Kenya after losing to Said Hemed during KANU's primaries and eventually proceeded to win the Kisauni parliamentary seat. Maitha was interviewed at his residence in Ukunda on 14 December 1997.
3. This information is based on interviews with several displaced victims of the violence in Mombasa conducted by a KHRC team between January 1 and January 7, 1998.
4. Ibid.
5. The terms 'upcountry-based' and 'coast based' are used to reflect the popular view about the location of the demographic strength of the respective parties.
6. Letter from the Registrar of Societies to the secretary general of the Kenya Federal Democratic Party-Shirikisho, dated 5 November 1997.
7. See, for example, the statement by SPK's parliamentary candidate for Matuga, Mwagomba Mwapeu, as reported in the *Daily Nation* of 22 December 1997.
8. Shakombo, an ex-district commissioner in the Rift Valley, is among those mentioned in various reports in connection with the violence in Mombasa and Kwale.
9. In separate interviews with Maitha (14 December 1997) and Shakombo (7 December 1997), both candidates claimed to have had audience with President Daniel arap Moi before their 'defection' to the DP and SPK, respectively.
10. In the recount conducted by Charles Hornsby, Katama Mkangi of KNC comes second with 2,655 votes as compared to Moi's 6,371 and Kibahi's 1,979. (see Appendix I).
11. Personal interview 27 January 1998.
12. Ali Mazrui developed and applied this concept in the context of the nation-state in Africa. Here I have extended its use to a sub-national situation.
13. Before the Akiwumi Commission on tribal clashes, MP Rashid Sajjad admitted he spent a total of Ksh. 17 million to fund the KANU election at the coast. Asked by commission chairman, Justice Akilano Akiwumi, what the money was for, he replied: 'buy votes, feast people, pay school fees for people and give some to elders to take to their families' (*Daily Nation* 23/10/98).

References

African Rights 1997, 'Violence at the Coast: The Human Consequences of Kenya's Crumbling Political Institutions', *Witness*, Issue 2, October-November 1997: 6-7.

IED 1997, *National Elections Data Book - Kenya 1963-1997*, Nairobi: Institute for Education in Democracy.

IED 1998, *Understanding Elections in Kenya: A Constituency Profile Approach*, Nairobi: Institute for Education in Democracy.

IED/CJPC/NCCK 1998, *Report on the 1997 General Elections in Kenya, 29-30 December, 1997*, Nairobi: Institute for Education in Democracy, Catholic Justice and Peace Commission, National Council of Churches of Kenya.

KHRC 1997, *Kayas of Deprivation, Kayas of Blood: Violence, Ethnicity and the State in Coastal Kenya*, Nairobi: Kenya Human Rights Commission.

KHRC 1997a, *Quarterly Repression Report*, July-September 1997, Nairobi: Kenya Human Rights Commission.

Mazrui, A. A., 1995 'The African State as a Political Refugee: Institutional Collapse and Human Development', *International Journal of Refugee Law*, Vol.7: 21-36.

RoK/CBS 1991, *Population Census 1989 Volume I*. Nairobi: Republic of Kenya, Central Bureau of Statistics.

RoK/CBS 1991a, *Population Census 1989: Analytical Report, Volume III - The Population Dynamics of Kenya*, Nairobi: Republic of Kenya, Central Bureau of Statistics.

RoK/MPND nd, *Kwale District Development Plan, 1994-1996*, Rural Planning Department, Ministry of Planning and National Development, Republic of Kenya.

Throup, D. and Hornsby, C. 1998, *Multi-Party Politics in Kenya. The Kenyatta & Moi States & the Triumph of the System in the 1992 Election*, Oxford: James Currey.

Wanjohi, N. 1996, *Political Parties in Kenya: Formation, Policies and Manifestoes*, Nairobi: Views Media.

11

Elections Among the Kenya Somali: A Conservative but Marginalised Vote[1]

Marc-Antoine Pérouse de Montclos

The paradox of the Kenyan government today is that it tends towards a centralised government yet leans on an alliance made up of pastoralist minorities on the periphery. This alliance consists of the Kalenjin (to which President Moi belongs), the Maasai, the Turkana and the Samburu, hence the acronym KAMATUSA.[2]

In this regard, the nomadic minority of the Somali in the North-Eastern Province (See map on p. 184) constitute a different case altogether. They do not belong to the KAMATUSA alliance but they, in majority, support KANU. In the seventh parliament of 1992-97, only one of the ten elected members of parliament from the province belonged to the opposition. The eleventh was nominated by the ruling party. This sole opposition MP was Farah Mohamed Maalim in Dadaab, Lagdera constituency, who in 1997 ran on a Forum for the Restoration of Democracy-Kenya (FORD-Kenya) ticket, because Safina, the party he belonged to, had not yet been registered by the government.

Two other MPs were bound to gain votes for the opposition in North-Eastern Province: Ahmed Khalif of Forum for the Restoration of Democracy-Asili (FORD-Asili) in Wajir West and Ahmed Sheikh Abdullahi of the Party of Independent Candidates of Kenya (PICK) in Mandera East. But the first one defected to KANU, while the second's election was cancelled in 1994 on procedural grounds and he was banned for five years from competing in an election. Ahmed Sheikh Abdullahi also defected back to KANU. In 1992 contenders in 80 per cent of North-Eastern Province constituencies took their case before the courts, a nation-wide record (Throup and Hornsby 1998: 313, 410).

In the 1997 elections, KANU retained its seats in nine of the eleven constituencies. The North-Eastern Province actually re-elected President Moi with a better score than even that of his own home stronghold: almost 74 per cent against less than 70 per cent in the Rift Valley (78 and 67 per cent respectively in 1992). Certain constituencies like Wajir North assured the KANU candidates of victories with percentages similar to those of a one-party system: more than 99 per cent of the votes!

In spite of this massive support, however, the Somali are a weak political link to the KAMATUSA alliance. Their vote, which is not void of contradictions considering the military repression of the KANU government in the region, is more a show of fidelity than an indication of access to power. On the Kenyan political scene, the Somali are marginalised. They live in a province which regularly falls victim to droughts and floods and which is always allocated the smallest share of the national budget, especially Wajir district, as compared to other regions in the country (see Rutten 1992: 110). Placed on the periphery of a very centralised state, the province lacks autonomous power to allow its local elite to manage local affairs without the supervision of the government in Nairobi. For the Somali, the central administration is an alien body and for the Christian elite in Nairobi, Koranic schools do not enable Muslims to qualify for the civil service. The administration is thus made up of 'expatriates' who are often sent to the North-Eastern for disciplinary reasons.

This political marginalisation has several explanations. Geographically, the Somali live on both sides of the Kenyan border and are often confused with illegal immigrants or refugees from Somalia.[3] The common resentment against them arises from racial and religious factors as much as from strategic reasons. The short-lived secession of the Somali in Northern Frontier District (NFD) at independence is still fresh in memory. Followed by a state of emergency which was partially lifted only in 1991, it paved the way for a kind of stigmatisation. Let us first have a closer look at this specific aspect of the political and economic position of Kenyan Somali.

The secession spectre

The nationalist unrest in Italian Somalia after World War II actually had repercussions on the Kenyan side (Turton 1972). The Somali Youth League, the main party in Mogadishu, set foot in the NFD in 1946 from where it was banned two years later. While the Lennox Boyd constitution of 1958 gave to Africans half of the seats in the Legislative Council in Nairobi, the political parties in the provinces were not admitted so until 1960. As a result, political groups demanding secession were formed. They included the Northern Province Peoples Progressive Party of Ali Adan, the Peoples National League of Guyo Dube and the Northern Frontier Democratic Party of Yussuf Abdi. Other groups in the north-east region, mostly of non-Somali origin, had a less firm stand towards the secession issue. For example, the Oromo dominated Northern People's National Union, the Northern Province United Association and the Galla Political Union were not favourable to the Somali and a number of them rejoined KANU.

The outcome of the 1962 survey on administrative boundaries emphasised the sociological complexity of the northern population. It showed that 87 per cent were in favour of secession, a percentage much higher than the proportion of Somali among the 40,000 inhabitants of the region at the time. The secession advocates did not align themselves according to a strict religious cleavage. The Turkana in the western part of the NFD were simply opposed to the secession for evident fear of being marginalised geographically and culturally. The Muslim Sakuye of the Waso Nyiro River favoured the Somali position and so did the non-Muslim Rendille who have close links with the Somali along language lines. The Boran were divided on the issue because of their affiliation with Islam. Wako Happi, the first chairman of the secessionist Northern Province Peoples Progressive Party, was a Boran Muslim, yet Boran from Marsabit and Moyale, who still believed in their traditional god (*Waaqa*), voted against the secession. So did related Burji, Konso and Gabbra communities in Marsabit district and Pokomo animists from Tana River district (Baxter 1966).

Meanwhile, the authorities in Mogadishu supported irredentism by extolling the five stars of their new flag, which represented the Italian Somalia, the British Somaliland, Djibouti on the French side, the NFD in Kenya and the Ogaden in Ethiopia (see e.g., Lewis 1963; Touval 1963; Fitzgibbon 1982; Asiwaju 1985). In the region, Somalia was the only country which did not sign the Organisation of African Unity (OAU) Charter which recognises the inviolability of colonial borders. The 1960 constitution followed the same principle as that of Israel in 1948. It gave Somali citizenship to all the Somali living outside the country, entitling them to the same rights as those living inside. This facilitated the integration of the refugees from the Kenyan NFD after 1964 and the Ethiopian Ogaden after 1978. One of the strong arguments of pan-Somalism was the linguistic unity in the Horn of Africa. The British did not show a strong opposition against the idea of a Greater Somalia. Richard Turnbull, who had served in the NFD for a long time before being appointed minister for Defence during the Mau Mau rebellion, did not hide his sympathy for the Somali. Ernest Bevin, the British Foreign Secretary in 1946, shared the same views. On the occasion of discussions on the Italian mandate in Africa after World War II, he proposed the creation of a Greater Somalia that would include disputed border regions in Ethiopia, Ogaden and Haud, but not the NFD in Kenya. An unfortunate slip of the tongue by Prime Minister Harold McMillan shortly before the independence of Kenya confirmed the feeling that London still supported pan-Somalism, an impression that was quickly annulled by what ensued.

The Lancaster House conference in 1962, which aimed at preparing the constitutional frame for an independent Kenya, led to the division of the NFD and the creation of a North-Eastern Province in March 1963. This move was meant to satisfy the ardent irredentist Somali by regrouping Garissa, Mandera and Wajir districts with the eastern part of Moyale, where they were also dominant (see e.g., Adar 1994; Drysdale 1964; Hoskyns 1969). The Kenyan nationalists categorically opposed the amalgamation of the North-Eastern Province with the Somali state. Both Jomo Kenyatta of KANU and Ronald Ngala of KADU were uncompromising about this issue when they met Mogadishu officials in July and August 1962. Kenyatta proposed a vast East African federation which would have included the Ethiopian and Somali enemies. The Somali government asked for a preliminary reunification with the NFD. The negotiations took a sharp turn and Mogadishu severed its diplomatic relations with Great Britain because of its alleged support for Nairobi. Disappointed, the Kenyan Somali boycotted the regional elections in April 1961 and the general elections in May 1963. In December 1963, the so-called *shifta* rebellion began.

During the Christmas of 1963, a state of emergency was declared with the approval of only 60 per cent of the Kenyan parliament, overriding the 65 per cent quorum required constitutionally. President Jomo Kenyatta at the time was afraid of an invasion by Somalia and asked for military assistance from Britain. Exceptional laws were made to cover the North-Eastern Province and the neighbouring Marsabit, Isiolo, Tana River and Lamu districts, in a way perpetuating the special status that Britain had given to this region. The bordering areas were evacuated and nomadic movements strictly controlled. Meetings of more than ten persons were prohibited. The possession of firearms entailed a death penalty. Consumption of *miraa*, the Somali stimulant equivalent of the Yemenite *qat*, was forbidden. Listening to foreign radio stations was prohibited, and transmissions from Mogadishu were cut off. The president governed as he pleased by way of regulations. Special tribunals replaced the Kenyan judicial system; the suspects did not have the benefit of presumptive innocence nor were they allowed a lawyer to defend them. They could be detained for 56 days in solitary confinement before they were brought to court.

The fighting led to 2,000 deaths in 1964. The first amnesty to be granted was at the end of the year, coinciding with the *Jamhuri* celebrations, a national holiday that marks the day when Kenya became a republic. Despite this, the army continued to carry out punitive raids and slaughter the cattle of those pastoralists suspected of supporting the guerrillas.[4] The fighting ceased officially in 1967, when in June, the new Somali Prime Minister Mohammed Ibraim Egal, initiated a political *détente* with Kenya. In October, the Arusha agreement put an end to the support Mogadishu was giving to the *shifta* guerrillas. Kenya-Somalia diplomatic relations, which had been severed in June 1966, were re-established. In 1968, Kenya pardoned the rebels who in turn agreed to lay down their arms.

The peace process was, however, jeopardised by the nationalist sentiments of the military junta of Siad Barre who came to power in 1969. At the beginning of the Ogaden war against Ethiopia in June 1977, 3,000 Somali soldiers attacked a Kenyan border post at Rhamu. Two years later, there were some rumours about the resurgence of a separatist Somali movement in Kenya, the Northern Frontier Liberation Front. Siad Barre was eventually forced to give up his territorial claims on north-eastern Kenya because of his defeat by Ethiopia in the Ogaden war in 1978, the pressure of his new American ally and the rise of the opposition in Somalia.

By virtue of a frontier agreement signed in 1981, Somalia and Kenya agreed not to support any opposition guerrillas rising up in their respective countries. The official visit of Siad Barre to Nairobi for the twentieth anniversary celebrations of the Kenyan's independence in 1983 and of Moi to Mogadishu the following year confirmed this reconciliation (see Musambayi 1995). In 1984, Kenya signed an amnesty for the last rebels who were in exile in Mogadishu. Public ceremonies of national reconciliation were organised to mark their return to the North-Eastern Province. From 1986, the Kenyan army hunted down Siad Barre's political enemies who operated in the north-eastern region. In 1989, the hostility against the Somali Patriotic Movement (SPM) existed partly because some of the rebels from the Ogaden clan had been involved in the *shifta* war. For example, General Aden Abdullahi Noor, nicknamed 'Gabio' had deserted the Kenyan army as a major and joined the SPM troops in Mogadishu in 1966.

However, when Siad Barre's dictatorship collapsed in 1991, the Kenyan government had to make some choices. It was assisting guerrilla groups in southern Sudan. So Moi's government supported General Mohamed Siad Hersi, 'Morgan', a son-in-law and former right-hand man of Barre who fought General Mohamed Farah Hassan 'Aidid', a Mogadishu warlord linked to the Islamist junta in Khartoum. Moreover, 'Morgan' pretended to be the heir of Barre. Last but not least, the Kenyan army chief of general staff was an Ogaden Somali who had facilitated the reconciliation between Presidents Daniel arap Moi and Siad Barre.

In May 1992 at Amuma near Liboi, the Kenyan army killed Colonel Bashir Ali Salad 'Bililiqo', an SPM commandant opposed to 'Morgan'. In September, the former soldiers from Barre's Marehan clan, regrouped under the Somali National Front (SNF), and the 'Morgan' faction of the SPM launched a joint attack on Somali territory with the help of the Kenyan military who provided them with arms. Driven off by the Americans at Kisimayu, 'Morgan' had to retreat to Dobley, where he re-organised his troops and continued to receive support from Nairobi (*Daily Telegraph* 27//01/93). The Harti clan of 'Morgan' distanced itself from the Marehan of Barre, and joined part of the Ogaden of

SPM, who were now divided into two factions: the one of Aden Abdullahi Noor 'Gabio' which supported 'Morgan' and the one of Colonel Ahmed Omar Jess which supported 'Aidid'. The SNF and its allies from SPM took control of Kismayu, Badhade, Bardera and Dobley regions. But at the end of 1993, it is said, the Kenyan army chief of general staff, Mahmoud, stopped helping 'Morgan' and the Marehan of SNF because the latter had stolen cattle from his own clan, the Abdwak.

The hope of reinstating Barre to power was lost anyway. The mediation that Nairobi claimed to lead in the peace negotiations in Somalia obliged President Moi to establish goodwill with the various factions which were now controlling the border area, especially those fighting against the rise of the Islamists in Lugh, whom Kenya was absolutely opposed to.

The government's aim was to maintain an impenetrable border. However, the Kenyan security forces could hardly control it. The authorities tried in vain to enter into an agreement with the SPM, so that the latter would return vehicles stolen from Kenya. The SPM leaders, Commandant Ahmed Hassan Abdi 'Qat' and Imam Said Hussein Abdalla were even allowed to receive medical attention in Garissa at the end of 1996 (Gomes 1997). This did not achieve much. At the beginning of 1998, a Kenyan police post at Hare was attacked and emptied of all its arms by the SPM, while al Itehad Islamists briefly took control of El Wak. Again in April 1999, the Kenyan security forces in Kolbio could not contain an Islamist detachment running away from Ras Kamboni where it was involved in the murder of a staff member of a humanitarian organisation.

The roots of stigmatisation

Beyond questions pertaining to strategic and military views, the elite Christians who hold power in Nairobi mistrust the Somali Muslims. Differences in lifestyles cause an exacerbation of negative attitudes. In a small town like Kakamega in western Kenya, local Luhya disdain the Somali for their eccentricity, their relatively high rate of illiteracy and their fertility that seems to produce idle youth, thieves and smugglers, etc.[4] The fear of one another causes suspicion and gives birth to stereotypes.

More than just a religious confrontation, the race argument of the 'Arabs' versus the 'Blacks' comes into play. In Mombasa, the United Muslims of Africa (UMA) led by Omar Masumbuko thus denounces the Arabs of the Islamic Party of Kenya (IPK). Perhaps we should add that UMA is pro-KANU while the IPK is in the opposition. On the other hand, the Somali are convinced of their superiority and do not hide their contempt for the Bantu who are categorised as descendants of slaves. This arrogance has its roots in a racial foundation. It goes beyond a simple suspicion against foreigners, the pagan *gal*, etymologically a word which comes from the ancient name Galla of the Oromo of Ethiopia (*Galti* is just an immigrant in Somali).

The heritage of the British segregation has a part to play in the establishment of this racism. Colonisation forced flexible communities to identify themselves according to criteria based on ethnic purity (Lonsdale and Berman 1992:38). It introduced a racial hierarchy with the Asians falling between the Whites and the Blacks. The Somali wanted to be treated as the equals of the Indians. They even went as far as demanding an increase in their taxes, so as to distinguish themselves from the locals who paid lower rates (Turton 1974). After being exempted by a 1919 ordinance from the forced labour that the indigenous people were subjected to, Kenyan Somali opposed the transcription of their language using the Roman alphabet, as this would have 'reduced' it to the level of the Bantu languages in Kenya. They put forward very uncertain Arab origins – and for the Isaaq clan a strong presence in Aden – as a reason to obtain Asian status in 1942 and 1947. This was not without contradiction since they were largely compelled by the clauses in the indigenous law and not those of the western penal code.

Moreover, the claims regarding Arab origin were exacerbated by members of the colonial authority. Before, the Somali were not ashamed of their African descent through the Galla, the present-day Oromo in Ethiopia. As a French explorer observed, for instance, at the end of the nineteenth century, the Mijertein, a Darod clan, remarked 'with pride that they used to be Galla and they [did] not seem to confess easily their Arab origin' (Révoil 1880: 257). It was the British who aggravated the differentiation between the Somali and the Bantu. Recalling his experience in Somaliland, an official could write that 'to pass from the administration of Somalis to the administration of African negroes must be like bestriding a donkey on Margate sands after riding a thoroughbred at Newmarket' (Jardine 1923: 23). Of course, such a colonial classification stirred up racial reactions in Kenya.

The stigmatisation of the Somali also corresponds to a certain political dynamism. The Kikuyu and the Luo in the opposition view the Somali as allies of the regime because they vote for KANU, and the Somali supported the Kalenjin clique of President Moi during the *coup d'état* of 1982. The failure of the 1982 coup, led by the Kenyan air force, presented a special opportunity for the minority Somali to gain political ground to the detriment of the Kikuyu who, during the Kenyatta era, had succeeded in securing half of the officers' posts in the armed forces in 1972 as compared to only a third in 1969. The air force had rebelled before in 1964. At the time, British troops came to the aid of the Kenyatta regime. In August 1982, it was a Somali, General Mahmoud Mohamed, who remained faithful to President Moi, taking over the command of the air force and then becoming the armed forces' chief of general staff in 1986, a post which he occupied until his retirement in 1996.[6]

The Kenyan Somali and the 1997 general elections

So the Somali are not only seen as irredentist troublemakers but also as conservative supporters of the government. More than Kenyatta, President Moi was to rely on Somali support, especially as a result of the 1992 multi-party general elections. The new rule for these elections made it compulsory for the presidential candidates to get at least 25 per cent of the votes in five out of eight provinces. It emphasised the importance of the north- eastern region. North-Eastern has the three least populated constituencies in the country: Ijara, Wajir North and Fafi. Still the number of constituencies in the low populated North-Eastern Province rose from eight to eleven between 1979 and 1996, whereas during the same period, those of Nairobi, an opposition stronghold, remained unchanged. But the eight Nairobi constituencies were inhabited by at least four times the population living in North-Eastern. By 1997, with 171,675 registered voters in North-Eastern Province every constituency represented an average of 15,606 votes against a mean of 90,704 registered voters per constituency for Nairobi.

The clan factor

Boundary reviews according to clans actually emphasise the collective patterns of the Somali vote as well as the leading influence of KANU big shots. North-Eastern Province is dominated by four main families, namely the Mohamed in Garissa district, the Sheikh Ali in Mandera, the Khalif and the Ogle in Wajir. The Mohamed represent an Ogaden clan, the Abdwak. They are led by a former general, Mahmoud Mohamed, whose lineage, the Rer Ugar, belongs to the Rer Yahye sub-clan. Before he retired to chair the Kenya Railways Corporation, Mahmoud Mohamed was the army's chief of general staff. The rewards were to benefit his kin and folk. His brother, Hussein Maalim Mohamed, became a minister and a nominated MP for Dujis, formerly Garissa Central constituency. Since 1983 up till now, he has regularly been re-elected. Other members of Mahmoud's extended family were also absorbed in the administration: Mohamed Yussuf Haji was appointed provincial commissioner of the strategic Rift Valley Province while Ali Yussuf Haji became the first Kenyan Somali to be in charge of the president's security.

In this regard, the Sheikh Ali in Mandera and the Ogle in Wajir present some similarities because they ran their constituencies as family businesses. From the 1960s to 1980, the MP of Mandera West has been a Gurreh, Mohamed Sheikh Ali, who ensured the election of his brother in Mandera East in 1969 and handed over his place to his son in 1980 (the latter to his uncle in 1988). It was not until the multi-party elections in 1992 that a new MP who was not of this family appeared on the scene. He was nonetheless a Gurreh. The behaviour of boundary gerrymandering along clan lines is not new. The Electoral Boundaries Review Commission of 1986 confirmed for Mandera East the domination of the Murilleh clan by removing the competing Gurreh of El Wak and Kotulo locations to a newly created Mandera Central constituency. In Ijara, formerly Garissa South, the Hulugho division was also transferred, to neighbouring Fafi constituency. In 1997, Ijara maintained a KANU stance while Fafi voted for the opposition.

As for the Makabul clan in Wajir South, the Ogle brothers, Ahmed Abdi and Noor Abdi, monopolised the constituency until 1992 when the former defected to the Democratic Party (DP) while the latter was ousted by a rival KANU contender.

The case of Wajir is a little different because Ahmed Khalif enjoyed a national stature as an MP and was a prominent political figure as an assistant minister and secretary general of the Supreme Council of Kenya Muslims. This position allowed him to be much more independent-minded and vocal than his KANU counterparts in Dujis, Wajir South or Mandera Central. In 1966, his eldest brother, Abdi Sirat Khalif, MP for Wajir North, had already participated in founding the Kenya People's Union (KPU) which was banned by the government in 1969. First elected in 1979, Ahmed Khalif became a champion of the rights of his constituents. He denounced the Wagalla massacre by the army in 1984 and the government's discriminatory policy that required the Kenyan Somali to have special identity cards in 1989. At this time, he was going to be expelled from KANU and was suspended from his post at the Supreme Council of Kenya Muslims (Supkem).

Ahmed Khalif had worked hard on the creation of a new in order to get rid of his political opponents. Ahmed Khalif belongs to the Degodia clan. Their rivals, the Ajuran, formed about 40 per cent of the voters in Wajir West before a constituency was created for them in the North. The division of the old in 1969 should have satisfied the Degodia in the east and the Ajuran in the west. But the latter lost the in 1979, regained it in 1988 and lost it again in 1992 which explains why some of them voted for the opposition (Gomes 1995). In 1996, the redivision of the Wajir West constituency contented one of their lineages, the Garen in the north, but disappointed another one, the Geelbaris in the south, who had to continue living under the domination of the Degodia in Wajir West.

Indeed, Ahmed Khalif was not re-elected in 1997. At the end of 1997 he was very critical of the dominant KANU-B faction, a stance which might be one reason why he lost his seat. Also, despite a wide political influence, he had not succeeded in representing the interests of the whole Somali community. The latter are divided into such a good number of lineages that local pundits and the press talk about controversial clan arithmetics (see Table 11.1).

The Somali are far from forming a united front and violent disputes are common. For example, among the Ogaden at the beginning of the twentieth century, the Mohamed Zubeir were fighting the Aulihan, and later the Abdalla and the Abdwak. Since that time, the struggle for control over pastureland and water sources took other forms. The control of constituencies has more or less replaced that of tribal areas during the colonial period and every Somali clan essentially has a representative in parliament. The confrontations started again when this status quo was interrupted by increasing demands from smaller and smaller sub-clans. Today, the hostility is foremost between two Hawiye clans, the Degodia and the Ajuran.

The December 1997 elections perpetuated this system of clan-based clienteles. In Mandera Central, for instance, the KANU candidate was the front runner for the Gurreh who represented 60 per cent of the population in the constituency. He managed to get the support of the Degodia and the minority clans by giving them positions in the local administration which, on the other hand, displeased the spiritual head of the Gurreh in Rhamu.

Table 11.1: The so-called clan arithmetics in North-Eastern Province

Constituency	Major Somali clan	Main sub-clans	Order of size (in %)	Main lineages in competition
Dujis	Darod (Ogaden)	Abdwak	+50	Rer Yahye Rer Harun
Lagdera	Darod (Ogaden)	Aulihan	+50	Mumin Rer Ali Rer Turade
		Abdalla	n.a.	Abokar Adan Hassan Adan
Fafi	Darod (Ogaden)	Abdalla	-25	n.a.
		Abdwak	+25	Rer Musa Rer Kassim Rer Yahye Rer Harun Guleid

Table 11.1 continued

				Mahat Daud
Ijara	Darod (Ogaden)	Abdalla	+50	Abokar Adan Hassan Adan Abdulkarim
Wajir North	Hawiye	Ajuran	80	Rer Mohamed Waqle Walamoge (Geelbaris & Garen)
		Degodia	10	n.a.
		Gurreh	10	n.a.
Wajir West	Hawiye	Degodia	80	Jibrail Rer Mohamed
Wajir East	Hawiye	Degodia	+50	Fai Massareh
Wajir South	Darod-Ogaden	Ogaden	90	Bah Geri Mohamed Zubeir Makabul
	Hawiye	Degodia	n.a.	n.a.
Mandera West	Hawiye	Gurreh	70	Tuf Kuranyo
		Degodia	n.a.	n.a.
Mandera Central	Hawiye	Gurreh	60	Tuf
Kuranyo		Degodia	30	n.a.
Mandera East	Hawiye	Gurreh	n.a.	Furkisha
		Degodia	n.a.	n.a.
		Murilleh	-40	Yabarsen Naabsoor
	n.a.	'Corner Tribes'	n.a.	n.a.

Source: *Daily Nation* 23/08/97: 22-23; 25/08/97: 25; 16/10/97: iv-v; 10/11/97: 26-27; 20/11/97: iv-v; *Weekly Review* 05/09/97: 12-18; 12/09/97: 13-17; 19/09/97: 15-20; *Economic Review* 25/08/97: 29-37.

This allegiance to lineages is not, of course, void of quarrels between individuals. It is possible to have two candidates from the same clan or the same family. For example, the Rer Yahye and Rer Harun of the Abdwak, an Ogaden clan in Garissa in the Dujis constituency. Or still, the Waqle and the Walimanga of the Ajuran, who dominate by 80 per cent, or the Fai and the

Massareh of the Degodia of Wajir East. Similarly, the Yabarsen and Naabsoor of the Murilleh, a Degodian clan which constitutes about 40 per cent of the Mandera East constituency since the Gurreh-dominated territories in El Wak and Kotulo were joined with Mandera Central in 1986.

In Lagdera the main Aulihan lineages have all managed to elect an MP, introducing a kind of rotation. Yet, in Wajir South, the Makabul did not respect the rule and re-elected a member of their lineage to the detriment of the other Ogaden in the constituency. The vote of the minority clans also proves quite influential: the Bah Geri decided between two predominant Ogaden lineages in Wajir South, the Mohamed Zubeir and the Makabul. In Mandera Central and Mandera West, the minority Degodia vote also determined the selection of an MP from the Gurreh majority. Eventually, it was the KANU logistics that made the difference between the candidates.

Opposition leaders find it difficult to enter this remote region and their local candidates are keen to be bribed in a poverty-ridden area. In 1992, North-Eastern Province registered the highest number of defections to KANU; 20 candidates rejoined the ruling party while four seats out of ten went unopposed during the elections. In 1997 two opposition candidates withdrew from the competition just a few days before the elections. In other words, the KANU primaries were crucial, perhaps even more so than the general elections. Many candidates joined the opposition only after losing the KANU primaries in a last resort bid to get elected.

Outside the North-Eastern Province the Somali are a minority, but in Eastern Province they constitute a contributive force that can be compared to the so-called 'Regabu' alliance, i.e., Rendille, the Gabbra and the Burji who front the Boran majority with the support of North Horr and Laisamis MPs Bonaya Godana and Robert Kochalle. In 1997, the Somali in Eastern Province sold their votes to the one who offered the most. Similarly, amongst the Boran in Isiolo North, the Degodia Somali clan, who came from Wajir, received from the local MP and KANU representative some rights to pasturelands, the recognition of three chiefs and the nomination of two municipal councillors. The Degodia vote, in spite of being small in the constituency, was all the more important to the KANU candidate, a Boran who had been elected with a lot of difficulties in 1992. The exercise had to be repeated four times and necessitated the consecutive deployment of three district commissioners in a few weeks. Confronted by the opposition of the Kiome (a Meru clan voting for the Democratic Party), this KANU candidate in Isiolo North had also to solicit the support of the Sakuye in exchange for his Boran clan votes (the Karayu) for the Isiolo South Sakuye candidate.

A façade of democracy?

By allowing KANU to divide the Somali and to patronise influential individuals, these alignments overshadowed any serious discussion on the pertinent problems facing the region: insecurity, drought, access to educational and health services, etc. The *baraza* convened by district commissioners are only for solving cases to do with clan issues, but do not allow the communities to follow up on their demands. While the Boran from the Eastern Province organised demonstrations in Nairobi in May 1997 to denounce the insecurity of which they were victims, the Somali took a low profile. And while the Meru businessmen of Isiolo (who were in the opposition) launched a campaign of civil disobedience in order to protest against fresh outbreaks of banditry, the Somali opted for self-defence, an attitude which is typical of them, and which cannot be compared with Boran rural vigilantes.

However, there exists a number of Somali grievances against a government which is accused of not protecting its citizens. The police, for instance, can be considered as conclusive evidence for this. For the North-Eastern Somali who remember the brutality that was used in the repression of the *shifta* secessionists (1963-67), the police are nothing but a foreign force of occupation in their land; and members of the community in Mbalambala can testify about how they were tortured recently (KHRC 1998). As for the colonial home guards, they continue to defend the chiefs installed by the government in places like Isiolo, Wajir and Lokichokio. The administration police has simply taken over the role that the British gave to the tribal police i.e., the protection of chiefs and, today, the protection of the big shots in KANU.

Given this sort of situation, the 1997 elections offered little else other than a façade of democracy. Only lobbies and clients could set out some clear demands. Hence, livestock owners in Mandera district lobbied their MPs for the construction of a giant abattoir that would help avoid transporting livestock to the slaughterhouses in Nairobi. In Garissa town, traders also criticised the incumbent Dujis MP, Maalim Mohamed, for failing to develop water facilities in an area where the Tana River passed and which was prone to severe periods of drought.

This kind of lobbying shows how poorly representative the elections could be. Most of the youth, the women, the destitute and the victims of drought vote according to the instructions of their elders. Whether belonging to KANU or Safina, all the 1997 MPs are wealthy members of the community: an insurance broker and a director of the National Housing Corporation in Wajir West, a district medical officer in Wajir North, two businessmen in Wajir East and South, a former teacher and district education officer in Fafi, a minister in Dujis, etc. Some of them are well-educated. The Fafi MP, Elias Shill, for example, got a scholarship to study at the University of London where he was the president of the African Students Union and the Wajir South MP Mohamed Abdi Afey is a graduate of Kenyatta University and was a leader of the North-Eastern Province University Students Association.

In the Kenyan context, one wonders if these elites can really be representatives of the masses. An analysis of the voter turnout tends to give negative answers. This is especially so considering that the 1997 elections were characterised by all sorts of malpractices: buying of votes, capitalisation on state monies by influential individuals, exclusion of the opposition and a doubtful legitimacy of the whole process. Since 1979, elections have been consistently rigged. Correspondingly, the turnout fell from more than 83 per cent in 1961 to less than 37 per cent in 1988 (Hornsby and Throup 1992). The North-Eastern Province's turnout, for instance, was only 37 per cent during the 1983 elections.

The 1992 elections, then, were different because of the introduction of multi-partyism. But the percentage of participation among the Somali and the Muslims at the Coast was still the lowest in the country: 51 per cent as compared to 81 per cent among the Kikuyu in Central Province. The fact that the mobilisation was a little better in 1997, with a turnout of about 55 per cent for the parliamentary and 56 per cent for the presidential elections, was due, to a certain extent, to the heavy rains of December, which forced the pastoralists to stay and vote in the constituencies where they had been registered. Yet, in Ijara and Wajir West, the helicopter in charge of collecting the votes could not land in some areas because of the floods.[7] Poor participation in the elections did benefit the ruling party in Mandera East where the discontented ones did not bother to vote. This is, nevertheless, symptomatic of the poor integration of the Somali in the political game.

A more detailed analysis further demonstrates that the voter turnout was seldom higher in the constituencies which recorded the tightest scores (see Table 11.2). This is especially true with regard to the opposition. Was it that the masses did not press for reforms or that they did not care? Or was it that the ruling party rigged the competition in such a way that the people did not believe in the process? Some facts are disturbing. First, the two constituencies that fell to the opposition in 1992, Lagdera and Mandera East, recorded the highest increase of registered voters in 1997. Second, by contrast, the two constituencies that fell to the opposition in 1997, Fafi and Wajir West, had recorded a negative or one of the lowest increases of registered voters, a possible counter-effect of some stuffing of neighbouring constituencies where KANU felt threatened. In Lagdera, for instance, the winners of the 1983, 1988 and 1992 contests had beaten their rivals by a margin of only a hundred votes. But in 1997, the number of registered voters in the constituency rose by 30 per cent and the KANU contender got almost two thousands votes more than his closest rival. Allegations have been made by the opposition that KANU was selling identity cards to Somali refugees in exchange for their vote.[8]

Table 11.2: Parliamentary voters turnout and winner's scores in North-Eastern Province (in per cent)

District	Constituency	Turnout in 1992	Winner's score (1992)	Turnout in (1992)	Winner's score (1997)	Increase of registered voters
Garissa	Dujis	40.8	86.1	60.07	61.7	10.5
	Lagdera	49.6	51.2	50.1	62.9	29.6
	Fafi	31.1	97.5	48.7	50.2	-17.3
	Ijara	36.4	96.1	70.1	54.8	-5.0
Wajir	Wajir North	n.a.	n.a.	53.6	99.2	n.a.
	Wajir West	60.9	51.2	54.0	50.8	4.7
	Wajir East	57.2	64.6	57.0	68.2	23.4
	Wajir South	52.8	65.3	43.3	51.7	32.4
Mandera						
	Mandera West	32.9	83.4	47.5	59.4	25.8
	Mandera Central	61.3	60.0	60.9	51.2	19.4
	Mandera East	64.7	53.6	47.5	64.8	32.7

Source: Author's tabulations from IED 1998

On the other hand, we need to mention the questions put towards the conduct of the count in the Fafi constituency, Garissa district. The current MP Elias Barre Shill of the Abdwak clan was running on a Safina ticket against the KANU candidate, Yussuf Issa Abdi, of the Abdalla clan. Ballot boxes from six polling stations were not counted although they were brought into the counting hall before the returning officer announced the result in which Shill won by only a 12 votes majority. It is said that four of the six polling stations that were not counted were strongholds of the KANU candidate. Protests from the KANU candidate were ignored and, since the counting hall was in Bura, the birth place and stronghold of Shill, the KANU candidate resorted to a court petition.

Once in parliament, Elias Shill seems to be in the opposition technically, but fully collaborates with the ruling party. As a result of his association with KANU, Shill, some claim, convinced the ruling party to withdraw its petition by prevailing upon its candidate. The case was withdrawn after a payment was made to the petitioner in the name of a cost refund.

There is still a long way to go before North-Eastern Province experiences some kind of electoral democracy. Mohamud Yussuf Haji, a member of the powerful Mohamed family in Garissa district, illustrates these difficulties. He took KANU to court in 1996, demanding that the party hold national elections, implying that the current apparatchiks were in office illegally. The 'Young Turk' angered his elder brother, Mohamed Yussuf Haji, the Rift Valley provincial commissioner, who is said to have summoned the rebel to his private residence in Nairobi and to have administered to him a number of lashes so that he could withdraw the suit. Back in Ijara, Mohamud Yussuf Haji had lost the support of the elders and got a total of three votes on behalf of Safina in 1997. At the same time, the 'old guard' managed a successful comeback with a veteran politician in Mandera West, Sayid Mohamed Amin. A younger brother of Mohamed Sheikh Ali, this MP was one of the first to be selected by the government in North-Eastern Province in 1964.

Conclusion

Elections in North-Eastern Province in 1997 did attest some improvements, especially when we compare the electoral process with the nomination system among the elders during the shifta state of emergency, when the population boycotted the one party's candidates. First of all, the push for reforms obliged KANU to nominate new faces on the political scene, e.g. six candidates out of the eleven in 1997. Moreover, the results confirm the notion that the big families' influence is waning. In Garissa district, the Mohamed family lost Fafi constituency in 1997 after it had lost Lagdera constituency in 1992. In Wajir South, the Ogle brother who defected to DP could not win while Ahmed Khalif was not re-elected in Wajir West. Last but not least, it was the first time that some women contested elections in North-Eastern, i.e., in Ijara, Wajir East and Mandera Central. Local pundits were quite confident that the youth were tired of the politics of patronage and were demanding a change of guard.

Still, 1997 was only a preliminary step in this regard. One of the main obstacles to reform comes from the government itself. More than Kenyatta, President Moi has to rely on Somali support especially as a result of the introduction of the multi-party elections in 1992. A new rule for these elections made it compulsory for the presidential candidates to get at least 25 per cent of the votes in five out of eight provinces. This emphasised the importance of the north-eastern region and explains why the Somali are part of the regime, yet remain poorly integrated in the political game on a national scale. KANU patronage in North-Eastern Province entertains clienteles and reinforces the power of the elites. The segmentation of the Somali society into clans and lineages is also of importance since it does not help to counter the manipulation of the periphery by the centre, especially if we take into account the remoteness of the province, its lack of good communications, its underdevelopment and its low education standards.

Power struggles existed during the KANU nominations but not so much during the elections. Despite the impressive results of Safina which won two seats (Fafi and Wajir West) and which followed KANU very closely in four other constituencies, the opposition overall did not represent a viable alternative. As long as the opposition contenders are only KANU 'leftovers' and the voters mobilise to pay a tribute rather than to defend political issues, the elections will not centre on real divergent political ideas.

Notes

1. I wish to thank Abdi Nunow, Nathalie Gomes and the editors of this volume for their critical review of this chapter.
2. Researchers have explained this paradox by describing KANU as a vague 'federation of local powers that are relatively autonomous . . . The minority ethnic groups are therefore not doomed to disappear as a result of being marginalised by the majority tribes. It suffices for them to affirm their control on a part of the periphery through a political machinery so that the Government is obliged to recognize their existence' (Bourmaud 1988: 102)
3. In English, the word Somali refers to either a nationality or an ethnic group. This is a source of confusion in that some 'ethnic' Somali in Kenya are Kenyan whereas others are refugees from Somalia who do not belong to Somali lineages (e.g the Bantu of Shebelle River). By analogy with French usage, the latter would be described as 'Somalian' and the use of 's' in the plural should be reserved for Somali nationals.
4. Unlike the Somali, the Boran, who lived right on the front line, were the most affected since they could not keep their cattle in safety on the other side of the border. The Boran lost up to 90 per cent of their cattle and were put in camps under the protection of the army (Hogg 1987:53). As for the Sakuye of Marsabit and Waso River in Isiolo district, they were suspected to betray both the government troops and the Somali rebels. They lost their cattle in the camps in which they were concentrated by the army and some of them were victims of the Boran militia's attacks (Schlee 1994:19).
5. In the mid-80s, the authorities tried to relocate them to the suburb of Amalemba. Today, they would rather like to move them to the Kakamega forest where the municipal council has a project . . . which is to build a cemetery (*Daily Nation* 01/02/97).
6. In 1998, it was a Muslim Boran from Isiolo district, General Aden Abdullahi, who became chief of army staff, another symbol of the northern support to the regime.
7. Communication N. Gomes.
8. Theoretically, the Foreign Investment Act and the Domicile Act give foreigners residential rights, but not citizenship. The clandestine Somali does not have the political refugee status of Ancient Greece, which was placed between the foreigner and the citizen (Balogh 1943:95).

References

Adar, K.G. 1994, *Kenyan Foreign Policy Behaviour towards Somalia, 1963-1983*, Lanham (Maryland): University Press of America.

Asiwaju, A.I. (ed.) 1985, *Partitioned Africans: Ethnic Relations Across Africa's International Boundaries, 1884-1984*, New York: St. Martins Press.

Balogh, E. 1943, *Political Refugees in Ancient Greece*, Johannesburg: Witwatersrand Press

Baxter, P.T.W. 1966, 'Acceptance and Rejection of Islam among the Boran of the NFD of Kenya', in Lewis, I.M. (ed.), *Islam in Tropical Africa*, London: International African Institute: 232-52.

Bourmaud, D. 1988, *Histoire Politique du Kenya*, Paris: Karthala.

Drysdale, J.W.S. 1964, *The Somali Dispute*, London: Pall Mall Press.

Fitzgibbon, L. 1982, *The Betrayal of the Somalis*, London: Rex Collings.

Gomes, N. 1995, 'Les revers de fortune des Ajuran', *IFRA Nairobi Newsletter* 3 (1): 9-13.

Gomes, N. 1997, 'Bandits du Nord Kenya: les contradictions d'une revendication politique', *Les Cahiers de l'IFRA*, No.4, 29-70.

Hogg, R.S. 1987, 'Development in Kenya: Drought, Desertification and Food Scarcity', *African Affairs* Vol.86, No.342: 47-58.

Hornsby, C. and Throup, D. 1992, 'Elections and Political Change in Kenya', *Journal of Commonwealth and Comparative Politics* Vol.30, No.2: 172-99.

Hoskyns, C. 1969, Case Studies in African Diplomacy: *The Ethiopia-Somali-Kenya Dispute 1960-1967*, (Institute of Public Administration, Vol.2), Dar es Salaam: Oxford University Press.

Jardine, D. 1923, *The Mad Mullah of Somaliland*, London: Herbert Jenkins.

KHRC 1998, *Where Terror Rules. Torture by Kenyan Police in North Eastern Kenya*, Nairobi: Kenya Human Rights Commission.

Lewis, I.M. 1963, 'Pan-Africanism and Pan-Somalism' *The Journal of Modern African Studies* 1 (2): 147-61.

Lonsdale, J. and Berman, B.J. 1992, *Unhappy Valley: Conflict in Kenya and Africa*, Oxford: James Currey.

Musambayi, C.I. 1995, The Politics of Regime Consolidation and Entrenchment. Moi's Foreign Policy, 1978-1994, *Working Paper* No.23, Nairobi: IFRA (French Institute for Research in Africa).

Révoil, G. 1880, *Voyage au cap des Aromates*, Paris: E. Dentu.

Rutten, M.M.E.M. 1992, *Selling Wealth to Buy Poverty - The Process of Individualization of Landownership Among the Maasai Pastoralists in Kajiado District Kenya, 1890-1990*, NICCOS, Saarbrücken-Fort Lauderdale: Verlag Breitenbach Publishers.

Schlee, G. 1994, *Identities on the move. Clanship and Pastoralism in Northeastern Kenya*, Manchester University Press.

Throup, D. and Hornsby, C. 1998, *Multi-Party Politics in Kenya. The Kenyatta & Moi States & the Triumph of the System in the 1992 Election*, Oxford: James Currey.

Touval, S. 1963, *Somali Nationalism*, Cambridge (Mass.): Harvard University Press.

Turton, E.R. 1972, 'Somali Resistance to Colonial Rule and the Development of Somali Political Activity in Kenya, 1893-1960', *Journal of African History* 13 (1): 117-43.

Turton, E.R. 1974, 'The Isaq Somali Diaspora and Poll Tax Agitation in Kenya, 1936-1941', *African Affairs* Vol.73, No.292: 325-46.

12

Breaking the 'Ngilu Wave': The 1997 Elections in Ukambani

François Grignon

For 35 years the Ukambani area (See map on p. 182) had not experienced a political excitement equal to what happened during the 1997 election campaign. For the first time since independence, when former detainee and radical anti-colonial leader Paul Ngei led the African People's Party (APP) against the Kenya African National Union (KANU), a Kamba leader was claiming national leadership, challenging both the ruling regime establishment and the main opposition parties. In Kitui Central, home of Charity Kaluki Ngilu, the first Kenyan woman to have declared herself presidential candidate, the local people could not stop thinking of the goods that their Kamba daughter would soon deliver: jobs, tarmacked roads, health and educational facilities were going to mushroom in the district, and its residents would not even be able to harvest all of it.

The presidential candidature of Charity Kaluki Ngilu, launched in June 1997, was indeed a surprise and one of the main attractions of the 1997 general elections. Ngilu was not only the first Kenyan and African woman to vie for the position of president, she definitely rocked the boat of Kenyan politics, symbolising to the extreme the need for political change that the unsatisfactory 1991-92 democratisation process had started. Indeed, Charity Ngilu embodied a wave of mobilisation and hope which went very far beyond the aspiration of her fellow Kamba to receive finally the *matunda ya uhuru* (the fruits of independence), that they never really enjoyed. Charity Ngilu wanted to represent a different way for Kenyan politics, and her personal background could easily lead to the belief that her candidature was different.

She carried the slogan that it was 'time to vote for a change'. This promise apparently was welcomed by other Kenyans as well. Ngilu does not belong to the ruling establishment. She does not come from a family of colonial chiefs, like so many leaders of the Kenyatta regime, or to one of the networks of the landed gentry. She is a self-made businesswoman who came very recently to politics and, therefore, does not bear the load of being associated with the Moi regime either.[1]

Charity Ngilu was elected at her first attempt in 1992 on a DP ticket, when she surprisingly ousted a former KANU cabinet minister, George Ndotto, to conquer the Kitui Central parliamentary seat. She had a difficult first term, suffering a lot from the harassment of the police and the abuse of the provincial administration. Yet, her tough stand and resistance to KANU's attempt to undermine her and then to compromise her to defect to the ruling party, gave her a solid reputation of an unbreakable political leader. She seemed moreover less interested in her own advancement or enrichment than in the welfare of her constituents, whom she helped through the financing of the Tungutu-Ithookwe water project and the donations she made to local schools, dispensaries and other self-help projects.[2] In other words, Charity Ngilu appeared as if she could combine the qualities of a new kind of leadership. She was not the product of the corrupt and flawed system that has characterised the country since independence. She seemed hardworking, determined, successful and to a great extent; she was the fresh face that the country desperately needed. Being a woman, her candidature, moreover, embodied the image of a different Kenya for the middle classes and the international community: progressive, non-violent and clean. As a Kamba, who form the fifth ethnic group of the country, she did not bear the load of the prejudices attached to Kikuyu, Luo or Kalenjin/Maasai leadership (greed, arrogance, violence). Being neither a dominant nor a marginalised ethnic group and living on the coffee growing highlands as well as in the semi-arid lowlands, the Kamba, 11 per cent of the population of the country, could articulate at the same time the expectations of accumulation of the cash crop growers as the demands of equal redistribution from the less favoured cattle-grazing populations. In other words, the 'Ngilu wave' was less the result of Charity Ngilu's own work than the crystallisation of very many different kinds of aspirations, coming as much from the Kamba, as from the urban youth and from the Kenyan middle class or even from the international community.

Yet, the historical trajectory of Kenya is such that there is no other politics than local. In order to become a national leader, a politician has first to win the support of his/her home area, then district and finally his or her people. The Kenyan polity is a complex system of interlocking political arenas where it becomes almost impossible to envisage a national career if you have not guaranteed first the support of your own backyard (see Grignon 1997). Therefore, despite the media frenzy that crowned Charity Ngilu's presidential bid, everything was going to be decided first of all in Ukambani, where KANU concentrated all its efforts to undermine systematically the 'Ngilu wave'. As in other parts of Kenya, politics in Ukambani under the old one-party system had been run by a number of 'big men' who not only could never imagine being led by a woman, but often based their political clout on the mobilisation of women's groups to their own benefit.

In the mostly semi-arid districts of Machakos, Makueni, Mwingi and Kitui, women's groups are the arms and economic lungs of rural development. They grow the food crops, harvest the cash crops, fetch water and firewood, keep the homesteads alive and send their children to school while their husbands work in towns, in the local markets or beat the pavement as their fathers-in-law drink the traditional brews. Organised on a neighbourhood, parish or sub-locational basis, following a social organisation of self-help called *miethya*, women often join forces to build benches and terraces, grow and sell tree-seedlings, make sisal bags and fetch firewood in order to generate the little income that will keep the homestead going (for more details see Hill 1991; Thomas-Slayter 1991; Asamba and Thomas-Slayter 1995). These women's groups, as well as the exclusive senior-male clan associations, which intervene in the daily resolution of land and inheritance conflicts and in any other matter of customary law, are the common mobilisation targets of politicians. Paul Ngei, one of the Kamba independence leaders, had created *Mbai Sya Eitu* (the women's clan) in Machakos district in the 1960s, an army of women's groups organised on clan lines which he protected against male clan associations and which, in return, gave him years of staunch support (Mutiso 1975). Banned in 1971, *Mbai Sya Eitu* was dissolved. However, the provincial administration and the New Akamba Union (NAU), a welfare association which had become the umbrella of all clan associations at independence, promoted the rebuilding of thousands of women's groups, this time to stay under strict male control. They were allowed to be organised on sub-locational or neighbourhood basis only and had to be registered with the chief's office. Women, who form up to 70 per cent of the rural electorate, are henceforth the regular target of food and money distributions in Ukambani as they provide a guaranteed source of electoral support.

Indeed, in the semi-capitalist environment of rural Ukambani, the moral economy of political leadership is still often based on the provision of food and welfare, as well as a good reputation, free from any sign of involvement with the forces of witchcraft. In Kenya, a good politician is often rated according to the amount of money he or she delivers during *harambee* meetings and the number of jobs made accessible to the constituents. If these goods are not delivered, one's re-election is jeopardised. Quantitative factors are henceforth believed to be the *ultima ratio* in understanding why, if not for rigging, a politician lost or won an election. An anthropological perspective, following James S. Scott's study on the moral economy of the peasant in South-East Asia (Scott 1976), would add that the politician is expected by the voters to 'deliver the goods' because it is his or her duty as a leader.

Representations on the legitimacy of leadership in pre-capitalist societies often require that the leader or the ruler is a provider, and more generally a food provider. Moreover, in Ukambani, to take food or money from a leader is a commitment that cannot be reversed on election day. 'Kula kwa KANU na kura kwa FORD' (Eat from KANU but vote for FORD), was one of the most popular slogans of the 1992 elections in the urban areas. Yet this disruption of the logic of political exchange is hardly conceivable for many rural voters. The moral economy of rural communities is such that they are faithful to those leaders who provide goods and services. To receive food implies a moral commitment that would not be the same in the semi-urban or urban context, where crowds often display very volatile political behaviour. In rural areas, however, where the market economy has not yet fully taken over the logic of pre-capitalist social exchange, the acceptance of food or money is a moral contract which ties the parties together. In this setting, handing out food or money, sometimes described as vote buying, takes another dimension. Contrary to what the democratic theory implies, the vote is not conceived as the expression of a rational choice independent from its social context. The vote is the confirmation of a commitment which was made earlier and, especially for rural women, this commitment cannot be easily challenged.

This is part of the equation Charity Ngilu had to deal with when she launched her presidential bid in June 1997. Before presenting how she tried to resolve it, we still have to recall briefly the shape that politics have taken in Ukambani since independence, and especially elaborate how the developments since the 1992 multi-party elections created the 'Ngilu wave'.

An outline of politics in Ukambani (1963-97)

Post-war anti-colonial politics in Ukambani took off at the end of the 1950s (for a detailed analysis see Grignon 1997). Prior to the re-authorisation of party politics by the colonial administration in 1955, in preparation for the multi-racial elections scheduled in the Lyttelton Constitution, very few Kamba had been involved in anti-colonial activities and even fewer in the Mau Mau uprising. The majority of the Kamba stayed loyal to the British Crown, even though they had been heavily involved in the Second World War fighting, during which many soldiers travelled abroad and were exposed to Asian and Middle-East emancipation mobilisations. Many were members of the armed forces and of the police, and even more took part in the war against Mau Mau than actually supported it. The Kamba Committee of the Mau Mau Central Organisation mobilised only railway workers and members of the unions led by Fred Kubai and Bildad Kaggia, a handful of urban dwellers who barely managed to get the support of the squatters and employees working in the ranches and coffee estates of Koma Rock, Lukenya and Kilima Mbogo, on the south-eastern part of the Thika 'whites-only' district. Paul Joseph Ngei, the Kamba political activist of the Kenya African Union (KAU), who was arrested together with Fred Kubai, Bildad Kaggia, Kungu Karumba and Jomo Kenyatta for organising Mau Mau, was not even a member of the Mau Mau Nairobi

Kamba committee. He stayed nine years in prison on flimsy grounds, but benefited politically greatly from his jailing.

Post-colonial politics in Ukambani

In 1961, the Kamba enthroned Paul Ngei their natural historical leader. One year later Ngei formed the African People's Party (APP) after being denied any leadership position within KANU or at the Lancaster House independence conference talks. His radical stance on land issues and his oversized ego could not be taken any more by Jomo Kenyatta and Tom Mboya. The APP frenzy took Ngei to parliament together with seven other Kamba MPs. This, however, lasted less than 15 months since Ngei was quickly offered a cabinet position after which he dissolved the party just before independence. As a result, Ukambani was kept at the periphery of national politics.

Within KANU, Paul Ngei never really managed to achieve his national ambitions. He was outsmarted by Tom Mboya during the 1960s and he became a victim of his own excesses. In 1969, after the Kisumu crisis when Jomo Kenyatta was roughed up by Oginga Odinga's KPU supporters, Ngei organised an extensive oathing campaign in Ukambani, forcing the population to swear their allegiance to the person of Jomo Kenyatta and his heir or suffer the wrath of the *kithitu* (traditional oath).[3] This bought him a passport to wealth and influence.

He became the deputy leader of government business in parliament and a close friend to Mama Ngina Kenyatta. After the 1974 general elections, Ngei was convicted of an electoral offence. He had threatened and abused one of his opponents. He was lost from his parliamentary seat and his cabinet position. But just before the subsequent by-election could be organised, parliament passed a constitutional amendment allowing the president to pardon electoral offenders. Ngei was pardoned and he vied for his Kangundo seat, which he won once again against his eternal rival, schoolmate and former friend, Henry Mulli.

But Ngei was never really enthroned as the uncontested spokesman of the Kamba, nor supported by the leaders of Machakos and Kitui districts, support which would have allowed him to vie for real positions of power at national level. During the 1960s, he had found on his way the 'Mboya boys' (Henry Mulli and William Mbolu Malu) in Machakos and Ngala Mwendwa in Kitui. Over the 1970s, his involvement in the clove scandal[14] of 1973, which cost several Kenyans their lives, his perennial womanising habits as well as his erratic and often violent behaviour never allowed him to rise to national leadership. Moreover, his position as spokesman for the 'change-the constitution-movement' soon thereafter put an end to his national career as the Vice-President Daniel arap Moi managed to stand firm in his chair and to ultimately became the second president of Kenya.

From 1978, Mulu Mutisya, the illiterate chairman of NAU, who had been nominated to parliament in 1969, became the official spokesman of the Kamba people within KANU. He was often allied to highly educated Kitui leaders, such as Kitili Mwendwa, the former chief justice, who died in a road accident in 1985, and Stephen Kalonzo Musyoka, a young advocate from Mwingi North who rose from the post of deputy speaker in parliament to minister for foreign affairs in 1992. As leader of NAU since 1964, Mulu Mutisya, a curio businessman from Wamunyu, in Machakos district, had become a kingmaker thanks to the financial clout of his welfare organisation. As early as 1969, potential parliamentary candidates in Ukambani were fighting to get the endorsement of NAU and to benefit from its development projects and harambee contributions. As the umbrella of all Kamba clan associations, NAU offered opportunities of electoral mobilisation that proved useful on election day. Nominated to parliament in 1969 as the representative of his ethnic association, Mulu Mutisya watched carefully the 'change-the-constitution-movement' and benefited directly from its failure. An executive from the KANU-Nairobi branch till then, he moved to Machakos in 1978 and, finally, managed to unseat Ngei in 1985 as he was elected chairman of the Machakos KANU branch.

Never has the control of Mulu Mutisya on Machakos politics and his influence on the other side of the Athi River in Kitui been seriously challenged from then on till 1992. Those who tried like former chief of general staff, Jackson Mulinge, or the youthful publisher elected MP for Mbooni in 1988, Johnstone Makau, soon learnt that Mulu Mutisya, *Ithe wa akamba*, (the father of the Akamba, his nickname), could not be easily unseated. A master orator in Kikamba and a generous donor to all women's groups of Machakos district, Mulu Mutisya knew how to use the former NAU networks to keep the support of the rural population, even though he kept the Kamba profile very low on the national scene. He kept it as a peripheral force which had never been able to rise to the much envied vice-presidency, let alone the presidency[6]. Mulu Mutisya owed his political success precisely to his limited capacities and ambitions. A king-maker in his own backyard, he could never threaten Daniel arap Moi or his close partners and would prove to be a useful ally in choosing and taming other Kamba leaders.

The return to multi-partyism and the 1992 general elections

With the exception of George Nthenge, a former Iveti MP allied to Martin Shikuku and Kenneth Matiba, the Kamba political elites were almost absent from the mobilisation for the return to multi-party politics. And since they were not observers of the battles that were taking place in the columns of the daily and weekly newspapers, and on the streets of Nairobi, they were staunch defenders of KANU and the Moi regime from which they were benefiting. Stephen Kalonzo Musyoka, who had been elected KANU national organising secretary and deputy speaker in parliament in 1988, after he had kept his seat of Kitui North, was one of the front runners of this group, systematically defending the government in the press.

It is only after the repeal of section 2(A) of the constitution, legalising opposition parties, that a number of frustrated former KANU MPs started to defect. Most joined the Democratic Party of Mwai Kibaki: Kyale Mwendwa, unseated by his sister-in-law Nyiva Mwendwa in Kitui West in 1988; Josephat Mulyungi, the perennial and unsuccessful opponent of Kalonzo Musyoka in Kitui North; Joseph Konzollo Munyao, another frustrated KANU leader who had been victim of Mulu Mutisya's schemes in his Mwala constituency in 1988; Jonesmus Kikuyu, an ally of Paul Ngei, in the cold since his public dismissal of President Moi's leadership in 1984; Frederick Kalulu, a former MP for Mbooni, convicted of an electoral offence in 1974, pardoned by Daniel arap Moi but a victim of Johnstone Makau's rising star in 1988; Paul Sumbi, another former MP for Makueni and former ally of Paul Ngei who had suffered from Mulu Mutisya's hostility and Agnes Ndetei, elected on a KANU ticket in 1988. She was a declared opponent of Mulu Mutisya; since she made public the Masongaleni Settlement Scheme scandal in 1990, revealing with her colleague from Makueni, Johnstone Makau, that the chairman of the KANU Machakos branch had grabbed for himself and his cronies hundreds of acres of land originally devoted to the resettlement of squatters in her Kibwezi constituency.

Mutisya managed thereafter to have Ndetei removed from the chairmanship of the Makueni KANU branch, and had Makau sacked from the cabinet. Kennedy Kiliku, the incumbent MP of the Mombasa Kamba-dominated constituency of Changamwe, had also joined the DP after the publication of his parliamentary reports on ethnic clashes, directly incriminating Daniel arap Moi's closest allies, Nicholas Biwott and the Vice-President George Saitoti.

Like the other parties, and notably the FORD-Asili which was capable of aligning candidates in almost all Kamba constituencies in 1992, the DP had attracted a number of newcomers, mostly independent businessmen who seized this opportunity of the opening of the political field to offer their professional experience to the benefits of their constituents: there was Joseph Mulusya in Kangundo, a quantity surveyor, land acquisition consultant and owner of the Buru Buru-based Wab Hotel in Nairobi; Jimmy Muthusi Kitonga in Mutito, a lawyer who was one of the sons of the late Chief Kitonga who had held the seat throughout the 1960s and 1970s; and of course Charity Ngilu. The DP had, therefore, managed to align a fairly strong opposition team in Ukambani and was expected to give KANU a very strong challenge even though it had itself managed to recruit new blood (Peter Kavisi in Mwala, Peter Maundu in

Makueni, Tony Ndilinge in the new constituency of Kilome). KANU had also managed to field some very strong candidates, such as (Rt.) Gen. Jackson Mulinge in the newly created constituency of Kathiani, (Rt.) Col. Ronald Kiluta in Masinga, former permanent secretary John Kyalo in Machakos Town, and veteran politician Gideon Mutiso in Yatta. Johnstone Makau, frustrated by Mulu Mutisya who had sidelined him in Mbooni, had quit KANU in July 1992 to create the Social Democratic Party, but after a few months in opposition and some promises about his ministerial future, he was back to KANU to lead the fight in the newly created Makueni district.

The 1992 elections in Ukambani were probably some of the most heavily rigged in the country. Needing his 25 per cent vote in Eastern Province, Daniel arap Moi could not let Ukambani go to Mwai Kibaki. Vote-buying was rampant. Set up in December, the general elections came up at a time when drought-induced famine was threatening. The short rains of October had failed to come. In Machakos, William Kivuvani, the director of intelligence, and Philip Kilonzo, the commissioner of police, were the chief distributors of relief food and campaigners for KANU. Philip Mbithi, head of civil service, had dispatched junior civil servants to campaign for KANU and threatened to have them sacked if the party did not win in their areas.[7] In October 1992, Mulu Mutisya, the Machakos KANU branch chairman, organised a huge *harambee* in the town's stadium. All the leaders of all the women's groups of the district were convened and given money and blankets so that each of their members got at least Ksh. 20.[8]

In their extensive investigation on the 1992 general elections, David Throup and Charles Hornsby delivered a damning analysis on KANU's rigging in Ukambani. If KANU ended up winning 12 of the 15 Kamba seats (Agnes Ndetei's Kibwezi, Charity Ngilu's Kitui Central and Joseph Mulusya's Kangundo went to the DP), there were 'extensive electoral abuses' in at least ten of them (Throup and Hornsby 1998:505). In Machakos Town, there were reports of KANU buying votes on election day. At one station people voted without ID cards and ballot boxes arrived with marking anomalies. In Mwala, for example, DP agents claimed that a ballot box had arrived open and DP lost the parliamentary seat despite having an 11 per cent margin in the presidential vote. In Yatta, DP alleged that KANU agents were counting votes, some boxes were only accompanied by KANU agents and there was organised oathing in support of the KANU candidate, Gideon Mutiso. Kilome, Mbooni, Makueni and Kitui West KANU victories looked equally fraudulent as in Mutito and Mutomo, where Mwai Kibaki surprisingly won the presidential elections against Daniel arap Moi but the DP lost the parliamentary seat (Throup and Hornsby 1998: 506-07). As the two analysts put it: 'the major question is whether KANU's Eastern Province results were inflated to bring the President over the 25 percent hurdle'. In Kitui North alone, the presidential results were probably inflated by more than 11,000 votes for Daniel arap Moi.

Through direct rigging and vote buying, KANU therefore managed to steal at least seven seats from the DP in Ukambani and might have inflated President Moi's results by 70,000 to 90,000 votes, almost half of the margin he had on his closest opponent, Kenneth Matiba, and more than enough to make him pass the 25 per cent level of votes in Eastern Province. With such a performance, the Kamba KANU leaders were in a good position to negotiate their share of the national wealth and claim a determinant role in the succession battle that was soon going to take place after the elections.

1993-97: Chasing the vice-presidency

With 12 MPs out of 15 seats, the Kamba legislators formed the second largest KANU parliamentary group after the Kalenjin's and were rewarded with four cabinet posts. Kalonzo Musyoka (Mwingi) became minister for Foreign Affairs; Gen. Jackson Mulinge (Rtd) (Kathiani) was chosen as the minister for Land Reclamation, Regional and Water Development; Johnstone Makau (Mbooni) got the Ministry of Information and Broadcasting, and John Kyalo (Machakos Town) was given the Ministry for Energy, under the unofficial control of Nicholas Biwott and its long-time aide, the ministry's permanent secretary, Crispus Mutitu. The Kamba MPs were also rewarded with three assistant ministers' positions: Agriculture, Livestock and Marketing (Peter Maundu, Makueni), Health (Gideon Mutiso, Yatta) and Public Works and Housing (Nyiva Mwendwa, Kitui West). The Kamba elites seemed never to have had so much influence on the destiny of the country since they also held a number of key civil service positions including its head and secretary to the cabinet (Prof. Philip Mbithi), the commissioner of police (Philip Kilonzo), the director of intelligence (William Kivuvani), the director of education (Sammy Kyungu) and the head of immigration (Frank Kwinga).[6]

Moreover by mid-February 1993, the political scene in Machakos district seemed to change dramatically. Mulu Mutisya was asked by President Moi himself to retire and give way to younger leaders. This dismissal of an old ally came up concurrently with the organisation of a meeting in Kitengela, Kajiado district where Jackson Mulinge and Johnstone Makau joined Vice-President George Saitoti to celebrate a newly created alliance of Maasai and Kamba leaders to promote the interests of KANU against the opposition. The infamous 'Kitengela Declaration' implied that Maasailand and Ukambani should be 'opposition-free zones', where DP, FORD-Kenya and FORD-Asili supporters (read Kikuyu, Luo and Luhya) would be hunted and chased away if necessary as had been done in Molo (Nakuru district) and as was going to take place in Enoosupukia (Narok district). Mulu Mutisya was believed by the KANU hawks to be too old a politician to successfully resist the opposition breakthrough in Ukambani and had to be replaced by a new breed of more abrasive and outspoken leaders. Behind this crude move, analysts also read the influence of Philip Mbithi, the influential head of the civil service and the real brain and strategist of a group devoted to the advancement of former chief of general staff Jackson Mulinge, but which could have supported, later on, his own vice-presidential ambitions.

Some signals of Mulu Mutisya's dismissal had already been sent right after the elections. Mutisya had not been re-nominated to parliament as had been the case continuously since 1969. Soon after Daniel arap Moi's request, the 64-year-old Jackson Mulinge was enthroned by his fellow MPs at a Kitui meeting as the new spokesman of the Akamba, seconded by the newly elected MP for Masinga, Col. Ronald Kiluta (Rtd) and the long-serving MP for Yatta, Gideon Mutiso. Mutisya was rewarded for his long service with a directorship at the Kenya Power and Lighting Company and chairmanship of the Presidential Commission on Soil Conservation and Afforestation (*Weekly Review* 26/02/93). The elections which were to take place soon thereafter at the Machakos KANU branch were supposed to confirm this change of leadership.

Yet, the ageing Mutisya could not accept his eviction from active politics. When the KANU Machakos branch delegates voted to choose their new chairman, Mutisya's supporters threw their weight behind an outsider, Henry Mulli, former chairman of the Co-operative Bank of Kenya who managed to beat Mulinge. In Makueni, Mutisya also managed to check Johnstone Makau's rise to power by supporting the acting branch chairman, Kasanga Mulwa, a lawyer and former MP (*Weekly Review* 13/08/93). Kitui, Machakos and Makueni KANU branches were, henceforth, led by politicians without any government posts whereas the cabinet members from the districts had failed to conquer the party local leadership positions. This resistance of the rank and file of the party in support of the former NAU chairman was not dismissed by the KANU headquarters. Daniel arap Moi himself came again to Machakos in October 1993 to confirm that he would not impose Jackson Mulinge or Johnstone Makau on the local branches of the party and dismissed rumours of the organisation of fresh KANU elections (*Weekly Review* 22/10/93).

Moreover, Mulu Mutisya could argue that he had listened to the president's call. He had managed to surround himself with the newly-elected and youngest elements of the party and his opponents now looked like the old guard. On one side, the Mulinge group included MPs John Kyalo (Machakos Town) and Gideon Mutiso (Yatta) from Machakos, Johnstone Makau (Mbooni) from Makueni, Nyiva Mwendwa (Kitui West) as well as George Ndotto (KANU branch chairman) from Kitui, and behind the scenes, the influential Philip Mbithi, head of the civil service. On the other side, the Mutisya group included

Kalonzo Musyoka (Mwingi), Isaac Muoki (Kitui South) and Mutinda Ndambuki (Mutito) from Kitui, newly elected Tony Ndilinge (Kilome) and Peter Maundu (Makueni) and Ronald Kiluta (Masinga) and Peter Kavisi (Mwala) from Machakos. With the exception of their leader, the Mutisya group members were barely 45 years old, but united the new breed of KANU MPs whereas behind Jackson Mulinge had rallied the more experienced and educated leaders who already had mandates in the 1970s or the early 1980s. Both camps were fighting to take over the local party apparatus and prompt up a possible candidate for the vice-presidency: Jackson Mulinge or Philip Mbithi on one side and Kalonzo Musyoka, on the other.

By the end of June 1994, Mulu Mutisya had again taken over the Machakos KANU branch chairmanship against an embattled Henry Mulli, this time supported by Jackson Mulinge, with Ronald Kiluta as his branch secretary (*Weekly Review* 01/07/94). Jonstone Muthama, a gemstone trader and vice-chairman of the International Gemstone Association, financier of most Machakos KANU parliamentary candidates allied to Mutisya, also came to the forefront of the district politics by being elected to the chairmanship, but the Mulinge camp did not disarm despite these initial setbacks. Indeed, after the death of John Kyalo, a Mulinge crony, Alphonse Musyoki, won the subsequent Machakos Town by-election in June 1995. One of its Kitui members, Nyiva Mwendwa, was one month later elevated to a cabinet position, the first woman to achieve this position in the country.

Yet, in January 1996, the Mutisya group finally took over. Kalonzo Musyoka became the party's national organising secretary as well as minister for Foreign Affairs. Branch elections were called in Kitui and Makueni districts. The Makueni KANU chairmanship was won by Tony Ndilinge against Johnstone Makau. Once she agreed to bury the hatchet with the minister for Foreign Affairs, Nyiva Mwendwa was also given the Kitui leadership to the detriment of an embattled George Ndotto.

Two months later, systematic attempts to dismantle the DP's encroachment in Ukambani also started to bear fruits. Tony Ndilinge engineered Agnes Ndetei's defection from DP back to KANU. After her success in the following by-election, she was appointed assistant-minister for Education. Almost at the same time, the Mulinge group suffered a heavy blow when Philip Mbithi was unceremoniously sacked from his position as head of the civil service and permanent secretary in the Office of the President.

With the appointment of Agnes Ndetei to the government, KANU seemed to have finally regained the influence conceded to the DP. After two years of systematic police and administrative harassment of the opposition MPs, from which Charity Ngilu particularly suffered (*Weekly Review* 17/09/93), KANU's tactics became more divisive than confrontational, banking on the DP's incapacity to satisfy its non-Kikuyu leaders. Divisions among the DP members had started soon after the 1992 general elections. The increasing influence of the former Gikuyu, Embu, Meru, Association (GEMA) establishment on the party affairs was heavily contested by its non-Kikuyu elements. In October 1993, despite a fairly wide distribution of the National Executive Council's positions, (Joseph Munyao was re-instated as deputy secretary general, Agnes Ndetei as second national vice-chair person and Charity Ngilu the party secretary for health), Kennedy Kiliku (Changamwe) joined Joseph Mulusya (Kangundo) and 12 other Kamba KANU MPs to warn against a possible revival of GEMA and the reformation of a parallel Akamba Union led by the DP deputy secretary general, Joseph Munyao. Charity Ngilu (Kitui Central) had also previously threatened to quit the party if it was to become a GEMA affair (*Weekly Review* 15/10/93). The KANU confrontational stance following the 'Kitengela Declaration' had contributed to uniting the DP MPs and making them stick to the opposition. But after almost two years of total inactivity by Mwai Kibaki and his failure to tame the collaborative tendencies of Njenga Karume who, on his own, led the GEMA-KAMATUSA talks with Nicholas Biwott in 1995 (see Peter Mwangi's contribution in this volume), as well as the ambitions of Ngengi Muigai, one of Kenyatta's nephews, to take over the party, the chairman's main non-Kikuyu allies started to let him down. Before Agnes Ndetei, John Keen, secretary general of DP, had defected back to the ruling party and the idea that 'nothing can be gained by collaborating with the Kikuyus. They will never relinquish the front seats', systematically hammered by KANU in Ukambani, started to take its toll. Soon after Ndetei's defection, rumours were rife that Kennedy Kiliku, Joseph Mulusya and Charity Ngilu would soon come back to the ruling party, where the Kamba had more to gain, especially if Kalonzo Musyoka got the vice-presidency (*Weekly Review* 23/02/96).

Over the 1993-97 period, KANU's preoccupation in Ukambani was not only directed towards harassing or luring the opposition politicians to defect to the government's side. Soon after the general elections a very systematic policy of punishment was set up towards the opposition electorate. In Machakos, locational and sub-locational administrative boundaries were systematically redrawn to carve the opposition's voting areas out of their KANU-dominated counterparts and channel development funds only to the latter. Rural electrification, dam building and road maintenance were organised only in the areas which had voted for the ruling party. The discrepancies between the allocation of resources between KANU and opposition areas went as far as the distribution of relief food. In the semi-arid environment of Ukambani, relief food is often very necessary to prevent the starvation of thousands of families who, in times of drought, cannot raise the financial resources to buy their food from shops, even if they are well supplied with maize from other parts of Kenya.

In Katangi location of Mwala division, Machakos district, after the failure of the long rains in 1994, the distribution of food relief took place three times weekly in KANU areas whereas only one was organised every two weeks in the opposition areas. The provincial administration was actually responsible for the starvation to death of several families. Still in Mwala, where the KANU candidate Peter Kavisi had been rigged in against the DP deputy secretary-general Joseph Munyao, the Kibaoni and Kalawa areas, who had elected DP councillors, suffered at least five confirmed deaths from starvation.

Father Francis Kunyusa from the Kibaoni Catholic parish reported that at least 20,000 people in the vast semi-arid area of Mwala were starving. Hundreds of families were trekking daily from neighbouring areas to seek relief food distributed by the church. The Kibaoni water project, which was to supply water to 30,000 residents and counter the consequences of rain failure through irrigation, had been stopped after the election. Some people were forced to travel more than 20 km in search of water from the Athi River (*Daily Nation* 22/07/94, 08/11/95 and 23/11/95)

The political vendetta of the provincial administration increased the dramatic consequences of drought and famine. Yet, with the coming of the 1997 polls, the objective of food distribution changed. After three years of punishment, the opposition electorate was again offered relief food by a merciful government in need of their renewed support. Andrew Mondoh, the Machakos district commissioner was reported in early June 1996 distributing 2,000 bags of maize in his district. The same operation was reproduced in Makueni, Kitui and Mwingi (*Sunday Times* 16/06/96). But as the excitement of coming elections was growing, relief food did not seem to be enough reward for some KANU Kamba leaders. In December 1996, during a fund-raising function in the administrative centre of Wote in Makueni district, Peter Maundu (Makueni), Tony Ndilinge (Kilome) and Peter Kavisi (Mwala) stated that the Akamba were fed up of being taken for granted by the government. Food relief was not enough to deliver roles to KANU; if the party wanted to remain the dominant party in the region, it would have to deliver roads, water and other desperately lacking infrastructure. This 'Wote Declaration' was heard loudest in the administrative centre of Makueni district which was not even equipped with an automatic phone exchange.

In the north of Ukambani, it remains equally doubtful whether Kalonzo Musyoka's patronage really benefited the inhabitants of Mwingi. With the coming of the elections, the Mwingi/Garissa highway was being reconstructed and a rural electrification programme took place in various divisions. The Kiambere water project gave hope to the residents that they would soon have piped water in their homes although the project had been re-activated only because of the forthcoming elections. The same opportunistic activities occurred with the Mwingi bus station building, but banditry and cattle rustling continued to plague the area. Hundreds of peasants had been forced to flee Ngomeni and Tseikuru locations owing to escalating banditry and in late 1996 the armed forces had to intervene to restore security after several people were killed by thugs. Locally, businessmen and elements of the security apparatus were accused of running a cattle-rustling syndicate which was allegedly benefiting from the protection of the minister for Foreign Affairs (*Daily Nation* 27/09/98). Mwingi, Mutito and Mutomo, all KANU-represented areas, are some of the poorest divisions of the region. Access to water there is the big issue. Over 70 per cent of the half-a-million inhabitants of Kitui district rely on rivers for their water. Piped water is non-existent. Only 39 per cent of the Mutito population are literate. 'About 30 % of . . . children suffer from chronic malnutrition or nutritional stunting, 6% from acute malnutrition or wasting and 34% from underweight' according to a UNICEF-funded government report (*Daily Nation* 25/09/98). The Kitui Teachers Training College in Kitui West had been under construction for the past six years.

The complaint of Maundu, Ndilinge and Kavisi quickly nicknamed the 'three rebel sisters' therefore touched a particularly sensitive chord all over Ukambani, where popular dissatisfaction was only increased by the ruling party leaders' blunders. In December, after the 'three sisters' had raised their voices on the threatening famine that was looming once again, Nyiva Mwendwa, Kalonzo Musyoka and Jackson Mulinge appeared in the press, violently denying that anything of the sort was happening. This denial of the obvious greatly angered the famine-stricken areas and in January 1997, Daniel arap Moi had to go himself to Ukambani for a damage control exercise, declaring the region a disaster zone requiring urgent food supply.

In this context, the initiative taken in February 1997 by the National Commission on the Status of Women to propose Charity Ngilu as the sole opposition candidate for the coming presidential context was welcomed more than positively in her home districts. By April, Ndilinge, Maundu and Kavisi were already campaigning unofficially for her in their respective constituencies and Nicholas Biwott had to organise a fund-raising in the Nairobi City Stadium for the benefit of all Kamba women's groups to counter-attack the growing popularity of the Kitui Central MP presidential bid (*Economic Review* 07/04/97). Ngilu had been groomed by Kenneth Matiba and Raila Odinga's opposition front to make sure Daniel arap Moi would not get his 25 per cent of the votes in Eastern Province. She was also welcomed by the Kenya National Congress in case of primary problems with Mwai Kibaki and endorsed by some fellow 'Young Turk' colleagues (Anyang' Nyong'o, Muite and Leakey) and clergymen (Rev. Njoya) as the only opposition candidate embodying real change. Ngilu had also received the support of the entire DP Kamba officials (*Business Chronicle* 18/07/97). In July, she finally defected from the DP where she would have had to face Mwai Kibaki, Benjamin Ndubai and also her fellow Kamba colleague Kennedy Kiliku in the primaries, to the little-known Social Democratic Party, she took with her the entire DP local Kamba apparatus.

One of the most formidable electoral challenges to the ruling party had been finally set up in Ukambani, threatening to deny Moi the possibility of getting 25 per cent of the votes in at least five of the eight provinces of the country. Nicholas Biwott, the chief political strategist for KANU and a key player in the Moi succession battle, seemed to be one of the very few national leaders to have realised the extent of the danger caused by Ngilu's presidential bid. He literally put the heat on the local KANU leaders, so that the rest of the electoral period in Ukambani was entirely devoted to ruin her chances.

Towards the 1997 general elections: gerrymandering and voter registration

The preparatory work of the electoral commission in Ukambani was, as in other parts of the country, geared towards easing KANU's success and President Moi's re-election. The creation of new constituencies, the modification of the existing boundaries, usually known as gerrymandering, and the registration of voters were the three main means in the hands of the ECK to give a head-start to Daniel arap Moi and KANU.

By September 1996, the electoral commission had finished its review and two new safe KANU constituencies had been allocated to Ukambani: Mwingi South, which brought a second constituency to the newly created district of Mwingi, and Kaiti, carved out from the constituencies of Kilome, Mbooni and Makueni, in Makueni district. The new district of Mwingi and the new constituency of Mwingi South were created thanks to the efforts of the local KANU baron and minister for Foreign Affairs, Stephen Kalonzo Musyoka. Yet locally, Musyoka's achievement was contested as the minister was accused of having worked hard on gerrymandering. Indeed, both Mwingi North and Mwingi South surprisingly share Mwingi town. Kanzanzu ward, the constituency of Kalonzo Musyoka's local ally, Mwingi town council chairman Musyoka Munyambu, had been posted in Mwingi North. No socio-economic or geographical argument can explain the resulting strange shape of Mwingi North's southern boundary, which seems to have been drawn only to cover the wards of Musyoka's strongest allies and therefore ease the control of the town council.

Moreover, the location of Migwani, which has by itself 17,530 registered voters and was formerly included in the neighbouring constituency of Mutito is now part of Mwingi South. Mutinda Ndambuki, the Mutito MP, found himself in an awkward position as his home was now placed in a different constituency. Ndambuki, who was a public opponent to Musyoka, had now to fight it out with former provincial commissioner David Musila, the most important local

KANU opponent of Kalonzo Musyoka. Musila's popularity and development record in Mwingi was a tremendous threat to the cabinet minister. Locally, it is believed that Musila opposed the creation of the new constituency as he wanted to fight with Kalonzo Musyoka during the KANU primaries and beat him.

Through the creation of Mwingi South, Kalonzo Musyoka seemed therefore to have killed two birds with one stone: he had produced an extra safe seat for the ruling party and had managed to have two of his opponents fight against each other during the ruling party primaries, thus securing his own smooth nomination. Kaiti, in Makueni district, was created in another safe KANU area to the direct benefit of businessman Gideon Ndambuki, chairman of the Garden Group of Hotels and a former director of the collapsed Trade Bank. A close associate to Nicholas Biwott, Ndambuki was pushed to enter politics by his godfather who was obviously not satisfied with the current KANU Kamba leadership and their national ambitions.

The other major pre-electoral responsibility of the electoral commission next to the creation and modification of constituencies was the registration of voters. As in 1992, the figures released in August 1997 showed some surprising results.

Table 12.1 indicates that about 350,000 potential Kamba voters did not register in the Kitui and Machakos districts' lists of the electoral commission. A benevolent interpretation of these figures could conclude that the registration situation had nevertheless improved. Indeed, the percentage of registered voters to the total potential electorate in 1997 was slightly superior compared to 1992: 68 against 65 per cent on average. Yet, a more critical analysis shows that, in 1997 as in 1992, despite the huge political excitement that stormed Ukambani, the registration figures were kept at an all time low compared to the previous electoral contests: 85 per cent of registered voters for Kitui and 78 per cent for Machakos in 1969, 89 and 78 per cent respectively in 1974, 81 and 78 per cent in the same order in 1979 and, finally, 91 and 82 per cent, respectively, for Kitui and Machakos in 1983. All socio-demographic factors being equal through time, it is reasonable to state that the usual level of voter registration in Ukambani is about 80 per cent of the total potential electorate. Therefore, in 1997 10 to 12 per cent of the Kamba electorate, 75,000 to 90,000 voters were probably not in the electoral commission's registration lists.

Table 12.1: Comparative levels of elector registration prior to the 1969, 1974, 1979, 1983, 1992 and 1997 elections in Ukambani

District	1969 total pop.	18 and over	1969 Reg. Vot.	Missing voters	% Registered
Kitui	339,850	142,737	122,159	20,578	85
Machakos	705,783	296,429	230,613	65,816	78
	1974		**1974**		
Kitui	407,549	171,171	153,160	18,011	89
Machakos	846,378	355,479	276,692	78,787	78
	1979		**1979**		
	total pop.	and over	Reg. Vot.		
Kitui	464,283	194,999	158,709	36,290	81
Machakos	1,022,522	429,459	334,711	94,748	78
	1983		**1983**		
Kitui	536,905	225,500	206,748	18,752	91
Machakos	1,182,462	496,634	411,689	84,945	82
	1992		**1992**		
Kitui	737,000	313,962	207,377	106,585	66
Machakos	1,590,000	672,570	429,614	242,956	64
	1997		**1997**		
Kitui	839,000	357,414	247,903	109,511	69
Machakos	1,795,000	759,285	514,217	245,068	68

Note

The figures for 1992 and 1997 are based on extrapolations of the 1989 Kenya population census, which was carried out when Mwingi and Makueni districts had not yet been created. The Kitui figures should therefore be read as including the current Kitui and Mwingi districts and the Machakos figures as including the current Machakos and Makueni districts. Both the 1992, 1997 total population figures, and the percentage of the 18 years olds and over were provided by the Kenya Bureau of Statistics in one of its latest reports on extrapolations of the 1989 census. The percentages of '18 and over' are 42.6 for Kitui and 42.3 for Machakos. The 1969, 1979 and 1983 figures are derived from the 1969 and 1979 Kenya census. The 1974 and 1983 figures have been calculated on the basis of a 3.7 per cent annual population growth between 1969 and 1974 and 1979 and 1983. The level of '18 and over' in 1969, 1974, 1979, and 1983 has been evaluated as 42 per cent of the total population.

Table 12.2: Distribution of registered voters by constituencies in 1992 and 1997

Constituency	Registered voters 1997	1992	Increase (%)	Constituency	Registered voters 1997	1992	Incr (%)
Mwingi district				Kangundo (68)	63,125	66,550	-5.1
Mwingi N (60)	45,373	60,959	31.7	Kathiani (69)	52,490	44,933	14.4
Mwingi S (61)	43,836			Mkos Town (70)	63,426	42,814	32.5
Kitui district				Mwala (71)	48,698	40,496	16.8
Kitui W (62)	46,603	44,268	5.0	**Makueni district**			
Kitui C (63)	52,525	51,675	0.2	Mbooni (72)	49,495	42,655	13.8
Mutito (64)	27,635	22,494	18.6	Kilome (73)	25,394	57,345	4.4
Kitui S (65)	31,935	29,892	6.4	Kaiti (74)	34,569		
Machakos district				Makueni (75)	55,846	41,766	25.2
Masinga (66)	33,657	26,021	22.7	Kibwezi (76)	49,837	37,912	23.9
Yatta (67)	37,688	29,931	20.6	**Total**	762,132	639,711	19.1

Moreover, the discrepancies in the increase of registration figures per constituency gives a more precise outlook of local reasons that may have guided the manipulation of the registration process (see Table 12.2). Between 1992 and 1997, the average increase of the registered population in Ukambani is about 19 per cent. Yet Mwingi district, a 'safe' KANU area, registered an increase of its electorate of 31 per cent whereas Kangundo in Machakos, a 'safe' opposition seat registered a decrease of 5.1 per cent. In those two specific cases, it is highly likely that the registration process was politically controlled in order to maximise KANU's presidential and parliamentary votes.

In Kitui Central, the relative stagnation of the electorate (0.2 per cent) is most definitely linked to the gerrymandering engineered by the electoral commission in the district and the under-registration of the generally pro-opposition youth. Indeed, Nzambani, a pro-opposition populous location of Kitui Central, was transferred to the peripheral area of Mutito. But this alone cannot explain the complete stagnation of registration figures, especially since the local MP's presidential bid generated a lot of excitement in the constituency. The 0.2 per cent increase in Kitui Central, as well as the meagre 5.0 per cent in Kitui West and 6.4 per cent in Kitui South, are clear expressions of the under-registration of the opposition electorate. Even the Mutito figures (18.6 per cent) are lower than what could be expected. Mutito lost the Migwani location to Mwingi South but got Nzambani from Kitui Central and Voo from Kitui South. A higher increase could have been expected. In Machakos district, the increase of Mwala (14.4 per cent) and Kathiani (16.8 per cent) constituencies are also surprisingly low whereas the low figures of Mbooni and Kilome in Makueni District can be attributed to the creation of the Kaiti constituency.

By the end of August 1997, four months before election day announced by Daniel arap Moi only at the last minute, the ECK and the Office of the President had, therefore, contributed to depriving Charity Ngilu and SDP of around 100,000 votes in Ukambani only, greatly increasing Moi's chances to achieve the 25 per cent figure of votes in the Eastern Province polls.

KANU's campaigning tools: relief food and women's fund

Relief food distribution, *harambee* meetings and the mobilisation of women's groups are the usual campaigning tools which have been used by Kenyan politicians since independence. The 1997 electoral campaign was not any different from this established tradition whose efficiency was to be tested by Charity Ngilu's presidential bid. By September 1997, presidential and KANU campaign teams had been set up. But suspicion by the KANU headquarters that incumbent MPs were unofficially supporting Ngilu for the sake of their own re-election brought a lot of tension within the management of this team. It ended up being closely supervised from Nairobi and composed, almost exclusively, of civil servants. Sammy Kyungu, the director of education, Frank Kwinga, the principal immigration officer, Prof. Kiambaa the vice-chancellor of Moi University, Prof. Munavu, the deputy vice-chancellor of the University of Nairobi in charge of finance and administration, provincial commissioner Simon Kiilu, David Masika the executive manager of the National Social Security Fund (NSSF), Reuben Mutisya and Alan Simu, two practising architects from Nairobi benefiting from government contracts, were some of its most important members. No expense was spared. Frank Kwinga is reported to have used a helicopter to supervise the campaign logistics, which were closely supported by the provincial administration and notably the Machakos district commissioner, Andrew Mondoh, who was also found several times attending KANU meetings.[11]

Compared to 1992, local observers of both electoral processes argue that, in 1997, KANU distributed more money than food, due to the good harvests that had followed the El Niño rains. The women's groups of Kyangwithya-East, the location of origin of George Ndotto, the nominated KANU candidate for Kitui Central, received, for instance, a total of Ksh. 3 million. An extra Ksh. 1.7 million was distributed within the neighbouring Misewani sub-location from the National Women's Fund.[12] At the end of November, the *Daily Nation* reported that Kalonzo Musyoka had distributed a total of Ksh. 1.2 million of the National Women's *Harambee* Fund to the 131 women's groups of the Mumoni division in his Mwingi North constituency and told his audience to reciprocate President Moi's gesture by voting for him (*Daily Nation* 23/11/97). Maize was also distributed in Kitui, Mwingi and the semi-arid areas of Machakos and Makueni, through the provincial administration or the local network of KANU supporters most maize was being made available at the back of their houses or in their shops (*Daily Nation* 25/11/97). And contrary to the constitutional changes voted in October, the chiefs, assistant chiefs and heads of department in the civil service campaigned heavily for KANU, often being threatened with sacking if their areas of origin did not support the ruling party.[13] Gen. Jackson Mulinge in Kathiani was also caught openly using the cars of his ministry for his campaigns (*Daily Nation* 26/11/97).

Comparatively, the SDP campaign benefited from fewer resources. Each district had its campaign team, but was dramatically limited in its movements and operations by the lack of financial resources.[14] Some of its staff worked on a purely voluntary basis as did members of the Ngilu national campaign team based in Nairobi. Like any other SDP parliamentary candidate, Charity Ngilu had to finance herself for her Kitui Central re-election bid. For her national campaign, she received financial backing from foreign sympathisers – for example SDP got Sh. 870,000 shilling from a European sister party – some wealthy Safina party members (Richard Leakey among others) and the Kamba business community, led concurrently by one of its most successful industrialists, Chris Musau, the executive manager of Nova Chemicals Ltd, the former KANU-Machakos vice-chairman, Jonstone Muthama, a group which had called itself 'young professionals from Ukambani', and an architect Norbert Musyoki. Muthama was absent from the country during the campaign but he is said to have helped substantially the SDP and even the DP presidential candidates.[15] He had quit the KANU Machakos branch in December 1996 over the drought denial debate. Otherwise, the main Ngilu fund raiser was Chris Musau who mobilised the Kamba business community and organised several fund-raising dinners in hotels and at his own home. For example, on 17 October the SDP presidential campaign team managed to raise one million shillings at a dinner at the Grand Regency Hotel (*Daily Nation* 03/12/97). A similar function was organised at the Blue Post Hotel in Thika, on 12 December, and another one at the Nairobi Wagon Hotel on 19 December (*Daily Nation* 15 and 19/12/97)).

Charity Ngilu's campaign was managed from the SDP Mountain View Estate headquarters in Nairobi and was closely supervised by her SDP colleagues Apollo Njonjo and Peter Anyang' Nyong'o, in addition to special advisers, such as the gender activist and University of Nairobi professor Maria Nzomo, and the *Daily Nation* columnist and theatre playwright Wahome Mutahi. Charity Ngilu's campaign was popularly summarised as WOMEN: 'Wipe Out Moi, Elect Ngilu', which also gave her the nickname of 'wiper' (*The Executive* December/January 1998).[16] The label 'wiper' was sometimes transformed to 'viper' by her opponents. Charity Ngilu's national campaign was extremely well covered in the media, including the influential *Daily Nation*.

Njehu Gatabaki, the editor of *Finance* magazine who later became an SDP member of parliament, ran a special issue on her presidential bid and on the SDP political programme in October. Ngilu also generally became the attraction of the international press based in Nairobi, groomed by the Anglo-Saxon gender activists, even though she was constantly accused of not campaigning enough on the gender aspects of her presidential bid and of being surrounded and advised by too many men.

Prior to the official nominations, one of the peaks of her campaign came in mid-November when, during a 'meet-the-people' tour of Nyanza Province, she claimed that militia-men had been dropped by helicopter at strategic points in Kitui district with the aim of attacking non-Kamba residents, especially Luo and Kikuyu (*Daily Nation* 11/11/97). This public outburst, which was quickly followed by accusations against Nicholas Biwott and Wilson Ndolo Ayah's plans to hurt her after an attack by KANU youth on her campaign trail in Kisumu, kept her in the news for several days, while she visited the clash-hit areas of Homa Bay, Migori, Gucha, and Kisii. In addition to her election programme, Charity Ngilu pledged during her campaign to free the economy from destructive male politics which provoked ethnic clashes and marred the country for the past few years. 'I decided to step in to tame the bulls who are fighting for State House and save millions of Kenyans who are languishing in poverty' was one of the most recurrent catch-phrase of her 'meet-the-people' tours (*Daily Nation* 14 /11/97).

By the end of November, her visit to Central Province had revealed one of her strategies: she had been welcomed in Murang'a by FORD-Asili supporters who pledged to vote for her and where she had promised to include the Kangema MP, John Michuki, in her government. Welcomed in Thika and Kiambu by Kenneth Matiba's followers, Charity Ngilu was obviously trying to capture the FORD-Asili electorate. She received the support of some of its incumbent MPs such as Stephen Ndichu (Juja), Njehu Gatabaki (Githunguri) and Robert Mungai (Makuyu) (*Daily Nation* 18/11/97). The support of some FORD-Asili supporters tremendously increased the credibility of her presidential bid, even if a number of the party's councillors made it clear that they would mobilise the electorate for one of their own, either Mwai Kibaki or Kimani wa Nyoike (*Daily Nation* 23/11/97).

Charity Ngilu, an Anglican, also received the tacit support of the mainstream churches which gave her opportunities to assert her national position. Twice, in the presence of President Moi, Mwai Kibaki and George Saitoti, Archbishop David Gitari invited her to speak to the audience during official functions (*Daily Nation* 24/11/97). In their pastoral letters or in their sermons, Catholic Bishops Urbanus Kioko and Boniface Lele of Machakos and Kitui dioceses equally urged the Catholic church followers not to sell their votes but to elect 'clean leaders', an unofficial endorsement for Ngilu.

Party nominations and the final week of campaign frenzy

At the end of November, the KANU nominations provoked a number of bloody skirmishes. In Kitui West especially, supporters of rival candidates Francis Nyenze and Nyiva Mwendwa stoned each others' cars and ended up killing a passing-by lorry driver in Kakeoni trading centre (*Daily Nation* 26/11/97). The KANU nominations nevertheless ended with a number of big surprises and the complete demise of the Mutisya-Musyoka opponents. Nominated unopposed, Kalonzo Musyoka managed to have the victory of his foe Nyiva Mwendwa overruled by the Nairobi headquarters and his ally Francis Nyenze win in the following re-run. Jackson Mulinge in Kathiani refused to have his contested nomination repeated despite obvious irregularities and a tiny margin of 438 votes. His opponent Kyalo Kaindi defected to the SDP. Johnstone Makau was beaten by an old foe and former Mbooni MP, Frederick Kalulu. In Makueni, two of the 'three sisters': Tony Ndilinge and Peter Maundu cruised through the KANU nominations easily whereas the third one, Peter Kavisi, in Machakos, could not resist Mulu Mutisya's assault on the Mwala nominations, through the former director of security intelligence, William Kivuvani. Mulu Mutisya's influence proved also determinant in the nomination of Wilson Musila for Machakos Town, despite Alphonse Musyoki's protest that the final results were announced before the results of all polling stations had come out (*Daily Nation* 04/12/97). Agnes Ndetei was a surprising loser in Kibwezi whereas veteran politician Paul Ngei failed to make his comeback and was severely beaten by his 1990 successor for the Kangundo seat, former deputy police-commissioner Joseph Ngutu.

Nominations within the SDP did not go through the electoral process and were endorsed by a 28-member-electoral college from the party headquarters. This opaque system did not initially cause too many problems, as the party was first of all struggling to have as many nominees in as many constituencies as possible. Just after the KANU nominations, Apollo Njonjo, the secretary general of the party, had declared that SDP would not accommodate defectors who had just lost their nominations in the ruling party. But this rule was not respected, as Kyalo Kaindi, for instance, obtained the SDP nomination for the Kathiani seat. Soon confusion set in and strong protests were expressed about the whole matter. It was even alleged that several KANU losers bribed the SDP secretary general to obtain the party's endorsement. It is only because of Chris Musau's strong opposition to it, that Johnstone Makau did not get the SDP Mbooni ticket (*Daily Nation* 02/12/97).[17] In Mombasa, SDP national chairman, Justus Nyang'awa had to intervene to clarify the situation as some KANU defectors had already paid their nomination fee. He had to rule that the procedure would vary according to constituencies, following the agreement reached by the main contenders and the local party officials. In Taveta,

Mwacharo Kubo was nominated through the delegate system while in Changamwe, William Makau Nduva got his SDP nomination through secret ballot (*Daily Nation* 05/12/97).

December saw a dramatic intensification of the campaign and an increase in the personal attacks on Charity Ngilu. The *Kenya Times*, the KANU daily, published an interview with Ngilu's mother declaring her daughter unfit for the presidential office. Ngilu answered this abusive manipulation of maternal authority by bringing her mother to Nairobi City Hall on presidential nomination day. *Kenya Confidential*, a DP news-sheet fighting her popularity in Kikuyuland, described her several times as corrupt and a spoiler of Kibaki's victory, because her husband's electrical engineering company had received contracts to operate on the construction sites of government buildings (*Sunday Nation* 07/12/97). While touring Ukambani, President Moi stopped calling her by her name, using instead the derogatory *mama* and Mulu Mutisya accused her of having ignored the Kamba elders, 'no house could have two husbands' (*Daily Nation* 21/12/97). Yet, Ngilu's popularity became a real threat for Moi and Mulu Mutisya. These men had to face hostile crowds on several occasions in Machakos and Makueni districts when they made nasty comments about the Kamba presidential candidate (*Daily Nation* 24/12/97).

While addressing the striking nurses, Ngilu endured the abusive use of force by the police who hurled tear-gas canisters at her crowds. She also confronted the police when she wanted to storm a KANU fund-raising luncheon at the Hotel Inter-Continental in Nairobi. The last days of her campaign were completely devoted to wooing the voters in Central Province. After a quick tour of the coast in mid-December she again toured Murang'a and Kiambu districts, before proceeding to Nakuru, promising to give Kenneth Matiba a cabinet position. The last days of the campaign equally saw an increase of violence between SDP and KANU supporters. Violent clashes were reported in Kisumu, Machakos and Kangundo and, at the Machakos town bus stage, all *matatus* were forced to bear the SDP colours and the Ngilu posters (*Daily Nation* 19/12/97).

In Kitui, the defeated KANU candidates who had taken part in the nomination process against George Ndotto (a former MP, cabinet minister, and director of the National Social Security Fund) formed a campaign team against Charity Ngilu. Going round the district as the six bulls of Kitui, former MPs and brothers Daniel and John Mutinda, the latter being also a director of Postbank, former cabinet minister and MP Titus Mbathi, Dr Mulinge, owner of the agricultural chemicals producing company Farmchem Ltd, Dr Kitheka, owner of a local clinic, and local petrol stations owner Anthony Kinyili, led the campaign against Charity Ngilu. They were supported by the provincial administration in allegedly buying votes. One week before voting day, Gideon Moi, one of the sons of the president and his cousin, former Kitui district commissioner Peter Lagat, were caught by a hostile crowd while allegedly delivering a full bag of banknotes to their local team. They sought refuge within the CPK St Martin's Cathedral but were not welcomed by the church and had to escape to the local offices of the Japanese International Co-operation Agency forestry programme. Vote buying became so widespread in Kitui Central during the last days of the campaign that Ngilu had to rush back to her constituency and campaign for her own parliamentary re-election, missing a key SDP political rally at Uhuru Park on 27 December (*Daily Nation* 28/12/97). On 29 December, Gideon Moi and Peter Lagat allegedly came back to Kitui to buy the voter cards of opposition electors for as much as Ksh.5,000 each, in her stronghold of Kitui town, Ithookwe, Kisasi, and Miambani and provoked the official protest of the Catholic Bishop Boniface Lele (*Daily Nation* 29/12/97). Joseph Munyao, DP's secretary general, allegedly suffered the same fate in Mbooni, Ngilu's birthplace. During the last three days of the campaign, Mutula Kilonzo, President Moi's lawyer, camped at Frederick Kalulu's home and distributed bread and money to all the women's groups in the district, mobilised by the local *Maendeleo ya Wanawake* chairlady, Grace Mueni Mwema.[18]

Voting day and the results

The multi-party presidential contest introduced for the first time in 1992 has somehow dramatically changed Kenyan elections. In some parts of the country, parliamentary candidates benefit from concurrent presidential and parliamentary elections. To a certain extent, such was the case in Ukambani where the 'Ngilu wave' delivered seats to SDP, whoever was the candidate. Yet in a number of cases, the strength of personalities and the specific socio-economic situation and history of a constituency prevailed over the 'Ngilu wave' which may have also been countered by a 'rigging wave' organised by the ruling party. KANU presented candidates in every constituency, SDP presented candidates in 16 out of 17 constituencies and DP in 13 out of 17. Yet, apart from DP's secretary general Joseph Munyao's Mbooni constituency, and Mwingi district where the SDP was almost absent, the DP and Mwai Kibaki's presidential bid found almost no support in the four Kamba districts. We will therefore mainly focus on the KANU versus SDP rivalry for this analysis of the results.

Mwingi: surprisingly good results for KANU
The parliamentary and presidential elections in Mwingi North and South did not bring any big surprise. Kalonzo Musyoka was re-elected and the first election of David Musila, the KANU candidate for Mwingi South, could hardly

be contested. A former provincial commissioner, Musila had been contributing to the development of Mwingi for the last 15 years by promoting the building of dispensaries and schools all over the area. His election to the Mwingi South seat was a plebiscite as he got 80 per cent of the vote, more than Charity Ngilu got in Kitui Central.

Yet, the Mwingi North parliamentary and presidential results were very intriguing. Despite the division of his constituency, which was left with roughly three quarters of the electorate of 1992, Kalonzo Musyoka increased his votes from 20,613 to 24,509. President Moi also performed exceptionally well, getting 21,808 electors compared to 21,047 in 1992, despite the division of the constituency into two and the competition from Charity Ngilu who barely performed better than Mwai Kibaki in 1992 (27.6 per cent to Kibaki in the entire Mwingi 1992; 31.7 per cent to Ngilu in Mwingi North 1997). This result is even more intriguing when we consider the good performance of Charity Ngilu in the neighbouring Mwingi South constituency where she beat Moi by more than 8,000 votes. Like in 1992, Kalonzo Musyoka and Moi seem to have over-scored.

These inconsistencies give a lot of weight and credibility to the complaint raised by the DP Mwingi North candidate, Josephat Mulyungi, about rigging in his constituency. Mulyungi stresses that the counting of the votes was far more regular in 1997 than in 1992, despite the inclusion by the returning officer, after two days of quarrels, of nine ballot boxes which had come unaccompanied by any party agents from Tseikuru, Kalonzo Musyoka's home. The problem came from the intimidation suffered by voters from the very tight network of chiefs and assistant chiefs working closely with KANU.

Since the creation of Mwingi district and after the redrawing of administrative boundaries, it is surprising that Mwingi North has twice as many locations and sub-locations as Mwingi South, coming to a total of 18 chiefs and 54 assistant chiefs, all clients of Kalonzo Musyoka, according to Mulyungi. The DP candidate alleges, moreover, that these provincial administration personnel were very instrumental in distributing relief food and intimidating the electorate. Voters were met on their way to the polling stations and bribed or threatened by the KANU agents to vote for Musyoka and the President.

They would then proceed to the polling stations, identify themselves to the ruling party men and systematically pretend that they could not read or vote without assistance of the deputy presiding officer. Ballot-box stuffing was also highly suspected. The local electoral commission team confessed that boxes used in 1992 had been given to KANU agents in Tseikuru 'for training purposes' prior to election day. Yet by 29 December they had not been recovered by the ECK. Allegations have also been made that the entire Mwingi North ECK team, composed exclusively of civil servants, had been bought and threatened by KANU to give a good result to Daniel arap Moi, so that he could help develop the district.

This is most probably the reason why all agents are reported to have been expelled from polling stations half an hour before closing time after two days of voting.[19] These reports are difficult to verify and to confirm. Yet, the general picture is clear. Charles Hornsby and David Throup had concluded that the 1992 Kitui North results had been inflated by at least 11,000 votes for Daniel arap Moi. There is no reason to believe that the same rigging scheme did not take place in Mwingi North in 1997. Daniel arap Moi scored 33,256 (49.7 per cent) in Mwingi district against 31,014 (46.4 per cent) to Charity Ngilu, surprisingly beating her by more than 2,000 votes in her ethnic backyard.

Kitui: operation Ngilu loses

Kitui, the home district of Charity Ngilu was of course one of the very hot spots of the 1997 elections. One of the strategies of KANU in the district was to beat Ngilu in her own constituency so that her presidential results could not become valid and therefore could not prevent Daniel arap Moi from getting the 25 per cent of the votes he needed in the Eastern Province.

Tensions ran very high during the campaign and on voting day, and testimonies that KANU activists bought hundreds of votes by distributing five hundred shilling notes abound. The provincial administration might even have been involved, by having voters summoned to the chiefs' and assistant chiefs' offices to sell their votes to KANU. On the first day of voting, a revealing incident occurred. Charity Nguli stormed the returning officer's office in Kitui Central and found evidence of rigging. The *Daily Nation* reported that she had run into thousands of hidden blank ballot papers, electoral cards and other documents, some of them half-burnt in the electoral office. Several electoral books had ballot papers plucked off and a number of them were from other constituencies. The returning officer Frederick Mutegi failed to explain the situation and some of the documents and papers she confiscated indicated that voter registration in Kitui Central had been going on secretly until 23 December. Ngilu confiscated the evidence and confronted the police for two hours, at gun point, challenging them to shoot her. The drama ended when former cabinet minister Nyiva Mwendwa convinced the Kitui officer in command of the police department to leave the matter to the ECK (*Daily Nation* 30/12/97). To a certain extent, the returning officer was perfectly entitled to have in his possession the voting cards which had not been collected and the ballot papers which had been wrongly sent to Kitui Central in the confusion of the polling organisation. Yet the documents showing the illegal extension of registration, the half-used ballot books and the burnt voters cards are strong evidence indicating the existence of a local ECK-supported rigging scheme against Ngilu. The revelation of this scheme on the first morning of voting day angered young SDP supporters in Kitui. They proved afterwards to be as violent as the KANU ones during the nomination process in Kitui West. They threatened and mistreated KANU activists on several occasions around polling stations and became disorderly.

Despite these incidents, the popularity of Charity Ngilu in her own constituency could not be tamed. She easily regained her seat and managed to have two other SDP candidates elected. One of them was a Jimmy Muthusi Kitonga a brother to the former Law Society of Kenya chairman Nzamba Kitonga and son of the long-standing Mutito MP Chief James Kitonga. The other was Samuel Kiminza in Kitui South, a young businessman operating in Mombasa, despite a strong resistance from the former MP running on a DP ticket, Patrice Ivuti. One of the district seats, Kitui West, went to KANU in dubious circumstances. Francis Nyenze, who had produced a big surprise by beating Nyiva Mwendwa during the KANU nominations won the seat with a very narrow margin of 563 votes (17,572 versus 17,009) over Nzuki Nzuki running on an SDP ticket. This result had been rightfully questioned with the knowledge that a total of 422 votes were rejected as invalid, but most importantly because it seemed to have suffered from the 'Westlands syndrome' where a returning officer does not add up the ballot figures to the same total as the agents and observers, but gives a seat to KANU even though it had lost. Moreover, Daniel arap Moi got only 13.7 per cent of the vote in Kitui West and nothing can explain such a huge discrepancy between the KANU presidential and parliamentary candidate scores. In the presidential contest, Charity Ngilu surprisingly did not perform as well in her own constituency as in the others, where she got 80 to 85 per cent of the votes. In total, despite all the efforts put in by the ruling party and contrary to 1992, KANU managed to steal only one seat from the opposition in Kitui district and Daniel arap Moi got only, on average, 19 per cent of the votes against 78.8 per cent for Ngilu.

Machakos: Mulu defeated
In Machakos district, other than the usual support by the provincial administration for the ruling party, reports of serious irregularities came up only for the Kangundo seat, where rampant intimidation, the distribution of food and money from the women's fund and vote buying were allegedly organised by the local district commissioner, Andrew Mondoh. The 'Ngilu wave' brought four clean seats to the SDP and a major upset: the defeat of outgoing cabinet minister Gen. Jackson Mulinge (Rtd.). Beaten by an almost 20 per cent margin, Mulinge seemed to have been sanctioned by the electorate for his poor defence of the Kamba interests within the government and the rigging out of his challenger, Peter Kyalo Kaindi, from the KANU nominations.

Kaindi finally made it on an SDP ticket. Surprisingly, and most probably thanks to some ballot box stuffing, Daniel arap Moi scored better than Gen. Jackson Mulinge in his own constituency. Former MP Jonesmus Mwanza Kikuyu also made the right choice by vying for the Machakos Town seat on an SDP ticket, as did unknown John Mutua Katuku, who beat the former director of security intelligence William Kivuvani in Mulu Mutisya's home seat of Mwala. The only legitimate resistance by KANU came from the popular Ronald Kiluta who managed to bank on the implementation of an irrigation scheme in his Masinga constituency and was re-elected.

The victory of KANU's Joseph Kimeu Ngutu against SDP's Joseph Mulusya in Kangundo can be seriously questioned. At a press conference a few days after the proclamation of the results, Mulusya detailed how he bumped into Florence Wambui Maingi, *Maendeleo ya Wanawake* national treasurer, in Kikambuani polling station as she was allowed to vote irregularly and had in her possession two empty ballot books and several pre-marked others, an ECK stamp and voters cards (*The Star* 08/1/99). Reports of Land-Rovers circulating under exclusive administration police surveillance which brought ballot boxes to the Tala counting hall, equally cast very serious doubts on KANU's parliamentary candidate's victory, especially since Daniel arap Moi lost by 11,000 votes to Charity Ngilu in the constituency and scored 7,000 votes less than Ngutu himself.

Overall, Mulu Mutisya and the local KANU branch seemed to have lost the grip on Machakos politics and could not resist the 'Ngilu wave', but Daniel arap Moi easily managed to garner 25 per cent of the votes in Machakos district. He was systematically beaten by Charity Ngilu (56.9 per cent) but his district campaign team had done what was necessary to score a rewarding 38.5 per cent.

Makueni: KANU's new stronghold?

By bringing back three of its five seats to the ruling party, Kilome, Kaiti and Mbooni, Makueni became KANU's strongest barrier against the 'Ngilu wave', even though the district is the home of the Kamba presidential candidate. The district moreover saw one big surprise: the defeat of the secretary general of DP, Joseph Konzollo Munyao, against his old KANU rival, Frederick Kalulu and the very poor score of the SDP candidate, Michael Illumbi (27.7 per cent), despite the 63.8 per cent garnered by Charity Ngilu in her home area. Compared to other presidential candidates in their home constituency, she is married in Kitui Central but born in Mbooni – Ngilu's score is even relatively low. Here again, suspicion of a large-scale rigging scheme involving local members of the ECK and the provincial administration are fairly high.

Rigging in Makueni had also been directly observed for the seat of Kilome, where the incumbent KANU MP, Tony Ndilinge, managed to have ballot boxes unsealed for more of his supporters to cast their ballots and bought the support of the local returning officer. Although one can argue that this rigging does not seem to have been decisive in helping Ndilinge keep his parliamentary seat, as he won with an almost 40 per cent margin, it was most definitely crucial for Daniel arap Moi to get more than 45 per cent of the Kilome votes. The constant intimidation of illiterate voters by KANU agents at polling booths, the systematic tricks used inside the booths to favour the ruling party by the presiding officers, and the open vote buying among women's groups and even outside polling stations should legally invalidate Ndilinge's re-election. On the SDP side, Paul Mulwa Sumbi, elected for the first time in 1969, was returned for the Makueni seat. A newcomer, Onesmus Mboko, took Kibwezi, formerly held by Agnes Ndetei, the colourful assistant minister who could not manage to go through the KANU primaries. On average, Charity Ngilu scored 65 per cent of the votes in Makueni and Daniel arap Moi 29 per cent.

With eight of the 17 Ukambani seats, KANU gave a relatively good performance during the 1997 elections. The ruling party definitely stole three seats from the opposition (Kitui West, Kangundo and Mbooni) and at least two others could have been invalidated if the elections had been 'free and fair' (Mwingi North and Kilome). The three seats alone gave the ruling party a majority in parliament that it should never have had. Yet the most crucial question still stands: did the systematic vote buying, food distributions, and support by the provincial administration allow Daniel arap Moi to decisively garner the needed 25 per cent in the Eastern Province or not? His score of 363,027 votes was 100,000 votes over the 262,724 he needed to reach the 25 per cent minimum requirement. His winning margin corresponds to an average of 5,900 votes per seat in Ukambani, roughly 14 per cent of the registered voters. The question, of course, is whether we can reasonably speculate that the pre-electoral under-registration of voters and KANU manoeuvres were responsible for this winning margin, just as in 1992.

Conclusion

The 1997 general elections in Ukambani may not have been as flawed as those of 1992. As many opposition parliamentary candidates admit, the campaign was far less violent than five years earlier and the activities of the electoral commission far more regular. Yet, these elections were neither free nor fair. Contrary to the constitutional changes voted three months before the polls, the provincial administration heavily supported KANU, for which the results could have been invalidated. Again, the presidential and parliamentary elections were seriously rigged so as to inflate President Moi's share of the votes in Eastern Province and guarantee an illegitimate KANU majority in parliament. The KANU Kamba politicians did not benefit as much from their efforts as they had in 1992. Kalonzo Musyoka made it back to the cabinet, but was only given the difficult Ministry for Education. Makueni district was rewarded by the appointment of the newly-elected Kaiti MP, Gideon Ndambuki, as minister of state in the Office of the President, and Machakos obtained the appointment of Joseph Ngutu as the minister for Labour and the return of Ronald Kiluta as the assistant minister for Energy. The good work of Grace Mueni Mwema in mobilising the women's groups of Mbooni in favour of KANU was also rewarded by her nomination to parliament on the KANU list. The prospect of Kamba contenders holding the post of vice-president has never seemed so distant. Despite their efforts and their well-organised campaign, they did not really manage to tame the 'Ngilu wave'.

Indeed, if Charity Ngilu failed to have an impact on the national scene, she definitely managed to bring back the Akamba to the polls. She completely failed in her bid to conquer Central Province (3 per cent) or other rural non-Kamba areas of the country (less than 1 per cent in the Rift Valley, North-Eastern and Western provinces, between 1 per cent and 2 per cent in Nyanza), and scored only 10 per cent in Nairobi and Coast provinces, where the pre-electoral polls had predicted that she would win up to one third of the votes. Her fifth rank on the list of the presidential candidates definitely reduced her performance to a Kamba affair. And indeed in Ukambani, she had real appeal. The increase in turn out which averaged 68 per cent against 58 per cent in 1992 speaks for itself. Moreover, the fact that so many young voters in Ukambani were not able to register naturally limited her performance. Yet, Charity Ngilu's score in Ukambani was very far from what Mwai Kibaki or Raila Odinga managed to achieve in Central Province and Luo Nyanza, respectively. The official presidential results of Mwingi North and Yatta cannot be taken into account to access Ngilu's performance in Ukambani since these were most probably manipulated and did not reflect the wishes of the voters (See above for Mwingi North and Appendix I for Yatta where the official presidential results were inverted).[20] Yet in eight of the constituencies, almost half of them (Mwingi South, Masinga, Kangundo, Kathiani, Machakos Town, Mbooni, Kilome, and Kaiti), she got very comfortable levels of support but still did not manage to block Moi from taking 35 to 45 per cent of the vote. In only seven constituencies (Kitui West, Kitui Central, Mutito, Kitui South, Mwala, Makueni and Kibwezi) did she get strong support and a genuine plebiscite in her own district.

Several factors can explain why the Kamba did not vote as a bloc for Charity Ngilu, and why she did not perform nationally as well as the national and international media expected. First, Charity Ngilu was probably the least well off of the big five presidential candidates and had barely the means to campaign all over the country. Her party, the SDP, did not have the capacity to financially help its candidates whose campaigns often even lacked posters. Her campaign team was very small, less than ten people in total, and they opened up an office only in November. Money is crucial to electioneering. Even without organised voter bribery, the resources and logistics necessary for the transportation of a presidential candidate and supporters all over the country, the printing of posters and payment of staff are as huge in Kenya as in European societies.[21]

Secondly, her gender and background might have embodied a real hope for change in the country from a cross-section of the press, the youth, the urban middle class and the international community, but these groups are not the backbone of Kenyan politics. In a male-dominated country where close to 75 per cent of the population is still rural, the usual prejudice against women's leadership greatly hampered her presidential bid. As in many Latin European or Latin American countries, a great majority of the electorate might enjoy the idea of a woman president, but when the time comes for casting the ballot, the weight of the individual's political socialisation which usually associates power with men's attributes does not play in favour of women candidates. Kenya is not unique in this respect.

Finally, some credit has to be given to KANU. It has, for almost 40 years, been involved in vote buying, bribing, intimidating, rigging, crowd pulling and manipulating the different facets of the electoral process. These combined with huge financial and administrative resources, had their effects. Ukambani was one of the key areas for President Moi. In Central Province or Nyanza he had absolutely no chance of reaching 25 per cent of the votes and had, therefore, to break at least partly the 'Ngilu wave' to get them in Eastern Province. We can be assured that he used all the resources in his power to reach that target, whether lawfully or not.

Notes

1. Charity Ngilu was born in 1952 in Mbooni constituency, Makueni district, the ninth child in a family of thirteen. Her father was a Christian preacher. After attending local Mbooni schools, she joined Alliance Girls High School, the cream of contemporary feminine elites, where she sat for her O levels in 1970. She later trained at the Government Secretarial College as a secretary and joined the Central Bank in 1973. In 1975 she left her secretarial job to attend the Kenya Institute of Administration where she trained in business management, before moving to Chase Manhattan Overseas Corporation in Nairobi in 1978 where she worked as an administrative manager till 1981. She resigned to start a bakery and a restaurant in Athi-River, then Anti-plastics Ltd, a company manufacturing water pipes and electrical conduits. Her husband is a consultant electrical engineer in Nairobi (see Verdier 1998:145-46).

2. She claims that 'her development record' is worth 18 dams, 2 fully-equipped dispensaries, a 76-bed-ward at the Kitui District Hospital, one borehole and 150 primary school classrooms with desks (*The Executive* December/January 1998).
3. To take an oath in Kikamba is translated by *kuia kithitu*, literally, to eat the *kithitu*. In the process of the administration of the oath, the oath takers indeed eat a piece of meat after having sworn. This piece of prepared meat is supposed to contain a force that oath-takers keep forever in their bodies. It kills them or their children if they betray it, unless they go through a cleansing ceremony.
4. Cloves were smuggled into Kenya from Zanzibar and exported abroad. When the revolutionary government of Zanzibar found this out and captured the culprits, they were executed.
5. After 18 years in parliament Mutisya, who cannot speak English and has also big problems of elocution in Kiswahili, is credited with a total of three interventions: one in October 1980, another one in March 1981 when he asked the government to arrest 'Karl Marx' who seemed to be responsible for the unrest at the University of Nairobi, and one in July 1992, to defend himself against attacks from Agnes Ndetei about his interference in her district's affairs (see *Weekly Review* 26/12/93).
6. There are also Sammy Mbova, permanent secretary in the Ministry of Land Reclamation, Regional and Water Development; Joseph Ngutu, the outgoing Kangundo MP who was compensated with the chairmanship of the National Hospital Insurance Fund (NHIF).
7. Interview T.O., Machakos, 25/04/94.
8. Interview W.K., Machakos, 04/05/95.
9. Interview returning officer, Machakos, 26/05/94.
10. Interview J.K.M., Nairobi, 28/01/99.
11. Interviews with J.K.M., Nairobi, 28/01/99; J.W.M., Nairobi, 29/01/99; J.M.M., Kitui, 20/02/99.
12. Interview L.N., Kyangwithya, 22/08/98.
13. Interviews with J.K.M., Nairobi, 28/01/99; J.W.M., Nairobi, 29/01/99; J.M.M., Kitui, 20/02/99.
14. Interview J.W.M., Nairobi, 29/01/99.
15. Interview A.N. by M.R., Nairobi, 03/02/98 and J.K.M., Nairobi, 28/01/99.
16. Interview with L.N., Kyangwithya, 22/08/98.
17. Interview J.W.M., Nairobi, 29/01/99.
18. Interview J.K.M., 28/01/99.
19. Interview with J.M.M., Kitui, 20/02/99.
20. The official ECK results for Yatta show 17,100 votes for Moi and 6,362 for Ngilu. The correct figures are 17,100 for Ngilu and 7,612 for Moi.
21. Interview A.N. by M.R., Nairobi, 03/02/98. A 'reasonable' parliamentary campaign without big distribution of money through harambees or vote buying costs from Ksh. 1.5 to 2.0 million ($25-35,000). Interview with J.W.M., Nairobi 29/01/99.

References

Asamba, I. and Thomas-Slayter, B.1995, 'From cattle to coffee: transformations in Mbusyani and Kyevaluki', in Thomas-Slayter, B. and Rocheleau, D. (eds), *Gender, environment and development in Kenya*, Boulder: Lynne Rienner: 221-57.

Grignon, F. 1997, *'Le politicien entrepreneur en son terroir. Paul Ngei à Kangundo, Kenya, (1945-1990)'*, Ph.D. thesis, Université Montesquieu-Bordeaux IV.

Hill, M. 1991, *The Harambee Movement in Kenya: Self-Help Development and Education Among the Kamba of Kitui District*, LSE Monographs in Social Anthropology, London: The Athlone Press.

Mutiso, G.C.M. 1975, *Kenya-Politics, Policy and Society*, Nairobi: East African Literature Bureau.

Scott J.S. 1976, *The Moral Economy of the Peasant. Rebellion and Subsistence in South-East Asia*, New Haven: Yale University Press.

Thomas-Slayter, B.P. 1991, *Traditional institutions in village management: erosion control in Kitheka, Kenya*, Nairobi: WRI/ACTS Press.

Throup, D. and Hornsby, C. 1998, *Multi-Party Politics in Kenya. The Kenyatta & Moi States & the Triumph of the System in the 1992 Election*, Oxford: James Currey.

Verdier I. (ed.) 1998, *Kenya: The Top 100 People,* Paris: Indigo Publications.

13

'Mix-and-Match Parties and Persons': The 1997 General Elections in the Meru and Embu Regions of Kenya

Karuti Kanyinga

Throughout much of the post-colonial period, 'ethnicity' has been a central focus in the analysis of Kenya's politics. Ethnicity has continually informed the organisation of politics and/or struggles to control state power in Kenya. The importance of ethnicity in the country's political economy is indeed bound to increase, given the widening socio-economic and political inequalities. Arguably, a deepening of both the economic and political problems has reinforced ethnic rivalries between and among different social groups. Relatedly, the state's capacity to deliver development has been on the decline and this has meant a decline in the 'development significance' of the state. This has had one important effect: activation of extant ethnic identities as each of the major groups struggles to out-compete the others in the race to control the state and therefore the diminishing resources.

On account of the above, analysts see an increasing role of ethnicity in elections. The mobilisation of groups on the basis of common culture, common language and habitation of a common territory is arguably a major factor behind the pattern of election results. That is, struggles to win elections are premised on a distinct ethnic foundation around which everything else related to politics in Kenya revolves (Berg-Schlosser 1994; Chege 1994; Oyugi 1998; Barkan and Ngethe 1998; Throup and Hornsby 1998).

With regard to the pattern of elections at the local level; however, there are other factors that combine to influence the final outcome or results. In some constituencies, individual leadership qualities and the ability to 'deliver development' and to contribute to the expansion of the democratic space, among other factors, are the bases upon which voters judge and support the candidates. As Cowen and Kanyinga (2000) have argued, the 'communal logic of politics' critically influences the pattern of voting. In this argument, the 'well-addressed' question of tribe, namely the territorial association between an ethnic group and a region, is conflated with the local issue of representation. It is as much the local as the tribal which has been brought into play to explain national contours of political power and opposition in Kenya. Questions of political association arise from the role of the 'local' in national politics (Cowen and Kanyinga 2000).

In the 1997 elections, local level communal issues influenced the reproduction of a 'mix-and-match' election pattern in which the electorate sometimes supported certain candidates in spite of the party with which these candidates were affiliated. In many constituencies and particularly those outside of the leading presidential candidates' home districts, the number of votes for the party's presidential candidates did not tie with the number of votes for the same party's parliamentary candidate. This 'mix- and-match' pattern was a big departure from the 1992 elections. In the latter, a 'three-piece-suit' pattern evolved in ethno-regional areas of the leading presidential candidates. The electorate voted in a uniform of the same party's candidates in the presidential, parliamentary and civic elections (Kanyinga 1994).

This chapter examines the significance of local level issues in elections in Kenya. The discussion highlights the need to understand factors beyond ethnicity. The argument here is that ethnicity alone cannot explain the pattern of election results in Kenya. Further, the discussion observes that although multi-party competition for control of 'high politics' tends to organise around ethnic and sub-ethnic identities, local issues outside ethnicity dominate the organisation of politics and elections at the base of the society. This 'local' element was responsible for the 'mix-and-match suit' in some of the constituencies. It has in turn a lot of influence on what happens in 'high politics'. Accordingly, one should not underline ethnicity as the single important determinant of election results in Kenya. It is ethnicity 'plus' something else that shaped the content, character and outcome of the 1997 elections in Kenya. The discussion is based on the author's research on the 1992 and the 1997 national general elections in two regions of the country: the Meru and the Embu regions (See map on p. 179). The significance of the two regions in the country's politics is explained below.

Meru and Embu: a socio-economic and political profile

Until the early 1990s, the Meru region had one administrative district – Meru. Today, as a result of subdivisions, it has four: Meru Central or Imenti; Meru North or Nyambene; Meru South or Nithi; and Tharaka (these districts comprise the Meru region discussed here). The Meru region borders Isiolo to the north and east; Kitui to the southeast; Embu to the south and southwest; Laikipia and Nyeri to the northwest. The Meru as an ethnic group comprises several sub-ethnic groups, which speak closely related dialects – the Imenti, Tigania and Igembe, Mwimbi, Chuka, and Tharaka. The Imenti occupy the high agricultural potential central region, which also borders the Mt Kenya slopes. The Mwimbi and Chuka occupy the Nithi district in the west of the area. The principal economic activity in both places is farming which includes tea, coffee, dairy production and horticulture. The Tigania and the Igembe sub-ethnic groups occupy the eastern part of Meru region. The Nyambene range of mountains divides the two. This area grows *miraa*, tea and coffee as the principal cash crops. The lower plains are mostly used for food crops and livestock farming.

The Embu region borders Meru to the north; Kirinyaga district to the south; Kitui district to the east; and Murang'a and Nyeri districts to the west. Embu district was subdivided into two just before the 1997 elections following demands by the Mbeere ethnic sub-group. The old Embu district comprised Manyatta and Runyenjes constituencies. It is a high potential agro-ecological area where farming of tea, coffee, dairy cattle and horticulture are the principal economic activities. The new Mbeere district comprises Gachoka and Siakago constituencies. It occupies the lower semi-arid part of the Embu region. Farming of food crops and grazing of traditional livestock is the mainstay of the area's economy. Both Embu and Mbeere districts are high potential agricultural districts.

The Meru and Embu regions are important in the Kenyan political space in one important respect. Together with the central region of Kenya, the heartland of the Kikuyu ethnic group, they formed the Gikuyu, Embu and Meru Association (GEMA). GEMA, on the other hand, was the most politically influential organisation throughout the 1970s and during the last years of the Kenyatta government. Indeed, in lieu of organised political life GEMA played an important political role, especially in central Kenya after KANU banned all other political parties.

The GEMA group has a long political history. The Kikuyu, Meru and Embu groups, related by language, cultural practices and share of territory, played a central role in the de-colonisation struggle. They were at the centre of the Mau Mau peasant rebellion and constituted the main groups in KANU at independence. Foremost, the Kikuyu, Meru and Embu integrated into the country's capitalist economic framework through the settler economy where they sold labour or engaged in commodity production. As a result, and in addition to their control of the government up to the late 1970s, these ethnic groups dominated the country's political economy. The GEMA group came to control a relatively large share of the indigenous capital in Kenya. Although the group's main economic occupation is agriculture, they have also invested in non-agricultural economic activities, such as banking, tourism, transport and manufacturing (Throup 1987; Cowen and McWilliams 1996; Cowen and Kanyinga 1999).

From the time Moi acceded to the presidency in 1978, however, there have been consistent attempts to deconstruct their political and economic base

(Throup 1987; Anyang' Nyong'o 1989). Political strategies have been consistently employed to erode their economic bases of strength in politics. The multi-party elections provided the Moi government with more opportunities to deconstruct the GEMA confederacy. That is, the ideology of ethnicity percolated to the local level with different consequences which are different from that of cementing identities. It has increasingly led to the disintegration of the GEMA identity and, therefore, provided the Moi government with more opportunities to erode the political base of the Kikuyu in the opposition group. This he has done by consolidating smaller agro-pastoralist communities related to his Kalenjin ethnic group. The Kalenjin, together with the Maasai, Turkana, and the Samburu or the KAMATUSA now comprise an important social category in both politics and the economy.[1]

High politics in Kenya: The 1997 general elections

As social realities and social classifications ethnic groups are often imagined by those who stand to gain politically from mobilising around them and are, therefore, a significant factor in shaping the pattern of local and national politics in Kenya as a social identity, ethnicity remains latent or dormant until it is triggered off by some external factors (Mafeje 1998: 14) such as inter-elite struggles for control of state power. Ethnicity thus is conspicuous in what Lonsdale (1986) calls 'high politics' which concerns the practice of politics at the level of the state. 'Deep politics', by contrast, concerns political relations outside the central state; it concerns relations between the rich and the poor, the powerful and the weak (Lonsdale 1986: 130). Ethnicity in high politics is important in one respect. Groups with different identities compete and, subsequently, conflict over the struggle to access and control of state power. Moreover, as Mafeje (1998) has argued, ethnic conflicts arise from social factors, which are extrinsic to their ethnic identity – external manipulation, discrimination, deprivation or marginalisation. Thus, the centralisation of state power and evolution of the state as the single most important institution in the political and social economic space are responsible for intensified ethnic conflicts during elections. Both the 1992 and the 1997 multi-party Kenyan general elections bear this out. Political parties formed and disintegrated along ethnic lines. The ethno-political elite mobilised their 'own' to win the elections or form a solid social constituency for bargaining after the elections.

One explanation for the saliency of ethnicity in the 'practice of politics' in Kenya is that the state, from the colonial period onwards, transformed into a means of 'social reproduction': 'statism' dominated the 'development space' and resulted in the state regulating and controlling most activities. The state evolved as the single most important engine for development. As a result, the control of the state became the focus and guaranteed access to political competition between different ethnic groups, because such control meant patronage resources, through which the ethnic elite maintained their hold on political power. Accordingly, 'how much development one delivered' to his or her constituency determined to a large extent the election results.[2] This had another consequence. It increasingly politicised ethnicity. Attached to this politicisation was also a 'zero-sum' result of political competition. Winners excluded losers from the evolving patronage networks (the new 'fields of accumulation') and especially from the centre of state power. This intensified struggles for 'inclusion' by the excluded ethnic elite.

In the ensuing competition, the ethnic elite would turn to mobilising those groups with whom their people shared a common identity in terms of language, culture or myth of origin. Ethnic cleavages, co-operation and incorporations gradually formed as each group sought to increase its numerical strength and the potential to win. But the politicisation of ethnicity should not be seen as a goal in itself. The constituencies also put pressure on their elite to locate themselves around the state so as to appropriate development resources. 'Ethnicity from below' thus has an overt social-economic content. It is driven by a desire to access state resources through 'one of their own' to enable them to 'eat'. It is 'our turn to eat because another group ate or has eaten' becomes the organising slogan around which other considerations revolve. This is particularly true of electoral politics among the numerically populous communities. They see their strength in numbers as a means to both economic and political power.

'Ethnicity from above' is an elite-project. Its aim is to help the elite maintain their political power as a means for both accumulation and self-perpetuation. This evinces itself in what Lonsdale (1993:94) has called 'political tribalism', a means through which the ethnic elite sustain themselves. Ethnicity is not only about conflicts; it is also about co-operation and incorporation. Again, the ethnic elite invoke a consciousness of being one in relation to others to bring together groups sharing a common heritage. Those speaking dialects of generic language groups, or even those sharing similar socio-political concerns, group together to enhance their competitive capability.

Results of the 1997 elections bear this out. Daniel arap Moi, KANU's candidate, got almost 2.5 million votes in the presidential elections. This represents slightly over 40 per cent of the 6.2 million votes cast. Moi and KANU obtained votes from a confederation of small ethnic groups and from certain of the Luhya 'sub-ethnic' groups. The combined opposition got about 3.7 million votes - almost 60 per cent. However, the latter was a 'wasted vote' since electoral rules require the winning candidate to get at least 25 per cent of the votes cast in at least in five of the eight provinces. The winner must also be the first among other presidential candidates. Meanwhile, DP's Mwai Kibaki was the second with about 31 per cent of votes, drawn especially from the Gikuyu, Embu and Meru (GEMA) groups. Raila Odinga (NDP) had 10.9 per cent from mainly Luo Nyanza; Wamalwa of FORD-Kenya had 8.2 per cent from especially the Bukusu and the Luhya diaspora; and Charity Ngilu (SDP) was fifth with 8.0 per cent obtained especially from her Ukambani area. Each of the minor presidential candidates got less than 1 per cent each. Some failed even to win parliamentary seats in their constituencies.

In terms of parliamentary seats, KANU won the elections, but lacked a decisive majority. The party acquired 107 seats against the opposition's 103 seats. Nonetheless, the results and the pattern that eventually evolved show that ethno-political factors influenced the outcome of the presidential elections. However, local issues such as individual ability to deliver development, social-cultural factors and clannism acted in the main as the most important factors shaping the actual outcome of elections at the local level. Party politics was not the main concern in some areas. Voters were concerned with the ability of candidates to deliver development and/or provide support in their struggle to dominate local rival clans and/or sub-ethnic groups. The 'we' versus 'they' of the national politics percolated – though in different forms – to the local level. Norms, values and philosophy of the community are main factors that direct local competition. The discussion that follows examines some of these issues in detail.

Deep politics in rural Kenya[3] - the Meru region

Jackson Angaine dominated politics in Meru in the post-colonial period until the re-introduction of multi-partyism in the early 1990s. Angaine was the only Meru senior politician, having been a cabinet minister in charge of lands and settlement during the Kenyatta period. He lost his parliamentary seat in the 1979 elections but recaptured it in 1983. He was appointed a minister in the Office of the President in charge of the provincial administration and internal security. Angaine had anointed himself the 'King of Meru' by virtue of his influence as the minister for lands who presided over the resettlement efforts in the former White Highlands and, therefore, clearly presided over the deconstruction of the colonial settler economy. His close association with Kenyatta and the inner court cabinet at the time meant that there was no other politician in Meru who could match his authority and influence (Kanyinga 1998). Politics in Meru was practised in reference to Angaine. Politicians lost or won their seats on this factor. Some, however, won on account of promising to go to parliament to fight the dominance of Angaine. In parliament, however, the 'king' was so powerful that no one would touch him or, if an attempt was made, it would have a backlash on the politician.[4]

After 1978 the Angaine factor in Meru declined in tandem with the rise of influence and the entry into parliament of youthful politicians, notably Karauri (in Tigania) and Nteere Mbogori in Angaine's constituency: North Imenti. Mbogori defeated Angaine in North Imenti in the 1979 elections. The defeat of Angaine evolved with a change in the political balance to issue-based politics. The theme now shifted to the politics of local development. Candidates began to mobilise around development concerns, and the influence of clan-based and sub-ethnic identities upon which Angaine's political life depended began to wane.

Politics of administrative districts
Both the 1992 and the 1997 elections were held in the context of changes in the administrative boundaries of Meru district. New districts and constituencies were created ostensibly to advance KANU's interests in the area owing to the fact that the area had a historical and political relationship with the Kikuyu through GEMA. Secondly, these districts and constituencies were created along sub-ethnic lines with a view to solidifying KANU's support in each region of the district. Tensions in the relations between the different sub-groups (some based on traditions and cultures) apparently dictated how the administration boundaries were to be drawn.

The creation of new districts started before the 1992 elections. Before the elections, the government created Tharaka/Nithi district. This divided the area into two separate administrative units (Meru and Tharaka/Nithi districts). The two areas are also distinguished by their distinct sub-ethnic identities and agricultural potential. Meru comprised the Tigania and the Igembe sub-groups on the Nyambene side, and the Imenti subgroup in the central region. Both have distinct dialects of the Kimeru language and distinct levels of infrastructure and development. A similar differentiation applied also in Tharaka/Nithi where the Tharaka have a distinct language and a relatively low level of development compared to the Mwimbi and the Chuka people who inhabit the Nithi part of the district. Nonetheless, Tharaka/Nithi was divided further before the 1997 elections. Moi and KANU launched a campaign for the presidency and the 1997 elections in the district where he began by ordering a further sub-division of Tharaka/Nithi into two: Tharaka and Nithi districts. The fact that this was done towards the election date (29 December) confirmed that it was meant to buy the two communities into KANU. The KANU elite argued that this had the advantage of bringing administrative services closer to the communities. True to this, the introduction of the new district was accompanied by an increase in the numbers of other administrative units such as divisions and locations.

Nyambene district was created from the remaining part of Meru district in 1993 immediately after the first multi-party elections. President Moi ordered the creation of Nyambene district after those elections as a reward to the Meru people for voting in three KANU MPs in spite of DP's influence and domination in the district's politics at the time. This decision had already been made as part of a bargain between Moi and the Meru elite (the Tigania/Igembe and Imenti) in a meeting held a few months before the 1992 elections. In this meeting they disowned Kibaki, Matiba and other Kikuyu elite with the argument that the latter 'invoked' GEMA anytime 'they had a political project to benefit from but dispensed with the Meru when it was time to eat'. The group present comprised prominent politicians, senior civil servants, and heads of parastatals from the larger Meru district. They specifically underlined that the Meru benefited least from the Kenyatta regime in spite of being associated with GEMA throughout the independence period and, therefore, the community was happy to identify with Moi and KANU. Moi promised to reward them with a district if they voted for him and KANU. He actually lived up to his promise. He created a new district after they voted in KANU candidates in Igembe, Central Imenti and Tharaka constituencies. Again the new district had its boundaries delineated along sub-ethnic identity lines. This tended to formalise the sub-ethnic identities and to fragment the Meru identity further. The result obviously was the erosion of a Meru identity, a result that ultimately contributed to further fragmentation of the GEMA identity.

Meanwhile, though KANU candidates won three parliamentary seats in the Meru region, in his presidential bid Moi got fewer votes than each of the KANU candidates got. This was true of all the three constituencies except in Igembe. Again, this meant that local level issues overlay other factors: the electorate was concerned with personalities and not party politics. A significant issue, however, is that KANU could access an area 'fenced off' by DP, an opposition party, and this convinced Moi to live up to his promise of rewarding the Meru people with a district. Arguably, the creation of several districts in the large Meru area, therefore, was part of a bigger project to weaken the GEMA coalition by providing a framework for the construction of a Meru identity separate from the GEMA one. GEMA was further weakened through the politics of administrative districts. This process of weakening the GEMA coalition had its internal contradictions, however. It did not solidify the Meru identity but fragmented them even further as a community. Consequently, the community straddled KANU and the opposition, each sub-group aligned with a different faction.

Besides the creation of new districts, there were several other factors that changed the configuration of politics at the local level. The 1992 multi-party elections in Meru, therefore, were conducted in a context in which local level issues played a critical role in the organisation of politics. This was unlike in the Kikuyu GEMA area, where party politics and opposition to KANU in particular influenced the outcome. KANU all the same managed to win three parliamentary constituencies in the area (Central Imenti, Igembe and Tharaka) in spite of the overwhelming influence of DP which owed much to the ethnic relationship and affinity between the Meru and the Kikuyu. The reasons for this are the overwhelming influence of local level issues and individual ability of the parliamentary candidates to deliver development or resolve constituency development problems, as discussed above. It mattered less whether an individual had led the struggle for political liberalisation. Deep politics required a menu that included this plus something else.

The 1997 elections did not alter the above. Parliamentary candidates lost or won on the basis of their individual ability and other 'items on the menu' of local politics. Indeed, by this time DP's influence, which had depended on the GEMA factor, had considerably declined, owing to the supremacy of local level issues over party politics. On account of this in 1997, out of nine parliamentary constituencies, DP won six, KANU two, and FORD-Kenya one. On the other hand, in the 1992 elections, out of eight constituencies, KANU won three seats, FORD-Kenya one and DP four. DP thus increased its seat margin in the 1997 elections.

The presidential elections had different results, however. In 1992, KANU (Moi) scored 21 per cent while DP (Mwai Kibaki) polled over 73 per cent in Meru district. In the 1997 elections, DP's strength at the presidential level reduced significantly and the party polled about 60 per cent while KANU (Moi) obtained almost 35 per cent of total valid votes. Tables 13.1, 13.2, 13.3 and 13.4 provide a summary of the presidential and parliamentary elections in 1992 and 1997 in the Meru region.

Table 13.2 on the 1992 parliamentary elections in Meru shows that KANU did not match DP's strength at the time. DP polled some 55 per cent in all constituencies, while KANU got 28 per cent. Moreover, the votes cast in the parliamentary elections did not fully correspond to those of their party presidential candidates. In Tharaka, for instance, KANU's parliamentary candidate, Francis Kagwima, got over 56 per cent of the valid votes while Moi, KANU's presidential candidate, scored 27 per cent. In Ntonyiri constituency, Joseph Muturia, the KANU parliamentary candidate, got 35 per cent while Moi made almost 50 per cent.

DP showed a similar pattern. For example, in South Imenti, DP's David Mugambi polled slightly below 39 per cent while Kibaki's score was double (over 78 per cent). Kiraitu Murungi won the South Imenti seat on a FORD-Kenya ticket and got 43 per cent of the parliamentary votes cast, while his presidential candidate Oginga Odinga, got less than 4 per cent.

The 1997 elections produced a similar pattern but also portrayed the declining influence of DP as an opposition party (see Tables 13.3 and 13.4). The 1997 general elections produced a 'mix-and-match' pattern: the electorate gave different votes to the parliamentary and presidential candidates of the

Table 13.1: Results of the 1992 presidential elections - Meru district (per cent)

Const. / Party	KANU Moi	FORD-K Odinga	FORD-A Matiba	DP Kibaki	KENDA Ng'ang'a	KNC Tsuma	KSC Anyona	PICK Mwau
Igembe	46.83	0.00	2.06	51.11	0.00	0.19	0.00	0.00
Ntonyiri	49.88	0.22	1.03	48.48	0.23	0.15	0.07	0.10
Tigania	21.56	0.82	2.73	74.13	0.03	0.17	0.53	0.11
North Imenti	16.04	1.62	3.50	78.43	0.04	0.29	0.08	0.00
Central Imenti	30.69	3.10	1.47	63.82	0.09	0.68	0.15	0.00
South Imenti	5.73	3.82	3.57	86.22	0.09	0.16	0.26	0.16
Nithi	12.57	4.47	4.14	78.07	0.07	0.17	0.22	0.29
Tharaka	27.09	0.47	2.18	69.66	0.08	0.17	0.19	0.16
Av. Meru	21.01	2.36	2.93	73.17	0.07	0.22	0.17	0.10

Source: NEMU 1993; IED 1997; author's calculations

Table 13.2: Results of the 1992 parliamentary elections - Meru district (per cent)

Party	KANU	FORD-K	FORD-A	DP	KNC	KSC	PICK
Const.							
Igembe	*J. Kalweo* 47.46	J. Kumeri 0.00s	I. Karunge 1.08	E. Mbaabu 41.88			J. Malebe 9.58
Ntonyiri	J. Muturia 35.38	J. Muriuki 0.09	W. Kigwathi 0.33	*M. Maore* 63.62	E. Mutuura 0.58		
Tigania	A. Karauri 23.42	N. Nkuraru 1.66		*B. Ndubai* 60.73		G. Mweneris 13.84	J. Mwongo 0.36
North Imenti	S.Rutere 25.86	N.M. Mukira 1.08	P. M'Mungania 1.02	*D. Mwiraria* 72.04			
Central Imenti	*K. M'Mukindia* 35.82	G. Imanyara 24.45		J. Muthamia 23.32	H. Kinyua 16.42		
South Imenti	K. M'Bijiwe 14.58	*K. Murungi* 43.10	K. Murugu 1.19	D. Mugambi 38.78	M. Kiome 0.69		
Nithi	M. Mureithi 21.39	G. Murungi 0.82	N. M'Muchai 2.85	*B.N. Mutani* 74.34		E. Mutunga 0.59	
Tharaka	*F. Kagwima* 56.28	D. Kauna 3.06	A. Muchee 1.99	N. Wakiondo 38.66			
Av.Meru	28.05	10.79	1.18	54.73	2.26	2.05	0.67

Source: IED 1997; author's calculations (Winners in italic)

Table 13.3: Results of 1997 presidential election - Meru District (per cent)

Party Const.	NDP Odinga	UMMA Ngethe	GAP Mwereria	UPPK Waiyaki	LPK Maathai	FORD-P Nyoike	KANU Moi	EIP Oludhe	KSC Anyona	KENDA Wamwere	KNC Mkangi	FORD-A Shikuku	DP Kibaki	FORD-K Wamalwa	SDP Ngilu
Igembe	2.02	0.04	0.15	0.07	0.12	0.12	60.34	0.06	0.03	0.09	0.07	0.08	35.35	0.05	1.51
Ntonyiri	1.02	-	0.17	0.07	0.03	0.14	44.87	0.00	-	0.09	0.02	0.17	52.33	0.07	1.01
Tigania W.	0.12	0.02	0.60	0.24	0.53	0.12	27.92	0.10	0.03	0.05	0.14	0.28	69.02	0.08	0.75
Tigania E.	1.05	0.15	3.93	0.09	0.40	0.07	46.28	0.04	0.03	0.05	0.08	0.17	47.18	0.03	0.44
N. Imenti	0.88	0.04	0.23	0.23	0.12	0.09	28.84	0.10	0.06	0.15	0.03	0.29	65.69	0.39	2.84
C. Imenti	0.17	0.05	0.27	0.14	0.10	0.07	37.60	0.07	0.06	0.13	0.07	0.35	49.16	7.46	4.30
S. Imenti	0.54	0.04	0.13	0.15	0.17	0.08	21.31	0.14	0.07	0.09	0.05	0.30	75.18	0.15	2.59
Nithi	0.69	0.03	0.16	0.19	0.22	0.15	28.01	0.19	0.09	0.09	0.06	0.37	67.73	0.11	1.90
Tharaka	0.51	0.02	0.10	0.08	0.32	0.08	35.59	0.11	0.04	0.07	0.13	0.21	61.77	0.05	0.91
Av. Meru	0.70	0.05	0.52	0.15	0.20	0.10	34.77	0.10	0.05	0.10	0.07	0.27	59.83	1.07	1.94

Source: IED/CJPC/NCCK 1998; ECK 1999; author's calculations

Table 13.4: Results of 1997 parliamentary elections - Meru District (per cent)

Party Const.	GAP	LPK	SAFINA	FORD-P	KANU	NDP	FORD-A	DP	FORD-K	SDP
Igembe					*Kalweo* 49.59	Muriungi 29.96		Mbaabu 16.22		Malebe 1.37
Ntonyiri				Mbiko 7.76	Munoru 30.42	Kangwani 1.15		*Maore* 60.67		
Tigania West		M'Imunya 1.24			Mukangu 46.87			*Ndubai* 51.89		
Tigania East	M'Mwereria 4.04				*Karauri* 51.22	Ringera 3.97		Nkuraru 40.72		
North Imenti					Meenye 34.30		M'Mungania 1.22	*Mwiraria* 64.47		
Central Imenti					M'Mukindia 29.43			Kinyua 4.60	*Imanyara* 65.98	
South Imenti					Riungu 24.90	Kinyamu 1.16		*Murungi* 73.94		
Nithi			Mbuni 20.66		Ntigwa 30.47	Murithi 3.47		*Mutani* 35.78		Ruchiami 1.32
Tharaka					Kagwima 42.44	Kaaria 0.64		*Mwenda* 56.31		Gaichura 0.60
AV Meru	0.35	1.45	3.89	0.59	35.53	4.17	0.19	45.16	8.21	0.40

Source: IED/CJPC/NCCK 1998; ECK 1999; author's calculations. (Winners are in italic)

same party. On average DP's overall parliamentary score of 45 per cent in 1997 in the Meru area fell far below Kibaki's presidential 60 per cent and also fell short of the 1992 DP result (55 per cent). The number of seats won rose from four to six, however.

As in 1992, parliamentary candidates scored differently from the party presidential candidates in 1997. In Igembe, for instance, Erastus Mbaabu of DP obtained 16 per cent while Kibaki polled 35 per cent. In Ntonyiri, Maoka Maore polled 61 per cent while Kibaki got 52 per cent. This was the trend in all constituencies in the large Meru district.

We have already noted the significant performance of Moi in the 1997 presidential elections results in the Meru region, especially in South Imenti, North Imenti, Nithi and Tigania. Interestingly, KANU performed poorly at the parliamentary level except in Nyambene. In 1997 the party got only two parliamentary seats in the region. They took the Tigania and Igembe areas but lost in Tharaka and Central Imenti to DP and FORD-Kenya, respectively.

The overall KANU parliamentary score improved by 8 per cent from 28 per cent 1992 to 36 per cent in 1997. The presidential score increased by about 14 per cent from 21 per cent in 1992 to 35 per cent in 1997. A point to emphasise is that in 1997 KANU got only three parliamentary seats in all of the GEMA areas. These were Tigania East and Igembe constituencies in Nyambene (Meru), Gachoka constituency in Mbeere (Embu). KANU had no seat in Kikuyu areas. The large Meru area with the exception of Ntonyiri and Igembe in Nyambene overwhelmingly supported DP and Mwai Kibaki. The large Meru district gave about 114,000 votes to Moi and 196,000 to Kibaki. This was the highest figure that Moi received in GEMA areas, more than the total number of votes that he got in the entire Central Province (56,000 votes). However, the Tigania and Igembe sub-ethnic groups gave KANU and Moi the highest number in comparison to other GEMA areas. Their four constituencies Tigania East, Tigania West, Ntonyiri and Igembe combined, gave KANU about 49,000 votes and Kibaki about 52,000 votes. Responsible for this trend was the internal contradiction in KANU's anti-GEMA strategy and particularly the strategy to evolve a new identity for the Meru. Owing to the contradictions mentioned earlier, the strategy did not facilitate a consolidation of a Meru identity. Instead, it fragmented the community and deepened the divisions among them. As a result, they straddled KANU and the opposition, depending on where each subgroup felt secure.

The variation between the parliamentary and the presidential election results also attests to the supremacy of local level issues and indeed the 'communal logic of politics' as argued earlier. It means that deep politics or issues about relations between and among the people at the local level are shaped by several factors, which are often different from the national ones.

South Imenti - the 'person-versus-money'

DP's influence spread, especially in Central Imenti, South Imenti, Nithi and Tharaka constituencies. With the exception of Tharaka, these constituencies are relatively well developed in terms of agriculture – dairy cattle, coffee, tea, and horticulture are the principle economic activities. This is one factor that tended to influence voters' loyalty to DP more than KANU. Noteworthy, farmers here were concerned with the collapse of the agricultural sector which, they argued, had its resources plundered through mismanagement by the KANU government. In South Imenti, for instance, the electorate voted for a DP candidate, Kiraitu Murungi, on the ground that Eliphaz Riungu, the KANU candidate, had irregularly accumulated his wealth when he worked with the Central Bank of Kenya. Riungu's wealth was rapidly translated into a 'mobile hotel' where the South Imenti electorate wined and dined throughout the campaign period arguing that they were 'eating' what had been stolen from them. Gangs of youth could be seen along the main highway waiting either for the 'hotel' or for material items, which the KANU supporters distributed in their endeavour to mobilise support.

Kiraitu Murungi, on the other hand, mobilised support on the basis of what he had delivered from 1992 when he was voted on a FORD-Kenya ticket, a party that had little support in the district. To the residents in the area, Murungi had become a custodian of justice and a leading light in the struggle for democratisation at both the local and the national levels. Often cited in the constituency was his ability to mobilise the residents for self-help development initiatives to start and complete basic service projects which the government had allegedly neglected owing to the failure of the residents to vote in a KANU candidate in the 1992 elections.

Murungi's campaign literature was widely distributed across the constituency. It spelt out the agenda for the development of the constituency, past achievements and the way forward. The literature counselled people against voting on the basis of bribes, threats and intimidation by the provincial administration. His campaign built on the platform of social justice, equality and popular participation.

The youth were solidly behind Murungi and DP, because of their concern for change. In their view, the old generation of politicians had contributed to the deepening of corruption which had in turn led to the inability of the government and the private sector to provide employment opportunities. Riungu's and KANU's mobile hotel finally failed to deliver results for KANU. He got 25 per cent of the valid votes while Murungi received 74 per cent. The electorate gave Kibaki, DP's presidential candidate, 75 per cent of the votes while Moi received 21 per cent. Developmentalism and individual character considerably influenced the voting behaviour in the area, far more than the ability to buy votes.

Central Imenti: clannism and the ability to foster development and democracy

For a long while, electoral politics in Central Imenti revolved around who among the Karuku and Abogeta clans could lead. This changed in 1988 with the entry of Kirugi M'Mukindia, another youthful politician. He re-configured politics in the area by de-emphasising clan bases of support and the Angaine factor. Local politics of development became more important with candidates getting elected on the basis of how much they delivered. M'Mukindia was elected on his promise to deconstruct clan loyalties in the political and economic arena.

In 1992, before the elections, he was appointed minister of commerce and industry after the defection of Minister George Muhoho to DP. This was an added advantage to M'Mukindia in that it enabled him to win amidst a strong opposition wave and against Gitobu Imanyara (FORD-Kenya) and Henry Kinyua (DP) the two main candidates in the opposition. Imanyara is a renowned advocate of human rights who had played an important role in the process that led to multi-partyism. Kinyua once headed the Kenya Planters Co-operative Union, the country's only umbrella coffee milling body – but was disengaged by Moi in the late 1980s. Although M'Mukindia had won and been given a powerful portfolio as minister, his re-appointment no longer served as a re-election weapon during the 1997 elections. He lost to Gitobu Imanyara, the secretary general of FORD-Kenya. Although in a relatively unpopular party, Imanyara got 27,112 votes (66 per cent) and M'Mukindia, 12,092 votes (30 per cent), only.

Several factors contributed to this vote margin. Notably, the political contest in the entire large Meru district had been reduced to a fight between KANU and DP. Several people argued that the Kikuyu were related to the Meru and, therefore, they did not see any point in voting for KANU and Moi. If Kibaki formed the government, the Meru would benefit as much as the Kikuyu. Others argued that although the constituency voted in a KANU MP in 1992, the locals got nothing in return. They had to punish KANU and Moi for not delivering. In addition, others charged that M'Mukindia abandoned the constituency after having been appointed to the cabinet. They observed that he held more *harambees* in Moi's Baringo Central constituency than in his own Central Imenti. M'Mukindia allegedly had the habit of postponing *harambees* in his constituency so that he could attend those in the KAMATUSA area with a view to endearing himself to the KAMATUSA elite.

Contributing to his 'downfall' also were family problems, which increasingly related to the politics of the area. His opponents charged that he not only attended to KAMATUSA's interests but had also got 'married' to a relative of a senior State House official. This meant neglecting his first wife who was central in the organisation of his 1988 and 1992 campaigns and winning the subsequent elections. The marriage issue increasingly weakened his base in the populous Kibirichia area where his first wife comes from. Furthermore, the loss of Kibirichia meant that he lost control over other locations in the constituency except Katheri and Githongo locations, his home area. The other locations slipped to Gitobu Imanyara of FORD-Kenya who won with a big majority.

Imanyara won for a number of reasons. Firstly, as mentioned earlier, was his role from the early 1990s in the struggle for the second wave of political liberalisation. As a publisher of the *Nairobi Law Monthly* journal, which was critical of the governance situation in the country, he had been arrested on false accusations several times in the run up to multi-partyism. Unlike other 'Young Turks' whom the electorate rewarded with parliamentary seats in the 1992 elections, Central Imenti did not vote him in because of a deep split in the ranks of the opposition supporters in the constituency who were divided between Imanyara and Kinyua. The 1997 period was, therefore, the time to reward Imanyara. Secondly, Imanyara, after losing the 1992 elections, continued to mobilise support in the constituency by organising *harambees* and sometimes by participating in civic education on people's rights.

In short, M'Mukindia busied himself with the KAMATUSA elite and created a space that Imanyara filled. Thirdly, the youth mobilised for 'change' of leadership arguing that the infrastructure and governance problems that continued to plague the constituency and the country in general were a KANU problem and, therefore, they needed change to facilitate both democratisation and economic growth. This became the organising theme of Imanyara's campaigns. To them it did not matter whichever party Imanyara affiliated with as long as it was not KANU.

The electorate apparently neglected Henry Kinyua although he was in DP, a popular party, and despite the fact that he fared very well in the 1992 elections. Kinyua got only 1,889 votes, which was less than 5 per cent, a significant drop from his 5,546 votes polled in 1992. The electorate all the same overwhelmingly voted for Kibaki in the presidential elections: 20,402 votes against Moi's 15,603 and Wamalwa's 3,094. Moi got more than M'Mukindia, the KANU candidate, while Wamalwa of FORD-Kenya got less than Imanyara which is a clear evidence of the dominance of local level issues. Kinyua also lost because of the youth factor. The emphasis was on routing the first and second generations of leaders whom the youth argued had no answers to Kenya's problems. Fundamentally, KANU and M'Mukindia had begun organising against Imanyara, pointing out that they were of the same age group with Imanyara and it was wise for people to vote M'Mukindia back to parliament since he already held a ministerial post. In order to avoid splitting votes, or confuse the elderly and the indecisive ones whom KANU was targeting, the youth and prominent opposition elite made a decision communicated constituency-wide by the mobile youth to sideline Kinyua.

Clan politics submerged under the need for political change. M'Mukindia lost and blamed it on the churches and NGOs that had conducted civic education in the constituency. Interestingly, he had an enormous amount of resources to facilitate his campaign which included several 4-wheel drive vehicles for the virtually impassable roads and a neat network of senior civil servants from the constituency. However, all this worked against him. He was accused of using such vehicles instead of using his ministerial influence to repair the roads.

Igembe constituency: personality and sub group rivalry

Nyambene district was hived off the old Meru district after the 1992 elections. Two closely related ethnic groups, the Tigania and Igembe live here. Coffee, tea and the lucrative *miraa* trade are the key cash crops. The region had three constituencies (Igembe, Ntonyiri and Tigania) in the 1992 elections, but got an additional one when Tigania was divided into two (East and West). In 1992 KANU won Igembe, the only seat out of the three. Jackson Kalweo won against a formidable force from the opposition. He was rewarded with a powerful cabinet position as minister of state in the Office of the President. KANU candidates Karauri and Muturia lost Tigania and Ntonyiri, respectively, to DP candidates Ndubai and Maore (see table 13.2).

The creation of Nyambene intensified power struggles among the elite and especially between Kalweo and Karauri, the then acting KANU branch chairman and an ally of M'Mukindia. This activated intense social-political rivalries between and among the Igembe and the Tigania ethnic groups in the area. The rivalry consequently eroded the social bases of party politics. Political competition in the area became more a matter of intra-community rivalry and personality conflicts rather than party identities and policies.

In the rivalry, the Igembe (including Ntonyiri) had Minister Jackson Kalweo on their side, and the Tigania had Mathew Adams Karauri on their side. The rivalry between the two had origin in Kalweo's desire to reconstruct his past political identity and patronage which had dissipated after losing in 1983. The electoral defeat of those who rivalled him - Karauri and Muturia - provided him with an opportunity to be the dominant figure in the new district. Kalweo thus emerged stronger than his past rivals with absolute control of the local provincial administration since he was the minister in charge. Consequently, through his appointed chiefs and district officers in the newly created administrative divisions in the area, he reconstructed his patronage to block the re-emergence of his 1980s rivals (Karauri and Muturia). He saw party elections for the new district as the framework on which to concretise this ideal. And since Karauri and Muturia were holding party positions on acting bases (branch chairman and secretary, respectively) and by virtue of having been Meru branch officials before the creation of Nyambene, Kalweo urged the KANU headquarters to call for elections in the new district hoping to win and reign. Each group lined up its candidates for different party ranks. This was followed by accusations and counter accusations of electoral fraud. The rifts emerged and factionalism spilt over.

The divisions that ensued compelled the KANU headquarters to indefinitely postpone the exercise. Although this was done, it was not before the conflict had transformed itself to that between the Igembe (represented by Kalweo) and the Tigania (by Karauri). The two mobilised support on the basis that the fight was between the sub-ethnic groups. It was over the control of politics and economics in the new district. Whoever won should help his group dominate not only the party but also other power structures in the district.

In the meantime, opposition parties lost support from area residents. Although DP had more following than any other party in 1992 elections, its popularity considerably subsided and several of its councillors decamped to KANU. The party apparently lost support because it did not do much after failing to capture the seat and also because of the creation of Nyambene district, which meant independence from the Imenti people who had dominated the Tigania and Igembe for a long time. DP activists and MPs went 'under' after the elections. Indeed, a majority of area residents agreed that, 'people wanted change or something different from Moi and KANU but after Moi won, people drifted back to KANU to avoid political backlash and opprobrium.'

The 1997 elections thus came at a time of deep divisions among the leading elite in the district and amidst an opposition lacuna, the opposition leaders having gone under. Kalweo's powerful cabinet position helped him retain his seat. His creation of administrative units as an example of development worked in his favour. So did his continued fight against the domination of Igembe constituency by the Tigania. Kalweo also claimed ownership of the activities of an international NGO in the area, emphasising that he had in the early 1980s brought the organisation into the area to help in the construction of schools and provision of piped water.

Afraid of a blind change, which the youth in the opposition fronted, elderly women and men rallied around him. To them, the opposition had fragmented and often disagreed over everything. They would similarly disagree on how to manage the state if they happened to win the elections. Others in gainful employment such as teachers and civil servants, especially chiefs, rallied around Kalweo because of the power he had demonstrated in the five years he was in office. Several chiefs, teachers and other civil servants opposed to him had been interdicted or sacked or retired in the public interest as a punishment for their opposition. This occurred in other parts of the district, i.e., Tigania and Ntonyiri.

The youthful electorate rallied behind Raphael Muriungi, an opposition (NDP) candidate who previously worked with the same NGO in the area but was sacked allegedly for showing ambitions to oppose Kalweo in Igembe. The need for a change characterised the opposition's campaigns but fear of Kalweo's influence translated into a decisive victory for him by getting him 15,943 votes against 9,633 by his NDP rival Muriungi. A DP candidate, Erastus Mbaabu, got only 5,216 votes despite the fact that the party's presidential candidate, Kibaki, got 11,194 votes.

Tigania East and West: agro-ecological zones, age-sets and political experience

Kalweo's hand was felt outside Igembe. The primaries for the KANU candidate in the Tigania East constituency in the 1997 general elections were riddled with allegations of rigging and fraud. Two candidates, Kamenchu Ringera and Kamundi Larama, with the help of those in Kalweo's faction, opposed Karauri at the KANU primary. They lost and subsequently appealed to the KANU headquarters, challenging the nomination of Karauri. The three carried with them different figures purporting to show what each candidate had obtained in the nomination exercise. KANU declined to accept their figures. The party ratified Karauri's nomination, thereby laying the basis for further divisions between the Karauri and the Kalweo factions in the new district.

In Tigania East and Tigania West, other local issues dominated the electoral politics. In Tigania East, the Karauri-Kalweo struggle for power in KANU and issues over the development of the area transformed into votes for Karauri. A majority of the constituents tended to argue that had they elected him in 1992 he would have become a minister like Kalweo in the neighbouring Igembe, and their constituency would probably have developed from state resources as well. This was an opportunity they should not lose. In their view, DP candidate Benjamin Ndubai, 'took off from the constituency immediately after the elections in 1992 and failed to address problems such as those about poor infrastructure.' The people were not ready to take chances with Ntai Nkuraru in DP, another opposition candidate in spite of the role he had played in the struggle for democratisation in the country. Moreover, Kalweo had demonstrated a vicious dislike for the Tigania in the district and had even assumed a position of an ex-official MP for the constituency after Ndubai took off. Citing instances of about three chiefs who had been sacked for allying themselves with Karauri, some of the Tigania 'nationalists' agreed to mobilise support for Karauri, because he was the only force that could contain Kalweo.

In the meantime, the Tigania economy and politics began to interlock as the campaign proceeded. The northern part of the constituency (the old Muthara and Karama locations) comprises agro-pastoral communities who graze in the Meru's northern grazing zone. Some are also small-scale coffee and tea producers, besides cultivating food crops. The lower parts of the constituency, Mikinduri and Thangatha, have coffee, tea, and food crops such as maize and beans and bananas as their main activity. These agro-ecological divisions began to bear on the area politics. Some of the agriculturalists had a grudge against KANU and Kalweo in particular, because they lost thousands of their livestock to Samburu cattle rustlers in 1996. Kalweo (in charge of internal security) failed to assist in retrieving those herds, probably because of the fear of retribution by the KAMATUSA elite. After they lost the livestock, the people requested the local elite to appeal to Kalweo for help, but his promise to do so did not yield anything useful. When Karauri was an assistant minister, he had implored the government to give them 'home guards' which considerably helped in keeping off the rustlers, but the intensity of the problem in 1996 required more guards which Kalweo did not provide. Accordingly, although this was a grudge against the government and Kalweo, the Karauri assistance gradually became a plus. Nonetheless, others wholly blamed the loss of their livestock on the country's general state of insecurity and subsequently shifted their support to the opposition which they hoped would form a government that would eradicate the rustling problem. This debate especially in Muthara and Karama reproduced itself in the final results: Muthara voted overwhelmingly for Ntai Nkuraru and Karama location chose to rally behind Karauri. This was an interesting result because Nkuraru comes from this upper zone. One would have expected him to get block votes in his two home areas.

The agricultural division had an even more interesting argument for supporting Karauri in the parliamentary elections and Kibaki in the presidential ones. To them Karauri tended towards arrogance, but demonstrated good leadership abilities before he lost to DP in 1992. In their view, he had initiated more development projects than the DP candidate they had elected in 1992. On the other hand, Moi had failed to revitalise the economy, especially the agricultural sector on which the local cash crop and cereal crops depended. Kibaki, an economist and a former finance minister under KANU, was best qualified for the position of president, if only to clean the economic mess Moi had brought about. Thus, in several meetings, they warned Karauri against campaigning for Moi and urged him to market himself because 'even mentioning Moi would lead to a walk out or generate a resolute backlash on him Karauri.' The agriculturalists in the cash crop areas thus 'mixed-and-matched' Karauri and Kibaki. Nonetheless, the influence of the opposition in the tea-growing areas of Mikinduri and Thangatha areas (Karauri's home zones) was enormous. Nkuraru polled more votes than Karauri in some of the polling stations, but not enough to fully impact on the overall influence of 'mix-and-match'. In the final results, Karauri obtained 14,421 against Nkuraru's 11,465.

Table 13.5: Results of 1992 presidential elections - Embu district (per cent)

Party	KANU	FORD-K	FORD-A	DP	KENDA	KNC	KSC	PICK
Const.	Moi	O. Odinga	Matiba	Kibaki	Ng'ang'a	Tsuma	Anyona	Mwau
Runyenjes	5.8	0.9	22.9	69.5	0.09	0.3	0.2	0.3
Siakago	6.9	1.9	30.7	58.7	0.07	1.2	0.2	0.2
Gachoka	20.0	1.1	39.2	38.6	0.05	0.8	0.2	0.1
Av. Embu dist.	10.7	1.1	29.3	57.8	0.07	0.6	0.2	0.2

Source: NEMU 1993; IED 1997; author's calculations

Table 13.6: Results of the 1992 parliamentary elections - Embu district (per cent)

Party Const.	KANU	FORD-Kenya	FORD-Asili	DP	KNC
Runyenjes	L. Kimani	M. Mugeni	N. Kathangu	*N. Ndwiga*	
	4.8	2.7	22.1	70.4	
Siakago	E. Mbogo	S. Mate	F. Njue	E. Njue	*G. Ndwiga*
	12.2	12.4	21.0	25.4	29.0
Gachoka	J. Maringah	B. Nyagah	K. Kagundu	*N. Nyagah*	N. Minigi
	25.5	3.8	32.0	33.5	5.2
Av. Embu dist.	12.1	4.2	25.1	53.3	5.2

Source: NEMU 1993; IED 1997; author's calculations.   Winners are in italic.

Other significant issues at the local level superseded Nkuraru's youthful age and radicalism. His participation in the struggle for political change did not appeal to all electorate. Indeed, the elderly raised concern about his youth and radicalism. They were concerned about the possibility of him going to parliament for confrontational purposes. The youth, however, were the majority of his supporters. They argued that his was the right approach to politics in Kenya given that KANU was not keen to change and improve on governance.

The Embu region: families, clans, and politics of social domination

The divisions between the Embu and the Mbeere invited the creation of Mbeere district, which was excised from the large Embu district. The division also reflected the already existing agro-ecological boundaries. The Mbeere's economic activities include the farming food crops while the Embu grow tea, coffee and dairy.

The creation of Mbeere district was also part of a bargain between KANU and the Mbeere elite. Influential in this regard was Ireri Ndwiga who won the 1992 elections on a Kenya National Congress (KNC) ticket. In 1995, Ndwiga switched to KANU and bargained for the creation of a separate Mbeere district. The Mbeere popular version of this request, like the Tigania and the Igembe, was based on the perception that the agriculturally rich Embu regarded them as inferior and backward and had dominated them in both the local economy and politics. To the Mbeere, only a district of their own could provide opportunities for 'group survival'.

Before the 1992 elections, politics in Embu revolved around long-serving former cabinet minister Jeremiah Nyagah and his family. Although he was the MP for Gachoka constituency, his influence spread without obstruction to other constituencies in the Embu region. His only match and main rival in district politics was the MP for Runyenjes, Kamwithi Munyi, who had served as an assistant minister for Foreign Affairs during the Kenyatta government. Jeremiah Nyagah retired from active politics after 35 years and, therefore, did not contest any seat in the area in 1992. That year, however, one of his sons, Norman Nyagah, vied for the Gachoka seat on a DP ticket and won amidst strong opposition from FORD-Asili and KANU (see Table 13.6). Interestingly, his father was still the district's KANU branch chairman. This familial factor had an important consequence in Embu. Some candidates lost on account of being associated with the Nyagah family while others gained from the same association. This was particularly true of electoral politics in Mbeere in 1997 where another of Nyagah's sons, Joseph Nyagah, vied for the Gachoka seat on a KANU ticket (see Table 13.8). He won on the strength of his father's influence and clan.

Table 13.7: Results of the 1997 presidential elections - Embu district (per cent)

Party Const.	NDP Odinga	UMMA Ngethe	GAP Mwereria	UPPK Wayaiki	LPK Maathai	FORD-P Nyoike	KANU Moi	EIP Oludhe	KSC Anyona	KENDA Wamwere	KNC Mkangi	FORD-A Shikuku	DP Kibaki	FORD-K Wamalwa	SDP Ngilu
Manyatta	0.49	0.02	0.09	0.16	0.30	0.11	11.87	0.10	0.06	0.17	0.04	0.41	82.95	0.37	2.86
Runyenjes	0.44	0.03	0.12	0.16	0.25	0.11	13.25	0.18	0.10	0.15	0.14	2.03	81.15	0.47	1.42
Gachoka	0.40	0.35	0.17	1.50	0.04	0.31	34.56	0.12	0.11	0.09	0.09	0.36	40.40	0.97	20.53
Siakago	0.52	0.06	0.05	0.00	0.17	0.10	37.56	0.06	0.05	0.07	0.12	0.13	59.42	0.07	1.61
Av. Embu	0.46	0.10	0.11	0.41	0.21	0.15	20.84	0.12	0.08	0.13	0.09	0.86	70.14	0.48	5.81

Source: IED/CJPC/NCCK 1998, ECK 1999; author's calculations

Table 13.8: Results of the 1997 parliamentary elections - Embu district (per cent)

Party Const.	NDP	UPPK	LPK	SAFINA	FORD-P	KANU	FORD-A	DP	FORD-K	SDP
Manyatta	Muguimi 1.03		Mbogo 1.32			Gachora 12.90		*Ndwiga* 81.18	Ndwigah 1.38	J. Njeru 2.19
Runyenjes	Kagondu 1.72			Njathika 1.50		Kathungu 14.67	*Kathangu* 55.03	Wamugunda 24.11	Mugeni 0.41	S.Nyagah 2.55
Gachoka	Cingano 1.63	Mbithi 36.48			Kagundu 13.57	*J. Nyagah* 40.73			B. Nyagah 3.81	A. Njeru 3.79
Siakago			Kago 0.29			J. Njoka 46.13		*Ita* 52.27		V. Njoka 1.31
Av Embu	1.21	7.48	0.49	0.46	2.78	24.26	16.91	42.56	1.37	2.49

Source: IED/CJPC/NCCK 1998; ECK 1999; author's calculations. (Winners are in italic)

In 1992, KANU's presidential candidate polled 11 per cent of valid votes in Embu. DP's Mwai Kibaki polled over half of the votes (58 per cent) and FORD-Asili's Kenneth Matiba obtained 29 per cent. KANU performed poorly in some constituencies, such as the agriculturally rich Runyenjes where Moi scored less than 6 per cent. The party, however, obtained over 25 per cent in the Gachoka constituency.

The 1997 elections showed that the creation of Mbeere district had helped KANU to make electoral gains at the expense of DP and the opposition in general. KANU's performance in 1997 improved significantly. As shown in Table 13.7, Moi increased his share of the vote from 11 to 21 per cent. KANU likewise doubled by polling 24 per cent in 1997 as against 12 per cent in 1992 (see Tables 13.6 and 13.8). KANU's performance in the new Mbeere district, which comprises Gachoka and Siakago constituencies, also improved. The party won 41 and 46 per cent, respectively. Moi obtained 35 and 37 per cent of the votes cast in the two constituencies. Kibaki increased his share of 1992 votes as well. In one constituency, Runyenjes, a candidate on a FORD-Asili ticket got 55 per cent, but the party's presidential candidate, Martin Shikuku, less than 1 per cent.

Several factors account for this 'mix-and-match' pattern in the Embu region. The Embu were as concerned about the state of the agricultural sector as the Meru were. In Runyenjes and Manyatta, for instance, farmers were concerned about delays in payment for their tea and coffee deliveries and the poor infrastructure in the area. Interestingly, the area had senior civil servants campaigning for KANU. Their resources and promises for development to the residents if they voted for KANU produced little results. DP won in Manyatta and FORD-Asili won in Runyenjes. The latter had an interesting outcome. FORD-Asili disintegrated owing to leadership disputes between Kenneth Matiba and Martin Shikuku, but this disintegration of the party at the national level had little consequence on the local scene. Njeru Kathangu, who had been jailed in the early 1990s over political charges, won the parliamentary seat. DP took the bulk of the presidential votes. Kathangu won for factors outside party politics. His crusade for good governance and his imprisonment rewarded him at this stage and he won despite the fact that the resource-rich KANU elite camped in the district to campaign and mobilise for KANU.

The rich agricultural communities clearly favoured the opposition candidates and political parties. Additionally, they appeared interested in an individual who would promote and champion the struggle for governance on the argument that, if there were a good government, the area would be more developed. Further, farmers would have their commodities delivered, paid for and on time without the embezzlement that characterised the Moi political regime. While these factors account for the success of the opposition in the upper Embu region and especially among the agriculturally rich areas, arguments in favour of KANU were evident in the new Mbeere district. Here, family, clan, and kinship issues influenced the pattern that evolved.

Siakago: 'person' and clan loyalties

The creation of Mbeere district separated the Mbeere from the Embu community. This supposedly marked the end of the social domination of the Mbeere by the Embu elite. As mentioned before , Siakago constituency voted for an opposition candidate, Gideon Ireri Ndwiga, who later defected to KANU in 1995. KANU made promises to revive the local economy, improve the infrastructure and support development in the area. By 1997 these promises had not been met and the 1997 KANU nominee, Justin Muturi Njoka, failed to sail through the sea of opposition. Njoka was challenged in the KANU nomination exercise by another candidate, Silas Ita. Njoka won the party nomination clouded by allegations of rigging and manipulation by the KANU elite who did not trust Silas Ita, because he was a self-made person (see below) and was difficult to patronise. Silas Ita switched to the opposition DP after he failed to win the KANU primary and the DP subsequently nominated him. Finally, Ita won the parliamentary seat with 52 per cent of the valid votes while Justin Njoka, KANU's candidate, got 46 per cent.

Silas Ita won because of his own personal ability to deliver development. He was the executive chairman of the Export Processing Zone and a former chief in Mbeere. His individual achievements accounted for his electoral victory. He was a self-made man who had educated himself up to a Master's degree level and had risen from an ordinary village man to a chief and then to a chief executive of a parastatal. This had a tremendous impact on local level politics.

Njoka is from the populous Irumbi clan and was a former senior resident magistrate. However, clan rivalry, in particular the rivalry between the Irumbi and the Thagana clans, did not prevent the person with the best credentials from winning the seat. Moreover, Njoka faced criminal charges over corruption. As in the case of Riungu in Meru, the irregular accumulation of wealth through the state framework endeared some candidates to KANU probably for fear of retribution if they attempted to contest on an opposition party ticket. KANU thus was a natural political canopy for individuals who had irregularly accumulated wealth via the state framework.

Gachoka: contesting for and against the Nyagah family

We have already seen how politics in Embu revolved around Jeremiah Nyagah until his retirement in 1992 and how his two sons won parliamentary seats.

Although it is not clear why the two sons decided to challenge each other, observers were of the opinion that this had to do with familial tensions and interest to fit the father's shoes. Some were also of the view that Joseph Nyagah was the father's favourite son because of his association with KANU, while the mother favoured Norman in order to maintain a 'political balance' at the family level.

With a focus on the Nyagah family, the hitherto instrumental clan factor in Gachoka waned. The Mururi clan is the most populous clan while Ndamata is less populous and less influential. Ndamata provided opposition to Nyagah throughout his 'reign' in Gachoka but could not dislodge him owing to the numerical strength of the Mururi clan and his general influence as the most senior politician in Embu district. The focus and shift towards the Nyagah family meant a change in the configuration of factors determining the outcome of elections in the constituency. Nonetheless, afraid that challenging each other at the family level would leave the family vulnerable to the father's rivals, Norman, who was then the MP for the area, shifted to Kamukunji constituency, Nairobi which he won on a DP ticket.

In Gachoka, Joseph Nyagah, the newcomer, won the seat on a KANU ticket. Joseph polled 41 per cent against Muyia Mbithi of UPPK who got 36 per cent. Muriuki Kagundu of FORD-People got slightly over 13 per cent. The contest here, therefore, was not one between the parties. It was one against the Nyagah family. The wave was against the Nyagah family: a candidate on a less known party (UPPK) challenged Nyagah and, had there been fewer candidates in the opposition, Nyagah's family would probably have lost. However, the field was crowded which made it difficult for the opposition to win.

In addition to the influence of his father, Joseph won on account of the fact that he was in KANU, which had promised to resolve problems in the constituency, especially problems around the Mwea Settlement Scheme. Notably, the landless in the settlement scheme had no control over the land and the rice produce. Colonial irrigation legislation was still based on regulating many activities in the scheme. Accordingly, the residents demanded change so that they could gain control of both the land and the produce. The creation of the new district also influenced the outcome of the elections in the area. The Mbeere saw the new district as a process of liberation and a reward from KANU. The emergence of a new district marked the end of the socio-political and economic domination of the Mbeere by the Embu. The new district thus paved the way for KANU to penetrate the heartland of the Kikuyu-led opposition in GEMA areas.

Conclusion: this is not ethnicity alone

John Lonsdale (1993) has succinctly observed that 'the politics of modern Kenya is an enigma. Looking at the same events and stories in Kenya, actors and observers "violently" disagree on what they mean.' In his view, Kenya is and has always been a deeply divided society (Lonsdale 1993:130). The above discussion clearly fits this observation, for while ethnicity is the factor dividing articulation of 'high politics', 'deep politics' owes much to local level issues which include clannism, personal abilities to address social economic concerns, and a fear to be dominated by 'others'. This clearly shapes organisation of electoral politics at the local level and again feeds into the dynamics of 'high politics' which is mediated to the local through 'deep politics'.

The agriculturally rich groups in these cases are infatuated with the opposition both at the presidential and at the parliamentary levels. On the other hand, the poor groups in the marginal agricultural zones have associated more with KANU. This appeared to be their weapon against the rich groups who dominated both the economic and the political spheres. It is clear that associating with an established 'authority' provides some 'momentary protection' against those identified as 'economic others'. Risks of marginalisation and exclusion from the state accounts for their 'affective relations' with those already in control of the state. Local economic development thus is an important political tool. Economically, strong communities can take the risk of supporting the opposition political party while vulnerable communities cannot.

The above suggests that, were the opposition to win, poor groups would also decamp to the winning group. The rich groups, on the other hand, would continue to use their agricultural produce in the 'carrot-and-stick' game with any major political actor – be it the opposition or the KANU government. In this case, their association with the opposition was a 'protest noise' against the state's inability to improve the agricultural sector on which their livelihoods depend.

On the whole, the discussion has also shown that national level presidential electoral politics seems to differ significantly from local level parliamentary politics in terms of content. Secondly, ethnicity is not the only factor that influences the outcome of elections in Kenya. It could be the main factor for the presidential but not the parliamentary elections. Thirdly, ethnicity in electoral politics has its own contradictions. It can be mobilised to either solidify or fragment social bases of support. Each of these has certain consequences. For instance, instead of the Meru forming a solid block in support of KANU after having been given several districts, they straddled KANU and the opposition. Ethnicisation of administrative districts as a political strategy, therefore, produced certain consequences that undermined the potential of KANU to gain support in the district.

As Mafeje (1998) has argued, ethnicity at the national level assumes the character of ideology. It is used to mobilise by those who have something to gain or lose from it. The ethnic identity of presidential candidates informed the pattern of voting at the presidential level, while the 'mix-and-match' pattern dominated parliamentary elections; several candidates got elected on account of their ability to deliver. Such qualities were not sought at the presidential level since 'acceding to State House', through an ethnic mobilisation, overruled other factors including party policy orientation. This has another implication. It reproduces ethnic or sub-ethnic nationalism, thereby making ethnicity an indispensable factor in 'high politics'. Its indispensability, in turn, has several implications for the organisation of local electoral politics. The elite who win, even on basis of advancing local interests, have no choice but to build ethnic alliances at the national level in order to paddle through the turbulent waters of 'high politics'. Responsible for this is the obvious fact that the state has remained the single most important agent of social reproduction. The powers and influence associated with the state from the colonial period onwards are largely reproduced, maintained and sustained through ethno-political support. This ethno-political support is in turn strengthened by opportunities for 'accumulation from above' through extra-economic coercion.

The implication of these issues for the consolidation of political liberalisation and governance are quite clear. The fear to lose out in the elections, for instance, saw KANU allowing those who had pending criminal cases to be nominated to advance KANU's interests in the opposition strongholds. Although some of them lost, it is clear that they were using KANU as a political canopy. Despite the fact that neo-liberalism tends to justify multi-party forms of democracy as a means of promoting governance and democratisation, the use of candidates who had criminal charges to contain the tide of opposition or to penetrate opposition strongholds clearly shows that multi-partyism, as practised in Kenya, is informed by factors outside conventional democracy and governance. To win and control the state and its prebends is the concern of the mainstream parties. In relation to this, KANU was more concerned with deconstructing the GEMA hegemony in central Kenya, the heartland of the Kikuyu opposition politics. This end led to choices of various means, including outright voter buying, promises for development, and the creation of new districts. Owing to the contradictions at the local level, however, this strategy did not bear fruits everywhere. The contradiction between the 'high' and the 'low' politics, nonetheless, clearly shows that politics in modern Kenya is an enigma: it is a deeply divided society and a 'heap of contradictions'.

Notes

1.   The process of consolidating the Kalenjin started early in the 1940s. Pre-independence ethnic nationalism resulted in the Kalenjin becoming a confederacy that articulated their interests. For details on the consolidation of these groups during the Moi period, see Kanyinga (1998) and Cowen and Kanyinga (1998).

2. Barkan and Holmquist (1979) provide an elaborate discussion on how the elite appropriated *harambee* (pulling together for self-help development projects) as a base for political capital.

3. This section on Meru draws extensively from materials for Mike Cowen and Karuti Kanyinga (1998): 'The 1997 Elections in Kenya: the Politics of Communality and Locality', Institute of Development Studies, University of Helsinki, Mimeo, and from Tostensen et al. (1998). I would like therefore to thank Cowen and Tostensen who supported me in different ways during the period.

4. This observation was made by several residents in the Tigania and Igembe region in 1996 while I was conducting field work for a study on the land question and politics in Meru. Some observed that the land administration problems were a creation of Angaine for the purpose of punishing his rivals in the area (Kanyinga 1998).

References

Anyang' Nyong'o, P. 1989, 'State and society in Kenya: the disintegration of the nationalist coalitions and the rise of presidential authoritarianism in Kenya, 1963-78', *African Affairs*, Vol.88, No.351: 229-51.

Barkan, J.D. and Holmquist, F. 1989, 'Peasant-state relations and the social base of self-help in Kenya', *World Politics*, Vol.41, No.3: 359-80.

Barkan, J.D. and Ng'ethe, N. 1998, 'Kenya tries again', *Journal of Democracy* Vol.9, No.2: 32-48.

Berg-Schlosser, D. 1994, 'Ethnicity, Social Classes & the Political Process in Kenya' in Oyugi, W. (ed.) *Politics and Administration in East Africa*, Nairobi: East African Educational Publishers: 244-93.

Chege, M. 1994, 'The Return of Multiparty Politics', in Barkan, J.D. (ed.) *Beyond Capitalism vs. Socialism in Kenya and Tanzania*, Boulder: Lynne Rienner: 47-74.

Cowen, M. and Kanyinga K. 1998, The 1997 Elections in Kenya: the Politics of Communality and Locality, Institute of Development Studies, University of Helsinki, Mimeo.

———————— 2000, The 1997 elections in Kenya; The politics of communality and locality', in Cowen. M and L. Laakso (eds), *Multiparty Elections in Africa*. Oxford: James Currey.

———————— 1997, *National Elections Data Book: Kenya 1963-1997*, Nairobi: Institute for Education in Democracy.

Cowen, M. and MacWilliam, S. 1996, *Indigenous Capital in Kenya: the 'Indian' dimension of debate*, University of Helsinki, Institute of Development Studies, Interkont Books 8.

Cowen, M. and Ngunyi, M. 1997, 'Prelude to the 1992 and 1997 Elections in Kenya: reconciling reform within a chain of events', University of Helsinki, Institute of Development Studies, *Working Paper* No.10.

IED 1997, *National Elections Data Book: Kenya 1963-1997,* Nairobi: Institute for Education in Democracry.

IED 1998, *Understanding Election in Kenya: A Constituency Profile Approach*, Nairobi: Institute for Education in Democracy.

IED/CJPC/NCCK 1998, *Report on the 1997 General Elections in Kenya, 29-30 December, 1997*, Nairobi: Institute for Education in Democracy, Catholic Justice and Peace Commission, National Council of Churches of Kenya.

Kanyinga, K. 1994, 'Ethnicity, Patronage and Class in a Local Arena: "High" and "Low" politics in Kiambu, Kenya, 1982-92', in Gibbon, P. (ed.) *The New Local Level Politics in East Africa-Studies on Uganda, Tanzania and Kenya*, Uppsala: Nordiska Afrika Institutet (Scandinavian Institute of African Studies), Research Report No.95: 89-117.

_____ 1998, *The Land Question in Kenya: Struggles, accumulation and changing politics*, Unpublished PhD. Dissertation, Roskilde University.

Lonsdale, J. 1986, 'Political Accountability in African History' in Chabal, P. (ed.) *Political Domination in Africa: Reflections on the limits of power*, African Studies Series No.50, Cambridge University Press: 126-57.

_____ 1993, 'The Political Culture of Kenya' in Frederiksen, B.F. and Westergaard, K. (eds) Political Culture, Local Government and Local Institutions, *Occasional Paper* No.7, Roskilde University, International Development Studies: 87-107.

_____ 1994, 'Moral Ethnicity and Political Tribalism' in Kaarsholm, P. and Hultin, J. (eds) Inventions and Boundaries: Historical and Anthropological Approaches to the Study of Ethnicity and Nationalism, *Occasional Paper* No. 11, International Development Studies, Roskilde University: 131-50.

Mafeje, A. 1998, 'Class and Ideology of Ethnicity in Africa: Proposals for a new paradigm', Dakar: CODESRIA, Mimeo.

NEMU 1993, *The Multi-Party General Elections in Kenya, 29 December, 1992*, Nairobi: National Election Monitoring Unit.

Oyugi, W. 1998, 'Ethnic Politics in Kenya' in Nnoli, O. (ed.) *Ethnic Conflicts in Africa*, Dakar: CODESRIA: 287-309.

Throup, D. 1987, 'The Construction and Destruction of the Kenyatta State' in Schatzberg, M.G. (ed.) *The Political Economy of Kenya*, New York: Praeger: 33-74.

Throup, D. and Hornsby, C. 1998, *Multi-Party Politics in Kenya. The Kenyatta & Moi States & the Triumph of the System in the 1992 Election*, Oxford: James Currey.

Tostensen, A., Andreassen, B.-A., Tronvoll, K. 1998, *Kenya's Hobbled Democracy Revisited: the 1997 general elections in retrospect and prospect*, Oslo: University of Oslo Norwegian Institute of Human Rights (Human Rights Report No.2).

14

The Culture of Politics and Ethnic Nationalism in Central Province and Nairobi

Kimani Njogu

If ethnicity refers to, among other things, a system of social classification that is ostensibly rigid, yet dependent on flexibility and manipulation at the individual and collective levels; a structure for the definition and interaction of sub-national power groups making up the national polity; a system of social inequality and a strategic network for redistribution, as Van Binsbergen (1997: 91) suggests, then it has been a major factor in Kenya's social, economic and political life. Ethnicity, as a form of consciousness, following Colin Leys (1975) and Haugerud (1995), does constitute a local theory of political causation. Furthermore, it functions as an ideology through which inequality and violence vis-à-vis other ethnic groups may be 'justified'. When effectively manipulated by those who wield power, it can be a major rallying point for gaining and maintaining political support. Equally, it may be a major tool for shaking the status quo and putting in place an alternative leadership. In a country where ascendancy to the highest office in the land translates into at times real and at times illusory feelings of social and economic promise among the members of the leader's community, ethnic solidarity can frequently be quite strong and compelling.

The invocation of a discourse of differences and similarities among ethnic groups may also lead to a regrouping of others in local and national elections. Consequently, in the 1992 polls, the Central Province and Nairobi voted overwhelmingly for FORD-Asili, led by Kenneth Matiba. The DP voted for Mwai Kibaki, especially in Nyeri and Kirinyaga. In the 1997 elections, the two provinces voted mainly for Mwai Kibaki in the presidential elections, while Nyeri, Nyandarua, Nairobi, and Kirinyaga went for DP parliamentary candidates (See map on p.174). On the other hand, Murang'a, Thika, Maragwa, and Kiambu voted for candidates from a wide range of parties. How can this voting pattern be explained? What factors contributed in the 1997 electoral practices in Central Province and Nairobi?

Immediately after the 1992 multi-party elections results, Daniel arap Moi set out to win much needed support in Central Province and Nairobi. He put in place strategies that would ensure that come the 1997 elections, Kenya African National Union (KANU) would win some seats in the opposition strongholds. For example, Moi encouraged the activities of an economic elite among the Kikuyu, dubbed the Central Province Development Support Group (CPDSG). He vehemently denied any involvement in the pre- and post-1992 politically instigated violence in the Rift Valley in which the Kikuyu people and other non-Kalenjin communities were specifically targeted and forced to flee their homes due to their opposition politics. During his trips to central Kenya, he invoked the history of the ruling party as originally a Kikuyu-led party that had brought independence. Furthermore, he invoked the spirit of the first president of Kenya, Mzee Jomo Kenyatta, and argued that the Kikuyu community had a responsibility of ensuring that the party of the founding father of the nation remained in power. The anxieties of the Moi government stemmed from the 1992 voting patterns which had shown that the majority of the Kikuyu people wanted an alternative government, preferably led by a Kikuyu, that would guarantee economic recovery, relative democratic practices, and security.

Between 1992 and 1997, political realignments had moreover been taking place in Central Province. Paul Kabugi Muite, MP for Kabete (formerly Kikuyu) constituency, had resigned his position as the first vice-president of the Forum for the Restoration of Democracy-Kenya (FORD-Kenya) and sought to have the Safina party registered, but the government would not initially relent. Besides, the ailing Kenneth Matiba, MP for Kiharu and leader of the FORD-Asili party, had insisted that the 1992 presidential elections were rigged in favour of Moi. He had consequently refused to participate in parliamentary debates and only made 'technical appearances' in parliament. Later, he was to call for a national boycott of the 1997 polls and to urge his supporters to burn their voting cards. Later it emerge in the long run that he had himself not registered as a voter and could not have run for political office, in any case. Meanwhile, Mwai Kibaki had been working to portray himself as the alternative leader from Central Kenya in view of Matiba's deteriorating health.

Central Province had seen a systematic decline in the social and economic spheres since the 1980s. In the political domain, by the mid-1980s the province had moved away from the centre of national political activity. Kanyinga (1994) has, for example, effectively argued that Kiambu had, in the 1970s, politically been Kenya's most central and influential district, yet by 1993 it was one of the most politically marginal in national politics. The Moi regime had systematically worked to dislocate and neutralise its hold in the national arena, inherited from the Kenyatta era.

Furthermore, although by Kenyatta's death coffee and tea had been generalised to smaller farmers and there had been major expansions in milk and horticultural products, the residents of Central Province witnessed excessive executive interference in the coffee and tea industries. The introduction of Nyayo Tea Zones and the mismanagement of the Kenya Creameries Co-operation (KCC), as well as the Kenya Tea Development Authority (KTDA) led to the poor performance of the agricultural sector. The manufacturing sector introduced in Thika and Ruiru in the 1970s stalled as the Nyayo regime sought to consolidate its base by establishing new coalitions and alliances. Central Province responded to this marginalisation by going oppositional in the 1992 elections. The KANU strategy to bring back the Kikuyu, after 'supervising' the collapse of the agricultural sector in central Kenya and taking their land in the Rift Valley, as well as doing very little to stop the politically instigated ethnic cleansing, was to put in place money that could be used to lure back the community.

The politics of money and development

According to Throup and Hornsby (1998), KANU won the 1992 elections due to three factors. First, the opposition was unable to present a united front and a single candidate to face Daniel arap Moi at the polls. Second, the elections took an ethnic and regional dimension and, third the state's bias and electoral malpractice worked to the advantage of the incumbent head of state. But money was an equally important factor, especially if one takes into consideration the role played by the Youth for KANU '92, under the leadership of Cyrus Jirongo, and related groups. In that move, university professors, including Henry Mwanzi, George Eshiwani and William Ochieng', among others, functioned as think tanks for the ruling party and helped in legitimising it, as well as churning out propaganda material disseminated through the local press. The KANU-funded lobby groups allegedly dished out money in order to weaken the opposition in their strongholds. In addition, they were reported to have bought and destroyed voters' cards in areas known to be opposition constituencies. Moreover, civil servants and government vehicles were used around the clock to campaign for the ruling party. There were reports that money was printed illegally for campaign purposes. In a country where half the population lives below the poverty line, it is also likely that money may have contributed to the outcome of the 1992 elections.

In a show of ethnic solidarity, voters in central Kenya voted for FORD-Asili and the Democratic Party (DP) in the 1992 polls. As a consequence, Joseph Kamotho, the KANU secretary general and faithful supporter of Moi, went home with only 14 per cent of the votes cast in Kangema, losing to John Michuki of FORD-Asili who polled 73.7 per cent of the vote.

Interestingly, voter turnout in Murang'a was extremely high and there was talk that voter registration may even have continued after the deadline. Furthermore, in Makuyu some returning officers did not allow agents to check seals or accompany boxes, and in Kandara count certifiers were blocked from entering the counting hall (Throup and Hornsby 1998: 472). Although the DP had the support of financial heavyweights in Kiambu, such as Njenga Karume of Kiambaa and George Muhoho of Juja, the shift of solidarity with Matiba meant that the DP economic and political elite would not be elected in the 'up-for-grabs' Kiambu and Nairobi. FORD-Asili political nonentities defeated those DP heavyweights. As a result, in Gatundu South Kamuiru Gitau collected 34,104 (56.7 per cent) votes beating his closest rival, Ngengi Muigai of DP, who polled 21,780 (36.2 per cent) votes. In Juja, former minister George Muhoho lost to Stephen Ndichu who had 35,187 (68.2 per cent) votes against Muhoho's 8,393 (16.3 per cent). In Githunguri, former Vice-President Josephat Karanja romped home with 34, 019 (79.7 per cent) against KANU candidate Arthur Magugu who got 4,498 (10.5 per cent) and Rose Waruhiu of DP who polled 3,450 (8.1 per cent). And in Kiambaa, millionaire Njenga Karume lost to JohnKamau Icharia who put together 34,209 (69.9 per cent) against Karume's 11,912 (24.3 per cent).

A similar scenario was evident in Nairobi and Murang'a. Apparently, it had become clear to the electorate in Central Province that Matiba was the one opposition candidate that could take Moi head-on. His pro-people rhetoric, his entrepreneurial skills and successes, his massive wealth portrayed him as an individual capable of bringing real socio-economic changes. In addition, he had the support of the *matatu* taxi operators who admired his uncompromising posture. The Democratic Party was viewed as a party of rich fence sitters, whose only interest is to protect their wealth and social status. In order to regain control in Central Province and Nairobi, the ruling party needed to put in place structures aimed at bringing the province back into the corridors of power. One strategy was to work out a system of rapprochement with the Kikuyu.

Prior to and immediately after the 1992 elections, resentment against the Kikuyu people among a powerful section of the Kalenjin elite had grown tremendously. But a section of Kalenjin politicians had become convinced that the interests of their community lay in forging a working relationship with the Kikuyu community. This group was behind the Gikuyu, Embu, Meru Association (GEMA) communities and the Kalenjin, Maasai, Turkana and Samburu (KAMATUSA) talks of 1995 and had developed a symbiotic relationship with Kikuyu KANU leaders who, as a lobby group, sought to ensure that the interests of the community were protected.

The GEMA-KAMATUSA talks were meant to defuse post-election tensions caused by politically instigated ethnic clashes before and immediately after the 1992 polls. They sought to bring relative amity between the GEMA and KAMATUSA communities and it was hoped that some form of alliance could be forged for mutual economic and political benefit. In reality, however, the Kikuyu KANU leaders were preparing a political base for themselves, come the 1997 elections, convinced that it was possible to wrest Central Province from the opposition by invoking the discourse of development. Nonetheless, the marriage was first to be tested in the 1996 Kipipiri by-election, in Nyandarua district, following the death of the FORD-Asili MP, Laban Muchemi. Could money and a discourse of development shift the electorate in favour of KANU? Could Nyandarua be persuaded to rethink its oppositional politics?

Nyandarua is the largest district in Central Province and its constituencies currently include Kinangop, Ol Kalou, Ndaragwa, and Kipipiri. The district mainly comprises migrants from Kiambu and Nyeri and occupants of former Settlement Fund Trustee farms. A significant number of the victims of the Molo and Enoosupukia violence have also settled here. Kipipiri constituency is made up of Wanjohi, Kipipiri, Lereshwa, and Geta locations. It is the heart of Nyandarua district due to its agricultural productivity. In the 1992 polls, Laban Muchemi of FORD-Asili emerged the winner after garnering 24,210 votes (61.3 per cent) against his closest rival Paul Mwangi of DP who collected 12,197 votes (30.9 per cent). In 1995, Muchemi died and a by-election had to be held.

According to the Institute for Education in Democracy, 'The death of Muchemi presented KANU with an opportunity to get a foothold in Nyandarua District and Central Province in general. KANU launched a high-level campaign promising development if the electorate opted for the ruling party' (1998:154). As it turned out, the September 1995 by-election was a big blow to the envisaged partnership and rapprochement that was being cultivated. KANU desperately needed an MP from Central Province since the only MP from the area, Joseph Kamotho, was a nominated legislator.

In the 1992 polls the province had overwhelmingly voted for FORD-Asili and DP. Furthermore, in 1993 after the defection of the then MP for Makuyu, Julius Njuguna Njoroge, to the ruling party, KANU had been humiliated when the seat was recaptured by FORD-Asili through Robert Mungai. In Kipipiri the ruling party campaigned hard and Daniel arap Moi spent three days in the constituency campaigning for the KANU candidate, Joseph Mwangi Maina. Money was distributed and development was promised. Horns were locked between Mwangi Githiomi of the DP and the KANU candidate, because the election's favourite, Kimani wa Nyoike, had been barred from contesting by the electoral commission on a technicality.

On the election day, KANU was totally rejected by the electorate. Paul Mwangi Githiomi, an engineer, obtained 14,858 votes (82.5 per cent) against Mwangi Maina's 3,144 votes (17.5 per cent). Events in Kipipiri badly strained the relationship between KANU leaders from Central Province and the government, because it was viewed as a betrayal of trust. Simeon Nyachae, the then minister for Agriculture, Livestock development and Marketing, told the president at a rally: 'You have been misled . . . which son will allow his father to drive on a road full of obstacles without warning him that the road was impassable." (*Weekly Review* 23/01/98).

Because of this poor showing by KANU in the Kikuyu-dominated areas, the ruling party had to come up with alternative strategies to make a comeback. Consequently, the Central Province Development Support Group (CPDSG), a KANU lobby group of wealthy and influential Kikuyu individuals, started holding meetings, at first secretly and later publicly, in order to chart ways in which the Kikuyu community could be wooed back into the ruling party. The leading members of this group were cabinet minister and KANU secretary general Joseph Kamotho; Samuel Gichuru, the managing director of the Kenya Power and Lighting Company; SamuelKamau Macharia, a Nairobi businessman; Joseph Kaguthi, the then Nyanza provincial commissioner; John Ngata Kariuki, a tycoon in the hotel business; Peter G. Muriithi, a wealthy insurance broker; Crispus Mutitu, the permanent secretary in the Ministry of Energy; a former permanent secretary in the Ministry of Commerce and Industry, Margaret Githinji, and others.

The group sought to popularise KANU in central Kenya and used every available opportunity to contribute huge sums of money for various projects. In addition, the group convinced Daniel arap Moi and the top KANU brass that time was ripe to change KANU leadership in the province. They hosted a KANU convention at·the Ruring'u stadium in Nyeri in which Moi was presented as a saviour of the Kikuyu people. Earlier he had been made a member of the Ambui clan at Gatundu, to which Jomo Kenyatta belonged, an elevation that was later denied by the elders who had conducted the ceremony.

The elders claimed that they did not have the cultural powers necessary for such an elevation, because they were not themselves members of the Ambui clan. Nevertheless, the CPDSSG embarked on a well-funded campaign to persuade the community to rejoin KANU, 'the party that had brought independence and for which the Kikuyu people had suffered so much.' They criss-crossed central Kenya conducting huge fundraising meetings and encouraged Daniel arap Moi and his close associates to support their initiative.

The KANU party polls in the province, preceding the 1997 elections, were clearly manipulated so that sympathisers of the CPDSG could capture seats. In Kiambu District, for example, Viscount Kimathi replaced the out-of-favour

Kuria Kanyingi as branch chairman and in Thika district Uhuru Kenyatta, son of Jomo Kenyatta, captured the chairmanship to make his debut into elective politics. In Murang'a and Maragwa districts, Joseph Kamotho clearly called the shots and determined who would be elected. The KANU elections were in preparation for the 1997 elections, which would show if the CPDSG had succeeded in shifting political gears in the province. A number of the members of the group were actually eyeing parliamentary seats. They included Joseph Kamotho, in the gerrymandered Mathioya constituency; Ngata Kariuki in Kerugoya/Kutus; Viscount Kimathi in Lari; Davidson Kuguru in Mathira; S.K. Macharia in Gatanga; Uhuru Kenyatta in Gatundu South; and former Nairobi mayor Stephen Mwangi in Kinangop. They were eager to spend any amount of money towards this end and they contributed generously at every opportunity. It is not clear how much of that money actually came from their pockets and how much from the government coffers. Suffice to say that Mathioya was, for example, a beneficiary of millions of shillings through fund-raising activities in 1997: Ksh.7.5 million for the Youth Fund and Ksh.16 million for women's groups. Together members of the CPDSG must have raised hundreds of millions of shillings in order to win support.

Another strategy used by the Moi regime in the run-up to the 1997 elections was the resort to the politics of fragmentation. During the 1992 polls there were 41 districts. They were increased by over 30 per cent before the 1997 elections. Interestingly, the constituency boundary reviews were not guided by demographic considerations, but a desire to maintain power, at whatever cost. The additional constituencies in Central Province were Ol Kalou, cut from Ndaragwa constituency in Nyandarua district; Kerugoya/Kutus in Kirinyaga district; Mathioya in Murang'a district; and Gatundu North in Thika district. Mathioya was created for Joseph Kamotho, the fiery KANU general secretary, when it became clear that he was unlikely to dislodge John Michuki in Kangema, and the Kerugoya/Kutus seat was created for Ngata Kariuki. Initially, it had been hoped that the former governor of the Central Bank of Kenya would be the one to bring Kirinyaga back to KANU. The realignment in Gatundu was expected to cater for Uhuru Kenyatta in his debut to elective politics.

Moreover, despite Central Province and Nairobi being densely populated, the government has been unwilling to favourably restructure the regions' constituency boundaries. Constituencies that have continued to benefit from the restructuring have been those where the electorate have been likely to vote for the ruling party. In the run-up to the 1997 elections, only four constituencies were created in Central Province and none was created in the demographically strong but oppositionist Nairobi Province. Equally, no single underpopulated seat was abolished. Nairobi, with 725,625 registered voters, has only eight constituencies (an average of 90,000 voters per constituency) while the Rift Valley has 49 constituencies (an average of 45,000 voters per constituency). Yet, the new constituencies in Central Province did not elect a single KANU candidate despite the economic power of the candidates presented by the ruling party. The balkanisation strategy did not have any effect here, as the results indicate.

When the votes were cast in December 1997, the lobby group was totally rejected by the electorate. This blow was equally a rejection of KANU and Daniel arap Moi, who obtained only 5.6 per cent of the presidential vote in Central Province. Nearly 80 per cent of the voters chose Mwai Kibaki for president. The lobby group was extensively ridiculed for this debacle despite the fact that they had obtained a total of 100,000 votes across Central Province for their candidates while Moi only received 55,822 votes. Dishing out money and invoking a discourse of development did not seem to impress the voters in Central Province. Clearly, KANU was a very difficult and expensive item to sell in that province. The difficulty may be due to a number of factors ranging from the collapse of the coffee, tea and dairy industries; the stalling of manufacturing industries; high unemployment rates; rising poverty; and politically instigated ethnic violence.

In fact, the political violence prior to and after the 1992 elections in the Rift Valley and that in the Coast Province before the 1997 multi-party elections, gives us an opportunity to reflect on the validity of retreating to notions of deep ethnic attachments as a way of explaining violent political events in Africa. In the absence of a national legitimatising ideology, ethnocentrism may be manipulated by the state as a more localised alternative ideology to win a measure of public support. This is especially so if the state is used, as is so often the case in Africa, as a locus of individual and group enrichment. Moreover, the experiences and images reminiscent of the colonial repatriations of the Kikuyu people, in the wake of the Mau Mau war of liberation, were quite vivid and telling. Voters in Central Province remembered these events in the 1997 elections. It was hard to convince people who had seen their relatives displaced and slaughtered as the government watched from the sidelines to vote for candidates affiliated with the ruling party. The politics of money and development could not erase the physical and psychological pain experienced when the electorate suspects that the government sanctioned the displacement and massacre of its citizenry.

Kiambu, Thika, Maragwa, Murang'a: the Matiba factor

During the dying minutes in the run up to the elections, Safina party was registered. The ruling party hoped that Paul Kabugi Muite would run for president and split the GEMA communities right down the middle. This would have been of tremendous advantage to KANU whose trump card has been the policy of 'divide and rule'.

Although prior to the elections Kenneth Matiba had called for a boycott of the polls, religious leaders and politicians in the province did not follow his cue and instead called on their followers to participate in the exercise. Whereas in 1992 Mwai Kibaki had polled 26,432 votes of the 321,000 presidential ballots cast in the seven constituencies of Kiambu district, in the 1997 elections he polled 270,000 votes from the same area. This translates into more than a ten-fold increase in an area that had overwhelmingly voted for Matiba in 1992. Equally in Murang'a and Maragwa constituencies, Kibaki took a big slice of presidential votes cast. For instance, in four of the constituencies the turnout was over 70 per cent although it was 63.3 per cent in Maragwa and 55.8 per cent in Matiba's former Kiharu seat where Kibaki took 30,211 of the 37,632 votes cast. Apparently, there was some abstention by Matiba's supporters but no major boycott of voting in Kiambu and Nairobi which had supported him strongly in the 1992 polls.

Inevitably, Matiba's call for a boycott of the 1997 elections and his refusal to participate in any way in the polls confused and destabilised his supporters. They were without a party and quickly needed to find solace somewhere. Most found refuge in the DP, SDP, Safina and FORD-People. George Nyanja, the MP for Limuru, was the only MP from central Kenya to end up in the National Development Party (NDP) led by Raila Odinga. It is instructive for a moment to reflect on Nyanja's narrative as it points to the absence of a strong ideological base for the parties and politicians as well as to the level of disorientation and disarray brought by Kenneth Matiba's absence from the election scene.

It would seem that a substantial number of elected leaders are willing to flirt with any party that ensures them access to political power. When Nyanja realised that Matiba was not going to contest in the elections because, among other reasons, he had no voting card and in view of his poor relations with Martin Shikuku, the leader of FORD-Asili, George Nyanja set out in November 1997, a month away from the general elections, to find a safe haven for his political activities.

Although he had initially been accepted in the DP, it quickly dawned on him that he might not be nominated by the party. Assuming that he could be easily embraced by Paul Muite and Richard Leakey of Safina party, he announced that he had shifted camp to the newly registered Safina. However, the Safina leadership did not admit him into the party because of his past utterances in reference to the Europeans and Asians living in Kenya. Safina was trying to carve an image for itself as a party of principled individuals with a vision for a united nation, free from ethnic and racial bigotry. George Nyanja quickly sought to join the SDP, but was not embraced by Charity Ngilu and Peter Anyang' Nyong'o. At this point he tried to rejoin the DP. When the DP shut the door in his face, Nyanja instantly and desperately turned to Raila Odinga and the NDP. As it turned out for the Limuru voters, it did not matter which party ticket Nyanja was going to run on so long as he did so on an opposition ticket. The legislator went on to become the only MP from central Kenya to win a seat on an NDP ticket. Nyanja's initial hesitation to seek NDP nomination had to do with ethnicity and the fear of rejection by his voters if he joined a Luo-led party.

If only three of the 31 FORD-Asili MPs elected in 1992 regained their seats in 1997, it is because Kenneth Matiba had withdrawn his support and resources. In any case, a number had been elected in 1992, not necessarily on the basis of their own credentials but, more so, on account of the three-piece-suit slogan in which Matiba called on his supporters to vote in FORD-Asili councillors and MPs as they had voted for him as president. In the absence of such rhetoric and a strong political base, a huge percentage of FORD-Asili MPs either abandoned elective politics altogether or defected to the more dominant parties, especially KANU.

The Starehe constituency, for instance, lost two MPs between 1992 and 1997: Kiruhi Kimondo and former Nairobi mayor Stephen Mwangi. Kimondo was not nominated by KANU when he defected in 1994 and Mwangi left the national assembly claiming that Matiba did not have a vision for the party. He sought to quit elective politics but was courted by KANU. Initially, he hoped to run for the Gatundu seat in the 1997 elections but, on realising that Uhuru Kenyatta would seek nomination on a KANU ticket, he moved on to Kinangop. He was nominated by KANU headquarters for the seat amid complaints by the local sub-branch. However, the seat was won by Mwangi Waithaka of FORD-People.

Mwangi Kirika Waithaka, a Nairobi-based lawyer, had run in the 1992 polls on a DP ticket, but lost to Mary Wanjiru of FORD-Asili, possibly as a consequence of the Matiba factor. Wanjiru had polled 20,144 votes, or 50.4 per cent of the votes cast against Waithaka's 9,814 or 28.4 per cent of the votes. In 1997, Mwangi Waithaka ran on a FORD-People ticket and garnered an impressive 23,141 votes or 60.8 per cent of the votes. His closest rival was Joseph Kuria Methu of DP who polled 9,583 votes or 15.2 per cent of the votes. Mary Wanjiru, the former member of parliament, could only manage an embarrassing 243 (0.6 per cent) votes. In Kinangop the issues revolved around developmet and she had clearly not delivered.

Murang'a

In Murang'a district, Matiba's support was still crucial in determining election results, although he had fallen out with his closest associates such as Philip Gachoka and George Kamuiru Gitau, former Murang'a mayor. His hold on the Wangu Investments in Kiharu, with a membership of over 10,000 members, meant that no candidate could succeed against him in that constituency. When he did not run in 1997, Ngenye Kariuki, a powerful Nairobi stockbroker, easily sailed through on a Safina party ticket by collecting 27,369 (72.4 per cent) votes, against Julius Gikonyo Kiano, a former powerful KANU minister, who polled 5,666 votes (15.0 per cent). In the 1992 elections, Matiba had a landslide victory over William Mbote of KANU by polling 57,000 (98.6 per cent) votes, against the latter's 784 (1.4 per cent). The people of Kiharu did not want to leave any doubts that Matiba was their favourite candidate.

Joseph Kamotho had for a long time represented Kangema constituency. However, with multi-partyism, he lost his grip on the constituency to John Njoroge Michuki, a descendant of an influential and powerful family that had served the colonial government in the pre-independence era. In fact, Kamotho quite often invoked the history of collaboration in his campaigns, as a strategy to discredit the candidacy of Michuki. Although for a time that invocation of history had an impact, it could not last and in 1992 Michuki, running on a FORD-Asili ticket, polled 38,620 (73.7 per cent) votes against Kamotho's 7,436 (14.2 per cent). During the 1997 elections, Michuki ran on a FORD-People ticket and collected 17,707 votes (80.4 per cent) against KANU's Naftali Ngeru who polled 4,308 votes (19.6 per cent).

KANU leadership had little choice but to nominate Joseph Kamotho to parliament. Kamotho has over time been the most visible and vocal secretary general of any party in Kenya. He will take every opportunity to articulate and defend his party's position, even at the risk of becoming unpopular in the eyes of the electorate. KANU recognises that if it has to maintain a semblance of presence in Central Province, then loyalist Kamotho is the indispensable flag-bearer. He has shown courage, consistency, and astuteness in his defence of the Moi government and this has made him extremely unpopular in his home district. Nominating him is a reward for his uncompromising position in the defence of KANU. This was the second time that Kamotho was rejected by the electorate but nominated by the president. Prior to the 1997 elections, Kangema constituency had been split into two to create Mathioya constituency, widely regarded as tailor-made for Kamotho's political survival. He was beaten at the polls by the little-known Francis Maina Njakwe, who had vied for the seat on a FORD-People ticket.

Whereas DP candidates did not have a major impact in Murang'a in the 1997 parliamentary polls, they seemed to call the shots in the neighbouring Maragwa district. In 1992, the Kigumo constistuency saw John Kirore Mwaura collect 50,527 votes (93.1 per cent) on a FORD-Asili ticket, defeating his closest challenger, J.K. Heho of DP, who polled 2,828 votes (5.2 per cent). However, during the 1997 elections Onesimus Mwangi of DP carried home 13,550 votes (67.2 per cent) against Obed Mburu of FORD-People who could only manage 1,897 votes (9.4 per cent). Maragwa, formerly Makuyu constituency, with parts of Gatanga and Kandara after the 1996 review, was the only constituency in Central Province to experience a defection to KANU after the 1992 polls when Julius Njoroge of FORD-Asili, who had been given 71.9 per cent of the votes cast, decamped to KANU in 1993.

In the resultant by-election, Robert Kinuthia Mungai of FORD-Asili won the seat after polling 8,791 votes (76.5 per cent). The seat was captured by the DP in 1997 when Peter Kamande Mwangi collected 8,547 votes, narrowly beating Maina Chege of FORD-People who polled 7,086 votes (25.4 per cent). The DP also took Kandara when Joshua Ngugi Toro polled 26,113 votes (65.9 per cent) against long time legislator George Mwicigi of FORD-People who had (18.8 per cent) 7,441 votes. CPDSG candidate David Muraya of KANU only managed 3,981 votes (10.1 per cent).

Thika

The poor showing by the rich lobby group was repeated in Gatanga, Thika district, where David Murathe of SDP beat Samuel K. Macharia by polling 14,306 votes (36.1 per cent) to 8,123 votes (20.5 per cent). In Kiambu and Thika districts, three of the six FORD-Asili MPs were re-elected: Philip Gitonga won in Lari for Safina; George Nyanja in Limuru for the NDP; and Njehu Gatabaki, the publisher of the politically controversial *Finance* magazine, who had been elected in 1994 as MP for Githunguri after the death of former Vice-President, Josephat Karanja, held the seat for the SDP against the rich former cabinet minister and KANU candidate, Arthur Magugu, who had this time round contested on a Labour Party Democracy (LPD) ticket. Apparently, Magugu had realised that it was only through an opposition party ticket that a successful re-entry into parliament could be made in Central Province. It did not matter that his ideological inclination and practice were at variance with that of oppositional politics.

Paul Muite, the Safina party leader and formerly FORD-Kenya's sole MP from central Kenya, re-captured the Kabete seat by polling 48,504 votes against KANU's 2,729. In Kiambaa, GEMA chairman and multi-millionaire Njenga Karume polled 37,091 votes for the DP while, John Kamau Icharia, the former FORD-Asili legislator in the constituency gained 5,561 votes for Safina, to which he had moved just a few weeks before the elections. Stanley Munga Githunguri, the wealthy Nairobi and Kiambu businessman and former chief executive officer of the National Bank of Kenya polled 6,901 for KANU. This poor showing was presumably due to his association with the CPDSG who, as we have seen thus far, were unpopular with the electorate.

In sum, therefore, Murang'a elected two FORD-People and one Safina party MPs; Thika district elected four SDP MPs; and Kiambu voted in one MP each for Safina, SDP, DP, and NDP. Apparently, voters in Kiambu, Thika, and Murang'a, unlike their counterparts in Nyeri and Kirinyaga, voted for individuals in the opposition and not necessarily for their party of affiliation.

Unbeatable Kibaki: politics in Nyeri and Kirinyaga

In Nyeri district, popular politicians were rejected for not running on a DP ticket. If the late Jaramogi Oginga Odinga called political shots in Luo Nyanza for decades, in Nyeri district Mwai Kibaki determines the political heart beat. Consequently, to campaign against Kibaki in that district is clearly futile, at least for the moment. In 1992, Kibaki had collected one million votes in the presidential polls, coming third after Moi and Matiba. In his Othaya constituency in Nyeri he had polled 31,536 votes (99.1 per cent) against those of his rival Kibira Wahome of KANU who could only manage 276 votes (0.9 per cent). This type of political presence was repeated in 1997 when he collected 31,637 votes (97.8 per cent) while his closest rival Stanley Maina Benjamin of KANU could only manage 610 votes (1.9 per cent). Kibaki's close associates did very well for the DP. Kieni, for example, an epicentre of nationalist politics hived off from Tetu constituency in 1988, and represented by Muruthi Muriithi of KANU between 1988-92, became a strong DP constituency and in 1992, was taken by Munene Kairu who polled 31,447 votes against Muriithi's 1,187 for KANU. Kairu was to recapture the seat easily in 1997 by polling 37,957 votes (93.0 per cent) against John Gitiche Mbao of KANU who took home 2,507 votes (6.1 per cent).

The environmentalist Professor Wangari Maathai contested the Tetu constituency on a Liberal Party of Kenya ticket. She made no impact either as a parliamentary candidate or a presidential contestant. The seat was taken by Paul Gikonyo Muya of DP, who polled 24,229 votes (89.0 per cent) against the 1,994 votes (7.3 per cent) of Nahashon Kanyi Waithaka of KANU's and Wangari Maathai's 905 votes (3.3 per cent). In the 1992 polls, Joseph Githenji had polled 28,085 votes (95.0 per cent) against Nahashon Kanyi of KANU who collected 1,469 votes (5.0 per cent). Tetu is the home of the late Dedan Kimathi, leader of the Mau Mau freedom fighters. The community bore the brunt of the liberation war during the colonial times and the shock is not over yet, especially because both the Kenyatta and Moi governments have not taken any steps to alleviate the glaring poverty in the constituency. According to Muthui Mwai:

Nearly 40 years after the end of the war that ushered in Kenya's independence, the constituency still looks stunned by the enormity of the struggle and the blood which was shed. One might even get the impression that the constituency is in deep political slumber. Yet this seemingly apolitical stance is misleading because the people of Tetu feel deeply about the stagnation of development in this area. (*Daily Nation* 09/08/99).

Tetu has very poor infrastructure, yet the area has great agricultural potential, especially in the production of coffee, tea and dairy products. The area has poor health facilities, a close to non-existent water supply, a deteriorating educational system and impoverished villages set up at the peak of the Mau Mau war. During the Moi era, further marginalisation of the constituency has occurred with the eviction of landless people who had occupied the Aberdare forest area. The constituents voted for Mwai Kibaki's party not only because he was a 'home boy' but also due to their disillusionment with KANU, which had failed to bring development to a constituency that had sacrificed heavily for the liberation of Kenya.

But Tetu was not alone in this call for change. Nyeri Town saw the entry of Wanyiri Kihoro as the new MP. This constituency had been targeted by the CPDSG, through the candidacy of Peter Gichohi Muriithi, a Nairobi insurance broker, as well as director of Kenya Power and Lighting Company, former chairman of the Nairobi International Agricultural Show, and Nyeri KANU branch chairman. There was hope that it would fall to KANU. In the 1992 parliamentary polls, Isaiah Mathenge, a former powerful provincial commissioner in the Kenyatta government, had won after polling 29,844 votes against his closest rival and former MP, the youthful Waihenya Ndirangu of Kenya National Congress (KNC), who collected 2,991 votes. When Wanyiri Kihoro was nominated by the DP, he went on to win after polling 30,629 votes (87.0 per cent) against Peter Gichohi Muriithi who polled 3,428 votes for KANU. Wanyiri had suffered detention without trial under Daniel arap Moi between 1986 and 1989 for his political activities. His detention experiences narrated in the autobiographical text *Never Say Die* attest to the man's resilience and fighting spirit.

One of the most politically charged constituencies in Nyeri district is Mathira. The constituency, whose politics revolve around the co-operative movement, has a track record of violence during election time. Since the 1980s, politics in the area have been dominated by two major players: the late Davidson Ngibuini Kuguru and Matu Wamae. Between 1969 and 1983, Kuguru had been the only political giant in Mathira and had served in the cabinets of Kenyatta and Moi. Matu Wamae was a parastatal executive with the Industrial and Commercial Development Corporation (ICDC) before joining elective politics. In the 1983 elections, there was unprecedented violence between the supporters of Kuguru and those of Wamae. Mwai Kibaki was accused of supporting Matu Wamae who went on to represent his constituency between 1983-88 and 1992-97. In 1992 Matu Wamae polled 47,256 votes (87.8 per cent) for the DP while Davidson Kuguru garnered 4, 310 votes (8.0 per cent) for KANU. When the elder Kuguru passed away in early 1997, Wamae remained the most experienced candidate in the constituency and in the 1997 election easily collected 38,349 votes (82.1 per cent) votes for the DP against Peter Ngibuini Kuguru of KANU who pocketed 4, 310 votes (17.3 per cent).

Table 14.1: Votes cast for the DP candidates in Nyeri district (per cent)

Constituency	Parliament 1992	Parliament 1997	Presidential 1992	Presidential 1997
Nyeri Town	83	87	90	92
Mathira	88	98	95	94
Tetu	94	92	97	96
Kieni	93	93	92	93
Othaya	99	98	98	97
Mukurweini	70	64	92	96

These percentages show the extent of the DP's popularity in Nyeri district. They are quite comparable to the party's performance in neighbouring Kirinyaga. Only in Mukurweini, does the party appear to be relatively weak. This is the constituency that is likely to go to a candidate not endorsed by Kibaki.

In Kirinyaga, the DP was the people's party of choice in 1992 and 1997, presumably because of the political influence of the Kibaki factor in Nyeri. In the presidential polls, the district gave Kibaki over 93 per cent of all the votes cast, just as he got in his home district of Nyeri. In the less developed multi-ethnic Mwea constituency, issues revolve around rice, horticulture, land tenure, health, and poor infrastructure. During the 1992 elections, Allan Njeru Murigu of DP took the seat upon polling 66.6 per cent of the votes against long-time legislator Stephen Kiragu of FORD-Asili who took 26.2 per cent of the polls. Again the DP came out victoriously in 1997 when Alfred Mwangi Ndiritu collected 27,373 (85.8 per cent) votes against Ibrahim Mutugi of KANU who garnered 2,253 (7.1 per cent) votes. Kibaki was given 93.5 per cent of the presidential votes. Equally, Gichugu constituency went to the DP through lawyer Martha Wangari Karua. Karua in 1992 beat long-time political rivals Geoffrey Kariithi and Nahashon Njuno by polling 57.2 per cent of the votes, and improved on the margin in 1997 by garnering 30,736 of the votes, (79.0 per cent) against her closest rival Harry Frederick Mugo who got 4,680 (12.0 per cent). Ndia and Kerugoya/Kutus constituencies followed suit and voted for DP candidates James Kareu Kibicho (88.8 per cent) and John Matere Keriri (59.5 per cent) respectively. The CPDSG candidate John Ngata Kariuki of KANU managed to take home 1,992 votes (6.5 per cent) in Kerugoya/Kutus. Clearly, Kirinyaga was a DP stronghold in every respect.

Nairobi: by any means possible

Nairobi remained an opposition orbit with Moi getting slightly more than 20 per cent of the votes and Kibaki above 40 per cent. The difference between 1992 and 1997 was that whereas in 1992 FORD-Asili dominated the elections in 1997 it was the DP that did. Clearly, the politics of Central Province affect the politics of the metropolis mainly because of its proximity. Except in Dagoretti, Lang'ata and Westlands, elections in Nairobi were a triumph for the DP, which captured five seats while Kibaki won seven in the presidential elections.

The capital city rejected KANU although Daniel arap Moi did better than expected. He obtained 20.6 per cent of all votes. DP won in Starehe, Makadara, Kamukunji and Embakasi comfortably, but had to struggle against the NDP in Kasarani where the main opposition party polled 35.0 per cent of the votes against 34.5 per cent polled by the NDP. It lost Dagoretti to Beth Mugo of the SDP; Lang'ata to NDP leader Raila Odinga and in Westlands the DP candidate Betty Tett was allegedly rigged out by KANU's Fred Gumo where the two parties obtained 36.3 per cent of the votes cast. KANU needed a seat in the capital city and Gumo would deliver it by any means possible.

Gumo's political career has always been full of controversy. He became the mayor of Kitale in 1974 at the age of 27 and held the position for six years. He left to pursue parliamentary politics in 1979 and upset Masinde Muliro in the polls which were claimed to be rigged. Moi appointed him an assistant minister. He recaptured the seat in 1983 but in 1984 the High Court ruled that his victory over Masinde Muliro in Kitale East was rigged and the results were nullified. He did not contest in the by-election, but re-emerged in 1989 in Kwanza and failed when he lost to Noah Wekesa. In 1989 Moi appointed him chairman of the Nairobi City Commission, during which period he supervised the demolition of Mworoto and Kibarage estates. Hawkers were constantly targeted for beating by the City Council *askaris* during his tenure of office. In the 1992 elections, Gumo shifted his base from Trans Nzoia to Bunyala, his original home, but lost to James Osogo. When in 1996 there was a by-election in Westlands, following the death of the KANU MP Amin Walji, Frederick Omulo Gumo went on to win by polling 1,204 votes in a very poor turnout of 6.3 per cent. During the 1997 elections, Gumo was committed to recapturing the Westlands seat.

It was widely claimed that Gumo had encouraged the Luhya community resident in Nairobi to register in Westlands where voter registration seems to have continued beyond the deadline. The count had been protracted and violent. In the final analysis, Kibaki narrowly took the presidential vote after three disputed boxes had been recounted. The DP presidential candidate polled 35.4 per cent votes in this constituency against Moi's 34.3 per cent, the highest for KANU in Nairobi. The parliamentary results were not announced until after four o'clock in the afternoon on Saturday 3 January 1998, 130 hours after votes had been cast.

Reports indicated that Gumo, shielded and assisted by the police, had allegedly assaulted Betty Tett's sister and other DP supporters, as the counting of presidential votes was under-way. International observers arrived in Westlands at about 1.30 pm on 3 January, 1998 to witness the final stages of counting the parliamentary election votes at the Railway Club, the counting centre. At about 1.45 pm the exercise was over, and the returning officer said that she needed an hour to check the results before she could make a formal announcement on the outcome. A huge number of armed riot police was assembled around the Railway Club. Moreover, Maasai moran armed with clubs and swords were also present. Journalists claimed that senior government officers – Njiru Kyanda and Joseph Ngala – had been talking with the returning officer, presumably so that she could tamper with the results. When the returning officer finally resurfaced at 4 pm after over two hours' absence, she announced that Amin Alibhai of NDP had secured 5,050 votes, Betty Tett 17,721 and Gumo 18,590.

Interestingly, all international observers and party officials from the SDP, FORD-Kenya, NDP and DP contested the results claiming that Betty Tett was the actual winner. Provisional figures released per polling stream had indicated that she had garnered 17,829 votes against 17,790 for Fred Gumo (*Kenya Times* 08/01/98). Thus, Gumo's figure had been inflated by 800 votes, and Tett's reduced by 69, DP officials claimed. They also stated that at one stage the deputy returning officer had congratulated Tett's agent on her triumph. KANU officials, however, had asserted to a foreign journalist after the release of the last stream count (but before the results were announced by the returning officer) that Gumo had won by five votes: from 17,885 to 17,880.

There was total chaos and the returning officer did not formally finish announcing the results. She actually did not make a declaration of the winner, as is legally required. Although the results from the polling stations had been accepted by all the parties, the final results were contested by all the opposition parties in the constituency. Their demand for a recount was denied. Funnily, the official results published by the ECK are again different from those announced by the returning officer and from those that appeared in the daily newspapers. The latter gave 18,590 for Gumo and 17,721 for Tett as announced by the returning officer (*East African Standard* 04/01/98). However, the ECK gave 17,882 to Gumo versus 17,877 to Tett – a five votes difference (ECK 1999:123).

There is little doubt that inefficiency, lack of leadership guidance and poor organisational capability from the DP headquarters had prevented the filing of an injunction in the high court against gazetting Fred Gumo as the MP for Westlands. They were far too undecided and slow. Disappointingly, by the time Betty Tett went to court to file an injunction on Thursday, 8 January, Fred Gumo had already been gazetted as the MP for Westlands. Speed had been crucial in determining the outcome of that seat and KANU had outsprinted the other parties in this vital race.

But what about Dagoretti? As the 1997 elections drew close, the FORD-Asili MP for Dagoretti Chris Kamuyu became closely associated with KANU because he was in financial problems and was no longer confident of Matiba's support. Moreover, Beth Mugo, initially associated with the DP and FORD-Asili before settling under SDP, had effectively consolidated her grassroots support. In the final analysis, Kamuyu received 6,027 votes against Beth Mugo's impressive 21,745 votes.

It had been assumed that the SDP under Ngilu would have a strong presence in Nairobi. In reality, the NDP and KANU did better although not well enough to dislodge the DP. The DP collected a total of 160,124 presidential votes (43.7 per cent) while KANU took 75,272 (20.6 per cent), the NDP 59,415 (16.2 per cent) and the SDP garnered 39,707 (10.9 per cent) of the votes cast. The opposition together collected around 80 per cent of the votes cast. But why this dismal showing by Charity Ngilu's party that had shown so much promise? First, just before the elections Mwai Kibaki held an extremely successful rally at Uhuru Park Nairobi in which he called on Kenyans to vote for the Democratic Party if they wanted the economy back on track. He called on Nairobians to vote for candidates nominated by the DP and he created the impression that he was the one candidate that had a real chance of wrestling the presidency from Moi. Although the electronic media had consistently ignored stories that had the potential to enhance the image of opposition candidates, the print media carried that story. It is plausible that Ngilu supporters in Nairobi changed their allegiance to Kibaki due to the latter's last campaign rally.

Secondly, Ngilu did not have a youthful constituency, drawn from the lumpen proletariat and the urban poor based in the slums, fully committed to her party. Over the years, there has been a deliberate ethnicisation and radicalisation of the youth in Kenya's urban centres. Because elections are seen as a platform through which individuals and constituents can be developed, socially and economically disadvantaged groups tend to congregate around individuals best suited to facilitate patronage resources. Significantly, powerful individuals drawn from one's ethnic group are more often than not viewed as 'the safest' patrons. For example, the Westlands MP Fred Gumo is associated with a group, predominantly Luhya in composition which has come to be known as *Jeshi la Mzee*. The *Jeshi* allegedly was responsible for privatised violence against opposition youths, mobilised political support, and eroded the social basis of individuals who were non-supportive of their favourite candidate. Although *Jeshi la Mzee* is the best known violent youth group, it is not the only one. It has been claimed that Raila Odinga has his own Luo-based youths that protect his interests in Nairobi. Moreover, Kenneth Matiba has full support of *matatu* touts in Nairobi and Central Province who are predominantly Kikuyu. When it became clear that Matiba was not running in the 1997 elections, the touts changed their allegiance to Kibaki and campaigned for him to the hilt.

Finally, there is the issue of ethnicity in Kenyan politics. Given the proximity between Nairobi and Central Province, it is evident that dominant voting patterns in Central Province will almost invariably be replicated in Nairobi. This had happened in 1992 when Nairobi overwhelmingly voted for FORD-Asili.

Raila Odinga is the only NDP member of the legislature in Nairobi. His Lang'ata constituency, comprising the plush Karen, the populous sprawling Kibera slums and Mugumoini, and the middle class Nairobi West, is an epitome of glaring contrast in living standards. It is multi-ethnic and multi-racial with the Luo, Luhya, Kikuyu and Kisii dominating political activity. In 1997 Raila Odinga, the then MP, defected to the NDP from FORD-Kenya and made history as the only opposition MP to defect from one opposition party to another. The others almost always defect to the ruling party 'for rewards and development' or resign altogether. In the 1992 polls, Raila had polled 24,261 votes (43.2 per cent) against Kimani Rugendo of FORD-Asili who took 13,430 votes (23.9 per cent) and Philip Leakey of KANU who collected 11,901 votes (21.2 per cent). Mwangi Maathai of the DP came a distant fourth with 6,282 votes (11.2 per cent).

In the 1997 by-election the voter turnout was very low (at 7,050 compared to 56,124 of the votes cast in 1992), as it normally is in by-elections because of, among other reasons, voter fatigue. Raila easily retained his parliamentary seat by polling 4,798 votes (68.7 per cent) against his closest rival Fred Amayo of KANU, who scored 1,874 votes (26.8 per cent). Kimani Rugendo of FORD-Asili could only manage 279 votes (4.0 per cent)

Raila Amolo Odinga, the son of the doyen of Kenya's oppositional politics, the late Jaramogi Oginga Odinga, has suffered detention under the Moi regime.

Ironically, since the 1997 elections he has worked closely with the ruling party under what is known popularly, though at times sneeringly, as the co-operation pact. For years, Raila had represented the radical, aggressive, confrontational thrust in Kenyan opposition politics. The Moi regime constantly portrayed him as a violent, underground operative closely linked to socialist regimes in Africa and abroad. Occasionally, he was shown as a close associate of the Mozambican and Ugandan revolutionary governments which were portrayed as leftist in inclination.

It has, therefore, come as a surprise to many Kenyans that Raila Odinga would choose to co-operate with KANU during the post 1997 election period. Raila's argument has been that co-operating with KANU would bring development to NDP-represented constituencies. However, critics of the co-operation pact, within and without NDP, point to an absence of tangible development attributed to the new cohabitation. They argue that the advantages are individual rather than collective and that it is only Raila Odinga who has reaped the benefits, if any. It is claimed that he is the only one who knows the terms of the engagement.

Raila Odinga's behaviour may be attributed to the outcome of the 1992 and 1997 elections. In both elections it was quite manifest that ethnicity was central in the shaping of Kenya's political landscape although it was not the only factor. In 1992, his father, Jaramogi Oginga Odinga, was placed fourth in the presidential polls after Daniel Moi, Kenneth Matiba, and Mwai Kibaki, respectively. It had been assumed that in view of Odinga's consistent contribution to the democratisation process during the Kenyatta and Moi eras, Kenyans would reward him with the presidency. The results were a shock to the old man and those closest to him. When Jaramogi died in 1993, his son, Oburu Odinga, took over the mantle of leadership in Bondo while Raila consolidated his base in Lang'ata.

Raila's opposition in Lang'ata before the 1997 elections was such that most political analysts thought he would be better off contesting the polls in Bondo instead of Lang'ata, because the latter was viewed to be a shaky political base due to, among other things, its ethnic diversity and migratory tendencies typical of urban constituencies. Moreover, Raila Odinga could not point to any specific projects he had initiated as a member of parliament. Observers argued that it would be suicidal for him to try and retain his seat, but the confident Raila Odinga went on to win the Lang'ata seat by collecting 22,339 (51.8 per cent) of the votes against his closest challenger Perez Malande Olindo of KANU who polled 11,883 (27.6 per cent) and George Njage Ngentu of DP who was a distant third at 4,667 (10.8 per cent).

Moreover, although Kibaki did quite well in the other Nairobi constituencies in the presidential polls, he only collected 8,664 votes (19.8 per cent) from Lang'ata, while Moi managed 11,420 votes (26.1 per cent) and Raila polled for the NDP 14,955 (34.2 per cent) of the votes cast. Clearly, Lang'ata was a closely contested constituency in 1997 but Raila seems to have been in control, sometimes through brute force, and to have legitimised his continued presence in parliament. After the polls, the radical, controversial, and sometimes violent Raila Odinga, started redefining his image and planning for the post-Moi era. His strategy is to co-operate with KANU and Kalenjin power brokers.

Raila's shift to the spirit of co-operation may have to do with his vision of the culture of politics in the post-Moi era. He had worked hard to get some form of endorsement from Kenneth Matiba in the run-up to the 1997 elections to no avail. Raila may well have reasoned that in the absence of the Kikuyu, Luhya, and Kamba support, he would be better off working with the minority Kalenjin, in the hope that they would one-day support a Luo presidency. He may have calculated that the Kalenjin are likely to welcome new ethnic alliances and, by accepting to co-operate with KANU, he would have a head start over his opponents.

The trouble with Raila Odinga's calculation is that it assumes that Moi will not want to endorse a KANU candidate in the 2002 elections. Furthermore, it takes for granted the commitment of KANU's power brokers to retain their hold on any future leadership. The operative questions are: who can they trust to protect their interests in the post-Moi era? The Odinga family has suffered immensely under the Moi regime, Can the power brokers support Raila's ascendancy to the presidency without fear of possible retaliation?

Another possible NDP constituency in Nairobi was Kasarani (formerly Mathare but renamed in 1996). It consists of Kariobangi North, Ruaraka, Kasarani, Roysambu, Kahawa South and North. Kasarani is an extremely poor constituency and has some of the most expansive slums, which include Mathare, Huruma, Kariobangi, Korogocho, and Githurai. The problems here include serious unemployment, poor housing, lack of health facilities, insecurity, and general poverty. In the 1992 polls, Muraya Macharia of FORD-Asili collected 23,836 (36.2 per cent) of the votes while Frederick Masinde of FORD-Kenya polled 19,579 votes (29.7 per cent), Andrew Ngumba of DP took home 15,147 (23.0 per cent) and Zachariah Maina of KANU could only manage 7,315 votes (11.1 per cent). It was a very close contest.

The constituency had two by-elections before the 1997 general elections. The first by-election was occasioned by a petition filed by FORD-Kenya's Frederick Masinde against FORD-Asili's Muraya Macharia. On the polling day, however, Masinde who was also a candidate in the by-election was involved in a tragic road accident and died before the election results were announced. He had been declared the winner after polling 6,609 (41.0 per cent) votes against Muraya Macharia who polled 5,984 for FORD-Asili and Andrew Ngumba who had decamped from DP to KANU and collected 3,533 (21.9 per cent).

The turnout was very poor at 16,126 (13.8 per cent) compared to the 1992 figure of 65,877 (56.5 per cent). A second by-election was held four months later and Ochieng' Mbeo of FORD-Kenya took the seat after polling 6,203 votes (42.1 per cent) votes against his closest challenger Andrew Ngumba of KANU who garnered 4,364 (29.6 per cent). Muraya Macharia polled 4,160 (28.3 per cent) for FORD-Asili.

In the 1997 elections, a new entrant Adolf Muchiri of DP collected 16,179 votes (35.0 per cent) against Ochieng' Mbeo of NDP who polled 15, 924 (34.5 per cent) in this closely contested seat. KANU's Pius Lee Kamau Muchiri carried 6,606 votes (14.3 per cent). Other than the phenomenon of ethnic voting, another feature of urban voting may help explain Ochieng' Mbeo's failure to recapture the Kasarani seat for the NDP. This is the feature of voter migration. It has been claimed that during the 1997 elections most of the Luo in Nairobi registered in Lang'ata in order to vote for Raila Odinga in the elections, leaving the NDP candidate with marginal votes. Although this claim cannot be verified, it is quite plausible. A related feature is that Central Province voters could easily register and vote in Nairobi if there is sufficient motivation, financial or otherwise, to do so. Consequently, voting patterns characteristic of Central Province, may easily seep into Nairobi.

Conclusion

Before the 1997 polls, KANU had assumed that the general disillusionment with opposition leaders would translate into votes for the ruling party. But Central Province is more integrated into the urban phenomenon of civil society leading to relatively higher levels of political consciousness, including an internalisation of notions of freedom, democracy, justice and accountability, and how these relate to economic growth at individual and collective levels; the region's awareness of the ethnicisation of politics locally and nationally; the possibility of re-establishing Kikuyu hegemony reminiscent of the Kenyatta era; the urge to resist the KADU-type of politics perpetuated by the Moi regime; and a real fear of further economic, political and social marginalisation from the centre of power. Voters in Central Province were therefore unyielding in their pursuit of oppositional politics. They were unwilling to embrace KANU, even at the risk of being cut off from 'development'. Furthermore, they were not ready to vote for candidates from outside the province in the presidential polls. At the local level, issues related to coffee and tea, unemployment, education, rising poverty, and a collapsing infrastructure were crucial. The qualities of individual candidates were assessed. Consequently, in some constituencies SDP, Safina, and FORD-People candidates registered victory.

Only time will tell if the politicians of Central Province can seek meaningful coalition with leaders from other communities in order to recapture power at the national level. Their pre-independence allies, the Luo and the Kamba, are likely to field their own candidates for the presidency. In the decision to chart paths for future polls, ethnicity will continue to play an important role, but it is pragmatism and the willingness to build alliances that may eventually determine the voting patterns at the national level. On the local front, however, local issues and organisational skills of individual candidates will dominate. Since the mid-1980s, the Kikuyu community has felt marked by KANU but they have, nevertheless, rallied behind their own opposition leaders. This happened in the 1992 and 1997 elections. In 1992, they were torn between Matiba and Kibaki in the presidential polls and, despite the huge sums of money that were poured into Central Province, KANU candidates did not make much headway. Similarly, in 1997 the community strongly supported Mwai Kibaki and rejected KANU. Local issues dominated decisions in the civic and parliamentary polls. However, it would appear that Nairobi and Central Province voters were uncompromising in their rejection of KANU as a party: electable candidates were rejected if they had been nominated by KANU. Party affiliation was an important factor.

The two regions also manifested another characteristic: namely, the ability to elect individuals even when they did not run on the most popular opposition party of the time. Consequently, in Central Province the DP, SDP, Safina, NDP, and FORD-People are represented. This is contrary to events in 1992 when the Matiba FORD-Asili wave swept the province. In those elections, Matiba had campaigned on a three-piece suit slogan; a slogan that sought to have FORD-Asili candidate elected at civic, parliamentary, and presidential polls. Given the high incidences of poverty, the collapse of basic infrastructure, and unemployment in the region, the ethnic regrouping evidenced in the 1997 polls in Nairobi and Central Province is likely to persist in the coming years.

References

Binsbergen, W. van 1997, 'Ideology of Ethnicity in Central Africa' in Middleton, J. (ed.) *The Encyclopedia of Sub-saharan Africa Vol.3.* New York: Scribner.

Haugerud, A. 1995, *The Culture of Politics in Kenya,* New York: Cambridge University Press.

IED 1998, *Understanding Elections in Kenya: A Constituency Profile Approach,* Nairobi: Institute for Education in Democracy.

IED/CJPC/NCCK 1998, *Report on the 1997 General Elections in Kenya 29-30 December, 1997,* Nairobi: Institute for Education in Democracy, Catholic Justice and Peace Commission, and National Council of Churches Kenya.

Kanyinga, K. 1994, 'Ethnicity, Patronage and Class in a Local Arena: "High" and "Low" politics in Kiambu, Kenya, 1982-92', in Gibbon, P. (ed.) *The New Local Level Politics in East Africa – Studies on Uganda, Tanzania and Kenya*, Uppsala: Nordiska Afrika Institutet (Scandinavian Institute of African Studies), Research Report No.95: 89-117.

Kihoro, W. 1997, *Never Say Die,* Nairobi: EAEP.

Leo, C. 1984, *Land and Class in Kenya*, University of Toronto Press.

Leys, C. 1975, *Underdevelopment in Kenya: The political economy of neo-colonialism, 1964-1971*, London: Heinemann.

NEMU 1993, *The Multi-Party General Elections in Kenya, 29 December, 1992*, Nairobi: National Election Monitoring Unit.

Scott, J. 1990, *Domination and the Arts of Resistance: Hidden Transcripts.* New Haven: Yale University Press.

Throup, D. and Hornsby, C. 1998, *Multi-Party Politics in Kenya. The Kenyatta & Moi States & the Triumph of the System in the 1992 Election*, Oxford: James Currey.

15

The Kenya 1997 General Elections in Maasailand: Of 'Sons' and 'Puppets' and How KANU Defeated Itself

Marcel Rutten

In early December 1997, a group of Maasai youngsters stopped the Peugeot car of the Kajiado District Commissioner Mutemi. Their aim was to admonish the administrator following interference by KANU in the nomination process for its parliamentary candidate in Kajiado Central constituency. The administrator was accused of being a party to the alleged rigging. After the car stopped, which did not carry the DC at the time, a conversation ensued in the following manner: Maasai: *'Sema Moi ni Mbwa'* (Say Moi is a dog). Driver: (refuses to answer). Maasai: *'Mimi nasema hivi, sema Moi ni Mbwa'* (I am telling you to repeat that Moi is a dog). Driver: (refuses to answer). The car was then set upon with clubs.

This story exemplifies the negative feelings towards KANU prevalent among many of the local people after the elected candidate Stephen ole Leken was dropped to give way for the incumbent MP David Sankori. Similarly, in Kajiado South constituency the same politics were played, thus bereaving Geoffrey Parpai his candidacy in favour of the incumbent Philip Singaru. This obstruction by KANU in the nomination of its candidates triggered a shock wave of anger and frustration. It caused an 'earthquake' that hit the political landscape in the Maasai area (See map on p. 190). As a result, KANU is no longer the natural option for the Maasai electorate. The 1997 elections ended the monopolistic position of the ruling party in Kajiado South constituency and in Kajiado Central the opposition party Safina almost won the seat. What remains to be seen is whether the turn away from KANU by the Maasai electorate is definitive. This chapter analyses the forces at work during the Kenya 1997 elections in the Maasai area.

Maasai politics in colonial days 1900-63

The Maasai of Kenya mainly inhabit the districts of Trans Mara, Narok and Kajiado in the southern part of the country bordering Tanzania. Before the arrival of the British colonisers they lived more to the north of their present position in an area which came to be known the White Highlands. Protests against the loss of their northern area have been raised since the 1904 and 1911 treaties between the Maasai and the British were signed. In return for giving up the northern pastures, the Maasai were guaranteed that the southern reserve would be closed to non-Maasai. Since then the process of land loss has continued and has become one of the main political issues in the Maasai setting (see Rutten 1992). In 1960, shortly before independence, the Maasai, fearing that the closed status of their districts would be lost, created the Maasai United Front (MUF). The driving force was John Keen, born in 1929 in Laikipia, the northern area, the son of a German father and Maasai mother. Stanley Oloitiptip, a Kisongo Maasai from the slopes of Mt Kilimanjaro, Kajiado district, became the first chairman. Within a year the two men had clashed. Keen, who was also the organising secretary of the Kenya African Democratic Union (KADU), the party that sought to rally support from all small ethnic groups in Kenya, called for dissolution of KADU-affiliated tribal organisations so that the party could devote its efforts to the independence question (see *Weekly Review* 15/11/76). In response Oloitiptip organised a protest to KADU's president Ronald Ngala and declared a vote of no confidence in Keen.

This marked the beginning of a long history of conflict between the two politicians representing Kajiado district. Keen left KADU to become an independent member of parliament before joining the Kenya African National Union (KANU) – which was mainly a Kikuyu-Luo body. Whereas KADU wanted some kind of *majimboism* (regionalism), KANU was considered to be a national party, which wanted freedom of settlement for every Kenyan in all parts of the country. Keen soon rose within KANU to become the organising secretary in 1962.

At the time of the Kenya constitutional conference at Lancaster House (March-April 1962) in London, which discussed Kenya's independence, the Maasai were represented by Justus ole Tipis, John ole Konchela (KADU parliamentary group) and John Keen (KANU). In addition, a Maasai delegation, which included five more Maasai representatives, also attended the conference.[1] This delegation expressed their wish to continue to enjoy security of tenure in their reserved area. In addition, they wanted their ownership of the lands which the Maasai had vacated as a result of the 1904 and 1911 treaties to be recognised as Maasai territory. They also demanded that the territory should revert to its original owners once it was vacated by the European settlers. The British government rejected these demands despite threats by Keen to go to the United Nations or the International Court of Justice. It also dismissed a proposal by Keen for financial compensation amounting to £5,800,000 and a further

£100,000 annually. The KADU members within the delegation were less willing to accept compensation: they wanted the return of the land. 'To the Maasai this was a matter of life and death' (KNA/MAC/KEN/52/11). In protest, all Maasai representatives i.e., Tipis, Keen and Konchela, refused to sign the final report of the conference, *The Framework of the Kenya Constitution*, because of 'the refusal of Her Majesty's Government to recognise the claim of the Maasai delegation that the land formerly occupied by the tribe in the Rift Valley should revert to them' (KNA/MAC/KEN/48/8). The loss of these high potential pastures and the loss of even more land later on are, as we will see, up till today major aspects of Maasai politics.

Post-independence politics in Maasailand: The early years 1963-83

In the 1960s Keen clashed with Oloitiptip several times. His outspokenness also landed him in problems with the authorities on several occasions. In 1967, he was detained for two months for blaming the heads of state of Uganda, Tanzania and Kenya for not making headway with East African unity. And in 1975 he was fired from the cabinet after a debate on killing of J.M. Kariuki. Likewise, on the issue of land he continued to criticise the establishment. In 1978 he warned that unless steps were taken to ensure its fair distribution, the potentially explosive land issue in Kenya would get out of hand. He pointed at corrupt individuals grabbing land in the Maasai area though at one time he himself was accused of favouring some friends and relatives in the Ngong Hills area. He blamed powerful individuals for misusing the funds meant for the conservation of wildlife in the Amboseli area (see e.g. *Daily Nation* 20/03/75; 17/09/81; 03/11/81; 03/06/82; *East African Standard* 31/05/79; 30/01/83; 10/11/84; *Nairobi Times* 24/09/78).

Although outspoken and fearless, Keen was blamed by his constituency residents for not bringing home the development they wanted. On his part, he accused the local Maasai of still wearing the traditional dress and keeping to traditional ways of life, including moranism (warriorhood). He urged them to send their kids to school and to modernise. His rival, Oloitiptip, by contrast, defended traditional Maasai customs and worked hard as assistant minister to bring development to the benefit of his family and friends in his home area.[2] By the mid-70s Oloitiptip's star was rising even further when he was made the first Maasai cabinet minister (for natural resources). Keen, however, continued to make life difficult for Oloitiptip. The latter's idea to revive the MUF in late 1976 was criticised and Keen demanded that his rival be thrown out of KANU for that idea. Eventually Oloitiptip lost his post of KANU district chairman (*Daily Nation* 15/11/76). In 1981, after Keen was re-appointed by Moi to the cabinet as assistant minister in the Office of the President, the two Kajiado politicians ended their feud.

Yet the peace agreement did not last long. Keen announced the beginning of the end of the road for Oloitiptip when the latter was publicly accused of active involvement in shady plot deals by the Olkejuado and Narok county councils (*Daily Nation* 05/02/83; 21/04/89; *East African Standard* 05/02/83; 27/03/83). County council land and forest land had been handed out to Oloitiptip and his political supporters since the mid-1970s. Maasai elders of the rival Matapato section of Kajiado South constituency openly rejected Oloitiptip by April 1983 (*Daily Nation* 28/04/83). The following day another group of Maasai elders protested, saying John Keen had incited them to undermine Oloitiptip (*Daily Nation* 29/04/83).

In May 1983 President Moi announced that the next general elections would be held a year in advance to enable the political system to elect honest and dedicated leaders (IED 1997: 124). At a KANU rally in July, Oloitiptip was accused of not being development conscious, practising divisive politics in the district and mismanaging public funds. Oloitiptip hit back at Keen saying he did not want to waste time and energy 'quarrelling with a dying horse' (*Weekly Review* 29/07/83:11). Each of the two warlords supported rival candidates in their respective constituencies. At one time the *Weekly Review* concluded: 'if there were any award given to the district with the longest record of political squabbling among its top politicians, then there is little doubt that Kajiado would hold the dubious distinction' (*Weekly Review* 26/08/83:17).

In neighbouring Narok district politics were dominated by Justus Kendet ole Tipis for Narok North and John Konchela for Narok West for most of this period. Like Keen both men had been to the Lancaster House conference. They also had their differences, but were not engaged in fighting each other as much as their Kajiado neighbours did. At one time Tipis was the president of the Maasai United Front. When KADU dissolved itself, he joined KANU and was made an assistant minister for Tourism and Wildlife before the 1967 elections which he lost to Moses Marima. He returned to parliament after beating Marima in 1974 and was appointed an assistant minister for Home Affairs. He also became KANU's national treasurer. By 1977 it seemed as if his political career was coming to an end (*Weekly Review* 10/01/77).[3] Tipis had tried to organise the elections in the middle of 1976 while prominent persons were not around. However, he was challenged and in the December 1976 Narok district party elections, he was defeated by William ole Ntimama, who until that date had kept a low profile in national politics but was building a strong empire in his Narok district. A few weeks later, KANU headquarters announced that it would allow petitions from a few branches in the country, including Narok. Tipis was a member of the appeals committee and a repeat was ordered. Ntimama's appeal to Kenyatta fell on deaf ears. However, he trounced Tipis a second time. When the general elections came in 1979, Ntimama was prevailed upon not to run against Tipis by President Moi (*Weekly Review* 31/01/97).

So, in 1979 ole Tipis was elected unopposed as MP for Narok North. He used his position to make life difficult for Ntimama who was then Narok county council chairman. This intensified when Tipis was appointed minister of state in the Office of the President in charge of internal security and the provincial administration. Though Ntimama survived a probe committee set up to investigate the affairs of the Narok county council, he was not able to withstand Tipis' harassment after he announced in early 1983 his intention to run against Tipis in the 1983 elections. He was arrested a few weeks before the polls and was charged with holding an illegal meeting. He appeared in court and returned home some days later to announce he would stand down in favour of Tipis. Again Tipis went in unopposed.

In both 1979 and 1983 elections, Francis Sompisha outvoted John Konchela, once an assistant minister for Works in Narok West, now Kilgoris constituency. The two had been competing over the seat since the early 60s. Narok West was also the home of the late Joseph Murumbi, Kenya's second vice-president, who had retired from politics earlier and died in 1990.[4] Narok South constituency had remained firmly in the hands of the late Meshack ole Nampaso from 1969 to 1988.

The rise of new political leaders in Maasailand (1983-92)

In spite of Keen's efforts, Oloitiptip survived the KANU elections in September 1983, backed by his Kisongo Maasai of Kajiado South constituency, and was re-appointed as minister in the cabinet. John Keen himself lost Kajiado North to Philip Odupoy who was appointed an assistant minister in the Ministry of Water Development. Odupoy was not well known by the people, especially the Maasai, but was politically and financially supported by Oloitiptip. Another person from Kajiado North constituency who marked his entrance into politics, was Prof. George Saitoti, a lecturer at the Department of Mathematics at the University of Nairobi. He was nominated MP and appointed the minister in the Ministry for Finance and Planning. It was the first time, in Kenya's history, that the post of minister for Finance was given to a nominated MP (*Daily Nation* 17/11/83).[5]

Oloitiptip's fortune did not last for long as he was dropped from the cabinet in October 1983. There were rumours that Oloitiptip was linked to Charles Njonjo's attempt to overthrow the government assisted by foreign mercenaries. Oloitiptip would have become vice-president had the operation to remove Moi from power succeeded (*Weekly Review* 30/03/89, 3-7). The MP for Kitui

West, Parmenas Munyasia, hit at the Kajiado South MP for claiming to be a Nyayo follower (Moi's) while he was named in the judicial commission of inquiry into the conduct of Njonjo (*Daily Nation* 28/03/84). Fred Gumo, the assistant minister for Transport and Communications, also accused Oloitiptip of plotting against President Moi (*Daily Nation* 03/03/84). The Olkejuado county council asked Oloitiptip to resign (*Daily Nation* 05/04/84). The following week Oloitiptip was named in a beach plot scandal in which he was said to have been illegally allocated 3.4 hectares in Malindi by the commissioner of Lands in the previous year (*East African Standard* 12/04/84). He was expelled by KANU in September 1984. After losing his political power, his financial base was also attacked by companies, hospitals, banks and the Olkejuado county council trying to settle unpaid bills by the now disgraced Oloitiptip. He was jailed and released on bail after one day (*East African Standard* 13/01/84; 25/05/84). In the end his property was saved from auctioning by his fellow Maasai, including John Keen. Oloitiptip died on 22 January 1985 and Moses ole Kenah became the new MP for Kajiado South.

In the 1988 elections, Kajiado district was divided in three constituencies: North, Central and South. In North, Saitoti backed by Keen was returned unopposed. Keen himself became a nominated MP and was appointed assistant minister in the Office of the President. To ensure Saitoti's election, the incumbent MP's life was made difficult (e.g, Philip Odupoy was charged with holding illegal meetings – *Daily Nation* 14/01/88), and so was Oliver Seki (threatened – *Daily Nation* 10/02/88). Odupoy's life as MP was thus short-lived. He had mainly made himself known for opposing land grabbers and political godfathers in Kajiado district (*Daily Nation* 19/08/85).[6] In Kajiado Central, Geoffrey Parsaoti beat David Sankori and Kiroken Mpoke during the secret ballot though initially the latter had gathered most votes at the queue-voting system. And with Oloitiptip gone, Singaru, married to Saitoti's sister, had an easy time in winning the 1988 elections in Kajiado South.

In Narok district, Ntimama finally was able to compete with Tipis. He defeated the former Minister in Narok North constituency by polling 14,240 to Tipis' 12,369 votes (*Weekly Review* 31/01/97). After Tipis died, the politics of Narok district remained divided. This time it was Harun Lempaka of the small Ildamat section crossing swords with Ntimama's powerful Purko Maasai. However, Ntimama's star rose quickly and he was appointed minister for Local Government and Physical Planning. Ntimama became known as a hawkish politician in national circles though he was defeated by Prof. Wangari Maathai by the end of 1989 over the intended construction of the 60-storey *Kenya Times* Complex in Uhuru Park, his ministerial position and influence notwithstanding (*Daily Nation* 09/11/89).

The 1988 elections marked the peak of regime consolidation under President Moi (IED 1997:153). Most of the regime's opponents had either been co-opted or were in prison or exile. In their respective positions of cabinet minister and assistant minister, both Saitoti and Keen stood together and condemned those Kenyan dissidents at several public functions. (*Daily Nation* 01/11/88). Their support for Moi and the party was rewarded on 1 May 1989 when Saitoti became vice-president, replacing Dr Josephat Karanja. Saitoti continued to hold the portfolio of minister for Finance (*Daily Nation* 02/05/88). Yet, as the sixth vice-president of Kenya, Saitoti soon learned that some politicians were not in favour of his vice-presidency. However, John Keen and Geoffrey Parsaoti came to his defence. By March 1990, in the wake of the Ouko murder, rumours spread that Saitoti had been shot dead (*Daily Nation* 04/03/90). Again Keen stood up against the inciters. Keen was also instrumental in defaming the opposition and the calls for multi-partyism (see *Daily Nation* 04/02/95).

Where Joseph Murumbi was quick to resign as vice-president from the Kenyatta regime, Saitoti, the second 'Maasai' son to become VP, decided to stay put and in due course became allegedly involved in numerous scandals. Among the most serious scandals was the infamous Goldenberg case.[7] Saitoti could no longer count on John Keen for support as the latter had run into problems with the anti-Saitoti KANU politicians who saw Keen as the main stumbling block to their designs against the vice-president. The *Weekly Review* called it the 'lone voice of reason' when Keen warned Rift Valley leaders going to Narok town not to associate the Maasai with irresponsible and inflammatory statements.

Keen said that the Maasai could not afford to isolate themselves from other Kenyans adding that 'the Maasai have spears, but the spears we have are for the protection of our livestock and families and we will never use them against other Kenyans' (*Weekly Review* 04/10/91:10). Keen became concerned that self-government for the Rift Valley Province would entrench the Kalenjin hegemony at the expense of his fellow Maasai (see Throup and Hornsby 1998: 96). KANU hawks like Biwott and Ntimama, who had started the renewed discussion on the *majimbo* system, as opposed to the centralised system Keen has been propagating since the early 1960s, attacked him.

The calls for political reforms in Kenya reached a height by the end of 1991. Out of fear for the post-KANU or post-Moi era, the clique of Rift Valley and Coast KANU hardliners propagated the introduction of a system whereby Kenya would be divided politically and economically, in a way that would safeguard their interests best. This independent stand, however, initiated the final fall of John Keen from his position within the Office of the President. Matters became worse when he accused 'mischievous' leaders of sniffing around offices and pretending to have barometers for gauging other leaders' loyalty to President Moi. In addition, his warning to leaders not to antagonise the American government and the US ambassador Smith Hempstone over issues of good governance was not welcomed by the hardliners (*Weekly Review* 18/10/91). Soon after, on 28 October, Keen, was dropped as assistant minister in the Office of the President. By November while still in KANU, he started to speak openly in favour of a multi-party system in Kenya.

It was at this time that Saitoti lost another, and even more important, friend. British Scotland Yard detective, John Troon named Nicholas Biwott as among the key persons in the killing of Foreign Affairs Minister Robert Ouko in February 1990 (*Weekly Review* 29/11/91). KANU was in a disarray after Biwott was arrested, jailed and sacked from the cabinet. On top of that, the World Bank and other donors decided to withhold development aid for Kenya, a measure used for the first time ever to link aid and good governance with regard to an African county. The pressure for change that had been initiated by the churches in early 1990 now mounted to its height. Money talked and on 2 December, President Moi summoned a special KANU national delegates' conference. Though most MPs wanted to continue with the single-party era, the president announced that he intended to repeal section 2(A) of the constitution, which had made Kenya a *de jure* single-party state in 1982.

The proposal allowing political pluralism in the country came into effect on 10 December. Apparently, Saitoti was among those in favour of political reform to pave the way for the resumption of Western aid. They were convinced that KANU could legalise opposition parties, call and win a snap election and keep the money rolling in (see Throup and Hornsby 1998:86-8). John Keen joined the Democratic Party that had been formed shortly after Christmas 1991 by former Vice-President Mwai Kibaki. Keen's divide with Saitoti was now complete.

To withstand the opposition KANU fought hard and used all means available to guarantee it remained in power. For its election campaign, it appropriated billions of shillings from such as the National Social Security Fund and the Kenyan Posts and Telecommunications and launched Youth for KANU '92 (YK'92) which was instrumental in mobilising money for KANU's campaign. KANU hard-liners also warned opposition politicians not to enter exclusive 'KANU zones'. Opposition supporters residing in these areas were intimidated and told to vote for KANU or face the consequences. The president himself informed the people in non-KANU zones, such as Luo Nyanza, that they would not get any development in their area for years to come if they voted for the opposition. The media was pro-KANU, and the provincial administration was also instrumental by frustrating opposition rallies or 'not-safeguarding' the lives of opposition leaders. Finally, the opposition itself disintegrated through infighting in FORD towards the end of 1992. KANU hastened this process by inviting opposition candidates to defect back to KANU in exchange for material wellbeing.

In Kajiado North, problems emerged when John Keen announced he wanted to oppose Saitoti on a DP ticket. He and his supporters were beaten up on a number of occasions between June and December 1992 (*Daily Nation* 14 /11/92). The provincial administration sided with the incumbent MP and Vice-President Saitoti. Another main challenger was Philip Odupoy for FORD-Asili, who this time around was not willing to step down for Saitoti. Challenged for the first time in his political history Saitoti issued a colour booklet reminding the electorate of all his virtues as a development-conscious leader.[8] It would appear that Saitoti won the Kajiado North elections as a result of a well-planned and conducted fraud rather than his development record. Voters had been trucked in from other constituencies. It is suspected that at the count ballot boxes that had initially been over ordered and withheld suddenly showed up (see Throup and Hornsby 1998: 499).[9] Saitoti scored 51 per cent against 22 per cent for both Odupoy and John Keen.

Kajiado Central and South were mainly a two-party battle between KANU and DP. In Kajiado Central, Saitoti tried to persuade his favourite's opponent (Moses Loontasati of DP) to step down in favour of Sankori. Loontasati refused. Sankori was supported by Leken (both of the Seuri age group). In the KANU party primaries they had beaten Peter ole Ntasikoi (Leken's brother) of the Kiseyia age group.[10] In both constituencies, KANU won the elections, albeit with a small margin of 10 only per cent. Singaru (also of the Seuri age group), with Sankori nicknamed 'Saitoti's puppets', kept ahead of DP's Geoffrey Parpai (a Kiseyia agemate).

In Narok North, Ntimama faced opposition from Harun Lempaka (FORD-Asili) and John Tiampati (DP). Both opponents claimed that YK'92 and Ntimama tried to kill them (*Daily Nation* 21/11/92; 26/11/92). Two opposition supporters were killed in Narok town and the FORD-Asili office destroyed. Ntimama himself threatened non-Maasai residents that they would face the consequences if they failed to support KANU during the 1992 elections. These were no empty threats. For instance, the village of Enoosupukia, foremost a Kikuyu settlement in the northern part of his constituency, was attacked by people in KANU youth uniforms, firing arrows at non-Maasai. The day before the elections vehicles carrying loudspeakers reminded the Kikuyu that they would be evicted if they did not support the ruling party. Ntimama gathered almost 63 per cent against 24 per cent for Lempaka and 11 percent for Tiampati.

In Narok South – the most traditional and pastoral of all the constituencies in Maasailand – KANU had a walkover. There are hardly any immigrants in this remote and mostly dry area. Moreover, the DP candidate was time barred during nomination day and thus could not stand during the elections. Accordingly, Samson ole Tuya went in unopposed.

Narok West was less easy to win for the local Maasai candidate because of the large number of Kipsigis living in the area. Their candidate, Richard arap Birir, narrowly lost the KANU nomination. On a PICK ticket he made life difficult, but could not beat newcomer Julius Sunkuli, a Moitanik Maasai. Yet both supported President Moi for president. Actually, with the exception of Kajiado North (48 per cent), Moi got an absolute majority of the votes in Maasailand in 1992, scoring between 60 (Kajiado South) and 97 (Narok South) per cent of the presidential votes.

The 1992-97 period: shifting alliances and the emergence of Maasai nationalism

After the 1992 elections, those who had dared to exercise their constitutional right to vote for the opposition became vulnerable to threats and intimidation from the ruling party and state functionaries. Threats uttered before the elections were turned into reality. At a rally in Kerio South early April 1993 Ntimama, backed by other Rift Valley politicians, including Saitoti, Tuya, Biwott and Kones, told the 'true' Rift Valley residents (the Kalenjin, Maasai, Samburu, and Turkana) to be on their guard against the opposition (see Human Rights Watch/Africa Watch 1993:15).

The warning was made a week after opposition supporters shouting 'Moi must go!' during the state opening of Parliament (*Daily Nation* 24/03/93) had been attacked by a Maasai moran squad. Policemen watched as if they were helpless bystanders.[11] The week after the Kerio rally Kamba and Maasai leaders, including Saitoti and Ntimama, gathered in Kajiado and repeated their war threats in what came to be known the Kitengela Declaration. This especially damaged Saitoti who was openly attacked by KANU moderates, including Cyrus Jirongo, the national chairman of YK'92. Concerned Kenyan citizen's construed the attack on Saitoti as a manifestation of the intra-KANU power struggle for the post of vice-president. Of course, if this was the underlying motive, the hard-liners, led by Biwott, won this internal KANU battle for the time being (see Throup and Hornsby 1998: 551-2).

By the middle of October 1993, clashes broke out in Enoosupukia, Narok district. Some 500 armed men wearing traditional Maasai dress (*shukas*) carrying knives, arrows, bows, clubs and sticks attacked Enoosupukia. Ntimama's threat was put into action. Houses were set on fire, at least 20 people were killed and some 30,000 people, almost all Kikuyu, fled the area (*Daily Nation* 16/10/93). Ntimama was accused of having personally led the evictions with his private army, assisted by the police (Kaiser 1995: 25). The

Maasai also attacked people who sought refuge in the nearby mission church.[12] Some 12,000 settled in Maela refugee camp, Nakuru district.

In parliament, opposition MPs attacked Ntimama and called for his resignation but he, backed by Moi, said he had no regrets about the events in Enoosupukia and defended the killings because, 'Kikuyus had surpressed the Maasai, taken their land and degraded their environment. . . . we had to say enough is enough. I had to lead the Maasai in protecting our rights' (Human Rights Watch/Africa Watch 1997:78).[13] By the end of 1994, the 8,000 refugees still in Maela forced the government to destroy the camp to avoid the embarrassment of starving refugees under the eyes of UNDP officials. Most of the internal refugees were dumped in Central Province or 'resettled' in Moi Ndabi (1,200 persons only). By late 1995 an estimated 5,000 people, the poorest of the poor, were still in the vicinity of Maela, in nearby farms and towns such as Ngondi and Ndabibi, hoping to one day return to their farms in Enoosupukia (Kaiser 1995:21-2).

The champion of Maasai rights, indeed, is how Ntimama portrayed himself. In the wake of the constitutional reform debate, he reopened the discussion on *majimboism*, once KADU's leading political ambition in the early 1960s.[14] He went as far as accusing the late President Kenyatta of undermining the independence constitution to favour one tribe. 'Kenyatta made sure that he prepared his people to dominate over other tribes'. He warned that the Maasai would not accept any constitution that failed to address the issue of land rights (*Daily Nation* 11/01/98). Once again, friend and foe attacked Ntimama, including President Moi, over his remarks. Only some KANU hawks like Shariff Nassir supported the minister (*Daily Nation* 15/01/95). The next day 'Maasai moran' killed ten Kikuyu in neighbouring Mai Mahiu in Nakuru district in revenge for the killing of a Maasai herdsboy. Fingers pointed at Ntimama as one of the instigators of the slaughter.

Then on 17 January, politics in Maasailand took an interesting turn. The DP secretary general John Keen stated that he supported the stand taken by Ntimama on the issue of Maasailand (*Daily Nation* 17/01/95) while, a week later, FORD-Asili national treasurer Harun Lempaka accused Ntimama of having installed a Maasai private army to evict non-Maasai from Narok District. Lempaka also mentioned the sacking of three chiefs who refused to co-operate in the eviction of non-Maasai (*East African Standard* 25/01/95). That same week Keen paid a visit to President Moi, ostensibly to discuss Maasailand rights. It was, however, no surprise to political commentators that John Keen soon after defected back to KANU. Keen was promised a position among KANU's kingmakers (*Africa Confidential* 26/05/95:4). Rumours say that he was also promised the return of the land that he once sold to the Government of Kenya and the waiving of huge debts (this money mysteriously disappeared after the 25 May rally in Kajiado town).

Ntimama and others (Parsaoti, Keen) campaigned against Saitoti mainly on the ground that, since he did not speak *Maa,* he was not qualified to be their representative. Furthermore, they accused Saitoti of being involved in shady land deals, favouring his 'fellow Kikuyu'. Believing they had Saitoti cornered, Ntimama and company travelled to Kajiado in Moi's entourage only to learn, when Moi mounted the podium, that Saitoti would remain local KANU chairman and, in effect, vice-president (*Africa Confidential* 26/5/95:4). As *Africa Confidential* rightly predicted, Saitoti was not be able to relax for long.

In September 1996 over 100 moran took to the streets of Nairobi to demonstrate against Vice-President Saitoti. The moran stormed the headquarters of the ruling party at the Kenyatta Conference Centre to demand audience with the secretary general of the party, Joseph Kamotho, a close ally of Saitoti. As they were demonstrating in Nairobi, simultaneous marches were taking place in Ngong town, where demonstrators claimed that the district officer for the area, Reuben Rotich, was causing rifts among KANU members in the district. Saitoti quickly convened a meeting in Ngong town, at which he and his supporters criticised the demonstrators, describing them as hirelings of a senior politician from Narok district. In December 1996, while addressing a meeting in Ewaso Kedong in Kajiado, Saitoti launched a scathing attack on Ntimama, accusing him of trying to bring bloodshed in Kajiado, and describing him as a tribalist. The *Weekly Review* reported that 'Saitoti was masterminding Lempaka's defection to hit back at Ntimama, who is suspected of organising and patronising a group of anti-Saitoti elements in Kajiado North constituency, including a former lecturer, Prof. G. Maloy, who is planning to run on a KANU ticket against Saitoti in the forthcoming elections' (*Weekly Review* 31/01/97:8). Saitoti persuaded Lempaka to defect back to KANU. Now the Maasai history of political infighting had shifted from Keen versus Oloitiptip to a major fight between the Kajiado and Narok Maasai leaders, and both cabinet ministers William ole Ntimama MP for Narok North and George Saitoti MP for Kajiado North, over control of politics in Maasailand. Each leader has considerable support and has sponsored a candidate against the other. In the Saitoti camp were the MPs of Kajiado South Philip Singaru, and Central David Sankori, as well as Julius Sunkuli of Kilgoris constituency, the single constituency in Trans Mara district (formerly Narok West).[15] Ntimama got support from Tuya (MP Narok South) and KANU-turned activist John Keen.[16] However, many elite Maasai, some of them MP candidates, supported Ntimama as well. Maasai nationalism had established itself firmly in the southern Rift Valley (see *Daily Nation* 02/06/97).[17]

Maasai traditional leadership: the role of sections, clans and age groups

The Maasai traditional leader is a respected community figure who is elected when a new age group is formed. This is done at the time of a big ceremony called *enkipaata*, when the boys gather to celebrate the start of circumcision. After this they can become young moran (warriors). The chief must be well known by all members of his age group. He should, preferably, come from a well known and wealthy family, to avoid any corruption in acquiring wealth. This wealth should also enable him to assist needy people. He should be a person of *esinyatisho* (purity), i.e., an incorruptible person with no physical deformities or any other abnormal marks on his body. This aspect is even more paramount than the family's wealth. Among the duties of the traditional chief are to control others, to link the elders and his age group, to have a say in important matters that touch upon the community (see ole Sekuda 1997:94).

Traditionally, the Maasai do not like people going for leadership. The family will cry foul when one is elected to be the *olaiguenani* (traditional Maasai leader). It means that the relative's interest is less with the family and more with the community at large. The Maasai also use the term *olkitokkitok* to refer to a big man. In the Maasai political arena it means that George Saitoti might be called an *olkitokkitok*, but not an *olaiguenani*. This is an important distinction as it implies that Saitoti lacks the traditional respect and network other Maasai leaders have. Where Maasai traditionally prefer not to be elected in a leadership position, nowadays the *ilnusui* (half-Maasai) think differently: they do have an interest in becoming councillor.

Some critics say this is to enrich themselves and their families, because their positions give them opportunities to make money. Some young Maasai elders claim that it will take their community at least ten years to appreciate educated persons in the age group members who are now in their 40-50s for leadership roles and positions.[18] At the moment, the Maasai prefer someone with no formal Western education but such a person has no chance in national politics.

The Kenyan Maasai are subdivided into 12 sections called *iloshon*.[19] The original meaning of the word *olosho* is plateau. Initially, in order to distinguish between the various 'plateaus', the inhabitants of each plateau were given a specific name. Gradually, the word acquired the extended meaning it has today whereby it refers to an independent group of people having their own name, specific territory with well-defined boundaries, peculiarities of dress, beadwork, speech, housing, celebration of ceremonies and even their own defence force (see Mol 1978:100).

Maasai society is also sub-divided along the lines of clans (*ilgilat*) and sub-clans (*ilponot*). The first division is in two major houses or moieties (*ink-ajijik*): *Orok Kiteng* (house of the black oxen) and *Odo Mongi* (house of the red oxen). Each of these is further subdivided into seven major clans (some say there are only four or five; see Mol 1996: 21). Theoretically, every clan can be represented in every *olosho*. The number and naming of clans show disparity among the various *iloshon*. The seven major clans again are sub-divided into a number of sub-clans (*ilponot*).

If a Maasai wants to go into politics, he needs, first and foremost, the support of the age group and, to a lesser extent, the clan. His age group and clan should ask the others to support their 'son'.

Preamble to the Kenya 1997 elections in Maasailand

Election fever started gathering momentum in early 1997. This was partly due to the fact that President Daniel arap Moi could announce the holding of elections any time in the year. This uncertainty meant that candidates had to be prepared for elections anytime within some six weeks after the announcement of polling day. On the ground, local candidates and their agents were doing a lot of work. Three main lines of interference were followed in the first half of 1997: influencing voter registration, building alliances between sub-clans and age groups, and pleasing the electorate by handouts; i.e. free food distribution in certain areas.[20]

In the Magadi area of Kajiado North, for example, many people were excluded from the register according to one informant. Not just young people but also people with old identity cards were not able to get new ones. Forms filled in January were never forwarded. The area near Magadi town is inhabited by immigrants working for the Magadi Soda Company. The nearby Nguruman cultivation area also has many immigrants. In preparation for election day local observer groups tried to recruit people, but failed in several polling stations. The local Catholic church refused to participate in the process despite the fact that all parishes had been ordered to do so. Fear of repercussions for queuing behind the 'wrong' candidate, as had happened in 1992, made them decide that observing and reporting would be too great a risk for anybody living in this small community.

Besides voter registration and observing problems, other 'preparations' were underway. For example, in Kajiado North constituency the Keekonyokie Maasai this time around had three candidates (Saitoti, Parantai, Maloi). The Kaputiei Maasai are a minority in Kajiado North constituency. The Keekonyokie insisted that the Kaputiei should support the sons of the majority without fail. A group of Maasai went to see the Kajiado district commissioner to make sure that Daniel ole Muyaa (chairman of the Olkejuado county council who has non-Maasai roots) would not bring his Kamba and Kikuyu friends from across the district boundary, using money to register and vote in Kajiado. Extra wards were created in this part of Kajiado North constituency. The last two wards would be for the Maasai. The others (near the flower company which employed many non-Maasai) was for the Kamba. Muyaa has a farm in Kitengela and would stand in that area. At the time of registration and thereafter reports from the area indicated that local chiefs and politicians handed out free relief food to village elders. More relief food was given than at the beginning of the year when it was needed most as a result of a serious dry spell.

Also in support of certain councillors Saitoti's hand was felt. He made life difficult for the opponents of his favourite candidates. For example, Andrew Nangurai stood for local councillor in Ololua ward on a KANU ticket. However, since his business companion, ole Leken, the MP candidate for Kajiado Central, was standing against ole Sankori of Saitoti's camp, Nangurai got a hard time. The Ololua ward has three main centres: Ololua, Embulbul and Kerarapon. Nangurai originates from Kerarapon. When the vice-president learnt of Nangurai's intentions to stand, he dictated that KANU nomination queuing would be done in Ololua and Embulbul only. Nangurai protested because he now had to stand in the strongholds of his opponents Mohammed Malambu, Henry Pulei and George Nyoike (a Kikuyu), the last being Saitoti's favourite. It is thought that Saitoti's assistant, Tanju, was influential in this decision.

In other constituencies of Kajiado district people were also working hard to ensure that their political lifespan would be extended after the 1997 elections or that they would take over from the incumbent councillors. Yet, in all areas, one force to reckon with was the vice-president. Saitoti allegedly interfered in the Namanga civic elections of Kajiado South constituency where his involvement had gone on for some years.[21] There had been a big fight over land in this area. A local Maasai candidate for the local council, Paul ole Olorkinyei, brought up the issue of grabbing commercial plots (up to 15 per person) by non-Maasai in Namanga town at the expense of the Maasai population. Saitoti was accused of assisting his friends to get this land. Tanju, who comes from nearby the area, initially offered Ksh. 500,000 and later Ksh. 1.2 million to silence Olorkinyei, but the latter refused.

For the parliamentary seat, three candidates were in the race in Kajiado South. Geoffrey Parpai had lost on a DP ticket to Singaru in 1992 and was this time prevailed upon by the people of Kajiado South to defect to KANU if he wanted to be elected to parliament. Though he did so on Madaraka Day 1997 (1 June), he was reluctantly accepted into KANU's fold. He was nevertheless nominated on the KANU ticket, so was Richard Oloitiptip. Each candidate belonged to the Kisongo Maasai, but represented a different clan: Singaru for *ilaiser*, Parpai *ilmolelian* and Oloitiptip *ilmosejua*.

These patterns were very interesting because people mixed themselves and formed the so-called *iltimito* (strong groups) which compete together. *Ilmolelian* and *ilmarmae* joined forces to back Parpai. *Ilaiser* and *ilmakuperia* supported Singaru and *ilmosejua*, a few *ilaitayiok*, and *ilmoshon* threw their weight behind Oloitiptip. This struggle took three good months with every group campaigning for victory. Initially, Singaru's camp seemed to be on the winning side. They went round during the night terrifying other groups by shouting a lot as well as travelling in cars and hooting to intimidate their rivals. Also dances used in circumcision ceremonies and other traditional activities were performed. But this time around Parpai's group enabled their candidate to win the race.[22]

In Kilgoris constituency, the main contestants were the incumbent Sunkuli and Gideon Konchela, a Uasin Gishu Maasai, son of the late MP John Konchela and former army colonel. Both had been able to secure funds from financial tycoons. The chairman of Co-operative Bank, Hosea Kiplagat, supported Sunkuli with millions of shillings, while Konchela, to a lesser extent, got support from Ntimama. Here the fight was less between clans, but more along lines of sections and between different ethnic groups: Maasai, Kipsigis and Kisii.[23]

The DC Kilgoris, Wilson Litole, who is a close friend to Sunkuli is thought to have been instrumental in ordering the police to disturb a *harambee* fundraising by Konchela in mid-1997. A political fight broke out between Sunkuli and Konchela on how to conduct the KANU primaries; whether they should be through the queuing system or by secret ballot as Konchela had requested. In the end, a compromise was found. KANU headquarters allowed the secret vote to be used in Kilgoris town only. It is in this constituency that ethnic cleansing was used as a fourth way of 'preparing' for the elections. Tension had already been on the rise in October and early November. Crossborder cattle-rustling related fights occurred between Kisii and Maasai.

On 20 November, however, Kilgoris town turned into a battle ground in which at least 12 people were killed, shops were looted and property destroyed (*Daily Nation* 22/11/97). The killing of nine Kisii residents in Kilgoris town began after an administration police officer shot dead a young Maasai a few metres from the DC's office. According to the DC, the killing was an accident by the policeman who tried to disperse marauding Maasai. Another two Kisii were killed along the border when the two communities clashed at 6 pm that same evening. Government vehicles were used to ferry thousands of Kisii who fled the area. Reports from local priests, however, state that not 12 but at least 21 people were killed. And although both Moitanik and Uasin Gishu Maasai have been fighting the Kisii, most fingers point to Sunkuli as the instigator of these clashes. First and foremost, he stood to benefit from the absence of a Kisii vote (*Economic Review* 01-07/12/97:23).[24] The Konchelas also have a history of expelling non-Maasai (i.e., Nandi). Whatever the truth of the matter, what is sure is that the attack on 20 November was well planned in advance.[25] On the morning of the attack, one informant reported that he had been told by a Maasai woman and passing young moran to stay away from town because problems were expected to erupt. Another informant stated that the officer commanding the station in Kilgoris town later told him that investigations into the case were somehow impossible, because the latter's hands were tied as 'the guy who did it is with the Office of the President, so he is somehow my boss.'[26]

The party primaries in Maasailand

On 27 November KANU held its party primaries. Reference has already been made to the fact that Maasailand was mainly a KANU-dominated zone. For this reasons we will restrict ourselves to the way KANU conducted its party election. The most interesting party elections were conducted in Kajiado Central and South. In Kajiado Central, Leken beat Sankori with a narrow margin of 88 votes (11,403 against 11,315). In Kajiado South, Geoffrey Parpai was declared the winner by the returning officer, Paul Ntiati, after garnering a total 8,884 votes to Singaru's 8,659 and Oloitiptip's 2,500. This victory was officially announced by KBC radio.

However, Parpai's and Leken's victories were nullified. There were complaints that Leken's agents rigged the results in Bissel and Lorngosua polling stations.[27] Fingers were pointed at Saitoti as the man behind the nullification. He himself had been nominated to vie for Kajiado North constituency on the KANU ticket.[28] People complained that he had manipulated the nominations to make sure that his 'puppets' won. This unprecedented move was well calculated and planned for. According to the Parpai and Leken camps, Saitoti used all his influence to convince KANU secretary general, Joseph Kamotho, and the head of party's nominations, Dr Njoroge Mungai, that his allies had genuinely won the nominations. The following plot was said to have been strategised carefully:

After the results were announced early Friday 28 November, it is said that Sankori and Singaru immediately met Saitoti in Nairobi to brief him of their defeat. On Saturday 29 November Sankori and ole Singaru spent half the day with the vice-president in Nairobi before going back to their respective constituencies later that day. On Sunday 30 November, the two went round meeting their supporters (mostly elected councillors) to organise demonstrations in Kajiado and Loitokitok. On 2 December, Sankori supporters demonstrated in Kajiado town denouncing the results and urging fresh nominations. John Keen was accused of working for Sankori's downfall and President Moi was given up to Friday 5 December to nullify the KANU nomination or they would defect to the opposition en masse (*Daily Nation* 03/12/97). Singaru and Sankori did not attend the demonstration as both were in Nairobi, KANU headquarters, to lodge their complaints.

On Wednesday 3 December, it was announced over the radio that the nomination exercise was to be repeated in Ilbissel Centre in Kajiado Central and Olgulului and Namanga centres in Kajiado South. The paradox here is that the announced centres were the strongholds for ole Leken (Kajiado Central) and Oloitiptip's son in (Kajiado South) and would not favour the former incumbent leaders whom the repeat was meant to favour. On Thursday 4 December, Richard Oloitiptip decided to step back and campaign in favour of Parpai so as to defeat Singaru. This move weakened Singaru's clan. The two leaders went to Namanga and Olgolului to campaign. Singaru was not seen in the two centres and is said to have been busy in other locations of the constituency campaigning.

In Kajiado Central, the area elite, namely John Keen, ole Leken, ole Polong (Public Service Commission under-secretary), ole Kipury (Registrar General), ole Tutui (prominent businessman in Nairobi) ole Nkaiserri (brigadier in the army), ole Ncharo (District KANU coordinator) and other prominent Maasai met in John Keen's home and strategised too for Leken. KANU supporters claim that the money given by Moi to campaign for him and KANU was actually used for Leken's campaign. Also the Club of 7 are said to have poured in Ksh. 200,000 each. In their view, Sankori had become too powerful and was overshadowing them. Job and chief allocations had not favoured their circles as much as they had Sankori's, they claimed.

Also lucrative business contracts, they feared, might be lost if Sankori stayed in power. To change the tides they went for Leken. Both men belong to the Seuri age group. This move was met with hostility by the Kingonde age group who stated that the Kiseyia age group in between them and their 'fathers', the Seuri, tried to break this natural bond between the Seuri and the Kingonde. In the months preceding the elections the Kingonde elite youngsters tried to convince their 'father' Leken that his standing would give the Kiseyia a chance, but they failed. By splitting the Seuri, the Kiseyia indeed tried their only chance to beat the more numerous latest-formed Kingonde age group following them.

Some of the elite backing Leken are said to have gone to Ilbissel town and campaigned for Leken. Sankori too, like ole Singaru, never showed up in the mentioned centre. Parpai appeared before the KANU disciplinary tribunal and successfully argued his case out. The KANU headquarters issued Leken and Parpai with valid party nomination certificates duly signed by the party's secretary general Joseph Kamotho. Leken and Parpai made copies of the certificate, on instigation from John Keen, and distributed them to their supporters.

Friday 5 December was marred by lots of confusion. It was not clear to Leken and Parpai whether there would be a repeat poll and what its status would be now with Leken and Parpai having obtained their papers. Leken was in Ilbissel town and Parpai was in Olgulului and Namanga in the early hours of the day. People arrived in the three centres and started queuing in favour of Leken and Parpai. Meanwhile, when this was going on, Singaru and Sankori were in other centres urging their supporters to queue. Leken and Parpai sensed danger and went to the KANU headquarters in their respective constituencies. Both the officials there could not clarify what the certificates issued the previous day were meant to be. Leken and Parpai, brandishing their nomination papers, urged their supporters to disperse and not to take part in the exercise, because the KANU headquarters did not sanction the repeat. The Singaru and Sankori camps capitalised on the confusion to their favour.

On Saturday 6 December, the party headquarters kept silent and maintained that Leken and Parpai were still the bonafide nominees. On Sunday 7 December, newspapers show that Sankori was nominated to vie for Kajiado Central and Singaru for Kajiado South. Both these leaders were issued with nomination certificates on this day.

During this week of confusion Leken and Parpai went to State House to complain about the rejection of their KANU nomination papers and the call for repeat polls.[29] They blamed the vice-president and Kamotho. Moi was not amused, but both Kamotho and Saitoti were able to convince the president that supporting Leken and Parpai would undermine KANU in the district.

In Narok district, the KANU primaries were of a less confusing character. The three main opponents for the KANU ticket in Narok North were William ole Ntimama, Harun Lempaka, and newcomer Jackson ole Mwaniki, a young man from Ntimama's Purko section. The latter mainly received his support from the Kiseyia age group and non-Maasai. All realised that not so much 29 December as 27 November would be the real election day. Thus, for example, in Narok town on the evening before the party primary, cars were driving up and down with campaigners telling people to come and vote next morning. Ntimama's opponents were shouting not to be afraid and 'to come to the funeral tomorrow'. This was meant to be the funeral of ole Ntimama who had been given the nickname Mobutu. 'Mobutu has died this week. Let us all come on 29 December to bury him'. In the year before the polls Ntimama had somehow fallen out with Moi and KANU headquarters and the non-Maasai in town felt they had a chance to elect somebody else who might be less aggressive to non-Maasai.

In Narok town all three contenders were physically present: Lempaka, Mwaniki and Ntimama. Administration police were present but kept a good distance in order not to interfere with the elections. Narok town elections were conducted in a well-organised and fair way. In the town, Mwaniki beat Ntimama and Lempaka with a landslide and the winner and his supporters started dancing in the streets. The fact that they had dared to come to the polling station and queue according to their wishes seemed to be a great relief since during the days and weeks before polling day some Ntimama supporters had been intimidating their rival's supporters. Still, altogether only 50 per cent of the registered voters in Narok town came to vote. But Mwaniki's celebration did not last long. As soon as the results came in from the 31 sub-locations of Narok North constituency, Ntimama took the lead and was declared the winner next morning.[30] The final results were: Ntimama: 21,291; Mwaniki: 12,516 and Lempaka: 3,864.

In Narok South, it was reported that identity cards and voters' cards were hardly checked during the KANU primaries. Even youngsters below 18 years of age were allowed to queue. Youngster Stephen Kanyinke ole Ntutu (36), son of former paramount chief Lelionkaole ole Ntutu defeated the incumbent ole Tuya who is in Ntimama's camp. The county council (read: Ntimama's) fight with the Loita Maasai over the sacred Loita forest, the control over the Maasai Mara Game Reserve revenues and lack of initiatives by Tuya were among the main reasons for his defeat. Also the fact that the Narok elite backed Ntutu was a setback for Tuya. As a last resort, Ntimama assisted Tuya to be nominated on the DP ticket.

In Kilgoris, Sunkuli beat Konchela 15,050 to 11,493. According to Konchela he was rigged in at least 16 polling stations.[31] Reports by more neutral observers confirm that especially in Sunkuli's area agents of Konchela were threatened and bought to co-operate with Sunkuli. Also, voters were threatened that if they queued in Konchela's line then bad things would happen. Elders from the area appealed to President Moi to order a repeat as 'the parliamentary nomination did not reflect what most Trans Mara residents expected'. The elders said Trans Mara is a KANU zone but the nomination results could force people to think otherwise (*Daily Nation* 03/12/97). After he was defeated, Konchela stated that he intended to bring back the Kisii using lorries on election day. He claimed that a secret ballot would have favoured him, as he would get all of the Uasin Gishu, the Siria and one third of the Moitanik and half the Kipsigis. Sunkuli, by contrast, claimed that he would have all the Moitanik, most of the Siria, some of the Uasin Gishu and most of the Kipsigis. However, a repeat was not ordered for Kilgoris constituency. Konchela defected to DP.

Parliamentary nominations on 8 and 9 December 1997

The nomination of candidates for parliament and civic councils was spread over two days. The candidates had to hand in their nomination papers to the electoral commission officials in each constituency. On Monday 8 December the 7 am news bulletins announced that the president congratulated all those who won in the repeat nominations. The names of Singaru and Sankori were mentioned among others. In Kajiado Central, Leken presented his KANU nomination papers first and the returning officer refused to accept them, saying that he was acting on a directive from KANU headquarters. Sankori supporters claim that Leken then contacted a military person at State House who instructed Leken's nomination papers to be admitted. Still the returning officer refused to accept the papers because 'if it was the president who had sent him, let him (Moi) call me directly.'

Parpai suffered the same fate. The reason for not accepting his nomination was that he was said to lack a language proficiency test. Both of them then announced their defections: Leken to Safina and Parpai to DP.[32] John Keen worked hard to organise their nomination papers by contacting Richard Leakey of Safina and DP headquarters. Keen also assisted Olorkinyei who once again was rigged out for the civic council seat after winning the elections as KANU candidate in the Namanga ward. The KANU headquarters issued nomination papers to the opponent who had been trampled in the party elections. Olorkinyei got DP papers as well. On Tuesday 9 December, Leken (Safina) and Parpai (DP) presented nomination papers for their respective parties to beat the deadline. Moses Loontasati (DP) and Sidney Quantai (SDP), formerly with KTN, were also cleared to vie for the Kajiado Central constituency.

In Kilgoris nomination was done in an orderly manner. The main problem was to hand in completed 'oath secrecy forms' which had to be done in front of a magistrate who was in Kisii town (51 km a way). Because of the tensions between the Kisii and the Maasai, however, transport was difficult and Maasai candidates feared going to Kisii town.

The campaign period: 10-28 December 1997

The political implications of KANU headquarters' interference were enormous. Not only did Leken and Parpai defect but also the outcry for justice to be done among many ordinary Maasai was revolutionary. Large numbers of people in both Kajiado constituencies were demoralised and angered by these developments. Their one and only party KANU had cheated them like small children. It was now that some realised that Kenya offered more than one party. This was bound to have detrimental repercussions on KANU as a party and Moi also realised this. Sensing danger, he called upon Leken and Parpai to come to State House for an impromptu meeting. They were accompanied by a group of Maasai leaders. Moi tried to cool down tempers and he sent his apologies to Parpai and Leken. He promised that should KANU win he would shake his tree and certainly some fruits will fall. District commissioner Mutemi was transferred immediately thereafter.

Saitoti himself personally experienced the anger among the Maasai when, on a meet-the-people-tour, he was chased away from Isenya town, bordering Kajiado Central constituency on 11 December. When he arrived at the shopping centre, the local people indicated that they were not ready to listen to him and he should therefore leave the area. Some even pretended to be vomiting when they saw him. They shouted pro-DP slogans at him and raised the DP symbol. Some days earlier both NDP and DP supporters had chased the vice-president from the Ongata Rongai quarry area. Some told him that he was wasting time by going to the area, and if he wanted their votes 'he should rig as he did in 1992 by marking ballots in his favour.' Almost a similar scene was repeated in Kiserian town, where interference in the KANU primaries occurred. County council chairman Muyaa feared that his fortunes would also dwindle and he made arrangements with a local businessman in the area to ensure that his employees would vote for him in exchange for money.

During a crowded rally on 17 December in Kajiado town, Parpai, Leken and Leakey and local councillors supporting Leken addressed hundreds of Maasai. They blamed Saitoti and his clique of KANU councillors, including county council chairman Muyaa, for interfering in the electoral process and for their involvement in corrupt land deals. Next, the team surrounding Leken went back to the drawing board and concluded that, though Leken had a good chance of winning on a Safina ticket, they feared that Loontasati, the DP candidate, might split the opposition vote.[33] The Leken team, including John Keen personally, talked to Moses Loontasati (DP) on several occasions urging him to step down, all in vain. The leaders went to a point of requesting Loontasati to mention his premium, but he refused to do so. Loontasati had simply been offered more money by Sankori, his critics claimed.[34] During the campaign the DP and KANU candidate went as far as advising voters that in case they did not vote for the KANU or DP candidates, then they should vote for Loontasati or Sanhari, respectively. All tricks were now being used to win the votes.

In the Dalalekutuk area of the Kajiado Central constituency, Sankori spread the story that Leken was planning to move back the border between the Dalalekutuk Maasai and Leken's Matapato section of the Maasai population if he became MP for the area. In 1978 a clash between the two sections over this border resulted in the death of many Dalalekutuk Maasai. In Kajiado town, the night before the elections, Sankori's men went round pretending to be Leken and warning that all non-Maasai would be kicked out after the elections. Leken, on his part, suggested Sankori was not a true Maasai and that by all means all Matapato Maasai should not vote for a Kaputiei 'Maasai'. Playing the *iloshon* card, backfired on Leken as it to some extent united the non-Matapato Maasai.

In Kajiado South, the situation was more relaxed as it was only a KANU versus DP fight, with KANU already having won in the first round with a clear victory. Tension was reported here and there in the area, but in general there was no chaos. The most interesting aspect was to see that the division among the Maasai became even more complicated after Oloitiptip (Kiseyia age group like Parpai) quit the race and also a number of *ilaiser* dropped their own MP (Singaru).[35] Instrumental in this were age group reasons and traditional Maasai chiefs now opposing their 'own son'. So people had made up their minds and stated 'KANU can't fool all people all the time.' The coming of DP activist Njenga Karume to Loitokitok was also warmly welcomed by the now DP-turned-Maasai and the large number of Kikuyu in the area.

In Narok North, Ntimama had an easy time after being elected the unopposed KANU MP as nobody dared to stand against him. Ntimama campaigned for Mwai Kibaki and made Tuya and Konchela defect to DP. Otherwise, he mainly stayed in Mombasa.

In Kilgoris, tension continued as the fighting and killing did not stop after the party nominations. According to informants, politicians from both sides were very active in the displacement of the Kisii from Trans Mara. Zaphaniah Nyang'wara (KANU MP for Bomachoge constituency, Kisii district) together with Sunkuli, were said to have been collaborating to safeguard their interests in the area. This was done, e.g. by Nyang'wara inciting the Uasin Gishu Maasai (home of the now turned DP candidate Konchela) to fight the Kisii. A local Kisii councillor was killed by youths from Uasin Gishu. The aim was to discredit Konchela among the Kisii and make them vote for Sunkuli. By 18 December, the campaign was further seriously hampered by President Moi's declaration of a security zone on the violence-torn borders of the clash-hit areas. It barred politicians from outside the area from campaigning. This move favoured Sunkuli. In spite of the 'security zone' on 26 and 27 of December many Kisii left Ngararu in Kilgoris constituency.

Election days: 29 and 30 December 1997 in Maasailand

Finally, after all these months of political intrigue and campaign, the candidates made the final step. Table 15.1 presents the number of those who registered to vote as well as those who actually did so. The figures are somehow consistent though, due to logistical problems such as the lack of ballot papers for either presidential or parliamentary (or both) elections, it is hard to make any firm statement about stuffing of ballot boxes or other irregularities at this level.

Table 15.1: Registered voters and valid votes for parliamentary and presidential Elections in Maasailand, 1997

Constituency	Registered	Presidential	Parliamentary	Difference
Kilgoris	47,624	35,226	34,456	770
Narok North	46,555	32,957	–	n.a.
Narok South	47,896	32,294	32,758	-464
Kajiado North	64,358	41,894	43,851	-1,957
Kajiado Central	28,319	22,460	23,335	-875
Kajiado South	32,139	24,271	24,030	241

Source: ECK 1999

Voting countrywide suffered from logistical problems due to heavy rains and for certain constituencies a lack or mix-up of ballot papers (Rutten 1998). This was especially so in Kajiado South and Kilgoris where some polling stations could not open until 2 pm (instead of 6 am) or had to close for some time when ballot papers got finished. Due to these problems the Electoral Commission of Kenya announced, though in a rather confusing way, that voting would continue next day, on 30 December. As far as irregularities were witnessed by the local and international observers during voting day, it was mainly in Kajiado North where some questionable events took place. Some of these are hard to prove while others are more obvious. Some were of a minor significance while others were of a more serious nature. In Ngong township primary school polling station, Saitoti was reportedly very angry with the presiding officer whom he accused him of 'rigging'. A lack of ballot papers delayed the voting. When Saitoti and Oliver Seki (SDP) announced by 6.30 pm that balloting was suspended, angry youths stormed the polling station and attempted to seize a ballot box. Police had to fire shots in the air to disperse the crowd and reclaim the box.[36]

At Eeno Matasiani in Kajiado North, ballot boxes were set on fire by a group of people who came in a pick-up twincab. The men demanded to bypass the queue and vote before the other people. When it proved impossible, the same group went round the building and broke the window to the classroom. The people inside ran out and a commotion ensued. In the mean time, the gangs jumped through the windows and poured petrol on the ballot boxes and set them ablaze. In the same station two men had a row over which of them was the presiding officer. Oliver Seki threatened to withdraw from the race on 30 December. He claimed that 19 ballot boxes had been sneaked into Ngong town (*Daily Nation* 31/12/97; 01/01/98).

As mentioned earlier, in the southern part of Kajiado North, i.e. in several polling stations in Magadi area, no observers were present. Also in certain areas (e.g., Korrompoi, Bulbul) KANU agents were allegedly bribing people, while a DP agent in Inkiito primary school was told to stop telling people who to vote for before entering the polling station. Two of Saitoti's agents, Tanju and Sultan, were seen going round monitoring what was happening on election day. Later they were named as the kidnappers of the deputy returning officer in the Ngong counting hall. The deputy returning officer, a Mr Simel, was put blindfolded in a car and dropped at Machakos.

In Kajiado Central constituency, KANU agents allegedly bribed voters in Enkaroni, while in Kajiado town voters were transported to the polling station by the KANU parliamentary and civic candidates. At Toroka (KMQ polling station) an official was found asking the illiterate voters questions, such as 'Who is your President?' and 'Who is your MP?', favouring the incumbent KANU politicians. This practice was stopped after opposition party agents complained. Also, in Ilmarba, Leken's stronghold, it was reported that some officials purposely invalidated ballot papers for those voters thought to be KANU supporters.

In Kajiado South no major irregularities occurred except that civic candidate Paul ole Olorkinyei's name was not followed by the DP symbol, but by the NDP logo (tractor). The people wondered about this and were confused. Many of them had apparently been told to go and vote for the DP's 'lamp'. Also many Kikuyu supporters of Olorkinyei changed their minds, preferring KANU to NDP. Olorkinyei lost to the KANU opponent whom he had beaten before with a landslide. Fingers pointed at Saitoti again.[37]

In Narok North's Olchorro location, the ballot papers for civic candidates were missing for the whole day and the community did not vote until the morning of 30 December. In Naisoya polling station the KANU agent, who happened to be the unopposed councillor of the area, used vernacular language. Agents of other parties were not present and observers were kept at a distance when illiterate voters entered the booth.

In Kilgoris, the DC was seen actively campaigning for Sunkuli in Enoosaen polling station; while in Sosio the presiding officer was caught influencing illiterate voters to vote for President Moi. In Olereko there was a switch of party symbol to the disadvantage of the DP candidate.

Table 15.2: Parliamentary and presidential results 1997 election in Maasailand (per cent)

Constituency	KANU parl.	Moi pres.	DP parl.	Kibaki pres.	Safina* parl.	Others parl.	pres.
Kilgoris	63.89	92.77	35.77	5.92	-	0.34	1.31
Narok North	unopp.	81.24	-	15.46	-	-	3.30
Narok South	79.19	91.12	20.81	8.33	-	-	0.55
Kajiado North	60.85	49.33	31.53	40.26	-	7.61	10.41
Kajiado Central	48.66	61.89	4.89	34.49	45.78	0.67	3.62
Kajiado South	42.58	43.08	57.42	53.23	-	-	3.69

Source: IED/CJPC/NCCK 1998
*Safina had no presidential candidate

Table 15.2 shows the winning parties and presidential candidates. Foremost, it is clear that, in spite of its still holding on to five out of six constituencies, Maasailand is no longer a KANU zone. Especially Kajiado Central was narrowly saved for the ruling party, due to the split of the opposition.[38] The next elections will tell whether this has been a one-time affair with the opposition or whether it is the beginning of a turnaround.

According to a councillor from Magadi, when some Maasai councillors paid Moi a courtesy call at State House soon after the swearing in of the president in Nairobi, he could not conceal his displeasure at the way the Maasai had voted in the 1997 elections. When the president rose to address them, he had very few words: 'I knew all along that I would win in this election. I also thought the Maasai to be mine and, hence, their votes. But you seem to have wavered somewhere and let the opposition wave sweep through your land. You seem not to be the Maasai I knew. You will never see me again in Maasailand, that's for sure.'[39] In spite of these emotional words, Moi returned in 1999 to Kajiado and Narok.

The first person to suffer was Saitoti who, shortly after the elections, was not reappointed as vice-president. One informant reported that Saitoti almost quit politics altogether in protest against Moi's decision. However, he remained in politics, and in the cabinet as minister for Planning and National Development and sought alliances to survive. On 27 January, he went to see Moi who promised that he (Saitoti) would soon regain his position as vice-president. This happened in April 1999 after many other candidates had been named to take the position.[40] Konchela defected back to KANU soon after the elections, while Mwaniki, who had not opposed Ntimama on 29 December, was rewarded with a post on the Kenya Wildlife Service board of governors.[41]

Ntimama was re-appointed to the cabinet. However, at the local level, the provincial administration and his Narok South counterpart had trimmed his power. They had worked hard to raise the number of wards in Narok South in spite of fewer people. The effect of this move was that in the Narok county council Ntimama's Purko no longer had a majority. Ntimama complained bitterly about it (see *Daily Nation* 01/04/98).[42] Since Ntimama had in the past used the same trick of creating wards in his Purko home area, this time round he was beaten at his own game.

In a surprise move at Parpai's victory party, Ntimama openly lined up with his political friends of the moment and tried to mend fences with the Kikuyu voters. In front of DP politicians and a large crowd of Maasai and Kikuyu of Kajiado district, he 'apologised' for Enoosupukia, claiming it to have been a 'misunderstanding'. This statement may not have made him popular with the Kikuyu deported from Enoosupukia, but it eased some of the tension among the remaining Kikuyu of Narok district. But the fact remains that Ntimama would most likely not have won his parliamentary seat had he not evicted the Enoosupukia residents.

For ole Leken the outcome was most dramatic. John Keen, who claimed he sponsored all opposition candidates in Maasailand, advised him to stay in Safina and wait for his turn.[43] The main problem is that Leken favours an active role in politics. Leken was one of the candidates for the post of secretary general of Safina but failed to win the post.[44] He accepted a government job as chairman of a committee of inquiry instead.

Conclusion

In the foregoing discussion, we have followed Maasai politics from the beginning of this century until the last general elections of 29-30 December 1997. A striking aspect of our journey along with the politicians and issues at stake is that in the end the power struggle among the Maasai is for safeguarding access to resources (land, water, jobs). Sections, sub-clans and age groups play a major role in the outcome of this political fight. However, no easy lines of voting can be pointed at, as individual interests play a major role. Secondly, most of the Maasai formal political elite have never held the position of a traditional Maasai leader. Almost all have mixed origins, yet some are considered to belong more to Maasai society than others.

The ethnicity factor has gained importance as a result of the opening up of the Maasai districts and the influx of non-Maasai voters, especially since the sub-division of group ranches, making land a commodity that could be sold to outsiders. It has changed the political landscape to the extent that soon there will be as many non-Maasai as Maasai living in Maasailand. This has multiple effects on the way politics is going to be conducted in the area in future. First, the newcomers are pointed at as those coming in to grab land. By trying to keep away other political parties, several KANU die-hards use this story. It is even used to chase away the 'newcomers' from their legally bought parcels of land (e.g., Enoosupukia). Secondly, although they still occupy the small towns and islands of high potential, the non-Maasai numbers are bothering the Maasai politicians, though less the ordinary pastoralist, because on voting day the non-Maasai might vote in their own representatives.

In Kajiado district the era of multi-partyism has opened the eyes of many firm KANU believers, when the ruling party they had supported for many years 'rigged' out their 'sons'. In almost all of these contests, though, the underlying fight was between two camps. At the surface it, might have appeared as Singaru versus Parpai, but in reality it was Saitoti versus Ntimama fighting for power. The fight was between those known to be involved in land deals (i.e., Saitoti who was instrumental in selling Maasailand to the Kalenjin elite, in collaboration with Muyaa) versus Ntimama's camp who had gained the questionable reputation of chasing away newcomers. Right now, with the exit of Simon Nyachae from the cabinet, the Ntimama faction in KANU has been seriously weakened.

Moreover, the age group issue is apparently at stake. The newcomers Sunkuli, Muyaa and Sankori might in the long run undermine Saitoti's and Ntimama's leadership.[45] The latest twists and turns underline the fact that Maasai politics are much influenced by the age group factor in addition to the issue of access to resources, especially land, jobs and contracts.

Whether the opposition will be able to consolidate its position in Maasailand and improve in the more Maasai-dominated regions remains to be seen. Kajiado Central could have been won if DP and Safina had co-operated. However, had Leken's nomination not been nullified he would have stood on a KANU ticket and Sankori would likely have 'defected' to the opposition. Leken might have ended up in parliament on a KANU ticket. The question remains whether in future a new brand of politicians, be it Maasai or non-Maasai, will be elected who, as in the Maasai tradition, are people of respect and dignity, who work hard for the good of the people they are supposed to represent faithfully and honestly.

Notes

1. These were: J. ole Sein, P. ole Lemein, P. ole Nampaso, Dr Likimani and J. ole Tameno (see KNA/MAC/KEN/47/5).
2. It needs to be stressed that both John Keen and Stanley Oloitiptip at times have condemned Maasai for 'backwardness'. For example in 1970, after Oloitiptip was made Maasai spokesman, they co-operated and spearheaded a campaign which was aimed at the

discontinuation of moranism (warriorhood) with young Maasai. They advised the Maasai to send their young children to school instead. Yet Keen was most extreme in this and even at one time gave an eight-month ultimatum to the Maasai to change dress otherwise he would quit parliament. Next day, Oloitiptip condemned him and the old fight between the two men started all over again.

3.　Ntimama was born in 1930 at Melili in Narok district. He attended the Narok Government School from 1937 to 1944 after which he went for a teacher training course at Kahuhia in Murang'a district. He taught from 1947 until 1958 when he joined Narok African District Council for about a year as a clerk. He had been a councillor in the council from 1954 to 1958 while he still served as a teacher, and from 1959 to 1960 he was a nominated member to the Legislative Council. In 1960 he joined government service and served as a district officer until 1964 when he quit to become one of the most prominent farmers in Maasailand. He was elected Narok county councillor and chairman in the 1974 local elections. In addition to his farm in Narok, he runs, among others, some business concerns in Nairobi and owns tourist lodges in Masai Mara Game Park (see *Weekly Review* 01/01/77).

4.　Joseph Murumbi, born in 1911 as son of a Goan father and Maasai mother. He was most instrumental in the early 1960s while in London to Kenya's fight for freedom. After returning to Kenya he would soon become minister of state for foreign affairs before becoming Kenyatta's right hand man in March 1966. In a letter dated 15 August 1966 addressed to Kenyatta, Murumbi indicated that he wanted to resign his position as VP as soon as possible. A mere eight months later he did. Murumbi made this step out of discontent of upcoming corruption in the regime, but foremost because of the assassination of his old and trusted friend Pio Gama Pinto, allegedly by the Kenyatta regime (*Daily Nation* 07/07/98; interview Mrs S. Murumbi, November 1997).

5.　George Saitoti was born in 1944 as George Kimuthia Kiarie in Ngong town, Oloolua location, of Kikuyu parents, the late Mr Zachary Muthengi Kiarie and Ms Zipporah Gathoni. He joined Oloolua Primary School, the only colonial school in Ngong in 1952. He was admitted to Mang'u High School in 1960, before going to Cambridge School, Western Massachusetts and later Brandeis University in the US in 1962. He graduated with a Bachelor of Arts degree in mathematics in 1967. He later went to the UK to Sussex University for his MA (1968) and a PhD at Warwick University (1971). He began teaching Mathematics at Nairobi University that same year. In 1978 he became a senior lecturer and chairman of the department. Later in the same year he was appointed chairman of Mumias Sugar Company and a director of Kenya Commercial Bank. In December 1982 he succeeded Philip Ndegwa as the bank's executive chairman (*Daily Nation* 02/05/89; Saitoti 1997: 16-7).

6.　Philip Odupoy was made boss of a vegetable firm in Naivasha.

7.　Goldenberg Ltd, was an Asian-owned company that received throughout 1991-92 some US$ 600 million in compensation for non-existing exports of gold and diamonds to fictitious companies in Switzerland and Dubai. According to the Law Society of Kenya (LSK) many people within government circles profited from this scandal. The LSK reasoned that, among others, the minister for Finance, George Saitoti at the time, should be brought to court. The society showed relevant documents to prove their case that the Treasury was involved. Also foreign donors have indicated that action has to be taken against the keyplayers involved. It is only in 1998 that detailed hearings started.

8.　Saitoti has been working hard to develop his constituency. He even used Treasury money directly to fund projects. For example he would call the Ministry of Water in Kajiado town to send an officer to a job in a certain location. These were unplanned projects. It is one of the reasons why expenditure in Kajiado rose after Saitoti came to power (see Rutten 1992: 109-12). It also explains one of the reasons for the failure of the District Focus Policy (see Rutten 1990).

9.   The trick of over-ordering boxes for Kajiado North constituency is one theory, but it might as well have been the case that extra boxes were available anyway. According to *Africa Confidential* (Vol. 33 No.20) 4: 'Britain had been under pressure from Kenya to assist KANU's plans for victory. As part of its support for the democratic transition, the UK has provided ballot boxes and will provide ballot papers too. But Nairobi has been demanding more boxes and papers than originally planned. This is widely understood in Kenya as a way of ensuring there are plenty of boxes filled with KANU votes. Britain pondered the request, while the USA pressured it not to provide any more papers or boxes. It has now agreed to provide 35,000 boxes, 5,000 more than originally requested. This was simply because the boxes were 'smaller than was expected', a Foreign and Commonwealth Office official told Africa Confidential, and there was 'no intention of favouring any party.' The Kenyan government has also been threatening to print its own papers and then hand the bill to Britain.

10. There were problems in the 1992 KANU nominations. Parsaoti won. Ntasikoi and Sankori petitioned. There was a repeat. Ntasikoi stepped down for Parsaoti but Sankori, backed by Saitoti won, to the chagrin of the Matapato elite Maasai. This made the Matapato to back Loontasati on a DP ticket.

11. It was later admitted by the KANU secretary general that the party had brought 3,000 youthwingers from Kajiado District and elsewhere. The policemen's duty had been to maintain peace and protect the youthwingers (*Daily Nation* 01/04/93).

12. Following independence, Kikuyu farmers began settling among the Maasai pastoralists in the Enoosupukia area. In 1977, the area was designated a land adjudication area and the government began to issue title deeds to purchasers. Many of those who bought land were Kikuyu. At the time, Maasai leaders welcomed the Kikuyu settlers and community relations thrived. Following the calls for a multi-party system, Maasai leaders from the area began to call for the expulsion of the Kikuyu from this area. In August 1993, Ntimama, a KANU minister for Local Government, declared the region 'trust land' and illegally conferred upon local authorities the power to evict people regarded as squatters. The official reason given for declaring the area 'trust land' was that the area was heavily degraded and as an important water catchment area it needed environmental protection (see Human Rights Watch/Africa Watch 1997:78).

13. The truth is that a group of Maasai elders visited Maela camp and requested the government to return the Kikuyu farmers. Most of these were not squatters but legal owners and renters.

14. As soon as KADU ceased to exist, *majimboism* was eliminated from the state structure. In the words of the late Joe Murumbi, regionalism was 'a ghastly character for inefficiency, corruption and ultimately poverty and suppression of our national aspirations' in which 'a few people want to carve out little kingdoms for themselves under the guise of protecting tribal interests' (Sanger and Nottingham 1964:16).

15. Narok West was carved off Narok district in 1994 and renamed Trans Mara district. In 1996 Kilgoris constituency, covering the whole of Trans Mara, was officially gazetted.

16. One of the most interesting stories about the opposing camps dates back to September 1996. It is said that Vice-President Saitoti invited a section of Maasai to his home in Kitengela. The aim was to have a discussion on what was termed as development matters in Kajiado North. In between, John Keen allegedly learnt of the arrangements and decided to capitalise on the gathering to fulfil his ambitions of humiliating the vice-president. He told the visitors that they had been selected and invited by the vice-president to be fed and then killed through use of the military personnel guarding his (Saitoti's) compound. The trick seems to have worked on the selected visitors and when Saitoti rose to address the gathering (after others had spoken), the armed Maasai rose with their simis and rungus in hand ready to beat (kill?) him. He finally managed to cool them down, but not before a high tensioned showdown which was aggravated by the storming of the military security

personnel into the meeting room, ready to strike and defend the VP. Finally the Maasai revealed the circumstances surrounding the confusion. Ironically, some of the influential and literate visitors had known beforehand what would happen, but did not inform their benefactor. Since then, no Maasai is allowed into the VP's compound with any weapons.

17. The Ntimama vs. Saitoti war was also extended to civic leadership wrangles. Pro-Ntimama supporters are said to have been rewarded with prime plots in Nairobi.

18. Interview Paul ole Nchake 16/06/97, Isinya, Kajiado.

19. The sections in Kajiado district comprise Loodokilani, Kaputiei, Keekonyokie, Dalalekutuk, Matapato, Kisongo, Ildamat and Purko. The latter two are also present in Narok and so are the Loita in the southern part of Narok district. In Trans Mara district we foremost find the Uasin Gishu, Moitanik and Siria Maasai.

20. For example, in the Olkinos area (Kajiado North constituency) free food was distributed to the people, including non-Maasai. The food was distributed by the chiefs and handed over to village elders. This went on until the end of June when more food was presented as at the time it was needed most (in early 1997 during a major drought). It was thought to be a political issue because of the elections coming and three people campaigning for votes to be elected in the county council and one MP seeking re-election.

21. In 1996, after intense lobbying by Olorkinyei a new ward was created in Namanga. Ntimama supported Olorkinyei. The VP campaigned for his man Matampash. However, Olorkinyei won. Saitoti ordered a repeat. Olorkinyei won again. Following this outcome the ward was de-registered. And if there is no ward, there cannot be a councillor. Olorkinyei initiated his anti-government (Saitoti) campaign. The nullification of plots allocated to non-Maasai has recently started.

22. The non-Maasai factor was also important in the struggle for votes. They mainly inhabit the urban centres such as Namanga, Loitokitok, Ngong and the like. In Namanga/Mile Tisa the non-Maasai (though in small numbers) supported Richard Oloitiptip. The Loitokitok and Entonet non-Maasai supported Singaru as he lives there. The Ilasit, Entarara and Rombo non-Maasai supported Parpai for the same reason.

23. The history of occupation of the area is of relevance here. To date the Trans Mara electorate covers some 20,000 Kipsigis, 8,200 Uasin Gishu, 8,100 Moitanik and 6,500 Siria. Traditionally, the Loita and the Siria Maasai used to live in what is now called Trans Mara district. The Loita lived in the plains while the Siria were in the now Maasai Mara game park. The Siria were pushed away by the Purko. These Purko came from the north. The Mau escarpment was too cold for livestock herding. Many animals died in that area. The Loita were pushed to more hilly areas and the Siria to the escarpments. One should keep in mind the fact that we are dealing with small populations. The Siria could be found near Lolgorien. The Uasin Gishu at that time were still around Nakuru and Eldoret. Only the Luo had some claims, e.g. above Migori (Awendo).

In 1922 the Maasai were given the option to move west to Kilgoris. Only a few Maasai families moved in that direction: ole Kaikai, ole Konchela, ole Maasai and chief Ntelamia. The latter kicked out Count von Dorenhoff (founder of Kilgoris) because of the war. This German was a dairy farmer involved in making cheese from Maasai herd's milk. He went to farm in Sotik. In 1952 Kilgoris was made a district officers station. The Moitanik are a strange lot. They are very much influenced by the Nandi, but also Baluhya and Baganda. Many speak Kalenjin, e.g., Sunkuli. The Moitanik had Nandi laibons (wise men). The Siria chased the Moitanik northwards. South of Kilgoris lived a group of Nandi workers (builders of the Catholic mission). These ones were kicked out by Konchela's father in 1968 (Billy Konchela – member of the Lancaster House conference in London discussing Kenya's independence). The reason must have been political, but Konchela (Uasin Gishu Maasai) could not kick out the Kipsigis. Battles along the Migori River are known to have occurred in the 1860s between the Maasai and Kipsigis. John Kaiser claims the

Kisii lived halfway between Lolgorien and Kilgoris upward from Lolgorien. Fights in the area were mainly between the Siria versus Kuria, Moitanik versus Kipsigis (over cattle) and the Uasin Gishu versus Kisii and Luo (interview with Father Frans Mol, Mill Hill missionary, 12/12/97).

24. On 23 November, Rail Odinga visited Kilgoris town on a fact-finding mission. He was soon ordered to leave by six moran who had been brought in by a police vehicle that had stopped some 200 metres from where the crowd had gathered. They were armed with *simis* and *rungus* and stated it was a KANU zone. One of the moran aimed his iron-studded club and seriously injured Odinga's bodyguard on the head. Damage was also done to the NDP vehicles by smashing windows and damaging bodywork. According to Odinga the police just stood by and watched (letter dated 25 November 1997 addressed to the Electoral Commission of Kenya). This story seems to confirm allegations that Sunkuli was the one orchestrating these attacks.

25. Evidence produced before the Akiwumi Commission seems to confirm the believed involvement of Sunkuli (see e.g., *East African Standard* 12/02/99; 13/02/99; 14/12/99; 22/04/99).

26. Interview conducted in Kilgoris town on 7 December 1997 by the author. Informants also narrated that Kisii had killed two Maasai boys recently. One boy, schooling in Kilgoris Secondary School, had his head cut off and impaled on a stick. The Maasai were furious. This happened in the border town Nangusa. The boy had gone to Nangusa to sell goats. He was in one of the hotels when Maasai looted cows from the market. The Kisii revenged on the boy. In addition, a small kid was killed by gunfire from a car. The Maasai took revenge on the Kisii by organising a raid on the market.

27. KANU supporters claimed that Leken's ally, one Tutui, was instrumental in changing the actual votes in his favour. One agent of Leken in Lorngosua polling station is said to have stated afterwards that he rigged over 88 votes.

28. After the KANU nominations, an acquaintance met Vice-President George Saitoti, and while congratulating him for his victory in Kajiado North, informed him that Kajiado had acquired a new brand of politicians. The VP was not amused and asked, 'What do you mean? Those guys are opposition *damu*. I cannot work with them'. The person retorted by saying, 'but they have won on a KANU ticket and are therefore KANU people. They could not have bothered for this kind of nomination if they are not interested in KANU.' 'No way,' replied the VP, 'those guys may have won in KANU. However, they will always have one foot in KANU and the other in the opposition and its masters. So I will have to do something in two days' time and revert the situation.'

29. When the Kajiado Central constituency KANU nomination results were nullified, Moi asked Leken to step down to give room for the KANU candidate. Some local people accompanied him on the journey, leaving a warning behind from the local people to the effect that: 'ole Leken, they are going to give you a job or money. If you agree to be cowed, do not come back here. Do not agree to be bribed. We need you as our leader and not Moi's servant.' When they arrived at State House, Moi offered Leken a job as a high commissioner in London, and acknowledged the fact that a mistake had been made in both Kajiado Central and South, 'but to error is human', he concluded. Leken is said to have replied that: 'Your Excellency, I am not refusing your offer. And I think that in the years that I have given (sic) you as an ambassador, I have done well. However, the people now want me to serve them in a different capacity and that is why they turned up in large numbers to queue for me. If you want me to serve you again, do come down to Kajiado Central and ask the people to allow me to. Otherwise, I am not able to do that on my own'. The president kept quiet and then said, 'Then, if you are going to campaign, then ask votes for me while you solicit for yours.' Councillor Osoi (from Mashuru) is said to have risen and told the president that, 'Let us be clear about this. The Maasai are very annoyed by what happened, and especially the role of the VP and the DC Kajiado. If you

really want the Maasai to co-operate in any way, first, do fulfil the following: Remove the DC within 48 hours, tell Saitoti to keep off Kajiado Central, and as for votes, come yourself and ask the Maasai to give you votes.' With these few words, the Maasai, picked their *rungus* by the gate and went home.

30. Results came in by sub-location, not by polling station. This was confusing, because the official gazetted list of the polling stations did not match with the sub-locations. The 'KANU' list also did not specify which polling stations were in which sub-location. Moreover the KANU list of registered voters per polling station was (slightly) different from the one carried by the domestic observers. This also brought forward questions, especially for a few polling stations where, according to Mwaniki supporters, the turnout was higher than the number of registered voters. Also Mwaniki stated that in at least six polling stations his agents were sent away by the local chiefs and presiding officers. He stated he would petition, but this never materialised (see also *East African Standard* 29/11/97).

31. Interview with G. Konchela 04/12/97.

32. Parpai had been the deputy clerk to the Kajiado county council. He was forced to resign in 1992 after he had raised a clenched fist, the DP sign, in a bar in Kajiado. This made him join the opposition in bitterness at the decision.

33. Sankori had full support in Kaputiei (his home area) and Dalalekutuk. He would do well among the Ildamat and the Ilpurko (though they are a minority in number). He has some support in Loodokilani (where he has married from) and some in Matapato. Leken had great support in Loodokilani, Matapato (home area) both of which are populous and has decided support in Dalalekutuk (nearly 50 per cent) and some in Kaputiei it was estimated.

34. Loontasati had contested in the 1992 elections on a DP ticket against Sankori where he got 8,543 votes to the winner's 11,262 votes. This time Leken asked Loontasati to support him in the KANU primaries for Leken to defeat Sankori. If Leken would fail he would, during the general elections, campaign for Loontasati and DP. When Leken defected to Safina, Loontasati felt betrayed and opted to co-operate with Sankori. Others claim that shortly after the KANU party nominations, Loontasati when asked to step down for Leken gave his terms to be compensated for the money used in his campaign. The Leken group delivered the money but Loontasati had meanwhile raised his price. The Leken group now decided to try the Safina ticket. It was a bitter moment for John Keen who had always been a very close friend to Loontasati's father (ole Nkoyo).

35. The *ilaiser* clan were divided by a sub-clan named *iloodo-kishu* (red cows) who did not want Singaru, simply because their clansman Somoire from the PADEP project was not in agreement with the former MP and so he used all means to convince his sub-clan to support Parpai to avoid the looter of his project. Likewise a sub-clan from *ilaitayiok* known as *isiria* (*ilmakuperia*) from the controversial Olgulului/Olallarashi group ranch backed Singaru so as to retain their group ranch positions.

36. Oliver Seki was seen actively campaigning in favour of George Saitoti. At 2.30 pm the voting had come to a complete standstill. Presidential and civic ballot papers were not available. The presiding officer went round but returned empty handed. Both candidates went and brought the returning officer (Taalam). He explained he had overdistributed the ballot papers to other stations. One of the ballot boxes for the civic elections was thrown out of the balloting room by an angry crowd planning to burn its contents. The police chased everybody out except agents and the deputy presiding officer. The boxes were sealed and voting continued the following day. The boxes were taken to the counting hall and returned next day. Agents agreed that the seals of the boxes were intact (IED observers' report).

37. KANU claimed that Olorkinyei's victory in the primaries was due to his bringing in Maasai moran, lacking ID and voter cards. When Godfrey Parpai defected to DP,

Olorkinyei also defected 'willingly' to DP though he could have stood on a KANU ticket. He, however, opted to campaign fully for his parliamentary candidate. KANU then cleared Moses Ketukei, supported by Saitoti, who had lost to Olorkinyei. On 29 December, Olorkineyi did agree to continue with the election with the wrong party symbol attached to his name and he signed a letter in this respect. Still, it is not clear whether the mistake was made in Kenya or in the UK. Finally, the fact that the moran could not vote in the general elections and that Olorkinyei is said to have threatened the non-Maasai if they engaged in the KANU primaries, this time around they did vote and most likely tilted the scale against the DP candidate.

38. Though Leken did not petition his defeat, long after one informant (a counting clerk), claimed that at the count he noticed that several ballot papers were folded tightly together. One would not expect this to be possible if ballots are put into the box one by one. The numbers stuck together could range from 5 to 15. Boxes from Dalalekutuk, Sankori's stronghold, especially showed this rare feature for the presidential and parliamentary elections, not so much the civic. Often all but one were votes cast for the KANU candidate. A possible explanation given for this was that if opposition supporters boycotted voting, the remaining papers could have been used and put in the box en masse. Of course one still needs an enabling environment to do so.

39. Informant's name withheld.

40. Moi and Saitoti were for a long time not on speaking terms. For example, Moi attended a party in 1998 organised by ole Muyaa to celebrate his recapturing the Kajiado county council chairmanship. According to witnesses Saitoti, who was also present as the MP of the area, was not allowed to speak.

41. A major factor in the voting pattern in Kilgoris constituency was the fact that a large number of Uasin Gishu (some 70-80 per cent) voters did not support 'their' man Konchela, because there is a fight over land. The Uasin Gishu want to be among the beneficiaries, like the Moitanik, of getting land from the Siria (in the Masurara area) and Konchela is not in favour of this. On 27 January 1998, tension among the Siria Maasai rose because of the Uasin Gishu and Moitanik Maasai, inciting them to join them against the Kisii. The call is that they are all Maasai and cannot sit on the fence. Yet, the Siria (the smallest group of Maasai in the area) are known to be a very gentle and peace-loving people. They will not support Sunkuli because, for example, in 1996 he tried to throw them out of an area (the Soit Escarpment) where the Siria had received a lot of revenue from some tourists lodges (one belonging to Moi) for allowing wildlife to roam the area. The idea was to allegedly put his Moitanik relatives and friends in the area to make them profit from the revenues. One Kijabe (a Siria) went to see Moi and threatened to sue the chief (Sunkuli's puppet) in court. The court case never materialised and Sunkuli failed.

42. In the county council Ntimama has a problem: the DC has influenced Ntutu to make sure his constituency got 25 wards as against the 17 in Narok North. Add the 6 and 4 nominated councillors and it will be 31 to 21. Most of the councillors in South are youngsters from another Maasai section and are not willing to co-operate with Ntimama. They now want full control of the resources of the Maasai Mara. They have appealed for the chairperson and the treasury to come from their side. The clerk already is. Altogether Ntimama will lose most of the Mara money. He has already indicated that Narok North still has the pyrethrum and wheat (interview in Narok town 23/01/98).

43. Interview with John Keen (18/01/98).

44. Interview with Richard Leakey (24/01/98).

45. Lately Muyaa is said to have been instrumental in an attempt to allocate the county council Livestock Holding Ground land near Ngong to State House-related persons. This should act as a stepping stone for an MP position. This would directly threaten Saitoti's position.

References

ECK 1999, *1997 General Election Report*, Nairobi: Electoral Commission of Kenya.

Human Rights Watch/Africa Watch 1993, *Divide and Rule. State-Sponsored Ethnic Violence in Kenya*, New York: Human Rights Watch.

Human Rights Watch/Africa Watch 1997, *Failing the Internally Displaced. The UNDP Displaced Persons Program in Kenya*, New York: Human Rights Watch.

IED 1997, *National Elections Data Book Kenya 1963-1997*, Nairobi: Institute for Education in Democracy.

IED/CJPC/NCCK 1998, *Report on the 1997 General Elections in Kenya, 29-30 December, 1997*, Nairobi: Institute for Education in Democracy/ Catholic Justice and Peace Commission/National Council of Churches of Kenya.

Kaiser, J. 1995, Maela (manuscript).

KNA/MAC/KEN The Murumbi Africana Collection, Nairobi: Kenya National Archives.

Mol, F. 1978, *Maa. A Dictionary of the Maasai Language and Folklore, English-Maasai*, Nairobi: Marketing & Publishing Ltd.

_____ 1996, *Maasai Language & Culture Dictionary*, Maasai Centre Lemek, Kenya.

Rutten, M.M.E.M. 1990, The District Focus Policy for Rural Development in Kenya. The Decentralization of Planning and Implementation, 1983-9, in David Simon (ed.) *Third World Regional Development – A Reappraisal*, London: Paul Chapman Publishing Ltd: 154-70.

_____ 1992, *Selling Wealth to Buy Poverty – The process of Individualization of Landownership Among the Maasai Pastoralists of Kajiado District, Kenya 1890-1990*, Saarbrücken:Verlag Breitenbach Publishers.

_____ 1998, Kenya General Elections 1997–Implementing a New Model for International Election Observation in Africa, report submitted to the Royal Netherlands Embassy, Nairobi, Kenya, Leiden: African Studies Centre.

Saitoti, G. 1997, *Saitoti – A Great Future for Kajiado North*, campaign brochure.

Sanger, C. and Nottingham, J. 1964, 'The Kenya General Election of 1963' *Journal of Modern African Studies*, Vol. 2, No.1: 11-24.

Sekuda, F.N. ole 1997, 'Maasai love peace and know how to make lasting peace', in Somjee, S. (ed.) *Honey and Heifer, Grasses, Milk and Water – A heritage of diversity in reconciliation*, Nairobi: Mennonite Central Committee: 81-100.

Throup, D. and Hornsby, C. 1998, *Multi-Party Politics in Kenya. The Kenyatta & Moi States & the Triumph of the System in the 1992 Election*, Oxford: James Currey.

16

Patronising the Incumbent: Kalenjin Unity in the 1997 Kenya General Elections

Adams G.R. Oloo

Elections represent the most formidable means of recruiting individuals into leadership positions and in this sense they form the very foundation of a political system that ascribes to liberal democracy. This chapter is concerned with the analysis of electoral politics in Kenya generally and in Kalenjin constituencies in the Rift Valley in particular (See map on p. 189).

Electoral studies can only be meaningful if they contribute to the understanding of political dynamics and behaviour in a specific system. With this in mind, the study attempts to explain why people voted or did not vote, and the factors which influenced the decisions of the voters. Moreover, this chapter analyses the relationship between the electoral process and the politics of parliamentary elections in Kenya.

The significance of elections is also dependent on how freely such elections are conducted. In a democracy elections enable the electors to vote on the basis of their free will. They also enable aspirants for elective posts to offer themselves for election without let or hindrance. The major test for free elections is the openness of a political system. Such openness implies that citizens are free to engage in political formations on the basis of their value preferences and that such formations enable the electors not only to choose between (or among) candidates, but also between or among competing policies and programmes.

Jean Blondel (1963) outlines the factors which he considers crucial to a voter's choice in a given political system. They include religion, demographic variables (age, sex), tradition and environment (social and family background), self assigned class and membership in interest or pressure groups. Out of the experience of the 1992 Kenyan elections we hasten to add ethnicity as one of the critical variables.

The Kalenjin community, which is our case study, is President Moi's ethnic group. Moi is also the chairman of the ruling party, Kenya African National Union (KANU). In Kenya, as elsewhere in Africa, often times the party in power tends to use its position to acquire electoral advantages over its opponents. Likewise the position of head of state is seen as beneficial to the community which the occupant of the office hails from.

The study covers all the predominantly Kalenjin inhabited constituencies in the Rift Valley Province including two constituencies in Nakuru district and one in Trans Nzoia. We shall also include Turkana district due to their allegiance to the Kalenjin although they are not a sub-group of that community.

The Kalenjin Rift Valley: a political profile

The name 'Kalenjin' is used in reference to a group of about eight highland Nilotic sub-groups related to each other by common migration origins, settlement patterns, language, tradition and culture. Those eight groups are the Kipsigis, Nandi, Keiyo, Marakwet, Tugen, Pokot, Saboat and Terik. The name, however, excludes other neighbouring Nilotic groups such as the Maasai, Turkana and the Samburu in the Rift Valley (see Kipkorir and Welbourn 1973).

The Rift Valley Province has a total of 17 districts of which nine are dominated by the Kalenjin. These are West Pokot, Uasin Gishu, Marakwet, Keiyo, Nandi, Baringo, Koibatek, Bomet and Kericho. The Kalenjin also have a significant presence in two other districts, namely Trans Nzoia and Nakuru, where the Luhya and Kikuyu dominate, respectively. Their presence in the remaining six districts is however minimal, with Laikipia being dominated by the Kikuyu while the Kalenjin allies, the Turkana, Maasai and Samburu, dominate the remaining five districts namely Turkana, Samburu, Trans Nzoia, Narok and Kajiado.

Among the Kalenjin in Uasin Gishu district, the Nandi sub-group are the majority and dominate most of the economic and political activities. Their predominance in the district has historical antecedents that go back to the colonial period. The Nandi together with the Kipsigis and some Maasai clans shared much of the district's expansive plains but the colonial state removed all the groups from the area and put them in their respective native reserves. The other significant sub-group in the district are the Keiyo who, despite being numerically smaller than the Nandi, wield more political influence than any other group in the district. Next with a significant presence in the area are the Kikuyu, who are found in the settlement schemes and in Eldoret town (Berman and Lonsdale 1992). Uasin Gishu has three parliamentary constituencies: Eldoret East, Eldoret North, and Eldoret South. During the 1992 elections they all returned KANU MPs.

Nandi district is predominantly dominated by the Nandi sub-group of the Kalenjin community. The Nandi are a proud people, who have throughout their history produced independent, principled and often articulate leaders such as the late Jean Marie Seroney, a formidable personality of Nandi politics, the late Bishop Alexander Muge, a fiery church minister of the Anglican church of Kenya, who died in a mysterious road accident, as well as the former deputy speaker of the National Assembly Samuel arap Ng'eny (*Weekly Review* 20/06/97). Nandi is one of the smallest districts in the vast Rift Valley Province covering an area of only 2,839 km². Until late 1996, when the electoral commission added Emgwen constituency, the district was divided into three constituencies, namely: Aldai, Mosop and Tinderet. Since 1978, when President Moi came into power, Nandi district has been characterised by a high turnover of members of parliament, mainly due to the strong influence of power brokers close to the country's power control, chiefly Mark Too, the chairman of Lonrho East Africa, and Ezekiel Bargetuny, the former Nandi district KANU chairman. Few elected MPs in Nandi have been able to get second consecutive terms, while those who have survived have been juggled around either being promoted or demoted from top government positions at the whims of the power brokers. The leaders include Samuel arap Ng'eny (Aldai), Stanley arap Meto (Mosop), John Cheruiyot (Aldai), Henry Kosgey (Tinderet), Kimaiyo arap Sego (Tinderet) all of whom have not been allowed to make a big impact in Nandi or national politics.

Mark Too, whose detractors have said that he is not a native of the district despite the fact that he was born and brought up in Nandi, is believed to have been influential in the 1992 election of the Nandi KANU MPs Henry Kosgey (Tinderet), Paul Titi (Aldai) and John Sambu (Mosop). Although the edifice of Kalenjin unity still exists, it has been put to the test mainly by the Nandi. The Nandi have been trying to assert themselves against what some of their leaders, such as Jackson Kibor, the former Uasin Gishu KANU branch chairman, and John Sambu see as dominance by the smaller Keiyo and Tugen groups.

In Nandi district more localised issues have assumed greater importance in the political calculations. Land is being sold at apparently exorbitant prices by the East African Tanning Extract Company (EATEC), a subsidiary of Lonrho East Africa. Second is the plight of squatters. An other is the perceived dominance of the Tugen and Keiyo in neighbouring Uasin Gishu district, which the Nandi consider as their traditional homeland (*Weekly Review* 20/06/97). Despite these issues, the district remained a KANU stronghold in the 1992 elections.

The Kipsigis are the most numerous among the Kalenjin sub-groups. Before Kericho district was divided into two to create a separate Bomet district, it had one of the highest turnovers of elected members of parliament. Bearing in mind their numerical strength, the Kipsigis of Kericho and Bomet districts feel that they have been short-changed specifically because they are unrepresented within the corridors of power. After the recent creation of Ainamoi constituency, Kericho district now has four parliamentary seats in addition to Belgut, Bomet and Kipkelion. Bomet district also has four constituencies: Bomet, Chepalungu, Sotik and Konoin.

And just like in Nandi, none of the Kipsigis personalities has been allowed to hold a strong independent political base since Moi came to power. For example, several personalities have been made cabinet ministers but have soon tumbled down. They include Prof. Jonathan Ng'eno (Buret), John Koech (Chepalungu), Taaita Toweett (Buret), Kipkalya Kones (Bomet), Timothy Mibei (Buret), former speaker of the National Assembly, Moses arap Keino, as well as the late Isaac Salat (Bomet). Out of these the only Kipsigis political leaders who have come close to wielding real political power at the centre since 1979 are the late Salat, who was a former MP for Kipkelion, Moses Keino and Kipkalya Kones. In the 1992 general elections, the Kipsigis overwhelmingly returned KANU candidates and President Moi with numerous votes.

The Keiyo are mainly to be found in Keiyo district, formerly Elgeyo Marakwet, before it was split into Keiyo and Marakwet districts in 1995. The Keiyo have also settled in large numbers in Uasin Gishu where they have made one constituency, Eldoret East, their preserve. The Keiyo, alongside Moi's Tugen, are said to have drawn the most benefits from Moi's presidency. This has been attributed to Nicholas Biwott who is a Keiyo and a powerful confidant of President Moi. In the neighbouring Uasin Gishu district, Biwott has been accused by the Nandi of trying to collude with the Tugen to dominate local politics and economic activities. Keiyo district has only two constituencies: Keiyo North and Keiyo South. Regarded as the most powerful man after Moi both in Kalenjin and Kenyan politics, Biwott has kept a tight hold on Keiyo politics and even Tabitha Seii, a former headmistress of Kapkenda Girls High School, has found him to be a stumbling block. He is the man who can be credited with KANU's and Moi's good showing in the district in the 1992 elections.

The Tugen are one of the smallest groups among the Kalenjin. Previously, they were mainly found in Baringo district but, since the creation of Koibatek district, they now straddle the two districts. President Moi hails form the Tugen sub-group and has to a large extent shaped Tugen politics since his sojourn in legislative politics in 1955. In spite of President Moi's lineage amongst the Tugen, they are a marginal force and even amongst the Kalenjin community they are smaller in population and economically less developed than their Nandi and Kipsigis counterparts (Throup 1987). Baringo and Koibatek have remained a safe haven for KANU and Moi. In 1992 most of the seats were returned unopposed on KANU tickets. Baringo has three constituencies: Baringo Central, Baringo North and Baringo East. Koibatek has two: Eldama Ravine and Mogotio.

As already mentioned, until 1995 the Marakwet and Keiyo belonged to the single Elgeyo Marakwet district. Since then Marakwet has been a district in its own right. Marakwet land is marginal and as a result the people mainly practise pastoralism. In the 1990s some Marakwet leaders have been quick to point out that they have not benefited from Moi's presidency. Their intermittent skirmishes with their Pokot partners in the Kalenjin coalition have not made matters any better. Marakwet district has two constituencies: Marakwet East and Marakwet West. Both voted KANU in 1992.

The Pokot are mainly found in West Pokot district, a semi-arid area which is only suitable for pastoralism. The area is also prone to cattle rustling emanating from their Kenyan as well as their Ugandan pastoral neighbours. Due to this problem the government in earlier years armed home guards to protect the community. However, this backfired as the Pokot homeguards have time and again been accused of terrorising neighbouring communities. The Pokot, Turkana, Samburu and Karamojong (Ugandan) have traditionally raided each other for cattle. Homeguards in West Pokot district first obtained guns in 1980 to defend themselves against Ugandan Sebei and Karamojong who had acquired guns during the chaos following Idi Amin's departure from power in Uganda in 1979. The area's politics currently revolves around the combative Cabinet Minister Francis Lotodo who time and again has come out to defend his community against cattle raid accusations. West Pokot constituencies are Kacheliba, Kapenguria and Sigor. During the 1992 general elections all the seats were won by KANU.

The creation of new constituencies: a boost to the Kalenjin kitty

The conduct of the Electoral Commission of Kenya in the 1992 general elections and subsequent by-elections was by and large seen to be partial to the ruling party. This has been attributed to the fact that the commissioners are directly appointed by the president and, therefore, they see themselves as serving at his pleasure. This has further been aggravated by the fact that the electoral commission lacks a sound institutional capacity.

This was the same electoral commission which launched the constituency boundary review exercise in preparation for the 1997 general elections on 28 September 1996. While launching the exercise its chairman, Justice Zachaeus Chesoni, called for written memoranda and submissions. The judge noted that the commission was limited by the constitution to distribute only 22 constituencies in addition to the existing 188.

After soliciting views from Kenyans, the commission created 22 new constituencies in September 1996. The Rift Valley Province got the highest number of additional constituencies (five) followed by Central, Eastern and

Western provinces which got four constituencies each, Nyanza three, while North-Eastern and Coast provinces ended up with one each.

After announcing the creation of the new constituencies, the commission expressed its wish that a further provision be made by parliament to give it authority to create 50 more constituencies to enable the country to enjoy adequate parliamentary representation. The chairman of the commission explained that his commission used proper criteria, such as population density and trends, means of communication, geographical features, community interest and boundaries of existing administrative areas in creating the new constituencies (*Weekly Review* 27/09/96).

According to some observers the electoral commission deliberately gave the highest number of the new constituencies to the Rift Valley Province which was considered the KANU stronghold. In otherwords, the new constituencies were created to benefit the ruling party. But even within the Rift Valley itself, there were feelings of disappointment as the five constituencies were all concentrated in five out of the 17 districts. Two of the new constituencies, Ainamoi and Sotik, were both in the Kipsigis-dominated districts of Kericho and Bomet, respectively, while one was in the neighbouring Nakuru district. The other two beneficiaries were in Nandi and Koibatek districts.

The Kipsigis group seemed to have benefited more than the other Kalenjin communities for, apart from the constituencies mentioned above, they were also generally considered the biggest beneficiary of the sub-division of Molo to create Molo and Kuresoi constituencies. The latter is predominantly inhabited by the Kipsigis and their Dorobo neighbours. Kuresoi seemed to have been created to ensure that the Kalenjin community won a seat in the predominantly Kikuyu-settled district.

Other constituencies created in the Rift Valley Province were all in predominantly Kalenjin areas where all the MPs were elected unopposed in the 1992 general elections. The Nandi were given Emgwen constituency while the fifth in the province was Eldama Ravine in the new Koibatek district which was carved out of the only constituency in that district formerly known as Baringo South and subsequently named Mogotio.

With four of the new constituencies geographically delineated in the Kalenjin heartland, and the fifth in Kalenjin inhabited Nakuru district, there was no doubt that KANU would have little problem winning all the new constituencies. It is interesting to note that although the Luhya and Kikuyu are heavily settled in Trans Nzoia and Nakuru districts respectively, no constituency was created in those areas that could directly benefit them.

Party primaries: canvassing for the KANU ticket

In the 1992 general elections, the Kalenjin Rift Valley was closed to opposition
parties through both intimidation and harassment by the majority Kalenjin
masses, who largely perceived opposition parties as ploys to undermine Moi's
leadership. Going by the 1992 general election results, most aspirants in the
Kalenjin Rift Valley viewed the real battle to be at the KANU primaries stage
rather than during the general elections. This was based on the belief that once
an aspirant won the KANU nomination ticket, the general elections would be
a mere formality since the area was a KANU stronghold. The massive interest
in the KANU nominations as compared to those of the opposition parties
attest to this.

Uashin Gishu district

While the above observation is largely true, the run-up to the 1997 elections
witnessed a lot of wrangling and misgivings from the Kalenjin coalition sub-
groups, mainly among the Nandi and Kipsigis and later the Marakwet.
Discontent first arose among the Nandi in Uasin Gishu district led by the then
district KANU branch chairman, Jackson Kibor. Kibor was later suspended
when he publicly asked Moi to name his successor. In the ensuing branch
elections, the Nandi once again rallied behind him, a move which the party
headquarters did not take lightly and which saw Kibor being suspended from
all KANU activities. In the subsequent elections, the three top positions were
shared equally among the three Kalenjin sub-groups in the district. The
chairman's position went to a Nandi, Reuben Siele, who was defending the
post, the secretary's position went to a Keiyo, Joel Barmasaai the then Eldoret
East MP, and the position of treasurer went to a Tugen, Reuben Chesire,
chairman of the Industrial Development Bank.

It was under these circumstances that Kibor took the unprecedented step
of moving to the opposition and vowed to wipe out KANU in Nandi and
Uasin Gishu districts. Kibor together with five councillors and a parliamentary
aspirant for the Cherangani seat in Trans Nzoia district, John Kirwa Rotich,
defected to the official opposition party, FORD-Kenya, at a public rally in
Kitale. The rally was addressed by the FORD-Kenya chairman, Kijana
Wamalwa. Kibor noted that although his heart was in FORD-Kenya, he would
work with all formidable opposition parties to field candidates in Nandi and
Uasin Gishu districts (*Weekly Review* 28/02/97).

Uasin Gishu district has its headquarters in Eldoret town – a fast growing
and increasingly politically significant metropolis in northern Rift Valley
that is usually quiet until election time. The dominant Kalenjin sub-ethnic-
group in Uasin Gishu district are the Nandi and past elections in the district

tended to revolve around the tussle between them and the Keiyo who are the other significant Kalenjin sub-ethnic group in the district.

Among the district's three constituencies, Eldoret North, which includes Eldoret town, comes across as the most volatile. This reputation goes back to the 1974 general elections, when Chelagat Mutai, then a 24-year-old fresh graduate of political science, came onto the scene after beating 11 other challengers. She was backed by the late Jean Marie Seroney, the respected Nandi lawyer and leader and the then MP for Tinderet. Eldoret North thus became a household name in the country largely due to Mutai's penchant for taking on powerful politicians in her crusade against corruption and her spirited contributions in parliament. Mutai's first tenure in parliament was, however, short-lived for she was charged in an Eldoret court with incitement to violence and subsequently jailed in 1976. By the time of the 1979 general elections Mutai was out of jail and she ran against Nicanor Kimurgor arap Sirma, the man who had taken over in her absence, and William Morogo Saina, a former MP of the area. Once again Mutai triumphed, but she was again taken to court towards the end of 1981, this time charged with falsifying parliamentary mileage claims. She was released on bond, jumped bail and fled to Tanzania. In the subsequent by-election, Kimurgor arap Sirma reclaimed the seat. Mutai was not in the running in 1983 when William Saina took the seat. Thereafter, the politics of Eldoret North took a new turn with the focus shifting to the rivalry between Saina and Reuben Chesire.

The Nandi are the dominant group in the constituency but there is also a substantial presence of other communities. That is certainly the case in the cosmopolitan Eldoret town which has a significant presence of Luhya, Kikuyu, Luo and other Kalenjin groups like the Keiyo, but whose role has never upset the equation in favour of a non-Nandi candidate. Among the contestants for the KANU ticket in the 1997 general elections were the two old guards, Saina and Chesire, alongside the youthful newcomer William Ruto. Saina happens to be a direct descendant of the legendary Nandi leader Koitalel arap Samoei who led the Nandi in the fight against colonialism and was assassinated by British forces. To the tradition-inclined Nandi, Saina is the embodiment of this warrior spirit and it is a legacy that he has never missed an opportunity to harp on. On 13 December 1993, Saina led Nandi legislators, Paul Titi and Henry Kosgey, Cherangani MP Kipruto arap Kirwa and the chairman of Lonrho East Africa, Mark Too, in passing the 'Kapkaben Declaration' at Kaptamok in Aldai constituency. The declaration was intended to bind the Nandi community in their hour of need. According to Saina the Nandi were at the time facing divisive forces (*Economic Review* 15/09/97).

Although Nandi supremacy reigned supreme in past elections, the 1997 general elections witnessed another angle whereby the younger Kipkoimet generation wanted to take leadership from the older Sawe generation. The Kipkoimet generation is made up of middle-aged people who were yearning to take over leadership of the community from the old guard. Despite the old-versus-the-young battle, the area also displayed its usual stand of rejecting the so-called outsiders. In the 1992 general elections the cry from Nandi nationalists was that they could not vote for two Tugen. That meant that they could not vote for Daniel arap Moi as president and have Reuben Chesire as their local MP. This question resurfaced in 1997 but the answer as to who was to become MP was found in the generation battle since both Chesire and the incumbent MP William Saina fell in the same *Sawe* generation which the young people, including William Ruto, had said outlived their usefulness in the Kalenjin leadership.

In Eldoret East, the Nandi/Keiyo dichotomy is quite visible. The constituency, which was created just prior to the 1988 elections, led to speculation that it had much to do with the significant Keiyo presence there. The focus immediately turned to and has lingered on powerful cabinet minister Nicholas Biwott, a Keiyo with vast business interests in Eldoret East and whose interest in the constituency the Nandi view with great suspicion. The first elections in Eldoret East were closely contested but in the end Francis Tarar narrowly edged out his arch-rival Joel Barmasaai who, however, beat Tarar during the KANU primaries in 1992. In the 1997 KANU primaries Barmasaai was challenged by Tarar, Eldoret businessman Michael Rono and the area KANU sub-branch chairman, John Chalunya. Barmasaai, who is a Keiyo, was considered to be at a disadvantage as it was perceived that non-Keiyo, particularly the Nandi, could translate the 'Kapkaben Declaration' to mean cleansing the entire Uasin Gishu district of non-Nandi leadership.

The third constituency in the district, Eldoret South, is host to a large immigrant community who bought land in the area. Apart from the majority Nandi, there is a significant presence of Kikuyu and Luhya communities. The incumbent Joseph Misoi was faced with a strong challenge which included Eldoret lawyer Paul Birech, a former primary school headmaster, Jesse Maizs, and the Uasin Gishu KANU branch chairman, Reuben Siele.

The Uasin Gishu district KANU nominations were held against a background of machinations by Kalenjin Rift Valley power brokers who wanted the three seats to be divided equally among the three sub-groups of the Kalenjin. Their wish was that Eldoret East should go to a Keiyo (Barmasaai), Eldoret North to a Tugen (Chesire) and Eldoret South to any of the successful Nandi candidates. However, the nomination results in Uasin Gishu showed that the goals of the KANU leadership and those of the electorate were not the same. First, all the incumbents lost and second, two of the nominees were Nandi with Eldoret North going to William Ruto, a former Youth for KANU 1992 (YK'92) operative, and Eldoret South to Jesse Maizs. Although a Keiyo, Francis Tarar won the Eldoret East nominations despite the leadership preference of Barmasaai over him. Thus, in Uasin Gishu, intra-ethnic infighting was the dominant factor in the nominations.

Nandi district

Nandi district elections have always been held under the guidance of power brokers such as former district KANU supremo Ezekiel Bargetuny and Mark Too. In Tinderet constituency, the incumbent Henry Kosgey was challenged by a string of youthful candidates for the KANU ticket. Kosgey first went to parliament in 1979 in a surprise win over the veteran of Nandi politics, the late Jean Marie Seroney. The upset was accomplished with outside intervention as President Daniel arap Moi sought to place his own men in the district soon after he came to power. Kosgey held the seat until 1988 when he was defeated by Kimaiyo arap Sego whose win was orchestrated by Ezekiel Bargetuny and Mark Too. Kosgey had by then managed to endear himself to the electorate and would have been a clear winner were it not for the blatant rigging which marked the 1988 KANU nominations. Kosgey however was re-elected in the 1992 elections.

In the newly created Emgwen constituency, several candidates were interested in the KANU ticket. In the Nandi language Emgwen means 'centre', an adequate name for the newly created constituency hived off from all the three previous constituencies in the district. The creation of Emgwen prompted speculation that it was meant to provide Mark Too with a launching path to parliament after a series of unsuccessful attempts. Too, who lost to John Sambu, the MP for Mosop, in the 1992 KANU nominations, first expressed interest in Emgwen but later shifted to Eldoret South constituency in Uasin Gishu district before giving up altogether. Among the aspirants for the KANU ticket in the new constituency were a former cabinet minister, John Cheruiyot, former deputy speaker of the national assembly, Samuel arap Ng'eny, former director of Kenya Co-operative Creameries, David Bett, and former head of the civil service Joseph arap Leting. However, in Aldai and Mosop no stiff competition was expected in the party primaries.

A common factor among the four Nandi district constituencies is the land problem. There was a feeling especially in Aldai and Emgwen that the African Inland Church, Moi's church, had been favoured with respect to land allocations at the expense of the locally more favoured Catholic church and Anglican Church of Kenya. The KANU primaries in Nandi district were thus held against a background in which the Nandi tried to resist a dominance by the smaller Keiyo and Tugen groups. Other local issues such as the plight of squatters and land being sold at exorbitant prices by the EATEC were also prominent. The battle was more intense in Tinderet where young politicians were preaching the gospel of change and turning up the heat on the incumbent Henry Kosgey

Three factors were at play. First, the interest of the youth in politics had reached unprecedented heights. Second, the overwhelming interests of the urban-based elite in the politics of the constituency and third, generous businessmen entered into the fray by organising huge fund-raisings occasions. Among the youths opposing Henry Kosgey were Tony Keter and David Lagat, both businessmen in Nairobi and Mombasa, respectively. Still, against all these odds, Kosgey won the KANU nomination.

In Mosop constituency John Sambu easily triumphed. This was mostly attributed to the fact that he had been fighting for the locals' rights both over the squatter problem and the EATEC land. His popularity increased when he was sacked over the Kenya Co-operative Creameries decentralisation saga.[1]

In Aldai constituency Simon Kiptanui Choge made a come back by beating youthful challengers while Mark Too's withdrawal in the newly created Emgwen constituency paved the way for Joseph arap Leting to win the KANU primaries.

Bomet district

In recent times Bomet district has seen battles between forces loyal to Kipkalya Kones the MP for Bomet and the previous MP for Chepalungu, John Koech, who also happened to be the Bomet district KANU branch chairman. The two rivals have been engaged in a war over the question of district supremacy and the title of Kipsigis spokesman. These two factors played a major role in the 1997 general elections whereby each supported protégés in other constituencies. The rivalry between the two intensified when Bomet was hived from Kericho district, with each of the antagonists trying to fill the gap left by the former powerful MP for Bomet the late Isaac Salat whose influence was felt across the former large Kericho district. The fight between Kones and Koech came out clearly in January 1997 when Kones was sacked as a cabinet minister and replaced with Koech. This made Kones change from an established party hardliner to a critic of the system appealing to the Kipsigis emotions in a way that threatened to endear the Kipsigis to their fiercely independent cousins the Nandi. But when Kones later on made peace with the powers that be, in July 1997, it was time for Koech to get jittery and this is said to have led to his dramatic three day's resignation, a decision which he later rescinded after persuasion.

In Bomet constituency Kones was expected to sail in smoothly despite the challenge from two serious rivals namely, Wilson Sitonik, the branch assistant treasurer and Wilson Langat, a lecturer at Moi University. In Chepalungu, Koech's challenger was 37-year-old Isaac Ruto, a Kones' crony, formerly of Egerton University, who was gunning for change and counting on his youthfulness. Koech had dominated the constituency since 1979 and cultivated strong grassroots support due to his previous image as a principled individual and a fighter for Kipsigis rights, which had led to his expulsion from KANU in 1989. Koech was thus seen as the front runner in the race for the seat.

Konoin constituency was created in 1988 from parts of Bomet and Buret constituencies. This gave Nathaniel Chebelyon, who had unsuccessfully contested the Bomet seat in the past, an opportunity to realise his parliamentary ambitions. Chebelyon, a former chairman of the Kenya Co-operative Creameries (KCC) and ally of the MP for Bomet, Kipkalya Kones, had kept a firm hold on the seat mainly due to the lack of a credible challenger. However, in 1997 he faced a determined duo for the KANU ticket from John Terer, a former MP, and Raphael Kitur, the Bomet district KANU secretary, who came second in 1988. The other contestant was Richard Rotich, a former accountant with Kenya Airways. Chebelyon was expected to benefit from his close association with Kones while his main opponent Kitur was expected to benefit from Koech's patronage.

Sotik constituency, which was carved out of Bomet and Chepalungu constituencies in 1996, attracted the most aspirants for the KANU ticket. Among them was Taaita arap Toweett, a former cabinet minister who was a nominated MP in the seventh parliament. Toweett, who had not won a parliamentary seat since 1979, decided to shift base to Sotik. Other contenders included Stephen Chelule, a Kericho-based lawyer, Justus Langat, a former headmaster, Alfred Kimunai Soi, a former MP for Chepalungu, Joseph Kibor, an insurance agent, Anthony Kimeto and Richard Kelong.

In Bomet district, success in the KANU primaries was expected to revolve around the support from Kipkalya Kones. In the district he was regarded more as a Kipsigis leader than as a mere MP. This was mainly attributed to his development record and his efforts to settle the landless during his tenure as a minister. Kones' support in his own Bomet constituency was solidified after his sacking from the cabinet. He therefore had an easier time winning the party ticket in the KANU elections. In Konoin constituency the incumbent Nathaniel Chebelyon represented the old political generation. Although his alliance with Kones brought him a considerable amount of political support, his undoing was that the Konoin voters went for a younger person and the youth factor prevailed. Raphael Kitur thus carried the KANU ticket. The youth factor was at work again in Sotik where the relatively young and unknown Anthony Kimeto won the KANU nomination against battle hardened aspirants such as Taaita Toweett and Kimunai Soi, both of whom defected to contest the same seat on opposition tickets of Party of Independent Candidates of Kenya (PICK) and Social Democratic Party (SDP), respectively. But it was in Chepalungu that the greatest upset occurred when the incumbent MP and minister of state John Koech lost to the youthful newcomer Isaac Ruto. Although most observers were quick to point out that Ruto was sponsored by Kones, the youth factor also seemed to have favoured him.

Kericho district

In the neighbouring Kericho district, all the three sitting MPs had a stiff challenge, arising from a combined force from a group of well-connected former top civil servants out to change the politics of the district. The focus was on Buret constituency where a big battle ensued during the KANU elections. The late Professor Jonathan Ng'eno, then a cabinet minister, was pitted against Josiah Sang, a former permanent secretary in the Ministry of Lands and Settlement. Earlier in 1997 Sang had deposed Ng'eno from the Buret KANU sub-branch chairmanship.

The battle between Ng'eno and Sang was interesting when viewed against the background of the wider national KANU politics and was directly linked with the battle for the presidential succession. On one end of the spectrum was the so-called KANU-A faction, associated with cabinet ministers Simeon Nyachae, William ole Ntimama and Kipkalya Kones. Until President Moi indicated his preference with a cabinet reshuffle in early 1997, KANU-A fought strongly for influence against the KANU-B faction grouped around the vice-president George Saitoti and cabinet minister Nicholas Biwott.[2]

Prior to his sacking from his strongly ministerial post in the Office of the President, Kones was emerging powerfully as the spokesman of the Kipsigis sub-group of Kericho and Bomet districts with very active support of other top Kipsigis figures like Ng'eno. After his sacking, he engineered a campaign that quietly spread word that the Kipsigis (Kones and his group) had, despite their numerical superiority, been short-changed by their Tugen and Keiyo counterparts (Moi's and Biwott's ethnic sub-groups respectively) who, it was added, were out to ensure that the Kipsigis were not effectively represented at the centre of power.

Thus, when Moi in February 1997 singled out the KANU branches in Kericho and Bomet district for fresh elections, it was perceived as a clear indication that he was seeking change in the party's leadership in the two districts. The new candidates in the political arena like Josiah Sang in Bomet, Kipng'eno arap Ng'eny in Ainamoi and Charles Kirui in Belgut were branded rightly or wrongly as aligned to KANU-B. By implication these men were seen as proxies of outside forces out to impose their own puppets in the Kipsigis political leadership.[3] The KANU elections for the branch leadership attest to this.

The battle in Kericho district for the party chairmanship was expected in Buret where Ng'eno and Sang were seen as the major contenders while Paul Kipkorir Sang, the former headmaster of Chebwagan High School, was considered a lightweight. During the February 1997 KANU polls it was a clean sweep for the anti-Ng'eno group as Josiah Sang took the sub-branch chairmanship. At the branch level, Kipng'eno arap Ng'eny took over the party leadership in elections which Ng'eno and his group claimed were flawed and clearly designed to favour his rivals. Ng'eno also accused some senior KANU officials of trying to shunt him out of politics and he hit out at some unnamed top KANU officials from outside the district for trying to impose leaders on the Kipsigis. Ng'eno's message was clearly a reference to the KANU-A and KANU-B rift and an indication that in his view it was the Sang-Ng'eny axis which was favoured by KANU's top organs.

Prof. Jonathan Ng'eno, who was the incumbent MP and also a cabinet minister, lost in the KANU primaries of November 1997. Ng'eno's loss had been expected since Josiah Sang, a former permanent secretary in the Moi government, joined the race. Sang was believed to be in the good books of the Moi government. But against all expectations, he too fell by the wayside to a former high school headmaster, Paul Kipkorir Sang.

In Belgut, no MP has ever held the parliamentary seat for two consecutive terms. In 1969 the seat went to Wesley Rono, who beat three other contestants, including Alfred Kerich and Ayub Chepkwony. Five years later, Kerich took the seat, but he lost to Chepkwony in 1979 in a closely contested fight with a newcomer, Kiptarus Kirior. The latter then turned tables on Chepkwony at the snap 1983 elections before Chepkwony recaptured the seat in 1988. However, towards the end of his tenure Chepkwony suffered a series of setbacks which severely affected his political career. First, he was sacked as an assistant minister for tourism and shortly afterwards he was ousted from the Kericho district KANU branch chairmanship. Hence, by the 1992 elections, Chepkwony could not withstand a determined challenge from Kirior who went in unopposed. In 1997 Kirior opted to contest in the new Ainamoi constituency in which his home location now falls. The four leading aspirants for the Belgut KANU ticket were, therefore: Chepkwony; the Kericho district KANU branch secretary, Charles Kirui; a veterinary doctor, Joel Chirchir; and Wilson Soi, a manager with Africa Highland Produce Company. Voters went for new blood and youthful newcomer Charles Kirui won the KANU ticket.

In the new Ainamoi constituency which was split from Belgut, Ng'eny was pitted against Kirior whom he supported during the KANU nominations in 1992. This was seen as a contest between Kirior's grassroot campaign skills against the financial base of Ng'eny. Ng'eny's rising star had earlier in the year been boosted when he was elected to the powerful post of Kericho branch KANU chairman. During the KANU primaries, he defeated Kirior who thereafter defected to the Democratic Party.

In Kipkelion constituency, the incumbent Bishop Daniel Tanui took on Samuel Rotich a former engineer in the Ministry of Public Works. The latter emerged as the winner.

Baringo district

Voters have been largely spared the luxury of election campaigns and elections in Baringo and Koibatek districts, home area of President Moi. In Moi's own Baringo Central constituency, for instance, save for 1997, voters had never cast a single ballot for a parliamentary candidate since independence because Moi went in unopposed. In neighbouring Baringo North constituency, the last time voters went to the ballot box was in the general elections of 1983. In Baringo East constituency, always predominantly inhabited by the Pokot, it goes even further back to 1974. Only Baringo South, since hived off to form Koibatek district (from which the new constituencies Eldama Ravine and Mogotio have been created), has witnessed animated political activity. The trend since the mid-1980s has been, by and large, the return of aspirants to parliament unopposed at the behest of KANU power barons, the idea being to avoid public displays of strife and dissension in the president's backyard.

Since ascending to power in 1978, Moi's authority and influence in Baringo has tended to revolve around his old and trusted friend, the mayor of Kabarnet, Councillor Philemon Chelagat. Equally powerful is the long serving Baringo KANU branch executive officer Hosea Kiplagat who, together with Chelagat, has over the years come to determine the direction of local politics (*Economic Review* 29/09-05/10/97).

Baringo Central constituency is unique in one particular respect. Its representative President Daniel arap Moi is Kenya's longest serving MP, having been first elected to represent the Rift Valley Province in the Legislative Council (LEGCO) in 1955. Since then, he has been returned to parliament unopposed as MP for Baringo Central in all subsequent elections except in 1997. The man who brought to a halt Moi's clean record was a former headmaster, 46-year-old Amos Kiprotich Kandie. In the 1992 general elections, Kandie was nominated by the DP to contest the same seat, but was waylaid on his way to present his nomination to the returning officer at Kabarnet. Armed mobs snatched the documents from him and warned him to keep off elections . The same fate befell Dr Njuguna Chege, a FORD-Asili aspirant. In 1997, Kandie entered the contest on an SDP ticket but not much was expected from his candidature.

Baringo North constituency is widely considered as the hotbed of Baringo politics. Its past MPs have included William Kiptui who served from independence to 1966 Henry Cheboiwo who served until 1979 and again from 1980 to 1988 succeeded him. In between Zephania Chepkonga took the position between 1979 and 1980 when his election was nullified. The other representative of the area was Willy Kamuren for the 1988-97 period.

In the 1992 KANU primaries Henry Cheboiwo stood against the incumbent Kamuren. However, the party primaries were heavily manipulated in Kamuren's favour and Cheboiwo decamped to join the DP. He did not, however, succeed in presenting his nomination papers as Baringo was declared a KANU zone. Apart from the incumbent Kamuren other contenders for the KANU ticket in the 1997 elections were Eric Bett, a Nairobi businessman, William Rotich, director of the Kenya Posts Authority, Reuben Yatur, a Kitale-based farmer and one-time aspirant Andrew Kiptoon.

The vast Baringo East constituency, bordered by Baringo North constituency and by Samburu, Turkana and West Pokot districts, is the largest of the three Baringo district constituencies. It is also the least developed, unlike the rest of Baringo and Koibatek districts where President Moi's Tugen predominate. The Pokot in Baringo East have always lived under the shadow of their more politically powerful Tugen neighbours even long before Moi came to power. The area's first post independence MP was William Kamuren who hailed from Baringo North constituency and was 'seconded' there at the age of 24, ostensibly because no local was up to the task. It was not until 1969, when Kamuren returned to contest at home, that a local, Stephen Lomeri Cheptai, took the seat. Cheptai lost the seat to James Kalegno in 1974, who in turn lost it to Samson Katurkana in 1979. Katurkana retained the seat until 1992 when he was ousted by Joseph Lotodo. In the countdown to the 1997 elections Lotodo faced a challenge from Asman Kamama, a former district officer, alongside former MPs Kalegno and Katurkana.

In the president's home turf of Baringo district, there were no meaningful nomination contests and Moi was nominated in Baringo Central while his lieutenants Andrew Kiptoon and Joseph Lotodo were nominated in Baringo North and Baringo East respectively.

Koibatek district

Eldama Ravine constituency is one of the two constituencies which were hived out of Baringo district. Until then the two constituencies, Eldama Ravine and Mogotio, comprised the larger Baringo South. For a long time, Eldama Ravine was represented by two MPs. Eric Bomett, served from 1963 to 1974 and Edward Kiptanui from 1974 to 1988. The latter was defeated by Lawi Kiplagat, but Kiplagat only served a single term losing in 1992 to William Morogo. Eldama Ravine is largely a settlement area with a relatively cosmopolitan electorate. The indigenous population in the two Koibatek district constituencies comprises mainly the Lembus and the Samor clans but there is also a large presence of Kalenjin immigrants from North Arror and a substantial number of Kikuyu who form the majority of the settler population, especially around Maji Mazuri and Timboroa. But leadership for a long time came from either Bomett's Lembus or Kiptanui's Samor clans.

The split of Baringo South changed the scenario dramatically. Among the most immediate repercussions was the moving of William Morogo to Mogotio constituency, prompting a myriad of declarations of interest in the Eldama Ravine seat. These included the Koibatek district forestry officer, Musa Sirma, Youth for KANU '92 activist Gerald Bomett, former Ministry of Lands surveyor Tom Ngoite, businessman Philip Koech and Joseph Leboo, a former trade-unionist and the eldest among those eyeing the seat. The battle was stiff with the two major contenders being Musa Sirma and Joseph Leboo. Sirma emerged the winner in the controversial nominations, which prompted Joseph Leboo to defect to the DP. In Mogotio constituency, the KANU ticket attracted, apart from Morogo, a Kiambu land court's clerk, James Chesire. William Morogo easily won.

Keiyo and Marakwet districts

Keiyo and Marakwet districts were in the countdown to the 1997 general elections considered KANU territories. One of the more recent significant developments in the region was that the Marakwet were separated from their dominant Keiyo cousins following the split of the former Elgeyo Marakwet district into Keiyo and Marakwet districts. The Marakwet, who mainly occupy the former Kerio West and Kerio East constituencies (now renamed Marakwet West and East), have been complaining about what they perceive as inequitable distribution of resources. They have also been fighting perceived domination by the Keiyo who mainly inhabit Kerio Central and Kerio South constituencies. These were renamed Keiyo North and Keiyo South, respectively. The central figure here is the powerful cabinet minister and MP for Keiyo South, Nicholas Biwott.

In 1992 the former Elgeyo Marakwet district was among the areas in the Rift Valley declared as KANU zones and closed to the opposition. Except for Kerio South, where Biwott faced a token challenge from the DP candidate Tabitha Seii, KANU candidates in Kerio East, Kerio West and Kerio Central went in unopposed. But in 1996 Biwott suffered a set-back following the demise of his right hand man Paul Chepkok, the former MP for Kerio Central. The ensuing by-election saw the entry of an independent-minded former deputy police commissioner, Elijah Sumbeiywo, who became the first person in many years to win a seat in the area without Biwott's blessings.

The contest for the Keiyo South 1997 KANU ticket was interesting in that it brought Biwott face to face with his former aides who were also Youth for KANU '92 operatives. The two were Moses Changwony, a motor vehicle dealer, and Micah Kigen a former technician with the Kenya Posts and Telecommunications Corporation. However the two challengers were not formidable and Biwott easily won the KANU nomination.

Keiyo North was in 1997 set for a major battle as several aspirants for the KANU ticket challenged the incumbent Elijah Sumbeiywo. Among them were the director of Keinan supermarkets, Gilbert Lagat, the managing director of Affiliate Security Services, Thomas Chesoi, the former managing director of Rivatex, Thomas Bore, a previous contestant, Tugut Keitany, and an Eldoret businessman Michael Rono. Sumbeiywo had also to contend with the lingering shadow of the self-declared 'Total Man' (Biwott) who, it was considered, was supporting Lagat for the party ticket. Still, Sumbeiywo easily won the 1997 KANU ticket for the Keiyo North seat.

Cattle rustling activities and violent exchanges between the Marakwet and Pokot preceded the KANU primaries in Marakwet district. In April 1997, attacks by Pokot cattle rustlers resulted in the death of many Marakwet and the loss of huge amounts of livestock. This prompted the then MP for Marakwet East, Fredrick Cheserek, to speak out emotionally against the government for failing to stop the persistent Pokot attacks. Although peace meetings were held between the two communities very little was achieved. This made Frederick Cheserek decamp to the DP. KANU aspirants positioned themselves to take advantage of the fallout between Cheserek and the party power brokers. These included former MPs Robert Kipkorir and Vincent arap Too, the KANU branch secretary Tina Chemuitut and John Kiptoo.

The KANU nomination in Marakwet West was a replica of the 1992 KANU primaries between the incumbent Boaz Kipchumba Kaino and his predecessor Francis Mutwol. Others in the race were David Sudi, a prominent Nairobi businessman and John Kendagor of the KCC. In the subsequent KANU primaries, John Kiptoo won the KANU primaries in Marakwet East, while David Sudi won Marakwet West, defeating the two frontrunners.

West Pokot district
West Pokot district, like neighbouring Marakwet district, is characterised by insecurity and perennial cattle rustling. The Pokot are distant cousins of the ruling Kalenjin and are known to take an independent stand. Pokot politics have of late revolved around the abrasive cabinet minister Francis Lotodo who was blamed for the clashes that took place in the district in the run-up to the 1992 polls and which effectively reduced opposition participation.

Lotodo was in the picture as far back as in 1984, when the state of insecurity in the area was at its peak. He was blamed for promoting war-like activities against other pastoralists, and this led to his sacking as an assistant minister for Information and Broadcasting and landed him in prison. The insecurity in the area has been aggravated by hostility against cultivating settlers from the Kikuyu, Luo, Luhya and Kisii communities with individuals like Lotodo often being accused of planning their expulsion. Due to the April 1997 skirmishes between the Pokot and the Marakwet, the government put in motion a security operation to disarm the Pokot. The residents were, however, opposed to disarmament claiming that it would put them at the mercy of the Turkana and Karamojong cattle raiders.

The then MP for Sigor, Philip Rotino, was subsequently arraigned in court on incitement charges. This followed the 'Kolongolo Declaration' in which Nicholas Biwott led a group of Rift Valley politicians that included Kipruto Kirwa, the MP for Cherangani, cabinet minister Henry Kosgey and Mark Too. The declaration was said to herald the end of cattle rustling in the area but was seen more as an attempt to bring down Lotodo. The plan was abandoned after the defiant Lotodo made it clear he was ready to lead the Pokot out of the Kalenjin coalition. Lotodo is the first Pokot to hold a full cabinet post (*Economic Review* 06-12/09/97).

In Kapenguria constituency, the incumbent Francis Lotodo has been a domineering figure since 1969 when he was first elected to parliament in the then Pokot West constituency, which then included the current Kacheliba constituency. Despite his dominance, Lotodo was challenged by the West Pokot *Maendeleo ya Wanawake* chairlady, Rhoda Rotino and Musa Tomno for the KANU ticket. Prior to the 1997 KANU primaries, Lotodo was quoted as publicly warning non-Pokot not to take part in the process or risk violence on nominations day. Lotodo's agents went round forcing non-Pokot out of the nomination centres, arguing that West Pokot was not their motherland. Armed police were also called in at Cheperena polling station where voters were being forced to stand in favour of Lotodo. It was under those circumstances that Lotodo won the KANU nomination for Kapenguria constituency.

In the neighbouring Sigor constituency, former Pokot East MP James Korellach dominated the political scene for nearly two decades until he was ousted in 1988 by Christopher Lomada. Korellach has since retired from politics but Philip Rotino, the man who emerged the winner in the 1992 KANU primaries, was set for a rematch with Lomada who ran on the PICK ticket during the 1992 elections. Lomada had defected to the opposition in 1992 after being defeated at the KANU nominations by Rotino, but crossed back to KANU in 1997. Observers attributed Rotino's victory to the support he received from Lotodo. Another aspirant for the KANU ticket was a former local DP official Christopher Lonyala. The war mongering Rotino was, however, defeated by Lomada. Finally, in the semi-arid Kacheliba constituency, the incumbent Peter Nangole was challenged by former MP and Daystar University lecturer Samuel Losuron Poghisio, a race which the latter won.

Turkana district

Although they are not a Kalenjin sub-group, the Turkana and their politics have revolved around this ruling group. In the arid and poverty-stricken Turkana district, drought and famine are the order of the day. Politics is usually relegated to the background as residents concentrate on survival. One of the poorest districts in the country, Turkana lacks sufficient health and educational facilities, faces acute water shortages and periodically relies on relief food. Persistent cattle raids in the region have also led to insecurity. NGOs and church organisations have come to play a significant role in providing food relief as well as community-based water, health and education projects. The NGOs include, among others, Oxfam (UK) and the Catholic Relief Services. KANU activists in the area have been suspicious of the wide reach and influence of these organisations which they have accused of campaigning for the opposition. Political hostility and interference has thus caused several NGOs to leave the area.

Due to the insignificant presence of other ethnic groups, clan rivalry is usually a factor at elections especially in Turkana South where clan solidarity is strong. Here the main contenders for the KANU ticket were Francis Ewoton and Eliud Longacha. Ewoton is a former manager with Turkana Fishermen's Co-operative Society and hails from the Ngisonyoka clan. He was banking on his incumbency to carry the day. On the other hand, Longacha, of the popular Ngisilae clan, had been active in the distribution of famine relief food in the area.

In Turkana North Japheth Ekidor was defending the seat which he had dominated since 1979. In the absence of the former MP for Turkana Central the late Peter Ejore, Ekidor who was also the district KANU chairman was considered the most powerful politician in Turkana district. Ekidor, who had been accused of intimidating his opponents for many years, was challenged for the KANU ticket by John Munyes, a former Oxfam project co-ordinator in Turkana district. Munyes had also been involved in several famine relief operations in the area. Ekidor was popular among the older generation while the youthful Munyes was targeting the youth. Observers were of the view that Ekidor's non-compromising and combative approach to politics was likely to cost him some votes. His critics accused him of frustrating civic education in the area. Ekidor was also at loggerheads with the local Catholic church, which he accused of supporting his opponents through the Catholic

Justice and Peace Civic Education Programme. He was, for example, accused of inspiring the government's hostility towards the Kenya Pastoralist Forum (KPF), an NGO which was striving to better the lot of the marginalised pastoralists.

The late Peter Ejore, who died shortly before the 1992 elections, had dominated the politics of Turkana Central constituency from 1974 until his death. His son, Patrick Ejore, succeeded him but also passed away in 1995. The by-election that ensued was won by Immanuel Imana who in 1997 faced a stiff challenge from David Ekwee, a former deputy county director of Oxfam. In the 1997 KANU primaries David Ekwee won in Turkana Central while Francis Ewoton took the ticket for Turkana South. In Turkana North, however, irregularities were reported and John Munyes defected to FORD-Kenya after Japheth Ekidor was declared the winner.

Trans Nzoia district

In the predominantly Luhya populated Trans Nzoia district, the resident Kalenjins have in the 1990s come to regard Cherangani constituency as a Kalenjin preserve. Thus, although KANU has time and again fielded Kalenjin candidates in Kwanza and Saboti constituencies, their main interest is usually in Cherangani.

The big question in the multi-ethnic Cherangani constituency once synonymous with the late veteran nationalist Masinde Muliro was whether the outspoken incumbent MP Kipruto arap Kirwa would overcome persistent attempts from within KANU to block his re-election bid. The youthful Kirwa, who controversially beat Muliro in the 1989 by-election, had cut a niche for himself within KANU as an established champion of the rights of his Nandi community. Kirwa, a former secondary school teacher, was at the time of the elections the Trans Nzoia district KANU chairman and was being challenged for the party ticket by a founder member of the defunct Youth for KANU '92 and wealthy businessman John Kiprono Kittony.

Kittony, a son to Zipporah Kittony, chairperson of *Maendeleo ya Wanawake* faced Kirwa, then an assistant minister who had early in January 1997 been rehabilitated after apologising to President Moi for remarks made earlier disparaging the president (*Weekly Review* 03/03/97). Initially, it appeared that Kirwa would not face any opponent until Kittony got the green light to contest.[4] Despite the published rhetoric that Kittony would give Kirwa a stiff challenge, Kirwa easily won the KANU ticket.

Nakuru district

In Nakuru district, as in Trans Nzoia district, KANU and the Kalenjin community have come to regard Rongai and the newly-created Kuresoi constituency as their preserve. Nakuru district is a multi-ethnic area in which the Kikuyu community are the majority. Various other groups such as the Kalenjin, Kisii, Maasai and Luo live in uneasy co-existence. The 1996 electoral boundary review which created Kuresoi constituency, brought the total number of constituencies in the district to six. Two constituencies, Nakuru East and Nakuru North, were renamed Naivasha and Subukia, respectively. The creation of Kuresoi from the larger Molo was perceived by the opposition as the ruling party's ploy to gain an extra seat in Nakuru, which was largely an opposition zone. It is in this light that we focus on Rongai and Kuresoi constituencies.

The Kabarak area in Rongai constituency is one of the homes of President Moi. The president therefore pays keen attention to political developments in the area. Rongai constituency was hived off the former Nakuru North (now Subukia) constituency in 1988 and was first represented by a former assistant minister for Lands and Housing, Eric Bomett, who went in unopposed but was shut out at the 1992 KANU nominations by Willy Komen. Both were members of Moi's Tugen. Komen's opponents for the KANU nomination were the Rongai party sub-branch chairman Joel Langat, a retired deputy director of intelligence, Hoseah Rono, and Eric Morogo, a farmer.

The newly created Kuresoi constituency was severely hit by the 1991 clashes which led to heavy losses of life and property. The Kalenjin, who make up more than half of the population, dominate the new constituency. Other communities present are the Kikuyu and the Kisii. Contenders for the KANU ticket included James Koskei, the Nakuru KANU chairman Wilson Leitich and Ezekiel Kesendany of the minority Ndorobo community. The winning KANU nominees for the two constituencies were Eric Morogo and James Koskei respectively.

As observed earlier, most of the KANU nominees were virtually sure of becoming members of parliament. However, this did not deter the opposition parties from fielding candidates in most of these areas. Unlike in 1992 when various Kalenjin constituencies in the Rift Valley were declared as exclusive KANU zones, a number of opposition parties did field candidates and their campaigns were more pronounced in the KAMATUSA-dominated Rift Valley Province in the build up to the 1997 general elections.

The campaign process: individual, party and intra-ethnic issues

In his study of the 1992 elections in Kenya, Oyugi (1997) explains how ethnicity was a major force that influenced the behaviour of politicians and voters alike. The elections, he observed, demonstrated how the elite can mobilise ethnic passions to defend and or promote what is otherwise their narrow sectional interest. The masses followed their leaders in the belief that only one of their 'own' could best serve communal interest if placed in a position of power.

The above situation did not change much in the 1997 general elections. With the exception of Jackson Kibor, who came out forcefully to challenge Moi's dominance in the Kalenjin Rift Valley and a few other former MPs who defected to opposition parties due to nomination irregularities, a majority of the Kalenjin community were satisfied with their kinsman Moi at the helm, despite some misgivings.

Kalenjin sub-groups who were somehow dissatisfied with the Moi regime include the Nandi in Uasin Gishu and Nandi districts, the Kipsigis and, to a lesser extent, the Marakwet. Central among the grievances of the Nandi was land belonging to EATEC, a Lonrho subsidiary. The company was reported to be selling most of the land under its lease ownership, spanning 18,182 hectares from north to south within Uasin Gishu district. The Nandi claimed that some of the land in question, especially in the south, which had traditionally been the grazing areas for their cattle, had been forcibly acquired by the British colonial government in order to give it to white settlers.

When the settlers began leaving the country during the early 1960s, they sold their farms to companies such as Plateau Wattle Company and Chester Beatty. After independence, Lonrho came into the picture by forming EATEC and acquiring some of the land left behind by departing settlers and companies. The land was used for growing wattle trees which produce an extract for leather tanning. Since this natural substance has increasingly been replaced by better and cheaper synthetic products for the tanning of leather, the importance of the wattle tree diminished (*Weekly Review* 23/05/97). In the 1980s, the company is reported to have returned to the government about 8,000 hectares of the leased land in the Uasin Gishu plateau and Kipkabus areas. What appears to have angered some Nandi leaders was the fact that much of the land was used to settle people from Elgeyo/Marakwet district free of charge while the Nandi were left out. Even after selling some of its land in the mid-1980s EATEC still had 18,200 hectares in the Soi and Nandi areas. While letting it be known that it would sell those parcels of land, it made clear that it would only sell 100-acre parcels to the highest bidders. The Nandi, interested in purchasing the 8,000 hectare EATEC land in the Kapsabet area, observed that ordinary people could not afford the prices demanded by Lonrho (*Weekly Review* 23/05/97).

Arising from the above, Nandi leaders such as Jackson Kibor, Kipruto Kirwa and John Sambu came out openly to condemn the government for marginalising the Nandi. Sambu was even quoted as warning the government that it stood to lose the support of the area's electorate if it did not tackle the

EATEC land issue. However, out of the three it was only Jackson Kibor who was technically ousted from KANU's decision-making organs. He quit the party and joined FORD-Kenya. Sambu on his part softened his stance as elections approached and remained rooted in KANU. Kirwa, who had by and large been the harshest critic of Moi amongst the three, had earlier in the year at the prompting of Mark Too beaten a retreat ostensibly because it was an election year. He seemed to realise that his continued stay as a parliamentarian could only be guaranteed if he mended fences with Moi.

The EATEC land issue, however, remained top on the agenda for the Nandi. And in the run-up to the 1997 elections the squatters and the labourers organised to raise their complaints with the president during his campaign tour of the district. They organised to shout out the name 'Tanning' in response to the KANU party slogan. The president responded by appointing a group of powerful individuals to look into the problem. In the group, however, there were the elite who had an interest in the land and on the whole these individuals became inaccessible, because it was an 'electoral season'. One of the unresolved issues on the EATEC land is how Lonrho came to own it since this was leased land which was supposed to have been returned to the government after the expiry of the lease. Their mandate to sell the land is therefore still shrouded in secrecy.

FORD-Kenya used the EATEC land issue as a campaign platform. In one of their meetings which sent strong signals to Moi, the FORD-Kenya chairman Kijana Wamalwa, accompanied by the party's national co-ordinator Jackson Kibor, got a heroes' welcome at Ziwa market in Uasin Gishu district. This was two days after rowdy youths heckled President Moi near the home of Jackson Kibor. Among other issues which fuelled the anger of the crowd against Moi in this earlier rally were the mismanagement of the agricultural industry including the Kenya Farmers Association, the National Cereals and Produce Board and the Kenya Co-operative Creameries. The crowd repeatedly invoked the names of the late Jean Marie Seroney and Alexander Kipsang Muge (Kanyinga 1998).

Overall, in Nandi and Uasin Gishu districts, Moi and KANU candidates campaigned on the platform of Kalenjin unity stressing the need to patronise Moi and KANU as a mechanism for continued benefits from the government. On the other hand, most opposition candidates under the leadership of Kibor drummed up their campaign on the platform of Nandi marginalisation and economic mismanagement of the dairy and cereals industry by the Moi regime. While Kibor did not appear to have the political weight to ferment a rebellion of the Nandi community against President Moi, it was believed that he had the potential to unseat other politicians in Uasin Gishu and Nandi districts by sponsoring candidates to oppose them.

Another group that expressed its disenchantment with the Moi regime in the countdown to the 1997 elections were the Kipsigis. Their discontent increased with the sacking of Kipkalya Kones from the cabinet in January 1997. Their grievances included claims that there was systematic removal of top Kipsigis civil servants from influential positions in the government. Another issue was the purchase of large tea estates by powerful non-Kipsigis establishment figures in various parts of Bomet and Kericho districts to the exclusion of the local people. And finally, they disliked the mismanagement of the maize and milk industry, the economic mainstay of the Kipsigis.

The Kipsigis, the largest sub-group among the Kalenjin, claimed that they had been short-changed by the minority Tugen/Keiyo axis, who were more represented at the centre of power. Before he was dropped from the cabinet, and at a time when Biwott was a backbench MP, Kones had carried himself around as the second most powerful Kalenjin after President Moi. In the succession battle, he was reportedly allied to the KANU-A faction which revolved around Simeon Nyachae. After he was sacked, Kones first played a high stakes gamble as a dissident within KANU, but as the 1997 election approached he pleaded for forgiveness which Moi promptly granted (*Daily Nation* 19/11/97; *East African Standard* 16/11/97).

Grouped together with Kones and Nyachae in the KANU-A faction was cabinet minister William ole Ntimama. Their opponents in the KANU-B faction coalesced around Vice-President George Saitoti, Nicholas Biwott and Joseph Kamotho. Until January 1997, the schism between the two groups was quite volatile. This ended somehow when President Moi showed his preference in a ministerial reshuffle. He dropped Kones from the cabinet and replaced him with Biwott, while other KANU-A faction members, such as Nyachae and Ntimama, were switched to relatively low-key ministries.

The pardoning of Kones, however, did not end the battles of the KANU-A and B factions. It instead shifted the battle to the KANU echelons in Kipsigis. Here lines were drawn between the KANU-A supported candidates versus the KANU-B supported candidates. In Kericho district the KANU-B fronted candidates such as Charles Kirui in Belgut and Kipng'eno arap Ng'eny in Ainamoi, while in Bomet there were mixed fortunes as both KANU-A and KANU-B candidates shared the seats.

Despite the disenchatment there were no signs that the Kipsigis were ready to abandon KANU. Disappointed individuals defeated in the KANU nomination who defected to opposition parties such as Kirior and Toweett soon found that the masses, although disenchanted on some issues, were still behind Moi and KANU.

The Marakwet's disenchantment with the Moi regime was not as substantive as that of the Nandi and the Kipsigis. Their grievances were mainly tied to the cattle raids and violence inflicted on their members by their Pokot kinsmen. The raids reached a crescendo, which saw the Marakwet led by the then Marakwet East MP Frederick Cheserek accuse the government of laxity in controlling Pokot raids. This remained a factor in the campaign process with Cheserek and the DP campaigning on the platform of insecurity and marginalisation of the Marakwet, while Moi and KANU campaigned on the platform of peaceful co-existence and the common goal of the Kalenjin groups.

In other Kalenjin areas there was little discontent especially in the president's home area and the Kalenjin constituencies in the diaspora. However, this did not stop KANU from intimidating opponents in areas which they considered as their strongholds. Several anomalies were experienced during the campaign period.

In Eldama Ravine the DP candidate, Joseph Leboo, was unable to hold campaign meetings due to intimidation and harassment by KANU youth wingers while in Baringo Central constituency, President Moi's opponent, Amos Kandie of the SDP, was barred from even residing in the constituency during the campaigns (IED/CJPC/NCCK 1998). Kandie complained that he was unable to conduct his campaigns due to harassment by KANU supporters. Indeed KANU officials, while addressing a presidential campaign rally in Kabarnet town, had asserted that they would make it impossible for Kandie to hold campaign rallies in the area. The group included the district KANU branch chairman Joel Bultut, executive officer Hosea Kiplagat, Baringo East MP-elect Joseph Lotodo and the branch secretary John Kiprono. Kandie also complained that some KANU agents were buying voters cards from his supporters and destroying them (NCCK/CJPC/IED 1997).

In the neighbouring Mogotio constituency, the SDP candidate, Christine Jebichii, was abducted and forced to write a letter indicating that she had surrendered from the race. By the time she was released, the damage had already been done. The KANU candidates also fanned threats against the Kikuyu ethnic community living in Maji Mazuri, Makutano and Timboroa. These were death and eviction threats (NCCK/CJPC/IED 1997).

Overall, the anomalies were mainly attributed to KANU with a few exceptions. In Turkana North government officers openly campaigned for the ruling party candidates while at the same time harassing the FORD-Kenya candidate. The situation was the same in Turkana Central where the deputy returning officer was openly biased and even tore down posters bearing Ekwee's symbol.

In Sotik, the presidential campaign motorcade consisted of government vehicles. The provincial administration was used to organise the crowd. And in the same constituency, stone-throwing incidents were witnessed after the SDP presidential candidate Charity Ngilu failed to give *kitu kidogo* (something small, i.e., money). In Chepalungu constituency, KANU youths erected roadblocks and inspected people's documents in an effort to fish out opposition aspirants and their supporters.

The 1997 election results

Despite pre-election rumblings of discontent among certain sections of the Kalenjin community, specifically the Nandi and the Kipsigis, the results of the 1997 general elections in the Kalenjin Rift Valley more than anything else confirmed the notion of Kalenjin solidarity. Moi obtained an overwhelming endorsement from all areas inhabited by the Kalenjin and from the Maasai, Turkana and Samburu areas.

His highest percentage tally was in Baringo North constituency where he received 99.6 per cent of the votes cast and his least in Kalenjin heartland was realised in Eldoret North where he scored 65.3 per cent of the votes cast. In the predominantly KANU constituencies of the Kalenjin Rift Valley, his lowest percentage tally was 50.2 per cent of the votes cast in Rongai constituency largely inhabited by the Kikuyu who voted for DP.

In the parliamentary elections, KANU swept all the seats in the Kalenjin Rift Valley and overall performed well in the whole province except in the Kikuyu settler districts of Nakuru and Laikipia, and Trans Nzoia district which is dominated by the Luhya community. Four of the six parliamentary seats in Nakuru district and both the seats in Laikipia district went to DP of Mwai Kibaki while two of the three parliamentary seats in Trans Nzoia were retained by FORD-Kenya of Kijana Wamalwa which also won Turkana North.

In the Kalenjin heartland of the Rift Valley, both President Moi and KANU had an easy time against a weak or non-existent opposition. Even before the polls KANU had already won nine seats unopposed in the Kalenjin constituencies. These were Baringo East, Baringo North, Bomet, Chepalungu, Belgut, Kipkelion, Eldoret East, Kapenguria and Sigor. This in itself was a solid indication that the Kalenjin were formidably behind their incumbent kinsmen. However, Moi's clean history as the unchallenged representative of Baringo Central was muddled when the little known retired schoolteacher, Amos Kandie, contested the same seat on a Social Democratic Party ticket. The two other constituencies in the district returned their MPs unopposed.

In Koibatek district, Mogotio constituency was easily won by KANU but there was a strong battle in Eldama Ravine constituency where Musa Sirma of KANU narrowly beat DP's Joseph Leboo by 14,390 votes to 10,707. This was an indication that Leboo was popular on the ground and the electorate voted for him against Sirma who was irregularly nominated. The fact that the same electorate voted for Moi in the presidential race at the expense of Mwai Kibaki (84.5 against 13.8 per cent) is a testimony to Leboo's personal popularity. Leboo's performance was the strongest of all opposition candidates in Kalenjin heartland. Other impressive performances by opposition candidates were witnessed in Keiyo North where Gilbert Lagat of Safina put up a formidable performance against Elijah Sumbeiywo, garnering 5,517 votes against the winner's 12,917 and in Marakwet East where DP's Frederick Cheserek posted 6,076 votes to John Marrirmoi's 11,193. Although the gaps in these tallies appear sizeable, we categorise them as impressive in comparison to the performance of other opposition candidates in Kalenjin heartland.

In the Kipsigis-inhabited districts of Kericho and Bomet observers expected KANU's dominance to be dented. However, contrary to these expectations, the Kipsigis voted overwhelmingly in favour of KANU. Out of a total of eight constituencies the two districts returned four MPs unopposed and in the contested constituencies KANU overwhelmed its opponents.

In Uasin Gishu district, the Kibor wave crumbled during the polls. In Eldoret East, predominantly inhabited by the Keiyo, Francis Tarar was returned unopposed. Kibor, who is a Nandi, failed to have any impact in this constituency. In Eldoret North, Kibor fielded his right hand man, Kipkorir arap Menjo who, although beaten by William Ruto, posted an impressive 16,303 votes against Ruto's 30,023. However, Kibor's handpicked candidate in Eldoret South performed poorly. The Kibor factor further crumbled in Cherangani constituency in Trans Nzoia district. Cherangani constituency had appeared to be shaky with Kibor prevailing upon Wamalwa to field John Rotich, a Kalenjin. However, KANU's Kipruto arap Kirwa easily held sway as he garnered 17,902 votes to his opponent's 8,474 votes. The disenchantment of the Nandi in Nandi district was also expected to translate into votes for opposition candidates but, as it turned out, KANU candidates trounced their opponents in all the four constituents.

In Turkana district, Moi has been a very important factor in the economic and political empowerment of the inhabitants. The Turkana also find no alternative to Moi in any of the opposition presidential candidates and, finally, the government interferes in the area's elections through the provincial administration. However, as opposed to presidential elections, the parliamentary race in Turkana is determined by many other variables which are not basically on party lines. The KANU MPs for Turkana Central and Turkana South were not in the president's favour and as for Turkana North, John Munyes won on an opposition FORD-Kenya ticket. The MPs for Turkana South, Francis Ewoton Echuka, and Turkana Central, David Ekwee Ethuro, won because of their popularity on the ground, despite the fact that ex-MPs Japheth Ekidor and Immanuel Imana still carry favour in State House corridors.

The Catholic church is also a key political player in Turkana. Any candidate opposed by the Catholic church has difficulties getting to parliament. This is attributed to the extensive educational and development activities carried out by the church in the district. For example, Japheth Ekidor harassed the area's Catholic bishop and got the wrath of lay catechists who worked as local FORD-Kenya agents. This was claimed by Ekidor himself who, after losing his seat, blamed the Catholic church which 'campaigned vigorously against me' (IED/CJPC/NCCK/1998).

The politics of cattle rustling have also determined the 1997 elections. Francis Ewoton (Turkana South) is immensely popular for his perceived toughness on Pokot while on the other hand Immanuel Imana and Japheth Ekidor were both accused of being too soft and hence heralding insecurity. They both lost. Relief food also played a hand in the area's politics. John Munyes, the FORD-Kenya MP for Turkana North, worked for Oxfam which distributed a lot of food in Turkana. This was at a time that the KANU government had failed to deliver relief food supplies.

Conclusion

From the foregoing analysis a number of conclusions can be made regarding elections in a developing multi-ethnic polity. In developed Western democracies, elections are a means not only of choosing the rulers but also the policies and programmes. However, in the majority of developing countries elections play three major functions: first, the legitimisation of the regime in power; second, the recycling of the elite and third, the patronisation of ethnic kinsmen. The 1997 elections in Kenya were foremost characterised by ethnic bloc voting expressed through political parties. In the Kalenjin Rift Valley, the elite and the incumbent president mobilised ethnic passions to defend or promote their interest in clinging to state power. The masses in turn followed their leaders in the belief that they stood to gain most from their own kinsmen. With Moi enjoying incumbency the Kalenjin proved to be the most solidified ethnic group in the 1997 Kenyan elections. The fact that no election petition was brought against the winning Kalenjin MPs attests to this.

Notes

1. Sambu was dropped after defending the then minister for Agriculture, Livestock Development and Marketing, Simeon Nyachae who was under siege from other Nandi leaders led by Mark Too over a raging controversy in the Kenya Co-operative Creameries.
2. This group also included a cabinet minister and secretary general of KANU, Joseph Kamotho.
3. These two candidates both won their seats with Ng'eny being appointed to the cabinet while Kirui was appointed as an assistant minister for Finance.

4. It had been assumed that Mark Too, who was the architect of Kirwa's change of heart, would prevail on the KANU power barons to let Kirwa get the KANU ticket unopposed. However, it happened that Zipporah Kittony was also lobbying for young Kittony to contest.

References

Berman, B. and Lonsdale, J. 1992, *Unhappy Valley. Conflict in Kenya and Africa*, London: James Currey.

Blondel, J. 1963, *Voters, Parties and Leaders: the social fabric of British politics*, Baltimore: Penguin Books.

IED/CJPC/NCCK 1998, *Report on the 1997 General Elections in Kenya - 29-30 December, 1997*, Nairobi: Institute for Education in Democracy, Catholic Justice and Peace Commission and National Council of Churches of Kenya.

Kanyinga, K. 1998, *The Land Question in Kenya: Struggles, Accumulation and Changing Politics*, Ph.D. dissertation, International Development Studies, Roskilde University.

Kipkorir, B. and Welbourn, V. 1973, *The Marakwet of Kenya – a preliminary study*, Nairobi: East African Literature Bureau.

NCCK/CJPC/IED 1997, The Pre-polls Report, Nairobi: unpublished report.

Oyugi, W. 1997, 'Ethnicity in the Electoral Process; the 1992 General Elections in Kenya', *Africa Journal of Political Science* (1997) Vol. 2, No.1: 41-69.

Throup, D. 1987, 'The Construction and Deconstruction of the Kenyatta State' in Schatzberg, M.G. (ed.) *The Political Economy of Kenya*, New York: Praeger: 33-74.

17

Gusii Politics: An Analysis of the 1997 Elections

Kenneth Samson Ombongi[1]

The Gusii are a Bantu-speaking people located in the southern parts of the cool and fertile western Kenya highlands (See map on p. 194). To the east and southeast they border the Maasai and Kipsigis with whom they have had mutual cross-border incursions over the years. To the south there are the Nilotic Luo who separate them from the Kuria with whom they have a striking linguistic similarity. Gusiiland is a high potential agricultural area, densely populated with an estimated population of 1.1 million people by 1989 (KPC 1989: 28).[2] It is made up of seven clans. The clans include Bobasi, Bogetutu, Bomachoge, Bogirango (Bogirango Maate), Bogusero (Bogirango Rogoro), Bonchari and Nyaribari (Ochieng 1978). The clans in turn are made up of several sub-clans and lineage groups.

Forces that shape electoral politics in Gusiiland are more or less similar to those elsewhere in Kenya. However, a number of mediating factors such as the local political rivalry and the region's stake in national politics, real or perceived, accord its electoral practice some peculiarity. This chapter is about the forces and mediating factors that influenced the 1997 general elections. It presents an analysis of the election in terms of key players, organisation, trends and conditioning factors.

Gusii politics in historical perspective

Electoral politics in Gusiiland since the 1960s have been dominated by the Kenya African National Union (KANU). Even during the short period of multi-party politics in the 1960s, KANU's predominance seldom waned in the region.[3] Attempts by Bensford Ainya Nyonkembo to popularise KADU, KANU's arch rival, at the grassroots in the early 1960s did not yield much. The latter's strong position, led by James Nyamweya, one of the pioneer Gusii politicians and MP for Nyaribari, stifled the lone efforts of Nyonkembo. It also laid the ground for a subsequent propensity towards intolerance to competitive inter-party politics among the Gusii (Omoro and Mutere 1979:11).

Things hardly changed with the short stint of Oginga Odinga's Kenya People's Union (KPU) whose mantle in the community was carried by Zephaniah Mugunde Anyieni, once the MP for Majoge Bassi.[4] Anyieni's defection from KANU to KPU in 1966 could not enhance prospects of his electoral victory in a subsequent election. His KANU opponent, John Mamboleo Onsando, trounced him. He rejoined KANU later and became the MP of the area in 1969 (*East African Standard* 25/11/97:E2). Since the reintroduction of multi-party politics in 1992 little has changed in Gusiiland to tilt things very much against KANU.

The dominance of influential politicians who have a stake in the status quo could, among other factors, account for KANU's monopoly among the Gusii. The electoral politics in the region, as in most parts of Kenya, revolve around personalities. Political party ideology or policy plays a minor role in determining individual or collective political action. Usually, dominant (KANU) personalities provide an umbrella under which individual and/or sub-clan interests compete. Little evidence from the 1992 and 1997 polls suggests that the opposition could thrive beyond politically marginal constituencies such as Bomachoge, Kitutu Masaba and West Mugirango.[5] Even in such areas contending forces from the KANU-dominated Nyaribari, the putative centre of Gusii politics over the years, fundamentally influence the nature, course and outcome of elections.

Thus, what has kept changing in Gusii politics over the years is not so much party affiliation or political ideology but the influence of individual politicians. Also, a trend in which sub-clan loyalties are giving way to communal solidarity is increasingly becoming noticeable in the politics of the community. Interestingly, however, in the 1992 and 1997 polls, the Gusii, unlike the Luo, Kalenjin and Kikuyu, did note vote as an ethnic block in the presidential elections.

The Nyachae factor in the Gusii elections

The current patterns in the electoral politics among the Gusii are determined by competition between forces and interests aligned to Simeon Nyachae, former minister for Finance, and those against him. The pro- and anti-Nyachae forces are not a function of any ideology or policy differences. The politics surrounding his personality and influence are often a complex array of inexplicable issues. However, his key role in determining Gusii politics could be explained by two main factors: patronage, and lineage relations.

Within the Gusii community, the politics of patronage constitute the core of the 'Nyachae factor'. The current politics is intertwined with his influence, so much so that clan or sub-clan issues, however significant, seldom overshadow him completely. Many politicians from the region, overtly or covertly, seek his blessings to bolster their positions to the extent that the 'Nyachae factor' is a common denominator conditioning the whole electoral process. The political role of Nyachae in Gusiiland did not begin in 1988 when he made his first abortive attempt to join politics. It goes back to his time as a senior civil servant in the Kenyatta and Moi eras. At the time, his influence was great although behind the scenes, and it resonated far and wide in the region. His impending retirement from the civil service in the mid-1980s, therefore, caused panic in the Gusii political landscape. There were signs that he would sooner or later venture into politics and it was only natural that his presence would destabilise the status quo at the expense of the contemporary politicians. The fear among incumbent MPs led to the 1987 'Kebirigo Declaration'. At the meeting in Kebirigo, a small and little known market centre in West Mugirango, Nyamira district, politician after politician denounced the 'big businessman' who was allegedly crusading against incumbent MPs. It was clear enough that the 'big businessman' was Nyachae. The declaration basically denounced his alleged intrigues and machinations detrimental to the MPs' interests (*Kenya Times* 18/10/96:12, 21). The sentiments against Nyachae during the Kebirigo meeting were part of the pressure that ultimately blocked him from contesting for the Nyabari Chache seat in the 1988 elections. This pressure was apparently championed by KANU.

A good number of Gusii politicians now, unlike in 1987, from KANU and opposition alike, seek his support to enhance their political fortunes. Equally, some of the incumbent MPs, like in the post-1992 election period, are his protégés and 'lieutenants'.[6] Compared to other district and regional king-makers, Nyachae's influence goes beyond local issues to make him impact on national politics. This further enhances his position at the helm of Gusii politics.

As the leader and spokesman of the Gusii community at the national level, Nyachae himself is a creation of the politics of patronage. Such politics were espoused by the post-colonial regimes of Kenyatta and Moi. It appears that this system goes back to the colonial days where the government nurtured and patronised a clique of loyal elite and chiefs to maximise its legitimacy. In the words of Berman, the colonial state in Africa ruled through 'alliances with local "big men"' (Berman 1998: 305). If there is any legacy Kenyatta and Moi have bequeathed to Kenyans, it is the 'big men' syndrome. The system is firmly grounded in the perpetuation of the allocation of national resources through either a self-made or state-made political clique in exchange for individual or collective, regional or ethnic subservience. Perhaps the key hindrance to multi-party politics in Kenya at the moment is the conservatism and political docility inherent in a political system built on the pillars of patronage.

It is within the context of patronage that the rise of Nyachae to national prominence could best be understood. At the advent of the strong wave of change that marked the end of single-party rule in Kenya in the early 1990s, Nyachae was a political asset. His political influence in Gusiiland made him indispensable to KANU if it wanted the community's support. The security of his widespread business concerns, however, as we shall see later, limited his options to supporting KANU. Nyachae all the same became the 'big man' through whom KANU sought to bolster its political position among the Gusii.

Furthermore, Nyachae combines a prominent family background and lineage, a long civil service career spanning more than three decades and personal wealth to wield power and influence among his people. He was born into a family of the eminent Nyaribari paramount chief, Musa Nyandusi, in 1932. He got his education at Nyanchwa Seventh-Day Adventist Primary School, Kereri Intermediate School and Kisii African Government School before he joined the colonial civil service as a clerk at the Kisii district commissioner's office (Leonard 1991: 47-48). In 1958 he was employed by the East African Breweries as a labour and welfare administrative assistant after obtaining a diploma in public and social administration from South Devon Technical College at Torquay, United Kingdom. He later rejoined the colonial administration as a district officer at Kangundo, Ukambani. At independence Nyachae was among the few African district officers in Kenya. He was appointed district commissioner, Nairobi, in 1964 after a nine-month training at the University of Cambridge. He rose thereafter to become the provincial commissioner (PC) for Rift Valley Province. In 1971 Nyachae was transferred to Central Province where he worked until November 1979 when Moi appointed him a permanent secretary in the Office of the President. In July 1984, he was appointed chief secretary, a post he held until his retirement in December 1986 (*Weekly Review* 14/02/92; 22/06/93).

While he was chief secretary, Nyachae consolidated his influence in his home region. He participated in fund raising in aid of various development projects. This was perhaps a pointer to his future political ambitions. It also enabled him to further enhance his posture as a 'son' of *Omogusii* (i.e., the Gusii community). That he took part in activities beyond Nyaribari, his home, enabled him to transcend, at least in the eyes of the public, sectional politics and clan cleavages common in Gusiiland. The elitist predisposition, flashy lifestyle and power (real or perceived) that went with his senior position in the civil service, became a source of social status among his people. His wealth from wide-ranging business concerns accorded him a coveted and formidable financial position in Gusiiland. The high social status and wealth, the two most important ingredients that enhance prospects of political success in Kenya, buttressed Nyachae's influence among his people. His advice and counsel were widely sought long before he joined politics. His success not only endeared him to his people but became a source of inspiration to many in Gusiiland.

On the other hand, however, wealth and an apparently privileged position is Nyachae's undoing politically, to some extent. They attract envy from his rivals and the poor sections of his people. Whereas his strict and popular workaholic image, traceable to his days in the civil service, is always associated with success in private business, it is also seen as arrogance of sorts on his part, a negative factor that compromises his local political standing.

It appears, although not easily made substantial, that his senior position within the administration facilitated the placement of his kinsmen in powerful positions in the civil service. He thus created necessary connections that would be of use in his future career in politics. Interestingly enough, it is widely believed in Gusiiland that some people whom Nyachae helped to secure jobs have been used by his detractors locally to undermine him. However, the authenticity of this belief is difficult to either prove or deny.

Nyachae's lineage, characterised by a large and prominent extended family, generated some support for him as it does today. Musa Barare Nyandusi, his father, was the longest serving chief in Nyaribari (1927-64). Benefiting from the early Seventh-Day Adventist missionary education, Musa was an aggressive chief-turned-teacher. Tactical and hard working, Nyandusi was able in the 1930s easily to outshine Chief Onsongo of Kitutu under whose jurisdiction Nyaribari fell. He soon assumed the role of a Gusii spokesman to the colonial government. No wonder that his son, Nyachae, would play the same role in post-colonial Kenya. Married to many wives, and with many children, Musa was a wealthy man with a coffee plantation, a car, large herds of cattle and several posho (flour) mills. He was a highly respected chief as he possessed the most coveted sources of high social status in the contemporary Gusiiland (Nyarang'o 1978: 12-38). Nyachae attained fame from his father, Nyandusi, early in life. His father prepared him for the kind of status he enjoys among the Gusii now. In 1951 Ayako, Nyandusi's favourite son and heir apparent to his position as chief of Nyaribari, died. He shifted his focus to Nyachae. As Leonard (1991: 49) reports, 'He would take him in his car to meetings, send him round to collect money from his several flour mills, and delegate him to report on coffee co-operative society meetings.' All these, undoubtedly, popularised the young Nyachae.

Such is Nyachae's background. It not only enables him to enjoy the prestige that goes with such a family but also support from all those linked to it. For example, during the 1992 elections, two of the Gusii MPs that strongly supported him were relatives. At the moment one of the incumbent MPs is related to him.[7] Like his father, Nyachae is a polygamist and this has further extended his lineage among the Gusii. In 1953 he married his first wife Esther Nyaboke from a prominent family in a neighbouring clan. In 1955 he married Druscilla Kerubo as his second wife, but she died shortly after. In 1957 he married Martha Mwango from a prominent family in Kitutu Chache. Mwango was a half-sister to Lawrence Sagini, the leader of the pioneer politicians from Gusiiland (Leonard 1991:49).

If the foregoing paragraphs suggest that Nyachae has had it easy all through in Gusiiland, or owes his influence wholesale to lineage connections, it is not true. At the Gusii community level, Nyachae's entry into politics engendered unity among the incumbent MPs. They felt threatened by his presence as alluded to earlier. Their unity, we have seen, culminated in the 1987 'Kebirigo Declaration', which sparked off a wave of anti-Nyachae campaigns in the entire Gusiiland. Nyachae was ultimately barred from contesting the Nyaribari Chache seat in the 1988 elections (*Kenya Times* 08/10/96:12). The elections saw the emergence in Nyaribari Masaba constituency of Samson Kegengo Ongeri, a professor of medicine, who became Nyachae's arch-rival and contender for Gusii political supremacy in the multi-party era.

That Nyachae was beleaguered in his home area was a function of the struggle for local political dominance between him and incumbent MPs in the second half of the 1980s. The events of 1992 confirmed the MPs' fears as most of them lost their seats, a move in which they saw Nyachae's hand. The local rivalry, apparently, provided an opportunity to the KANU establishment to neutralise Nyachae's ambitions through local 'sponsored opposition'.[8] 'Sponsored opposition' has been a strategy used by the powerful KANU clique to check prominent and potentially formidable politicians from various regions. The clique usually fans political bickering at the district level against a prominent politician. This often results in a division of the local leaders into contending camps. These camps are kept busy craving for recognition by the president, while always being loyal to him. This strategy took a strong root in Kenya's politics particularly from the late 1980s when Moi sought to neutralise any potential challenge through 'a new order whose fulcrum was his control over the [KANU] party and civil service, and the circulation of favoured men around' (Southall 1998: 102). The system of 'sponsored opposition' was further buttressed as KANU, in Moi's era, became the most influential and powerful political organ in Kenya.

In Gusiiland, the emergence of Nyachae shook the political equilibrium maintained by Dr Zachary Onyonka, an economist and long time minister in Kenyatta's and Moi's regimes. Onyonka, with a long political career and experience spanning more than three decades, constantly checked Nyachae's influence. He (Onyonka) helped maintain the traditional stable binary pattern of Gusii politics in which always two big men are in competition.[9] In Onyonka's absence, after his death in early 1997, there was no politician of his political muscle and stature to take up his mantle. This enabled Nyachae to go in unchecked unlike before. Further, the death of the octogenarian Gusii politician Lawrence Sagini earlier (1995) left a vacuum in the KANU chairmanship in the Kisii sub-branch. Nyachae, as expected, became the new chairman of the sub-branch. The new position and rumours in the region that he was a serious contender in the Moi succession dispute furthered his prospects as the bearer of the Gusii banner in national politics. This helped to stifle anti-Nyachae forces, to some extent, at the local level. That many of the anti-Nyachae MPs led by Ongeri lost in the 1992 elections gave Nyachae ample time to consolidate his position. He persuaded the incumbent MPs into a united front with subtle overtones of consolidating his position locally and advancing his cause in national politics (*Weekly Review* 15/09/97:13).

After the 1992 polls, Moi's succession became a significant issue in intra-KANU conflicts. This propelled Nyachae to the national limelight, pitting him against other KANU stalwarts, potential contenders in the succession dispute. Nyachae got embroiled in the dispute for two main reasons. First, the marginal political status of his community made political parties jostle for support from it during the 1992 and 1997 elections. For the survival of KANU in Nyanza, the Gusii vote was vital and Nyachae's influence was a crucial asset. It appears that this might have fuelled the rumoured promise of the vice-presidency to Nyachae, if ever made, from the powers that be in KANU as a bait to retaining the Gusii vote.

Secondly, the non-existence of a strong and dominant opposition party among the Gusii to necessitate voting as a bloc further exacerbated the struggle for their support from various parties during the multi-party era. Anyona's KSC did not, in 1992 as today, have a strong ethnic base in Gusiiland as FORD-Asili did in Kikuyuland and FORD-Kenya in Luoland. The inter-party jostling for the Gusii votes put Nyachae, the de facto spokesman of the community, squarely on the spot. Consequently, at the national level the line, if any, between his individual political posture and views and those of his community became increasingly thin. His ambitions, real or perceived, were often seen as the community's and vice versa.

During the 1991 wave of defections from KANU, Nyachae ironically did not defect to any of the extant opposition parties. He gave three reasons for this, namely: 'Kanu was the party that brought independence and of which he has been a member. He was not convinced that the emerging opposition parties had answers to the country's numerous problems. Improvement in management of national affairs could not be brought about by revenge and vengeance or joining the opposition' (*Weekly Review* 14/02/92:3). Much as these reasons quelled the curiosity of Nyachae's admirers and enemies at that momentous period, they blurred the intricate and fundamental issues that were core to his resolution to remain in KANU.

The Gusii, unlike the Luo, have never constituted pressure formidable enough to form a strong opposition. The want of an ideologically inclined opposition leader like Oginga Odinga made much of the politics of the region localised. Today the community is as characterised by bickering among politicians as it was during the Kenyatta era. With such precedence, it is plausible that Nyachae was left with the option of supporting the status quo. Signs of a fractured opposition in the run-up to the 1992 election gave credence to his position among his people.

It is difficult, however, to exonerate completely personal ambition as a cause of Nyachae's decision to remain in KANU. And this is so for two reasons. Politically, it is possible that he was clear that the chances of acquiring any meaningful prominence for himself and by extension for his community under the Kikuyu-led opposition rule were minimal. KANU appeared to be the only party that could enable him to become president, if ever he was to be one, as his people are numerically the biggest of the smaller ethnic groups. That Moi, during the single party era, dismantled the Kikuyu-dominated state 'and constructed a new alliance of minority ethnic groups' apparently offers credence to Nyachae's position (Southall 1998: 101). In this way Nyachae, with a strong base among the Gusii, a strong group among minorities, could stake a claim to the presidency. On the other hand, Nyachae's stance had an economic overtone, however subtle. That economically he could have had less control of other major players in Kenyan politics, particularly the Kikuyu, if he joined the opposition, appears undeniable. Further, he feared that the security of his wide-ranging and geographically spread business concerns would suffer if he backed the 'wrong horse'. At that time, the opposition was apparently the 'wrong horse'. It showed clear signs of division and leadership wrangles too early. It soon became clear, especially after the split of the original FORD into FORD-Kenya and FORD-Asili, that the opposition was too divided to win against KANU in the impending elections. With the benefit of hindsight, it is true to say that Nyachae read the signs of the opposition's destiny well.

Nyachae's resolution to support KANU reinforced the Gusii community's swing/marginal political status where the opposition and KANU jostled for votes in 1997 as in 1992 (Throup and Hornsby 1998: 290). If KANU was to enhance its victory among the Gusii, Nyachae had to be taken seriously. Serious in the sense that he had to be seen, by his people, to be wielding national influence with the support of the powers that be within KANU. Therefore, in the course of luring the Gusii community in 1992 to vote for KANU, the 'Nyachae factor' became crucial in the party's national politics.

The succession struggle within KANU intensified in 1997 with Moi's impending exit from its leadership. Simply put, it generated succession fever (Southall 1998: 101). The dispute in KANU took the shape of the forces for and against George Saitoti, Moi's vice-president. Nyachae, at the time the minister for Land Reclamation, Regional and Water Development, was dubbed one of the main contenders for the vice-presidency. The ensuing political rivalry crystallised into what the media termed KANU-A versus KANU-B.[10] The Nyachae-Saitoti rivalry worked to the advantage of Nyachae in Gusiiland. At least to the local public, the ambition of having one of their own as president after Moi's retirement was gradually becoming a 'reality'. Nyachae's attempt to unite Gusii MPs under his leadership in the run up to the 1997 elections added further impetus to this ambition (*Weekly Review* 15/09/97:13). With time, the political siege on him, either at the local or national levels, came to signify forces bent to marginalise the entire Gusii community (*Weekly Review* 17/01/97:8).

Whether the idea that offence against Nyachae is synonymous with an onslaught on the Gusii people is true is open to debate. In any case it is outside the scope of this analysis. In passing, however, such argument could be understood in the context of political patronage mentioned earlier. In Kenya political power is a main source of wealth accumulation and social mobility for individuals and their communities. For a community to have one of its own at the powerful office, the presidency, is a sure way, at least to the common people, of good things to come. Moi is rendering credence, as Kenyatta did, to this popular notion by appointing people from his community to key and strategic public, military and parastatal positions. Kenyatta's appointments enabled a clique of Kikuyu politicians to amass fabulous wealth at the expense of efficient service to the nation and employment based on merit. Under Moi's presidency, the Kalenjin elite have done the same thing. With such wealth, a number of these individuals were able during Kenyatta's era, as today, to donate huge sums of money in *harambees* (fund raising) in aid of development projects and the education of some of their people overseas. In so doing they demonstrated that they were capable of 'bringing development' from Nairobi.[11]

The participation in *harambees* has turned out to be a crucial gauge of who is, and who is not, a development conscious leader in Kenya.[12] Thus, that the support and influence of Nyachae among the Gusii people is a function of the direct relationship between political power and social mobility and wealth accumulation cannot be gainsaid. It is further reinforced by politics of clan, lineage, and personal wealth. The combination of all these factors enabled Nyachae to impact on the 1992 and 1997 elections.

Preparations for the 1997 elections and party primaries

In the run-up to the 1997 elections, events in Gusiiland involved alignment and realignment either around or away from Nyachae. Few incumbent MPs, the opposition and KANU alike, did not seek his blessings. So did potential contestants from various constituencies. His opponents, mainly the losers in the 1992 elections, sought to consolidate their positions in their respective constituencies. They did so by either whipping up clan loyalties and rivalry or belabouring proof of their proximity to President Moi. The few potential parliamentary candidates, if any, who operated outside these two blocks, one around Nyachae and another against him, were either of too little consequence to be noticed or political loners on the fringes of Gusii electoral politics.

The opposition's influence in the region was minimal. This meant that the main activities in preparation for the 1997 elections focused on KANU as much as they did in 1992. Like in 1992, the opposition parties provided a haven to losers of KANU nominations or their close associates.[13] However, SDP, one of the opposition parties, almost became a social movement of the youth, especially in Kisii and Keroka towns. This is perhaps an indication that Gusii politics is capable of transcending personality, clan and patronage issues during elections. But the euphoric reception of SDP was not peculiar to Gusiiland. It was equally noticeable among young people elsewhere, particularly in Nairobi, at the beginning of election campaigns in late 1997.

It appears that the meteoritic rise and presence of Charity Ngilu as the party's presidential candidate could account for the ecstatic reception among the youth in urban centres. That she was the first female presidential candidate in Kenya's political history was something new and exciting to the young (see also Chapter 12). Ngilu's rise was revolutionary; her 'youthful' physique and actions were an epitome of the energy and revolutionary thinking of young people. Her promise of *mwanzo mpya* (a new start) as a herald of a better tomorrow, a tomorrow with hope, was characteristic of the efforts of loving Kenyan mothers struggling to better the plight of their young ones. Other promises with popular overtones such as the selling of the luxurious presidential jet as a priority (as soon as she became president) struck a deep chord among the impoverished youth. They loved Ngilu. They were enthusiastic about their future in her hands. Nothing could be more attractive to young people.

However, this euphoria could not translate into votes. SDP was weak. It was wanting in money and other logistical support to make an impact vis-à-vis the 'formidable' KANU. It lacked KANU's solid social base of current and retired civil servants particularly in Kisii town. Its base was fragile, mainly made up of youths with immediate concerns such as solutions to unemployment and lack of money which it did not have the means to solve straight away.

Worse still, the provincial administration was to say the least not favourably disposed to SDP. Accordingly, the party's influence in many parts of the country died as fast as it had started. Whether this was due to the male prejudice of the old, conservative and traditionally-inclined opinion makers in Kisii town and indeed elsewhere in the country towards Ngilu as a female candidate is hard to prove. But it is equally difficult to deny its influence without further investigation, especially by those concerned with the influence of gender in politics.

The tempo and course of political activity in Gusiiland, shortly before elections in 1997, was determined by Nyachae's moves. In particular, his effort to unite incumbent MPs under the banner of 'Omogusii unity and development' was a crucial and determinant force.[14] At the beginning of 1997 Nyachae had transcended inter-personal differences to rally a majority of the 11 Gusii MPs. This culminated in the July 1997 Tombe rally in Kitutu Masaba. That the rally was held in George Anyona's constituency, an all-time champion of opposition politics in Gusiiland, was a milestone. It served as a demonstration that a new era characterised by KANU-opposition cooperation was dawning among the Gusii. Equally, it was an indication of the beginning of political ethnic solidarity of a magnitude never witnessed in Gusiiland before. The Tombe rally brought together Nyachae's supporters among the Gusii MPs. In this meeting a rallying clarion call, *ime yegetwanga* (inside the anklet), was coined. By August 1997 Nyachae and his supporters had held such rallies in seven of the ten constituencies in the region (*Weekly Review* 15/09/97:11-12).

Ime yegetwanga rallies had two main underlying implications. For the incumbent MPs they were a source of confidence of enhanced prospects of victory in their respective constituencies. The widely held opinion then was that any anti-Nyachae sentiments were synonymous with poor performance in the impending elections. Ironically, however, a majority of the MPs in Nyachae's camp lost during the nominations. Reuben Oyondi (South Mugirango), Atebe Marita (North Mugirango/Borabu), Stephen Manoti (Bobasi), and Hezron Manduku (Nyaribari Masaba) were all trounced at the KANU primaries (*East African Standard* 25/11/97:E3). Sub-clan politics, an apparent need for change among the electorate, and the contentious issue of deciding the headquarters of the new Gucha (South Kisii) district seem to have played a prominent role in these constituencies.

In 1996 a new district (Gucha) had been hived off from Kisii to form the third of the current three districts of the Gusii people: Nyamira, Kisii and Gucha. The government earmarked Kenyenya, a small market in Bomachoge, as the new headquarters of Gucha district. However, due to considerations of geographic distance and commercial and political advantages, a majority of the people in Bobasi and some sections of Bomachoge rejected the market in support of Ogembo. Ogembo was then the divisional headquarters beside the Gucha River valley.

Nyachae was perceived to support the location of the Gucha district headquarters at Kenyenya apparently for economic reasons. His opponents such as Christopher Obure, former MP of Bobasi, naturally took a stance to the contrary. It is possible that Nyachae's perceived anti-Ogembo position tilted things against contestants believed to be in his camp. For example, some of his supporters such as Stephen Manoti, then MP for Bobasi, were put in a difficult position. In the case of Manoti, he had to choose between siding with his constituents by supporting Ogembo or Kenyenya which was apparently Nyachae's preference. Manoti ultimately supported Ogembo, but perhaps he had been lukewarm enough on the issue to save his face before the people of Bobasi. However, the pro-Nyachae opposition candidates such as Henry Onyancha Obwocha, FORD-Kenya (West Mugirango), and George Anyona, KSC (Kitutu Masaba) regained their seats in the elections and so did KANU's Jimmy Angwenyi (Kitutu Chache). Their victory seemed to be partly a function of the strong popular base enjoyed by these contestants in their respective constituencies. Also, newcomer Zaphaniah Nyang'wara (Bomachoge) won in the KANU primaries despite his outright support for Nyachae (*Daily Nation* 30/12/97:17, 20-21).

On the other hand, there was an apparent general upset with incumbent MPs in Gusiiland regardless of their party affiliation, the support for Nyachae and the Moi succession issue. This, also, could account for their poor performance. People simply thought that their representatives were not delivering (by either giving out money or 'bringing development'). The year 1997 was a difficult one in Kenya due to a devastating fiscal crisis. This might have affected the private coffers of MPs, a majority of whom depended on business, and/or handouts from the state/KANU which seemed to be dwindling or simply not forthcoming. Nyachae, perhaps the only one with a formidable financial position, was fairly confident of regaining his Nyaribari Chache seat. He, therefore, did not seem to have invested much money to bolster the positions of his local supporters among the incumbent MPs. This was either because of the fiscal crisis or maybe because of diverting money into cementing a national level coalition to counter his detractors.

At another level, *ime yegetwanga* rallies sought to isolate the anti-Nyachae camp in Gusiiland. This, it was believed, would enable Nyachae to assume a complete posture of a spokesman of the community. Also, there was a popular belief that as a spokesman of the Gusii Nyachae could enhance his prospects in national politics at a time when his opponents seemed to be gaining a firm ground against him. His transfer to the less significant ministry of water and regional development from that of agriculture, livestock development and marketing in January 1997 signalled the intensity of the forces against him nationally. The anti-Abagusii move in KANU, real or imagined, was manifested in the transfer. The Nyachae siege generated a lot of euphoria in Gusiiland. It enabled him to garner more support in the region. It also led to the dubbing of the anti-Nyachae camp as political 'hirings' out to betray one of their own to his enemies outside Gusiiland (*Weekly Review* 15/08/97: 11-12).

On the eve of the KANU nominations, it was common to depict the anti-Nyachae contestants as merely traitors out to lose. This proved a crucial tool at the hands of Nyachae's supporters and politicians perceived to be in his camp. Whether it delivered any dividends or not is open to debate but the dismal performance of Nyachae's supporters in KANU nominations alluded to above, suggests the contrary. Overall, therefore, the KANU nominations brought back the losers of 1992 and a number of them won the subsequent elections. Prof. Samson Ongeri (Nyaribari Masaba) and Christopher Obure (Bobasi) regained their respective seats. The elections also brought in newcomers such as Joseph Kiangoi (North Mugirango) who trounced Atebe Marita, Nyachae's confidant (*East African Standard* 25/11/97:E3).

That Nyachae was in KANU, with influence transcending administrative boundaries and the KANU-opposition divide, made the 1997 elections a tussle between two personality-based contending camps in Gusiiland. First, there was the Nyachae-led camp apparently with material affluence and tactical manoeuvres, often associated with its leader. Second, there was the Ongeri-led camp believed to enjoy the KANU headquarters support. Prof. Ongeri, a former reputable don in the College of Health Sciences of the University of Nairobi, and a close confidant of President Moi, joined politics in 1988 after the creation of Nyaribari Masaba constituency. He won the Nyaribari Masaba seat against Manduki and joined the cabinet immediately as the minister of Science and Applied Technology (*Economic Review* 19-25/05/97:23).

As in 1992, the 1997 KANU primaries were hotly contested. They were characterised by irregularities and physical confrontation. In a number of places local interests clashed with those of the headquarters. Furthermore, the discrepancy between the number of registered voters and the number who turned up for the primaries was a source of serious disputes in a number of nomination centres. KANU nomination re-runs were done in Bobasi, Kitutu Chache, and in seven polling stations of West Mugirango (*East African Standard* 29/11/97:4, 6).

The primaries resulted in a few surprises and some expected outcomes. It was a surprise when a number of MPs perceived to be in Nyachae's camp were defeated. On the other hand, the defeat of candidates such as Protus Kebati Momanyi (Bonchari) was expected. Momanyi was the first to defect to KANU from DP after the 1992 elections. He recaptured the Bonchari seat in a subsequent violent by-election. In 1997 he was trounced at the KANU primaries by a newcomer, John Zebedeo Opore, who finally won the seat (*Sunday Nation* 30/11/97:8). It appears that Momanyi's defeat was not so much due to his support for a group opposed to Nyachae, but the woes he caused his constituents after his defection to KANU. The chaos that characterised the by-election was too much. Blood was shed and some lives lost. His constituents were also far from being satisfied. His defection and subsequent victory did not yield much from KANU in terms of development projects. His elevation to the post of the minister for Tourism and Wildlife in 1996 did not enhance his prospects of electoral victory as the press predicted (*Economic Review* 19-25/05/97:25).

The defeat of Nyachae's allies in the party primaries of 1997 seemed to spell doom for his efforts to marshal support through uniting Gusii MPs under his leadership. Further, the fact that he was perceived to be a factor in the Moi succession dispute pitted him against other contenders from other communities. These events reinforced the two dimensions of Nyachae's problems since he had left the civil service for politics. One is the local political rivalry and the other is the siege from the centre of the political establishment. His post-election appointment to head the ministry of finance may have endeared him to the donor community but it brought him nothing but trouble in national politics. It brought him into conflict with the former director of the Kenya Anti-Corruption Authority, John Harun Mwau. Mwau sought to prosecute treasury officials, accusing Nyachae of shielding them in their alleged corrupt deals. Nyachae, as expected, saw this move as a political affront against him. With his characteristic style of 'speaking his mind', on issues directly affecting him, Nyachae dismissed Mwau. But Nyachae himself then lost the finance portfolio and fell out of favour with Moi's inner circle.

Elections and thereafter

After the hotly contested KANU primaries, the 1997 polls in Gusiiland were generally in a low key, marred by sporadic incidents of violence and logistical, structural, administrative and political problems. It appears that sub-clan politics took a centre stage during the campaign period in a number of constituencies and determined to some extent the election outcome. In Bobasi, for example, Stephen Manoti from the small Bogesaka sub-clan could not defeat Christopher Obure from the large Boigesa sub-clan. Manoti's defection from KANU to Safina after the party primaries did not improve his performance in the polls (*Daily Nation* 30/12/97:7). It is probable, as popular opinion indicated earlier, that in Kitutu Chache, Jimmy Angwenyi (KANU) combined a strong support from Nyachae and maternal links to the prominent sub-clan in the constituency, Mwabogonko, to win during the primaries and subsequent election (*Economic Review* 19-25/05/97:28).

Of the logistical problems, transport was the most serious. Gusiiland is known for badly damaged roads. A majority of these are murram roads whose condition was worsened by overnight rain in a number of places on polling day. The polling stations such as Gesima Primary School (Kitutu Masaba), Mwongori (North Mugirango), Kirwa (Nyaribari Chache) and Borangi SDA (Bobasi) were severely affected by rain. Most of the roads in these places were impassable (NCCK/IED/CJPC No. 204, 206, 208, 210). Consequently, there was a delay in the opening of polling stations as officials, ballot papers and boxes did not reach the stations at the intended time. Most of the stations opened two hours late. But in Gesima (Kitutu Masaba) polling started at 10 am. Election observers reported that people started coming to the station as early as 6 am, only to find polling not yet begun but went back home to come later in the evening (NCCK/IED/CJPC No. 208). The delay caused much inconvenience to the entire electoral process. It resulted in the closing of the polls very late, overworking the polling officials, security personnel and party agents.

The fatigue on all those involved in the elections was most likely worse in areas where vote counting was delayed due to disagreement among politicians. For example, at Nyamira Technical Institute, West Mugirango constituency counting centre, David Onyancha (DP), Tom Sagwe (KANU) and Mathews Ondeyo (KSC) disputed the counting of ballot boxes from a polling station where voting had taken place throughout the night of 29 December 1997. This delayed the vote counting exercise (*Daily Nation* 31/12/97:27). It is possible that the intolerance from election officials, security personnel and party agents which was witnessed in vote counting halls in some constituencies, stemmed from the physical fatigue caused by such delays. These delays combined with the chilly and rainy nights of the Gusii highlands to make the whole exercise cumbersome. Inadequate transport to move all poll observers, party agents, security personnel and polling officials from polling stations to counting centres simultaneously, created loopholes that made the safety of ballot boxes open to manipulation.

True, election violence marred the 1997 Gusii polls but perhaps not to the same extent as in 1992. In many polling stations there were sporadic cases of rowdiness and drunkenness of voters, which interrupted the polling. In Nyamecheo (Nyaribari Chache), for example, a poll observer complained of harassment. The DP candidate, Peter Maragia Nyamweya, in the same constituency, claimed that his agents were violently evicted from the counting hall (*Daily Nation* 06/01/98:9; NCCK/IED/CJPC No 206). Undue interference in the electoral process, which took various forms such as bribery and intimidation on polling day, exacerbated violence-related problems. In Nyaboterere (Bobasi), agents of some opposition candidates, for example, openly bribed voters and chanted party slogans within the polling station (NCCK/IED/CJPC No. 204).

In general terms, it is arguable that the triumph of the majority of the 1992 poll losers at the KANU primaries in 1997 neutralised much of the tension that had built up during the run-up to the elections. Compared to the KANU primaries there was minimum tension on polling day. However, it is difficult to generalise as the situation differed from one constituency to another.

The situation in Bobasi, for example, was tense particularly during the primaries. It was characterised by reciprocal violence involving people close to the incumbent MP, Manoti, and his arch-rival, Obure. There were organised militias who regularly fought it out in various places prior to the election in the constituency. It is possible that such high tension prevented candidates such as Hezron Nyangito, who took part in the first round of KANU primaries, from the re-run. He left it to Manoti and Obure, who dominated the contest, to battle it out. In other constituencies, KANU particularly in Nyaribari Chache and Nyaribari Masaba had a 'zone' mentality.[15] The overwhelming dominance of Nyachae, however, apparently minimised the tension in Nyaribari Chache since his re-election was not at risk. The opposition in his constituency was feeble and wanting in grassroots support. In the polls, Nyachae got 83.3 per cent of the votes cast as opposed to 6.8 per cent for Isaac Nyamache Rwenyo (FORD-Kenya) who became second (IED 1998:358). In Nyaribari Masaba constituency, Ongeri's extra efforts and subsequent victory at the KANU primaries over Hezron Manduku, the incumbent MP, thwarted much violence. Manduku's apparent quick surrender, unlike Ongeri in 1992, from staking claim to political supremacy in the constituency, averted violence of the magnitude witnessed in 1992 during the KANU primaries re-run.

Voting secrecy was practically impossible in many polling stations due to the fact that Gusiiland has a high level of illiteracy. Illiterate voters were asked to verbalise their preferences for presidential, parliamentary and civic candidates, which made their right to vote for candidates of their choice open to abuse and manipulation. Besides, as observers from many constituencies reported, a number of voters' names were missing in the registers and, therefore, these persons were not allowed to cast their vote (NCCK/IED/CJPC No. 204-210). Why these names were missing is difficult to tell. The missing names were either a result of human error or purposeful rigging, but the former is most likely for two reasons. First, there were no bitter complaints from candidates or the general public about the missing names, probably because the human error involved was fairly understandable.

Second, errors of omission and commission in filling registration forms is a common occurrence, particularly where and when the electorate is largely illiterate electorate and the registration clerks are semi-literate.

Another interesting phenomenon in the 1997 Gusii polls was the high number of contestants in all constituencies. In many constituencies candidates ranged from four to eight. Four of the ten seats in Gusiiland had eight candidates, two had six, another two had five while the remaining two had four candidates. Some candidates, particularly in KANU, may have sponsored their agents on opposition tickets to weaken political rivals in Gusiiland. On the other hand, joining opposition parties was a way of expressing dissatisfaction with the KANU primaries. In Bobasi, the incumbent MP defected to Safina mainly for this reason.

In 1997 the Gusii overwhelmingly supported KANU candidates in the parliamentary elections. The election results revealed an overwhelming victory for KANU in two of the three Gusii districts. All the seats in Gucha and Kisii districts, except South Mugirango, went to KANU. In Nyamira district, as in 1992, KANU did not have a complete monopoly. KSC, FORD-Kenya and KANU took a seat each (*Daily Nation* 01/01/98:20-21). With Sam Ongeri's (Nyaribari Masaba) and Obure's (Bobasi) success in the primaries, KANU's prospects of victory were enhanced. Therefore, in 1997 KANU did not depend on Nyachae alone to trounce the opposition as it did in 1992, but also on Ongeri and Obure also (see Throup and Hornsby 1998:507).

Thus, whereas Nyamira district remained the heart of the opposition, Kisii district emerged a predominantly KANU zone with all its four seats going to its candidates. In the politically marginal Gucha district, KANU was dominant also, save for the South Mugirango seat which went to a FORD-Kenya candidate. Kisii district, the traditional centre of Gusii politics, gained much more than the other two districts if subsequent cabinet appointments are anything to go by. The two ministerial positions held by Gusii MPs went to Kisii district: Ongeri was named minister for Local Government and Nyachae minister for Finance. Such appointments for years have been dominated by MPs from Nyaribari and Kitutu Chache constituencies, all in the current Kisii district. It was only Protus Momanyi from Bonchari constituency (Kisii district. also) who 'spoiled' the trend when appointed minister for Tourism and Wildlife. Even then this only came as a reward for his defection from DP to KANU after the 1992 elections, and the death of Dr Zachary Onyonka which left vacant the second cabinet seat 'meant' for the Gusii.

Kisii district has been home for dominant figures and kingmakers in Gusiiland who have maintained a stable binary pattern competition. These strong men include the late Sagini, minister and KANU staunch supporter during Kenyatta and Moi eras, the late James Nyamweya, a long-time minister during Kenyatta's time and strong DP supporter after the advent of multi-party politics, the late Zachary Onyonka, the longest serving minister and MP of the Gusii politicians, Samson Ongeri, the current minister for Local Government and, above all, Nyachae.

In 1997, KANU faced a more feeble and fragmented opposition in Gusiiland than in 1992. The death of James Nyamweya (DP) before the 1997 elections left a gap in the Nyaribari Chache opposition that could not be filled by his son, Peter Nyamweya. The young Nyamweya came third after Nyachae (KANU) and Isaac Rwenyo (FORD-Kenya). Anyona (Kitutu Masaba) retained his seat. He remained the key opposition leader with his counterparts Henry Obwocha (FORD-Kenya) for West Mugirango, and Enock Magara (FORD-Kenya) for South Mugirango constituencies. This trio carries the banner of opposition politics among the MPs from Gusiiland.

Unlike in 1992, in 1997 Anyona faced challenges from KANU and opposition candidates in his constituency. His rivals sought to capitalise on his dismal development record, particularly his apathy towards fund-raising drives to aid projects in the constituency. Playing a more meek and reconciliatory role as opposed to his traditional radicalism, Anyona emerged as one of the key supporters of Nyachae. His agenda, as Nyachae's, was to champion 'Omogusii unity' on the eve of the elections. His new political posture seemed to be his main undoing during the campaign. It smacked of compromise of his old socialist ideals and long-drawn anti-establishment sentiments that had earned him many admirers within and outside Gusiiland. His support for Nyachae and his role in the resolution of the conflict surrounding the location of the headquarters of the new Gucha district accorded him Gusii-wide support to some extent. The media publicity he got as the secretary of the IPPG kept his name in the public limelight.

If the above gives an impression that Anyona won his seat in 1997 as easily as in 1992, as predictions had indicated, that is wrong (*Economic Review* 19-25/05/97:29). His opponents, Samson Nyang'au Okioma (FORD-Kenya) and Nelson Gichaba Simba (KANU) concentrated on development issues through numerous fund raising activities at the constituency level to counter Anyona's rhetoric. Although their efforts did ultimately not translate into votes, they gave Anyona a harder time than ever before. It is likely that Anyona was caught in the 'web' of people upset with the incumbents alluded to earlier in the chapter. His traditional tools of electioneering, eloquence and appeal to the poor (farmers), proved less rewarding in 1997 than before. It appears that many people were not satisfied with popular persuasion. Simply put, they refused to just 'eat words' in hard times. People needed money or huge donations in *harambees* to support development projects. That electoral concerns in Kitutu Masaba are gradually changing cannot be gainsaid. It is probable that in future a politician's development record rather than populism will be at the heart of the constituency's politics. Given the undeveloped state of infrastructure, particularly roads, in the constituency, the emphasis on development is hardly surprising. Such a fundamental shift in local electoral concerns is likely to undermine Anyona's position.

Yet, his active role in the on-going constitutional review process has helped to keep his name in the national limelight as did his IPPG position before elections. Also, it is apparent that, with his current brand of politics of reconciliation and minimal anti-establishment outbursts, Anyona has cut a new image of an 'elder politician' for himself. The new posture could be more appealing particularly to old people in his constituency and Gusiiland in general as opposed to his 'youthful' radicalism of the 1970s and 1980s (Omore and Mutere 1979: 19). In the absence of the late Onyonka, Sagini and Anyieni (who is currently at the brink of political oblivion) his long stay in politics makes him the most experienced of the current crop of Gusii politicians. If Nyachae's position in Gusii politics is bolstered by the twin foundations of lineage and wealth, Anyona's rests on experience and a past record as a spokesman of the poor.

Henry Obwocha (FORD-Kenya) combined his radical stance, oratory and the numerical strength of his Abasamaro sub-clan to retain his West Mugirango seat. Like the majority of the incumbent MPs, he reconciled with Nyachae during *ime yegetwanga* rallies. This put him in a good electoral position. His objection to President Moi's appeals to defect to KANU in the historic public rally at Nyamira township in the run-up to the 1997 polls became his 'trademark'. It endeared him to the electorate for demonstrating rare courage to say 'no' to Moi, particularly when sharing a political platform. 'Mr. President Sir', said Obwocha, 'like previous speakers who have said they are Kanu "damu" (true Kanu)[,] I would like also to inform you Mr. President that I am in Ford [Kenya] *kamili halisi* (directly and sincerely)' (*Daily Nation* 21/07/97:26).

Within KANU, Ongeri's (Nyaribari Masaba) and Obure's (Bobasi) victories put them at the forefront of Gusii politics. The victory strengthened their Ongeri-led alliance against the pro-Nyachae forces. Consequently, the results of the 1997 polls maintained the two 'big men' competition pattern, which has been a constant in Gusii politics over the years. It is now manifested in the Nyachae-Ongeri rivalry. This pattern dates back to the Lawrence Sagini days, once MP for Kitutu Chache, and James Nyamweya, MP for Nyaribari.[16]

The binary pattern in Gusii politics has been fairly stable over the years. Maybe it is a more or less 'natural order of things' politically. Whereas this 'order' has something to do with the inevitability of challenge to whomever appears dominant it may also have something to do with the habit of appointing two cabinet ministers from Gusiiland in every government since independence. It was once Sagini and Nyamweya, Onyonka and Nyamweya, then Onyonka and Omanga, Onyonka and Ongeri. After the 1992 elections, ministerial appointments went to Onyonka and Nyachae; and after the 1997 elections to Ongeri and Nyachae. This structure has helped over the years to ensure the binary pattern and conditions characteristic of the Gusii-wide competition. The so-called KANU-A and B division pitting Ongeri against Nyachae locally reinforced the pattern particularly during the 1997 elections. There were no signs from the poll results that the two 'big men' pattern will disappear soon. The polls rather demonstrated that in future bickering on similar lines might continue to be the hallmark determining the local political allegiance.

However, it appears that this will depend on two main variables. First, if KANU continues to hold political sway in the region after the Moi era, it is possible that its internal wrangles will revolve around a prominent personality who will go without a rival. Second, the binary pattern competition is likely to cease if the Ongeri camp gets swayed by the current wave of communal solidarity in Gusiiland revolving around the Nyachae attempts on national politics. The events of early 1997, manifested in *ime yegetwanga* rallies, that reconciled former opposition die-hards such as Anyona and Obwocha with Nyachae, are a pointer to the fact that it is possible for the Ongeri faction to put community interests before their own political survival.

In the presidential race interesting trends emerged in Gusiiland. As referred to earlier, the community did not vote as an ethnic bloc. Unlike the parliamentary race in which the majority of the seats went to KANU, the presidential one demonstrated not only the divisions associated with the region's politics but also the careful choice of personalities as opposed to parties. The contest was basically between Moi (KANU) and Kibaki (DP). Raila Odinga's poor showing was due to the long-standing cultural and political differences between the Luo and Gusii which have kept the two communities separate in all matters requiring joint action. Wamalwa was simply not a factor because very few people knew him for want of grassroots campaigning. As a presidential candidate Anyona got little support despite Gusiiland being his home area, ironically because people were aware of the fact that his impact nationally was minimal at best. In Kenya where ethnicity is a salient factor in determining voting patterns, this rare practice is a clear indication that it is possible for electoral politics to transcend ethnic allegiance.

Moi (KANU) did better than many people expected. This is because Moi has always done better in rural areas where the electorate is less informed than in urban centres. But it may also have something to do with the influence of key KANU supporters as well as a history of a strong KANU dominance in

Gusiiland. In four of the five constituencies where he defeated Mwai Kibaki (DP), Moi won with more than half of the cast votes with the best performance in Bonchari of 63.1 per cent. Other Moi supporting constituencies included Bobasi (59.7 per cent), Kitutu Chache (55.2 per cent), Nyaribari Chache (50.3 per cent) and Nyaribari Masaba (48.9 per cent) (IED/CJPC/NCCK 1998: 205, 207). The strong influence of KANU personalities such as Nyachae (Nyaribari Chache), Ongeri (Nyaribari Masaba), Obure (Bobasi) and Angwenyi (Kitutu Chache) were also instrumental to KANU's victory. Unlike in areas such as Kitutu Masaba and West Mugirango, which have always been in the opposition since 1992, the above constituencies have been predominantly KANU. Their MPs, particularly Nyachae and Ongeri, had high stakes in ensuring a Moi victory.

Kibaki did equally well, winning more than half of the votes cast in four constituencies with a very outstanding performance of 84.6 per cent in Bomachoge. Other places where Kibaki defeated Moi included South Mugirango (68.1 per cent), Kitutu Masaba (53.4 per cent), West Mugirango (53.0 per cent) and North Mugirango/Borabu (45.8 per cent) (IED/CJPC/NCCK 1998: 205, 208). A majority of these areas had voted for opposition MPs in 1992, such as Kitutu Masaba (Anyona) and West Mugirango (Obwocha). Others, such as Bomachoge, South Mugirango and Borabu, which are among the least developed in Gusiiland particularly in terms of transport infrastructure, supported the opposition because they felt that they had been neglected by the KANU government.

The overwhelming vote for Kibaki can be explained by the nationwide anti-incumbency popular feeling in vogue in the run up to the 1997 general elections. This was exacerbated by the wrangles involving the location of the new Gucha district headquarters, which Moi's government had earmarked for Kenyenya as opposed to Ogembo, against the wishes of the majority of the people in Bomachoge and Borabu. No wonder Moi's performance in Bomachoge was dismal. He only got 11.2 per cent of the votes cast as opposed to Kibaki's 84.6 per cent.

The Gusii-Maasai border insecurity to some extent contributed to the anti-Moi attitude, mainly among the Bomachoge and Bobasi border sub-clans. Apparently, many people along the Gusii-Maasai border in Bobasi did not vote for Moi despite the fact that he got 59.7 per cent of the cast votes compared to Kibaki's 37.1 per cent. The apparent bias of the provincial administration, real or imagined, in favour of the Maasai in quelling the clashes induced the common people to vote against Moi.

Conclusion

Generally, the 1997 elections demonstrated that the future in Gusii electoral politics would be as controversial and tension-packed as the past. Clanism, patronage and personality will be the determining variables of the nature and course of the electoral process for a long time to come. The polls equally saw the rise of new issues that do not fit in these three categories, however dominant they were. Questions touching on decaying infrastructure and social services, the location of the headquarters of the new Gucha district, insecurity on the Gusii-Maasai border and a politically biased provincial administration determined, to some extent, voting trends. This is perhaps an indication that local electoral concerns have, albeit gradually, started to include issues outside the realm of clan, personality and patronage.

Chances of the Gusii community doing away with its current marginal status in national politics appear slim. If Nyachae does not fare well in the Moi succession dispute to enable the Gusii to support KANU as a bloc in future, rallying together the politically fragmented community will be difficult. Consequently, they will not be in a position to offer united support to any other option that may be available then. If Nyachae joins the high echelons within KANU, say the vice-presidency, the community risks isolation from others. The Luyha and Kamba, who also hope to have one of their own to succeed Moi, are not likely to support the Gusii in case of a national contest where Nyachae will be involved. Furthermore, the community's numerical weakness vis-à-vis the Luo, Luyha, Kamba and Kikuyu will thwart any attempts to create a formidable opposition to any government of the day. It appears that the Gusii cannot be a crucial factor in Kenya's electoral politics without co-operation and collaboration with other communities.

Nyachae, by and large, seems to have limited options in terms of political choices if dropped from the race for the vice-presidency. As long as KANU is in power, he will have no choice but to support it to ensure the security of his business concerns. Thus, neither defection nor making a splinter group from KANU will be an option to him. If he survives and ascends to the vice-presidency, the time ahead of him in national politics will not be as easy as it will be in Gusiiland. To mend fences with the Saitoti-Biwott clique in order for him to enhance his prospects of succeeding Moi will be an uphill task. Whether or not he will stake claim as Moi's successor by forging a coalition of small ethnic groups such as the Taita, Turkana, Somali, Boran, Mijikenda, Kuria and various Luhya sub-groups remains to be seen.

It was clear from the 1997 polls in Gusiiland, like in many parts of Kenya, that multi-party democracy grounded in 'free and fair elections' is largely elusive. The legacy of a monolithic political system still lingers on. KANU holds sway because of the extant pre-multi-party structures that enable it to stifle the media, use public resources and servants for its ends, and exploit mass parochialism to its advantage. The patron-client relationship between the state and its people on one hand, and between leaders and their people locally on the other, is embedded in Gusii politics as in the entire country to an extent that negates democracy based on alternative and equally competing policies. The thoroughly divided opposition has not been able to devise any strategies beyond the immediate power struggle to nurture democratic practices at grassroots level. Thus, it seems the development of a multi-party democracy in Kenya will be as difficult in the future as it has been in the past.

Notes

1. I am grateful to Frank Holmquist, Charles Hornsby, Mary Okioma and Macharia Munene who read and made useful comments on the earlier draft of this chapter. Peter Nyaosi's service as a research assistant was invaluable, but I am solely responsible for all the contents.
2. Note that these are figures of the then Kisii district, which was the sole district of the Gusii people. Today the area is divided into three administrative districts namely, Kisii, Gucha and Nyamira, which are also called Central Kisii, South Kisii and North Kisii, respectively.
3. Kenya first witnessed an era of multi-party politics between 1961 and 1964, and 1966 to 1969.
4. Majoge Bassi was at the time used to refer to present constituencies of Bobasi and Bomachoge combined.
5. In Bobasi, that voted for a KANU MP in 1992, the majority of the votes went to Oginga Odinga of FORD-Kenya.
6. Of the incumbent Gusii MPs Zaphaniah Nyang'wara (Bomachoge), Jimmy Angwenyi (Kitutu Chache), George Anyona (Kitutu Masaba), and Henry Obwocha (West Mugirango) are believed to be Nyachae's strong supporters.
7. Hezron Manduku (Nyaribari Masaba) and Atebe Marita (North Mugirango/Borabu) were Nyachae's relatives who won the 1992 elections and in 1997 there is Zaphaniah Nyang'wara (Bomachoge).
8. 'Sponsored opposition' is a term popularised by the media to describe a mechanism used by KANU's powerful clique to check the influence of other politicians within the party seen as over ambitious and thus a 'danger' to the status quo (see *Weekly Review* 31/1/97:4).
9. I shall come to this later in the chapter.
10. KANU-A is believed to be made of Nyachae, Kipkalyia Kones and William ole Ntimama and KANU-B of Joseph Kamotho, George Saitoti and Nicolas Biwott.
11. Supporting projects funded either by the central government or through harambees.
12. The idea of gauging leaders, particularly politicians using not only the amounts of money they contribute to *harambees*, but also how regularly they attend them, has largely led to the misuse of the originally well-intentioned spirit of pooling together private resources to support indispensable projects that could not be funded by the exchequer. It has further reinforced the popular concept of 'bringing development from Nairobi', to use economic analyst David Ndii's words. Bringing 'development from Nairobi' means facilitating the implementation of development projects in the constituencies level through

the central government funding or fund raising that is usually associated with politicians by their constituents in rural areas. Consequently, this has fundamentally changed the MPs' role from concentrating on legislative affairs to development facilitators in their respective localities (see *Daily Nation* 13/09/98:8).

13. In 1997 Stephen Manoti, the incumbent Bobasi MP, defected to Safina after he was defeated by Christopher Obure in a re-run of the KANU primaries marred by chaos and irregularities (see Throup and Hornsby 1998:320).

14. Addressing a funds drive he presided over in North Mugirango/Borabu, for all primary and secondary schools, Nyachae said: 'In am holding joint harambees together with opposition MPs not because I want to defect but because I want Omogusii unity and development' (see *Daily Nation* 21/07/97:26).

15. A 'zone' mentality refers to a practice in which some areas are declared by politicians to be predominantly for a specific party in exclusion of others. Also, because of the influence of ethnic elements in Kenya's voting trend, some provinces or districts are 'meant' for a certain party/parties to the exclusion of all others.

16. Before the Nyaribari Chache and Nyaribari Masaba division, Nyaribari was one big constituency and this is one where Nyamweya was the MP for a long time (*Weekly Review* 15/08/97:11-12).

References

Berman, B.J. 1998, 'Ethnicity, Patronage and African State: The Politics of Uncivil Nationalism', *African Affairs*, Vol. 97, No.388: 305-41.

IED/CJPC/NCCK 1998, *Report on the 1997 General Elections in Kenya, 29-30 December, 1997*, Nairobi: Institute for Education in Democracy/ Catholic Justice Peace Commission/National Council of Churches of Kenya.

IED/CJPU/NCCK 1998a, *Understanding Elections in Kenya: A Constituency Profile Approach*, Nairobi: Institute for Education in Democracy/Catholic Justice Peace Commission/National Councils of Churches of Kenya.

KPC 1989, *Kenya Population Census*, Nairobi: Central Bureau of Statistics.

Leonard, D.K. 1991, *African Successes: Four Public Managers of Kenya Rural Development*, Berkeley: University of California Press.

NCCK/IED/CJPC, Observers/Poll Watchers Checklist, Nos. 204-210.

Nyarang'o, O.B. 1978, *Biography of Chief Musa Nyandusi*, BA dissertation, University of Nairobi.

Ochieng, W.R. 1978, 'The Gusii before 1900', in Ogot, B.A. (ed.), *Kenya before 1900*, Nairobi: East African Publishing House.

Omoro, B. and Mutere, A. 1979, *Guide to politics in Kisii*, Nairobi: Stellascope.

Southall, R. 1998, 'Moi's Flawed Mandate: The Crisis Continues in Kenya', *Review of African Political Economy*, No.75: 101-11.

Throup, D. and Hornsby, C. 1998, *Multi-party Politics in Kenya. The Kenyatta & Moi States & the Triumph of the System in the 1992 Election*, Oxford: James Currey.

18

A Strategic Seclusion – Yet Again! The 1997 General Elections in Luo Nyanza

Wambui Kimathi

'Luo Nyanza' describes the area of Nyanza Province predominantly inhabited by the Luo people of Kenya (See map on p. 193). This area voted solidly for the opposition during the 1992 elections. Other groups present are the Gusii, Suba and Kuria. The latter two are usually pro-KANU. The area consisted of four districts during the 1992 elections sub-divided into seven shortly before the 1997 general elections with a total of 22 constituencies.[1] Lake Victoria borders a large portion of this part of the province which shares a boundary with Western Province to the north-west of Lake Victoria, the Rift Valley Province to the east while Kuria district lies on the boundary with Tanzania. The province also shares a border with neighbouring Uganda.

The rationale of elections in Kenya: a community perspective

Whereas from a national outlook the electoral environment is largely influenced by the electoral system, the legal and constitutional framework of the state and the incumbent leadership, this changes significantly from a community level perspective. From a community perspective the decision to vote for candidate 'A' or 'B' seems to be embedded in the more circumscribed 'sites of power' politics that are preoccupied with the questions of 'Who is the candidate associated with in the community's political leadership?' 'Is the candidate in the "right" party?' And in some communities, 'Which clan does the candidate come from?' The emergence of such sites of power and their delimitation is largely a consequence of ethno-historic experiences and an expression of a group's expectations for the future.

This chapter contends that these experiences and expectations are predominantly economic and are based on voters' perceptions regarding the link between themselves and state resources. To the extent that the state sets the terms of competition for resources between groups, then it inevitably becomes 'an object of group struggle' (Lake and Rothchild 1998: 9). In Kenya the state control over the economy is so entrenched that the premium for controlling political power is very high. For that reason political parties and ethnic groups are willing to pay whatever it takes to acquire this power or, at least, have meaningful access this power. For those who already have it, its preservation or retention becomes their dominant preoccupation. This preoccupation is given a life of its own by the envy and sometimes resentment that those without power have for those who do.

Consequently, election time is seen as an opportune time for ethnic groups to have a chance to take control of political power, consolidate their hold, or engage in such contracts as will allow them to organise to found new 'sources of power' (different from sites of power). Sources of power are supposed to allow for meaningful political participation as they 'create, sustain and transform the production and distribution of power' (Held 1995:173).

This scenario provides the drive to the enhancement of social construction of ethnic identity. Voters want to place their political leaders in positions that will put them in good stead to compete for resources such as land, jobs, training and scholarships, admission to national education institutions, government contracts, improved infrastructure, ministerial positions, etc. They believe that this will confer tangible benefits on individuals from their own ethnic group and the ethnic group at large. As Kiraitu Murungi (1995: 8) argues, '. . . [Kenyans] vote the way they do primarily for economic reasons . . . they voted for them (Moi, Kibaki, Matiba and Jaramogi in 1992) on the basis of traditional economic theory that '*inoragia haria igwite*' (when the elephant dies, it is the grass near it that grows tallest)'.

During the 1997 election campaigns this was well captured by the KANU candidate in Karachuonyo constituency, Lazarus Amayo. He explained that being in KANU was strategic for the whole Luo community.

> Luos should give President Moi a couple of MPs to work with, because this will be to our advantage [observing] that political arithmetic requires that Luos, like Luhyas, Kisiis and Kambas spread their leaders among the main political parties . . .Vote like Luhyas who in 1992 made sure that they had MPs in Kanu, FORD Asili, and FORD Kenya. They have ministers, an Attorney-General and can get almost anything they want from the government . . . Tribes like Luyhas eat from each side. (*Daily Nation* 09/10/97:v).

Such political 'entrepreneurs' and ethnic activists understand the efficacy of ethnic mobilisation. As Murungi (1995:6) further argues, 'it is difficult to mobilise rural people around broad issues related to the overall development of society. They have to be mobilised around concrete local demands.' The prospect of a group's collective ability to extract goods and services from the state or other sector gives ethnic mobilisation a rational appeal in that the rational voter supports the party or individual who stands for what is closest to her or his own preferences – specifically economic wellbeing.

Whether the economic wellbeing is ever realised is another matter altogether. However, it suffices to observe that in formulating political and election strategies, the political elite recognises that any group derives power from its ability to mobilise its own members in a way that may enable it to take action either individually or in concert with other friendly groups to serve its particular interests. This has not escaped Kenya's political 'entrepreneurs' which probably explains why voting trends remain largely ethnic, as the analysis of results in subsequent pages will show.

The illusory transition

The two multi-party general elections in Kenya (1992 and 1997) have been dubbed transitory elections. This description mollifies all the shortcomings that have characterised them and provides some optimism that these elections constitute change in the right direction. Whereas this may be true in some ways, it is also true that voting patterns and results in the two general elections reflect some deep-seated cleavages that make the transitory description seem illusory. For example, political party support has remained largely ethnic based while candidate support is largely clan or proximal based.

Consequently, 'ethnicity becomes the single most effective predictor of political preferences.' (Throup and Hornsby 1998:44). Whatever other factors that come into play are quickly absorbed into this matrix.

In 1992, there was a discernible trend of a realignment of ethnic alliances similar to that on the eve of independence. Then, minority ethnic groups found a home in the Kenya African Democratic Union (KADU) while the majority ethnic groups were in KANU. In 1992, KANU took in the so called KAMATUSA (Kalenjin, Maasai, Turkana and Samburu) and other minority groups in North-Eastern and Coast provinces while the other parties, DP, FORD-Kenya and FORD-Asili were constituted by the larger ethnic groups— the Kikuyu, the Luo and Luhya. The 1997 general elections had similar alliances, although the parties of the larger ethnic groups had mutated into a myriad of other smaller parties as groups of individuals sought autonomy from the leadership of those parties. The National Development Party (NDP) was revived under a search for autonomy for Luo/Raila leadership aspirations when it became apparent that Kijana Wamalwa, although weak in his home area in western Kenya, as testified by the loss of by-elections in Luhyaland, was not going to relinquish the leadership of the party.

In this chaper, we examine the circumstances and events that have shaped the 'coalescing' of the Luo as a strong political unit, how national politics have responded to this, how local relationships play out in Luoland and how this impacted on the 1997 elections.

The moulding of the Luo political identity

This analysis is more enumerative and illustrative than a systematic one, as the factors identified as impacting on the 1997 general elections have a synergy that makes it difficult to analyse them in any systematic order.

The Luo identity has largely been shaped by shared values borne of a rich range of cultural practices and activities. These provide them with unique social interactions such as burial rituals that allow for prolonged periods of community mourning, an outspokenness that keeps the community at the leadership of most labour unions, and love for fun (music and football). Their linguistic uniqueness (unlike the Kikuyu whose language is easily understood by the Embu, Meru and Kamba or the Luhya who have a number of different dialects) makes them more cohesive when one considers the 'close relationship between a common language and effective political community' (Simala 1996:32).

The fact that the larger part of the Luo population has remained in their indigenous location (around Lake Victoria) unlike, for example, the Kikuyu who have migrated to various parts of the country also allows, for example, relatively easy diffusion of ethnic aspirations and the formation of a more cohesive pan-Luo political identity. Where common descent coincides with territorial boundary, language, cultural heritage, which are the other objective indicators of an ethnic category, the ingredients for ethnic mobilisation fall in place. As Goran Hyden (1987) further argues, in such economies, familial and communal bonds provide the keystone of organised activity. Ethnic mobilisation is, therefore, shown by the closed bloc voting patterns among the Luo.

Because of their population size – third largest community in Kenya according to the 1989 Population Census Report – the Luo feel they have a legitimate claim to a high office in the state political hierarchy. They also recognise they have to organise in order to capture it as history has shown them that the office is unlikely to be handed out to them. Table 18.1 highlights some of the events that have further facilitated and enhanced the Luo identity.

Table 18.1: Significant historical events that have solidified the Luo political identity

Event	Date	Outcome	Effects on the community
The 'little' general election.	1966	Kenyatta government isolates Oginga Odinga. Oginga resigns as VP. A number MPs follow him to found KPU.	The emergence of Luo as a political bloc fighting a community's apparent marginalisation. The bloc was divided between Tom Mboya and Oginga Odinga.
Tom Mboya's assassination.	July 1969	The young promising Luo politician who had worked with Kenyatta to isolate Odinga, and was now assassinated in the streets of Nairobi.	The Luo saw this as another onslaught on their community. Luo bloc, therefore, further consolidates.
Coup attempt and the subsequent arrest and detention of leading Luo politicians.	Aug. 1982	Oginga Odinga is put under house arrest, his son Raila is detained and several Luo are arrested with accusations of participating in the failed coup.	The Luo see themselves as besieged community.
S.M. Otieno burial case.	1987	A prominent Luo criminal lawyer married to a Kikuyu woman passes away. A dispute between the wife (Wambui Otieno) and Otieno's clan, Umir Kager, disagree on the burial site – Otieno's Nairobi home or in his ancestral Luo home in Nyalgunga	The tensions of the two largest ethnic groups – Kikuyu and Luo come to the fore. Luo public opinion is supportive of the clan while the Kikuyu opinion is supportive of Mrs Otieno. The Court ruling, in favour of the Luo, is seen as political and it is rumoured that President Moi who is wooing the Luo for support and is anti-Kikuyu, influenced the court decision.
Assassination of Foreign Affairs Minister Robert Ouko.	Feb. 1990	A senior Luo (Foreign Affairs) minister is murdered. The subsequent inquiry points as well placed people in the government as responsible for the murder	Though the whole country rises in anger with anti-government demonstrations all over, the Luo feel particularly wronged and see this as a political move to hurt the community's political prospects.

Other factors that ethnicise electoral mobilisation

Presidential vote: the 25 per cent rule

The introduction of the requirement that a presidential candidate must garner 25 per cent of the vote in at least five out of the eight provinces has increased the relative political worth of ethnic groups. Organised ethnic associations have become a 'much needed' political currency. Ethnic contracts have been formed on the basis of the assumed importance of a particular group's vote in the national political power equation. The communities that have displayed a good measure of cohesion in terms of being either pro-KANU or pro-opposition, or vice versa, have largely been left to vote their own way thus carving out safe ethnic electoral districts. For example, Moi did not campaign as vigorously in Luo Nyanza or Central Province just as Raila did not campaign strongly in Baringo, Pokot or Central Province areas compared to those regions that were relatively available for 'grabs'.

This hands-off approach on other political entrepreneurs' turf is captured by Moi's appeal to the residents of Kasipul Kabondo during the build-up to elections when he told them that he did not want victory there, but 'to get more votes from you this time' (*Daily Nation* 09/10/97). Consequently, all the major political parties have directed their energies towards intensive regional support (first and foremost) as opposed to extensive nation-wide support. Their central locus, therefore, becomes the ethnic support without which a party may seem 'illegitimate' or risks becoming a 'Kombi party' (one whose leaders and membership can comfortably be transported in an eight-seater vehicle). Each party has legitimised itself by establishing safe electoral blocs: NDP in Luo Nyanza, DP in Central Province, KANU in Rift Valley, North-Eastern and Coast provinces, FORD-Kenya in Bungoma district and Kitui district for SDP. This has significantly removed competition in such areas from parliamentary or presidential level elections to nomination level, hence giving room to the entry of ethnicised voting, personality patronage and clanism as some of the major factors influencing voting patterns.

Declaration of autonomy

Besides introducing a measure of competitive politics, multi-partyism has also provided Kenyans with a new community-based need for autonomy. This ethno-nationalism has slowly developed as a consequence of a realisation that conditions and patterns that open up the space for political action and access to state resources have been premised on excluding others. For example, it is largely believed that the Kikuyu owe their economic success to the Kenyatta presidency just as the Kalenjin owe theirs to the Moi presidency.

'Social closure' is therefore seen as a necessary political currency and ethnic bidding as the means of acquiring it.

This political currency becomes intensely desirable during election time. As President Moi told FORD-Kenya MP, Henry Obwocha, while addressing a rally on 6 July 1994, his contributions in parliament would remain unhelpful and there would be no development in his constituency unless he defected to KANU (*Daily Nation* 20/11/194). Though Obwocha did not defect, the message was clear. 'be in KANU or find a way of contracting with it or you are out in the cold!'

The search for autonomy can also be explained by what has been described as the 'fear of the future lived through the past', which has exacerbated during the Moi rule following ethnic clashes in 1992/93 and again in 1997. Clashes have given rise to the fear that the state has lost its ability to provide security and protection to groups. Different groups, therefore, feel obliged to organise themselves in ways that can respond to counter such situations in the future. The small ethnic communities that have enjoyed some relative protection under KANU fear that with the end of Moi's term of office in 2002, the larger ethnic communities may take over and marginalise them once more. The large communities are shifting alliances for similar reasons. They would like to ensure that the delimitation of constituencies, for example, is based on population figures, a factor that would assure them of electoral and, therefore, political dominance. The 1997 election results reflected such fears and the forging of 'autonomous' communities is an emerging strategy to prepare ethnic blocs that can negotiate access to state resources and protection with whoever takes over from Moi.

Delimitation of constituencies

As ethnic groups began to redraw or revoke their 1992 contracts with each other, the KANU government sought to weaken some of the previously safe opposition parties' voting blocs by drawing new constituency boundaries. This increased the number of constituencies from 188 to 210. Out of the 22 new constituencies, Luo Nyanza was allocated three – Uriri in Migori district, Kisumu East in Kisumu district and Gwasi in Suba district. A close look at the way these constituencies were created reflects the use of two discernible gerrymandering strategies. The first was 'fragmenting' which saw the creation of Suba district and Gwasi constituency. This was intended to isolate this Bantu group from the Luo, thus institutionalising their ethnic label, reshaping their identity and influencing the way they voted. However, some doubt the potential success of this move as the Suba people still hold the government responsible for the 1969 killing of Tom Mboya, who hailed from this community.

In the 1997 elections the KANU parliamentary candidate in Gwasi constituency got 5,657 or 34.6 per cent of the vote while Moi obtained 4,506 or 27.5 per cent, his highest vote in any of the constituencies in Luo Nyanza. Raila scored 11,774 or 71.9 per cent. In 1992 when the whole of Suba district was still part of Mbita constituency, Moi obtained a mere 572 votes (2.1 per cent), while the KANU candidate scored 2,114 (7.8 per cent) votes. Given these results, one may safely argue that had the Luo been ardent supporters of KANU, the emergence of the Suba as an ethnic group might never have arisen.

In drawing constituency boundaries KANU used the gerrymandering strategy in order to minimise opposition parliamentary representation. This is known as 'packing'. It was obvious from the outset of the election campaign that the NDP and Raila would get the Luo vote delivering a maximum of 21 constituencies. The designs of the post-1997 election co-operation between KANU and NDP may have been hatched by KANU well before the elections took place given this predicable outcome!

Coming of age: the adult stage of the Luo political identity – party politics and patronage in Luoland

The period preceding the 1997 elections marked a departure from attempts to form ethnic contracts similar to those witnessed just before the 1992 general elections when the Luo/Kikuyu/Luhya alliance was seen as a great source of strength. Subsequently, by fielding presidential candidates from all the large ethnic groups at one stage, the opposition felt strong enough to deny Moi an outright victory or at least to ensure that he did not get a minimum of 25 percent in five of the eight provinces thus forcing a run-off. If this happened, many predicted, then the opposition would have forged a new grand coalition to run Moi off the presidency. Raila and NDP went ahead after the elections and entered a contract probably meant to access state resources for the Luo community, but in anticipation that one of the Inter-Parties Parliamentary Group (IPPG) proposals that the president may appoint ministers from other parties other than his own would be implemented.

The 1994 death of the well-respected Jaramogi Oginga Odinga had reshaped the Luo political landscape. The loss for the Luo community was double edged; they lost the 'grand old man' and with him the leadership of FORD-Kenya. Politically, the loss was seen as a step backwards for the Luo who were the party's mainstay as it became clear that the leadership would go to the first chair, Kijana Wamalwa. In the line-up of the major political parties, Luo leadership had once again been eclipsed, the interpretation being that under Kijana Wamalwa top leadership and whatever else comes with it would be for the Luhya who did not support the party as solidly as the Luo. The Luo demanded either a take-over of FORD-Kenya's leadership or to form a political organisation of their own. Raila Odinga's fraternisation with Kenneth Matiba in 1996/97 could be seen in this light.

A new sage?

That the Luo's search for a leadership position fell on Raila Odinga was not unexpected. Oginga Odinga, his father, had for a long time been the political rallying point for the Luo, having shared the political limelight during independence days with other great leaders like Jomo Kenyatta, Eliud Mathu, Achieng' Aneko and others. The name Odinga certainly worked to the advantage of Raila in terms of assuming his father's mantle. His type of politics endears him to the masses and helps him keep a vibrant media profile. Secondly, those, like James Orengo, who could have challenged Raila in the contest for the leadership of the Luo community, lacked the type of style, personal charisma and sound financial base enjoyed by the Odinga family.

Raila first came to the fore of national politics when he was detained after the 1982 abortive military coup. In 1992 he ran for a parliamentary seat in Lang'ata constituency in Nairobi. He was then elected on the FORD-Kenya ticket. Before his term was over, and as politicians began making overt preparations for the 1997 elections, Raila defected from FORD-Kenya in December 1996 and joined his newly 'purchased' and little known party, NDP.[3] He won the subsequent by-election in March 1997 to become the first opposition MP to resign, join another opposition party and make it back to parliament since the re-introduction of multi-partyism.

This autonomy-seeking move put Raila in the centre stage of Luo politics. He assumed the community's leadership and guardianship, a role his father had played so successfully for over 40 years. His departure from FORD-Kenya to the nondescript NDP was seen as a bold and strategic move by the Luo, similar to that of his father who resigned as vice president in 1966 and formed the opposition Kenya People's Union. Raila's move was a politically well-engineered manoeuvre. Several MPs from Luo Nyanza declared their support for the new party although they did not defect from FORD-Kenya until the end of their parliamentary term towards the end of 1997.

To the Luo community, a new political identity had been born. They believed that the NDP would offer them opportunities to participate in national politics and, hopefully, to gain access to national resources. Although support by members of other communities was considered secondary, it was still welcome. With the new party and being at its helm, Raila had succeeded in obtaining the political currency crucial for political patronage. Loyalty to the new identity was effectively demonstrated during the 1997 elections. There was an unprecedented number of candidates seeking nominations on the party ticket with some constituencies having up to 15 candidates. Though eventually the Luo did not vote for NDP as solidly as they had done for FORD-Kenya in 1992, their support for Raila was clearly demonstrated.

Electioneering in Nyanza

As alluded to above, an implied decision among the Luos had been made on who they were, in Kenya's political lingua NDP *damu* (NDP supporters by blood). It did not matter that President Moi reminded them of the isolation this would bring to them when he talked of the Luo being made 'political nomads'. What mattered most was that, through this party, the community's ethnic 'nationalism' had once again been restored.

It therefore became clear to any candidate that the NDP party ticket was the key to winning the parliamentary elections in Luo Nyanza. The elections were therefore fought at the nomination stage. It is not surprising that the NDP nominations became a major battle. These were conducted on 29 November 1997, using a queue voting system and were marred by all sorts of problems from disagreement over procedures, lack of co-ordination as well as proper membership identification among others.

The process in Kisumu Town East and West was chaotic although it was little better in Gem, Ugenya or Kisumu Rural. Many young men in the queues were truculent and drunk, and large crowds of other presumably unregistered youths exacerbated the problems from the sidelines. NDP's organisation was weak and many presiding officers failed to turn up. Local church leaders were drafted by exasperated voters in the mid-afternoon to preside over the polls in Kisumu town. Much of the tension centred around the civic nominations. The parliamentary primary aroused less violent emotions except, for example, for Gem and Karachuonyo. In Karachuonyo the outgoing MP Phoebe Asiyo and her supporters said they would vote for SDP following rigged NDP nominations which, she claimed, her favourite candidate John Opar won but was sidelined (*The People* 19-23/12/97).

On nomination day, 8 and 9 December, problems mainly arose in Alego and Gem constituencies of Siaya district. Peter Oloo Aring'o, ex-cabinet minister and Luo political heavyweight, who had defected from KANU to NDP, was arrested when he went to present his nomination papers in Siaya town. In the scuffle, one person was killed. He ended up in the Kakamega prison but was allowed under escort to present his nomination papers on 9 December. Oloo Aring'o was charged with robbing a rifle, 20 rounds of ammunition and a Seiko watch from an administration police constable on 8 December. Aring'o denied the charges claiming that these were mere fabrications to deny him the opportunity to participate in the general elections (*East African Standard* 10/09/97).[4]

In Gem, NDP complained that KANU was attempting to plant a mole (Modek Asimba), who would defect to KANU immediately after the closure of the nominations. To prevent this, the NDP held fresh elections on 7 December and selected Booker Odhier as its candidate. Modek Asimba, who had won an earlier contest, served a court injunction on Odhier, thus preventing him from presenting himself as the NDP candidate. Another aspirant, Obare Asiko, was put forward by NDP. However, on nomination day, the returning officer rejected Asiko's papers stating that three of the mandatory seven supporters had signed forms for a civic aspirant and were therefore ineligible to again sign the NDP's parliamentary candidate's forms.[5] Consequently, the Gem battle was left for Grace Ogot (KANU) and Joe Donde (FORD-Kenya) (*East African Standard* 11/12/97). Nomination day saw more irregularities in Luo Nyanza as a result of the anomalies that bedevilled the NDP nominations, including the presentation of nomination papers by the losers in the party primaries.

Although the party greatly relied on volunteer support from members, the bulk of the funding came from Raila Odinga himself with some subsidy from Shem Ochuodho, who was a candidate for Rangwe constituency. The party also received donations from Kenyan NDP supporters based in the United States and Scandinavian countries, the majority of whom were Luo.[6]

Clanism came to the fore during the nomination process. The dominance of a given clan played well in favour of the candidate of the particular clan. Clan dominance may be in two forms: the most prevalent dominance is in population. As Rongo MP, Ochillo Ayako said, 'The nominee would invariably come from the biggest clan'.[7] For example, where a candidate hailed from a larger clan, he or she had a greater chance of winning the nomination. This mirrors a similar cleavage at the national level where voters feel that a politician who is their own is likely to bring constituency-bound resources closer home to his clan first and then to the rest of the community.

The other type of dominance is one associated with the leadership history of a particular clan or individual. According to Ayako, his counterpart in Mbita constituency, Otieno Kajwang', superseded the clan factor because of his long association with the second liberation struggle and support from the party chair. Eventually, those candidates who came from the larger clans won, as did those that had the blessing of the party chair Raila Odinga. Raila sparked off major complaints from supporters prompting him to apologise at one point though the nominations were never revoked.

Infighting in KANU between the old guard and a group of young and wealthy party operatives weakened KANU's strength in the area. Former Nyanza provincial commissioner Joseph Kaguthi is named as the one who orchestrated the take-over bid. However, no contest at the primaries took place since Moi named seven parliamentary aspirants in Luo Nyanza to contest on the party ticket unopposed (Ugenya, Alego, Bondo, Kisumu Town West, Nyando, Muhoroni, Rangwe). Except for Edwin Yinda (Alego Usonga), all appointees belonged to the old line-up headed by the Luos' sole cabinet minister Wilson Ndolo Ayah.[8] In Siaya district the former cabinet minister, Archbishop Stephen Oluoch Ondiek (Ugenya) was originally exempted from the nomination battle although his nomination was later nullified and won by William Omoga Nyahor who had been doing much groundwork for many months, but failed to take the seat in the 29 December general elections.

The South Africa peace mediator Prof. Washington Okumu, who stood in Bondo on a FORD-Kenya ticket, described KANU's move as an insult to the Luo community and a tacit message that President Moi did not recognise the Luo community as people capable of choosing their own leaders (*Economic Review* 01-07/12/97:9). Following the move, some KANU aspirants defected to the opposition, e.g. William Odongo Omamo. He contested in Muhoroni on the NDP ticket and won convincingly.

Victors and losers in the Luo Nyanza 1997 general elections

For the Luo Nyanza presidential elections, Raila Odinga took 515,234 (79.4) per cent of the votes. He was followed by KANU's Daniel arap Moi who scored 102,288 (15.8 per cent), FORD-Kenya's Kijana Wamalwa (8,889 half from Ugenya 1.4 per cent), SDP's Charity Ngilu (7,420-1.1 per cent) and DP's Mwai Kibaki (4,794 – half from Kuria – 0.7 per cent).

It is interesting to compare Raila's performance with that of his father Oginga Odinga. In 1992 Jaramogi Odinga scored 92.2 per cent in Luo Nyanza, followed by Moi (6.4 per cent), Matiba (0.8 per cent) and Kibaki (0.4 per cent). Also, outside the core Luo area, Raila is less popular than his father was. In 1997 Raila scored 57 percent in the whole of Nyanza Province, whereas in 1992 his father took 74 per cent. Like his father in 1992, Raila became fourth in the whole of Kenya, scoring 667,825 (10.8 per cent) against 944,197 (17.5 per cent) for the father.

In the general elections of 29/30 December 1997, all Luo Nyanza constituencies supported the NDP candidates, except for Kuria (lacking a Luo majority), Gem (no NDP candidate) and Ugenya (the Orengo factor). However, the ability of KANU to reinvent itself and make inroads in Nyanza cannot be underestimated. Unlike in the past, KANU headquarters allowed branches in this area to pick their candidates. This way they were able to attain over 25 per cent of the votes in eight Luo Nyanza constituencies (see Table 18.3).

Table 18.2: Luo Nyanza parliamentary results 1997 general elections

	NDP	%	KANU	%	FORD-K	%	SDP	%
Ugenya	7,433	20.5	4,375	12.1	24,504	67.5		
Alego	29,346	70.1	12,329	29.5	119	0.3		
Gem	6,743	40.4	6,743	59.6	9,953	59.6		
Bondo	23,830	88.4	2,406	8.9	719	2.7	124	0.5
Rarieda	19,953	82.2	2,793	11.5	614	3.5	378	1.6
Kisumu Town (East)	20,475	84.6	2,549	10.5	807	3.3	1,377	3.8
Kisumu Town (West)	26,233	73.0	6,118	17.0	1,285	3.6	4,935	19.7
Kisumu Rural	13,508	54.0	6,596	26.3			4,935	19.7
Nyando	23,229	85.3	1,867	6.9	981	3.6	1,169	4.3
Muhoroni	25,510	83.9	3,474	11.4	349	1.2		
Nyakach	23,113	86.6	3,580	13.4				
Kasipul Kabondo	31,746	82.9	4,984	13.0			1,582	4.1
Karachuonyo	19,867	61.3	10,885	33.6	136	0.4	1,503	4.4
Rangwe	26,030	71.7	7,561	20.8	1,542	4.3	1,061	2.9
Ndhiwa	29,644	93.3	1,355	4.3	105	0.3	682	2.2
Rongo	23,881	66.7	11,397	31.8	542	1.5		
Migori	19,681	64.1	8,900	29.0	1,728	5.6	163	0.5
Uriri	16,104	77.9	4,579	22.1				
Nyatike	19,351	71.9	6,327	23.5			79	0.3
Mbita	13,853	78.9	3,502	19.9			212	1.2
Gwasi	10,683	65.4	5,657	34.6				
Kuria	2,970	12.1	12,493	51.0			8,240	33.6

Source: ECK 1999

Table 18.3: KANU candidates with over 25 per cent of the vote

Constituency	Candidate	Votes	Per cent
Alego	Edwin Yinda	12,329	39.46
Gem	Grace Ogot	6,743	40.39
Kisumu Rural	Ndolo Ayah	6,596	26.34
Karachuonyo	Lazarus Amayo	10,885	33.61
Rongo	Dalmas Otieno	11,397	31.82
Migori	Charles Owino	8,900	28.99
Gwasi	Zaddock Syongoh	5,657	34.62
Kuria	Shadrack Mwita	12,493	50.99

Source: IED 1998

Eventually, well experienced and well financed KANU candidates delivered 15.9 per cent of the Luo Nyanza vote for President Moi, compared to 5.7 per cent in 1992. It is possible too that the KANU vote was improved by constituents who wanted to ensure that Luo could 'eat' from both sides by having NDP and KANU MPs, which is one message that the KANU candidates sought votes with.

The other constituencies worth singling out are Ugenya and Gem. These two seats were won by FORD-Kenya, the former through constituents' support and the latter by default. Since James Orengo entered parliament in the early 80s, he had been able to cultivate a solid profile not only in his constituency, but also nationally. He was, therefore, well rooted to survive the NDP wave. Secondly, his constituents appear to have decided to keep both Raila and Orengo. They gave the two almost equal votes – Orengo with 24,504 at parliamentary level and Raila with 27,080 in the presidential contest. Orengo did not campaign for his party's presidential candidate, Kijana Wamalwa. This way he did not appear disrespectful of the 'people's choice'. Orengo's participation had been uncertain for a long time. Initially, he seemed to have ditched FORD-Kenya, among others, over the party's participation in the IPPG discussions. Orengo was of the opinion that the party should have supported mass action. Also, as a 'matter of principle', along the lines of the Matiba reasoning of non-level playing field, Orengo did not want to stand in the 1997 elections. However, after last-minute negotiations he returned to FORD-Kenya only a week before nomination day. In fact, Orengo was told by his supporters that they would re-elect him on any party ticket except KANU (*The People* 19-23/12/97).

In Gem, following the technical knockout of the NDP candidate, the community opted for the next closest opposition party, FORD-Kenya.

However, its disappointment was clear in the low voter turnout (46.7 per cent) which was the lowest in Luo Nyanza.

Kisumu Rural was a special case that contrasts with the Ugenya constituency of Orengo. The incumbent, Prof. Peter Anyang' Nyong'o, was not able to stop the NDP wave despite his development record and distinguished national stature. Once a founder member of the original FORD party, he decamped to SDP in 1997. Some observers labelled his move as suicidal. Backing the Kitui presidential candidate Charity Ngilu instead of a fellow Luo Raila Odinga cost Anyang' Nyong'o numerous votes. As one villager stated, 'We have not gone to school like him, but there is no way he will convince us to elect a woman who is an outsider to lead our country at the expense of our own son, Raila' (*Daily Nation* 18/10/97:22-3). NDP youths disrupted an SDP rally in Kisumu town on Saturday 6 December. SDP presidential candidate Charity Ngilu did not attend the rally as scheduled. Next day Raila, while addressing a rally at the Kericho Green stadium, stated that Kenya was not ready for a woman president. He urged women to rally behind him instead (*Daily Nation* 08/12/97).[9]

Intense pressure from his constituents to abandon the SDP and join Raila's bandwagon were fruitless. Anyang' Ngong'o, it was rumoured, would rather vacate parliament than abandon a party dear to him for political convenience. Ironically, Anyang' Nyong'o was never regarded as an enemy of Raila and indeed backed him during the latter's battle with Kijana Wamalwa over the FORD-Kenya leadership (*Economic Review* 28/04-04/05/97). So the opposition vote was split between NDP and SDP. KANU hoped to profit from this situation.

The analysts' predictions on Anyang' Nyong'o's fate were right. He lost to Winston Ochore Ayoki (NDP) and even got less votes than KANU's Wilson Ndolo Ayah. One indeed wonders how the electorate would have voted had Anyang' Nyong'o stayed in the better-known and 1992 Luo-supported FORD-Kenya. In the 1992 elections Anyang' Nyong'o scored 91.1 per cent on the FORD-Kenya, as compared to the meagre 19.7 per cent in 1997. A man of principles paid his price. Still Anyang' Nyong'o was returned to parliament as a nominated MP for SDP.

Oloo Aring'o had no problem winning the Alego constituency although polling day was marred by severe violence that erupted over bribe money, leaving in the end two KANU youth wingers dead. Three more election-related deaths occurred in the area in the following days. Youths stoned vehicles and looted shops belonging to Kisii people in Kisumu town, accusing them of voting against Raila Odinga (*Daily Nation* 01/01/98). One person was killed in Kisumu Town East. At one polling station in Kisumu Town West, half of the voters could not cast their ballot because their names were not on the list. In Kisumu Rural a lack of ballot papers at a number of polling stations was reported by domestic observers. In Rangwe, where seven ballot boxes were rejected after being found ope, the count was controversial. The NDP candidate, John Onchiri, was accused by his opponents of rigging the elections (*East African Standard* 01/01/98). The police shot two people.

Conclusion

In the 1997 general elections, FORD-Kenya lost most of its seats in Luo Nyanza. The death of Jaramogi Oginga Odinga and the subsequent wrangles between his son Raila and Wamalwa resulting in the departure by Raila to the dormant National Development Party (NDP) turned out to be the end of the road for FORD-Kenya among the Luo. Coupled with the bloc voting is the community's perceived fear of possible political marginalisation and hence the motivation to coalesce together as a bloc.

For all the cohesion that the Luo attained over the years, the 1997 election results demonstrated that the bloc is penetrable. This time more votes went to KANU and President Moi than in 1992. Also, not all Luo were happy with the political leadership of Odinga's son. Although Raila did not deliver the Luo vote as solidly as his father had done before him, the fact that his party had been only a few months old by the time the general elections took place speaks of his centrality in Luo politics. Ethnic activists will continue to play a significant role in Kenyan politics for as long as ethnic 'sites of power' remain the basic determinants of access to political power.

Notes

1.   The 22 constituencies in Luo Nyanza Districts are: Ugenya, Alego, Gem, Bondo, Rarieda (Siaya district); Kisumu Town East, Kisumu Town West, Kisumu Rural, Nyando, Muhoroni, Nyakach (Kisumu district); Kasipul Kabondo, Karachuonyo (Rachuonyo district); Rangwe, Ndhiwa (Homa Bay district); Rongo, Migori, Uriri, Nyatike (Migori District); Mbita, Gwasi (Suba district); Kuria (Kuria district).

2.   The year 1966 is critical to the prominence of Luo politics in Kenya. President Jomo Kenyatta created and fanned rivalry between Odinga who became a 'rebel' on the one hand and the 'progressive' Tom Mboya on the other. This rivalry between the two over leadership of the Luo community and the succession of Kenyatta created a wedge within the community. Mboya was instrumental in effectively shutting out Odinga's KPU candidates from the local authorities and parliamentary elections then. Not until his assassination in 1969 and the banning of KPU did the Luo unity and pervasive homogeneity as we now know it today come into being (for more details see IED 1997).

3.   Media reports said that Raila bought the party from a Mr Omondi Oludhe who proceeded to step down from the party's chair on 8 January 1997 in favour of Raila. The process of registering a political party was then a strict one and one never knew whether a party would be registered or not. Buying a registered party was, therefore, a clever way of going around this KANU government-designed impediment (see Held 1995).

4. According to an eyewitness trouble started when Aring'o went to see the district commissioner, before presenting his nomination papers, over a land -grabbing issue in Siaya, involving him. When the DC asked the administration police (AP) to throw Aring'o out, a supporter beat up the AP. Aring'o had left for the polling station, but the DC caught up with him there, arrested and charged him with stealing a weapon and conducting violence. On 9 March 1998, the State dropped the robbery charge against Aring'o and 10 of his supporters.

5. Later Obare Asiko filed a petition challenging the election of Jospeh Donde on grounds that the ECK did not follow the law when it refused to accept his nomination papers.

6. Interview with the party secretary general, Dr Maranga, on 18 February 1999 at the party's rather scantily equipped office on Tom Mboya Street in Nairobi did not yield any details about the party funding. He could only say that the supporters and volunteers and other unnamed donors financed the party. He however was specific on the funding from membership which, he said, was upwards of Ksh 200,000 or slightly over US$3,000 at the time.

7. Interview with Hon. Ayako, 22 September 1998.

8. Edwin Yinda, Mombasa businessman and Siaya branch chairman, was considered to easily bag the KANU party ticket (see *Economic Review* 17/12/97). However, another KANU aspirant for the Alego Usonga seat, Ms Margaret Anyango Owegi, reported to human rights groups in Nairobi that her life was threatened by a group who called themselves 'Delta Force'. She linked the threats to her political opponent Yinda. On 22 November a group of about ten men entered her home and claimed that they were to be her bodyguards. A reliable source from Yinda's camp informed her that they had actually been sent to kill her. They insisted on accompanying her to Siaya town. She managed to trick the group and went into hiding.

Other informants, including KANU defectors, have also alleged that Yinda is the organiser of the Delta Force terror group. Small groups of 20-50 youth wingers had been recruited per location among idle 'rough' youths since 1995. They received a monthly allowance. The idea, among others, was to make them vote for KANU and afterwards hang around the polling station intimidating opposition voters.

9. On 10 December, Odinga issued a statement distancing himself from the press reports over the Kericho rally but attacked Ngilu's claims that she was the opposition's compromise candidate for the presidency (*Kenya Times* 11/12/97).

512 Out for the Count

References

ECK 1999, *1997 General Election Report*, Nairobi: Electoral Commission
of Kenya.

Held, D. 1995, *Democracy and Global Order*, Stanford University Press.

Hyden, G. 1987, 'Capital Accumulation, Resource Distribution, and
Governance in Kenya: The Role of the Economy of Affection' in
Schatzberg, M.G. (ed.), *The Political Economy of Kenya*, New York:
Praeger: 117-136.

IED 1997, *National Elections Data Book Kenya 1963-1997*, Nairobi: Institute
for Education in Democracy.

____ 1998, *Understanding Elections in Kenya. A Constituency Profile
Approach*, Nairobi: Institute for Education in Democracy.

____ 1998a, *Political Party Organisation and Management in Kenya, An Audit*,
Nairobi: Institute for Education in Democracy.

IED/CJPC/NCCK 1998, *Report on the 1997 General Elections in Kenya, 29-
30 December 1997*, Nairobi: Institute for Education in Democracy,
Catholic Justice and Peace Commission, National Council of Churches
of Kenya.

Kasfir, N., Explaining Ethnic Political Participation, (unknown date and
source).

KHRC 1998, *Killing the Vote: State sponsored Violence and Flawed Elections
in Kenya*, Nairobi: A Kenya Human Rights Commission Report.

Lake, D. and Rothchild, D. (eds) 1998, T*he International Spread of Ethnic
Conflict*, New Jersey: Princeton University Press.

Murphree, M. 1986, Ethnicity and Third World development: Political and
academic contexts in Rex, J. and Mason, D. (eds), *Theories of Ethnic and
Race Relations*, New York: Cambridge University Press: 153-69.

Murungi, K. 1995, *Ethnicity and Multi-Partyism in Kenya, Thoughts on
Democracy Series*, Issue III, Kenya Human Rights Commission.

NEMU 1993, *The Multi-Party General Elections Kenya*, Nairobi: National
Election Monitoring Unit (NEMU).

Simala, I.K. 1996, 'Ethnolinguistic Nationalism and Identity in Africa: Its
Evolution and Implications to Nation-States', in Ogot, B.A. (ed.) *Ethnicity,
Nationalism and Democracy in Africa*, Institute of Research and
Postgraduate Studies, Maseno University College: 28-39.

Throup, D. and Hornsby, C. 1998, *Multi-Party Politics in Kenya. The Kenyatta
& Moi States & the Triumph of the System in the 1992 Election*, Oxford:
James Currey.

19

By Ballot, *Pesa* or *Rungus*: The Dialectics of the 1997 Electoral Politics in Western Province and Trans Nzoia District of Kenya[1]

Musambayi Katumanga

This chapter[2] attempts an examination and discussion of the electoral process within the wider continuum of the electoral chain – from pre-election, election and post-electoral activities – in the Luhya districts of Trans Nzoia[3] and in Western Province (See map on p. 191).[4] It seeks to capture and provide an understanding of the social process that undergirded and influenced the electoral process. It also seeks to analyse the gap between formal institutional changes manifested through legal amendments and the actual institutional behaviour during the elections.

Symbols of Luhya political culture

The gizzard and the moral economy of Luhya leadership

To understand the voting trends in Luhyaland, one needs to examine the moral economy of the Luhya leadership which emanates from three elements highly regarded in their culture. These are the *luhya*, the gizzard and the leopard. *Luhya* refers to both a place where in the past administrative, judicial and conflict issues affecting the community were addressed and resolved, and also to a constituted administrative or judicial council made up of respected elders known for their independence, courage, negotiation skills and patience. The head of a constituted *luhya* was usually the most senior and respected elder: *mukhulundu*[5]. As long as such an elder was alive, he formally became the head of the clan. However, critical in the recognition accorded to him, was the fact that he had to be the eldest son of a respected and wealthy family within the clan. He also ought to have demonstrated courage as a warrior, intelligence as a counsellor and wit in his role as an arbitrator. It was a combination of the foregoing and seniority[6] that facilitated ascension to this position of moral leadership of the clan.

It must be noted that the function and nature of the *luhya* changed depending on the issues at hand. It could assume a legislative role, in which case the deliberations would be open to the public. The converse was the case whenever a *luhya* was constituted for judicial or matters related to war. To complete its constitution, in cases of conflict, conflicting parties were allowed representation. Such representation was made up of good public speakers, who could courageously articulate the interests of the parties they represented. Such representation included those who had proved their worth in war, as well as intelligent and honest men. Salient in the *luhya's* deliberations was the freedom of expression, the right for everybody's voice to be heard, whether meek or mighty. This orientation, which is ingrained in the psychic of the Abaluhya, tends to influence their negative reactions to those who attempt to deny it. Those who attended *luhya* were regarded as neighbours[7], members of a family and therefore referred to as Abaluhya (those of *luhya*).

To the Abaluhya, *imondo* (gizzard) is perceived as the most delicious part of the chicken, that is why it is reserved for the eldest male member of the family present at meal time. The pecking order surrounding the provision and eating of the gizzard structured power relations in a family and ensured peaceful political succession, process of deliberation and decision making in the event that a recognised elder member was absent in a family. *Imondo*, thus, was (is) a repository of the leadership institution and conversely authority. One is able to locate the centre of authority in a family merely by locating it on a given plate. A person bestowed with that honour of eating *imondo* was, in the moral setting of the community, allowed to represent them in *luhya* deliberations. Regarded as *mwana wamberi* (the first born), he was expected to be responsible, hardworking, honest, courageous and a guardian of the family's heirlooms. His other ceremonial and religious roles included pinpointing, with the help of the elderly, the likely burial sites of family members, sitting in dowry deliberations and authorising payments of family social security systems (cattle) to his nephews and nieces.

The embodiment, the symbol of courage, struggle and determination for the Abaluhya, is the leopard. Given its cunning nature, agility, ruthlessness, courage and speed, the leopard was perceived to be a tough animal to tame or kill. It took an equally courageous and determined man to wrestle it. Among the Abaluhya, those who had the knack to take up challenges and fight for certain principles were considered to be leopards. Such persons were praised in song *nisiye ingoi yavakhayanga khumakhayo* (I am the leopard that warriors struggle with, unable to chew its muscles from the hardened skin) analogised as leopards. In the Abaluhya psychic, they were deemed heroes regarded as first borns. Logically, therefore, in the pecking order they were entitled to the gizzards as a mark and demonstration of authority. In the *luhya* seating and order of speech, they were given the first preference to address and give advice to people.

While the gizzard and the leopard stored the hidden moral ethic of leadership, power, organisational structure, the leopard symbolised courage. *Luhya* on the other hand was and still is a manifestation of the people's sovereignty. Salient in *luhya's* role was its strife to evolve consensus by engendering a win-win situation for all its participants. Underlying this was the tribe's sense of justice, fairness and equality for all those participating in the process. It is this process of meting out justice that evolved and provided it with legitimacy in the eyes of the Abaluhya polity. *Luhya* had the authority to mete out punishment ranging from fines to death sentences (in extreme cases). The salience and utility of these three elements lies in their socialisation and evolution of social codes, relations between leaders and their subjects. Essentially, the three institutions have over time evolved what the Abaluhya consider to be one's duties and obligations.

Facilitating the institutionalisation of these moral codes was the structure of the family made up of a husband, wife (wives) and children. These institutions like *luhya* could be constituted of the family before being finally being pushed to the clan. To mediate conflict and engender resolution, the role of aunts and uncles was emphasised. The next immediate unit was, and is, the clan (*oluhia*). Given that the right of expression was guaranteed, the Abaluhya grew up respecting and expecting that the same should be granted to all. A good leader was the one who could not only listen patiently but who was also willing to courageously stand up for the rights of his people.

Luhya ethic also demanded that those who went to visit a leader took him some gifts in the form of food. The leader was in turn expected to cater for their needs, ranging from provisions to resolution of their problems. To discourage either of the two, extreme sayings such as *ukhumechera akhwaya khumoni* (he who gives you favours seeks to control you) and *ulia shititi navutsa ulavimba inda* (eat little or else you risk ending up with a swollen stomach) were commonly repeated. This was used to socialise and warn children. A composite leader was thus not only honest, wise, articulate and endowed with a fighting spirit but also a provider for his people's needs. An aggregation of these values is what Abaluhya perceived as *mwami* (leader) whom in return they gave *luyali* (reverence and honour). Such kind of *avami* (leaders) existed in Luhyaland before the advent of colonial rule. Individuals who distinguished themselves in community service emerged as leaders by consensus of the elders of clans. They in turn led by consultation and consensus. They did not thus need to deploy force but were instead backed by the moral force of taboos, mores, traditions and *luhya*.

On the other hand, such leaders were given the role of spokesmen at any *luhya* seating and thus symbolically regarded as the torchbearers of the community, therefore entitled to eat the ethnic gizzard. The advent of colonialism in Luhyaland mutated the logic of these institutions and perceptions without eliminating them. The institution of *luhya* was for instance, expropriated and mixed with new formal structures of chieftancies without restraining moral codes. The entire colonial experience equally distorted perceptions on leadership. The fact that those who had collaborated and perverted moral codes of the 'tribe' had turned out to be the beneficiaries of the new cash economy that colonialism had engendered, bifurcated the perception on leadership into a dual clear-cut logic. That is, the leopard logic – which encapsulated the traditional values of courage, honesty and outspokenness – and the logic of resource distribution.[8] The underlying logic in the latter is that a good leader was expected to be courageous enough to grab resources and distribute them to his people. This logic would inform the subsequent behaviour orientations of Abaluhya leadership. It also underlay the perceptions of the ordinary Abaluhya voters and thus in a way explains their tendency to bifurcate their votes at one level and over the years to vote for both radical and ultra conservative politicians like Martin Shikuku and Burudi Nabwera, respectively.

The leopard logic or the state gizzard: 1963 elections and bifurcation of the Luhya soul

The 1963 voting trends reflected these two dominant orientations. The Bukusu (Trans Nzoia and Bungoma), Isukha, Idakho, Batsotso, Bawanga, Bakisa, Marama and Banyore (Kakamega district) voted for Masinde Muliro and Martin Shikuku's Kenya African Democratic Union (KADU). These areas voted for KADU partly because Shikuku and Muliro were regarded as the best guarantors of strong Catholic roots, partly because of their Luhya interests against the hegemonic tendencies of the Kikuyu and the Luo in KANU. On their part, the Maragoli, Tiriki (in Kakamega) and the sub-nationalities in Busia voted for Joseph Otiende's Kenya African National Union[9] (KANU) in support of the local sons. In the then Vihiga division, the Quakers played a wider role in swinging the vote to Joseph Otiende. There was also a wide level perception that they would gain access to resources from the centre if KANU won the elections. Out of the 13 seats in Western Province, KADU took seven while KANU won five, leaving Mt Elgon to the independent parliamentarian Daniel Chepnoi. Out of these seats for KADU and KANU, five and three respectively were from Luhya areas, the remaining four coming from the Kalenjin and Teso nationalities (see IED 1997:26).

From Kenyatta to the Moi state: the politics of granting state gizzards to undermine the leopards

Both the Kenyatta and Moi regimes sought to undermine radical Luhya leadership. Kenyatta went to the extent of not only sacking Masinde Muliro and Martin Shikuku as ministers, but also detaining and jailing Shikuku and the trade unionist Peter Kibisu. Even then, his tolerance of some form of associational life in the civil society realm facilitated the mobilisation of the Luhya around their pride, Abaluhya Football Club (AFC) and the Abaluhya East Africa Association (AEAA), a welfare organisation. The same could not be said of Kenyatta's successor. While starting off as an accommodating ruler, Daniel arap Moi ended up not only banning Abaluhya East Africa Association, but also constricting the effectiveness of the Abaluhya Football Club.[10]

While Kenyatta facilitated the construction of Pan Paper Mills, Nzoia and Mumias sugar factories, in the process engendering employment, the Moi regime has attempted to prop up certain Luhya political leaders with state gizzards in a bid to undermine authentic leaders at one level, and the literal plundering of the sugar industry on the other, for patronage purposes. Moi also deployed the electoral and provincial administration instruments of the state to rig out those who espoused the leopard logic. It was, therefore, not surprising that Martin Shikuku and Masinde Muliro were successfully rigged out in the 1988 elections.

By 1992 President Moi's policies of benign negligence had effectively resulted into acute levels of poverty that placed the four Luhya districts of Kakamega, Busia, Bungoma and Trans Nzoia in the category of the ten poorest districts in the country.[11] In 1981/82, for instance, Kakamega district had 62.6 per cent incidences of poverty rising to 67.8 per cent in 1992. Trans Nzoia district's poverty rose from 58.6 per cent to 84.4 per cent over the same period. Bungoma stood at 67.3 per cent in 1981/82 and scored 78.5 per cent in 1992. Busia went from 74.0 per cent to 87.1 per cent. Likewise these districts showed an increase in the depth of poverty over the same period (see Mukui 1994). Such poverty levels entrenched a dependency syndrome that provided a healthy ground for KANU's tumbo[12] politics in the subsequent era of plural politics.

Who is the leopard who gets the ethnic gizzard? 1992 elections in the Luhya country

The formation of the Forum for the Restoration for Democracy (FORD) by Martin Shikuku, Masinde Muliro, Mohamed Bamariz, Oginga Odinga and Philip Gachoka, not only elicited opposition excitement in Luhyaland, but it also helped to undermine the KANU hawks in the province who were led by Elijah Mwangale and Burudi Nabwera.[13] This animation became buoyant as both Martin Shikuku and Masinde Muliro toyed with the idea of tendering in their presidential bids. Naturally, it was assumed that Masinde Muliro, being Martin Shikuku's senior, was the legitimate owner of the ethnic gizzard (leadership).

Apart from the high levels of unemployment and poverty that characterised the province, KANU was also undermined by the politically instigated ethnic clashes that displaced thousands of Luhya in Trans Nzoia, Kakamega and Bungoma. However, the bifurcation of FORD into Asili and Kenya factions effectively trifurcated Luhyaland. FORD-Kenya's initial gains, in terms of the number of senior and notable Luhya leaders who had followed Masinde Muliro, took a nose dive when disagreements over divisions of leadership positions and KANU's campaign – to woe most of them back by bribery – ensured that Peter Kibisu (new Vihiga district) and James Osogo[14] (Busia district) trooped back to KANU. The net impact of this was that the opposition's moral standing and legitimacy was immediately undermined in this part of Luhyaland. The fact that both FORD-Kenya and FORD-Asili were unable to attract any other notables explains their near dismal performance in the two districts.

To undermine the opposition further, KANU formed the Youth for KANU '92 (YK'92) and armed it with billions of shillings[15] which the lobby group flooded into Luhyaland. Some of these monies were used by the party to bribe and curtail any further hopes of notable Luhya moving out of the ruling party to the opposition. At any rate, in the 1992 elections, Trans Nzoia and Bungoma went solidly to FORD-Kenya. Out of the three predominantly Luhya constituencies in Trans Nzoia, two went to FORD-Kenya and one to KANU. In Bungoma, FORD-Kenya took three out of the four Luhya seats, with one going to FORD-Asili. KANU won the fifth seat courtesy of the Kalenjin sub-nationalities in the then Elgon sub-district. Martin Shikuku's FORD-Asili reigned supreme in Kakamega where it took six out of the seven seats in the district. KANU, on the other hand, took all the four parliamentary seats in Busia district.

Despite the opposition victory in Hamisi, KANU carried the remaining three seats in the Vihiga district. At the level of presidential elections, Matiba's FORD-Asili took Kakamega district as Odinga took Trans Nzoia and Bungoma, leaving Moi with Busia and Vihiga. The opposition won a total of 60 per cent of the presidential vote, compared to Moi's 40 per cent in Western Province alone.

An issue equally salient in the 1992 elections and effectively used by all parties was the vice-presidency 'pie'. In Kakamega, Martin Shikuku made it a point of reference, reminding the Luhya of his succeeding the ailing Kenneth Matiba as president. In Vihiga, Moi made it a point to remind the Luhya that this was a seat reserved for Musalia Mudavadi while in FORD-Kenya areas Odinga dangled the same carrot at Kijana Wamalwa, his second vice-chairman.

The tug of war over the Luhya soul

The ascent of Kijana Wamalwa onto the pedestal of FORD-Kenya leadership, following the resignation of the first vice-chairman, Paul Muite, and the subsequent death of Jaramogi Oginga Odinga, not only elicited excitement in Luhyaland, but also anxiety and fear in KANU and among other Luhya presidential aspirants. For many Luhya plebeians, this prospect was a function of Elijah Masinde's prediction[16] that a Luhya would ascend the presidency in Kenya via support from Luo Nyanza. KANU's fear of Kijana Wamalwa's candidature lay in the possibility of this bid not only denying President Moi the critical 25 per cent vote in the Western Province, but also the possibility of his being able to galvanise a credible national coalition outside the Luo-Kikuyu axis. With this in mind, KANU and other Luhya presidential aspirants sought to undermine him.

A combination of these machinations and Kijana Wamalwa's own blunders and leadership style began to undermine and erode the potency of his bid. Salient in this were financial scandals linking him to notorious money launderers like Ketan Somaia and Kamlesh Pattni at one level, and protracted struggles over FORD-Kenya leadership with Raila Odinga.[17] While scandals eroded his appeal among other nationalities in Kenya, his inability to stand up to the provincial administration's repressive tendencies undermined his appeal among the sections of the Luhya people who believed in the leopard logic.

With his legitimacy on the wane, it became easy for KANU to blackmail his potential allies in Luhyaland against rallying behind Wamalwa. Thus, when the by-elections in Lugari, Shinyalu, Lurambi and Ikolomani occurred, Wamalwa was unable to attract popular candidates (and was hence forced to contend with defectors and unpopular characters like Burudi Nabwera). He also fell victim to the hegemonic rock made up of the provincial administration and KANU-sponsored thugs. Even then, a case can still be made that his inability to attract popular candidates explains his poor performance in these constituencies.

Of the five by-elections in which his party contested, Wamalwa lost four. His inability to popularise himself, despite his front-runner status among the Luhya, ensured that by the time he entered the presidential race, he was unknown to many Luhya outside his native Trans Nzoia and Bungoma districts. For all practical purposes, he entered the race seriously bruised, tainted, and on a near equal footing with KANU's Musalia Mudavadi, notwithstanding the fact that Mudavadi was not even a candidate. He equally had to constantly reckon with the foreboding and destructive shadow of Martin Shikuku, which sought to question his 'Luhyaness' and, by inference, authority, moral ethnicity and legitimate claims over the ethnic gizzard.

Discontent in the Luhya country and the 1997 elections

As the 1997 elections approached, the Luhya country was engulfed in a wide range of crises. In Trans Nzoia, the salient issues revolved around ethnic violence engendered by the cattle rustling activities of the Pokot. This had not only resulted in the displacement of thousands of the Luhya and Nandi people, but also engendered the loss of property (see *Economic Review* 18-24/08/97; IED 1997). In Bungoma, the core issues revolved around not only the displaced victims of state-instigated ethnic violence of 1992, but also the stalled Kibabii Teachers' Training College and the collapsing Nzoia Sugar Company as a result of corruption by state elite and illegal importation of sugar by the politically correct. This collapse had engendered wide levels of impoverishment of farmers in the district.

There was also discontent revolving around the collapse of the coffee factories and Malaba/Malakisi cotton ginnery and the running down of the Kitinda Dairy Project in Bungoma. This was blamed on the KANU regime (*Economic Review* 18-24/08/97). Thus, despite Wamalwa's weaknesses, the Bukusu sub-nationality, dominant in the districts of Bungoma and Trans Nzoia, felt that only Wamalwa's presidency could remedy these problems, and thus went all out to embrace his candidature. It can thus be argued that Bungoma and Trans Nzoia were solidly behind Wamalwa as elections approached. Discontent in Kakamega revolved around high levels of poverty and unemployment, which KANU had failed to alleviate, farmer problems resulting from illegal importation of sugar, the mistreatment of Luhya 'sons' in KANU[18], FORD-Asili[19] and FORD-Kenya[20], and the assassination of Solomon Muruli[21]. versus Shikuku rivalry seemed to undermine both the two as it engendered apathy. Kakamega seemed to smoulder with a heavy anti-incumbency sentiment as elections approached.

In Vihiga district, the only incumbent who seemed safe was Musalia Mudavadi (minister for Finance). Several factors seemed to endear him to many Maragoli voters. Salient in this were his huge successful fund-raising for schools and women's groups, increasing machinations against him over the Moi succession and his completion of projects, such as the Mudete Tea Factory which had been initiated by his father, the late Moses Mudavadi. The same could not be said of other incumbents including the president himself, given the levels of excitement Kijana's Wamalwa candidature seemed to elicit. But thanks to his inability to crystallise this process through popularisation in the districts, KANU went into elections in Vihiga District as front runners.

In Busia district, core issues revolved around KANU's non-fulfilment of promises such as the earmarked new sugar factory and the localisation of the new district headquarters. The latter seemed to generate a near civil war in KANU between ministers Moody Awori and Philip Masinde.

In the new Malava/Lugari district, the core issues revolved around the site of the new district headquarters, the Jirongo factor and the government's unfulfilled promises. These ranged from the completion of Malava Health Centre and construction of a new sugar factory to the building of a new all-weather road in the constituencies and the stalled rural electrification programme and the controversy surrounding Ksh. 3.8 million funds raised for Malava Boys High School (*Economic Review* 11-17/08/97). Worse still for Minister Joshua Angatia and KANU was the banning of the production and selling of jaggery in the area. KANU's campaign machinery equally came under a serious onslaught from a strong opposition leadership in the district fronted by people like Maxwell Shamalla (former AFC Leopard's secretary general). Maxwell Shamalla had been instrumental in re-organising FORD-Kenya institutional structures and popularising its leader in the Malava/Lugari district.

Constituency gerrymandering and voter registration politics in Western Province and Trans Nzoia

Despite Kijana Wamalwa's buckling of his presidential bid, KANU did not want to take any chances and thus went all out to neutralise his impact. One variable KANU sought to utilise was the clan issue. It tried to animate clan sentiments by creating new constituencies, if only to undermine the opposition. Thus, although based on the 1992 election registration figures and a 40,000-population mean, Western Province deserved only one extra seat. It was given four. These comprised two in Kakamega effectively dividing the Kisa (Khwisero) and Marama (Butere) sub-nationalities, and the two Wanga clans, Bakolwe (Matungu), Bashitsetse (Mumias) and one each in Busia and Bungoma. The division of Butere was instrumental in splitting up Shikuku's political base, thus making his support tenuous.

However, what affected the process further was the low levels of registration in the province. Since most of the youth who had attained the voting age tended to identify with the opposition, the state was reluctant to issue identity cards to them. Equally delimiting was the inability of the politicians to mobilise people to register as voters. As a result, about one million people did not register as voters. In Bungoma and Trans Nzoia, politically instigated cattle rustling activities not only displaced over 20,000 people but also ensured that they as well as those displaced prior to the 1992 elections were not registered as voters (see *Expression Today* September 1999).

The politics of nomination

Six political parties nominated candidates to contest parliamentary seats in Western Province. These were KANU, FORD-Kenya, FORD-Asili, FORD-People, Safina, DP and SDP. Of these, only FORD-Kenya and KANU actually held party nominations in the province and Trans Nzoia. Like in other parts of the country, none of the parties held organised nomination processes. The nominations were characterised by chaos. Not only were party rules flouted, but also the regulations were not followed. The worst hit nomination process was that of KANU. KANU's decision to opt for a queue voting method for its nomination generated chaos and violence across the province.

Constituencies most affected included Shinyalu, Malava, Lugari, Butere, Khwisero, Nambale, Funyula, Lurambi, Ikolomani and Vihiga. The queuing method allowed non-party members to infiltrate the nomination process, consequently engendering disputes. The undemocratic nature of the candidates, especially their inability to accept defeat even in cases where they clearly had no demonstrable support, saw most of them instigate violence once it dawned on them that their queues were shorter than those of their opponents.

In addition, both the KANU and FORD-Kenya nomination processes equally lacked proper co-ordination, especially at counting centres, proper identification certificates for their members and lacked co-ordination between party headquarters and grassroots. It was thus not surprising that, despite carrying out the nomination exercise on 27 November, KANU was forced to carry out repeat nominations in various constituencies like Vihiga, Shinyalu, Funyula and Nambale where ministers and assistant-ministers such as Ligale, Shamalla, Awuori, and Masinde had lost in the first round in the initial nominations.[22]

However, even after repeat elections in places like Shinyalu some of the candidates could not accept the nomination results and hence opted to go to court to challenge the results. On the other hand, those defeated in primaries merely switched and sought nomination on other party tickets. To this extent, they demonstrated their non-commitment to any particular party policy programmes or ideals. The provision and acceptance of clearance certificates to and from such candidates equally demonstrated lack of commitment to party policies and ideology by the party leaders. For instance, Charles Gimose shifted base from KANU only to be nominated by Safina to contest the Hamisi seat, Fred Kimani from FORD-Kenya sought nomination on FORD-Asili (in Shinyalu) and Julia Ojiambo moved from KANU to FORD-Kenya (in Funyula). In the end, the anti-incumbency wave ensured that out of all the five sitting MPs in Kakamega, only three survived the nomination battle. Among the casualties were Javan Omani (Lurambi), Benjamin Magwaga

(Ikolonami), and Elon Wameyo (Mumias). In Busia district, only two assistant ministers, Moody Awori and James Osogo, survived. In Vihiga district two ministers out of three survived the nominations. These were Musalia Mudavadi and George Khaniri. The other minister, Andrew Ligale, lost out to Yusuf Chanzu. In Malava/Lugari district, only Minister Joshua Angatia survived the Malava nominations while his KANU colleague in Lugari constituency lost. In Trans Nzoia all the sitting members of parliament (Kijana Wamalwa, George Kapten and Kipruto Kirwa) were nominated.

One discernible phenomenon that emerged in the nominations was the level of intra-party fights. This saw certain factions within the party's front for and against certain core individuals they considered enemies. This phenomenon was carried out despite the fact that they shared parties. In Kakamega, for instance, the Nicholas Biwott faction sought to back Japheth Shamalla in Shinyalu and Reuben Nyangweso against Japheth Lijodi and Javan Omani. In Busia, Moody Awori went out of his way to back Chris Okemo against Philip Masinde. The losers, on their part, opted to support the opposition candidates. Thus as elections approached two levels of contestation seemed to emerge. That is, contestations for the Moi succession and for electoral seats. Notably, however, these contestations were neither mutually exclusive, nor were they limited to the parliamentary seats alone. On the contrary, they extended to the presidential contest too. Cyrus Jirongo, for instance, is said to have funded FORD-Kenya's presidential and parliamentary candidates in a bid to fight his opponents in KANU.

The struggle between Wamalwa and Daniel arap Moi

In the end, the election process in western Kenya narrowed down to a struggle between Kijana Wamalwa and Daniel arap Moi. Going for Wamalwa were his ethnic roots as a Luhya from the Bukusu sub-nationality. Even then, to a large extent, Daniel arap Moi was able to neutralise that advantage. He used money and promises to appoint Musalia Mudavadi as a vice-president to undermine Wamalwa. The two factors helped to sway a substantial number of voters mainly in the districts of Busia and Vihiga and, to some extent, Kakamega. Wamalwa, on the other hand, held sway in Bungoma and had a substantial following in Kakamega. At stake from the onset, were the 25 parliamentary seats in addition to the presidential vote.

For Moi, Western Province was critical given the 25 per cent rule. He needed the province if only to cross the five province minimum requirement. (Nyanza, Central and Nairobi provinces were practically out of his reach). Also working to Moi's advantage in Kakamega district was Martin Shikuku's anti-Kijana Wamalwa campaign. Such a message was so telling in places like Butere and Khwisero where Moi garnered a total of 9,648 and 10,891 to Wamalwa's 798 and 2,158.

Understanding the importance of the province to his chances of winning the presidential race, Daniel arap Moi from the onset sought to limit his involvement in the nomination process. He allowed the anti-incumbency feeling to take its course in order to stem anti-KANU feelings in the province while engendering the party's self re-engineering and reproduction process. It is indeed this orientation that facilitated Cyrus Jirongo's nomination and his clearance by KANU, despite its initial intention to deny him the party ticket. In Teso[23], he ensured that the popular Albert Ekirapa was nominated at the expense of Oduyo Oprong. In Nambale, Chris Okemo, who comes from a larger clan, was preferred to Minister Philip Masinde.

In Vihiga constituency, Yusuf Chanzu was preferred to Andrew Ligale. In Butere, KANU presented Amukowa Anangwe. Arap Moi thus preferred to use his popular leaders to do much of the campaigning for him at the grass-roots level with the help of the provincial administration. In his campaigns, Daniel arap Moi called on Luhyas to elect him on the account of the peace, progress and stability he had engendered. He promised to build a new sugar factory in Busia district. Kijana Wamalwa, on the other hand, credited himself for the IPPG (Inter-Parties Parliamentary Group) reform programme while condemning the Moi government for corruption, bad foreign policy that marred relations between Kenya and Uganda, refusal to build a new factory in Busia, and the poor economy of Kenya. Even then, he was unable to relate these issues to the day-to-day lives of the Luhya in Western Province. For instance, while taking credit of the IPPG programme, he was unable to relate the same to the existential situation for the Luhyas. Neither was he able to demonstrate to them how different his government would be. If anything, he went around merely asking Luhyas to vote for him on the ground that he was one of them and it was their turn to produce a president. Unlike Moi, who had the advantage of incumbency and finances, Kijana Wamalwa did not have sufficient resources to effectively cover the province. Worse still, Wamalwa was unable to attract leading personalities in the districts of Kakamega, Busia, Vihiga, and Malava/Lugari who would have provided useful and necessary entry points into their areas.[24]

The revolt from below: the plebeian participatory process in the elections

Given the high levels of poverty, Luhya political participation has been in a way reduced to that of receiving handouts from politicians seeking votes. This has worked in favour of KANU given its huge sources of funds.

Reinforcing KANU's financial advantage has been the commitment to religion, especially among the Luhya peasantry. But despite their strong religious inclinations, most Luhya peasants tended to support those who give them some cash.

In 1997, however, politicians from both sides of the political spectrum were increasingly faced by peasants who, over time, had come to realise that their votes only mattered during the time of elections. Many peasants came to see elections as an activity in which politicians participate in order to win seats in parliament. But once they are elected these politicians disappear from their constituences. The Luhya's electorate, therefore, sought to have politicians buy their votes. Once it was realised that KANU had held a successful funds drive, in which Ksh.100 million had been collected, some KANU politicians, candidates included, sought to gain access to these funds. In places like Kakamega, faulty fund distribution networks ended up turning some KANU agents and voters against the party after they failed to get those funds. Where those networks were streamlined like in Ikolomani[25], Mumias, Butere and Khwisero, KANU candidates literally purchased the votes. In Butere, for instance, the party allegedly used both the Church of the Province of Kenya and the provincial administration networks to distribute money.[26] In places like Shinyalu, the public rejected the little amounts of money passing around. People had been advised, by way of propaganda, to demand more money since the candidates in this constituency received as much money as other constituencies.

Other constituencies that were flooded with money were Lugari, Bumula, Vihiga, Sabatia, Malava, Nambale and Funyula. In areas like Sirisia constituency and Teso and Mt Elgon districts, voters had their cards purchased with cash amounts ranging from Ksh. 1,000 to Ksh. 5,000. Unlike in previous elections, in which politicians addressed huge rallies at market places and schools, the 1997 elections were characterised by low turnouts of *wananchi*. The population refused to attend such rallies and instead preferred to sit on roadsides and wait to be given money. As a result, politicians had to resort to what became known as 'meet-the-people' tours in which they were forced to go to trading centres looking for people to address. In most cases, crowds at trading centres were seen changing allegiance, shouting slogans in favour of one candidate present and changing to somebody else, the moment that candidate left.[27]

This behaviour, therefore, points to the fact that many ordinary Kenyan citizens have a clear and rational understanding of the political process. Knowing the lies that characterise the political process, which in most cases does not impact positively on their lives, many Kenyans in Western Province opted to make the best of the situation by selling their votes to political candidates.

On the other hand, there were those in the region who saw the elections as a chance for their son Kijana Wamalwa to win the presidency, and were willing to back him in any way. They rationalised this in the Luhya ethnic morality arguing that *shienu ni shienu* (what is yours is yours). This rationalisation was informed by Wamala's weaknesses as a candidate. He had been weakened by schisms in his party which had seen him wage a protracted battle against Raila Odinga over the chairmanship of the party and also the defection of many Luo members of his party to NDP. For this group of Luhyas, Martin Shikuku was seen as a spoiler and in many 'meet-the-people' tours, he was told as much. In one tour, at Shihuli market in Shinyalu constituency, Martin Shikuku was asked why he thought he should be trusted as a shepherd to be given additional sheep when he had not brought back home the previous ones he had been given.[28] Shikuku was also asked which Luhya clan Kenneth Matiba (a Kikuyu) belonged to.[29] It is on this account that he was chased away. Despite his inability to keep time, loyal supporters of Kijana Wamalwa kept vigil for him for as long as eight hours in some trading centres. Besides, despite his inability to effectively cover all Luhya areas, Wamalwa was still able to receive half of the Luhya votes and beat Moi even in some of the areas where KANU members of parliament were elected.

In Bungoma district, inhabited predominantly by the Bukusu sub-nationality, a majority of the Luhya electorate did not desert Wamalwa, given the fact that he was identified as a Bukusu and, therefore, one of them. In Busia district, the majority of the people preferred to mirror and interpret politics within the clan matrix. And here, in constituencies like Funyula and Nambale in Busia district, those from larger clans like Moody Awori and Chris Okemo were advantaged. This explains why in Funyula, for instance, Moody Awori and Chris Okemo won the elections on KANU tickets. In Butula and Budalang'i (in Busia district), despite KANU's winning of the parliamentary seats, Wamalwa was still able to win on the presidential race garnering 9,913 and 8,521 to Moi's 8,254 and 6,338.

In Kakamega, on the other hand, the opposition still carried sway and here, unlike other districts in Western Province, incumbent members of parliament except Joshua Angatia, were voted out in the nominations, due to their unpopularity. But while in places like Ikolomani this made a difference, it did not in Shinyalu, Lurambi and Kabras. Underlying KANU's problems in Shinyalu was popular bitterness regarding the death of a university student blasted in his room by a mysterious explosion as well as the unpopularity of Japheth Shamalla as a candidate.

By ballot or *rungus*: the dialectics of electoral violence

In the Kenyan electoral process, three levels of electoral violence are discernible. The first level is violence instigated, sponsored and directed by the ruling elite from the centre (i.e., state sponsored). This kind of violence is characterised by its sophistication, the kinds of armament used, its organisational designs and the benign negligence exemplified by the state's institutions of law and order. The second level is that which is carried out by the local elite (favoured parliamentary candidates or councillors) with the blessing of the ruling elite. This level of violence is characterised by a wide level of local mobilisation.

This level of violence can also be discerned from the kinds of armament and favouritism exemplified by institutions of law which in most cases tend to favour supporters identified with such elite. The third level of violence is usually that of ordinary supporters of political actors but, unlike the first two, this form of violence is spontaneous in nature, lacks organisational structure and is limited in terms of mobilisation. This level of violence is usually swiftly contained by the security forces. The weapons of war used at this level of violence are usually primitive in nature (mainly *pangas*, machetes and axe handles).

Unlike the 1992 electoral process, in which the first level of violence was prevalent and seriously affected the districts of Kakamega and Bungoma, consequently displacing over 100,000 potential voters, the 1997 elections were mainly marred by the last two forms of violence. Violence affected the entire chain of the electoral processes ranging from registration period, nomination, campaign, voting and result declaration period. The salience of associational space in facilitating political participation in the electoral process is inherent in the ability of the system to facilitate accessibility to information by voters and candidates, accessibility of candidates and voters to each other, freedom of association, movement, organisation and expression. If the political system and its actors, both candidates and the public, mutate the electoral environment by way of violence, effective political participation for purposes of free and fair elections is automatically constrained.

In the 1997 elections, not only did certain actors encourage and organise violence, they also engendered an opposite and equal reaction from their opponents. Violence here was a tool geared towards limiting the number of votes cast for opponents. Forms of violence ranged from the beating up of opponents, kidnapping and threats of death to actual death. Nomination violence, for instance, was widely spread in Shinyalu, Malava, Lurambi, Budalang'i, Webuye, Vihiga, Hamisi, Funyula and Nambale. Unlike in the 1992 elections, in which nomination violence tended to assume an inter-party orientation, the 1997 violence was intra-party in nature, with KANU nominations taking the lead.

In Shinyalu, for instance, a man was stabbed to death at Iloro polling station, thus spawning heavy fighting between supporters of Japheth Shamalla and Japheth Lijodi. At Nambale's St Joseph Primary School the police had to intervene and contain the violence that broke out between Labour Minister Philip Masinde and Chris Okemo when Masinde's supporters tried to disrupt voting queues. A standard eight pupil and a man were stabbed in Lurambi constituency in violent incidents involving supporters of various KANU candidates. Attempts by supporters of Basil Khalumi to force those of Javan Omani and Reuben Nyangweso degenerated into lawlessness as people fought each other (*Daily Nation* 28/11/97). In Malava constituency, a chief was beaten for interfering in the nomination process on behalf of Joshua Angatia. In his bid to bribe people, that chief was set upon with sticks and stones and it took scores of administration policemen to restore order. In Hamisi, supporters of KANU candidate George Khaniri fought it out with his opponents using stones and sticks.

In Vihiga, supporters of KANU candidates Andrew Ligale and Yusuf Chanzu fought it out in various polling stations with one group detaining polling agents of the other. The use of intimidation and violence did not end with the party nominations. It also characterised the electoral process in the said constituencies, just as it did in Mumias, Sabatia, Sirisia and Bumula constituencies. In Shinyalu, a policeman was seriously injured as security forces attempted to facilitate the presentation of Japheth Shamalla's nomination papers following the blockage of the nomination route by Lijodi's supporters. Violence engulfed Shinyalu town as pro-Lijodi supporters fought it out with police, leading to scores of injuries. But if it was assumed that levels of violence would come down in the post nomination period, this did not happen. As a matter of fact, in constituencies like Shinyalu, Webuye, Malava, Mumias, Bumula and Sirisia, inter-party violence continued to increase.

In Shinyalu, for instance, there were zones like Isukha East, which were declared no-go areas for certain candidates. The most affected candidate was Japheth Shamalla who was targeted by both Japheth Lijodi and supporters of Daniel Khamasi of FORD- Kenya. This is not to argue that Japheth Shamalla's supporters were above violent behaviour. His supporters were involved in violence up to the eve of elections. In one such incident, a vehicle carrying FORD-Kenya election agents was burnt and the occupants were seriously injured. In another incident, a person was burnt to death (*Daily Nation* 30/12/97). In Malava, a supporter of Joshua Angatia was kidnapped and murdered by unknown people. In Webuye, KANU supporters fought it out with FORD-Kenya supporters and at another point a brother to the FORD-

Kenya candidate of Webuye constituency was injured. In addition, the NDP presidential candidate Raila Odinga was stoned and his rally disrupted at Nabakholo by KANU youth. Condemning this incident, FORD-Kenya candidate for Malava, Shitanda Soita threatened to counter KANU's violence with violence. In Mumias, an attempt by KANU supporters to disrupt Wamalwa's rally at Mumias town was defeated as FORD-Kenya launched a full scale war on them chasing them out of town (*Daily Nation* 29/12/97).

In Sabatia, agents of the Finance Minister Musalia Mudavadi subjected the FORD-Kenya candidate to intimidation and harassment. The FORD-Asili presidential candidate, Martin Shikuku, was prevented from fuelling his vehicle and was chased out of Kakamega town by over 50 youths, who accused him of sabotaging Kijana Wamalwa. His rally was also disrupted by FORD-Kenya youth.

Provincial administration, the civil service and the electoral process in Western Province

If the Inter-Parties Parliamentary Group (IPPG) was supposed to disengage the civil service and the provincial administration from the electoral process, it did that merely at the level of direct and overt involvement as an institution. This, however, did not stop the participation of provincial administration officers and civil servants on behalf of KANU. Most of the chiefs and their assistants in Shinyalu, Ikolomani, Malava, Mumias, Butere, Khwisero, Vihiga, Sabatia, Emuhaya and Hamisi constituencies participated in the process on behalf of KANU.[30] In places like Ilesi (Shinyalu), the chief was cited as threatening opposition supporters for not supporting KANU. This was also the case in Muranda (Shinyalu) and Kambili (Malava), where the chiefs were seen not only harassing and intimidating the opposition supporters but also canvassing and bribing people to vote for KANU.

The Director of Betting Control and Licensing Board, Charles Shikanga, was involved in the campaign process on the KANU side in Mukomari, Shidodo, Mukhonje, and Khayega stations.[32] The provincial administration equally helped in recruitment of election campaigners for Daniel arap Moi.[33] Most KANU candidates seemed to have privatised state machinery on the ground, making it impossible for them to effectively guarantee law and order as necessary for free and fair electoral activities. The provincial administration provided intelligence support to KANU, including areas where the ruling party was weak and strong. The nerve centre in Kakamega district was apparently at the district commissioner's house.[34] At one point, the police stopped Raila Odinga from addressing people apparently acting on a district commissioner's orders.

The electoral commission and the conduct of the electoral process in western Kenya

Like in the rest of the country, the organisational process of the elections was seriously flawed. Despite being given powers to disqualify the parties and candidates who engaged in violence, the electoral commission did very little to engender compliance with the electoral code of conduct. It is therefore not surprising that a FORD-Kenya candidate for Malava was quoted as saying that, there was very little the electoral commission could have done to curb electoral violence (*Sunday Standard* 04/01/98). The conduct of the voting process in very many parts of Western Province was also flawed.

In almost all constituencies, not only did the ballot papers arrive late, but the polling stations themselves did not open on time. In Shinyalu constituency, it was apparent that most of the electoral commission officers did not understand the rules governing the process and nearly caused conflicts through their inability to control those who sought to enter the premises as agents of various parties. In places like Butere, presiding officers and polling clerks were seen marking papers in favour of KANU. They also refused to conduct the polling exercise at Maondo polling station following the confusion created by non-availability of voting materials. This was despite the assurances the previous day that the exercise would be continued (see *Sunday Standard* 04/01/98).

The situation was worse in many parts of Busia, especially in the border towns of Port Victoria and Budalang'i where 23 people had died from cholera caused by floods that had displaced hundreds of people. In Malava constituency, for instance, the electoral commission was unable to provide adequate ballot papers. So disorganised was the process that Joshua Angatia, a former cabinet minister, called for the involvement of the provincial administration in the organisation of subsequent elections arguing that they had a better logistical capacity than the electoral commission.

Analysis of the results

Despite the weaknesses that characterised his campaign, Kijana Wamalwa retained a substantial level of fidelity in almost all the Luhya districts. For instance, despite FORD-Kenya winning only one seat in Busia district, Wamalwa was able to beat Daniel arap Moi in two out of four constituencies. He was able to beat Daniel arap Moi on the presidential vote in Emuhaya constituency of Vihiga district. In Kakamega district, FORD-Kenya was able to win two seats and Wamalwa beat Moi in three of the seven constituencies. It is noteworthy that he performed very poorly in Butere and Khwisero constituencies. This is not surprising given the negative campaign against him by Martin Shikuku.

In the Malava/Lugari district, FORD-Kenya won one seat while Wamalwa beat Moi in the two constituencies. In Bungoma, FORD-Kenya won all the seats while its leader beat Moi in the presidential race.[35] In Trans Nzoia, the party won two seats while Wamalwa equally beat Moi in the presidential vote in two constituencies. He garnered a total of 338,120 which accounted for 48.0 per cent of the total valid votes cast in the province and 53.0, 29.0 and 58.8 per cent in Kwanza, Cherangani and Saboti, respectively (in Trans Nzoia), compared to Moi's 314,669 accounting for 44.7 per cent in Western and 39.8, 51.8 and 24.8 per cent in the three constituencies in Trans Nzoia, respectively.

Not many people turned up to vote in Western Province. Out of a total 24 seats in Western Province, only 10 had a voter turnout of over 70 per cent in the legislative elections. Only 70.9 per cent turned up to vote in the presidential elections. Total valid votes were 704,430 compared to the total number of registered voters amounting to 1,019,455. Out of the 24 seats in the province, KANU won 14 while FORD-Kenya took 10.

Several factors account for this relatively low, though still above the national average, voter turnout. Foremost among these was the feeling that little would change, given the likelihood of KANU returning to power and that Kijana Wamalwa was unlikely to win the 1997 elections given the defections from his party by the Luo members of FORD-Kenya to Raila Odinga's NDP. Equally salient was the high level of violence that characterised most constituencies in Western Province and Trans Nzoia. Other factors which accounted for low turnout included the heavy rains in parts of the province and the incompetence that characterised the organisation of the elections themselves.

Towards a meaningful participation in the electoral process in Western Province

Genuine representation can only emerge out of a fairly open and regular competition for office. The environment in which this process takes place must ensure not only a sense of fairness among political actors but among the voters. It is the evolution of such an environment that can engender the growth of a political culture that enables winners to accept victory with humility and losers to admit defeat with dignity. The foregoing discussion has demonstrated the fact that such an environment is far from being established in Western Province.

For a start, the decision to rush into an electoral process without putting into place supportive institutions both at party and electoral commission levels could not ensure free and fair elections. The Electoral Commission of Kenya, for one, must take advantage of the powers under its disposal to exclude those who engage in violence. It is only through serious demonstration of opposing violence that political actors will be dissuaded from using it in subsequent elections.

In future, it will be necessary to compel political parties to institutionalise their politics. To this end, it is important that a political party code of conduct is put into place to limit campaign expenditure while setting rules and conditions under which political parties can be funded. This code should equally ensure that parties demonstrate by way of ideology and action (membership registration) that they are set out for purposes of encouraging good policy discourse and national cohesion. Given the fact that parties have some committed followers, it might serve the purpose of effective monitoring if some of the funds for election observation are accessed to them. However, this is not to belittle the role of observers in limiting excesses of electoral malpractices.

Essentially, it would enable parties to adduce credible evidence for electoral malpractices in courts of law, something observers do not do. We only hasten to add that, to the extent to which observing as an activity does not have the legal sanction that can be marshalled up for prosecution in a court of law, the salience of observers remains limited. If anything, there is an extent to which the ruling party uses the very presence of observers to legitimise otherwise flawed elections.

It is also important for the electoral commission to ensure that state institutions such as the provincial administration are not deployed in the electoral process either in favour or to the disadvantage of certain actors. State security institutions must take responsibility for their acts of commission and omission that engender violence in the electoral environment. On the other hand, given the low levels of participation in the electoral process in Western Province, there is a need for concerted efforts geared towards understanding electoral apathy for purposes of putting into place mechanisms to reverse the same. It might perhaps be necessary to encourage a constitutional amendment to empower people to recall members of parliament who do not articulate people's interests. Such action, it is presumed, would raise stakes at the level of representation and in participation. One of the reasons for non-participation in the electoral process is the people's lack of confidence, not only in their representatives, but also in the entire political process. Elections, like any competitive game, must have rules of engagement agreed upon *ab initio* by contestants.

To this end, efforts must be made to encourage political actors to commit themselves to the spirit of free and fair elections. To facilitate such a situation, there will be a need for the referee in the electoral game, the electoral commission, to be seen acting within the agreed framework. The political elite must be encouraged to enter into agreements that engender consociational politics for purposes of creating an inclusive political society in a bid to end the 'winner-take-all' mentality. There is also a need for constitutional reforms that will allow for an inclusive level of power sharing and devolution from the central government to the regions. In seeking to construct such a consociational structure, it must be borne in mind that any power balancing acts must be driven by the understanding that the process is more of a geometrical progression than it is an arithmetical one.

But fundamental to any meaningful participatory process in the elections is the economic environment within which the process takes place. Given the levels of poverty in Western Province, it goes without saying that politicians will continue to buy votes in order to access power. There is, therefore, need for concerted efforts to reduce levels of poverty by putting into place structures that not only access but also facilitate economic production.

Notes

1. *Pesa* = money; *rungus* = *clubs*.
2. Interviews with key agents, observers, and actors – those who participated in the process as agents of various candidates and some members of the public. Specifically, a total of 40 respondents was interviewed. Among these were Martin Oloo (Aga Khan Foundation), John Katumanga (chairman National Union of Teachers), Gerald Bulinda (headmaster), Mulele Mboya (teacher), Simon Hussein (leader of 66 Group), Lijodi. Mbala (election observer) and a district officer in Kakamega.
3. Although situated in Rift Valley Province, it is a predominantly Luhya-populated area.
4. Made up of the six districts of Kakamega, Bungoma, Busia, Mt Elgon (populated by Kalenjin and Maasai sub-nationalities), Vihiga, Malava/Lugari. The post-election addition is the new Butere/Mumias district bringing the total to seven.
5. In some Luhya sub-nationalities, he was referred to as *mukasa munene* (The great arbitrator) or *iligutu linene* the great clan elder or *omukhulundu munene* (great elder).
6. The Luhyas put emphasis on respect of age grades and age-sets acquired by way of birth and rite of passage. This could be derived from the period of circumcision or a critical role played in certain events. The age set system fitted well into the traditional political organisation of the Luhya that was essentially hierarchical and centralised within the clan, which constituted a territorial unit. One could talk of centralised diversity, i.e., while critical decisions could be taken at clan level, internal patterns of decision making were (are) based on kinship ties inherent in the family relations.
7. Luhyas attach a lot of value on neighbours and visitors who are said to engender luck. Notably, visitors tend to get the first preference in seating and pecking order.
8. Referred to as *uvwami ni miandu* (leadership is wealth) meaning the moral role of acquiring leadership is to acquire wealth for the people.
9. The four Luhya districts as they existed in 1963 (Trans Nzoia, Kakamega, Bungoma, Busia).
10. This he did by forcing the club to change its name to minimise its cohesive ethnic appeal at one level, while forcing institutions to withdraw employees who played for both AFC Leopards (Abaluhya Football Club) and Gor Mahia.
11. Here, we are referring to the four districts before their division by President Moi.
12. Politics of the stomach characterised by bribery of political elite.

13. The hard-line secretary general of KANU.
14. Both Osogo and Kibisu had been instrumental in setting up opposition networks in their respective districts. These structures decamped to KANU once the two rejoined the ruling party.
15. Acquired mainly from parastatals like the NSSF (Cyrus Jirongo, the then chairman of YK'92 admitted as much to the Public Accounts Committee in 1999). These billions were also used to buy the then newly-elected FORD-Asili MPs into re-defecting to KANU in Kakamega district.
16. Founder and spiritual leader of *Dini ya Msambwa*, a green movement whose agitation for agrarian demands is articulated in quasi-religious modes.
17. Son and MP for Lang'ata and now chairman of the National Development Party.
18. The sidelining and mistreatment of Jirongo and the abuse tagged on the Luhya as 'cooks and watchmen' by KANU's secretary general Joseph Kamotho.
19. Mistreatment of Martin Shikuku by Kenneth Matiba.
20. Mistreatment of Wamalwa by Raila Odinga.
21. A university student leader from Shinyalu who died mysteriously in his university hostel room.
22. Interviews with John Katumanga, Lijodi, Mbela, Jerald Bulinda, Simon Hussein, Mulele Mboya.
23. Though in Western Province the Teso, who dominate Amagoro constituency, and Sebei and Sabaot in Mt Elgon district are not Luhya. To this end, essentially Luhya parliamentary seats amounted to 22 in Western Province and 3 in Trans Nzoia.
24. Based on actual fieldwork observations in Western Province during the electoral process.
25. Interviews with Gerald Bulinda.
26. Interviews with Martin Oloo and one of the Kakamega district officers who co-ordinated this process.
27. Witnessed by the author in Kakamega town (Lurambi), Chavakali, Mbale (Sabatia) and Khayega (Shinyalu).
28. This is in reference to the MPs elected in Luhyaland on FORD-Asili on account of Shikuku.
29. A reference to his declaration that Wamalwa was not a Luhya to be given votes by them.
30. Information from a district officer who was based in Kakamega provincial commissioner's office.
31. Interview with one of the election observers: Lijodi Mbala.
32. Interview with Lijodi Mbala.
33. Interview with one of the agents recruited by a district officer in Kakamega provincial commissioner's office. This information also corroborated by two district officers interviewed.
34. Information based on interviews with some of the individuals involved.
35. The Bukusu who happen to be his sub-nationality predominantly occupy Bungoma.

References

IED 1997, *National Elections Data Book, Kenya: 1963-1997*, Nairobi: Institute for Education in Democracy.

Mukui, J.T. 1994, *Kenya Poverty Profiles, 1982-92*, Consultant Report Prepared for the Office of the Vice-President, Ministry of Planning and National Development, Nairobi.

PART 4

POST-ELECTION PROSPECTS

20

'Fresh Killings': The Njoro and Laikipia Violence in the 1997 Kenyan Election Aftermath

Marcel Rutten[1]

The period before, during and after the December 1997 general elections was marred by harassment, intimidation and violence in many parts of Kenya. In the months leading up to the elections, public demonstrations in Nairobi and other urban areas in favour of constitutional changes were sometimes violently dispersed by the Kenyan authorities. Some of the bloodiest acts of violence before the elections took place at the coast and along the border of Trans Mara and Gucha districts (see Chapters 4, 10 and 15). This chapter will mostly concentrate on the violence that erupted after the 1997 elections. In the month of January 1998, 'ethnic' violence flared particularly in the Ol-Moran and Njoro regions of Laikipia and Nakuru districts, respectively. We will try to provide an answer to why these clashes erupted. Many indeed wonder 'why they break out and why they can't be stopped immediately.' (*Daily Nation* 06/05/98).

Awakening from the 1997 general elections

In the early days following the general elections it became clear that President Daniel arap Moi was heading for a renewal of his term. Surprising to some, though, was the good performance of runner-up Mwai Kibaki of the Democratic Party (DP). However, on 4 January 1998, the Electoral Commission of Kenya (ECK) officially proclaimed Daniel arap Moi as the elected president of Kenya. This statement was made while the results from nine constituencies were still not known. Still the ECK announced the winner because President Moi would win even if all remaining votes went to Kibaki.

Sensing defeat, two days before the commission's announcement, presidential candidates Mwai Kibaki, Raila Odinga and Charity Ngilu had rejected the results and demanded a repeat of the elections within 21 days. But on 6 January President Moi was sworn in to the position he had held since 22 August 1978. In the following days, opposition leaders Wamalwa and Odinga publicly accepted the results, though stating the elections were flawed. They announced a number of petitions regarding the parliamentary contest.

Whereas the presidential race had come to a fast conclusion, for parliament the outcome was less clear till the last seats. On 6 January the ECK gazetted that the Kenya African National Union (KANU) had captured 107 seats against 103 seats for the combined opposition. And some of the last wins for KANU (e.g., Westlands) said to have been won by irregular interference during the count were heavily contested (see Chapter 14). Thus, Kenya was set for a hung parliament and both political camps realised that Kenya's political future had entered a stage of uncertainty if the opposition could stand united and successfully petition the election results.

On 8 January, tension was further heightened when Mwai Kibaki, who vowed never to accept that President Moi had won fairly, filed a petition challenging Moi's re-election. At a public rally in Narok town on 17 January, cabinet ministers Kipkalia Kones and William ole Ntimama warned of possible violence if Kibaki did not abandon his election petition.[2] More KANU assistant ministers (e.g., Kosgey, Choge) rushed to the defence of their president, stating that the petition was an affront not just to Moi but to the entire Kalenjin community and they warned of bloodshed nationwide. Condemnation towards these utterances not only came from opposition politicians, local churches and the international community but also from within KANU, for example in the Nandi area (*Economic Review* 02-08/02/98:9).

It was this mixture of animosity, frustration, anger and hawkish threat-warning that characterised the Kenya social and political atmosphere in the election aftermath of early 1998. Some people were awakening from a bad dream. But real life for some innocent Kenyans soon turned into a nightmare. The two most hard-hit areas were to be found in Laikipia and Nakuru districts. Actually, the troubles had already started before the Narok meeting, i.e., on 13 January at about 5 pm shortly after a reconciliation meeting between groups of Kikuyu and Kalenjin in Ol-Moran, Ng'arua division, Laikipia district. Towards the end of the same month these troubles spread to Njoro division, Nakuru district, another strong Kikuyu immigration zone in the Rift Valley. Let us review the chronology of events as they occurred day by day in these two areas in the months of January and February 1998 before trying to explain the reasons for these happenings.

The chronology of the Laikipia and Njoro clashes

Laikipia

The reconciliation meeting of 13 January in the Laikipia area was held by Jonathan Soi, district officer (DO) of Ng'arua division, to discuss an incident that had occurred on Monday 11 January. That Monday, a group of Pokot stole 15 goats from Esther Njeri Mburu and raped the woman and her daughter. That same night some Kikuyu revenged and set four huts on fire and killed 52 goats and 12 head of cattle thought to belong to the Pokot raiders (*Daily Nation* 04/02/99).[3] At the 13 January reconciliation meeting, the Kikuyu pledged to compensate the damage with 70 bags of maize.

After the meeting ended, raiders from the Pokot and Samburu communities, supported by a few Turkana, attacked the Magadi, Survey, Miharati, and Merigwit areas using sophisticated firearms as well as traditional weapons, killing three elderly people, raping a woman and torching houses. The attackers retreated to two nearby hills where they had put up structures on land that belonged to the Kikuyu. Since the severe drought of 1984/85 some pastoralist groups had been allowed to graze in this area for compassionate reasons.[4] Reports of the killings only appeared in the newspapers of 18 January.

On 14 January another person was killed at Survey and the looting continued. At least 63 buildings were looted or set on fire in Ndemu Samaki, Magadi, Miharati and Survey that same day. Cereals, furniture, household goods and clothes were lost. Some 1,700 people fled the area and sought refuge at the Ol-Moran Catholic mission and National Council of Churches of Kenya (NCCK) compounds (CPK/PCEA/CC 1998).

However, on Friday 16 and Saturday 17 January, a group of some hundred Kikuyu men from Sipili, Kinamba and Ol-Moran areas took up traditional arms to defend and to revenge. Apparently, this time the community was no longer willing to resign from counteraction and accept a re-enactment of the 1992 post-election violence.[5] The Kikuyu, most of them in their 20s and 30s, were poorly armed with traditional weapons such as machetes, spears, bows and arrows, and one home-made gun only. On 17 January they counterattacked in the Suguta Mugie valley. This attempt was easily repulsed by the Kalenjin/ Samburu group who cornered the Kikuyu and butchered at least 30 of them in the Ngoisus area. In addition, 11 Kikuyu were killed at their homes and some 50 houses were looted or torched that same day. The following day in the Magadi, Ndemu Samaki, Miharati and Kakuho areas more killings continued. A mass exodus to the Sipili Catholic mission and National Cereals and Produce Board compound 20 km away followed these violent events. Six policemen stationed at the deserted Survey market and another seven at Ol-Moran could not cope. Father Sandro of Tarbor Spirituality Centre near Nyahururu later stated before the Akiwumi Commission that the police had fled from Ol-Moran division, although fully armed, towards Kinamba location. On 17 January, Father Sandro went to see the Kinamba officer commanding station (OCS) who stated he had visited Ol-Moran earlier in the day and that the security situation was under control. After the police station commander failed to give assistance, he went to see the Ol-Moran district officer Jonathan Soi at 8.30 pm to implore him to dispatch security reinforcement to the area. However, the district officer stated that he had visited the area earlier that day and was tired. He would visit the area the next day. He also declined to see a delegation of Catholic priests on 19 January (*East African Standard* 06/02/99; *Daily Nation* 06/02/99; 11/02/99).

On 19 January newly-elected Laikipia West MP Chege Mbitiru accused the government of laxity in dealing with the situation. His call for action was repeated by G.G. Kariuki, Laikipia KANU chairman, who urged the government to arrest perpetrators of clashes in the district. He blamed the clashes on the politics of doom advanced by some known personalities bent on causing mayhem among the members of the Kikuyu community living in Ng'arua division. Also, the Rev. Mutava Musyimi, the NCCK general secretary, urged the government to stop violence in Laikipia district..

On 21 January, the government belatedly deployed a heavily armed contingent of 100 men of the General Service Unit (GSU) to Ol-Moran. The provincial commissioner, Nicholas Mberia, visited the affected *manyatta* of the Pokot family and the camp of the displaced, but was not taken to see the torched houses. A meeting was held but many members of the Kikuyu community left in protest as no questions were allowed to be posed and the provincial commissioner's address put more emphasis on the killing and stealing of livestock and less on the killing of people, the rape of women, torching of houses, etc.

In the following days more bodies were discovered and the death toll for the Laikipia clash victims rose to 55. In spite of the deployment of security personnel, attacks continued and people were killed in neighbouring Rumuruti division. The raiders came in groups of six to ten, armed with AK-47 rifles, mostly wearing white T-shirts bearing the KANU symbol (*East African Standard* 09/02/99). Accusations were made that a white Mercedes Benz lorry which the villagers claimed belonged to a former senior military officer was used to carry away most of the looted property. (*Daily Nation* 23/02/98). DP leader Mwai Kibaki said the GSU personnel sent to Laikipia were instructed to stay in their camps without making any patrols to restore peace and hunt the killers. He blamed President Moi for keeping silent over the clashes and stated that the innocent people had a right to fight back for their defence (*Daily Nation* 27/01/98).

By the end of January, the post-election killings had stopped in Laikipia. On 30 January, 19 victims were buried in a mass grave in the Sipili area. The final number of people killed stood at 57, one Turkana, one Pokot and 55 Kikuyu, while 5,000 people had fled their homes (*Daily Nation* 06/05/98). By the end of April 1998 almost all the people had returned to their homes.

According to a report by the Catholic church, 109 houses and 73 stores were destroyed and 122 had lost their iron sheets. A total of 683 families, in which there were 2,663 children, had been camping in Ol-Moran and Sipili.[6]

Njoro

No sooner had the killings in Laikipia stopped than the so-called 'fresh killings' started in the Njoro division of Molo constituency, Nakuru district. During the night of 25-26 January, without warning signs and in a well-organised way, Kalenjin i.e., Kipsigis and Ndorobo raiders attacked the Kikuyu in the Stoo Mbili trading centre, Mutukanio farm area and Kihingo trading centre along the Njoro-Mau Narok road.[7] A group of police officers headed by Stephen Chiteka, the Njoro Deputy OCS, went to the area and found about 100 Kalenjin raiders torching 40 houses belonging to the Kikuyu (*Daily Nation* 14/08/98). Three persons were killed and scores injured. The police arrested seven Kalenjin attackers. The population, carrying their belongings, fled the area on foot or by *matatu*. Women, children and elderly men took refuge in various churches, such as St-Joseph Larmudiac's Catholic church, along the Njoro-Mau Narok road. Men who had stayed behind, armed with machetes, bows and arrows and picks, stood in groups on the main road, waiting for the attackers.

In the following days raiders, mostly men in small groups of ten, operated in different places along the Njoro-Mau Narok road. The fighting soon spread towards the south of the valley bordering the Eastern Mau forest and even beyond Mau Narok in the Meta and the Kianjoya area. Some attackers had their faces painted to prevent recognition. Still, some victims said they recognised their assailants (*Daily Nation* 27/01/98:18). On 27 January, the author witnessed how raiders armed with machete, arrows, picks and guns and mostly wearing white T-shirts moved in the valley west of the roadside. According to some informants, the raiders used houses on top of the hill as a shelter.

Three raiders were seen burning houses of non-Kalenjin without encountering any significant interference from the security forces. A group of about 10 administration police (AP) moved into the 15-metre zone next to the road while a few GSU stood on the road. According to informants, the attacks were taking place in Njeri Kleopa, Mutukanio, Ndeffo, Likia, Mau Narok and Kinanjoya. Irish priests confirmed that the raiders attacked Kikuyu people and also mentioned that on that day, 27 January, the Kikuyu retaliated on local Kalenjin in the Likia area and houses belonging to the latter had been set ablaze.

Between Likia and Mau Narok, the Kikuyu complained furiously about the behaviour of the police and claimed that the police prevented them from defending their property. In Mau Narok, some 100 people had taken refuge near a school. Further down the road, in the Meta area, the author witnessed a group of about 80 Kikuyu marching in a long line towards the attackers, trying to chase them away from a farm and prevent a house from being set ablaze. They managed to reach the house, but after a short while the Kikuyu, in spite of their big numbers, fled from a small group of ten raiders only. One Kikuyu was killed in the attack.[8]

According to police reports, 22 people had died by 27 January of whom 7 were found by the police. Also 16 suspects had been arrested. That day, 200 Catholic priests, nuns, monks and brothers from the Nakuru diocese, led by Bishop Peter Kairu, presented a protest note to the Rift Valley provincial commissioner, Nicholas Mberia, in which they accused the state of complicity and linked the renewed violence to recent remarks by KANU leaders in Narok. Also the MP-elect for Njoro, Kihaki Kimani (DP) said the Kikuyu community had been pushed to the wall for too long and warned they would go to war to defend themselves (*Daily Nation* 28/01/98).

On 28 January, Nakuru town shopkeepers shut their premises to protest at the on-going violence in Njoro. The police dispersed demonstrating residents by shooting in the air. Transport was paralysed as *matatu* operators withdrew their vehicles to mourn the dead (*East African Standard* 29/01/98). That same day, Kenya police commissioner Duncan Wachira directed security officers in the clash-hit areas of Njoro and Laikipia to arrest and disarm raiders. Officers in these areas had been reported in the press complaining that they had not been instructed to arrest or disarm suspected raiders. DP legislators asked President Moi to sack four cabinet ministers (Ntimama, Kones, Biwott and Lotodo) for fanning ethnic animosity and break 'his long silence on the matter as it may be interpreted to mean he does not care about the regrettable developments taking place.' (*Daily Nation* 29/01/98). In its editorial the *Daily Nation* wrote: 'The President's silence is particularly perplexing, indeed untenable, coming as it does hardly three weeks after he has sworn afresh to protect all the citizens of this country. . . . Not even condolences to the bereaved have issued from the politico-bureaucratic hierarchy.' (*Daily Nation* 29/01/98).

The following day, 29 January, President Moi in a statement from State House ended his silence and asked all *wananchi* in the clash-hit areas, regardless of their ethnic and political party affiliations, to stop hostilities against each other. He thanked KANU MPs for preaching peace and said it was unfortunate that some DP leaders were on record making inflammatory remarks, which fuelled hostilities (*East African Standard* 30/01/98).

That same day, the author again visited the Njoro area, when people were still fleeing the area, albeit in a less massive way. Civilians, still armed, waited in groups by the side of the road. According to the Larmudiac Catholic church priest, Simon Githere, 'there are a lot of policemen and security personnel here, but they are positioned along the road to arrest armed residents instead of pursuing the raiders into the forests and disarm them.' (*East African Standard* 30/01/98). Towards Mau Narok, five police 4-wheel drive cars and three empty army trucks could be seen on the road. From the talks with local informants, it became clear that local Kalenjin were increasingly attacked out of retaliation by groups of young Kikuyu.

On 30 January, the police released the names of 45 clash victims in he Njoro area (25 Kikuyu, 1 Kamba, 1 Kisii, 18 Kalenjin, 12 unnamed bodies). This confirmed the reports that the people murdered were not from the Kikuyu community alone. Increasingly, Kalenjin names appeared on the list of clash victims. A reconciliatory meeting was organised by the Nakuru DC, Kinuthia Mbugua, outside the Mauche trading centre. At the same time opposition MPs threatened to disrupt the opening of parliament on Tuesday, to block the election of the speaker and compel President Moi to end ethnic violence in the country. In spite of these attempts to stop the killings, organised violence spread to Mwariki, one of the outskirts of Nakuru town, following the same pattern of killing. Raiders with faces painted in white and red came from the forests and speared people while the police just watched (*Daily Nation* 31/01/98). Eight houses were burnt and two people killed.

On 31 January the death toll rose to 58. In Larmudiac Secondary School a mass burial service was held bringing together both communities. Also 20 Nandi KANU officials led by Kenneth Saina that day spoke out against cabinet assistant ministers Kosgey and Choge for inciting the Nandi against the Kikuyu and Luo. Political pressure intensified in the following days with the SDP in a press statement going as far as 'giving' President Moi an ultimatum to stop the killings, failing which the SDP would 'begin giving technical assistance to the victims so they can defend themselves.' (*Daily Nation* 01/02/98).

While speaking on 1 February at Kamasai in the Barut area, where 400 displaced Kalenjin from Njoro were camping, a section of KANU Rift Valley leaders claimed that the clashes were hatched and executed by some opposition elements still smarting from their humiliating defeat by KANU (*Kenya Times* 02/02/98). On 2 February police in the Njoro area recovered four more bodies of people killed bringing the death toll to 65. Rift Valley provincial police officer Joseph Cheruiyot was then replaced by James Warsame. The Nakuru divisional police boss Peter Kavila was also moved. In Nakuru town, Christians, Muslims and others held a two-hour long procession to protest the violence. KANU MPs of Kuresoi, Rongai and Eldama Ravine asked church leaders not to be partisan. They claimed the picture portrayed by the clergymen was that only one community had been adversely affected by the clashes, yet people from all communities had suffered (*East African Standard* 03/02/98).

With the news spreading that the Kalenjin were also victims of the Njoro clashes tension rose in other parts of the country. Some 60 non-Kalenjin people fled to the Kabernet Catholic church in Baringo and sought refuge for ten days after two bodies of Kalenjin victims of the Njoro killings were brought home for burial. Also reports in the newspapers appeared of one person tossed into the crocodile-infested River Keiyo in reaction to the Njoro violence (*Daily Nation* 03/02/98).

On 2 February, the Kenya Law Society, among many others, called for an independent investigation into the causes of the ethnic violence in parts of the Rift Valley. In a letter to the secretary general of the United Nations, the society said such independent investigations 'devoid of our municipal politics and acrimonies' were the only way of establishing the truth (*Daily Nation* 03/02/98).

That same day Raila Odinga rejected the call by DP's Kibaki to disrupt the opening of parliament to protest the ongoing clashes. FORD-Kenya also decided to deny the call. The non-DP/SDP/Safina opposition MPs supporting the call were Mukhisa Kituyi (FORD-Kenya) and George Nyanja (NDP). Indeed the, following day, the protesting MPs showed placards saying 'Moi Resign Now', 'Enough is Enough', 'Moi we want Peace', 'Leave Death to God'. They sang '*Oh, Oh Moi avunja nchi, Oh oh Kanu Yavunja nchi*' (Moi and KANU are destroying the country). When they finished singing they started chanting slogans such as 'No more killings, no more killings, Moi, we are tired of killings' (*Daily Nation* 04/02/98; *East African Standard* (04/02/98). An attempt to discuss the violence was rejected by the speaker. Outside parliament a group of about 100 people were violently dispersed and 10 arrested by riot police (*Daily Nation* 04/02/98).

In Njoro and neighbouring Molo areas, arsonists continued torching houses at Belbut, Moto and Kongoi farms. The death toll rose to 69 after four more bodies were found in Likia and Ndeffo (*East African Standard* 04/02/98). The political fire was kept burning by new allegations by 41 Rift Valley MPs who claimed that ethnic violence was part of a DP plot 'to topple Moi'. In a rejoinder, the DP dismissed the claims as 'incredible and an arrogant attempt to play around with matters of life and death' (*Daily Nation* 05/02/98).

The government deployed five new district officers for Njoro and Nakuru, and on 5 February placed Nakuru district under a partial curfew, effectively closing all business in the region's urban centres between 9 pm and 6 am. Violation of the curfew would cost one a fine of Ksh. 1,000 or one month in jail. The move was criticised by some stating that this would benefit the raiders and hamper self-defence groups. The political accusations intensified with more KANU MPs blaming the opposition for the violence and with President Moi blaming religious leaders for supporting aggressors and the opposition for wanting to create a Rwanda-like situation. But DP MP Njeru Ngigwa for Manyatta constituency said that if President Moi wanted to end the violence, he could do it in one hour (*Daily Nation* 06/02/98).

On 6 February 15 members of the Kalenjin community killed in the Njoro and Mau Narok area were buried in a mass grave in Naishi. The funeral was attended by KANU MPs and cabinet ministers Kones and Ntimama, among NCCK for being biased. The latter announced that it would hold a memorial service on 19 February in remembrance of all people killed.

On 7 February new attacks left one Kalenjin soldier seriously wounded by unknown assailants and one former Kikuyu soldier dead at Mutitu as he fled from his attackers who had descended from Mutitu Hill. For the police these were 'ordinary' cattle rustlers/looters. Others injured at Mutitu were four Kikuyu. In Ndeffo, one house was burnt and more looted. Earlier that morning some 40 youths were arrested in the Likia area (*Daily Nation* 09/02/98). A new attack took place on Sunday night 8 February in the Chukuiyat area which left six Kikuyu wounded. Trouble also spread to Loriani centre, Burnt Forest areas, Uasin Gishu district. Sixteen families (2 Kalenjin and 14 Kikuyu) were left homeless after their houses were torched by ten young men.

On 8 February, the US special envoy for the promotion of democracy in Africa, the Rev. Jesse Jackson, arrived in the country as part of a three-nation African tour, including the Democratic Republic of Congo and Liberia. Upon his arrival he invited the president to accompany him to the violence-hit areas, but the president 'chose not to come' (*Daily Nation* 09/02/98). Upon his return from the Njoro area, the Rev. Jackson said it was up to President Moi to end the violence. Also, on 10 February, the American ambassador Bushnell expressed her government's concern over the ongoing clashes and pleaded to the government to restore peace and unity.

That same day a police inquiry was started into the cause of the tribal clashes in Njoro and Laikipia areas. Tension remained high in these areas with more people in Njoro fleeing from the Gachuni area. Some residents of Ng'arua division in Laikipia complained that more than 20 innocent people who had been involved in transporting families from the area to safer grounds had been arrested, detained and their cars confiscated. Also, two chiefs (Kalenjin and Kikuyu) from Barut and from the bordering Lare location, respectively, in Nakuru were arrested for inciting people to set ablaze houses belonging to the other community. In addition over 100 curfew breakers were arrested. Finally, hundreds of families were fleeing their homes for fear of attack in Uasin Gishu district. They said they had been warned to leave or perish following the death of a woman in unclear circumstances at Kiptingia trading centre (*Daily Nation* 11/02/98).

The following day, 11 February, President Moi toured the Njoro area. He gave the police firm instructions to arrest and prosecute warmongers and to facilitate the resettlement of the displaced families. By mid-February, some 1,200 people were still camping in the Larmudiac church compound and other centres in the Njoro area. In Laikipia, President Moi ordered a committee of genuine and impartial elders to reconcile members of the warring communities. The Central Province Development Support Group praised President Moi's visits and messages 'which clearly demonstrate his commitment to peace, harmony and security of all Kenyans' (*Daily Nation* 18/02/98). In contrast, the religious community held a one-and-a half-hour procession in Nairobi, blaming the government for failing to end the violence (*East African Standard* 12/02/98; *Daily Nation* 12/02/98).

In reaction, the churches accused the government of lack of moral legitimacy to lead, called for the suspension of the constitutional review process and asked the United States and Britain to exert pressure to effect change. The names of 272 victims of the clashes were read out, drawn from victims of the Likoni, Trans Mara, Gucha, Migori, Nyambene, Tharaka/Nithi and the more recent Laikipia and Njoro violence. The churches also announced donation days for the violence victims. In response, President Moi said that the churches were on a smear campaign against the government and warned them that a Philippines-like revolution would not succeed in Kenya (*Daily Nation* 16/02/98; 20/02/98; 21/02/98). The Nakuru chiefs were released on bail and a High Court application was sought to lift the Nakuru curfew.

In Njoro and the surrounding area tension remained high for a long time. People mistrusted and feared members of other ethnicity. From the beginning of January Kalenjin and Kikuyu travelling along the Njoro-Mau Narok road had to use separate *matatus*. As late as April 1998 attacks were carried out by raiders and people were hacked to death.[9] As in Laikipia, the loss of life and property was high. A report compiled by the Catholic diocese of Nakuru in February indicated that at least 2,000 families had been displaced, 250 houses and some 5,000 bags of maize destroyed and 1,500 animals were stolen in the Njoro area.[10]

The clashes kept the churches and NGOs searching for funds to assist the displaced. In Laikipia the Catholics, the Anglicans and the Presbyterians formed a co-ordinating committee to solicit for material support. Through the committee, food and medication for the displaced were distributed. At the same time, the Catholic church and the NCCK offered temporary shelter to the refugees while in Nakuru they provided temporary shelter for most of the victims from Mau Narok, Larmudiac, Likia and Njoro areas. The reconstruction of houses was also part of the assistance scheme. NGOs such as *Medicins sans frontierès* and the Kenya Red Cross, with assistance from the International Committee of the Red Cross, provided food, seed, tools, fertiliser, blankets, jerrycans and other utensils. Initially short-term relief was provided in February-March and more structural support by early June 1998. Over 9,000 people received assistance worth Ksh. 13.2 million (*Daily Nation* 08/06/98). The Red Cross was also involved in sanitation and water activities. It turned out that water development was especially instrumental in the reconciliation efforts in the Laikipia area.

When trying to explain post-election violence in Kenya one needs to answer specific questions such as 'Who started the violence? For what reason? Was it spontaneous or organised? Who were the group(s) targeted initially? Which roles were played by local residents, outsiders, politicians and the police? In the following section of this chapter we will look for answers to these questions from four main sources. First, (un)published statements by stakeholders such as the churches, politicians and human rights groups. Second, the hearings of the Akiwumi Commission as reported in the local print media. Third, archive material and other scientific publications on Kenya's Rift Valley and, fourth, personal observations and discussions with residents, human rights watchers, journalists, politicians and church representatives.

The fundamental discussion was whether the violence was ethnic, politically instigated or land-related. To understand the importance of the land factor let us turn to the land history of the Laikipia and Njoro parts of the Rift Valley.

History of land occupation and politics in Laikipia and Nakuru districts

At the end of the last century, Maasai pastoralists occupied an area of some 100,000-200,000 km^2 located at a latitude of between 1° north of the Equator to about 6° south. Both the Laikipia and Njoro areas were part of the northern Maasai territory.

In the previous two centuries the Maasai had descended from southern Sudan assimilating some of the Okiek, Sirikwa and Kalenjin groups (Newman 1995:172; Ochieng 1985:28). They found the Kalenjin and Kikuyu already settled in most of the western and eastern highlands of the Rift Valley, respectively. The Maasai broke through them, colonising the arid trough in between the western and eastern highlands. This action deprived the Kalenjin of their eastern grazing lands in the Rift and forced them to contract within the western highlands. The Kikuyu were stopped in their move out of the fertile highlands, at that time located east of the Aberdares, ranging from Ngong in the south to Nyeri in the north and the Rubingazi River in the east, towards the Kabete south-western frontier.

In the course of the nineteenth century, trouble started to build for the Maasai. Inter-sectional wars, known as *Iloikop* wars weakened the Maasai. In addition, severe droughts, rinderpest and smallpox killed huge numbers of cattle and many Maasai during the 1890s. The Maasai could no longer control their vast pastures because of the disparity in manpower between the Maasai and their neighbours. Kamba, Kikuyu and Kalenjin increasingly encroached on Maasai grazing areas (see Waller 1976:532).

This growing imbalance in military and political force would, however, soon be interfered with by the arrival of the British colonisers by the end of the nineteenth century. The colonial administration actively tried to interest settlers in Kenya by making large areas of land available and promoting a 'settler-friendly' land policy and legislation. In 1902, the First Crown Lands Ordinance proclaimed that all unoccupied land was crown land. In practice, this meant a denial of traditionally established African rights in land. A few large concessions in the Rift Valley were granted to some rich British aristocrats. Lord Delamere obtained 100,000 acres; Grogan and Lingham 120,000 acres of the Eldama Ravine forest and the East Africa Syndicate obtained a lease of 400 square miles of pasture land in the Naivasha area, the heart of the Maasai country.

It was decided by the colonial administration that the Maasai had to be 'given' an area of their own. Two reserves were planned outside the Rift Valley: the Laikipia Plateau (12,350 km²) in the north and another reserve south of Ngong and the railway (11,250 km²). A treaty was signed to this effect in 1904. The total area of the two new Maasai reserves was some 40 per cent of the original Maasai-controlled territory. Soon the settler community, aware of the superior potential of the Laikipia plateau for livestock keeping, showed an interest in the northern reserve and a second Maasai treaty that resulted in the removal of the northern Maasai to an extended reserve south of the railway was signed in April 1911. Also other groups, especially the Kikuyu living in Limuru and Kiambu, were pushed towards their own reserves. 'The loss of lands that had once belonged to the Kikuyu, but especially the drawing of boundary lines around the Kikuyu land unit, jeopardized the traditional processes of political and economic expansion' (Tignor 1976:29).

The Laikipia and Njoro[11] areas played major roles for the settler economy in livestock ranching, wheat farming, pyrethrum growing and woodlogging (Weight 1955:341-49). Roads and rail were constructed and swamps drained. The question of the alienation of the land, though, remained a key subject of interest. For example, the annual report of Laikipia district for 1928 states:

> the Samburu occupy provisionally as an addition to their reserve the Northern portion i.e. [the north of Laikipia] of what was originally Masai country. The feeling is that the Maasai were moved to an extended

Southern Reserve in order to make way for white settlement. The war [1914-18] intervened so that settlement was delayed for about six years. In this interval the Samburu were allowed into Laikipia, then empty of inhabitants, as a result it is understood, of rearrangements of the tribes in the Northern Frontier (KNA/DC/LKA/1/15 1928:1).

This northern portion, the well-grassed Leroghi plateau, was a dry-season grazing area for the Samburu. According to Chenevix Trench (1993: 92-3) the settlers claimed the plateau had been promised to them, and called it 'The Promised Land'. The Laikipia settlers were plagued by Samburu moran (warriors) stealing cattle. The moran's usual victims were Kikuyu labourers employed by Laikipia ranchers.

The highlands became a 'White man's Country' (Rutten 1992: 174). By 1928 some 605,000 acres were in the hands of 83 European farmers out of which only 5,666 acres were under cultivation in Laikipia (KNA/DC/LKA/1/15/1928:22). In the whole of Kenya there were some 2,000 European farmers cultivating some 593,000 acres out of 5 million acres reserved for white settlement. Some of the land was grazed but a considerable portion was put to no effective use (Tignor 1976: 25). Also in Laikipia, several unalienated surveyed farms amounting to some 200,000 acres existed by the late 1920s. A committee was set up to look into the problem. It recommended selling suitable farms by auction, while unsuited blocks should be disposed of by tender. The third class consisted of poor land with thin grazing and much bush to be leased on special terms. It also stated that the greater part of the Ndaragwa area was unsuited for small mixed farming although some thought that wheat could possibly grow there. 'They were however not prepared to accept the responsibility of approving it being disposed as small mixed farms, the success of which is problematical in the extreme' (KNA/DC/LKA/1/15/1928: 2-3). The area of land still available for European occupation was estimated to well over 2,000 square miles.

The Maasai, however, hoped to regain their lost pastures one day and protested before the Carter Land Commission. This body was set up in the early 1930s on request of a British parliamentary committee to look into African grievances. Among other issues the Maasai complained about the Mau Likia area. However, the commission claimed the land never belonged to the Maasai but was part of an area outside the reserve boundaries and in the hands of (i.e., leased by) a Mr Powys Cobb. In fact, at the time, all of the Njoro area was in the hands of Lord Delamere and to a lesser extent Powys Cobb (see KLC 1934: 526). Otherwise the commission recommended some exchanges between Europeans and Kikuyu with the Maasai such as on the southern extremity of the Eastern Mau Forest Reserve, Ndeiya and near the Marmanet River.

Claims by the Tugen (Kamasia) for land east of the Molo River were dismissed. '. . . the piece of country east of the Molo river and south of Lake Hannington [Elmenteita] was not permanently inhabited by any natives, but was definitively looked upon by the Maasai, as their country.' (KLC 1934: 253). The Tugen stayed in the hills and did not go down out of fear of the Maasai. They only came down when the Maasai did not need these plains. The commission was of the opinion that even if the Tugen had lost land west of the Molo River, they were compensated by additional land elsewhere. For economic reasons only the commission recommended that an area of 74 square miles, formerly used by Uasin Gishu Maasai, should be added to rest the 'over-stocked' Kamasia Reserve. It also recommended that some neighbouring alienated farms near the Esagiti River (23 sq. miles) should be leased by the government for this purpose (see KLC 1934:527). This way the Tugen got access to most of the area north of Rongai stretching from west of the Molo River towards the Mau Summit, all in today's Baringo district.

As for the Kikuyu, the commission stated that 'an addition of land was required in order to reduce the pressure of population on the land . . . we have therefore recommended a substantial addition of the Mwea area (132,000 acres) and another 21,000 acres to the Kikuyu Reserve mainly to be found in forested zones.' (KLC 1934:129).[12] By 1930 it was estimated that some 110,000 Kikuyu lived outside their Reserves, for the most part on European farms, while some 500,000 stayed inside the Kikuyu Reserve (KLC 1934: 144; 351). The district commissioner Laikipia wrote in 1935:

> of the native population of the district about 63% is resident (i.e. squatters) the remaining 27[sic] is temporary labour . . . another question is arising from the squatter's situation and that is the ultimate position of the numbers of squatter children . . . who are to all intents and purposes detribalised. They know no other homes beyond the farms where they were born. The Kikuyu on the farms appears to be a colonist not a squatter. . . . . The majority of the labour is Kikuyu but there is a sprinkling of Masai, Lumbwa, Turkana, Wandorobo and Kamasai. (KNA/DC/LKA/1/16/1935:12).

By 1945 it was estimated that 90 per cent of the squatters in Laikipia were Kikuyu (KNA/DC/LKA/1/16/1945:6). The need for land among African cultivating groups in the reserves had grown tremendously. In Kikuyuland, population densities had increased from 254 persons per sq.m. in 1902 to over 500 in 1944/45 (see Kohler 1987:36). There was a growing class of landless people. The African population looked for alternatives in neighbouring scheduled areas, as temporary labourers or squatters. Resettlement away from the reserves was discussed by the authorities, but no proposals were ever made as to where it should take place. The White Highlands were out of the question for African settlement in the mid-1940s although African political leaders had made it quite clear by then that the Africans needed more land, and that this land could only be got from the scheduled areas (Bogonko 1980: 35). In the words of the DC Nakuru: 'the future of the ever increasing numbers of detribalized Africans who have lost all connection with, and for whom there is no room in their reserves presents a problem incapable of solution save on a Colony-wide basis.' (KNA/DC/NKU/2/4/2-1948: 2). The same annual report noted that an 'association designated Maumau, emanating from the Kikuyu Reserve started branches at Naivasha and Ol'Kalou . . . This association is probably affiliated to the Kikuyu Central Association.' (KNA/DC/NKU/2/4/2-1948:4).

This eventually escalated towards an armed struggle between the so-called Mau Mau movement and the colonial government. In October 1952 a state of emergency was declared, which lasted officially till January 1960. Disunity among the settlers as to how to respond to African grievances allowed the British foreign office to press for reforms. Among the most important initiatives was the *Plan to Intensify the Development of African Agriculture in Kenya of 1954* (the Swynnerton Plan). This plan must mainly be seen as a reaction to the Mau Mau revolt and the problem of land in the densely populated Central Province. Within Kikuyu society

> the strongest supporters [of land consolidation] were not unnaturally the larger landowners, particularly those who had come out on top in the litigation before the Emergency. They saw in consolidation a means of obtaining a final validation of their titles. . . The bitterest opponents of consolidation were landless . . . consolidation and registration confirmed their landlessness. Government had hoped that consolidation and improved farming would provide these people with regular employment but as this failed to materialize they had to be moved out of the Kikuyu country as quickly as possible. (Sorrenson 1967 : 243-50).

By early 1957 the few remaining Mau Mau fighters in the Nakuru area were either eliminated or thought to have left the district. Ex-detainees were released and returned to Londiani, Mau Summit, Mau Narok and the Bahati forest (see KNA/DC/NKU/2/1/2- April 1957). Many Kikuyu families were engaged locally by the forest department following their discharge from saw mills in the Elburgon and Molo areas. And in 1960 even more large numbers of Kikuyu moved to Nakuru and Laikipia following the lifting of the emergency restrictions. Unemployment rose by leaps and bounds owing to economic stagnation, especially in the building (including timber) industry. For example,

> Amalgated Sawmills alone signed off some 600 employees from their stations at Mariashoni, Nessuit and Maji Mazuri, but most of these were absorbed by the Forest Department. Several new Forest villages were started. . . . Many European farmers took time to recover from the shock

of the Lancaster House proposals, and morale was further weakened by the events in the Congo. . . . Animosity between the Kikuyu and the Kalenjin tribes increased as the year wore on. As the General Election approached political loyalty became more and more synonymous with tribal loyalty. The main lines-ups were the Kikuyu/Luo for K.A.N.U. and the Kalenjin/Abaluhya for K.A.D.U. (KNA/DC/NKU/2/4/2-1960: 1-2, 8).

These developments made J. Howard, DC Nakuru at the time, state that 'The growth of political intimidation is the curse of Africa, including Kenya' (KNA/DC/NKU/2/4/2-1960:11).

It was not until the last years of colonial rule that the government finally took steps towards African settlement in the European areas. In 1960, the British government passed an Order in Council ending the original reservation of the 'White Highlands' for farming by Europeans only. A report published in 1960 that looked into land available for settlement mentioned among others Ol Arabel in Laikipia and the good 'underused' land in the Mau of Narok district. This is between Olenguruone in the west and the Mau Narok European farms in the east. It stated that the plans for the settlement of Africans on farms purchased in the highlands would provide a useful outlet for people from the more densely populated districts (see CPK 1960).

That same year Kipsigis and Ndorobo people in the area complained about the lack of land holdings to which they could retire in their old age. Outside the Central Province, land enclosure programmes were started as early as the 1930s in the Kipsigis and other Kalenjin areas on a voluntary basis. None of these groups, however, evinced the same desire as the Kikuyu for titles; indeed with the Kipsigis it was not until 1960 that government persuaded them to register titles at all (Sorrenson 1967:252).

Land transfer schemes, based on 'willing buyer-willing seller' basis, were constructed to promote the gradual purchase of land by Africans. The most important and best known of these was the Million-Acre Settlement Scheme (see e.g., Leo1984:70). This settlement programme benefited Africans of all classes, although in later years larger and more fertile tracts were accumulated by rich, prominent, successful Kenyans. One of the less successful endeavours in aiding the unemployed landless of Nakuru was a scheme for the Kikuyu to emigrate to the Mpanda Settlement Scheme in Tanganyika. KANU set up a political boycott (for fear of losing voters) and was particularly successful but 410 families defied the boycott and went. That same year a relocation of Tugen people in the Sabatia Settlement of the district was carried out and a five-year purchase plan whereby European farms would be purchased for settlement was announced (KNA/DC/NKU/2/4/2-1962).

By the early 1960s relations between the Kikuyu and the Kalenjin/Maasai grew more tense. The Kikuyu 'Land Freedom Army' was revived in 1961. It had little support in Kikuyuland but it won a great deal of support in the Rift Valley and other European farming districts (see Sorrenson 1967: 250). Political activity increased. The authorities feared trouble especially in the border areas such as in the Eldama Ravine area where many Tugen, mostly KADU supporters, came over daily from the Baringo reserve to work while the residents of the township mostly supported KANU (KNA/DC/NKU/2/3-HOR 1962). But also inside Nakuru district a fear of fights was noticed. District officers at Molo and Njoro received large numbers of applications from farmers for native arms permits for their employees, all Kalenjin. This request was made after the return of Jomo Kenyatta to Gatundu from prison in August 1961.

And when in the Mau Narok area negotiations for the sub-division and sale of land to Kikuyu were underway, the Maasai indicated growing discontent, feeling that should this area be vacated by the Europeans it should revert to the Maasai (KNA/DC/NKU/2/1/2 - Sep. 1961).[13] Finally, in August 1962 the Regional and Constituencies Boundaries' Commission arrived in Nakuru. The commission spoke to several interest groups, including political parties. The KADU Laikipia branch stated that the Ndorobo, Samburu and Maasai wanted to be in the Rift valley region with the Kalenjin. 'They can never live together with the Kikuyu who came to Laikipia and Nanyuki merely as workers on the farms.' The KANU-Laikipia branch wanted the regional boundaries to follow the existing provincial boundaries to 'prevent tribal clashes in the future'. The KADU Nakuru branch stated that the Nakuru, Laikipia and Naivasha districts should be part of the Rift Valley region together with the Maasai, the Samburu, the Uasin Gishu and the Kalenjin districts. The branch predicted that otherwise 'there will be another Congo in Kenya' (RBC 1962). This line of thinking was also expressed by the Rift Valley Kalenjin Political Alliance of Daniel arap Moi. 'The Kalenjin do not want anything to do with the Kikuyu who take oaths at night.' Indeed, by September 1962 reports of oath-taking and gun-making by members of the Kikuyu community caused a lot of tension and anger among other Africans, especially the Kalenjin. 'Tribal tension is such that you only need to strike a match and anything at all can start.' (see KNA/DC/NKU/2/1/2-Sep 1962).

The KANU-Nakuru branch stated that the existing boundaries should not be altered one inch. KANU argued that since the ultimate goal of independence was to unite all tribes in Kenya, there was no need to redraw the boundaries along ethnic lines. The European farmers of the Njoro Settlers Association said that the Njoro mixed farming area should be in the region centred on Nakuru. Areas such as Kinangop, Kipipiri and Ol Kalou, apparently earmarked for future Kikuyu settlement, should be excluded from the Rift Valley region, and be included in whatever region is predominantly Kikuyu.

In its report the commission referred to the many delegations wishing to be united with groups of similar customs and habits. It also stated that before the British handed over to an independent Kenya, they should put their house in order and redraw the boundaries in a manner more closely corresponding to the position as it was when they first came to the country. It decided to include in the central region areas of land capable of being made available for settlement schemes. As a result, Nanyuki district was split, whereby the western and eastern high potential areas were added to Central and Eastern provinces respectively and the northern ranching areas to the Rift Valley Province.

In the opinion of the district administration, the report of the commission was accepted by the majority of the Nakuru inhabitants as fair and just.

> However, in Molo, Londiani and Njoro areas most of the Kikuyu did not like the report because they feared they might be thrown out from these areas by the Kalenjin. They talk of destroying these boundaries at a later date. The Luo living in these areas shared the Kikuyu views to a large extent. The Kalenjin were quiet but happy about the Rift Valley boundaries.
> . . To the European farming community in the District it may well have resulted in a return of confidence in the future (KNA/DC/NKU/2/1/2 Dec. 1962).

Still, a section of the European community decided that the time had come to go, but the actual exodus was limited to some 12 per cent of the Europeans in the Nakuru region (KNA/DC/NKU/2/4/2-1962). Others waited till they could get an acceptable price for their farms. In the last year before independence the Nakuru area witnessed many groups settling illegally, especially Kalenjin, as less than 10 per cent of the applications for land could be awarded on official settlement schemes.[14] Other well-organised groups made joint efforts and applied for loans to take over the farms from leaving Europeans. This way, Kalenjin squatters bought the 1,000 acre Sach-Ang'wan farm near Mau Summit by 1965. In the early 1970s it was sub-divided into 10-acre plots. Another such farm up for sale was Gicheha which, however, ended up in the hands of Jomo Kenyatta. So did Tangi Sita, opposite Gicheha, which was taken by Margaret Kenyatta. Other high-ranking officials followed suit including a permanent secretary who acquired Mukinyai farm. The rocky other half of the ranch was bought by a group of Kikuyu from Central Province (Sang 1997). The concentration of land in the hands of wealthy elements in Kikuyu society did not restrict itself to Central Province only. Even in the migration zones the powerful battled the poor. Ex-freedom fighters such as the Njoro-based Ndeffo (Nakuru District Ex-Freedom Fighters Organisation) also settled in the area.

In Laikipia, animosity developed between the Kalenjin and Kikuyu. 'This tribal feeling arose through fear, but was undoubtedly fanned and encouraged by the example of certain leading national members of K.A.N.U. and K.A.D.U.' (KNA/DC/LKA/1/11/8-1961: 2). Indeed, feelings of mistrust were exacerbated during the elections of 1961. It is interesting to recall the then DC Laikipia's words in view of the 1997 post-election violence:

> The prime motive was fear on the part of the Kalenjin minority in the district of the prospect of domination by the Kikuyu and Luo. In reaction to distorted messages about the disturbances in Nakuru in January, the local branches of K.A.N.U. and K.A.D.U. took steps to arm groups of supporters for defence against each other. The situation was quickly restored to normal on the intervention of the District Commissioner. In Rumuruti, however, the local K.A.D.U. Chairman went too far, and was arrested and convicted for setting out for Nakuru in a vehicle full of bows and arrows and other arms. On the 1st October a large number of K.A.D.U. Youth Wing members turned up at a K.A.D.U. sponsored political meeting in Thomson's Falls carrying an assorted collection of arms, apparently as a precautionary measure, in view of well founded rumours that the K.A.N.U. Youth Wing intended to break up the meeting. All were disarmed by the Police. At the meeting Mr. Towett strongly advocated Regional Autonomy as insurance against Kikuyu/Luo domination (KNA/DC/LKA/1/11/8-1961:7).

In Laikipia the first of the government-initiated settlement programmes was not carried out until 1967/69 (Kohler 1987: 30).[15] Under these public schemes, only 277 km² of land or 3 per cent of the district was transferred to small-scale settlers by 1980. These settlements are located in the wetter western section of the district, adjoining the forest reserves around Nyahururu and extending toward Ol Arabel/Ndindika. Other schemes such as Shirika schemes in Ndindika and Kalalu and a Haraka scheme in Marmanet were created in 1978 (Kohler 1987:30).[16]

Thus, by the early 1980s large-scale ranching still covered over half of Laikipia district and rested in the hands of non-Africans, mostly British and non-African Kenyans (see Kohler 1987:28). Other large-scale ranching such as the ADC Mutara Boran Breeding Station and the LMD livestock holding ground in the north bordering Samburu area was under state or parastatal ownership. But since the 1980s these areas have not been used for vaccination or fattening purposes, they are used by squatters and neighbouring pastoralists for grazing their livestock.

This leaves us with the small-scale settlements created by private initiative and self-help (*harambee*). Self-help groups of varying sizes, whether companies or co-operatives, were formed by people in need of land in order to pool enough money to buy the large European-owned farms. The 'patrons', such as Kihika Kimani and G.G. Kariuki, were often influential businessmen or politicians. Shares were issued to the group members. Land purchase loans were also involved. Sottas (1992:260) describes the way these groups operate and the crucial roles played by the leaders. In the words of Kohler (1987: 39): 'These people had to think about getting votes, and settling land-hungry citizens was a safe method of getting them.' By so doing, the leaders often safeguarded their long-lasting political interests besides direct financial gains. Sottas also points at the misbehaviour of certain land-buying groups by way of, for example, issuing more shares than land available (e.g., the Ngwataniro Company). Other bogus, land-buying groups only collected the money and never bothered to buy land.

In Laikipia 44 self-help groups were known to have purchased land in the district by 1981 (Kohler 1987:33). Most of these bought land in the late 1960s on a small scale, especially east of Salama, east of Ng'arua, and north and south-west of Nanyuki. Larger areas were acquired in the 1970s when settlement shifted to the drier regions of Laikipia district such as south and north of the Mutara ranch, west and east of Rumuruti, north of Sipili and north of Timau. By the 1980s buying land slowed down. '. . . obviously the reservoir of non-African land owners willing to sell has been exhausted, and it seems at present as if potent and influential land-buying personalities or pressure groups capable of rallying the political support needed to effectuate land transactions do not exist' (Kohler 1987:33).

The strain on natural resources, especially water, has increased and some argue that rainfed agriculture is not suited to these dry zones better equipped for extensive livestock keeping. Also cattle rustling-related insecurity is a problem for the immigrant mixed farmers. For example, in the 1990-97 period Samburu and Kalenjin attackers killed 21 people, mainly Kikuyu, in the Magadi, Kahuho, Survey and Merigwit areas. Some 300 people were injured, 8 women raped and 400 cattle and 2,300 goats stolen (CPK/PCEA/CC 1998). Though initially spears and bow-and-arrows were the main weapons, guns became more common in later years.

In spite of these natural and man-made insecurities, the immigrants were determined to stay on and continued to settle in Laikipia. The need for land to make a livelihood, a home and finally to secure the children's future is a driving force to this end. Sottas (1992: 224) also refers to the Kikuyu tradition whereby the new 'house' will become the new 'home' for the next generation.

In retrospect, migration towards the Rift Valley was noticed for the intercensal period of 1948-62.[17] In Laikipia, the number of agricultural employees increased more than 50 per cent between 1954 and 1961. Indeed, by 1962 almost two out of three inhabitants were born outside the district (RoK 1966: 41-76). A majority of the Kikuyu migrants to Laikipia were born in Nyeri district. Turkana, Kalenjin and Samburu immigrants were small minorities.

Population totals for Laikipia district were estimated to be 41,574 and 68,643 people for 1948 and 1962 respectively (RoK 1966). Densities were low. Laikipia population densities increased from 13 to 24 persons/km² for 1979-89. Especially the central (12 to 23) and western (18 to 28) parts of the district showed huge increases. The eastern area (Mugokondo) had a stable population density for the period (9 to 10). By contrast, Nyeri and Baringo population densities for this period increased from 148 to 186 and from 20 to 32, respectively.

Population estimates for Nakuru in 1948 and 1962 were 90,301 and 185,241 respectively (KNA/DC/NKU/2/4/2-1962). This meant population densities of 12 and 25 persons per km², respectively. A 1960 estimate put the percentage of Kikuyu, Embu or Meru (KEM) at 53. For Njoro it was 61 per cent. Mau Narok scored 65 per cent. Other so-called KEM-dominated areas were Elburgon (75), Eldama Ravine (66), Londiani (61), Dundori (57), Subukia (55), Solai (54) and Nakuru town (50). In Molo (42), Elmenteita (34), Rongai (33) Kampi-ya Moto (27) and Olenguruone (2) they formed a minority (KNA/DC/NKU/2/4/2-1962). By 1989 the Nakuru district share of KEM stood at 60 per cent. Population density increased from 40 in 1969 to 118 by 1989. For the Njoro division the overall density in 1989 was estimated at 148, ranging from 86 (Mau Narok) to 234 (Lare location) (see RoK 1994). Most Kikuyu immigrants came from the Murang'a and Kiambu areas.

Table 20.1: Ethnic composition of Laikipia district 1969-99

	Kikuyu	Maasai/ Ndorobo	Turkana	Kalenjin	(Kenyan) Europeans	Others	Total Pop	Land (km²)	Density (p/km²)
1969	38,223	8,440	4,277	7,406	431	7,729	66,506	9,723	7
1979	86,603	10,116	9,568	11,795	272	16,173	134,527	9,718	13
1989	146,607	11,821	14,396	15,690	211	30,232	218,957	9,162	24
1999 (pr)	290,000	15,000	26,000	23,000	150	60,000	414,000	9,162	45

Source: Kenya Population Census 1969, 1979, 1989; author's 1999 projection based on 69-89 average growth rates. Boundaries of Laikipia district were adjusted in 1962. A portion on the western side was transferred to Baringo district while in the east part of Nanyuki was added. This might, among other reasons, explain the apparent reduction in population size from 1962 to 1969.

Table 20.2: Ethnic composition of Nakuru district 1969-99

	Kikuyu	Maasai/ Ndorobo	Kalenjin	Luhya	Luo	(Kenyan) European	Others	Total	Land (km²)	Density (p/km²)
1969	169,363	14,528	37,354	24,154	20,606	2,102	22,746	290,853	7,291	40
1979	317,855	8,519	81,651	36,142	36,217	1,438	40,887	522,709	7,200*	73*
1989	506,499	16,650	127,163	63,020	61,660	1,043	73,061	849,096	7,190	118
1999(pr)	875,000	25,000	235,000	100,000	105,000	500	124,500	1,465,000	7,190	204

Source: Kenya Population Census 1969, 1979, 1989; Statistical Abstract 1982; authors' 1999 projection based on 69-89 average growth rates. The 1999 projection does not take into account the Molo and Njoro clashes and the Kalenjin settlement schemes of the 1990s.* The Nakuru land area used in the 1979 population census is 5,769 km² resulting in a 90 persons per square kilometre density. Most likely this is due to leaving out the gazetted forested areas in the Molo south and Mau Summit zone estimated to be some 1,523 km².

Table 20.3: Average annual growth rate of Laikipia and Nakuru districts 1969-89 (per cent)

	Laikipia Kikuyu	Laikipia Kalenjin	Laikipia Others	Laikipia Total	Nakuru Kikuyu	Nakuru Kalenjin	Nakuru Others	Nakuru Total
1962-1969				1.2*				6.7
1969-1979	8.5	4.7	5.9	7.4	6.5	8.1	3.9	6.0
1979-1989	5.4	2.9	4.6	5.0	4.8	4.5	5.7	5.0

Source: Kenya Population Census 1969, 1979, 1989; Ominde 1984; author's calculations.
*Estimate by Ominde.

Table 20.3 shows that in both Laikipia and Nakuru the average annual growth rate slowed down in the 1980s, from 7.4 and 6.0 to 5.0 per cent. The figures for the Kalenjin group seem to underline the claim that in the 1980s ordinary Kalenjin in the two districts did not profit from the 1978 change of presidency. Others, however, point at the influence of the Kalenjin-dominated government in the settlement of Kipsigis in the Salama (Lorien farm) region of Laikipia district (Sottas 1992: 228, 264). Sottas also claims that the groups of Turkana, Mukogodo Maasai, and Pokot pastoralists did not get access to land as easily as the Kipsigis mixed farmers. The former at best remained squatters on the farms not yet settled. However, in recent years government-owned land (e.g. research stations, livestock holding grounds) and gazetted forests has been transferred to these groups. For example, in the Ol-Moran area of Laikipia the Maundu ni Meri farm is utilised by the Tugen community from Kaptito and Mochongoi:

> With the coming of new multiparty era these privately-owned areas together with Lonyiek (whose ownership passed from ADC to the Pokot community) have started to be more and more inhabited by the pastoralists namely Samburu, Masai, Pokots and Tugens. Their attitude becoming more and more overbearing on the original settlers with unjustified grazing in the cultivated areas, carelessness and destruction of water infrastructures put up by the settlers and especially with increasing of cattle theft and level of violence (CPK/PCEA/CC 1998:1).

In Nakuru district, Bishop Ndingi Mwana a' Nzeki noted in April 1996 that 'strange people' had been taken to Teret, Likia and Sururu forests on 9 March of that year and a helicopter was seen landing there. The bishop also wanted to know why access roads in the area bordering Lusiru (Ndeffo farm and Mauche Settlement at Likia) were closed, why an explosion took place on 5 April 1996 in Likia and Teret forests and a local councillor visited Teret area at night (see *Clashes Update* 30/04/96). The non-Kalenjin residents in these areas confirmed the bishop's statements and questioned the role played by Kipkalia Kones, the minister in the Office of the President, in settling the Kipsigis immigrants.

Another land conflict worth mentioning is that, as early as November 1995, members of the Ndorobo community of Mau forest questioned, in a memo to parliament, the circumstances under which part of the forest in which they live near Sururu, Likia, Teret and Sigotik areas, was being treated as though it had been de-gazetted and converted into agricultural land and allocated to people from other districts, i.e., Bomet and Kericho. The government in conjunction with the British ODA had been resettling the 'Ndorobo' since 1996. In addition, the Ndorobo community would like to have part of Mau forest set aside for their special use arguing that at no time have they endangered the trees as is happening in the Mauche Settlement Scheme in Sururu forest, which had started in 1993 (see *Clashes Update* 30/11/96).

People who settled in the Marishiani area of Nakuru district were referred to by the locals as aliens from the neighbouring districts masquerading as members of teh Ndorobo community. 'Those being resettled are not genuine Dorobos but senior government officials and families drawn from Kericho and Bomet districts.' (*Clashes Update* 30/11/96:2). This also caused problems. In protest the genuine Ndorobo set on fire five houses belonging to Maasai. The leaders of the genuine Ndorobo were arrested and jailed. By June 1997 the High Court allowed the genuine Ndorobo living in East Mau Forest to block the provincial administration's attempt to evict them from their ancestral land.

In March 1997, Molo MP Njenga Mungai (FORD-Asili), applied to the Kenyan government to settle the Olenguruone 1992 clash victims. President Moi suggested Likia and Mau Summit. 'The President's suggestion confirmed the fear that the number of displaced people has increased due to the escalating cases of illegal land transfer, secret demarcations and change of boundaries. It also confirms another fear from the increasing zoning off of areas for specific communities.' (*The Update* 31/08/97:12). From the foregoing discussion it is clear enough that politics and land, especially in the Njoro area, were closely linked during the period leading up to the 1997 elections.

Searching for explanations of the 1997 post-election violence

During and shortly after the clashes in Njoro and Laikipia, stories appeared in the press trying to explain clashes which erupted in the Rift Valley. Next to political rhetoric, some journalists either by conducting investigative journalism or by way of deductive reasoning tried to explain what sparked the violence. For example, the *Economic Review* (02-08/02/98: 6-10) concluded that:

> The outbreak of violence in Njoro and Laikipia areas of the Rift Valley followed very much the pattern witnessed from 1991. Well organised gangs of raiders attacked homesteads and market centres in broad daylight killing looting, burning and leaving destruction in their wake. They appear confident, probably with foreknowledge that security forces called in will either arrive long after they have left, or merely look on helplessly firing impotently into the air... It appeared as if the Kalenjin community was psyched to defend the presidency by resorting to violence. Thus it might not be wrong to conclude that after the Kikuyu, both in Central Province and the diaspora, again decisively rejected Moi and KANU, some in the establishment might have felt it was time for reprisals. . . One should keep in mind that even after peace was restored following the earlier clashes thousands of displaced particularly from Molo, Burnt Forest and Enosupukia areas, were never given the opportunity to go back and thus the objective of ethnic cleansing was achieved.

Likewise *The Star* journalist Kamau Ngotho, in an article 'Why political killings are taking place in Laikipia', explained the genesis of the political killings as follows: 'One, a criminal programme of political zoning pursued by a hawkish faction of Kanu and two, failure to resolve, in fact make political capital out of the problem of pastoralism and insecurity in northern Rift Valley.' (*The Star* 23-26/01/98). Ngotho points at two rival sections within KANU, one led by G.G Kariuki and the other by a Mr Barno arap Some, a young Kalenjin backed by anti-Kariuki political rivals such as the commissioner of Lands, Wilson Gachanja, and Nicholas Biwott. He claims that the day the election results were announced – concluding that the Kariuki faction failed to deliver the Laikipia West seat – the Some faction started the build-up of the forcible eviction of Kikuyu people in Laikipia (see *The Star* 23-26/01/98:20).

According to the same author, the Some faction had earlier lobbied to have the constituency boundaries in Laikipia reviewed in order to have an ethnically-configurated Laikipia North and Liakipia South. This set-up would mostly favour the non-Kikuyu inhabitants living in the northern zone of the district. To increase these numbers, it is alleged, the group, assisted by Laikipia district commissioner Mohammed Saleh, was instrumental in allowing large numbers of Pokot and Samburu pastoralists to graze in the government-owned Lonyiek and TND Mugie ranches, respectively. The Kariuki faction proposed a third (Rumuruti) constituency. The ECK, however, decided to ignore both proposals.

A *Daily Nation* journalist, Ken Opala, toured the Njoro area in February 1998 and expressed, in a series of articles, his doubts about 'land differences as the source of the conflict' (*Daily Nation* 12/02/98). However, the argument that 'Kikuyus settled in the area in 1974 while the majority of the Kalenjins started flocking there seven years ago where they occupied the forested highlands' as evidence for dismissing the 'land' factor, is not satisfactorily. In the light of the historical overview showing the strong links between land and politics it is questionable, to say the least. Opala stresses politics as the only cause of the violence: 'There is no doubt the violence was instigated. The plot was hatched in Nairobi and Nakuru months before the actual mayhem, long before the general election. The violence seems to be the fall-out of a shrewd attempt by prominent Kalenjin politicians to patch up their stratified community before the polls.' (*Daily Nation* 12/02/98). However, Opala provides no proof to support his claim. In fact, in an interview with a Kalenjin and Kikuyu elder, he was told that besides multi-party politics, 'the creation of many farms' was considered to be a cause for the violence. The Kalenjin elder claimed that thugs had been brought from elsewhere – without elaborating which group of thugs and the location they came from – whereas the Kikuyu elder stated that since the raiders came from the forested highlands, they must have been Kalenjin as these were settled in the forests. 'It was a plan hatched outside the area. . . . This is not an ethnic conflict; it is politics' (see *Daily Nation* 14/02/98). Opala also points at the late arrival of police reinforcements after the raiders had almost left. 'Most times police just watched as raiders torched houses and assaulted the helpless. The security and administration personnel were plainly partisan in their operations' (*Daily Nation* 13/02/98). Opala blamed opposition politicians and clerics for being biased against the Kalenjin community, stating they wrongly blamed the community for the mayhem and as a result did not take care of the Kalenjin victims as (much as) the Kikuyu ones.

On 30 June 1998, President Moi announced that the government would set up a Judicial Commission of Inquiry to probe the ethnic violence which started in 1991. The Akiwumi Commission, named after its chairman Justice Akilano Molade Akiwumi, opened on 20 July 1998 and held 194 hearing sessions over a period of 11 months. It wound up on 11 June 1999. Unfortunately so far, the commission has not made its findings available to a wider audience. In this the commission follows in the footsteps of many other official government appointed bodies which were set up to look into similar problems.

However, in retrospect and with the full hearings published in Kenya's dailies providing information discussed before the Akiwumi Commission, we are now able to conduct a more in-depth exercise in the post-election violence of 1998 thereby directing more specific questions such as: Who were the likely instigators? Is there hard proof that politicians were involved? Was the outbreak of the violence the work of outsiders? What happened in the run-up to the first attack? Was the initial attack well-organised or an accident that got out of hand? Which people conducted the violence? How did police and security forces behave? Was there organised retaliation? Can the violence be attributed to multi-party politics only or to other, fundamental, causes as well?

Laikipia

Political developments in Laikipia before the 1997 elections revolved around G.G. Kariuki's efforts to win the Laikipia West seat for KANU. Having been one of the most important Kikuyu politicians in KANU since the 1960s, Kariuki believed he had the best chance to win the Kikuyu vote in the constituency although he had failed against DP's Kihika Kimani in 1992. In 1997 his score almost doubled, but Kariuki failed again; this time beaten by Francis Chege Mbitiru, the Laikipia DP branch youth affairs co-ordinator and a farm inputs wholesaler in Nairobi. He made a name for being in the forefront of pro-reform rallies (see *The Star* 23-26/01/98:20).

The circulation of letters warning against the Kikuyu community in Kinamba trading centre, shortly before the elections, 'to take tea in Nyahururu if they failed to vote for Kanu and President Moi' (*The Update* 31/01/98) may have been the fore runner for a planned attack on the Kikuyu community. Other non-Kalenjins stated that before the fighting started they had received a letter warning them to leave Ol-Moran or have their heads chopped off. This suggests that the problem had moved from cattle rustling to land ownership disputes (*Daily Nation* 06/02/99).[18] Also, questions were raised why the raiders were earmarked by government officials as ordinary cattle raiders whereas they attacked schools and bars (*Daily Nation* 26/01/98). A total of six teachers were killed in Laikipia and all but three primary schools in the area had been closed by this time. In an interview with *The Update* (31/01/98) G.G. Karuiki stated that 'although he was not aware of any political motive behind the clashes, he could not rule out that the Kikuyus were being punished for voting against President Moi and Kanu.'

Before the Akiwumi Commission, Father Sandro stated that, in his opinion, ethnic cleansing in Laikipia was orchestrated to create political power bases in preparation for the Moi succession. The shedding of blood was intended to make the affected communities take a definite position in support of certain politicians. According to him there was an intention to create a third constituency in Laikipia to encompass areas such as Doldol, Lonyiek and Rumuruti, which have pockets of pastoralist communities supporting KANU (*Daily Nation* 09/02/99). He blamed the administration for inactivity and non-co-operation with the church never experienced before. In particular the

DO, Jonathan Soi, and the late Jeremiah Ndahi, the OCS Ng'arua station, were mentioned as failing to protect the people.[19] A Kikuyu village elder, Robert Kamau, told the commission that the Ol-Moran clashes escalated because there were very few policemen on the ground to control the situation. He also claimed that the policemen who were later dispatched to the area did not pursue the raiders (*Daily Nation* 05/02/99). For many this was a sign of a cover up.

Before the Akiwumi Commission, senior superintendent Mutinda Ngunguni stated he received reports from OCS Ndahi on livestock killed by Kikuyu youths, the killing of two Kikuyu elderly people and the burning of Kikuyu houses. However, he claimed that he did not receive any report about Kikuyu making preparations for revenge. He said neither the DO nor the OCS informed him that they had seen Kikuyu youngsters singing war songs on their way from Sipili to Ol-Moran and neither spoke of having seen Kikuyu women preparing large quantities of food for the youths who had gone to attack the Samburu. Ngunguni told the commission that the Laikipia DC did not call any district security committee (DSC) meeting to discuss the causes of the incidents which had led to the violence. He denied being negligent and told the commission that he had called the then Rift Valley provincial police officer, Philip Cheruiyot, and asked for reinforcements (*Daily Nation* 18/02/99). He further stated that police were overwhelmed (*East African Standard* 17/02/99).

Former DO Jonathan Soi, in his evidence before the Akiwumi Commission, said he had received information from the Ol-Moran chief, Wilson Lemoi Lule, and some local elders that Ol-Moran aspirant councillor Francis Ndung'u (defeated in the KANU primaries and on election day once more on an SDP ticket by his KANU rival David Gichiga) had for political reasons incited Kikuyu youths to slash the goats belonging to Loshau. Ndung'u was named as one of three people who organised transport for the Kikuyu youngsters to the 'valley of death'. Soi also quoted the illegal occupation of Kikuyu-owned land by Samburu and Pokot pastoralists as the main cause of the 1998 clashes at Ol-Moran in Laikipia district. The DO claimed that the Kikuyu were bitter over the loss of their livestock and illegal grazing by the pastoralists communities yet Mutukanio farm, where the Samburu and Pokot herdsmen were grazing their livestock, belonged to the Kikuyu and was bought through a land-buying company. The witness said that only a small number of Samburu had bought land from Kikuyu in the area. The rest were living on Mutukanio farm illegally. These resource-related problems and the political scheme are said to be the underlying causes of the clashes.

The cattle rustling only started the fighting according to Father Sandro (*Daily Nation* 09/02/99). The fact that the Turkana, Samburu and Pokot teamed up to revenge the attack on a Pokot family was questioned by Father Sandro. He also pointed at the lack of a clear land policy in Ol-Moran which was causing trouble between the communities. For example, the Mutukanio farm shareholders had no title deeds yet and as a result others, i.e., pastoral communities, were using the land. In addition, the communities clashed over water. The clashes in Ol-Moran ended only after the IMF, the church and the press pressurised the government to stop the violence (*Daily Nation* 11/02/99). Altogether this took more than two weeks.

Isaac Naitiri Muthuri, the deputy acting commissioner of police, who investigated the clashes in Laikipia also mentioned cattle rustling as the initial cause of the fight. Before the Akiwumi Commission, he narrated how the attack and theft of Esther Njeri's goats triggered off the clashes.[20] The revenge attack by the Kikuyu killing the animals belonging to a Pokot from Nagum village in Ol-Moran location, Lochau Apalunginya, made the Pokot and other pastoral communities very bitter.[21] In return, the Pokot and Samburu killed two elderly Kikuyu and set houses on fire. According to Muthuri, supporting Father Sandro's view, the local police and administration did not act promptly. No reinforcements were called. When on 16 January the OCS and DO witnessed the Kikuyu youths travelling from Sipili to Ol-Moran they warned the youths to go back.[22] According to Muthuri the massacre was only reported three days after it had happened. The crucial question regarding police operations in the district in this respect is whether the lack of action was deliberate, out of sheer neglect, fear, or lack of manpower.

The KANU T-shirts the attackers wore is said to be proof that these people had been given instructions by the party hierachy to hit at the Kikuyu community. According to some victims, the raiders were transported to the villages by lorries that did not have number plates (*The Update* 31/01/98). An Amnesty International report (1998: 7) also argues that the Pokot attack was well-planned and differed from 'normal' cattle raids in that a woman was raped and guns used. Finally, according to a *Daily Nation* (06/05/98) report Simon Kanyaman, a Pokot elder, told a reconciliation meeting that some of the raiders were from outside the area although many were his tribesmen (*Daily Nation* 27/07/98).

Still, in our view the claim that the attack in Laikipia was well planned and organised a long-time before does not necessarily hold. First, as a result of the initial attack Pokot raiders took goats and raped two women. The eight cases of rape that were registered in Laikipia West from 1990 to the beginning of 1998 (CPK/PCEA/CC 1998) negate the claim that raping is not common in cattle raids. Likewise, because almost all the deaths in Laikipia were from bullet wounds, Amnesty International (1998:7) believes that outsiders were involved. 'Normal' raiders would not have used guns. However, it is known that the pastoral communities do possess AK-47 rifles and, over the 1996-97 period, the use of guns in raid incidents was registered (see CPK/PCEA/CC 1998:1). According to Kikuyu clash-victims, the guns were mainly used to scare people although in some cases they were also used to kill (see *The Star* 23-26/01/98). The bloody massacre on 17 January 1998, killing 36 people (all Kikuyu), was the result of a revenge attack by a large group of Kikuyu ambushed by the raiders in the Rum Rum valley near Survey township. According to one eyewitness, the Kikuyu went to the Pokot and Samburu manyatta perched on the hills determined to get even. 'The Pokots and Samburus then went into the bush and came out with guns. After that it was every man for himself.' (see *Daily Nation* 01/02/98). This narrative does not suggest that Kikuyu lives were lost as a result of an organised attack by the Pokot and Samburu groups.

It is relatively easy to hire terror groups in the Laikipia area, especially in the northern provinces where cattle rustling is very common. Some of these gangs, as claimed by Mwai Kibaki, are for hire and are linked to certain government officials (*The Update* 16/08/97).[23] The normal scenario is that stolen livestock is sold to Uganda at high prices. Not only do the small-scale Kikuyu farmers suffer from these gangs, but the Turkana, Samburu and Marakwet pastoralists as well. Hiring a few 'professionals' to team up with local groups seems to be an option easily put into practice. This could explain the statement by the Pokot elder that it was mainly his Pokot, assisted by a few outsiders, who attacked the Kikuyu.

As for the police laxity, the Akiwumi Commission found that police in the area were both understaffed and poorly equipped, i.e., lacking vehicles and weapons. Also it is known that police stations such as Rumuruti and Ng'arua have difficulty in getting from Nanyuki, the district headquarters and prefer to seek assistance from Nyahururu in Nyandarua district (see *Daily Nation* 13/05/98).[24] Finally, a question remains whether high-ranking officials were behind the clashes. If so, it turned against them; for example, among the teachers killed was Timothy Mwangi, a teacher at Ol-Moran and nephew to ex-commissioner of Lands Wilson Gachanja (see *The People* 29/01-05/02/98).

Thus, in spite of all the arguments claiming the killings were planned, organised and instigated by outside forces, no hard evidence has been brought to support those arguments. In any case the possibility that the Laikipia violence was a consequence of Pokot cattle raids which have been ongoing for long cannot be completely ruled out.[25] Perhaps, one such raid went out of hand, firstly because Kikuyu youngsters retaliated and killed livestock belonging to the Pokot who, in turn, revenged with a massacre of Kikuyu youngsters who had come ill-armed to an area inhabited mainly by well-armed Pokot and Samburu. After this massacre the Kalenjin, Turkana and Samburu raiders purposely tried to increase the mayhem and fear among the Kikuyu people by specifically attacking schools and bars in other parts of Laikipia district.

Trouble in Laikipia was dormant by the end of January 1998. However, in October 1998 tension was high again when two MPs, Chege Mbitiru (Laikipia West) and Thirikwa Kamau (Ndaragwa), led the protest against the grabbing of some 5,000 acres of the Gitundaga section of Marmanet forest allocated to well-connected individuals. Land problems continued to cause trouble. For example, in March 1999 Laikipia East MP Mwangi Kiunjuri announced he would acquire poisoned arrows for his constituents to protect themselves against elephants destroying crops and killing people. In April 1999 Kiunjuri called for government intervention and warned that clashes might erupt among land allottees who had been given title deeds by a land-buying company for the same plots. And in January 2000, he requested the government to stop Samburu pastoralists pulling down fences and poisoning dogs belonging to Kikuyu cultivators in order to let loose livestock on the crops.

Njoro

Among the first witnesses to appear before the commission was Philemon Abong'o, the deputy commissioner of police, who led the February 1998 investigations into the causes of the clashes in the Rift Valley. For the Njoro area, the police report points at an incident that occurred between 7 and 9 December 1997 whereby a disagreement between two drunkards at Ndeffo trading centre led to the death of a Mr David Bii, a Kalenjin. This provoked Kalenjin revenge upon the Kikuyu who were accused of having killed David Bii. This resulted in the death of Robert Waweru, a Kikuyu. Also seven shops, seven hotels and three butcheries were set on fire. Abong'o stated that the incident was reported to police headquarters by the Njoro police station (see *Daily Nation* 28/07/98). Abong'o also stated that although the provincial security committee had made good recommendations to prevent the eruption of violence, some of them were not implemented (*Daily Nation* 31/07/98). Among these recommendations was a close monitoring of politicians. Kihika Kimani was said to have advised local Kikuyu to defend themselves by whatever means possible and even threatened to organise hundreds of Kikuyu youths to 'beat up Kalenjins until President Moi sheds tears' (*Daily Nation* 12/08/98). Other witnesses before the commission also mentioned this aspect (see below). However, these utterances, Abong'o claimed, did not cause the clashes and were mostly prompted by the bitter experiences of the 1992/93 ethnic clashes.

In addition, Abong'o referred to land issues in Njoro division as another possible cause. 'Before the elections, the Kikuyu were saying the Kalenjin got their land free and the first move, when the Democratic Party of Kenya took over, would be to revoke the allocations of those farms. At the same time . . . the Kalenjin had threatened the Kikuyu with eviction from their land if they did not vote for Kanu' (*Daily Nation* 31/07/1996). Abong'o referred to a letter written on 23 January by Kihika Kimani to Kipkorir Siele, the Nakuru district special branch officer, alerting him of an imminent attack on the Kikuyu by the Kalenjin (*Daily Nation* 31/07/98). Siele was posted to Nakuru by 13 November 1997. Kimani wrote the letter because a group of 70-80 people, looking like Kalenjin warriors, had invaded his farm, erected structures and divided it among themselves by placing beacons. They had also forced two Europeans who had bought land from Kimani to leave. This information, apparently, was never forwarded from Siele to other relevant authorities such as Nakuru district commissioner Kinuthia Mbugua and the Nakuru police boss, Peter Kavila. Abong'o mentions poor working relations for this lack of communication. Siele's action, backed by district criminal investigations officer (DCIO) John Maritim, to prevail upon Peter Kavila to release an elderly Kalenjin man who was among the group of seven attackers arrested, was questioned (*Daily Nation* 14/08/98). Kavila said that his decision not to release the suspect apparently did not go down well with Siele who refused to let his motor vehicle be used to carry arrested armed warriors (see *East African Standard* 31/10/98).

Also, Kiraitu Murungi, who cross-examined Siele before the commission (and who appeared for MP Kihika Kimani), questioned why the intelligence officer left Njoro for Nakuru in the dead of the night shortly after the clashes started on 25 January, thus incriminating himself as the architect of the clashes (*East African Standard* 22/08/98; *Daily Nation* 22/08/98).

Siele, for his part, said he left for urgent personal matters and also claimed he informed the provincial security committee. On 24 January Kihika Kimani informed Siele and his deputy Philemon Opiyo that, after reporting to Kavila, he was referred to the Njoro officer commanding police division (OCPD). Kimani was annoyed at the laxity of the government. According to Siele, the MP told him he had met 40 Kikuyu elders from various locations in Njoro and discussed the invasion. The meeting had resolved to organise vigilante groups for self-defence against possible Kalenjin attacks. With regard to the outcome of this meeting, Siele claimed he had also informed the OCPD and the DC and requested the OCPD to send security men to Teret when he realised tension was high and tribal clashes were likely to break out any time (*East African Standard* 22/08/98).

However, when clashes erupted in Njoro only five APs and three regular police constables were present despite a resolution that security be beefed up. In addition, according to Peter Chiteka, deputy OCS Njoro, the officers' efforts were hampered by impassable roads as well as lack of communication equipment and transport. Some 10 police stations lacked vehicles and the only lorry at the Nakuru police station had broken down (*Daily Nation* 14/08/98; 15/08/1998).

Finally, Abong'o stated that he had not indicated in his report which group started the clashes, yet he agreed that given the higher number of casualties from the Kikuyu community in the first two days of the clashes, 'it was apparent that the Kikuyus were taken unaware but re-grouped later and launched counter-attacks.' (*Daily Nation* 12/08/98).[26]

Before the commission, Petkay Miriti, former Rift Valley provincial security intelligence officer (PSIO) and Siele's boss, said he was for long aware about tension building up between the Kalenjin and Kikuyu. He referred specifically to the some 500 'land speculators' from Bomet and Trans Mara who had been settled in Ndoinet forest.[27] Miriti said these were the people who attacked in the night of 25 to 26 January at Stoo Mbili and who had also invaded MP Kihika Kimani's farm (*Daily Nation* 15/08/98).

Other incidents had contributed to the tension in the area before the clashes broke out by late January 1998. First, leaflets had been pinned on trees in Nakuru district issuing an ultimatum to non-Kalenjin to leave the Rift Valley before Sunday 26 October 1997 (*The Update* 31/10/97). Second, Njenga Mungai, the former MP for Molo was chased away from a public rally in the Ndeffo area by mid-December. Following this incident Mungai allegedly warned the Kikuyu community that their women would carry their children on their backs if they refused to vote for KANU and President Moi (*The Update* 28/02/98).

Third, his opponent Kihika Kimani was also accused before the commission of instigating Kikuyu voters and to have foretold the Njoro clashes at several meetings. For example a Mr Michael Maathai, a Molo watchman, claimed before the commission that on 19 September 1997 the Molo MP convened a meeting at Ndeffo area where he urged members of the Kikuyu community not to vote for President Moi. The MP observed that KANU had a tendency to rig elections and warned that Kenya could plunge into a bloodbath like Rwanda if KANU won the elections (*Daily Nation* 19/11/98).

Another witness, Priscilla Chepkirui Lelaitich, said the warning of an imminent war, if KANU was voted back to power, was made by the DP legislator at a public rally at Kihingo centre a few weeks before the 29 December general elections. This frightened many non-Kikuyu living at

Sinendet Settlement Scheme which was predominantly a Kikuyu zone (*East African Standard* 18/10/89). And a Mr Stanley Kiplagat Maritim stated that Kihika Kimani, during a meeting at his Njoro farm, threatened to kill Kalenjin who had invaded his farm. According to Maritim, Kimani revealed that he had formed a gang of 5,000 youths to drive out Kalenjin settled in Sululu area (*Daily Nation* 17/12/98). Kimani dismissed the claim and also denied that he had incited the Kikuyu against the Kalenjin. He said he had informed intelligence officers that the Kikuyu would retaliate for the killing of their people. He conceded that he had asked Kikuyu to form self-defence groups before ethnic clashes broke out (*Daily Nation* 14/04/99).[28]

Fourth, leaflets distributed by Wangari Maathai calling for a united Kikuyu community stand in electing one presidential candidate and other leaflets circulating in Nakuru town warning the Kalenjin that they would be sacked from the civil service within two weeks after DP won the elections apparently angered and worried the non-Kikuyu in the area (*East African Standard* 20/08/98; *Daily Nation* 11/11/98).

Fifth, the Kalenjin were said to be unhappy about the election counting process in Molo that led to a conflict in which four people were killed. Sixth, DP and KANU youths had clashed in Nakuru over who was allowed to collect the levy at the bus station. According to *The Star* bi-weekly this trouble was organised by the KANU branch chairman, Raphael Korir, and Musa Kiyai, the deputy State House comptroller in charge of Nakuru State House. They allegedly revived the notorious Nakuru KANU youth to harass non-Kalenjin in Nakuru town. This plan was discussed at a meeting on 3 January 1998 at the KANU Nakuru campaign office at the Agricultural Society of Kenya showground. 'In attendance at the meeting which our sources dubbed "the war council" were, among others, the Nakuru District presidential campaign co-ordinator Jackson Rutto, Egerton University Vice-Chancellor Japheth Kiptoon and the district Kanu boss, Korir.' (*The Star* 27-29/01/98). In another edition *The Star* claimed that the involvement of Molo KANU chairman Joseph Kibenei, KANU activist Jackson Sang, Mau Narok and Njoro DOs Kingsley arap Too and Peter King'ola, respectively (see *The Star* 3-5/02/98). In revenge for failing to vote for KANU and humiliating President Moi, the paper claims, non-Kalenjins were attacked.

Seventh, on Sunday 25 January 1998 at Ndeffo farm, two Kalenjin youngsters, who were drunk, abused a Kikuyu shopkeeper. The man then refused to sell the boys cigarettes. On their part, the Kalenjin claimed that Kikuyu shopkeepers refused to sell them goods. As most shopkeepers in the area are Kikuyu, the Kalenjin are disadvantaged. In turn, the Kikuyu stated that some Kalenjin youths did not pay for the goods sold. Also Amnesty International reported that several Kikuyu shops were burned at the beginning of December 1997 and that, as a consequence, some Kikuyu shop owners refused to serve Kalenjin (Amnesty International 1998:8).

In the end, the Njoro clashes left over 70 people dead and many wounded and some 1,500 people displaced. The majority of the people killed were Kalenjin. The retaliation by the Kikuyu mostly affected the ordinary Kalenjin living in the Lare area. Amnesty International reported that the Kikuyu's violent response did not appear to have involved outsiders. Kalenjin witnesses recognised most of the attackers, often neighbours, wearing normal clothes and carrying *pangas* and *rungus* (Amnesty International 1998: 8).[29] However, one of our informants stated that youths from as far as Nyeri district came in to assist their Kikuyu brethren.

By contrast, the Kikuyu survivors stated that the Kalenjin raiders were mostly outsiders who worked in groups with the local Kalenjin who identified the houses of the Kikuyu. The attackers moved in groups: one engaged in fighting and burning, a second one in looting and a third, made up of women, assisted in removing the looted goods. It should, also, be mentioned that the Kikuyu and Kalenjin neighbours did not always fight each other but sometimes assisted each other during the clashes. For example, members of a Kikuyu family living in Njoro near Egerton University complex were advised by their Kalenjin neighbour to run for their lives when he heard attackers coming near the home speaking Tugen. The Kalenjin neighbour guarded the Kikuyu's home. Likewise Amnesty reported that a Kikuyu neighbour rescued two children of a Kalenjin woman in the Lare/Naishi area when she had fled her house after being attacked by Kikuyu (Amnesty International 1998:6).

On 30 January, a team of *The Star* succeeded in penetrating the Sururu forest and managed to talk to a group of Ndorobo raiders. While moving towards the raiders, accompanied by two APs, the journalists saw a white Land-Rover Discovery (KYF 293) belonging to Egerton University. The vehicle could only have come from where the raiders were hiding, and was most likely being used to ferry supplies to the fighters. This, according to the bi-weekly, was proof of the involvement of Professor Japheth Kiptoon in particular in the ongoing clashes (see *The Star* 03-05/02/98). The team met some 200 warriors. The group complained that the Kikuyu had grabbed all land and owned everything (shops, matatus, posho mills).

> We have been depending on the sale of timber and charcoal since 1994 when we were settled here and the forest is now depleted. . . . Kiprono, the gang leader, told The Star that they had been told on Sunday, January 25, that ethnic skirmishes had erupted in Ndeffo and that Dorobos had been killed. He said they were instructed to arm themselves and invade homes of Kikuyus. . . . They could not say from whom they were taking instructions, but they said word would 'come from Nakuru' (*The Star* 03-05/02/98).

Three days earlier, on 27 January, another journalist, who prefers to remain anonymous, located attackers near burning houses in the Meta area who identified themselves as Kalenjin. Within less than a minute a GSU officer in uniform arrived and interrupted the discussion. He then admonished the Kalenjin saying they were tarnishing Kenya's reputation. After the short speech, the GSU officer ordered the journalist to leave the area. Asked whether those standing right next to burning houses would be arrested, the GSU officer said there was not enough evidence to justify such action. When the journalist asked if some of the people present would be interrogated, at least in connection with the two Kalashnikov guns which the Kalenjin had in their hands, the officer replied that the Kalenjin held farming tools (others had *pangas* and picks) and as such there was no evidence to warrant taking them for questioning.

Testifying before the Akiwumi Commission, Nakuru police boss Kavila said he could not rule out the possibility that government officers, including senior police officers, took sides in the clashes. This statement supports the observation by the journalist mentioned above that on 28 January he witnessed at a roadblock, supposedly manned by the raiders, three green Mercedes lorries hidden behind bushes and people in plain clothes, yet wearing GSU raincoats (because it was raining) and holding G-3 rifles (which are known to be GSU weapons and need training to operate). Another informant (name withheld) claimed that a military officer who had been posted in the area after the clashes erupted was reprimanded for trying to keep order.

This might confirm a remark by Kavila who said he and other officers were surprised to learn that Siele had intercepted a contingent of GSU personnel which was on its way to the troubled area and ordered it not to proceed. He instead deployed the GSU personnel in Ndeffo where there were no clashes at the time (*East African Standard* 31/10/98). Shortly after Kavila was posted to the area, Siele was transferred to Uasin Gishu district. This was described by the Akiwumi Commission judges as accelerated promotion from an acting superintendent of police (before the clashes) to a senior superintendent of police after the clashes. Also Justice Akiwumi summarised Siele's behaviour in front of Kavila as follows: 'Here is a man who gets information and fails to pass it on; then disappears when there is high tension and resurfaces when clashes broke out; then prevails upon you to release one of the suspects; and then disappears again during patrols and even refuses to release his car to you. What do you comment about this kind of conduct?' (*Daily Nation* 31/10/98).

The trouble in Njoro ended abruptly, especially after national and international outcry intensified. The fact that the Kikuyu hit back very hard might have contributed to this even more. Still, by May some revenge killings had taken place and tension and suspicion remained high. Reconciliation initiatives and national and international aid to the victims tried to address this situation. Most interestingly, in this respect, was the stand taken by Kihika Kimani.

In August 1998 Kimani criticised those opposing peace talks between Kikuyu and Kalenjin leaders in the Rift Valley. Kimani spoke at his Engashura farm where the first in a series of planned meetings was held. More than 300 leaders, political and religious, from both communities drawn from Nakuru, Laikipia, Baringo, and Koibatek districts attended (*Daily Nation* 17/08/98). Yet, when Kimani decided to vote in favour of KANU in parliament, over the no-confidence motion, party leaders questioned his behaviour (see *Daily Nation* 20/10/98; 21/10/98). His position became even more critical when in May 1999 he threatened to mobilise more than 3,000 members of the Mungiki sect assisted by KANU youth wingers and NDP youngsters to violently disrupt a planned opposition meeting in Nakuru town. 'We shall not allow any Opposition meeting in Nakuru, even if it means shedding blood, to preserve the peace currently prevailing in the district' (*Daily Nation* 23/05/99). By 27 May 1999, the DP (Nakuru branch) had decided to suspend its Molo MP (*Daily Nation* 27/05/99).

That peace had not yet fully returned became even more clear when that same month Okiek elders claimed that warriors who had settled in the area after 1992 were being trained at Gongogeri Settlement Scheme in Mau South forest. They also protested at the massive logging and selling of trees by politicians, civil servants and businessmen (*Daily Nation* 12/05/99).

Conclusion

Violence broke out in Laikipia and Njoro areas after the 1997 Kenya general elections. Questions were raised and answers given to the cause of the clashes. Ethnicity. land problems and partisan politics were mentioned. Many people claimed that involvement of the Kenyan state was evident or at least most likely. In this chapter, different sources were analysed including press reports, archive material, the Akiwumi Commission hearings, interviews and last but not least the author's personal observations of the clashes during the month of January 1998. Different conclusions were drawn with regard to the Laikipia and the Njoro violence. For Njoro there is hard proof that Kenyan authorities or politicians were involved in the instigation or coordination of the attacks. For Laikipia, it is hard to prove that the authorities were involved on the basis of the presently available evidence.

Arguments such as the rape does not come along with 'ordinary' cattle rustling do not hold. Raping has occurred long for a time and has intensified since 1995. Also in the 1990-97 pre-election period 21 people, all Kikuyu, were killed in Laikipia cattle raids. This time, in retaliation, the Kikuyu youth killed so many Pokot animals, a traumatic experience for the pastoralists, that a strong revenge was unavoidable. These people do not need an army or any other group to assist them in planning and executing cattle raids-related violence. Firstly, the Pokot are known to possess huge numbers of sophisticated weapons and they regularly attack neighbouring groups (Turkana, Marakwet, Samburu as well as Kikuyu) and are capable of causing havoc. A combination of a young local Pokot KANU civic aspirant who lost the nominations and a few police reservists can easily turn the area into hell. It should also be kept in mind that most Kikuyu died in the Rum Rum valley when they pursued the Kalenjin and Samburu raiders. This differs significantly from a pre-planned attack by the pastoral groups executed on Kikuyu homes.

But how come the Pokot were assisted by Turkana and Samburu? Had the political competition united these groups to act together? Did the pastoralists continue seeking compensation by extra looting of Kikuyu property? Or did loose gangster groups come in to profit from the hectic situation, threaten, loot and kill people in other parts of the district? Or was there a co-ordinated militant army, sent by top politicians taking the conflict to other (political) levels, to force the Kikuyu community to drop the election petition and vote wisely next time or leave the area as earlier attacks in Enoosupukia and Olenguruone among others had shown to be 'paying-off' for KANU politicians? The Narok Declaration has been mentioned in this respect. But this meeting took place after the Laikipia trouble had started. Why did the provincial administration and police act the way they are said to have done? Was it cowardice, unwillingness to risk their lives for non-Kalenjin, instructions from elsewhere, lack of personnel? A mixture of these possible reasons, each weighing differently over the 10-day span of violence, cannot be ruled out. Whatever the case, the Laikipia violence evidence might have been politically coordinated, but that does not necessarily mean that political leaders or their handmen were involved.

For Njoro we believe that the attack was organised by KANU and the participation of government related individuals is irrefutable. Proof was provided by informants who were able to speak to the attackers. Also, before the Akiwumi Commission much evidence and arguments were brought forward pointing at planned violence orchestrated by a team of intelligence officers and KANU political activists and directed at the Kikuyu residents. This involved Kalenjin immigrants, especially those settled in the forests in the 1990s, assisted by a part of the security forces. The attack in Njoro was not spontaneous and seems to have been well planned and implemented.

Whether we should call the violence political, ethnic or land-related depends on the relative position of those involved: the politician, the immigrant, the land buyer. In the end, for all parties involved, access to and control over resources were critical. This control and access is either acquired by political power, economic wealth or brute force. To a certain extent it is not necessary to try to single out one reason why the clashes erupted. In our historical analysis, it became clear, in the words of Sorrenson (1967:250), that 'with the Kikuyu it is still not possible to divorce politics from the land.' Lack of land was a driving motive for the independence movement. Likewise, land and politics were linked in that political leaders gained their support from their positions in land-buying companies or the other way around. The big men (both Kikuyu and Kalenjin) win. The small ones lose, but put their hopes in the hands of the former either by giving votes or financial support (political parties/land buying companies).

In the nineteenth century, flexible boundaries between groups had always existed, depending on the strength of a group and interethnic mobility. The vacuum left by the Maasai as a result of their society's collapse enabled an easy take-over by European settlers of the white highlands. The coming of the British froze the land use pattern. Reserves sealed off areas into which new Kikuyu bands would probably have expanded. However, the European farmers employed many Kikuyu labourers, some of whose descendants bought the land after independence. Original Maasai claims were futile. By contrast, the land consolidation, leading to a push away from the Central Province and backed by an enabling political environment in the 1960s and 1970s, allowed many Kikuyu, to 'jump their father's fence' and migrate to the Rift Valley. They occupied the semi-humid/semi-arid border zone between the humid fertile hills and dry plains of the Rift Valley.

From the 1980s onwards, the enabling political environment shifted from the Kikuyu to the Kalenjin. But these new political favourites still lacked financial power, except for a small elite. These numbers became even more important in a multi-party constituency model. Elections might initiate a change in political and thus economic power and fortune. For the common man, it is land that matters most because it allows him to graze his livestock or to grow crops. Access to and development of the land depends on economic and political power. Here the local MP's personal interest comes in most strongly. As long as voting for certain parties follows the ethnic lines, simple calculations will teach that losing land to immigrants in the end will result in the loss of political power. This, first and foremost, affects the individual politician, but by pointing out to 'his' or 'her' community the danger of losing more land (i.e., pastures and water) to the immigrants, he/she consolidates his/her position as the spokesperson of the people and creates tension between the local communities. Among the pastoral communities of the Rift Valley, one easily finds a listening ear by mentioning the threat of losing land, mostly to the Kikuyu immigrants.

The ever-growing need for land, the ability of well-off Kikuyu to buy it, and the resulting change in the political supportive strength in the area of immigration is a doom-spelling scenario. The Kikuyu discovered that only by hitting hard at the attackers, including innocent Kalenjin neighbours, were they able to stop the clashes. Come next time they might prepare themselves with more sophisticated weapons than their *pangas*, sticks and bows and arrows.

In the 1990s most victims of violence were poor innocent Kenyans. The perpetrators, when it was not the government security apparatus itself, were mostly organised vigilante groups, sometimes well armed, who operated with total impunity. Violent acts committed by agents of the state, or people acting on their behalf or with their acquiescence or complicity, involved serious breaches of human rights including: the right to life; the right to physical integrity; the right to liberty and security of person; the right to freedom of movement; the right to freedom of opinion and of expression; and the right to property. The price paid for these forms of freedom has been too high for a few hundred Kenyan families whose relatives were butchered in an orgy of killings. Thousands lost their belongings and were rendered refugees in their own country.

Some people, and President Moi is among the main proponents of this stand, claim that the introduction of multi-party politics is responsible for the clashes that have occurred in Kenya in the 1990s (see *Clashes Update* 31/08/93). The claim that multi-party politics will lead to ethnic violence could find support from the happenings in Kenya in the early 1960s and 1990s. In both cases, a shallow analysis of reasons behind the trouble that erupted in the Rift Valley between Kalenjin and Kikuyu, backed by KADU versus KANU, and in later years KANU versus DP, might lead to such a superficial conclusion. However, a more in-depth breakdown shows that the access to land, water, pastures, i.e. access to a livelihood for ordinary people and access to economic positions, business etc, for the elite, especially in later years, is the real cause of fights between groups. In times of potential loss of these resources, political interference heightens because the interests of political leaders are at stake.

Another argument against the 'multi-party linked to ethnic violence' reasoning is that fights between ethnic groups during the period of single party rule also occurred. Moreover, the violence between Pokot (Lotodo) and Marakwet or Maasai (Sunkuli) and Kipsigis, all within KANU, are ongoing. The most powerful minister is able to put his or her men (e.g. chiefs) in place to control and frustrate local happenings. In the latter cases, the access to land is again crucial and the backing by a hawkish minister claiming supremacy in his constituency, leads to ethnic strife and misery, whatever the political system, i.e. single or multi-party.

In my view, less the multi-party aspect but more the constituency system, indeed, seems to be the cause for ethnic violence. As a result of this 'winner-take-all' system, failing to win the elections will result in an economic cold for first and foremost the political leader and possibly his supporters. Politicians thus have an interest to ignite mistrust or revert to violence to reach their goals and stay or get into power. In extreme cases, this means removing people physically from the specific constituency. The moment these goals match with those of the ordinary people's longing for land and jobs, the conditions are set for a potentially, dangerous situation. In January 1998, with more light weapons around, and a police force less well equipped and apparently more biased and/or less willing to interfere than in the 1960s, violence was witnessed in Laikipia and Njoro.

A strong lesson on curbing the violence can be learned from the 1961 election tension. As we saw this was stopped immediately by a firm police effort, altogether lacking in 1998. Even more important, to strictly keep law and order and to reconcile rival groups are good ways to prevent clashes from erupting. When asked by the Akiwumi Commission for recommendations on how future conflicts in Ol-Moran could be avoided, a witness proposed that in addition to disarming groups, the government should sink boreholes and build dams in areas occupied by pastoralists to avert disagreements over water during the dry season (*Daily Nation* 05/02/99).

As KANU activist John Keen elaborated before the commission: 'If we are to avoid tribal clashes, ethnic animosity and hatred, the government must come up with a land policy or establish a land commission with proper terms of reference to look into the issue of land tenure' (*Daily Nation* 06/11/98). Unfortunately, efforts to this end by the Kenyan government so far do not allow for firm optimism. As a result, clashes, irrespective of the political system in the country, are likely to occur more often in the years to come. Serious trouble might occur in Kenya soon, whether politically instigated or not, between the powerful and the less strong, between man and wildlife, between different ethnic groups or among members belonging to the same group.[30]

In this respect, it is also important to realise that the troubles of the 1990s have produced a group of young Kenyans, sons and daughters of innocent clashes victims. They witnessed the killing of their fathers and mothers by vigilante groups and sometimes neighbours. Their crime? Just being another Kenyan. The 1992-98 clashes in Kenya might have prompted the minds of young Kenyans to a hatred that could one day ignite massacres never witnessed in the country before. Yet the Mois, Biwotts, Lotodos, Ntimamas, Kibakis and Odingas will not be the victims of Kenya's future killing fields. It will be the ordinary Mwangis, Kiptanuis, ole Saronis, i.e., innocent Kenyans, struggling to make a daily living by cultivating the soil, picking tea leaves or keeping livestock, whose lives will be ruined.

Notes

1. I am indebted to Peter Kagwanja and Catherine Duhamel for reviewing this chapter.
2. For long, the Kones/Ntimama faction of KANU had kept a low profile while President Moi and KANU-B (Biwott and Saitoti) had put in time and money, much against KANU-A's wishes, trying to reach an accommodation with the Kikuyu. The rapprochement failed and was sealed in KANU's poor performance in Central Province and even more so by Kibaki's petition.
3. This part of Laikipia is prone to cattle rustling. So, that Monday evening the villagers responded as the raiders drove away the animals. They were able to recover eight of the goats. The raiders, however, escaped into the hills with the remaining animals. The villagers continued their search and revenged (*Daily Nation* 21/01/98).
4. Since the introduction of multi-partyism these mostly Kikuyu-owned Narok ranches, together with the former government-owned Agricultural Development Farm of Lonyiek, which was passed on to the Pokot, the TND Mugie ranch that went to the Samburu, and the Maundu ni Meru ranch, occupied by Tugen foremost, the northern Laikipia zone became more crowded and less secure. The pastoralists in particular have been blamed for unjustified grazing in cultivated fields, destruction of water structures set up by the immigrants, especially increasing cattle theft and violence. From 1990 to 1997 193 cattle raids resulting in 21 deaths, 8 cases of rape and some 300 injured persons occurred (see CPK/PCEA/CC 1998).
5. *The Star* reports that on 21 January its reporters witnessed a bitter young man who moved an emotional crowd in the streets of Nyahururu town to donate money in order to defend themselves against the ethnic cleansing (*The Star* 23-26/01/98:3).
6. In addition, more than 280 families lost their beddings, 362 lost their utensils, 217 clothes, 172 farm implements and 124 lost their furniture. At the same time, 1,324 bags of maize were stolen from 315 families while 213 bags of beans and 39 bags of potatoes were looted. Some 477 acres under maize, beans and potatoes and other crops had been destroyed through grazing by Pokot and Samburu herdsmen after the families fled. Also 28 cows, 565 goats and 3,513 chickens were stolen (*Daily Nation* 6/01/98).
7. Mutukanio is the Kikuyu equivalent of unity, togetherness. The name was coined because of the area's ethnic mix. The majority of Mutukanio farm shareholders are Kikuyu but Kisii and Luyha also bought plots. According to Amnesty International, the Njoro clashes started as early as 9 on 24 January 1998 when Kalenjin raiders attacked unarmed Kikuyu in their homes in Mauche and later Stoo Mbili (see Amnesty International 1998: 6). Thereafter, attacks by Kalenjin took place at Mwureri, Mutukanio, Mauche (25 January), Kihingo, Milimani, Likia, Kinyanjoya (26 January), Barut (28 January), while the Kikuyu retaliated on 25 and 26 by attacking unarmed Kalenjin in their homes at Naishi/Lare.
8. This killing raised anger among the group of Kikuyu watching the scene from a distance and questions were raised whether the Kikuyu should continue this way, having their people killed and the survivors only going down to collect the dead bodies instead of trying to chase the attackers once and for all. Two other men suffered arrow injuries. On returning to the farm, the attackers shouted war cries (in Kipsigis). On our way back from Mau Narok towards Njoro, we met the OCS, who was with three other police officers, on the side of the road. We told him that we had just witnessed someone being hacked to death and asked about police presence. He replied that 60 of his men had been deployed and that everything was under control.

9. On 27 April a watchman, Godfrey Njuguna Ndindi, was hacked to death in Ndeffo, one day after a lecturer at the Nakuru Medical Training College, Karuri Kimbo, was killed when the pick-up in which he was travelling was stoned and the driver forced to stop by the roadside. The driver managed to flee. This stoning of *matatus* belonging to Kikuyu was done at Mauche by members of the Kalenjin community while at Ndeffo the Kikuyu were stoning those belonging to the Kalenjin. In yet another attack, raiders killed 20-year-old Hellen Njeri Mbuthia at Mathangauta farm in Mau Narok (*Daily Nation* 06/05/98).

10. According to the report in Kianjoya, Likia and Sururu, 156 houses and nine shops were burnt and 175 sheep and goats and 215 donkeys stolen. More than 2,000 90 kg bags of maize were destroyed after the granaries were torched. At least 200 families were displaced in this area alone and were forced to seek refuge in church compounds and trading centres off the Nakuru - Mau Narok road. In Barut, Mwariki, Ingobor and Kwa Ronda areas, which are within the Nakuru municipality, at least 400 families were displaced and 85 houses torched. More than 185 sheep and goats were stolen and 15 bicycles, 11 TV sets and household property of unknown value burnt. In Larmudiac, Ndeffo and Mau Narok 1,170 families were displaced and more than 3,000 bags of maize burnt. Stolen animals here included 400 head of cattle and 500 sheep and goats. At least 167 families were placed in Kongasis, Kapyemit and Kiptangwany areas (*Daily Nation* 06/05/98).

11. Njoro is a Maasai term meaning small spring, (anglicised from en-corro). Laikipia refers to the Laikipiak Maasai section that used to roam this area.

12. No direct recommendations were made for the Laikipia area, except for some bordering areas such as the Churo area west of Laikipia. Pokot laid claims to the area, but C. Adams, DC Laikipia (1909-10) stated that this area was occupied by the Maasai and not the Suk (Pokot). According to the commission the Churo, an area of some 140 sq. miles, should be added to the Pokot Reserve, yet a fence be erected to prevent trespass by the Pokot in the direction of the Laikipia settled area (KLC 1934: 251). Likewise the Chamus (Njemps) claimed an area of 78 sq. miles east of the Njemps reserve towards Ngelesha, the western tip of the Laikipia escarpment.

    In the north the commission stated that the Leroghi Plateau should not be assigned to any group but treated as land in which Africans had prior interest, i.e. the Samburu taking over from the northern Maasai who had been removed to the Southern Maasai Reserve (see KLC/Evidence 1934: 1202). Finally, in the eastern portion of Laikipia the commission recommended be detached the Mukogodo area and from the Kikuyu Province added to the Northern Frontier Province and make arrangements for sufficient land for the Maa-speaking groups of Mukogodo, Mumonyot, Tikirri and Ng'wesi.

13. At the Lancaster House Conference in London, dealing with Kenya's independence, a Maasai delegation stated that they did not want to evict Europeans who were willing to stay, but expected to receive the rents from the lease of the land. Likewise, they expressed their discontent a possible loss of the special status of their territory. The British confirmed the security of tenure on the lines of the treaties but disagreed on any claim for compensation for the loss of land outside the present Maasai reserves. The Maasai '. . . had given up land under the 1904 and 1911 agreements and could not now claim it back.' (KNA/MAC/KEN/47/5). In response all Maasai, including KANU's John Keen, refused to sign the final Lancaster House agreement.

14. By early 1963 a total of 9,530 applications for land on settlement schemes had been received in the Nakuru district. Only 820 were selected (KNA/DC/NKU/2/1/2-Jan/Feb 1963). By August the scramble for land at Menengai by Kalenjin took everyone by surprise. Between 300-400 plots were demarcated and a good number of huts built. These were eventually pulled down and the area completely cleared of illegal occupation. 'The motive behind the demonstration would appear to be more social and economic

rather than political. Hence, a recurrence of the problem in the near future is not unlikely.' (KNA/DC/NKU/2/1/2-Aug 1963).

By 1964 illegal squatting in Rongai and Solai areas of Nakuru by Tugen pastoralists was reported. 'This unwelcome move was well balanced by more Africans taking over farms, particularly in Dundori/Subukia and in Molo areas' (KNA/DC/NKU2/1/2-Jan 1964). Finally, the Ndorobo in the East Mau forest discussed ways of moving to the Tinet Forest Reserve and Olenguruone.

15. By the late 1950s, Europeans owned 80 per cent of Laikipia. At independence this started to change. In Laikipia there was much talk of leaving the country mainly among the Afrikaans farmers in the Ol Kalou, Ol Arabel and Leshau areas. During 1961, some 14 farmers left and the farms concerned were leased or otherwise taken up locally. More would have left if able to do so but the majority of the farmers decided to stay (KNA/DC/LKA/1/11/8/1961:1).

16. *Haraka* is a Kiswahili word meaning hurry. *Shirika* means divide. Kohler (1987: 30-1) claims that increasing political pressure was most likely one of the reasons for the small plots (2 acres) offered in the Marmanet scheme. Also campaign tactics leading up to the 1979 elections – the then MP for Western Laikipia, G.G. Kariuki, held a key position in the 'Ministry of Lands and Settlement'– may have been another.

17. Ten districts showed increases of the African population of more than 60 per cent during this period: Narok (193 per cent), Elgeyo-Marakwet (150), Kajiado (133), Nairobi (126), Kisii (116), Mombasa (102), Kericho (82), Nanyuki (68), Baringo (68) and Laikipia (65). Naivasha-Nakuru district scored 12th position with 54 per cent.

18. Njeri's neighbour later recalled that only a few raiders attacked and one shouted, 'We shall push you to Kiambu and then take all your livestock'. This apparently confirms the motive of the land as well as cattle-rustling motive.

19. Father Sandro visited the DO at his house in Kinamba at about 8.30 pm on 17 January 1998 to inform him that houses were being torched in Ol-Moran. In response the DO said he had visited the area earlier in the day and that he was tired. The DO told him that he would visit Ol-Moran the following day. Earlier Father Sandro had gone to see the Kinamba police station commander who told him that he had visited Ol-Moran earlier in the day and that the security situation was under control (see *Daily Nation* 11/ 02/99). Father Sandro he had also met some policemen driving towards Kinamba from Ol-Moran and when he informed them about the two incidents they told him that they could not go back to Ol-Moran without instructions from their boss in Kinamba.

20. Another witness, Ms Lamarias Lomuna, a Samburu who is the KANU chairlady in the Ol-Moran area, told the commission that the clashes in Ol-Moran started after animals were slashed by the Kikuyu. She also stated that the relationship between the Samburu and the Kikuyu soured after a KANU civic candidate, Francis Ndung'u Gachau, described the Samburu as primitive (*Daily Nation* 04/02/99).

21. The traumatic experience of killing of one's animals was expressed by two Samburu elders who said they regretted the raids but blamed both sides for the flare-up. 'The Kikuyu youths should have waited for the police to handle the matter as promised.' 'On the other hand, the other combatants should not have started war cries after being addressed by the Government officials', said one elder. 'You know with us the pain of the death of livestock can be more unbearable than that of a child' said Mzee Stanley Lesaigor. He denied any knowledge of politics behind the killings although he admitted there was friction during the campaigns over the different parties the communities were supporting.' (*Daily Nation* 04/02/98).

22. Before the Akiwumi Commission, Jonathan Soi denied the report and claimed he never saw bands of Kikuyu youths marching towards Ngoisus to attack the Samburu. Soi said he learnt that Kikuyu youths had been killed in Ngoisus area in Ol-Moran division

several days after the incident when he was informed by assistant chief John Kimaiyo of Sipili (*Daily Nation* 20/02/98).

23. Likewise on 26 September 1998, when visiting Laikipia district, President Moi called for the communities to co-exist peacefully. He told Samburu West MP, Peter Leenges, and his Baringo East counterpart, Joseph Lotodo, that he would hold them responsible for livestock stolen from Laikipia and driven to their respective areas. He called on the leaders from all the communities to form committees of elders to curb the menace (*Daily Nation* 27/09/98).

24. In September 1995 Nyahururu was ceded from Nyandarua district in Central Province to Laikipia in the Rift Valley Province through a presidential decree.

25. For example, on 24 June 1997 Laikipia West MP, Kihika Kimani, while in parliament said more than 40 people had been killed and thousands of cattle stolen by bandits in his area. As a result over 15,000 acres of land had been abandoned (*The Update* 30/06/97).

26. According to Abongo's report, on 26 January seven Kikuyu and three Kalenjin were killed. On 27 January 11 Kikuyu and four Kalenjins. Two days later, the scenario changed: On 28 January three Kalenjins and one Kikuyu were killed. On 29 January 29, three Kikuyu and three Kalenjin and on 30 January five Kikuyu and eight Kalenjin were killed (*Daily Nation* 12/08/98).

27. On 20 August a meeting was held by the DCs of Narok and Nakuru to settle a dispute between Maasai from Narok who protested about Kalenjin who had settled in Likia forest. In the last few years more than 8,000 Kalenjin families had been settled in parts of Likia, Sululu, Tinet, Ndoinet, Teret and other forests (*Daily Nation* 21/08/98).

28. In this respect three local Kikuyu elders, Josephat Chege, Benjamin Mara and another called Joab, were named by witness Joseph Kimani Mboi, a 1997 KANU campaigner and poll agent, as advising youths in Njoro to drive away Kalenjins. In September 1997, he claimed before the commission that he had overheard three meetings in Peacock Hotel (Bagari trading centre, Lare location) in Njoro division of Nakuru district. The purpose of the meetings was to arrange for an oath to be administered to members of the Kikuyu community 'to bind them together and reject President Moi and Kanu.' (see *East African Standard* 22/12/98; 23/12/98; 07/01/99). Joseph Mboi also named Lare location chief Sammy Kivuthu Kimani as warning the Kikuyu youths that their survival depended on defeating the Kalenjin and urging them to arm themselves in readiness for a protracted war. Witness Michael Maathai said that Kivuthu ordered the Kikuyu to attack Kalenjin in Sululu Settlement Scheme. The chief later congratulated the Kikuyu for killing Kalenjins in the area, Maathai claimed (*Daily Nation* 19/11/98).

29. In Likia, resident David Gacheru reported that some of the raiders were strangers but others were neighbours. Julius Kuria in Kianjoya said that the attackers included people who settled in the area only a few years ago. Joseph Kinyanjui in Mutukanio stated that some of the attackers were known and had been living with the victims in a friendly way (see *Daily Nation* 31/01/98:12).

30. For example, in February 2000 eight Kikuyu KANU leaders from Kenya's Central Province accused the government of not protecting members of the province. They called on the government to protect the community and its investments and urged the government to sack and charge cabinet minister Francis Lotodo for spearheading a hatred campaign against non-Kalenjin. They vowed to 'recover whatever is snatched from us through unfair means even if it takes 200 or 500 years' (*Daily Nation* 04/02/00).

References

Amnesty International 1998, *Kenya – Political violence spirals*, London: AI International Secretariat.

Bogonko, S. 1980, *Kenya 1945-1963. A Study of African National Movements*, Nairobi: Kenya Literature Bureau.

Chenevix Trench, C. 1993, *Men Who Ruled Kenya – The Kenya Administration 1892-1963*, London: The Radcliffe Press.

CPK/PCEA/CC 1998, Report on clashes at Ol Moran and part of Sipili location and also cattle rustling in parts of Kinamba and Gitwamba locations, Laikipia District: Church of the Province of Kenya, Presbeterian Church of East Africa, Catholic Church.

KLC 1934 Report of the Kenya Land Commission – The Evidence, Nairobi: Government Printer.

Kohler, T. 1987, *Land Use in Transition. Aspects and Problems of Small Scale Farming in a New Environment: The Example of Laikipia District, Kenya*, Berne: Geographica Bernesia Vol. A5.

Leo, C. 1984, *Land and Class in Kenya*, University of Toronto Press.

Newman, J.L. 1995, *The peopling of Africa – a geographic interpretation*, New Haven: Yale University Press.

Ochieng, W.R. 1985, *A history of Kenya*, Nairobi: Macmillan Kenya.

Ominde, S.H. (ed.) 1984, *Population and Development in Kenya*, Nairobi: Heinemann.

RBC 1962, Kenya: *Report of the Regional Boundaries Commission, Presented to Parliament by the Secretary of State for the Colonies by Command of Her Majesty*, London: HMSO, Cmnd 1899.

Republic of Kenya 1966, *Kenya Population Census 1962, Volume III African Population*, Statistics Division Ministry of Economic Planning and Development, Nairobi: Government Printer.

_____ 1970, *Kenya Population Census 1969, Volume I*, Statistics Division Ministry of Economic Planning and Development, Nairobi: Government Printer.

_____ 1981, *Kenya Population Census 1979, Volume I*, Central Bureau of Statistics Nairobi: Government Printer.

_____ 1994, *Kenya Population Census 1989, Volume I*, Central Bureau of Statistics, Nairobi: Government Printer.

Rutten, M.M.E.M. 1992, *Selling Wealth to Buy Poverty – The Process of the Individualization of Landownership Among the Maasai Pastoralists of Kajiado District, Kenya, 1890-1990*, Saarbrücken: Verlag Breitenbach Publishers.

Sang, J. 1997, 'Kenyatta's Grabbing of Gicheha Farm/Pipeline to Kabarak', mimeo.

Sorrenson, M.P.K. 1967, *Land Reform in the Kikuyu Country – A Study in Government Policy*, Nairobi/London: Oxford University Press.

Sottas B. 1992, *Afrika Entwickeln und modernisieren. Paradigmen, Identitätsbildung und kleinbaüerliche Überlebensstrategien*, Studia ethnographica Freiburgensia 18, Freiburg, Schweiz: Univ.-Verl.

Tignor, R.L. 1976, *The Colonial Transformation of Kenya – The Kamba, Kikuyu, and Maasai from 1900 to 1939*, Princeton University Press.

Waller, R. 1976, 'The Maasai and the British 1895-1905, the origins of an alliance', *Journal of African History* Vol.17, No.4: 529-53.

Weigt, E. 1955, *Europäer in Ostafrika – Klimabediengungen und Wirschaftsgrundlagen*, Doppelheft 6/7 Selbstverlag des Geografischen Instituts der Universität Köln.

21

After the Count...

François Grignon, Marcel Rutten

As in 1992, Kenya woke up from the 1997 general elections with a serious political hangover. Once again President Moi was sworn in to protect the lives and property of all in Kenya and once again this oath, taken in front of the Tanzanian and Ugandan Presidents, Benjamin Mkapa and Yoweri Museveni, respectively, proved to be nothing more than a meaningless ritual. The two neighbouring presidents asked Kenyans to avoid chaos and bloodshed at all costs. However, by the end of January operations of ethnic cleansing had resumed in Njoro and Laikipia (Chapter 20) while, on the political front, half of the opposition was negotiating its co-operation with the newly formed government. Even Mwai Kibaki's DP, which had initially rejected the results together with Raila Odinga's NDP, finally took up its seats in parliament. Still, Kibaki filed a petition to challenge Moi's election and another 26 election petitions were taken to court by people looking for the nullification of the election results (see Appendix 5). However, despite the well documented rigging of elections in at least seven constituencies, which invalidated KANU's majority, the international community led by the United States lauded President Moi's re-election and acknowledged the formation of his government. Still, the foreign countries, especially the Europeans, aired a more critical opinion than the domestic observers who in a surprising report had claimed as early as 3 January that the 'results represented the wishes of Kenyans despite numerous anomalies'. Only opposition politician Kenneth Matiba, who had opted not to join the 1997 presidential race and declared these elections as rigged from the start, called for a constitutional review to be followed by fresh elections. He also registered a new party Saba Saba Asili.

Over the following two years, Kenya appeared to shrink a little more in a state of economic, political and administrative decomposition that will be remembered as the trademark of the last years of the Moi era. Even three successive reshuffles and the appointment of a World Bank-inspired 'dream team', led by Richard Leakey at the helm of the civil service, could not shake off the status quo and the image of gloom and doom.

'If you can't beat them, join them'. This popular saying became, with the opening of the eighth parliament, the guideline of two opposition parties:

FORD-Kenya and NDP. KANU's tiny majority in parliament was quickly reinforced by roughly three dozen MPs and managed to have its incumbent speaker, Francis ole Kaparo, easily re-elected. As a reward for its collaboration, the NDP had its own candidate, Joab Omino, elected as a deputy speaker. He is a former football player and executive of the Kenya Football Federation turned businessman and MP for Kisumu Town East.

Despite the few skirmishes that welcomed the opening of the debates of the eighth parliament, as early as February 1998, it became obvious that the main political battle in the country did not take place within the national assembly, but within the government over the succession to President Moi. The rift between KANU-A and KANU-B leaders quickly resurfaced even though the latter had been humiliated by the electorate and beheaded by the non-reappointment of Prof. George Saitoti as vice-president. KANU headquarters were repeatedly pressed by their backbenchers to have party polls to line up a leadership in accordance with the supporters' wishes, but that became another of President Moi's empty promises.

By February 1998, Joseph Kamotho, one of the main contenders of the KANU-B faction, was re-appointed to the cabinet as minister for Trade, together with Shariff Nassir, the long-time hawkish and sabre-rattling 'king of Mombasa', who was given the home affairs ministry. On the other side, KANU-A's Simeon Nyachae, who was apparently given the Ministry for Finance so that he could be blamed for the non-resumption of international aid to Kenya and therefore become unpopular while raising taxes and laying off civil servants, managed to do away with his KANU-B watchdog, permanent secretary Sally Kosgei who was transferred in February back to the Office of the President over personal differences with her minister.

Two months later, after a meeting convened in Mombasa by an independent NGO on the strategy to be adopted for the economic recovery of the country, daggers were drawn in public. Nyachae, one of the key speakers, led a government delegation to confess to the nation that the government was 'broke'; that it would have to reduce public expenditure by roughly Ksh. 20 billion in the coming months; and that this could only be achieved through the tightening of every civil servant's belt. The latter would not only lose most of his/her allowances and the use of 'GK' cars for private business but would have to accept a drastic review of President Moi's pre-electoral promises to increase civil service salaries.

Indeed, the financing of the budget deficit through treasury bills and bonds had brought the stock of government domestic debt to Ksh. 158 billion (26.7 per cent of the estimated GDP) which alone consumed 15 per cent of the national revenue (EIU 1998:14). On target for cancellation was also the 150-200 per cent salary increase promised by the government to its teachers over three years. With an overall civil service salary slip amounting to 35 per cent of government revenue, and the current vicious circle of financing debt service though more endebting, Simeon Nyachae rightly predicted that the government would go bankrupt before the end of the just opened parliamentary term.

This bold and straight talk, together with the confession that corruption was rampant within the government, made in front of the opposition, the diplomatic community and three quarters of KANU MPs, enraged Daniel arap Moi, who claimed he had not been informed of the meeting, had not authorised it and would not enforce its recommendations. According to the president, the state of the economy could not be discussed publicly, 'with every Tom, Dick and Harry'. The president summoned the KANU Parliamentary Group (PG) to an urgent meeting in Nairobi. Yet, over the subsequent PG meeting, more than 80 KANU MPs refused to condemn Nyachae for his speech in Mombasa and strongly expressed their support for drastic economic reforms in the country. In a face-saving public relations exercise, President Moi officially reached the same conclusions at a meeting hurriedly organised in Mbagathi, Nairobi, which recommendations were to become the government's programme of action for the months ahead. Desperate for cash and for the resumption of international support for its balance of payments, the president finally gave in to the international community's agenda. It started the process of privatisation of key public assets, such as the posts and telecommunications services and Kenya Commercial Bank, and re-activated the Goldenberg trial, and re-launched the activities of the Kenya Anti-Corruption Authority (KACA), led by former 1992 PICK presidential candidate, John Harun Mwau. The media was also partially liberalised. For example, the BBC was granted a frequency to broadcast on FM and the Nation Group (publishers) finally received its TV and radio licences despite some initial reluctance. In order to render broad-casting services, the Nation Group first acquired the East African Television Network, which organisation was granted an operating license by the government. However, when the group took over its subsidiary that license was revoked. However, after a few months of legal tussle and protest, the Nation Group was finally granted the rights to broadcast in the Nairobi area.

This goodwill attitude was acknowledged by the Paris donor's club, which agreed in June to reschedule Kenya's loan payment of Ksh. 4.2 billion in foreign aid and grants after a three-year grace period. In July, the World Bank also decided to advance a Ksh. 2.4 billion loan to deal exclusively with El Niño-related destruction of public infrastructure in 23 districts. Already in January 1998, Central Bank governor Micah Cheserem had called for reopening the talks with the IMF to guarantee loans to repair the country's devastated infrastructure. The government had, nevertheless, to agree that the loan would be administered by an independent body and not by the Ministry for Public Works.

Six months after his appointment, Finance Minister Simeon Nyachae looked as if he had managed to establish himself as the strongest candidate for the Moi succession. His tight monetary policy, control of post-electoral inflationary trends and good working relations with Central Bank Governor Cheserem and the IMF began to build an international statesman's credibility which was threatening the interests of KANU-B which in response launched desperate attacks against him within and outside the ruling party.

The first one came from John Harun Mwau's anti-corruption team which claimed to have uncovered mismanagement by close Nyachae aides at the Treasury, including Samuel Chebii, the respected former commissioner of customs whose removal from office in July 1997 had triggered the suspension of IMF and World Bank support. An enraged Nyachae displayed a rare show of power when he quickly dropped all charges against his associates by Attorney General Amos Wako and managed to have Mwau suspended from his job and submitted to a public investigation in the misuse of his powers. One of Nyachae's wives was then accused of obtaining favours to market tea bags privately, but the combative Nyachae easily sailed through these attacks. By September, he had even demonstrated that he could efficiently flex his political muscle and that he was seriously committed to his Budget Day promises of streamlining public expenditure. The successive labour actions in August and September of the bankers and the teachers had to abort and they had to accept government's increased taxation and a salary freeze without any compensation.

Second on the list of possible successors was the minister for Agriculture Musalia Mudavadi who had improved his credentials in September by successfully mobilising the unhappy backbenchers of the party against a motion of no-confidence brought against the government by rebel FORD-Kenya MP James Orengo. A possible leader of a KANU-C faction, composed of young Nandi and Luhya leaders and other backbenchers from the Rift Valley, Western and North-Eastern provinces he mobilised for a change of guard within the party. Mudavadi also positioned himself as a possible alternative to Nyachae or Saitoti for vice-president. With co-operation between KANU, NDP and FORD-Kenya bringing obvious benefits and minimum costs to the regime in parliamentary matters, the chances of KANU-A's front runner, former VP George Saitoti regaining his automatic successor's seat looked dimmer and dimmer.

This intense politicking nevertheless looked increasingly cut off from the reality of the country. In addition to the coffee, tea, rice, dairy and sugar industries being in total disarray owing to mismanagement, there were other problems such as corruption and violent actions of desperately impoverished farmers, the road network being in shambles after the horrendous El Niño rains, and the 7 August bomb blast, thought to have been executed by Muslim extremists from outside the country. The blast destroyed the American embassy and neighbouring buildings, killing some 250 people and brought an extra economic disaster by heavily undermining the recovery chances of the tourism industry. GDP growth for the year 1997 had already fallen to 2.3 per cent from an expected 5.0 per cent, and it did not climb higher than 1.7 per cent for 1998. Tight monetary policies followed by the government eased the control of inflation but the high cost of credit and high interest rates made it impossible for other than speculative investments to take place and revive the economy through national consumption.

Moreover, with time the reformist credentials of the government appeared to be closer to a public relations exercise than a strong commitment. The constitutional review process was initially launched by Attorney General Amos Wako within the limits of an Inter-Parties Parliamentary Group (IPPG) in accordance with the flawed Act voted the previous year. It was then opened to other stakeholders (churches, NCEC, NGOs) during all inclusive internationally-funded negotiations at Safari Park Hotel in Nairobi, after heavy protests and international pressure. But they were finally stalled by the government once an agreement had been reached on a three-tier consultation and power-sharing review process between district, parliamentary and civil society representatives. After months of silence on the issue, President Daniel arap Moi finally announced, at the end of April 1999, that the process should once again be referred to the KANU-dominated parliament. By the end of 1999, Raila Odinga had taken over the mantle and was leading consultations over the necessary reform process, assisted by a team of NDP and KANU colleagues. An IPPG flawed scenario was slowly taking shape.

Similarly, in June Daniel arap Moi had announced his commitment to establish the truth on the ethnic clashes by instituting a presidential commission of inquiry chaired by the respected Judge Akilano Akiwumi. Yet, even though the proceedings of the commission's hearings confirmed a number of public suspicions on the involvement of the KANU leadership in the Coast and Rift Valley violence over the past few years, the report submitted to the president in June 1999 was never published and no prosecutions were ever attempted against the culprits. Surprisingly, nominated KANU MP Rashid Sajjad had confessed that the funding of 'KANU youth activities might have led to the violence' and Catholic Father John Kaiser directly incriminated cabinet ministers William ole Ntimama, Nicholas Biwott and Julius ole Sunkuli in the clashes of Narok and Trans Mara districts. After a few months of proceedings, Bernard Chunga, the director of public prosecutions (DPP), had even been rushed to lead the cross-examinations in Nakuru, apparently because his young predecessor appointed to assist the commission was giving too much leverage to the victims. Old habits of violence and graft die hard and the hopes that the final mandate of Daniel arap Moi would be different from the two previous ones clearly vanished.

In February 1998, Prof. Kivutha Kibwana, one of the NCEC co-convenors had been kidnapped for a few hours, physically threatened by individuals identified as special branch officers and told to mellow his stand on constitutional review. In May 1998, opposition and KANU MPs who had teamed up to diffuse ethnic tensions in the Rift Valley were violently attacked by the police and KANU youths. Then, as Lamu West MP Fahim Yasin Twaha was accused of stealing and dumping 160,000 bags of sugar from Say Enterprise in Shimanzi, Mombasa, and was subsequently sacked from the government, a serious financial crisis hit the country and once again damaged its credibility. In August, the Central Bank of Kenya had to put five political banks under statutory management for failure to respect their cheques' clearing requirements (Trust Bank, Bullion Bank, Reliance Bank, Prudential Bank and City Finance Bank) due to insider lending and loan defaulting from politicians or politically connected directors. By November, the two biggest countrywide banks, Kenya Commercial Bank and National Bank of Kenya (NBK) were shaken by revelations on the amount of their non-performing loans, most of them having been attributed to politicians or politically connected individuals. In December NBK, the second banking operator in the country, announced a loss of Ksh. 2.8 billion and a total of outstanding non-performing loans of Ksh. 18.8 billion, close to 84 per cent of its loan base. By April 1999, the government had to bail out NBK twice, amidst public outcry, injecting a total of Ksh. 4.5 billion into the financial institution to keep it afloat.

As the list of the most important debtors was presented in parliament and included names such as Prof. Sam Ongeri the minister for Local Government, Kipkalya Kones, minister for Public Works, KANU Baringo secretary Hosea Kiplagat, former State House comptroller Abraham Kiptanui and presidential aide Joshua Kulei, the government decided to cover for them, endorsing once again the misappropriation of public resources and the impunity of the culprits. The released names of other bank debtors provides an interesting who's who of the KANU establishment crossing widely through the civil service, the judiciary, the ruling party and the politically connected private sector (for full list of names see *Daily Nation* 28/11/98).

Meanwhile, Kenya had also woken up to the Karura forest land-grabbing saga. In October 1998, the revelation of an allocation of 80 ha of Nairobi prime forest land to private interests as a reward for electoral funding sparked a heated debate in parliament, demonstrations and violent confrontations in the city centre and on the developer's allocated site, close to the Gigiri United Nations Centre. After the Karura files had mysteriously disappeared from the registry, Land Settlement Minister Noah Katana Ngala exacerbated the tension when he refused to name the allottees *in personae*, and only provided the public with the list of companies fronting for individuals suspected to be June Moi, Rashid Sajjad and other KANU financiers. Yet, despite the national outrage, Natural Resources Minister Francis Lotodo remained unmoved and announced the de-gazetting of 930 ha additional land across the country in January 1999.

By the end of 1998, the unbreakable Kamlesh Pattni of the Goldenberg scandal was again in the news. He publicly denounced an extortion of Ksh. 20 million organised against him by the former limelight of Kenya's radical opposition, Kikuyu MP Paul Muite, to keep secret damning evidence in the Goldenberg trial. The indebted politician, incapable of exonerating himself from the allegation soon became a parliamentary outcast. Yet, Kamlesh Pattni also suffered from his outbursts. In March, the former executive of Goldenberg International was re-arrested as new evidence was brought against him in the never-ending trial that saw his lawyers sinking in more paperwork. Nassir Ibrahim Ali, the owner of the Duty Free Complex, which was supposed to have received the gold exports, swore in an affidavit presented to the court that he had never received any shipment, confirming that the claims made by Pattni to the Treasury for export compensation were indeed fake. Pattni blamed Muite for this new development.

Throughout 1998, the Kenyan government had seemed totally paralysed by its internal wrangles on the presidential succession. Despite the success over no-confidence motions brought against the government, the absence of internal party elections due since 1993 and the persistent domination of a highly unpopular KANU-B establishment at the helm of the party had caused regular outbursts of protest from the KANU backbenchers who threatened to undermine the action of the government.

The only political will Daniel arap Moi finally managed to display at the beginning of 1999 appeared to be the continuation of his past choices despite their electoral failure and a total retreat on any commitment to reforms. In February, an attempted reshuffle turned into a battle. Simeon Nyachae resigned from the government after refusing to be demoted to a junior ministry and he was replaced by Francis Yekoyada Masakhalia, a former civil servant and MP for Butula, who was close to Moi's long-time aide, Nicholas Biwott.

Similarly, the youthful mayor Najib Balala had to resign from office in Mombasa after KANU councillors blocked his widely acclaimed plan to revamp the city. Two months later, on 2 April 1999, scandal-ridden George Saitoti was finally re-appointed vice-president, and his leadership endorsed by the party. In July he survived a motion of no-confidence brought by rebel NDP MP Otieno Kajwang'. Saitoti's reappointment ended a period of over 15 months during which Kenya had been without a vice-president.

From January to June 1999, KANU increased its strength in parliament through its usual use of force and bribery to win three consecutive by-elections, Makueni, Kitui South, and Tigania West. It subsequently also won two more in September, Nithi and Siakago, to increase its share of the National Assembly to 118 MPs (see Appendix 4). As the severe public beating of Rev. Timothy Njoya and other NCEC demonstrators by *Jeshi la Mzee* men on Budget Day revealed, the regime had again come back to its old habits, resolved to deal violently with its opponents and guaranteed total impunity to its troops. It similarly deported Nassir Ibrahim Ali at the end of July after the controversial Pakistani businessman had presented to the press an affidavit directly implicating President Moi, Joshua Kulei, and George Saitoti in the Goldenberg scandal. In addition to being the official Dubai recipient of the gold shipment, Ali claimed that he had a letter from President Moi asking him to seek funding for KANU's 1992 electoral campaigns from the Middle East and Far East political leaders.

Yet, the reassertion of KANU-B front men's influence in national politics proved to be short sighted for the management of the economy. In March, Kenya had defaulted its debt repayment only for the second time in its history. Bankruptcy was looming and this finally prompted President Moi to engage in secret negotiations with the IMF and the World Bank on the conditions to resume international support of the country and its weakened balance of payments. Richard Leakey, the Safina-nominated MP (re-appointed head of the Kenya Wildlife Service in October 1998), was sent by Moi and brokered the deal with World Bank President James Wolfensohn whom Moi met secretly in London in May. On 7 August 1999, President Moi announced his third reshuffle in two years. Richard Leakey was appointed head of the civil service with the mission to trim down public expenditure, reduce the 250,000-strong civil service by at least 60,000 and eradicate corruption. He brought with him what was quickly castigated as a reformist 'dream team' composed of Martin Oduor-Otieno, a former banker at Barclays Bank Kenya who was appointed permanent secretary in the Treasury; Mwaghaza Mwachofi, a resident representative of the World Bank group's International Finance Corporation in South Africa, who was appointed financial secretary in the Treasury; Titus Naikuni, managing director of Magadi Soda Co., appointed permanent secretary in the Ministry for Transport; Dr Shem Migot-Adholla, a World Bank official in Washington was appointed permanent secretary in the Ministry for Agriculture. In addition to these international technocrats, Leakey engineered an extensive reshuffle of permanent secretaries in key ministries. Among them were the replacement of Crispus Mutitu, permanent secretary in the Ministry of Energy, Philemon Mwaisaka, permanent secretary in the Ministry for Health, Francis Awuor, permanent secretary in the Ministry for Trade, Stanley Murage, Ministry for Transport andCommunications. The shuffles were quickly followed by a swap between the ministers of Finance and Energy (Chris Okemo, a Canada trained economist with experience in the oil industry and outgoing incumbent minister for Energy took the position of minister for Finance Francis Masakhalia and vice-versa.

Yet, if Richard Leakey proved, upon his arrival at the head of the civil service, to be more determined than Justice Aaron Ringera, the former director of public prosecutions appointed head of KACA at the beginning of the year, it was not certain that he had the necessary political clout to seriously implement his programme of reforms. KACA had indeed been paralysed initially by lack of staff and funding. But even after it managed to constitute a 35-strong investigating team, it remained almost toothless as it lacked obvious determination and its mandate proved to be extremely limited. It could only deal with the cases of bribery through lengthy public prosecutions and had no authority to refer individuals for indictment for theft, fraud, embezzlement or tax-evasion as demanded by the IMF (EIU 1999).

Leakey began his term in office by bringing in new managers at the Kenya Tourist Board (Eliud Mahihu replaced by Uhuru Kenyatta), and the National Hospital Insurance Fund (Paul Lang'at replaced by Peter Matui). Yet, the long-expected reshuffle that took place in September illustrated how vain Richard Leakey's efforts could be when he had to deal with KANU-B. All but one minister was re-appointed and squeezed into an officially reduced government of 15 ministries. They were 27 before, which now had three to four heads each. Nicholas Biwott was given the influential Ministry for Trade and Industry; George Saitoti was reverted to the vice-presidency and Joseph Kamotho was put in charge of the Ministry for Local Government which controls all allocations of trust land in the country.

Newly appointed Chris Okemo quickly showed the kind of pressures he was under, when he announced that the reduction of the number of ministries would not lead to budget cuts and subsequently refused to reveal the list of the Kenya Commercial Bank's Ksh. 9.6 billion loan defaulters to parliament. The only result the reshuffle had reached was to have 15 incumbent permanent secretaries retired. Moreover, when Bernard Chunga, a hawkish former public prosecutor was appointed chief justice, thus replacing the deceased Zacchaeus Chesoni, it became obvious that the regime was protecting itself against any misadventure. Kamlesh Pattni could legitimately seek the nullification of his trial as, in addition to Chunga's removal from the prosecution, the judge presiding over his case, Uniter Pamela Kidullah, was appointed the new DPP.

In 1998 and 1999, there were additional signs of the total decomposition of Kenyan administration and of the need for radical change. In April 1999 the *Daily Nation* revealed that passports, birth and death certificates, logbooks, primary school slips, and other official documents were freely on sale in downtown Nairobi, barely one year after it had uncovered that Kenyatta University degree certificates, abstracts and diplomas were also put on sale by unscrupulous officials. Even the intelligence, judiciary, police and security services seemed paralysed by graft. In January 1998, CID officers had been arrested over the systematic rackets of Asian businessmen. By August, speculations were rife that corruption within the immigration department had tremendously eased the work of the terrorists, some of them having left the country with Kenyan passports. In September, a raid from Ethiopian Oromo pastoralists on their Somali neighbours in Dagalla claimed close to 300 lives. The capture of more than 1,000 young girls and the seizure of 15,000 head of cattle without a single reaction from the security forces days after it had been reported were all surprising.

In October, Justice Richard Otieno Kwach released a damning report on the situation of the judiciary in the country, revealing how corruption and favouritism had deeply compromised the administration of justice. The report called for radical reforms and the dismissal of the most corrupt judges. In February 1999, intelligence services handed over Kurdish rebel leader Abdullah Ocalan to the Turkish government, after being tipped off by Israeli intelligence of his presence in the country. Rumours circulated that the Turkish government had paid a 'delivery fee' of Ksh. 270 million to State House and security individuals. By May 1999, an explosion of a land mine on the Marsabit-Moyale road confirmed that the Ethiopian army's conflict with the Oromo Liberation Front was freely taking place on Kenyan territory. The department of defence had to send a troop of 2,000 soldiers to secure the area and remove minefields from the road, suspected to have been put there by the Ethiopian army to block the OLF retreat into Kenya. Finally, in August, Somali warlords freely came into the country and attacked isolated posts of the Kenyan army to steal its materials, weapons and ammunitions. President Moi threatened to retaliate and officially closed the border with Somalia. Through negotiations with the warlords, the military equipment was recovered.

By the end of the 1999, and despite the public relations efforts of Richard Leakey, few reliable indications had been given that his recovery programme would indeed be implemented and it was not clear the IMF would resume its funding in the months ahead. Believing that nothing but violence, graft and politicking would be achieved as long as Daniel arap Moi was in power, Kenya was impatiently waiting for his retirement.

References

EIU 1998, *Kenya Country Report*, 2nd Quarter 1998, Economist Intelligence Unit.

EIU 1999, *Kenya Country Report*, 4th Quarter 1999, Economist Intelligence Unit.

22

Conclusion

François Grignon, Alamin Mazrui, Marcel Rutten

On 29 December 1997, Kenyans went to the polls to choose their presidential, parliamentary and civic representations. These multi-party elections offered an opportunity for the Kenyan voters to choose between candidates from different political parties. However, the Kenyan 1997 general elections were a knockout in which the counting exercise was a crucial part. *Out for the Count!* the title of this book describes its contents. Notwithstanding other shortcomings, it was the flawed ballot count of the parliamentary votes in at least three constituencies (Westlands, Changamwe, Kitui West), that enabled KANU to secure a majority in parliament. In other words, the 107-103 KANU majority should have been at least a 106-104 victory for the opposition, notwithstanding its own sometimes shady victories (i.e., Fafi). Indeed, in the end it was through the counting exercise that the opposition was denied a majority.

This book is somehow the story of how KANU manipulated the 1997 general elections. This may have been in many ways, but three of them stand out above the rest. First, through the government, KANU enjoyed total control on the issuance of ID cards which enabled the party to exercise extensive influence on voter registrations. Secondly, the use of the same black ballot boxes as in 1992, including the 150 which were never recovered by the Electoral Commission of Kenya in 1993 was open to abuse by the party. Thirdly, KANU party agents were not only able to intimidate some voters, but they also manipulated the law by 'helping' the illiterate voters to mark the ballot papers. Needless to say, this was the highest violation of the rule of 'secret ballot' and put the electors at the mercy of the violence so systematically deployed by foremost, though not solely, the KANU youth surrounding the polling stations.

The book gives a far broader list of the necessary changes in the electoral system for it to become genuinely 'free and fair'. It also gives a number of other highlights on Kenya's electoral politics, which are revealing of its culture of politics.

Like justice in the courts of law, elections are a democratic exercise that must not only be done, but must also be seen to be done. But the sample of serious flaws in the electoral process which has been described in this book –

from the initial phases of constituency determination to the later phases of actual voting and vote counting – did little to accord it even a modicum of legitimacy in the eyes of the Kenyan public. In spite of all these flaws and irregularities, however, election observers concluded that, on the whole, the results of the elections reflected the wishes of Kenyan voters. But how were these wishes of Kenyan voters determined in the first place? The logic adopted was that even after statistically factoring in all the irregularities – often a cover-up term for rigging – into the counting of the votes, the election results would still favour Moi and KANU. This is a logic that essentially views democratic elections as outcome rather than process. And it is precisely the logic that lent political legitimacy to the 'Out for the Count' culture in electoral politics. Nothing else really matters beyond the final numbers of votes, no matter how those numbers were eventually arrived at. Are observers, therefore, contributing, even if unwittingly, to the entrenchment of the prevailing mood of satisfaction with the appearance of democracy devoid of any real substance?

Sometimes, there have also been the patronising sentiments expressed by sections of the foreign diplomatic establishment that in spite of the serious lapses in the process, its results should stand because it constitutes a major step towards democracy. A relativist twist is thus invoked to justify the acceptance, in the African context, of what would otherwise have been totally unacceptable in Europe and America as part of the liberal democratic package. Moreover, some diplomats in need of influence, usually competing for the marketing of their institutional set-ups, are often hit by a strange kind of amnesia and oversized self-confidence in the superiority of their own political system.

Ask them about election rigging, campaign violence, corruption and they will half-heartedly admit that, indeed, in certain circumstances these unfortunate irregularities occur in their respective polities, but they cannot seriously be compared with what happens in Africa. Their polities are mature, complex, based on ideological debates nurtured by the class and religious divides of the Western societies, not on 'primary' or utilitarian patterns of identification such as ethnicity.

Learning from the 1992 and 1997 general elections, it is easy to draw the conclusion that the principle of 'free and fair elections' will be better upheld by solving the myriad of technical and logistical problems associated with administrative corruption and inefficiency come the next round of elections. Important and necessary as these changes are, however, they will amount to little if the entirety of the process continues to be seen by the electorate as less than 'free and fair'. No amount of administrative efficiency, for example, would have convinced the majority of Kenyans of the fairness of the process as long as its administration (the electoral commission) was directed by a person

(Z. Chesoni) who, in their eyes, lacked both independence and the will to be independent, as well as political credibility.

A real challenge in the consolidation of democratic elections in Kenya, therefore, lies partly in greater transparency and accountability of the process in a way that will foster public perceptions, trust and confidence that the elections were truly 'free and fair'.

The verdict that the results of the elections were a fair reflection of the wishes of Kenyans, the many flaws notwithstanding, brings us directly to the question of election observation. The end of the Cold War precipitated major changes in the global political arena which led to the emergence of an 'international consensus that assistance in the organisation of free elections is a new phase in state-building' (Gershman 1993:10).

In addition to economic liberalisation and performance, therefore, the political performance of countries receiving aid from the West now became a condition for continued support. And, as a result, international monitoring and observation of elections in these countries assumed new importance in evaluating the degree of compliance by recipient nations with the political conditionality that was demanded by international donors for the disbursement of aid. International observation and monitoring thus became part of the new agenda of globalisation of Western forms of democratic electoral practice.

Earlier international observation attempts, however, soon revealed a number of problems. Most international governments and agencies could not afford to send more than a limited number of observers to the election and most of these tended to establish a presence for only a few days before and after elections. Their small numerical size imposed limitations on the size of the terrain they could cover and on how closely they could observe the process. Lack of proficiency in the local languages and lack of familiarity with local cultures also impacted on how well they could comprehend what they observed. Finally, the observers' task was too narrowly focussed on the election process to the exclusion of the wider political context and process within which the elections were taking place.

To remedy some of these problems, international organisations sought to support and encourage the complementation of international observation with the more extensive network of domestic observation through co-ordination with local non-governmental organisations. In Kenya, this collaborative venture was first attempted in 1992, and as explained in the introduction, it was tremendously improved upon in the 1997 general elections through a number of innovative strategies. In a country like Kenya where the regime has been openly hostile to election observation, the relationship between international and local observers proved to be particularly useful and symbiotic.

The institutionalisation of domestic observation holds some promise for democratisation in Kenya. At the very minimum, its active presence reaffirms local commitment, among the elite as well as the general citizenry, to the principle of free and fair elections, democratic procedure and due process. This affirmation, in turn, has the potential of galvanising the society, leading it eventually towards a new electoral culture of greater transparency and accountability. This potential development is particularly feasible in contexts like Kenya, where domestic observation is becoming an accepted feature of electoral politics.

But to what extent are local observers seen to be neutral enough to gain legitimacy in the eyes of the electorate? Unlike international observers, domestic observers are often considered to be vulnerable to local political pressures from various interest groups. The fact that the local observer group rushed to give its stamp of approval to the results of flawed 1997 general elections raised serious questions about its non-partisanship in carrying out its mission. But how realistic would the quest be for total political neutrality on the part of local observers? Would it not make better sense to strive for greater representation in the domestic observation machinery of different stakeholders who can then act as checks and balances in relation to each other?

But, if domestic observers are seen to represent particular interest groups in the political process, international observers are often suspected of harbouring a hidden agenda on behalf of their respective countries. And because the sincerity of the Western nations' own commitment to genuine democratisation in Kenya is deemed suspect, international observers are often regarded as 'imperialist' pawns who have come to endorse a pre-determined outcome of the election exercise. Commenting on the 1992 general elections, for example, Emeka Nwokedi has noted that 'despite the criticism of the flawed election in Kenya, especially by the United States, the unanimous opinion expressed by the international observers that the results should stand, set the tone for western policy towards democratization in Kenya' (1995:203). To the extent that the objective assessment of elections is not seen to be genuinely a part of the agenda of donor countries, their representatives are not likely to be seen as credible observers and monitors of the election process.

Like domestic observers in the local context, however, it would probably be naive to expect foreign observers to act in a manner that is unmediated by the politico-economic interests of the Western world. At the same time, however, one notices greater intra-EU competition, on the one hand, and competition between the USA and other EU allies, on the other. In this respect, the USA stood on their own throughout the election observation exercise and only came back actively within the DDDG Election Observation Centre in the end, in support of the British, the Japanese and the Canadians in order to block the 'undiplomatic' proposition to reveal immediately and publicly the findings on the most blatant frauds and instead produce more of a government-to-government document (*Economic Review* 23/02-02/03/98).

But let us assume for the moment that the election observers were right that, everything else being equal – which it certainly was not – the election results were indeed stacked against the opposition. How, then, can we explain the election outcome in favour of a regime that is decidedly unpopular? The chapters in this volume have provided several explanations for this seeming anomaly, some of which are shared by the Kenyan public at large. Prominent among these is the thesis of a divided opposition. There were indeed several attempts behind the scenes – all of which came to nought – to get various opposition parties to field one presidential candidate against KANU's Daniel arap Moi.

Even when this initiative did not succeed, however, it was anticipated that, with strong presidential contenders in Central, Eastern, Nyanza and Western provinces, Moi was unlikely to garner the required minimum of 25 per cent of the votes in at least five provinces. This indeterminate outcome would have forced a run-off election between Moi and one candidate from the opposition. Indeed an opinion poll on presidential popularity conducted in June and July of 1997 among some 1,600 Kenyans covering all eight provinces concluded that the only likely candidate to beat Daniel arap Moi in a run-off would be Charity Ngilu. All other aspirants would not receive the much-needed support from other opposition zones. In a run-off against Wamalwa, Matiba, Raila or Kibaki, Moi would score from 60 to 64 per cent, whereas versus Ngilu he would lose, gaining no more than 35 per cent of the votes (see ACCORD 1997). The voting pattern in both Eastern and Western provinces, however, failed to meet this expectation of the opposition.

For whatever it is worth as a 'strategy' for ousting Moi, however, the electoral politics of a united/divided opposition essentially betrayed the narrow vision of democracy prevalent in much of the country. Generally, there was much less concern with democratic practices and processes than with blocking Moi and KANU from winning the elections. Sections of the opposition were often willing to accept blatant flaws in the election process well before the polling day as long as it appeared to them that they stood some chance of being the eventual victors – a status, which they have always been in a hurry to attain. Well before the elections, the 25 per cent rule was repeatedly attacked not because it was undemocratic in any principled manner, but only because it was seen to favour Moi. Moi and KANU, rather than democracy, turned out to be the real issue: and because it was simply 'Out for the Count', the opposition became a cause for its own undoing. It is, nonetheless, true that by reason of internal divisions within the opposition, the (illegitimate) narrow win for KANU became possible. Had there been better co-ordination between the opposition parties in the fielding of their candidates, the fraudulent counts would not have been able to make up for the loss of some 15 seats where the combined opposition gathered more votes than KANU. The constituencies where much of this fraud took place are mainly to be found in the Coast, Eastern and Western provinces.

Then there was KANU's own capacity to reinvent itself. In its bid to ensure its own survival as a ruling party, KANU has incorporated into its organism a blend of new politicians – some well educated and highly motivated – who, as long as they support Moi, have had the space to demonstrate their leadership potential. Even once avowed enemies of KANU and the establishment, like Jembe Mwakalu of Bahari constituency, have not only been accommodated in the party and allowed to pursue their own brand of politics, but they have actually been rewarded by their landslide victories in their respective constituencies. In other words, KANU has allowed its own political face to change in conformity with the changing political reality.

And the fact that the leading opposition parties were not at all different from KANU in ideological orientation, made its transformation that much easier: opposition parties seemed to provide the promise of new leadership without the potential of new direction. Its new guise, after all, need not be substantially different from the old one in order to be at par with opposition parties in offering a 'new kind' of leadership.

Finally, there was the ethnic factor. Chapter after chapter in this book has demonstrated how much force ethnicity has in electoral politics, sometimes, as in the case of the Rift Valley and the Coast, with tragic and bloody consequences. KANU as much as the opposition parties has continued to gravitate around the ethnic pole. It continued to play on the fears of the so-called ethnic minorities in places like the Coast and North-Eastern Province. And even in Western Province Moi's success was perhaps partly attributable to the 'ethnic minority card' to the extent that the region's ethnic profile is a lot more heterogeneous than it is often presumed to be. On the other hand, despite the millions of shillings that were poured into the Central Province by the Central Province Development Support Group of tycoons like Stanley Githunguri and S.K. Macharia in support of KANU, the party lost miserably to the seemingly Kikuyu-based party, the DP.

But as indicated in the introduction and demonstrated in several of the chapters, it would be naïve to interpret these results simply as manifestations of an uncompromising ethnic consciousness on the part of the Kenyan electorate. At the bottom of it all is a struggle for the distribution of power and resources in a political system which, over the decades, has been designed to thrive on the politics of inclusion and exclusion. Voters, therefore, see elections as a way of attracting resources to their own communities but, in a multi-party context, they often do so '. . . by voting for the party that most community members believe represents the interests of the geographic region in which they reside. Because geographical attachments and considerations of ethnicity are the defining attributes of voters' interests, political parties invariably emerge that purposely appeal to the inhabitants of some region more than others' (Barkan 1997:14). The pursuit of multi-party elections in Kenya, in other words, has taken place in a context where ethnicity has either been exploited for political gain or is a manifestation of underlying struggles between communities based on material interests necessary for collective survival. The regional distribution of the support for political parties also reflects this factor. Extreme caution must be exercised, however, when making general statements on the interplay between ethnicity and party politics. There is currently no real sociology of political parties in Kenya. How KANU, DP or FORD-Kenya really interact with their electorate is still, to a great extent, an enigma. It is only when politicians and their audiences will be recorded and understood when expressing themselves in their mother tongues, that it will be possible to establish a credible pattern of data analysis and have a clear picture of the actual changes within Kenya's culture of politics (see an attempt in Grignon 1998a and 1998b).

An adjustment of the 'winner-take-all' constituency system is called for. Proportional representation seems to be able to prevent some of the disadvantages of the constituency system as it has developed in the Kenyan setting. As for now, losing an election is economically a disadvantage. Politicians thus have an interest in igniting mistrust or reverting to violence to reach their goals and stay, or get into, power.

What seems to be needed most is to de-link the narrow interests of politicians from those of their respective regions. Moreover, the current system is blocking a voter from choosing the party he or she wants to support in the parliamentary or presidential contest since not every party is able to field a candidate in each constituency.

In a proportional electoral system KANU would have won 93 parliamentary seats in the 1997 general elections, i.e, without an absolute majority (see Table A2.1 page 629). This would have allowed KANU, with the largest number of parliamentary seats, to try to form a coalition government, for example, with DP, NDP, FORD-Kenya or any other combination resulting in a majority of MPs supporting the cabinet. This way a government would have been formed backed by a real majority of the Kenyan electorate; a government, moreover, forced to deliver to more, if not all, Kenyans.

The argument that minorities' interests are not taken care of in a proportional system is false. On the contrary, the proportional system favours the minorities since by combining efforts they can make a major player and, as KANU showed, could easily win the elections. The price to pay, some argue, is political instability characterised by frequent collapses of the cabinet. But coalition governments exist all over the world and, in general, it seems many Kenyans would prefer this road towards greater democracy, especially as it is more likely to prevent a future scenario of all open violence. Otherwise, several elections recently conducted in Africa, e.g., South Africa in 1999, illustrate that violence and corruption do not necessarily come with voting. No single election is worth the loss of human lives, anywhere. As long as Kenyans die simply because of state-organised or 'spontaneous' violence, basic democratic rights are still at peril.

Under the circumstances and limitations of interpretation described above, what conclusion can be drawn on the prospects of democracy in Kenya? How far have Kenyans liberated themselves from the peculiar 'mindset' and social relations precipitated by decades of a system of corruption and brutal dictatorship? The opinion of many observers of the political scene in Kenya, in particular, and in Africa in general, has been one of discouragement and frustration. In the words of Lemarchand (1995:1) 'After raising hopes of a major political renewal, Africa's "second wave" of democratisation seems to be running out of steam. Afro-pessimism is again in fashion and many feel that the emergent trends are better captured by the incessant bloodshed in Liberia, Somalia, and Burundi than by the few success stories represented by South Africa, Botswana and Benin.'

The seeming failure of the transition to democracy has been attributed to many factors, including an opportunistic opposition whose only objective is to capture the state to promote its own interests, the divisive and disintegrative effects of multi-partyism in an ethnicised political context, and the continuing state of underdevelopment in the economy and the infrastructure. And, above all, there have been the international forces which, in a hurry to globalise democracy in the post-Cold War period, have reduced it '. . . to the crude simplicity of multiparty elections to the benefit of some of the world's most notorious autocrats, such as Daniel arap Moi of Kenya and Paul Biya of Cameroon, who are now able to parade democratic credentials without reforming their repressive regimes' (Ake 1996:130).

Of course, there are many other factors that can be cited as possible explanations for this seeming growth of electoral systems without democratic foundations. In spite of this gloomy political picture, however, the wave of political liberalisation that has come with the struggle for political pluralism has led to certain developments whose combined effect on the direction of politics in Kenya promises to be positive. Of greatest significance, of course, has been the end of the culture of fear and silence which has forced open the political space and created the possibility for the expression of alternative political voices and for the articulation of different interests as well as individual and collective anger.

Regime autocracy has never experienced a more resolute challenge to its legitimacy than in the recent years of multi-party politics, its many flaws notwithstanding. While it is true that the political positions expressed in this new dispensation have not been as ideologically distinct (and polarised) as they were in the earlier phase of multi-partyism in Kenya, a wide range of hitherto marginalised groups, including women, the unemployed, ethnic and religious 'minorities', have become relatively more visible.

In the meantime, more traditional bodies, like trade unions, that were either muzzled or co-opted, have now found room for recomposition and self-rejuvenation. And organisations that were once pro-establishment or claimed to be apolitical, like the Supreme Council of Kenya Muslims (Supkem), have been politicised in a new direction, often being forced to participate in challenging authoritarian and repressive rule. This is a conquered space that Kenyans are unlikely to ever surrender again, at least not without a major political battle.

An accompanying attribute of this reconfigured political arena has been the destruction of the wall of invincibility of Daniel arap Moi, in particular, and of the Kenyan presidency, at large. At one time, it was virtually unthinkable to imagine the president facing opposition on an election platform or serving a term that is not life-long. In 1997 as in 1992 he was not only challenged by several presidential candidates, but was actually forced to go around the country begging for votes from the electorate to allow him complete his final term of office. The president is attacked and ridiculed at public platforms, is made a subject of litigation, and is routinely challenged and contradicted in many of his pronouncements. Even when it has sometimes assumed a crude form, this process is giving rise to the kind of political psychology that is unlikely to accommodate a rebirth of the political strongman syndrome that had bedevilled the nation since independence

For these gains to be consolidated and deepened and for new ones to be won, however, there is much more that needs to be done as part of the process of establishing a democratic system and culture in the country above and beyond the periodic elections. Both the legislature and the judiciary need to be strengthened and institutions for the articulation of collective interests must be developed. There needs to be a shift of emphasis in the struggle for rights, from individual to collective. The very scope of rights must itself be expanded to include not only rights of a political nature, but also economic, social and cultural rights, and in a manner that is integrative. Without paying greater attention to its socio-economic content, democracy is not likely to find root and become sustainable in Kenya.

References

ACCORD 1997, June/July 1997 Presidential Polls Survey – Presidential poll; run-off scenarios, Nairobi: ACCORD.

Ake, C. 1996, *Democracy and Development in Africa*. Washington DC: The Brookings Institution.

Barkan, J.D. 1997, 'African Elections in Comparative Perspective.' in *Elections: Perspectives on Establishing Democratic Practices*, Produced by the United Nations Department for Development Support and Management Services, New York: 2-29.

Gershman, C. 1993, 'The United Nations and the New World Order.' *Journal of Democracy*, Vol.14, No.3: 10-11.

Grignon, F. 1998a, 'Espace public, démocratisation et imaginaires politiques: remarques théoriques et méthodologiques à propos d'une recherche sur le Kenya' in Martin, D.-C. (sld), *Nouveaux langages du politique en Afrique orientale*, Paris: Karthala: 15-28.

Grignon, F. 1998b, 'La démocratie au risque du débat? Territoires de la critique et imaginaires politiques au Kenya (1990-1995)', in Martin, D.-C. (sld), *Nouveaux langages du politique en Afrique orientale*, Paris: Karthala: 28-112.

Lemarchand, R. 1995, 'Four Models for Resolving Ethnic Conflicts: How Can Democratic Institutions be Strengthened Where Conflict Threatens Their Survival?' *Africa Voices*, Vol.4, No.2: 1-2.

Nwokedi, E. 1995, *Politics of Democratization: Changing Authoritarian Regimes in Sub-Saharan Africa*, Hamburg: Lit Verlag.

Appendices

Appendix 1: 1997 Presidential election results

Constituency	NDP Raila	UMMA Ngethe	GAP M'mwereri	UPPK Waiyaki	LPK Maath	FORD-P Kimani	KANU Moi	EIP Oludhe	KSC Anyona	KENDA Wamwere	KNC Mkangi	FORD-A Shikuku	DP Kibaki	FORD-K Wamalwa	SDP Ngilu	TOTAL VALID	TOTAL REJECT	REGIS TERED	%TURN-OUT
001 Makadara	7138	23	14	12	11	36	8628	6	109	71	9	214	19147	3070	7117	45605	846	90986	51.05
002 Kamukunji	3760	11	22	51	18	47	7349	22	44	75	19	133	17076	1095	3604	33326	833	65397	52.23
003 Starehe	5406	16	14	34	23	89	9973	17	96	81	39	251	25403	2611	5808	49861	1587	107128	48.02
004 Langata	14955	22	11	25	18	1386	11420	14	96	51	17	548	8664	1968	4575	43770	1355	80888	55.79
005 Dagoretti	2115	18	22	24	23	43	6480	12	118	51	22	264	21773	3168	3280	37413	1087	69216	55.62
006 Westlands	3168	16	25	54	21	38	16651	12	131	62	26	295	17154	6826	4005	48494	1497	101571	49.22
007 Kasarani	14462	33	28	38	16	43	6267	15	66	89	30	442	20809	2646	3046	48030	970	91271	53.69
008 Embakasi	8411	19	17	114	18	25	8504	16	158	79	37	195	30098	3587	8272	59550	1392	113848	53.53
NAIROBI	59415	158	153	351	149	1707	75272	124	818	559	199	2342	160124	24971	39707	366049	9567	720305	52.39
009 Changamwe	6235	8	13	26	6	22	10588	13	66	65	301	143	5728	2660	8662	34536	170	76567	45.33
010 Kisauni	3288	12	16	29	17	24	12865	19	48	48	995	98	8696	1948	3666	31769	811	74246	43.88
011 Likoni	1877	12	15	11	8	27	6371	8	28	28	2655	68	1979	1092	1549	14309	328	40414	36.22
012 Mvita	3029	12	19	30	7	19	14570	13	60	53	521	64	5011	1227	3333	27968	801	64938	44.30
013 Msambweni	1037	15	36	68	29	65	21765	25	77	45	6286	166	5372	481	3026	38493	656	59922	65.33
014 Matuga	222	15	13	43	12	47	16421	11	44	26	5158	29	561	54	1646	24302	509	37365	66.40
015 Kinango	366	17	14	16	17	13	16841	11	11	16	683	12	992	20	884	19898	147	33478	59.88
016 Bahari	1528	24	27	25	17	38	23528	15	47	35	2299	47	2422	1560	1113	32725	436	63580	52.16
017 Kaloleni	1288	18	15	33	2	24	19456	18	35	20	1285	31	1790	133	4956	29104	1270	54736	55.49
018 Ganze	48	7	17	15	7	19	10009	8	13	7	76	5	988	10	942	12167	117	27243	45.09
019 Malindi	1240	5	12	22	3	44	17661	8	33	26	300	23	3631	507	1706	25225	410	52150	49.16
020 Magarini	93	2	9	15	7	12	11492	1	2	3	764	3	375	1120	162	14066	306	27780	51.74
021 Garsen	39	2	7	4	1	9	12602	2	4	8	17	3	134	34	60	12926	46	22049	58.83
022 Galole	335	1	3	10	2	8	9555	5	5	9	8	8	405	90	126	10567	343	16334	66.79
023 Bura	1676	4	8	5	2	2	5824	3	11	5	2	8	830	26	303	8703	136	15192	58.18
024 Lamu East	1056	3	3	8	4	16	5156	1	12	5	4	5	249	29	60	6602	123	9039	74.40
025 Lamu West	268	17	22	51	13	120	7403	16	33	28	55	87	5271	60	185	13613	399	22635	61.90
026 Taveta	441	7	10	12	3	19	6460	20	29	15	21	29	1301	65	634	11379	193	16542	69.96
027 Wundanyi	102	12	18	33	8	21	8544	15	17	14	35	26	2029	60	624	11574	308	20685	57.44
028 Mwatate	304	14	12	51	9	35	10667	12	30	22	83	32	1802	81	624	13768	396	22572	62.75
029 Voi	372	9	13	39	7	23	9287	12	30	8	28	20	2343	60	1504	13755	368	24532	57.57
COAST	24844	228	302	555	164	607	257065	242	606	486	20145	901	51909	11306	38089	407449	8273	781999	56.32
030 Dujis	118	2	5	5	2	7	12213	3	13	7	2	10	3949	67	195	16596	88	27250	61.23
031 Lagdera	24	–	–	–	–	1	5556	1	3	3	2	6	1324	8	9	6938	40	13665	51.06
032 Fafi	3	–	–	–	–	1	3974	–	2	2	1	1	127	1	4	4115	19	8429	49.04
033 Ijara	62	2	1	2	2	3	3549	–	2	–	–	6	1604	4	–	5236	14	7445	70.52
034 Wajir North	7	–	–	–	–	–	3901	–	2	3	–	6	159	–	1	4081	17	7577	54.08
035 Wajir West	18	–	–	–	–	2	7110	2	2	3	–	6	3077	5	7	10260	56	18693	55.19
036 Wajir East	1	1	1	1	–	3	6823	2	2	1	–	–	2615	13	52	9509	62	16247	58.91
037 Wajir South	1	–	–	–	–	–	4196	3	3	231	–	15	2511	–	19	6953	116	15896	44.47
038 Mandera West	16	1	2	2	–	2	5439	–	1	1	1	12	935	1577	8	7997	79	12043	67.06
039 Mandera C.	34	1	4	4	–	5	7572	–	–	1	–	17	704	2550	–	11006	153	17081	65.33
040 Mandera E.	23	2	6	6	2	2	10173	2	2	–	2	58	3399	206	134	13941	122	21456	65.54
NORTH-EAST	307	8	17	19	40	32	70506	10	28	249	13	128	20404	4431	440	96632	766	165782	58.40

Constituency	NDP Raila	UMMA Ngethe	GAP M'mwereri	UPPK Waiyaki	LPK Maatha	FORD-P Kimani	KANU Moi	EIP Oludhe	KSC Anyona	KENDA Wamwere	KNC Mkangi	FORD-A Shikuku	DP Kibaki	FORD-K Wamalwa	SDP Ngilu	TOTAL VALID	TOTAL REJECT	REGISTERED	%TURN-OUT
041 Moyale	21	1	-	5	-	6	14201	9	3	4	1	28	885	1492	61	16708	232	22379	75.70
042 North Horr	2106	5	3	3	-	3	5691	-	-	4	1	-	-	10	4	7848	11	11999	65.50
043 Saku	40	-	2	-	-	-	9285	-	3	3	2	1	443	11	64	9855	147	12534	79.80
044 Laisamis	12	1	-	2	1	2	7225	-	2	4	-	-	62	1	14	7327	8	11850	61.90
045 Isioʃo North	134	4	12	10	5	13	10239	4	2	11	-	16	4157	68	284	14957	165	25325	59.71
046 Isiolo South	9	7	10	-	4	1	5517	-	2	9	2	7	504	415	16	6503	56	8165	80.33
047 Igembe	641	14	49	22	37	38	19159	18	9	29	22	26	11194	15	481	31754	252	49265	64.97
048 Ntonyiri	254	-	42	17	8	36	11185	1	-	22	6	43	13046	18	252	24930	454	38732	65.54
049 Tigania W	26	5	127	50	112	26	5926	-	7	10	30	59	14649	16	159	21224	541	32265	67.46
050 Tigania E	293	43	1092	26	111	20	12857	7	7	14	21	48	13105	9	121	27778	201	35637	78.51
051 N Imenti	466	23	120	121	65	50	15263	22	34	82	16	152	34761	207	1504	52916	470	73996	72.15
052 C Imenti	69	21	111	59	41	28	15603	11	26	54	30	146	20402	3094	1783	41498	1084	52901	80.49
053 S Imenti	271	20	66	75	85	41	10632	71	34	47	24	149	37515	77	795	49902	1446	62214	82.53
054 Nithi	396	18	91	109	123	86	15987	108	52	51	37	212	38652	62	1086	57070	813	78676	73.57
055 Tharaka	105	4	20	66	66	17	7328	23	8	14	27	43	12718	11	188	20588	174	26844	77.34
056 Manyatta	198	9	38	64	122	45	4806	42	23	70	15	165	33578	150	1157	40482	528	51847	79.10
057 Runyenjes	167	11	46	61	93	43	4975	67	37	55	53	761	30473	177	533	37552	1451	49425	78.91
058 Gachoka	98	87	42	11	11	77	8520	29	26	23	21	89	9961	240	5061	24654	508	31936	78.79
059 Siakago	97	12	10	-	31	18	6963	12	9	13	22	25	11015	13	298	18538	152	23159	80.70
060 Mwingi N	80	10	15	26	6	19	21808	31	45	15	20	47	1570	18	11016	34726	526	45288	77.84
061 Mwingi S	76	44	15	13	2	38	11448	27	101	7	18	22	350	18	19988	32167	426	43768	74.47
062 Kitui West	81	10	27	24	5	54	4523	20	171	23	26	52	210	14	28084	33324	449	46498	72.63
063 Kitui Cent.	122	5	12	16	23	31	10602	20	214	10	23	43	273	48	27337	38779	152	51293	75.90
064 Mutito	32	5	15	10	5	18	2154	13	82	2	11	62	73	8	17176	19666	125	28728	68.89
065 Kitui South	48	6	15	14	6	27	4313	13	102	4	10	39	2545	32	16816	21700	274	31879	68.93
066 Masinga	108	18	10	23	6	47	9462	17	152	13	36	55	303	32	13638	23920	382	33620	72.28
067 Yatta	65	11	11	17	10	29	7612	19	31	16	22	64	912	19	17000	26070	295	37683	69.96
068 Kangundo	118	36	28	49	6	75	16747	56	374	30	73	79	734	69	27212	45711	1137	63122	74.22
069 Kathiani	619	8	11	33	6	38	14690	32	256	15	28	40	1455	311	17460	35002	600	51877	68.63
070 Machakos T	241	21	21	55	23	65	15642	35	383	24	21	81	843	112	27472	45039	806	63212	72.53
071 Mwala	107	9	28	47	47	71	9911	38	281	16	59	65	471	107	31125	42382	540	48647	88.23
072 Mbooni	80	12	14	13	16	53	11172	10	324	-	26	54	578	34	21867	34263	749	49447	70.81
073 Kilome	73	17	2	28	16	36	7284	10	130	7	32	16	143	13	8218	16024	204	25374	63.96
074 Kaiti	69	10	18	31	16	27	8694	21	156	16	4	15	197	18	12366	21658	645	34521	64.61
075 Makueni	56	8	19	32	6	60	7667	42	385	20	36	60	291	24	28632	37338	665	55695	68.23
076 Kibwezi	409	17	-	19	-	46	9035	16	379	18	381	37	548	54	21124	32083	1064	49709	66.51
EASTERN	7787	532	2142	1459	1140	1284	370954	924	3848	761	1155	2802	296335	7017	349754	1047894	17732	1459510	72.58
077 Kinangop	147	5	18	43	9	162	1332	26	12	24	19	151	34614	114	363	37039	559	47273	79.53
078 Kipipiri	72	51	48	120	63	679	705	59	48	106	50	194	19352	27	112	21686	338	26301	82.43
079 Ol Kalou	188	8	30	31	39	146	1029	42	18	64	18	206	35478	72	455	37824	477	48569	78.86
080 Ndaragwa	24	4	14	15	9	43	812	17	4	29	14	57	20697	12	161	21912	312	27424	81.04
081 Tetu	13	4	7	29	64	13	709	15	2	11	7	49	26298	14	42	27277	169	31298	87.69
082 Kieni	30	13	30	14	23	32	2546	11	11	55	10	69	37809	29	155	40855	314	49449	83.26
083 Mathira	93	14	34	52	32	39	2521	53	10	49	106	92	48093	51	203	51440	370	61079	84.82
084 Othaya	24	3	6	7	32	3	658	6	-	21	12	40	31352	20	57	32241	174	36069	89.87
085 Mukurweini	16	14	21	37	35	9	892	23	6	29	28	36	27545	7	85	28783	126	33419	86.50

Constituency	NDP Raila	UMMA Ngethe	GAP M'mwereri	UPPK Waiyaki	LPK Maath	FORD-P Kimani	KANU Moi	EIP Oludhe	KSC Anyona	KENDA Wamwere	KNC Mkangi	FORD-A Shikuku	DP Kibaki	FORD-K Wamalwa	SDP Ngilu	TOTAL VALID	TOTAL REJECT	REGISTERED	% TURNOUT
086 Nyeri	296	4	24	21	22	16	1711	25	10	66	12	63	32259	194	456	35179	100	44431	79.40
087 Mwea	75	8	26	37	48	34	1341	22	5	36	29	73	29931	24	334	33023	278	43132	74.89
088 Gichugu	119	16	32	50	110	63	1940	21	20	47	31	140	35660	23	292	38564	596	48547	80.66
089 Ndia	87	2	7	18	9	11	666	5	7	39	6	72	25555	38	277	26799	375	33854	80.27
090 Kerugoya/K	80	8	3	24	64	9	908	14	7	21	164	92	28965	20	374	30759	456	43385	71.95
091 Kamgema	73	21	31	51	93	225	1541	55	31	72	76	192	18636	17	676	21790	488	29167	76.38
092 Mathioya	40	20	28	32	36	219	6464	44	71	54	37	351	19917	17	251	27530	584	36683	76.64
093 Kiharu	256	85	82	90	323	149	2921	138	71	225	176	376	30211	72	2457	37632	1042	66630	58.04
094 Kigumo	49	14	34	39	54	71	783	50	25	49	29	106	29516	28	478	31325	591	42700	74.74
095 Maragua	129	51	48	120	63	175	1250	59	69	106	50	194	24360	27	1174	27854	856	42445	67.64
096 Kandara	54	460	60	51	100	196	1604	64	26	67	63	273	36343	31	411	39803	708	52417	77.29
097 Gatanga	306	21	43	51	46	110	4306	87	69	84	66	185	31542	152	2485	39553	818	55473	72.78
098 Gatundu S	36	18	27	68	36	22	2150	33	29	44	13	96	30482	47	802	33903	620	43173	79.96
099 Gatundu N	156	10	18	34	38	17	514	22	14	74	7	77	25979	36	629	27625	419	33861	82.82
100 Juja	2496	24	30	35	32	51	5342	34	96	252	32	332	34504	1005	4264	48529	602	88400	54.60
101 Githunguri	91	20	56	44	58	78	861	40	57	121	34	227	40974	108	1396	44165	813	53840	83.54
102 Kiambaa	503	24	39	83	41	171	3908	55	69	253	30	280	40763	403	3961	50583	853	68461	75.13
103 Kabete	704	11	53	53	58	93	2887	97	68	191	33	302	39575	283	5779	50187	867	68558	74.47
104 Limuru	1263	11	30	28	32	25	2402	30	81	129	19	284	26946	496	1265	33041	41	45069	73.40
105 Lari	100	15	26	43	20	59	1937	53	24	43	24	146	28548	47	460	31545	715	39079	82.55
CENTRAL	6812	918	886	1218	1540	2718	55822	1190	843	2235	1180	4606	885382	3067	29473	997890	14661	1340186	77.18
106 Turkana N	50	6	6	12	1	5	7161	2	2	3	-	27	196	5911	34	13414	89	26425	51.10
107 Turkana C	83	13	10	24	1	9	15802	8	6	6	3	19	255	443	58	16740	103	33471	50.32
108 Turkana S	12	22	6	46	2	1	6196	3	2	1	-	13	219	1366	21	7910	60	18237	43.70
109 Kacheliba	3	-	-	-	-	-	9206	1	-	-	-	-	17	29	1	9259	6	13666	67.80
110 Kapenguria	152	-	1	2	1	7	28221	7	11	6	2	10	285	718	173	29596	111	36259	81.93
111 Sigor	11	-	-	2	-	-	24976	5	5	2	3	3	88	98	13	25199	32	31645	79.73
112 Samburu W	70	-	1	2	2	2	22045	4	4	3	-	6	4535	19	27	26716	27	30793	86.85
113 Samburu E	30	-	3	4	-	-	5602	-	1	-	-	3	1723	7	21	7394	28	10757	69.00
114 Kwanza	150	21	3	19	11	18	14608	2	10	5	6	68	2222	19455	121	36719	764	48759	76.87
115 Saboti	1586	40	19	51	36	60	14538	16	28	20	9	310	6976	34504	532	58725	1056	81766	73.11
116 Cherangani	82	30	11	19	5	23	14715	12	27	7	11	84	4959	8244	168	28977	545	36990	78.24
117 Eldoret N	3316	17	15	28	12	23	41759	9	96	47	8	345	9331	8235	736	63977	1386	90363	72.33
118 Eldoret E	378	4	7	13	3	11	34096	18	15	12	7	11	3426	1144	219	39364	371	51654	76.93
119 Eldoret S	1346	8	12	8	17	23	28130	9	98	15	4	106	7517	1880	299	39472	642	52345	76.63
120 Marakwet E	74	-	2	3	-	-	12670	1	2	-	3	2	4619	25	16	17424	65	20965	83.42
121 Marakwet W	37	6	1	6	1	32	22406	3	6	3	2	17	724	319	28	23598	154	27998	84.83
122 Keiyo N	63	1	4	1	2	7	18185	3	4	2	2	7	168	54	34	18534	93	21921	84.97
123 Keiyo S	28	2	12	2	3	7	26877	5	8	4	2	6	585	51	24	27615	373	32974	84.88
124 Mosop	123	8	-	3	3	20	32164	13	27	29	12	43	756	481	182	33848	197	40138	84.82
125 Aldai	123	11	3	10	9	17	30324	6	6	8	2	23	261	2955	70	33836	257	40353	84.49
126 Emgwen	365	31	11	16	11	50	33897	7	8	10	8	44	1094	3169	192	38938	409	49930	78.80
127 Tinderet	1765	24	10	27	10	26	34562	18	18	44	12	50	1088	2447	128	40278	741	52842	77.63
128 Baringo E	4	1	-	19	-	-	13115	1	1	-	4	-	85	9	16	13253	8	15362	86.32
129 Baringo N	9	-	-	11	1	-	27541	-	-	-	-	-	68	6	22	27649	22	28683	96.47
130 Baringo C	84	-	1	2	1	-	37972	2	2	8	-	3	181	24	37	38317	29	42956	89.27

Constituency	NDP Raila	UMMA Ngethe	GAP M'mwereri	UPPK Waiyaki	LPK Maath	FORD-P Kimani	KANU Moi	EIP Oludhe	KSC Anyona	KENDA Wamwere	KNC Mkangi	FORD-A Shikuku	DP Kibaki	FORD-K Wamalwa	SDP Ngilu	TOTAL VALID	TOTAL REJECT	REGISTERED	%TURNOUT
131 Mogotio	33		-	1	1	3	15288	-	4	2	3	2	141	7	98	15583	260	18389	86.15
132 Eldama Rav	174	5	34	12	5	11	21582	11	5	8	3	37	3533	119	43	25552	221	31124	82.81
133 Laikipia W	234	10	29	14	16	25	9677	19	14	29	17	54	39978	66	208	50395	703	65820	77.63
134 Laikipia E	380	9	29	20	8	37	7757	29	7	27	18	89	21815	138	439	30802	454	45280	69.03
135 Naivasha	3644	27	21	57	31	67	8310	39	87	127	55	302	40354	1823	889	55841	1175	89368	63.80
136 Nakuru T	8627	12	13	27	8	20	13012	8	187	156	13	493	28426	4479	1689	57178	890	89592	65.55
137 Kuresoi	110	3	66	10	8	8	38762	10	8	11	10	277	8984	58	66	48433	430	54536	89.60
138 Molo	958	21	26	37	45	94	11658	74	67	67	24	364	43550	632	432	58089	1284	75763	78.37
139 Rongai	2394	8	26	18	13	20	17587	20	20	53	9	122	14356	257	116	35019	640	44759	79.67
140 Subukia	277	12	26	36	15	53	2854	74	31	475	14	200	30926	101	201	35295	728	45224	79.65
141 Kilgoris	283	1	1	7	1	1	32717	1	5	6	2	16	2089	30	66	35226	155	47624	74.29
142 Narok N	450	1	-	6	15	14	26775	8	50	23	9	39	5096	214	247	32957	352	46555	71.55
143 Narok S	45	-	10	5	3	2	29427	7	13	5	1	7	2691	32	56	32294	247	47896	67.94
144 Kajiado N	1889	6	11	27	12	21	20665	12	43	38	8	126	16865	495	1676	41894	856	64358	66.43
145 Kajiado C	134	1	1	6	1	8	13900	3	9	6	3	5	7746	38	599	22460	256	28319	80.21
146 Kajiado S	174	1	-	10	-	7	10457	5	11	5	2	17	12919	49	604	24271	229	32139	76.23
147 Bomet	56	-	3	2	2	10	48000	15	13	10	5	8	743	19	133	49025	148	55563	88.50
148 Chepalungu	9	2	3	7	5	8	35157	5	5	5	5	4	730	11	41	35999	57	39830	90.52
149 Sotik	143	1	15	7	3	5	37179	5	18	5	3	11	474	45	108	38010	189	43966	86.88
150 Konoin	2178	8	2	18	5	22	29278	11	62	35	11	404	1301	355	71	33774	183	43941	77.28
151 Bureti	39	7	2	9	-	8	33934	2	-	4	5	9	147	32	107	34298	99	38377	89.63
152 Belgut	1103	6	2	8	6	8	40853	5	38	11	9	26	655	296	49	43075	142	50063	86.33
153 Ainamoi	1936	14	6	10	4	21	35468	12	23	21	2	31	2770	636	159	41113	521	53167	78.31
154 Kipketion	808	4	17	17	7	20	43044	24	23	16	3	48	5862	653	76	50599	465	57600	88.65
RIFT VALLEY	**36022**	**406**	**468**	**688**	**451**	**837**	**1140109**	**529**	**1140**	**1397**	**370**	**3885**	**343529**	**102178**	**11345**	**1643354**	**18252**	**2145505**	**77.87**
155 Malava	169	42	5	2	1	-	14032	18	55	107	-	119	174	20536	147	35435	1702	53745	69.10
156 Lugari	170	37	34	52	52	51	15829	9	6	18	12	234	2508	17787	223	37016	808	51277	73.60
157 Mumias	2628	23	34	16	16	49	18627	9	12	19	12	3373	462	9241	167	34720	840	51354	69.24
158 Matungu	114	10	4	4	4	23	10593	3	4	2	-	403	755	11484	422	22840	603	33630	72.68
159 Lurambi	1047	71	32	19	10	73	15817	19	9	15	10	1192	738	25297	261	44670	965	69064	66.08
160 Shinyalu	87	37	18	10	3	39	10832	8	6	9	6	195	87	13892	65	25347	616	41795	62.12
161 Ikolomani	28	-	2	3	6	15	10112	11	-	3	1	115	76	8272	40	18734	486	28818	66.69
162 Butere	336	23	84	19	4	15	9648	3	2	4	13	9849	125	796	125	21053	1884	33412	68.65
163 Kwishero	574	16	17	21	6	48	10891	91	6	9	7	3138	42	2158	115	17018	137	27502	62.38
164 Emuhaya	250	23	86	129	8	30	13888	21	12	13	37	239	289	14331	284	29806	210	53709	55.89
165 Sabatia	113	35	7	112	8	22	25229	7	8	11	4	163	109	3689	143	29682	993	41625	73.69
166 Vihiga	264	25	1	63	17	40	15038	32	1	10	4	54	102	3639	74	19321	599	28856	69.03
167 Hamisi	118	49	22	72	12	22	18301	6	36	30	15	235	271	11722	133	31088	981	47597	67.38
168 Mt Elgon	162	22	-	27	10	55	25091	11	3	9	1	23	22	6950	46	32394	263	39685	82.29
169 Kimilili	125	79	8	105	37	46	4027	7	26	17	7	175	909	39827	197	45585	473	54548	77.46
170 Webuye	510	212	8	77	36	48	9162	4	17	10	7	133	625	26646	174	37681	1224	50829	71.32
171 Sirisia	68	59	3	66	17	36	6228	8	2	6	6	63	224	32752	68	39611	1538	41443	80.96
172 Kanduyi	684	74	8	65	8	42	3311	10	4	21	7	224	963	22443	181	27998	467	39447	68.68
173 Bumula	90	47	5	59	14	10	3366	7	4	26	6	197	33	27708	52	31517	425	52923	80.97
174 Amagoro	2706	11	5	32	5	39	33672	8	7	16	8	66	656	2625	143	39867	333	45341	75.96
175 Nambale	1959	38	1	69	12		17935	10	3		12	75	757	10683	125	31783	1015		72.34

Constituency	NDP Raila	UMMA Ngethe	GAP M'mwereri	UPPK Waiyaki	LPK Maath	FORD-P Kimani	KANU Moi	EIP Oludhe	KSC Anyona	KENDA Wamwere	KNC Mkangi	FORD-A Shikuku	DP Kibaki	FORD-K Wamalwa	SDP Ngilu	TOTAL VALID	TOTAL REJECT	REGIST ERED	% TURN-OUT
176 Butula	1001	17	3	20	5	17	8254	1	7	8	8	110	53	9913	187	19604	296	28576	69.64
177 Funyula	145	10	-	20	6	8	9551	1	1	2	43	58	124	8212	41	18222	345	25221	73.62
178 Budalangi	149	9	5	4	1	3	6338	3	3	2	1	28	15	8521	16	15091	164	19594	77.86
WESTERN	13458	932	344	1267	338	695	314669	265	228	357	212	20361	9755	338120	3429	704430	17053	1019455	70.92
179 Ugenya	27080	15	1	-	6	21	4050	4	-	63	7	70	53	4508	180	36057	1056	54485	68.12
180 Alego	31135	11	1	20	2	22	10530	14	6	52	4	18	24	101	242	42182	261	56887	74.61
181 Gem	25314	10	5	13	2	14	2536	11	6	68	1	43	20	581	226	28850	432	41942	69.82
182 Bondo	24856	1	-	3	1	10	1764	3	4	43	2	3	17	157	93	26955	252	38488	70.69
183 Rarieda	22372	5	4	11	3	7	1610	1	-	61	-	36	5	234	124	24445	229	33467	73.73
184 Kisumu TE	20801	2	11	7	2	8	1966	4	14	48	3	36	434	527	444	24300	274	36808	66.76
185 Kisumu TW	27636	14	10	17	11	24	5017	15	32	67	5	95	834	1198	965	35941	278	61355	59.03
186 Kisumu R	18986	16	3	19	3	11	4606	5	22	46	6	14	19	242	1116	25121	219	35436	71.51
187 Nyando	25550	10	6	6	-	10	1268	2	12	52	1	6	27	83	486	27517	335	36401	76.51
188 Muhoroni	27309	7	2	10	3	19	2520	6	11	79	4	31	286	353	289	30933	309	43637	71.60
189 Nyakach	24763	5	5	2	-	11	2020	9	1	64	2	4	15	29	173	27098	317	36245	75.64
190 Kasipul-Ka	35390	6	-	7	4	13	2327	3	11	82	2	8	30	31	305	38224	421	51748	74.68
191 Karachuonyo	24849	4	8	8	2	5	7158	5	13	65	-	8	10	55	238	32415	410	42930	76.46
192 Rangwe	32451	9	-	14	29	3	3604	4	9	111	2	8	75	169	672	37168	316	52579	71.29
193 Ndhiwa	30409	-	5	6	2	8	918	-	-	40	-	14	10	37	265	31709	102	42870	74.20
194 Rongo	29055	21	4	13	-	25	6382	5	9	103	2	15	66	151	302	36155	266	50937	71.50
195 Migori	22411	10	1	10	2	18	6317	7	5	84	6	20	324	235	260	29711	750	44617	68.27
196 Uriri	16083	4	2	6	2	3	4396	4	3	35	2	4	21	83	51	20698	44	28482	72.82
197 Nyatike	21894	-	2	4	1	15	4390	1	-	23	-	6	96	29	95	26560	157	36579	73.04
198 Mbita	14307	2	-	2	-	6	2977	5	5	32	2	6	18	30	174	17567	277	25321	70.47
199 Gwasi	11774	1	6	4	-	2	4506	-	-	21	5	2	7	27	24	16366	391	23444	71.48
200 Kuria	809	6	5	4	4	14	20557	1	16	13	4	109	2403	29	696	25540	301	35117	73.87
201 Bonchari	92	7	2	10	32	26	11018	7	227	21	30	27	5024	175	756	17457	637	26850	66.14
202 S. Mugiran	60	5	-	6	-	14	6256	2	194	7	10	33	15543	560	140	22832	803	34927	67.19
203 Bomachoge	67	-	19	34	15	11	3053	14	155	10	40	97	23145	405	297	27354	484	42707	65.93
204 Bobasi	88	10	17	21	5	33	20110	36	215	18	8	64	12499	83	500	33709	484	45322	75.44
205 Nyaribari M	223	9	53	32	11	31	11588	32	245	35	15	60	10128	115	1146	23687	886	37407	65.69
206 Nyaribari C	417	33	19	70	66	155	12470	41	463	40	11	86	9616	140	1739	24817	444	41024	61.58
207 Kitutu Cha	1070	28	41	41	24	61	18123	37	750	22	17	99	10097	698	172	32825	991	51945	65.10
208 Kitutu Mas	305	39	25	55	31	68	6790	45	5533	147	50	142	16182	697	459	30298	399	49779	61.67
209 W. Mugiran	422	22	33	51	12	12	9410	24	341	21	7	122	15309	2625	1516	28862	718	41977	70.47
210 N. Mugiran	1202	38		41	50	48	14817	43	590	45	14	113	15865	236		34651	1828	53114	68.68
NYANZA	519180	361	290	547	327	728	215923	389	8892	1618	255	1367	138202	14623	15301	918003	14987	1334827	70.12
TOTAL	667825	3543	4602	6104	4149	8608	2500320	3673	16403	7662	23529	36392	1905640	505713	487538	6181701	101291	8967569	66.97

Source: ECK 1999

Note: Figures in italics are corrections by Charles Hornsby after checking "box-by-box". However, we have not corrected the constituency, provincial and Kenyan

Appendix 2: 1997 parliamentary election results

Constituency		Party	Candidate	Votes scored	% Votes scored
NAIROBI AREA					
001	MAKADARA	DP	Paul Kamau Mugeke	17,916	39.40
		KANU	Vincent Shimoli Lugalia	9,644	21.21
		NDP	John Kiema	7,013	15.42
		SDP	Joe Owaka Ager	5,164	11.36
		FORD-K	Wafula Musamia	3,596	7.91
		SAFINA	George Kabuthi Kamau	1,167	2.57
		LPK	Beatrice Mbithe	493	1.08
		FORD-A	Jane Wilunda Daisy	482	1.06
				45,475	
002	KAMUKUNJI	DP	Norman M G K Nyagah	10,477	32.10
		KANU	Hassan Ali Adams	6,545	20.06
		SAFINA	Clement Muturi Kigano	5,909	18.11
		NDP	Wambui Otieno	3,974	12.18
		SDP	Anne Ndunge Bittock	1,986	6.09
		FORD-P	James Kuria Njine	1,736	5.32
		FORD-K	Eliakim Malumbe Victor	983	3.01
		FORD-A	George G Wilson Nthenge	607	1.86
		LPK	Douglas Kamau Githumbi	255	0.78
		KENDA	Nicholas Gathu Mbugua	152	0.47
				32,624	
003	STAREHE	DP	Maina Kamanda	23,780	47.39
		KANU	Gerishon Kamau Kirima	11,166	22.25
		NDP	Ratib Hussein	6,033	12.02
		SDP	Francis Kirubi	4,632	9.23
		FORD-K	Hannington Zebedy Apudo	2,748	5.48
		SAFINA	Richard Maina	1,018	2.03
		LPD	John Akuk Okech	277	0.55
		UPPK	Christopher Kamau Kariuki	214	0.43
		KENDA	Joseph Ngacha Karani	200	0.40
		LPK	Waqambo-Qambo	108	0.22
				50,176	
004	LANGATA	NDP	Raila Amolo Odinga	22,339	51.79
		KANU	Perez Malande Olindo	11,893	27.57
		DP	George Njage Ngentu	4,667	10.82
		FORD-K	Ernest Sogwe Muhonza	2,000	4.64
		KSC	Fatma Abeyd Anyanzwa	1,070	2.48
		FORD-A	John Musunji Khiyaniri	523	1.21
		LPK	Margery Nduta	386	0.89
		RRP	Lihanda Kemeni Savai	252	0.58
				43,130	
005	DAGORETTI	SDP	Beth Wambui Mugo	21,745	57.36
		KANU	Christopher Kariuki Kamuyu	6,027	15.90
		DP	James Gichuru Kirubi	3,944	10.40
		FORD-K	Ferdinand Kevin Wanyonyi	2,872	7.58
		NDP	Waiharo Gitau Thiongo	1,950	5.14
		FORD-A	Alex Jimmy Mukabwa	681	1.80
		KSC	Jephita Oeke Otuke	436	1.15
		FORD-P	Pius Njogu Nguo	180	0.47
		DAP	Hezron Nyerere K Magunza	74	0.20
				37,909	
006	WESTLANDS	KANU	Frederick Omulo Gumo	17,882	36.39
		DP	Betty Njeri Tett	17,877	36.38
		NDP	Amin Mohamed N Alibhai	5,104	10.39
		FORD-K	Batroba Chang'eda Kemoli	4,137	8.42
		SDP	Eddah M Rubia	2,536	5.16
		SAFINA	Dr Kariba J Charles Muniu	783	1.59
		FORD-A	Wanguhu Ng'ang'a	685	1.39
		LPK	Simon Karanja Kamoni	140	0.28
				49,144	

007	KASARANI	DP	Adolf Isaac Muchiri	16,179	34.0
		NDP	Ochieng Gilbert Mbeo	15,924	33.4
		KANU	Pius Lee Kamau Muchiri	6,606	13.8
		SDP	Isaac Waihenya Ndirangu	3,630	7.6
		FORD-A	Francis Njuru Ngugi	1,953	4.1
		SAFINA	Gitau Kinyanjui Gachui	1,634	3.4
		FORD-P	Samson Mugacha Mwangi	1,349	2.8
		LPK	Alice Ngima Githae	273	0.5
				47,548	
008	EMBAKASI	DP	David Solomon Kamau Mwenje	23,953	39.9
		NDP	Agnes Nyaboke Ogari	9,702	16.1
		KANU	Godfrey Muhuri Muchiri	9,159	15.2
		SDP	Florence Adhiambo Awuoche	4,884	8.1
		SAFINA	Henry Ruhio Muriama	4,776	7.9
		FORD-K	Jael Ogombe Mbogo	3,801	6.3
		UPPK	Dr Munyua Waiyaki	2,541	4.2
		KNC	Onesmus Musyoka Mbali	879	1.4
		KSC	Omari Nixon Nyairo	327	0.5
				60,022	

COAST PROVINCE
MOMBASA DISTRICT

009	CHANGAMWE	KANU	Ramadhan Seif Kajembe	9,703	27.6
		DP	Joseph Kennedy Kiliku	9,192	26.2
		NDP	Joseph Okoth Waudi	6,500	18.5
		SDP	William Makau Nduva	5,331	15.2
		FORD-K	Mohamed Faki Mwinyihaji	3,735	10.6
		KSC	Loise Ndunge Nzioka	340	0.9
		FORD-A	Lukas Adams	279	0.8
				35,080	
010	KISAUNI	DP	Emmanuel Karisa Maitha	10,074	31.0
		KANU	Said Hemed Said	9,540	29.3
		NDP	Rashid Muhammed Mzee	7,526	23.1
		SDP	Rahab Wanjiku Mwendwa	2,832	8.7
		FORD-K	Abubakar A Mohamed Awadh	2,035	6.2
		SPK	Thomas Lewanga Mwaingia	481	1.4
				32,488	
011	LIKONI	SPK	Suleiman Rashid Shakombo	5,297	33.4
		KANU	Hisham Abdulla Mwidau	4,860	30.7
		NDP	Abdulkadir Abdullah Mwidau	2,039	12.8
		FORD-K	Khalif Salim Mwavumo	1,665	10.5
		DP	Dr Sammy Kents Wafula	906	5.7
		SDP	Salim Mwakutsuma	634	4.0
		FORD-A	Grace Wakarima Gituma	431	2.7
				15,832	
012	MVITA	KANU	Shariff Nassir	14,426	51.35
		NDP	Ahmed Salim Bamahriz	7,261	25.85
		FORD-K	Omar Mwinyi Shimbwa	1,998	7.11
		DP	Gabriel Kinda Ngala	1,939	6.90
		SDP	Juma Omar Aly Bedzimba	1,509	5.37
		SPK	Mbwana Ali Warrakah	961	3.42
				28,094	

KWALE DISTRICT

013	MSAMBWENI	KANU	Marere Mwarapayo Wa-Mwachai	17,168	44.89
		DP	Yusuf Hassan Mubwana	10,692	27.96
		SPK	Kassim Abdalla Juma	5,664	14.81
		NDP	Kassim Athuman Choka	2,362	6.18
		SDP	Samuel Chege Kamau	1,297	3.39
		KSC	Lennox Victor Telle	1,062	2.78
				38,245	

014	MATUGA	KANU	Sulleman Mwaronga Kamolleh	13,681	59.15
		SPK	Mwagomba Mwinyi Mwapeu	7,773	33.61
		KSC	Mohammed Soud Beti	776	3.35
		SDP	Masudi Ali Mwakileo	663	2.87
		NDP	Omari Abdallah Gakesho	237	1.02
				23,130	
015	KINANGO	KANU	Simeon Mwero Mkala	16,389	80.72
		NDP	Batso Daniel Nyanje	2,831	13.94
		DP	Mlagwa Saakumi Kubwa	735	3.62
		KSC	Samuel Ndupha Mangale	349	1.72
				20,304	

KILIFI DISTRICT

016	BAHARI	KANU	Jembe Mwakalu	23,196	70.77
		DP	John Safari Mumba	3,201	9.77
		NDP	Geoffrey Sadi Chimega	2,806	8.56
		FORD-K	Timothy Mtana Lewa	2,521	7.69
		SPK	Maurice Mboja	1,053	3.21
				32,777	
017	KALOLENI	KANU	Mathias Benedict Keah	17,165	59.59
		SDP	Edwin Githire Muinga	4,986	17.31
		DP	Japhet Kahindi Chea Shaha	2,534	8.80
		NDP	Anderson Chibule Watsuma	2,113	7.34
		KSC	Prof Katama George C Mkangi	1,127	3.91
		SPK	Leslie George Mwachiro	721	2.50
		FORD-K	Samson Vidzo Petero Mwaro	160	0.56
				28,806	
018	GANZE	KANU	Noah Katana Ngala	9,130	74.26
		SDP	Moses Kitsao	1,789	14.55
		DP	Kenneth Karisa Baya	1,308	10.64
		FORD-K	Morris Wasi Hare	67	0.54
				12,294	

MALINDI DISTRICT

019	MALINDI	KANU	Abubakar Mohammed A Badawy	10,550	42.75
		NDP	Fredrick Kazungu Diwani	6,768	27.43
		DP	Francis Bobi Tuva	5,070	20.54
		SDP	Naomi M Sidi Kumbatha	1,302	5.28
		FORD-K	Jamal Mohamed Sheikh	988	4.00
				24,678	
020	MAGARINI	KANU	David Noti Kombe	9,982	69.96
		FORD-K	Joseph Kasena Yeri	2,279	15.97
		KSC	Harrison G Kombe Mali	1,246	8.73
		DP	Katana Ndzai	353	2.47
		NDP	James Kirimo Menza	323	2.26
		SDP	Morris Yaa Mangi	85	0.60
				14,268	

TANA RIVER DISTRICT

021	GARSEN	KANU	Molu Galogalo Shambaro	7,471	57.67
		SAFINA	Mandara Barisa Badiribu	4,086	31.54
		NDP	Said Mohamed Rhova	858	6.62
		SPK	Omara Abae Kalasigha	540	4.17
				12,955	
022	GALOLE	KANU	Tola Kofa Mugava	7,993	76.57
		NDP	Japhet Zakaria Kase	1,141	10.93
		DP	Davidson Maina Kariuki	1,038	9.94
		FORD-K	Mark Timona Maro	267	2.56
				10,439	
023	BURA	KANU	Mohamed Abdi Galgallo	2,917	33.32
		NDP	Ali Wario	2,790	31.87
		SDP	Ali Shebe Said	1,781	20.34
		DP	Mahadh Ali Loka	1,214	13.87
		FORD-K	Hussein Falama Wario	35	0.40
		KSC	Hassan Shora Odha	17	0.19
				8,754	

LAMU DISTRICT					
024	LAMU EAST	KANU	Mohamed Hashim Salim	5,039	75.68
		NDP	Abudi Omar Mohamed	1,353	20.32
		DP	Bwanahamadi Mohamed Bwanahamad	184	2.76
		FORD-P	Mohamed Kussoma Bunu	47	0.71
		FORD-K	Salim Ali Mohamed Fani	35	0.53
				6,658	
025	LAMU WEST	KANU	Fahim Yasin Twaha	8,851	64.41
		FORD-P	Rishad Hamid Ahmed	4,373	32.82
		KSC	Bwanakheri Bakari Musa	518	3.77
				13,742	
TAITA DISTRICT					
026	TAVETA	KANU	Basil Criticos	7,803	68.34
		SDP	Mwacharo Kubo Tayo	3,615	31.66
				11,418	
027	WUNDANYI	KANU	Darius Msaga Mbela	6,951	58.48
		DP	Mborio Mashengu Wa Mwachofi	4,531	38.12
		FORD-K	Wisdom Mwakudua Nyange	252	2.12
		NDP	Lucas Wamwandu Mwanjila	153	1.29
				11,887	
028	MWATATE	KANU	Marsden Herman Madoka	9,410	66.35
		DP	Calist Andrew Mwatela	4,238	29.88
		NDP	Allen Peterson Mbela	408	2.88
		FORD-K	Philip Mwawaza Mombo	127	0.90
				14,183	
029	VOI	DP	Basil Nguku Mwakiringo	6,377	46.46
		KANU	Khamis Chome Abdi	6,303	45.92
		SDP	Richard Mwambi Mwangeka	1,047	7.63
				13,727	
NORTH EASTERN PROVINCE					
GARISSA DISTRICT					
030	DUJIS	KANU	Hussein Maalim Mohamed	10,218	61.74
		SAFINA	Aden Sugow Ahmed	4,425	26.74
		DP	Abdikadir Hassan Yussuf	1,722	10.40
		NDP	Hassan Jelle Hussein	81	0.49
		SDP	Abdulahi Haji Muhamed	68	0.41
		KSC	Mahamed Jama Ali	24	0.15
		FORD-P	Yussuf Mohamed Bare	12	0.07
				16,550	
031	LAGDERA	KANU	Mohamed Muktar Shidiye	4,355	62.86
		SAFINA	Farah Maalim Mohamed	2,552	36.84
		DP	Hassan Mohamed Aress	16	0.23
		NDP	Ali Abdulahi Gure	5	0.07
				6,928	
032	FAFI	SAFINA	Elias Bare Shill	2,070	50.17
		KANU	Yussuf Issa Abdi	2,056	49.83
		SDP	Abdullahi Sirat Osman	-	0.00
				4,126	
033	IJARA	KANU	Mohamed Dhahir Werah	2,876	54.83
		FORD-A	Sophia Abdi Noor	2,355	44.90
		DP	Abdi Salat Agalab	5	0.10
		FORD-K	Abdirahamaan S Mahat	5	0.10
		SAFINA	Mohamud Yussuf Haji	3	0.06
		NDP	Abdul Ahi Mahat Daud	1	0.02
				5,245	
WAJIR DISTRICT					
034	WAJIR NORTH	KANU	Abdullahi Ibrahim Ali	4,047	99.22
		FORD-K	Osman Yusuf Abdullahi	32	0.78
				4,079	

035	WAJIR WEST	SAFINA	Adan Keynan Wehliye	5,204	50.75
		KANU	Ahmad Khalif Mohamed	4,985	48.62
		SDP	Abdi Birik Abdinur	36	0.35
		DP	Abdullahi Abdi Ali	15	0.15
		NDP	Khalif Abdullahi Mohamed	11	0.11
		KSC	Yussuf Mohamed Abubakar	3	0.03
				10,254	
036	WAJIR EAST	KANU	Mohamed Abdi Mahamud	6,476	68.15
		FORD-A	Mohamed Irshat Hassan	2,360	24.83
		SDP	Abdi Sheikh Mohamed	594	6.25
		DP	Adan Sheikh Omar	36	0.3
		NDP	Ahmed Jelle Madey	24	0.2
		SAFINA	Hassan Dahiya Bardad	7	0.0
		KSC	Mahat Issak Hussein	6	0.0
				9,503	
037	WAJIR SOUTH	KANU	Mohamed Abdi Affey	3,582	51.7
		DP	Ahmed Abdi Ogle	3,050	44.0
		KENDA	Sahal Sheikh Ali Muhumed	286	4.1
		NDP	Abdirashid Mohamed	7	0.1
				6,925	

MANDERA DISTRICT

038	MANDERA WEST	KANU	Sayid Mohamed Amin	4,761	59.3
		SAFINA	Hassan Aden Osman	3,203	39.9
		FORD-K	Kulow Maalim Hassan	28	0.3
		NDP	Jaafar Mohamed Sheikh	17	0.2
		DP	Maalim Issack Adan	11	0.1
				8,020	
039	MANDERA CENTRAL	KANU	Adan Mohamed Nooru	5,661	51.1
		SAFINA	Abdikadir Adan Abdulla	3,588	32.4
		FORD-A	Mohamed Ali Farah	1,709	15.4
		FORD-K	Alihaji Ali Abdi Baricha	85	0.7
		NDP	Abdi Haji Yussuf	5	0.0
		FORD-P	Alikheyr Abdi Mohamed	5	0.0
		LPK	Ali Haji Hassan Husseini	5	0.0
				11,058	
040	MANDERA EAST	KANU	Shaaban Ali Isaack	7,180	64.8
		FORD-K	Abdi Hassan Haji	3,400	30.6
		FORD-A	Abdirahaman Abdinoor	363	3.2
		DP	Abdi Issak Ahmed	111	1.0
		LPD	Abdullahi Sheikh Ahmed	15	0.1
		FORD-P	Adan Maalim Abdullahi	12	0.1
		LPK	Mohamed Abdullahi Omar	-	
				11,081	

EASTERN PROVINCE
MARSABIT DISTRICT

041	MOYALE	KANU	Dr Gurrach Boru Galgallo	11,102	66.1
		FORD-K	Qalicha Diba Elema	4,244	25.3
		DP	Osman Abajilo Araru	1,348	8.0
		SAFINA	Ali Issak Ibrahim	82	0.4
				16,776	
042	NORTH HORR	KANU	Bonaya Adhi Godana	5,404	68.8
		NDP	Wario Hukha Ali	2,441	31.1
				7,845	
043	SAKU	KANU	Abdi Tari Sasura	6,737	68.2
		DP	Danso Barako Guyo	3,138	31.7
				9,875	
044	LAISAMIS	KANU	Robert Iltaramatwa Kochalle		

ISIOLO DISTRICT

045	ISIOLO NORTH	KANU	Charfano Guyo Mokku	7,151	45.43
		DP	Tache Wako Gaji	6,771	43.01
		SDP	Tarcisius Kobia	1,065	6.77
		FORD-K	Sebastian Muthaura Kiome	474	3.01
		NDP	Fatuma Hassan M Iman	148	0.94
		FORD-P	Ali Mohammed	133	0.84
				15,742	

046	ISIOLO SOUTH	KANU	Abdullahi Haji Wako	3,791	58.24
		FORD-K	Dida Jaldesa	2,622	40.28
		DP	Adam Wako Bonaya	96	1.47
				6,509	

NYAMBENE DISTRICT

047	IGEMBE	KANU	Jackson Itirithia Kalweo	15,943	49.59
		NDP	Raphael Muriungi	9,633	29.96
		DP	Erastus Mbaabu	5,216	16.22
		SAFINA	Franklin Mithika Linturi	918	2.86
		SDP	Joseph Mwenda Malebe	442	1.37
				32,152	

048	NTONYIRI	DP	Richard Maore Maoka	15,117	60.67
		KANU	Andrew Kainga Munoru	7,580	30.42
		FORD-P	Andrew Mbiko	1,934	7.76
		NDP	Abdalla Mohammed Kamwana	286	1.15
				24,917	

049	TIGANIA WEST	DP	Benjamin Ravel Ndubai	11,001	51.89
		KANU	Stephen Mukangu	9,937	46.87
		LPK	James Turibu M'imunya	262	1.24
				21,200	

050	TIGANIA EAST	KANU	Mathew Adams Karauri	14,421	51.22
		DP	Ntai Nkuraru	11,465	40.72
		GAP	Godfrey Kaibiria M'mwereria	1,149	4.08
		NDP	Simon Kamenchu Ringera	1,119	3.97
				28,154	

MERU DISTRICT

051	NORTH IMENTI	DP	Daudi Mwiraria	33,722	64.47
		KANU	Gideon Kaumbuthu Meenye	17,942	34.30
		FORD-A	Peter Kiunga J M'mungania	640	1.22
				52,304	

052	CENTRAL IMENTI	FORD-K	Gitobu Imanyara	27,112	65.98
		KANU	Joseph K Laiboni M'mukindia	12,092	29.43
		DP	Henry Kinyua	1,889	4.60
				41,093	

053	SOUTH IMENTI	DP	Kiraitu Murungi	38,153	73.94
		KANU	Eliphaz Riungu	12,851	24.90
		NDP	Leon William Kinyamu	597	1.16
				51,601	

THARAKA /NITHI DISTRICT

054	NITHI	DP	Bernard Njoka Mutani	20,620	35.78
		KANU	Capt. (Rtd) Eustace Ntigwa	17,560	30.47
		SAFINA	Basil Ntwiga J Nyaga Mbuni	11,906	20.66
		LPK	John Bosco Mputhia Muthamia	4,791	8.31
		NDP	Murithi Murithi	2,001	3.47
		SDP	Kiruja Ruchiami	759	1.32
				57,637	

055	THARAKA	DP	Cicilio Murango Mwenda	11,975	56.31
		KANU	Francis Nyamu Kagwima	9,025	42.44
		NDP	Solomon Ikunga Kaaria	137	0.64
		SDP	Samuel L Mugwira Gaichura	128	0.60
				21,265	

EMBU DISTRICT

056	MANYATTA	DP	Peter Njeru Ndwiga	32,949	81.18
		KANU	Samuel Phinehas Gachora	5,235	12.90
		SDP	John Njagi Njeru	887	2.19
		FORD-K	Nemasius M Ndwigah Kenyan	562	1.38
		LPK	Agatha Muthoni Mbogo	535	1.32
		NDP	Justus Nyaga Muguimi	420	1.03
				40,588	

057	RUNYENJES	FORD-A	Augustine Njeru Kathangu	20,547	55.03
		DP	Benjarnin Geteria Wamugunda	9,003	24.11
		KANU	Cosmas Namu Evans Kathungu	5,479	14.67
		SDP	Silas Nderi Nyagah	952	2.55
		NDP	Hoseah Njeru Kagondu	643	1.72
		SAFINA	Japhet Nyaga Njathika	560	1.50
		FORD-K	Margaret Waveti Mugeni	152	0.41
				37,336	

MBEERE DISTRICT

058	GACHOKA	KANU	Joseph William N Nyagah	10,147	40.73
		UPPK	Andrew Muyia Mbithi	9,089	36.48
		FORD-P	Elikana Muriuki Kagundu	3,382	13.57
		FORD-K	Beatrice Kanini Nyagah	948	3.81
		SDP	Albert Mugire Njeru	943	3.79
		NDP	Justin Gatiti Cingano	405	1.63
				24,914	

059	SIAKAGO	DP	Silas M'njamiu Ita	9,764	52.27
		KANU	Justin Muturi Njoka	8,617	46.13
		SDP	Vincent Ngari Njoka	244	1.31
		LPK	Francis Njue Kago	55	0.29
				18,680	

MWINGI DISTRICT

060	MWINGI NORTH	KANU	Stephen Kalonzo Musyoka	24,509	68.58
		DP	Josphat Musyimi Mulyungi	9,835	27.52
		SDP	John Hunter Musee	1,395	3.90
				35,739	

061	MWINGI SOUTH	KANU	David Musila	25,599	80.05
		DP	John Mung'ei Nzambou	6,379	19.95
				31,978	

KITUI DISTRICT

062	KITUI WEST	KANU	Francis Mwanzia Nyenze	17,572	50.40
		SDP	Nzuki Mwinzi Nzuki	17,009	48.78
		NDP	Charles Katana Mbuvi	287	0.82
				34,868	

063	KITUI CENTRAL	SDP	Charity Kaluki Ngilu	28,172	72.61
		KANU	George Mutua Ndotto	10,628	27.39
				38,800	

064	MUTITO	SDP	Jimmy Muthusi Kitonga	10,612	54.30
		FORD-A	Jacob Kilunda Mulatya	4,821	24.67
		KANU	Julius Kiema Kilonzo	3,805	19.47
		DP	Daniel Konzi Mwove	189	0.97
		PICK	Joseph Ndunda Wambua	81	0.41
		FORD-K	Titus Musyoka Muungami	36	0.18
				19,544	

065	KITUI SOUTH	SDP	Samuel Kalii Kiminza	8,623	40.24
		KANU	Isaac Mulatya Muoki	6,621	30.89
		DP	Patrice Ezekiel M Ivuti	6,012	28.05
		NDP	Anne Munyao	175	0.82
				21,431	

MACHAKOS DISTRICT

066	MASINGA	KANU	Col Ronald John Kiluta	12,886	54.26
		SDP	Peter Masilu Katu	10,861	45.74
				23,747	

067	YATTA	SDP	Francis Philip Wambua	16,003	66.42
		KANU	Joseph Munyao Mutisya	6,926	28.74
		DP	Dr James F Suva	1,016	4.22
		LPK	Charles Nduli Mbatha	150	0.62
				24,095	

068	KANGUNDO	KANU	Joseph Kimeu Ngutu	23,698	51.70
		SDP	Joseph Wambua Mulusya	20,499	44.72
		DP	Joshua Musyoka Kitonga	1,639	3.58
				45,836	

069	KATHIANI	SDP	Kyalo Peter Kaindi	20,630	59.07
		KANU	Jackson Kimeu Mulinge	14,297	40.93
				34,927	

070	MACHAKOS TOWN	SDP	Jonesmus Mwanza Kikuyu	27,093	60.18
		KANU	Wilson Masila Muema	16,058	60.18
		DP	John Elijah Wambua	1,382	3.07
		NDP	Bernard Kilonzo Katiku	486	1.08
				45,019	

071	MWALA	SDP	John Mutua Katuku	16,748	42.04
		KANU	William Kivuvani Mbatha	12,193	30.61
		FORD-K	Joseph Musyoki Ndolo	3,923	9.85
		DP	John Philip Luusa	3,443	8.64
		PICK	Boniface Mutua Musyoki	3,248	8.15
		NDP	Benson Mwathi Lemba	283	0.71
				39,838	

MAKUENI DISTRICT

072	MBOONI	KANU	Frederick Mulinge Kalulu	16,133	46.43
		SDP	Michael B Mulli Ilumbi	9,614	27.67
		DP	Joseph Konzollo Munyao	9,001	25.90
				34,748	

073	KILOME	KANU	Antony Wambua Ndilinge	10,368	68.00
		SDP	Benjamin Kyalo Muthoka	4,559	29.90
		DP	John Muange Ngui	320	2.10
				15,247	

074	KAITI	KANU	Gideon Musyoka Ndambuki	11,159	52.02
		SDP	Adelina Ndeto Mwau	8,853	41.27
		NDP	Dave D Musyoki Muumbi	810	3.78
		DP	John Kaleli Kavali	505	2.35
		LPK	Faustine King'ola Mutisya	126	0.59
				21,453	

075	MAKUENI	SDP	Prof Paul Mulwa Sumbi	21,420	57.64
		KANU	Peter Eliud Mutua Maundu	14,896	40.08
		DP	David Sila Nzioki	846	2.28
				37,162	

076	KIBWEZI	SDP	Onesmus Mutinda Mboko	14,219	48.72
		KANU	George Mutua Makwattah	6,932	23.75
		KSC	Thomas Musyoki Mutuse	6,360	21.79
		DP	Wilson Musembi Ndetei	920	3.15
		NDP	Seth Kakusye Mweu	755	2.59
				29,186	

CENTRAL PROVINCE
NYANDARUA DISTRICT

077	KINANGOP	FORD-P	Mwangi Kirika Waithaka	23,141	60.81
		DP	Joseph Kuria Methu	9,583	25.18
		KANU	Stephen Flavian Mwangi	2,935	7.71
		SDP	Thiongo Kagicha	1,486	3.90
		SAFINA	Leonard Gugu Njoroge	666	1.75
		FORD-K	Mary Wanjiru	243	0.64
				38,054	

078	KIPIPIRI	DP	Paul Githiomi Mwangi	11,371	52.76
		FORD-P	Nyoike Wa Kimani	7,631	35.41
		KANU	James Kabingu Muregi	1,451	6.73
		FORD-A	Edward Gachigu Ndiritu	640	2.97
		SAFINA	Simon Peter Mburu	460	2.13
				21,553	
079	OL KALOU	DP	Karue Muriuki Muriuki	29,034	74.56
		SAFINA	James Irungu Wakaba	6,766	17.37
		KANU	Stephen Kimani Gakenia	1,704	4.38
		FORD-P	Ezekiel Karanja Ndune	1,436	3.69
				38,940	
080	NDARAGWA	DP	Kamau Thirikwa Thirikwa	19,464	88.49
		KANU	Gabriel Thumbi Ndungu	1,709	7.77
		FORD-P	Geoffrey Gachara Muchiri	822	3.74
				21,995	

NYERI DISTRICT

081	TETU	DP	Paul Gikonyo Muya	24,229	89.00
		KANU	Nahashon Kanyi Waithaka	1,994	7.32
		LPK	Wangari Muta Maathai	905	3.32
		SDP	Peter Wachira Muchemi	95	0.35
				27,223	
082	KIENI	DP	David Munene Kairu	37,959	93.02
		KANU	John Gitiche Mbao	2,507	6.14
		KENDA	Eustace Maina Wachira	340	0.83
				40,806	
083	MATHIRA	DP	Eliud Matu Wamae	38,349	82.05
		KANU	Peter Ngibuini Kuguru	8,096	17.32
		LPK	James Weru Maina	296	0.63
				46,741	
084	OTHAYA	DP	Mwai Kibaki	31,637	97.78
		KANU	Stanley Maina Benjamin	610	1.89
		NDP	Dr Paul Macharia Ndirangu	109	0.34
				32,356	
085	MUKURWEINI	DP	David Muhika Mutahi	19,360	67.52
		SAFINA	Godfrey Kariuki Mwangi	7,141	24.90
		KANU	John Waweru Kamau	2,000	6.98
		SDP	Frank Njururi Maiyani	172	0.60
				28,673	
086	NYERI TOWN	DP	Wanyiri Kihoro	30,629	86.99
		KANU	Peter Gichohi Muriithi	3,428	9.74
		KENDA	James Kariuki Githinji	509	1.45
		NDP	Kenneth Kimara Nguru	421	1.20
		LPK	Peter Gitari Weru	223	0.63
				35,210	

KIRINYAGA DISTRICT

087	MWEA	DP	Alfred Mwangi Ndiritu	27,373	85.75
		KANU	Ibrahim Reuben Mutugi	2,253	7.06
		SAFINA	David Njue Kabugo	944	2.96
		LPK	Kibugi Kathigi	694	2.17
		SDP	James Mwangi Mugo	657	2.06
				31,921	
088	GICHUGU	DP	Martha Wangari Karua	30,736	78.95
		KANU	Harry Fredrick Mugo	4,680	12.02
		LPK	Phinehas Njeru Njuno	3,189	8.19
		FORD-P	Allan Mbogo Mugwimi	197	0.51
		KSC	John Ndungo Murandi	129	0.33
				38,931	
089	NDIA	DP	James Kareu Kibicho	24,411	88.82
		KANU	John Githui Mithamo	1,199	4.36
		SDP	Dickson Karume Kariuki	945	3.44
		NDP	Silas Gachanja Kinyeki	794	2.89
		LPK	Stephen Aurelius Gachua	134	0.49
				27,483	

090	KERUGOYA/KUTUS	DP	John Matere Keriri	18,149	59.51
		KSC	Lazarus Munyi Mugo	6,638	21.77
		SDP	Nicholas Kinyua Mbui	2,770	9.08
		KANU	John Ngata Kariuki	1,992	6.53
		FORD-A	David Chrispo C Weru	580	1.90
		LPK	James Njagi Njiru	366	1.20
				30,495	

MURANG'A DISTRICT

091	KANGEMA	FORD-P	John Njoroge Michuki	17,707	80.43
		KANU	Naftali Ngeru	4,308	19.57
				22,015	

092	MATHIOYA	FORD-P	Francis Njakwe Githiari	13,009	46.57
		KANU	John Joseph Kamotho	11,517	41.23
		FORD-A	Maina Wanjigi	3,409	12.20
				27,935	

093	KIHARU	SAFINA	Ignatius Ngenye Kariuki	27,369	72.38
		KANU	Dr Julius Gikonyo Kiano	5,666	14.98
		DP	John Gocho Kimani	2,929	7.75
		SDP	Kihoro Cerere	1,438	3.80
		LPK	William Ngara Mwangi	411	1.09
				37,813	

MARAGWA DISTRICT

094	KIGUMO	DP	Onesimus Kihara Mwangi	13,550	55.92
		SAFINA	Simon Mwangi	4,522	18.66
		FORD-P	Obed Gathuya Mburu	1,897	7.83
		LPK	David Kiragu W Wanjagi	1,871	7.72
		KANU	John B Mwaura	1,416	5.84
		SDP	Gibson Macharia Gachuru	976	4.03
				24,232	

095	MARAGWA	DP	Peter Kamande Mwangi	8,547	30.68
		FORD-P	Maina Chege	7,086	25.44
		UPPK	S K Kariuki	4,734	16.99
		SAFINA	Kariuki Leonard Nduati	4,627	16.61
		SDP	James Ngigi Njangi	1,495	5.37
		KANU	Rebecca M Mwangi	1,370	4.92
				27,859	

096	KANDARA	DP	Joshua Ngugi Toro	26,113	65.93
		FORD-P	George Ndung'u Mwicigi	7,431	18.76
		KANU	David Muraya Thuo	3,981	10.05
		FORD-A	Ephantus Ngugi Kariuki	1,023	2.58
		UMMA	David Waweru Ngethe	734	1.85
		LPK	Fredrick Kinyanjui Kiruthi	327	0.83
				39,609	

THIKA DISTRICT

097	GATANGA	SDP	David Wakairu Murathe	14,306	36.11
		DP	Samwel A Macharia	8,752	22.09
		KANU	Samuel Kamau Macharia	8,123	20.50
		FORD-P	Julius W Mwangi Njunu	7,095	17.91
		SAFINA	Francis Mbugua Mwihia	1,114	2.81
		LPK	Jerad Amos Kabugi	233	0.59
				39,623	

098	GATUNDU SOUTH	SDP	Moses Ng'ang'a Muihia	22,637	66.03
		KANU	Uhuru Muigai Kenyatta	10,632	66.03
		SAFINA	Joseph Kimani Kagombe	1,014	2.96
				34,283	

099	GATUNDU NORTH	SDP	Patrick Kariuki Muiruri	7,115	26.83
		DP	Nahashon Ngugi Gatarua	6,090	22.97
		LPD	Clement Benson Gachanja	5,018	18.93
		SAFINA	Anthony Kamuiru Gitau	4,386	16.54
		NDP	Samuel Muciri W'njuguna	2,820	10.64
		LPK	Julius Mbugua Bacha	571	2.15
		KANU	Moshe Mutua Kihu	515	1.94
				26,515	

100	JUJA	SDP	Stephen Ndicho Ndabi	26,842	52.63
		DP	Charles Ng'ang'a Muchai	10,655	20.89
		KANU	Paul Hato Kigamba	7,035	13.79
		NDP	Isaac Nyamane Masese Nyagaka	3,055	5.99
		FORD-A	Benard Nganga Theora	1,180	2.31
		FORD-K	Gitu Wa Kahengeri	1,033	2.03
		SAFINA	Peter Wangai Kiama	922	1.81
		KENDA	Winston Kimani Kange'the	279	0.55
				51,001	

KIAMBU DISTRICT

101	GITHUNGURI	SDP	Njehu Gatabaki	20,129	45.38
		LPD	Kinyanjui Arthur Magugu	19,694	44.40
		DP	David Ndua Thuo	1,835	4.14
		FORD-P	Paul Karuga Njuguna	1,020	2.30
		KANU	Godfrey Njoroge Wanjihia	817	1.84
		SAFINA	Muhia David Gitau	590	1.33
		KSC	Daniel Kago	159	0.36
		KENDA	James H Gitau Mwara	108	0.24
				44,352	

102	KIAMBAA	DP	James Njenga Karume	37,733	67.06
		KANU	Stanley Munga Githunguri	7,191	12.78
		SAFINA	John Kamau Icharia	5,626	10.00
		SDP	Lawrence Nginyo Kariuki	5,342	9.49
		NDP	Samwel Maina K Nganga	376	0.67
				56,268	

103	KABETE	SAFINA	Paul Kibugi Muite	48,504	89.90
		KANU	Joseph Njung'e Mukirae	2,976	5.51
		DP	George Njenga Wakahiu	1,162	2.15
		FORD-A	Martin Wainaina Kenyanjui	1,134	2.10
		FORD-P	Benjamin Kamau Kiroga	238	0.44
				54,014	

104	LIMURU	NDP	George M Nyanja	20,319	61.35
		FORD-A	Simon Kanyingi Kuria	7,145	21.57
		DP	Joseph Kimani Munyaka	3,243	9.79
		KANU	Samuel Ngigi Mwaura	1,445	4.36
		SDP	Paul Ng'ang'a Njugunah	501	1.51
		SAFINA	Joseph Magu Gitau	344	1.04
		KENDA	Joram Kariuki	123	0.37
				33,120	

105	LARI	SAFINA	Philip Gichuru Gitonga	11,565	37.58
		DP	Joseph Ndegwa Duncan	9,838	31.97
		KANU	Viscount James Kimathi	5,805	18.87
		SDP	Samuel Thinguri Warwathe	2,730	8.87
		FORD-P	Peter Mbugua Wainaina	441	1.43
		KSC	Tiras Mburu Chege	392	1.27
				30,771	

RIFT VALLEY PROVINCE
TURKANA DISTRICT

106	TURKANA NORTH	FORD-K	John Munyes Kiyonga	7,098	53.30
		KANU	Japheth Ekidor Lotukoi	6,218	46.70
				13,316	

107	TURKANA CENTRAL	KANU	David Ekwee Ethuro	15,005	95.77
		FORD-K	Peter Derick Ejore Emase	662	4.23
				15,667	

108	TURKANA SOUTH	KANU	Francis Ewoton Achuka	6,086	77.71
		FORD-K	Anton Jeremia Etheri	1,746	22.29
				7,832	

WEST POKOT DISTRICT

109	KACHELIBA	KANU	Samuel Losuron Poghisio	8,943	99.16
		FORD-K	John Loinit	76	0.84
				9,019	

110	KAPENGURIA	KANU	Francis Pollis Loile Lotodo	-	-

111	SIGOR	KANU	Christopher Motoywo Lomada	-	-

112	SAMBURU WEST	KANU	Peter Steve Leenges	13,696	61.09
		DP	Moses Mayo Lanairoshi	8,349	37.24
		NDP	Lawrence Sebastian Lorunyei	315	1.41
		KENDA	George Kanyaro Lalaikipian	42	0.19
		FORD-K	Kennedy Letoona	16	0.07
				22,418	
113	SAMBURU EAST	KANU	Sammy Prisa Leshore	4,602	63.76
		DP	Job Moika Lalampaa	2,587	35.84
		NDP	Peter Lasaari Kupanai	29	0.40
				7,218	

TRANS NZOIA DISTRICT

114	KWANZA	FORD-K	George Welime Kapten	22,790	61.52
		KANU	Samuel Kisoro Moiben	13,451	36.31
		NDP	Richard Mutai Tumwet	520	1.40
		SDP	Mary Jeruto Kirwa	286	0.77
				37,047	
115	SABOTI	FORD-K	Michael Christopher Wamalwa	37,944	65.35
		KANU	Justina Nasambu Sitti	13,444	23.15
		DP	Jackson Ruiru	4,728	8.14
		NDP	Joel Kibiwot Mutwol	1,424	2.45
		FORD-A	Peter Sammy Onani	526	0.91
				58,066	
116	CHERANGANY	KANU	Kipruto Rono Kirwa	17,902	63.43
		FORD-K	John Kirwa Rotich	8,474	30.02
		DP	John N Joshua Nasila	1,848	6.55
				28,224	

UASIN GISHU DISTRICT

117	ELDORET NORTH	KANU	William Ruto Samoei	39,023	61.26
		FORD-K	Shadrack Kipkorir Menjo	16,303	25.59
		DP	Job Kibiwot Mutai	4,240	6.66
		NDP	Tom Simiyu Mapesa	3,211	5.04
		FORD-A	Emmanuel Marava Lichuma	533	0.84
		SDP	Jason Ambe Miroya	390	0.61
				63,700	
118	ELDORET EAST	KANU	Francis Kipkoech Lagat	-	-
119	ELDORET SOUTH	KANU	Maizs Jesse Kibet	28,528	73.20
		DP	Jean Jeeptar Tanui	7,801	20.02
		FORD-K	Kimari Karanja	2,643	6.78
				38,972	

MARAKWET DISTRICT

120	MARAKWET EAST	KANU	John Kiptoo Marrirmoi	11,193	64.35
		DP	Freddie Kisang Cheserek	6,076	34.93
		NDP	Johnstone Barmargony Kassenge	99	0.57
		FORD-K	Francis Cheptile K Smith	20	0.11
		SDP	Jebii Linah Kilimo	6	0.03
				17,394	
121	MARAKWET WEST	KANU	David Kiprono Sutter Sudi	21,991	93.88
		FORD-P	John Kosgei Chebii	1,434	6.12
				23,425	

KEIYO DISTRICT

122	KEIYO NORTH	KANU	Elijah Kipkosgei Sumbeiywo	12,917	70.07
		SAFINA	Gilbert Koech Lagat	5,517	29.93
				18,434	
123	KEIYO SOUTH	KANU	Kipyator Nicholas K Biwott	25,799	93.72
		DP	Tabitha Jeptoo Seii	1,504	5.46
		FORD-K	Moses Kiplagat Changwony	224	0.81
				27,527	

NANDI DISTRICT

124	MOSOP	KANU	John Kipkorir Sambu	32,808	96.70
		NDP	Felicity Irene Magut	1,119	3.30
				33,927	

125	ALDAI	KANU	Simeon Kiptum Choge	20,609	64.88
		SAFINA	Sammy Kipcho Choge	9,529	30.00
		FORD-K	Benjamin K Wambok	1,629	5.13
				31,767	
126	EMGWEN	KANU	Joseph Tendenei Leting	32,688	85.04
		FORD-K	Patrick Kipkemboi Rop	4,312	11.22
		NDP	Henry Kiplagat Arap Kemei	910	2.37
		FORD-P	Dorcas Jepkemboi	530	1.38
				38,440	
127	TINDERET	KANU	Henry Kiprono Kosgey	33,891	83.89
		NDP	Raymond Kipkoech Chelulei	4,471	11.07
		FORD-K	Paul Kipngetich Belio	1,857	4.60
		SDP	Everlyn Chepkemooi Kiprotich	181	0.45
				40,400	

BARINGO DISTRICT

128	BARINGO EAST	KANU	Dalldosso Joseph Lotodo	-	-
129	BARINGO NORTH	KANU	Chepkoiywa Andrew Kiptoon	-	-
130	BARINGO CENTRAL	KANU	Daniel T Arap Moi	38,015	99.45
		SDP	Amos Kiprotich Kandie	210	0.55
				38,225	

KOIBATEK DISTRICT

131	MOGOTIO	KANU	William Cheruiyot Morogo	13,426	86.09
		SDP	Christine Jebichi Ndoigo	2,170	13.91
				15,596	
132	ELDAMA RAVINE	KANU	Musa Cherutich Sirma	14,390	57.35
		DP	Joseph Leboo Rop	10,701	42.65
				25,091	

LAIKIPIA DISTRICT

133	LAIKIPIA WEST	DP	Francis Chege Mbitiru	38,193	71.65
		KANU	Godfrey Gitahi Kariuki	13,911	26.10
		SAFINA	Bartholomew Gichuru Gathuo	1,199	2.25
				53,303	
134	LAIKIPIA EAST	DP	Festus Mwangi Kiunjuri	22,795	70.59
		KANU	Rashad Mahmud Butt	8,448	26.16
		FORD-P	Austin Kiguta Mung'atu	1,049	3.25
				32,292	
135	NAIVASHA	DP	Paul Samuel Kihara	25,845	46.62
		SAFINA	Rumba Kinuthia	8,491	15.32
		KANU	Dr George Gicheru Ngatiri	7,664	13.83
		NDP	James Kahora Kuria	4,636	8.36
		FORD-K	Stanley Kimani Njenga	4,351	7.85
		SDP	Julius Muranga Gichure	3,353	6.05
		KENDA	James Keffa Wagara	1,094	1.97
				55,434	

NAKURU DISTRICT

136	NAKURU TOWN	DP	David Manyara Njuki	22,173	38.85
		KANU	Alicen Jematia Ronoh Chelaite	12,970	22.72
		NDP	Joseph Mbuthia Gichuru	9,076	15.90
		KENDA	Mirugi Kariuki	5,705	10.00
		FORD-K	Protas Kangwana Nyandika	4,689	8.22
		FORD-A	Joseph Lwali Oyondi	1,439	2.52
		SDP	Julius Okong'o Okinda	762	1.34
		FORD-P	Isaac Wacira Waweru	263	0.46
				57,077	
137	KURESOI	KANU	James Cheruiyot Arap Koske	36,481	77.83
		DP	Geoffrey Kiplangat Kenduiywa	10,392	22.17
				46,873	
138	MOLO	DP	Dickson Kihika Kimani	42,397	73.17

138		MOLO	DP	Dickson Kihika Kimani	42,397	73.17
			KANU	John Njenga Mungai	12,802	22.09
			SAFINA	Njuguna G G Ngengi	2,041	3.52
			LPK	George Wainaina Ng'ang'a	401	0.69
			FORD-P	Anne Wangeci Murage	301	0.52
					57,942	
139		RONGAI	KANU	Erick Toroitich Morogo	17,256	51.47
			DP	Patrick Miri Gichuhi	15,199	45.33
			SAFINA	Kennedy Karungu Ngigi	529	1.58
			FORD-K	Jonathan Mbuthia Kameana	304	0.91
			FORD-P	Peter Ngugi Njuguna	240	0.72
					33,528	
140		SUBUKIA	DP	Joseph Mukera Kuria	20,637	58.18
			KENDA	Koigi Wa Wamwere	10,334	29.13
			KANU	Onesmas Kimani Ngunjiri	3,380	9.53
			FORD-A	Bishop Joseph Kamau Kimani	645	1.82
			FORD-P	Gabriel Gitau Waweru	476	1.34
					35,472	

TRANS MARA DISTRICT

141		KILGORIS	KANU	Julius Lekakeny Sunkuli	22,015	63.89
			DP	(Col,) Gideon Sitelu Konchela	12,324	35.77
			PICK	Daniel Talengo Kiptunen	117	0.34
					34,456	

NAROK DISTRICT

142		NAROK NORTH	KANU	William Rongora Ole Ntimama	-	-

143		NAROK SOUTH	KANU	Stephen Kanyinke Ntutu	25,942	79.19
			DP	Samson Kituiyian Tuya	6,816	20.81
					32,758	

KAJIADO DISTRICT

144		KAJIADO NORTH	KANU	George Saitoti	26,682	60.85
			DP	Lepish Phillip Odupoy	13,828	31.53
			NDP	Prof Geoffrey M Ole Maloiy	2,311	5.27
			SDP	Lemachon Oliver Oleseki	651	1.48
			FORD-K	William Gisairo Obwaya	379	0.86
					43,851	

145		KAJIADO CENTRAL	KANU	David Lenante Sankori	11,354	48.66
			SAFINA	Stephen Kapaai Ole Leken	10,683	45.78
			DP	Moses Loontasati M Ololouaya	1,142	4.89
			SDP	Sidney Tawuo Toirai	156	0.67
					23,335	

146		KAJIADO SOUTH	DP	Geoffrey Mepukori Parpai	13,798	57.42
			KANU	Philip Lampat Singaru	10,232	42.58
					24,030	

BOMET DISTRICT

147		BOMET	KANU	Kipkalya Kiprono Kones	-	-

148		CHEPALUNGU	KANU	Isaac Kiprono Ruto	-	-

149		SOTIK	KANU	Anthony Kipkosge Kimeto	34,622	92.01
			SDP	Kimunai Arap Soi	1,494	3.97
			PICK	Taaitta Toweett	1,089	2.89
			DP	Joseph Ivor Korir	423	1.12
					37,628	

150		KONOIN	KANU	Raphael Kiprono Arap Kitur	26,713	80.65
			NDP	Ronald Kipng'etich Ngeny	5,218	15.75
			DP	Francis Kipsiele Too	691	2.09
			FORD-K	Kipkemoi Peter Cheruiyot	499	1.51
					33,121	

151	BURET	KANU	Kipkorir Marisin Sang	31,223	92.11
		SDP	Edwin Kiprotich Kimeto	2,247	6.63
		DP	Philip Kipkorir A Sigei	429	1.27
				33,899	

| 152 | BELGUT | KANU | Charles Davy K Arap Kirui | - | - |

153	AINAMOI	KANU	Kipng'eno Arap Ng'eny	32,824	81.91
		DP	Kiptarus Arap Kirior	4,429	11.05
		NDP	Didacus Kipchirchir Ngetich	1,844	4.60
		FORD-K	Peter Kipkorir Birgen	977	2.44
				40,074	

| 154 | KIPKELION | KANU | Samuel Kimutai Arap Rotich | - | - |

WESTERN PROVINCE
LUGARI DISTRICT

155	MALAVA	FORD-K	Peter Soita Shitanda	19,719	54.98
		KANU	Joshua Mulanda Angatia	14,427	40.23
		KSC	Benjamin J S S S Imbogo	1,241	3.46
		FORD-A	Nyikuli Mukaramoja Jacob	266	0.74
		DP	Abraham Walingo	210	0.59
				35,863	

156	LUGARI	KANU	Shakhalaga Khwa Jirongo	19,983	54.51
		FORD-K	Simon Walwanda Washiko	16,265	44.37
		SDP	Florence Andenyi Machayo	412	1.12
				36,660	

KAKAMEGA DISTRICT

157	MUMIAS	KANU	Wycliffe W Osundwa	18,917	54.42
		FORD-K	John Paul Shikunyi Mandu	9,679	27.84
		FORD-A	Augustine Nyamwoma Sakwa	3,910	11.25
		NDP	Beatrice Auma Wafula	2,256	6.49
				34,762	

158	MATUNGU	KANU	Joseph Pius Wamukoya	10,678	45.61
		FORD-K	Charles Victor Okumu Okwalo	7,568	32.33
		SDP	Samuel Echessa Buluma	3,421	14.61
		DP	Shaban O, Mabuko	1,744	7.45
				23,411	

159	LURAMBI	FORD-K	Newton Wanjala Kulundu	25,457	57.89
		KANU	Sechele Reuben Nyangweso	15,809	35.95
		FORD-A	George W Magomere	1,195	2.72
		NDP	Juma Ali Makabila	807	1.84
		DP	Nashon Joshua Ambundo	574	1.31
		FORD-P	Moses H S Bwonya	130	0.30
				43,972	

160	SHINYALU	FORD-K	Daniel Lyula Khamasi	12,676	50.96
		KANU	Japheth Galagati Shamalla	11,161	44.87
		FORD-A	Fred Maxwell Andole Kimani	1,039	4.18
				24,876	

161	IKOLOMANI	KANU	Joseph Jolly Mugalla	11,471	61.17
		FORD-K	Dr Bonny Dixon Khalwale	7,068	37.69
		DP	Philip Jasper Wishaminya	215	1.15
				18,754	

162	BUTERE	KANU	Dr Amukowa Fredrick Anangwe	10,811	50.31
		FORD-A	J Martin Shikuku Oyondi	10,260	47.75
		FORD-K	George Arunga Sino	416	1.94
				21,487	

163	KHWISERO	KANU	Harrison Aywa Odongo	11,840	69.15
		FORD-A	Wilson Shikanda Opembe	3,690	21.55
		FORD-K	Livingstone Maina Ombete	1,501	8.77
		SDP	James Ameyo Okusimba	90	0.53
				17,121	

163	KHWISERO	KANU	Harrison Aywa Odongo	11,840	69.15
		FORD-A	Wilson Shikanda Opembe	3,690	21.55
		FORD-K	Livingstone Maina Ombete	1,501	8.77
		SDP	James Ameyo Okusimba	90	0.53
				17,121	

VIHIGA DISTRICT

164	EMUHAYA	KANU	Washington S Sakwa Muchilwa	14,297	44.91
		FORD-K	Nehemiah Ayub Ochiel	13,697	43.03
		LPK	Dr Reuben Indiatsi Nasibi	1,646	5.17
		FORD-A	Chief Newton Osborne Ambuyo	803	2.52
		DP	Joab Ombima Wesa	697	2.19
		SDP	Peter Wells Yambusi	693	2.18
				31,833	

165	SABATIA	KANU	Musalia Mudavadi	26,305	89.65
		FORD-K	Nancy Kahera Lidubwi	2,563	8.73
		SDP	Isaac Nadolo Jami	243	0.83
		NDP	Hudson Mudogo Chahale	231	0.79
				29,342	

166	VIHIGA	KANU	Yusuf Kifuma Chanzu	13,531	69.64
		FORD-K	Bahati Musira Semo	5,627	28.96
		NDP	Absai Johnson Angote	271	1.39
				19,429	

167	HAMISI	KANU	George Munyasa Khaniri	14,440	46.45
		SAFINA	Charles Gumini Gimose	9,222	29.67
		FORD-K	Elijah Gideon Asubwa	6,778	21.80
		FORD-A	Laban Benard Musoga	494	1.59
		DP	Joash Lovi Liyosi Kidiavai	153	0.49
				31,087	

MT ELGON DISTRICT

168	MT ELGON	KANU	Joseph Naibei Kimkung	21,835	68.56
		FORD-K	Enos Saulo Chemobo	7,607	23.88
		NDP	Bramwel Murgor Serebemuum	2,408	7.65
				31,850	

BUNGOMA DISTRICT

169	KIMILILI	FORD-K	Dr Mukhisa Kituyi	39,127	88.01
		KANU	Rajab Waliaula	5,328	11.99
				44,455	

170	WEBUYE	FORD-K	Musikari Nazi Kombo	25,935	67.73
		KANU	Bernard Alfred W Sambu	12,354	32.27
				38,289	

171	SIRISIA	FORD-K	John Barasa Munyasia	31,073	78.76
		KANU	Moses Masika Wetangula	8,211	20.81
		DP	George Makali Nabukhale	167	0.42
				39,451	

172	KANDUYI	FORD-K	Athanas Misiko Wafula	23,136	80.88
		KANU	Joseph Wafula Khaoya	4,654	16.27
		DP	Dickson Wafula Kakalukha	816	2.85
				28,606	

173	BUMULA	FORD-K	Lawrence Simiyu Sifuna	24,375	78.08
		KANU	Pius Isaiah Khaoya	6,157	19.72
		NDP	Maurice Murenga Mandila	685	2.19
				31,217	

TESO DISTRICT

174	AMAGORO	KANU	Albert Alexander A Ekirapa	28,825	72.29
		NDP	Sospeters Odeke Ojaamongson	11,050	27.71
				39,875	

BUSIA DISTRICT

175	NAMBALE	KANU	Chrysanthus Okemo	20,137	66.81
		FORD-K	Gervase Mathias K B Akhaabi	10,002	33.19
				30,139	

176	BUTULA	KANU	Yekoyada Francis O Masakhalia	10,343	53.19
		SDP	Clement O Odhiambo	5,376	27.65
		FORD-K	Erick Amakombo Obuya	3,247	16.70
		FORD-A	Bonventure Eric P Acholla	478	2.46
				19,444	
177	FUNYULA	KANU	Arthur Moody Awori	9,842	53.97
		FORD-K	Patrick Kalori Afwande	7,580	41.57
		DP	Washington Ohanya Masinde	814	4.46
				18,236	
178	BUDALANGI	FORD-K	Raphael Wanjala S Bitta	8,343	54.96
		KANU	James Charles N Osogo	6,765	44.57
		NDP	Nicholas Wanyama Okada	55	0.36
		KSC	Peter Gabriel O Akilewo	16	0.11
				15,179	

NYANZA PROVINCE
SIAYA DISTRICT

179	UGENYA	FORD-K	James Aggrey Orengo	24,504	67.48
		NDP	Paul Otieno Nyamodi	7,433	20.47
		KANU	William Omoga Nyahor	4,375	12.05
				36,312	
180	ALEGO	NDP	Peter Oloo Aringo	29,346	70.12
		KANU	Edwin Ochieng Yinda	12,329	29.46
		FORD-K	Hannington Wamera	119	0.28
		EIP	Stephen W Omondi Oludhe	59	0.14
				41,853	
181	GEM	FORD-K	Joseph Akech Donde	9,953	59.61
		KANU	Grace Emily Akinyi Ogot	6,743	40.39
				16,696	
182	BONDO	NDP	Robert Odinga Oburu	23,830	88.41
		KANU	Arthur Dedan Sewe	2,406	8.93
		FORD-K	Washington Jalango Okumu	719	2.67
				26,955	
183	RARIEDA	NDP	George Odeny Ngure	19,953	82.20
		KANU	Henry Ouma Okendo	2,793	11.51
		FORD-K	Ramogi Achieng' Oneko	614	2.53
		SAFINA	Eliazaro Agoya Ochieng	584	2.41
		SPK	Oiro Obwa	172	0.71
		SDP	Florence Adhimbo Awuoro	124	0.51
		LPK	Bethwel Allan Omondi Okal	34	0.14
				24,274	

KISUMU DISTRICT

184	KISUMU TOWN EAST	NDP	Eric Gor Sungu	20,475	84.58
		KANU	Zebby Palme Odhiambo	2,549	10.53
		FORD-K	Michael Odongo Jobita	807	3.33
		SDP	Maurice Odawo Onduru	378	1.56
				24,209	
185	KISUMU TOWN WEST	NDP	Joab Henry Onyango Omino	26,233	72.99
		KANU	Aloys Obunga Aboge	6,118	17.02
		SDP	Billy Mark Menya Kariaga	1,377	3.83
		FORD-K	Gwela Jakandango	1,285	3.58
		PICK	Jack Oraro Owiddo	930	2.59
				35,943	
186	KISUMU RURAL	NDP	Winston Ochoro Ayoki	13,508	53.95
		KANU	Wilson Ndolo Ayah	6,596	26.34
		SDP	Peter Anyan'g Nyong'o	4,935	19.71
				25,039	

187	NYANDO	NDP	Geoffrey Paul Orwa Otita	23,229	85.26
		KANU	Paul Debacko Gogo	1,867	6.85
		SDP	Clarkson Otieno Karan	1,169	4.29
		FORD-K	Lukas Akoth Owaga	981	3.60
				27,246	
188	MUHORONI	NDP	William Odongo Omamo	25,510	83.93
		KANU	Samwel Onyango Okello	3,474	11.43
		PICK	Mathew C Onyango Midika	1,063	3.50
		FORD-K	Ogeka Justus Aloo	349	1.15
				30,396	
189	NYAKACH	NDP	Peter Ochieng Odoyo	23,113	86.59
		KANU	Phares Odhiambo Kouko	3,580	13.41
				26,693	

RACHUONYO
DISTRICT

190	KASIPUL-KABONDO	NDP	William Oloo Otula	31,746	82.86
		KANU	Peter Otieno Owidi	4,984	13.01
		SDP	Dr Otieno Kopiyo	1,582	4.13
				38,312	
191	KARACHUONYO	NDP	Dr Adhu Awiti	19,867	61.33
		KANU	Lazarus Ombai Amayo	10,885	33.61
		SDP	Daniel Rachuonyo Mboya	1,503	4.64
		FORD-K	Peter Lieta Odhiambo	136	0.42
				32,391	

HOMA BAY DISTRICT

192	RANGWE	NDP	Shem Odongo Ochuodho	26,030	71.68
		KANU	Phelgona Okoth Okundi	7,561	20.82
		FORD-K	Prof Joseph Ouma Muga	1,542	4.25
		SDP	Francis Ogolla Kagoro	1,061	2.92
		LPK	Tom Mboya Oloo	118	0.32
				36,312	
193	NDHIWA	NDP	Joshua Orwa Ojode	29,644	93.26
		KANU	Tom Elvis Okello Obondo	1,355	4.26
		SDP	Elisha Akech Chieng'	682	2.15
		FORD-K	Nobert Omolo Odero	105	0.33
				31,786	

MIGORI DISTRICT

194	RONGO	NDP	George Mbogo Ayako Ochilo	23,881	66.67
		KANU	Dalmas Anyango Otieno	11,397	31.82
		FORD-K	John Linus Aluoch	542	1.51
				35,820	
195	MIGORI	NDP	George Henry Owino Achola	19,681	64.10
		KANU	Charles Oyugi Owino	8,900	28.99
		FORD-K	Jack Baraza Baraza	1,728	5.63
		DP	Ibrahim Owino Opiyo	232	0.76
		SDP	Gilbert Oginga Okeyo	163	0.53
196	URIRI	NDP	Herman Odhiambo Omamba	16,104	77.86
		KANU	Rev Fr Peter Arunga Indalo	4,579	22.14
				20,683	
197	NYATIKE	NDP	Tom Otieno Onyango	19,351	71.88
		KANU	Zablon Owigo Olang'	6,327	23.50
		PICK	David Adundo Oyao	1,163	4.32
		SDP	Jacob Ouma Orem	79	0.29
				26,920	

SUBA DISTRICT

198	MBITA	NDP	Gerald Otieno Kajwang'	13,853	78.86
		KANU	Eliazar Ochieng Ochola	3,502	19.94
		SDP	John Olang Sana	212	1.21
				17,567	
199	GWASI	NDP	Felix Useru Kanyauchi	10,683	65.38
		KANU	Zaddock Madiri Syong'oh	5,657	34.62
				16,340	

KURIA DISTRICT 200	KURIA	KANU	Shadrack Roger Mwita Manga	12,493	50.99
		SDP	Dr Wilfred Gisuka Machage	8,240	33.63
		NDP	Nelson Mahanga Mwita	2,970	12.12
		DP	Martin Omahe O'mwita	563	2.30
		FORD-A	Chrispinus Weiria Gibagiri	236	0.96
				24,502	
KISII DISTRICT 201	BONCHARI	KANU	John Zebedeo Opore	9,264	54.32
		SDP	John Mochama Orwochi	4,533	26.58
		DP	Luke Maurice Maangu	1,675	9.82
		FORD-P	Philip Obote Motonu	497	2.91
		NDP	Richard Nyamao Mbeche	408	2.39
		FORD-K	Francis Oluoch Morema	299	1.75
		KNC	Alex Bill Momanyi	212	1.24
		KSC	John Peter Nyakundi Motende	167	0.98
				17,055	
202	SOUTH MUGIRANGO	FORD-K	Enock Nyankieya Magara	11,176	50.65
		KANU	David Ondimu Kombo	9,962	45.15
		DP	Charles Nyakundi Marua	520	2.36
		KSC	Job Ochari	321	1.45
		NDP	Peter Mauti Nyakweba	54	0.24
		KNC	Esther Kerubo Nyangate	31	0.14
				22,064	
203	BOMACHOGE	KANU	Zaphaniah Moraro Nyang'wara	13,337	49.75
		FORD-K	Ferdinand Ondabu Obure	8,450	31.52
		DP	Zedekiah Mekenye Magara	4,150	15.48
		KSC	Josiah Nyaega Gori	299	1.12
		SDP	David Marcos Rakamba	167	0.62
		KNC	Ogembo Masese	149	0.56
		UPPK	Justin Omwoyo Nyaberi	128	0.48
		NDP	Ibrahim M A Siekei	126	0.47
				26,806	
204	BOBASI	KANU	Christopher Mogere Obure	18,336	59.38
		SAFINA	Stephen Kengere Manoti	10,603	34.34
		DP	Oguta Daniel Matoke	791	2.56
		SDP	Henry Nyangechi Nyanchoka	391	1.27
		KSC	Daniel Nyanchiri O Oenga	304	0.98
		FORD-K	David Moracha Nyareru	258	0.84
		FORD-P	Joseph Ratemo Maua	150	0.49
		LPK	David L Oyieko Ratemo	46	0.15
				30,879	
205	NYARIBARI MASABA	KANU	Prof Samson Kegengo Ongeri	14,935	62.09
		SDP	Zablon Ratemo Ouko	5,820	24.19
		DP	Davinson Areba Mairura	2,336	9.71
		NDP	Dr Charles Maranga Bagwasi	692	2.88
		FORD-K	Charles Mirwoba Ayieni	272	1.13
				24,055	
206	NYARIBARI CHACHE	KANU	Simeon Nyachae	20,550	83.33
		FORD-K	Isaac Nyamache Rwenyo	1,683	6.82
		DP	Peter Maragia Nyamweya	1,541	6.25
		NDP	James Oira	887	3.60
				24,661	
207	KITUTU CHACHE	KANU	Jimmy Nuru Ondieki Angwenyi	25,168	75.25
		FORD-K	Leo Blasius Obweri Matundura	4,992	14.93
		NDP	Justus Onsongo Mochoge	1,773	5.30
		SDP	Daniel Rasugu Mokaya	1,031	3.08
		FORD-P	George Ondieki Manyara	482	1.44
				33,446	

NYAMIRA DISTRICT

208	KITUTU MASABA	KSC	George Moseti Anyona	14,653	48.69
		FORD-K	Samson M Nyang'au Okioma	6,487	21.56
		KANU	Nelson Gichaba Simba	6,095	20.25
		DP	Francis Omurwa Manyibe	1,162	3.86
		FORD-P	Elijah Nyabuti Mamboleo	687	2.28
		NDP	Hezron Oira Kiage	537	1.78
		SDP	Augustus H Otieno Momanyi	471	1.57
				30,092	

209	WEST MUGIRANGO	FORD-K	Henry Onyancha Obwocha	14,731	50.60
		KANU	Sagwe Thomas Morwabe	8,729	29.98
		DP	David Anasi Onyancha	5,091	17.49
		NDP	Evans Ondieki	384	1.32
		KSC	Mathew Ondeyo Nyaribari	179	0.61
				29,114	

210	NORTH MUGIRANGO BORABU	KANU	Joseph Kiangoi Ombasa	17,323	49.51
		DP	Godfrey Masanya Okeri	14,243	40.70
		SDP	Frank Patty Ndubi	2,327	6.65
		NDP	Nemwel Peter Mogaka	1,098	3.14
				34,991	

Table A2.1: Representation in parliament - constituency versus proportional

Party	Elected	Nominated	Total Seats (1997)	% Votes Cast (adjusted)	Total Seats (proportional)
KANU	107	6	113	41.65	93
DP	39	2	41	20.72	46
NDP	21	1	22	10.65	24
FORD-Kenya	17	1	18	9.77	22
SDP	15	1	16	7.83	18
Safina	5	1	6	3.87	9
FORD-People	3	0	3	1.76	4
FORD-Asili	1	0	1	1.28	3
KSC	1	0	1	0.62	1
SPK	1	0	1	0.37	1
				0.41	1 (LPD)
Total	210	12	222	98.52	222

Note: the percentage votes cast has been calculated by including the KANU, DP, NDP, FORD-K and SDP scores of the presidential elections for 11 constituencies where KANU won the parliamentary seat unopposed. A threshold of 20,000 votes is taken as a minimum to make it to parliament. Two 'rest seats' are added, one each, to KANU and SDP.

Table A2.2: Parliamentary votes by province (absolute and per cent)

Province	Nairobi		Coast		N. Eastern		Eastern		Central		Rift Valley		Western		Nyanza		TOTAL		TOTAL(adjust)	
Party	Abs	%	Abs	%	Abs	%	Abs	%	Abs	%	Abs	%	Abs	%	Abs	%	Abs	%	Abs	%
KANU	78922	21.56	218528	53.33	56197	59.93	415294	39.85	109355	10.83	759144	59.00	328121	46.52	274169	30.46	2239730	38.52	2569733	41.65
DP	118793	32.45	63586	15.52	4966	5.30	253714	24.34	482731	47.81	299345	23.26	5390	0.76	32304	3.59	1260829	21.69	1277932	20.72
NDP	72039	19.68	47469	11.58	151	0.16	20626	1.98	27894	2.76	35183	2.73	17763	2.52	432399	48.04	653524	11.24	656516	10.65
FORD-K	20137	5.50	16164	3.94	3550	3.79	40073	3.85	1276	0.13	116993	9.09	309439	43.87	91732	10.19	599364	10.31	602533	9.77
SDP	44577	12.18	26871	6.56	698	0.74	241730	23.19	109636	10.86	11906	0.93	10235	1.45	36245	4.03	481898	8.29	482901	7.83
Safina	15287	4.18	4086	1.00	21052	22.45	13466	1.28	126560	12.53	37989	2.95	9222	1.31	11187	1.24	238849	4.11	238849	3.87
FORD-P	3265	0.89	4420	1.08	29	0.03	5449	0.52	89151	8.83	4293	0.33	130	0.02	1816	0.20	108553	1.87	108553	1.76
FORD-A	4931	1.35	710	0.17	6787	7.24	26008	2.50	15111	1.50	3143	0.24	22135	3.14	236	0.03	79061	1.36	79061	1.28
KSC	1833	0.50	5435	1.33	33	0.04	6360	0.61	7318	0.72	-	-	1257	0.18	15923	1.77	38159	0.66	38159	0.62
SPK	-	-	22490	5.49	-	-	-	-	-	-	-	-	-	-	172	0.02	22662	0.39	22662	0.37
LPD	277	0.08	-	-	15	0.02	-	-	24712	2.45	-	-	-	-	-	-	25004	0.43	25004	0.41
KENDA	352	0.10	-	-	286	0.31	-	-	1359	0.13	17175	1.33	-	-	-	-	19172	0.33	19172	0.31
LPK	1655	0.45	-	-	5	0.01	5919	0.57	9220	0.91	401	0.03	1646	0.23	198	0.02	19044	0.33	19044	0.31
UPPK	2755	0.75	-	-	-	-	9089	0.87	4734	0.47	-	-	-	-	128	0.01	16706	0.29	16706	0.27
PICK	-	-	-	-	-	-	3329	0.32	-	-	1206	0.09	-	-	3156	0.35	7691	0.13	7691	0.12
KNC	879	0.24	-	-	-	-	-	-	-	-	-	-	-	-	392	0.04	1271	0.02	1271	0.02
GAP	-	-	-	-	-	-	1149	0.11	-	-	-	-	-	-	-	-	1149	0.02	1149	0.02
UMMA	-	-	-	-	-	-	-	-	734	0.01	-	-	-	-	-	-	734	0.01	734	0.01
RRP	252	0.07	-	-	-	-	-	-	-	-	-	-	-	-	-	-	252	-	252	-
DAP	74	0.02	-	-	-	-	-	-	-	-	-	-	-	-	-	-	74	-	74	-
EIP	-	-	-	-	-	-	-	-	-	-	-	-	-	-	59	0.007	59	-	59	-
TOTAL	366028	100.0	409759	100.0	93769	100.0	1042206	100.0	1009791	100.0	1286778	100.0	705338	100.0	900116	100.0	5813785	100.00	6167055	100.00

Source: ECK 1999, author's calculations

Note: The adjusted total is derived from corrected figures for propotional representation.

Appendix 3: 1997 Civic Election Results

PARTY	PROV. Nairobi	Coast	N. Eastern	Eastern	Central	R. Valley	Western	Nyanza	TOTAL
DP	28	8	4	109	164	94	1	17	**425**
FORD-ASILI				2	7	3	6	1	**19**
FORD-PEOPLE	1	1	4	11	1	36	110	23	**187**
FORD-KENYA	2				28			3	**33**
KANU	15	197	199	281	9	763	162	133	**1759**
KNC								1	**1**
KENDA			1						**1**
KSC		1	1			1		4	**7**
LPD					4				**4**
LPK			2	3	2				**7**
NDP	5	7	2	9	4	7	4	255	**293**
PICK						1			**1**
SAFINA		1	3	3	27	1		2	**37**
SPK	1	4							**5**
SDP	4	5	1	97	23			10	**140**
UPPK					1			1	**2**
Total	**56**	**224**	**217**	**515**	**270**	**906**	**283**	**450**	**2921**

Source: ECK 1999

Appendix 4: Members of the eighth parliament

Constituency	Members of Parliament	Modifications by 01/05/2000

NAIROBI
1 Makadara	Paul Kamau Mugeke	DP	-
2 Kamukunji	Norman Nyagah	DP	-
3 Starehe	Maina Kamanda	DP	-
4 Lang'ata	Raila Amolo Odinga	NDP	-
5 Dagoretti	Beth Wambui Mugo	SDP	-
6 Westlands	Frederick Omulo Gumo	KANU	-
7 Kasarani	Adolf Isaac Muchiri	DP	-
8 Embakasi	David Kamau Mwenje	DP	-

COAST
9 Changamwe	Ramadhan Seif Kajembe	KANU	-
10 Kisauni	Emmanuel Karisa Maitha	DP	-
11 Likoni	Suleiman R. Shakombo	SPK	-
12 Mvita	Shariff Nassir	KANU	-
13 Msambweni	Marere wa Mwachai	KANU	-
14 Matuga	Sulleman M. Kamolleh	KANU	-
15 Kinango	Simeon Mwero Mkala	KANU	-
16 Bahari	Jembe Mwakalu	KANU	-
17 Kaloleni	Mathias Benedict Keah	KANU	-
18 Ganze	Noah Katana Ngala	KANU	-
19 Malindi	Abubakar M.A. Badawy	KANU	-
20 Magarini	David Noti Kombe	KANU	-
21 Garsen	Molu Galogalo Shambaro	KANU	-
22 Galole	Tola Kofa Mugava	KANU	-
23 Bura	Mohamed Abdi Galgallo	KANU	-
24 Lamu East	Mohamed Hashim Salim	KANU	-
25 Lamu West	Fahim Yasin Twaha	KANU	-
26 Taveta	Basil Criticos	KANU	-
27 Wundanyi	Darius Msaga Mbela	KANU	-
28 Mwatate	Marsden Herman Madoka	KANU	-
29 Voi	Basil Nguku Mwakiringo	DP	-

NORTH EASTERN

30 Dujis	Hussein Maalim Mohamed	KANU	-
31 Lagdera	Mohamed Muktar Shidiye	KANU	-
32 Fafi	Elias Bare Shill	Safina	-
33 Ijara	Mohamed Dhahir Werah	KANU	-
34 Wajir North	Abdullahi Ibrahim Ali	KANU	-
35 Wajir West	Adan Keynan Wehliye	Safina	-
36 Wajir East	Mohamed Abdi Mahamud	KANU	-
37 Wajir South	Mohamed Abdi Affey	KANU	-
38 Mandera West	Sayid Mohamed Amin	KANU	-
39 Mandera Central	Adan Mohamed Nooru	KANU	-
40 Mandera East	Shaaban Ali Isaack	KANU	-

EASTERN

41 Moyale	Gurrach Boru Galgallo	KANU	-
42 North Horr	Bonaya Adhi Godana	KANU	-
43 Saku	Abdi Tari Sasura	KANU	-
44 Laisamis	Robert Iltaramatwa Kochalle	KANU	-
45 Isiolo North	Charfano Guyo Mokku	KANU	-
46 Isiolo South	Abdullahi Haji Wako	KANU	-
47 Igembe	Jackson Itirithia Kalweo	KANU	-
48 Ntonyiri	Richard Maore Maoka	DP	-
49 Tigania West	Benjamin R. Ndubai (+09/01/99)	DP	Stephen Mukangu(DP) since 24/04/99
50 Tigania East	Mathew Adams Karauri	KANU	-
51 North Imenti	Daudi Mwiraria	DP	-
52 Central Imenti	Gitobu Imanyara	FORD-K	-
53 South Imenti	Kiraitu Murungi	DP	-
54 Nithi	Bernard Njoka Mutani (-)	DP	Eustace M. Ntigwa (KANU) 04/09/99
55 Tharaka	Cicilio Murango Mwenda	DP	-
56 Manyatta	Peter Njeru Ndwiga	DP	-
57 Runyenjes	Augustine Njehu Kathangu	FORD-A	-
58 Gachoka	Joseph William Nyagah	KANU	-
59 Siakago	Silas M'Njamiu Ita (+)	DP	Justin Muturi (KANU) 04/09/99
60 Mwingi North	Stephen Kalonzo Musyoka	KANU	-
61 Mwingi South	David Musila	KANU	-
62 Kitui West	Francis Mwanzia Nyenze	KANU	-
63 Kitui Central	Charity Kaluki Ngilu	SDP	-
64 Mutito	Jimmy Muthusi Kitonga	SDP	-
65 Kitui South	Samuel Kalii Kiminza (>)	SDP	Samuel Kiminza (KANU) 24/04/99
66 Masinga	Ronald J. Kiluta	KANU	-
67 Yatta	Francis Philip Wambua	SDP	-
68 Kangundo	Joseph Kimeu Ngutu	KANU	-
69 Kathiani	Kyalo Peter Kaindi	SDP	-
70 Machakos Town	Jonesmus Mwanza Kikuyu	SDP	-
71 Mwala	John Mutua Katuku	SDP	-
72 Mbooni	Frederick Mulinge Kalulu	KANU	-
73 Kilome	Antony Wambua Ndilinge	KANU	-
74 Kaiti	Gideon Musyoka Ndambuki	KANU	-
75 Makueni	Paul M. Sumbi (+ 15/09/98)	SDP	Peter Maundu (KANU) 16/01/99
76 Kibwezi	Onesmus Mutinda Mboko	SDP	-

CENTRAL

77 Kinangop	Mwangi Kirika Waithaka	FORD-P	-
78 Kipipiri	Paul Githiomi Mwangi	DP	-
79 Ol Kalou	Karue Muriuki Muriuki	DP	-
80 Ndaragwa	Kamau Thirikwa Thirikwa	DP	-
81 Tetu	Paul Gikonyo Muya	DP	-
82 Kieni	David M. Kairu (+04/04/98)	DP Christopher Murungaru (DP) 16/09/98	
83 Mathira	Eliud Matu Wamae	DP	-
84 Othaya	Mwai Kibaki	DP	-
85 Mukurweini	David Muhika Mutahi	DP	-
86 Nyeri Town	Wanyiri Kihoro	DP	-
87 Mwea	Alfred Mwangi Ndiritu	DP	-
88 Gichugu	Martha Wangari Karua	DP	-
89 Ndia	James Kareu Kibicho	DP	-
90 Kerugoya/Kutus	John Matere Keriri	DP	-
91 Kangema	John Njoroge Michuki	FORD-P	-
92 Mathioya	Francis Njakwe Githiari	FORD-P	-
93 Kiharu	Ignatius Ngenye Kariuki	Safina	-
94 Kigumo	Onesimus Kihara Mwangi	DP	-
95 Maragwa	Peter Kamande Mwangi	DP	-
96 Kandara	Joshua Ngugi Toro	DP	-
97 Gatanga	David Wakairu Murathe	SDP	-
98 Gatundu South	Moses Ng'ang'a Muihia	SDP	-
99 Gatundu North	Patrick Kariuki Muiruri	SDP	-
100 Juja	Stephen Ndicho Ndabi	SDP	-
101 Githunguri	Njehu Gatabaki	SDP	-
102 Kiambaa	James Njenga Karume	DP	-
103 Kabete	Paul Kibugi Muite	Safina	-
104 Limuru	George M. Nyanja	NDP	-
105 Lari	Philip Gichuru Gitonga	Safina	-

RIFT VALLEY

106 Turkana North	John Munyes Kiyonga	FORD-K	-
107 Turkana Central	David Ekwee Ethuro	KANU	-
108 Turkana South	Francis Ewoton Achuka	KANU	-
109 Kacheliba	Samuel Losuron Poghisio	KANU	-
110 Kapenguria	Francis Pollis Loile Lotodo	KANU	-
111 Sigor	Christopher M. Lomada	KANU	-
112 Samburu West	Peter Steve Leenges	KANU	-
113 Samburu East	Sammy Prisa Leshore	KANU	-
114 Kwanza	George Kapten (+25/12/99)	FORD-K Dr Noah Wekesa (FORD-K) 17/04/00	
115 Saboti	Michael Ch. Wamalwa	FORD-K	-
116 Cherangani	Kipruto Rono Kirwa	KANU	-
117 Eldoret North	William Ruto Samoei	KANU	-
118 Eldoret East	Francis Kipkoech Lagat	KANU	-
119 Eldoret South	Maizs Jesse Kibet	KANU	-
120 Marakwet East	John Kiptoo Marrirmoi	KANU	-
121 Marakwet West	David Kiprono Sutter Sudi	KANU	-
122 Keiyo North	Elijah K. Sumbeiywo	KANU	-
123 Keiyo South	Kipyator N. K. Biwott	KANU	-
124 Mosop	John Kipkorir Sambu	KANU	-
125 Aldai	Simeon Kiptum Choge	KANU	-
126 Emgwen	Joseph Tendenei Leting	KANU	-

127 Tinderet	Henry Kiprono Kosgey	KANU	-
128 Baringo East	Joseph Dalldosso Lotodo	KANU	-
129 Baringo North	Andrew Ch. Kiptoon	KANU	-
130 Baringo Central	Daniel T. arap Moi	KANU	-
131 Mogotio	William Cheruiyot Morogo	KANU	-
132 Eldama Ravine	Musa Cherutich Sirma	KANU	-
133 Laikipia West	Francis Chege Mbitiru	DP	-
134 Laikipia East	Festus Mwangi Kiunjuri	DP	-
135 Naivasha	Paul Samuel Kihara	DP	-
136 Nakuru Town	David Manyara Njuki	DP	-
137 Kuresoi	James Cheruiyot arap Koske	KANU	-
138 Molo	Dickson Kihika Kimani	DP	-
139 Rongai	Erick Toroitich Morogo	KANU	-
140 Subukia	Joseph Mukera Kuria	DP	-
141 Kilgoris	Julius Lekakeny Sunkuli	KANU	-
142 Narok North	William R. ole Ntimama	KANU	-
143 Narok South	Stephen Kanyinke Ntutu	KANU	-
144 Kajiado North	George Saitoti	KANU	-
145 Kajiado Central	David Lenante Sankori	KANU	-
146 Kajiado South	Geoffrey Mepukori Parpai	DP	-
147 Bomet	Kipkalya Kiprono Kones	KANU	-
148 Chepalungu	Isaac Kiprono Ruto	KANU	-
149 Sotik	Anthony Kipkosge Kimeto	KANU	-
150 Konoin	Raphael Kiprono arap Kitur	KANU	-
151 Buret	Kipkorir Marisin Sang	KANU	-
152 Belgut	Charles D. K. arap Kirui	KANU	-
153 Ainamoi	Kipng'eno arap Ng'eny	KANU	-
154 Kipkelion	Samuel Kimutai arap Rotich	KANU	-

WESTERN

155 Malava	Peter Soita Shitanda	FORD-K	-
156 Lugari	Shakhalaga Khwa Jirongo	KANU	-
157 Mumias	Wycliffe W. Osundwa	KANU	-
158 Matungu	Joseph Pius Wamukoya	KANU	-
159 Lurambi	Newton Wanjala Kulundu	FORD-K	-
160 Shinyalu	Daniel Lyula Khamasi	FORD-K	-
161 Ikolomani	Joseph Jolly Mugalla	KANU	-
162 Butere	Amukowa F. Anangwe	KANU	-
163 Khwisero	Harrison Aywa Odongo	KANU	-
164 Emuhaya	Washington S. Muchilwa	KANU	-
165 Sabatia	Musalia Mudavadi	KANU	-
166 Vihiga	Yusuf Kifuma Chanzu	KANU	-
167 Hamisi	George Munyasa Khaniri	KANU	-
168 Mt. Elgon	Joseph Naibei Kimkung	KANU	-
169 Kimilili	Mukhisa Kituyi	FORD-K	-
170 Webuye	Musikari Kombo	FORD-K	-
171 Sirisia	John Barasa Munyasia	FORD-K	-
172 Kanduyi	Athanas Misiko Wafula	FORD-K	-
173 Bumula	Lawrence Simiyu Sifuna	FORD-K	-
174 Amagoro	Albert Alexander A Ekirapa	KANU	-
175 Nambale	Chrysanthus Okemo	KANU	-
176 Butula	Yekoyada F. Masakhalia	KANU	-
177 Funyula	Arthur Moody Awori	KANU	-
178 Budalang'i	Raphael Wanjala S Bitta	FORD-K	-

NYANZA

179 Ugenya	James Aggrey Orengo	FORD-K	-
180 Alego	Peter Oloo Aringo	NDP	-
181 Gem	Joseph Akech Donde	FORD-K	-
182 Bondo	Robert Odinga Oburu	NDP	-
183 Rarieda	George Odeny Ngure	NDP	-
184 Kisumu T. East	Eric Gor Sungu	NDP	-
185 Kisumu T. West	Joab H. Onyango Omino	NDP	-
186 Kisumu Rural	Winston Ochoro Ayoki	NDP	-
187 Nyando	Geoffrey Paul Orwa Otita	NDP	-
188 Muhoroni	William Odongo Omamo	NDP	-
189 Nyakach	Peter Ochieng Odoyo	NDP	-
190 Kasipul Kabondo	William Oloo Otula	NDP	-
191 Karachuonyo	Adhu Awiti	NDP	-
192 Rangwe	Shem Odongo Ochuodho	NDP	-
193 Ndhiwa	Joshua Orwa Ojode	NDP	-
194 Rongo	George Mbogo A. Ochilo	NDP	-
195 Migori	George Henry O. Achola	NDP	-
196 Uriri	Herman O. Omamba	NDP	-
197 Nyatike	Tom Otieno Onyango	NDP	-
198 Mbita	Gerald Otieno Kajwan'g	NDP	-
199 Gwasi	Felix Useru Kanyauchi	NDP	-
200 Kuria	Shadrack Roger M. Manga	KANU	-
201 Bonchari	John Zebedeo Opore	KANU	-
202 South Mugirango	Enock Nyankieya Magara	FORD-K	-
203 Bomachoge	Zaphaniah M. Nyang'wara	KANU	-
204 Bobasi	Christopher Mogere Obure	KANU	-
205 Nyaribari Masaba	Samson Kegengo Ongeri	KANU	-
206 Nyaribari Chache	Simeon Nyachae	KANU	-
207 Kitutu Chache	Jimmy Nuru O. Angwenyi	KANU	-
208 Kitutu Masaba	George Moseti Anyona	KSC	-
209 West Mugirango	Henry Onyancha Obwocha	FORD-K	-
210 N. Mugirango Bor.	Joseph Kiangoi Ombasa	KANU	-

NOMINATED

211 Peter Anyang' Nyong'o	SDP	-
212 Richard Leakey (withdrawn)	Safina	
	Josephine O. Sinyo (Safina) since 27/10/98	
213 Maryam Mohammed Matano	NDP	-
214 Tabitha Seii	DP	-
215 Joseph Munyao	DP	-
216 Mohammed Galgalo	FORD-K	-
217 John Joseph Kamotho	KANU	-
218 Zipporah Kittony	KANU	-
219 Yusuf Haji	KANU	-
220 Rashid Mohammed Sajjad	KANU	-
221 Grace Mueni Mwewa	KANU	-
222 Mark Too	KANU	-

(+) = deceased
(-) = election nullified
(>) = defected

Appendix 5: Presidential and Parliamentary Election Petitions

HIGH COURT REGISTRY NO.	COURT OF KENYA AT	PARTIES	CONSTITUENCY
E.P. 1/98	Nairobi	Mwai Kibaki (Petitioner) versus Daniel Toroitich arap Moi, S.M. Kivuitu Electoral Commission of Kenya (Respondents)	Presidential

Outcome: dismissed 11/12/99

E.P. 2/98	Nairobi	Abubakar Dubow, Abdi Mohamed, and Abdille Abdi (Petitioners) versus Said Adan Warsame (Returning Officer/1st Respondent) Mohamed Abdi Affey (2nd Respondent)	Wajir South

Outcome: pending

E.P. 3/98	Nairobi	Betty Njeri Tett (Petitioner) versus Rosemary Moraa (Returning Officer/1st Respondent) Fredrick Omulo Gumo (2nd Respondent) Electoral Commission of Kenya (3rd Respondent)	Westlands

Outcome: dismissed 28/07/99

E.P. 4/98	Nairobi	Said Hemed Said (Petitioner) versus Emmanuel Karisa Maitha (1st Respondent) Hotham Nyange (Returning Officer/ 2nd Respondent)	Kisauni

Outcome: recount ordered and won by Maitha (new 10,013 vs 9,963 old 10,074 vs 9,540), but suit goes on

E.P. 5/98	Nairobi	Mohammed Abdi Ali (Petitioner) versus Adan Keynan Wehliye (1st Respondent) Abdi Rahim Haji Abbas (Returning Officer; 2nd Respondent)	Wajir West

Outcome: withdrawn 25/11/98

E.P. 6/98	Nairobi	Joseph Kennedy Kiliku (Petitioner) versus Mary Mwamondo (Returning Officer/1st Respondent) Seif Ramadhan Kajembe (2nd Respondent) Electoral Commission of Kenya (3rd Respondent)	Changamwe

Outcome: dismissed 27/07/98

E.P. 7/98	Nairobi	Tache Wako Gaji (Petitioner) versus Omar Sheikh (Deputy Returning Officer/1st Respondent) Charfana Guyo Mokku (2nd Respondent) Electoral Commission of Kenya (3rd Respondent)	Isiolo North

Outcome: dismissed 21/07/98

E.P. 8/98	Nairobi	Alexander Kipaiyn Sialala (Petitioner) versus Daniel Tallam (Returning Officer/1st Respondent) George Saitoti (2nd Respondent) Electoral Commission of Kenya (3rd Respondent)	Kajiado North

Outcome: withdrawn 16/06/99

| E.P. 9/98 | Nairobi | Yussuf Issa Abdi (Petitioner) versus Enow Adawa (1st Respondent) Elias Barre Shill (2nd Respondent) Electoral Commission of Kenya (3rd Respondent) | Fafi |

Outcome: withdrawn 01/12/98

| E.P. 10/98 | Nairobi | Perez Malande Olindo (Petitioner) versus Joseck Tsuma (Returning Officer/1st Respondent) Electoral Commission of Kenya (2nd Respondent) Raila Amolo Odinga (3rd Respondent) Charles Maranga Bugwasi (4th Respondent) | Lang'ata |

Outcome: dismissed 22/06/99

| E.P. 11/98 | Nairobi | Samwel Kamau Macharia (Petitioner) versus Electoral Commission of Kenya (1st Respondent) Naphtali H. Chomba (Returning Officer/2nd Respondent) A. Samwel Macharia alias Samwel Macharia alias Sammie Macharia | Gatanga |

Outcome: dismissed

| E.P. 12/98 | Nairobi | Ernest Eugine Osogo (Petitioner) versus Bahati Shikanga (Returning Officer/1st Respondent) Raphael Wanjala S. Bitta (2nd Respondent) Electoral Commission of Kenya (3rd Respondent) | Budalang'i |

Outcome: dismissed 23/10/98

| E.P. 13/98 | Nairobi | Ochieng Gilbert Mbeo (Petitioner) versus Thomas Ochieng (1st Respondent) Adolf Isaac Muchiri (2nd Respondent) | Kasarani |

Outcome: dismissed

| E.P. 14/98 | Nairobi | Japheth Galagati Shamalla (Petitioner) versus Philip Wekesa (Returning Officer/1st Respondent) Daniel Lyula Khamasi (2nd Respondent) | Shinyalu |

Outcome: dismissed 15/12/98

| E.P. 15/98 | Nairobi | Meshack Luchendo Libasia (Petitioner) versus Philip Wekesa (Returning Officer/1st Respondent) Daniel Lyula Khamasi (2nd Respondent) Electoral Commission of Kenya (3rd Respondent) | Shinyalu |

Outcome: dismissed 15/12/98

| E.P. 16/98 | Nairobi | Abdi Waticho (Petitioner) versus Rophin Mwakio Ndau (Returning Officer/1st Respondent) Mohamed Abdi Galgalo (2nd Respondent) | Bura |

Outcome: pending

Outcome: pending

| E.P. 17/98 | Nairobi | Wario Hukha Ali (Petitioner) versus Stephen Miriti Muguna (Returning Officer/1st Respondent) Bonaya Adhi Godana (2nd Respondent) | North Horr |

Outcome: withdrawn 06/12/98

| E.P. 18/98 | Nairobi | Stephen Kimani Gakenia (Petitioner) versus Francis Mwangi Kimani (Returning Officer/1st Respondent) Karue M. Muriuki (2nd Respondent) Electoral Commission of Kenya (3rd Respondent) | Ol Kalou |

Outcome: dismissed 29/05/98

| E.P. 19/98 | Nairobi | Abdi Hassan Haji (Petitioner) Mohammed Abdullahi Omar (2nd Petitioner) versus Shaban Ali Isaack (1st Respondent) Ibrahim Mohammed Hussein (Returning Officer/2nd Respondent) Mohammed Korow Nur alias Sheikh Burhan (3d Respondent) Mohammed Khalif Ali (4th Respondent) Richard Rakuomi (5th Respondent) | Mandera East |

Outcome: withdrawn 06/04/98

| E.P. 20/98 | Nairobi | Stephen Mukangu (Petitioner) versus David K. Kituku (Returning Officer/1st Respondent) Electoral Commission of Kenya (2nd Respondent) Benjamin Ravel Ndubai (3rd Respondent) | Tigania West |

Outcome: dismissed 15/06/98

| E.P. 1/98 | Meru | Eustace Mbuba Ntigwa (Petitioner) versus Julius Musyoki (Returning Officer/1st Respondent) Electoral Commission of Kenya (2nd Respondent) Samuel Kivuitu (Chairman, Electoral Commission of Kenya) (3rd Respondent) Bernard Njoka Mutani (4th Respondent) | Nithi |

Outcome: outcome nullified and Ntigwa new MP (KANU)

| E.P. 11/98 | Mombasa | Khamis Chome Abdi (Petitioner) versus Francis Chibwara (Returning Officer/1st Respondent) Basil Nguku Mwakiringo (2nd Respondent) Electoral Commission of Kenya (3rd Respondent) | Voi |

Outcome: withdrawn

| E.P. 1/98 | Kakamega | Alfred Muhadia Ngume (Petitioner) John Sitati Teka (Petitioner) versus George W. Sitati (1st Respondent) Peter Soita Shikanda (2nd Respondent) Electoral Commission of Kenya (3rd Respondent) | Malava |

Outcome: dismissed 28/10/98

| E.P. 2/98 | Kakamega | Harry Roger Keya (Petitioner) William Nandwa Anjiru (Petitioner) Peter Leo Omurunga (Petitioner) versus Amukowa Fredrick Anangwe (Respondent) J.B. Omatete (Respondent) Bishop Horace Etemesi (Respondent) | Butere |

Outcome: dismissed 23/09/98

| E.P. 1/98 | Kisumu | Elijah Obare Asiko (Petitioner) versus Electoral Commission of Kenya (1st Respondent) Walter Juma Absaloms (2nd Respondent) Joseph Aketch Donde (3rd Respondent) | Gem |

Outcome: dismissed 08/07/98

| E.P. 28/98 | Kisii | David Ondimu Kombo (Petitioner) versus Oburu Obara (Returning Officer/1st Respondent) Enock Nyakeya Magara (2nd Respondent) | South Mugirango |

Outcome: dismissed 10/08/98

| E.P. 1/98 | Nakuru | Alice J.R. Chelaite (Petitioner) versus David Manyara Njuki (1st Respondent) Simon K. ole Kerore (Returning Officer/2nd Respondent) Electoral Commission of Kenya (3rd Respondent) | Nakuru Town |

Outcome: dismissed 16/10/98

| E.P. 2/99 | | MakueniMaurice Musamba (petitioner) versus Peter Maundu (incumbent) | Makueni |

Outcome: dismissed 05/06/99

Index

639